IN HARM'S WAY

A HISTORY OF THE AMERICAN MILITARY EXPERIENCE

Gene Allen Smith
David Coffey
Kyle Longley

NEW YORK   OXFORD
OXFORD UNIVERSITY PRESS

Oxford University Press is a department of the University of Oxford.
It furthers the University's objective of excellence in research, scholarship,
and education by publishing worldwide. Oxford is a registered trade mark of
Oxford University Press in the UK and certain other countries.

Published in the United States of America by Oxford University Press
198 Madison Avenue, New York, NY 10016, United States of America.

© 2020 by Oxford University Press

Library of Congress Cataloging-in-Publication Data
Names: Smith, Gene A., 1963- author. | Coffey, David, 1960- author. |
    Longley, Kyle, author.
Title: In harm's way : a history of the American military experience / Gene
    Allen Smith, David Coffey, Kyle Longley.
Description: New York : Oxford University Press, [2020] | Includes
    bibliographical references and index.
Identifiers: LCCN 2018032486 (print) | LCCN 2018052490 (ebook) | ISBN
    9780190929404 (eBook) | ISBN 9780190210793 (pbk.)
Subjects: LCSH: United States--History, Military.
Classification: LCC E181 (ebook) | LCC E181 .S564 2020 (print) | DDC
    355.00973--dc23
LC record available at https://lccn.loc.gov/2018032486

9 8 7 6 5 4 3

Printed by Sheridan Books, Inc., United States of America

CONTENTS

LIST OF MAPS *xi*

ISSUES IN MILITARY HISTORY *xiii*

PREFACE *xv*

ACKNOWLEDGEMENTS *xvii*

ABOUT THE AUTHORS *xix*

INTRODUCTION   **An American Way of War** *1*

CHAPTER **1**   **Surviving in a Wilderness, 1585–1676** *3*

English Contact in North America *4*

Trade, Shipping, and Colonies *5*

A Foothold in America *7*

Jamestown *8*

The Reality of Indian War *10*

The Militia Tradition and War *14*

Praying for Peace and Providential Protection *16*

Pilgrim Separatists *17*

Puritan City on a Hill *18*

The Pequot War *19*

A Rising Discontent *20*

The English Civil War *21*

Bacon's Rebellion *21*

Metacom's (King Philip's) War *26*

Conclusions *30*

CHAPTER **2**   **Competing for a Continent, 1565–1763** *33*

Prelude to Conflict *34*

From the Sea *34*

Anglo-Dutch Wars *36*

Wars for North American Empire   *37*
    Fighting Over Furs   *37*
    King William's War   *38*
    Queen Anne's War   *39*
    Tuscarora and Yamasee Wars   *43*
    War of Jenkins' Ear   *45*
King George's War   *47*
Great War for Empire   *49*
    The Ohio River Valley   *49*
    A World War   *51*
    Albany Congress   *52*
    Braddock's Campaign   *54*
    British Commitment   *55*
Global War   *57*
    Local yet Imperial Dimensions   *58*
    William Pitt Takes Charge   *58*
    1758: The Year of Decision   *60*
    Quebec   *62*
An Empire on Which the Sun Never Set   *66*
Conclusions   *66*

CHAPTER **3**   **'Tis Time to Part, 1763–1776**   *69*
A Changing Relationship   *70*
    Pontiac's Rebellion   *70*
    Salutary Neglect   *72*
    Sugar and Stamps   *74*
Revenue Acts   *76*
The Boston Massacre   *77*
Troubles over Tea   *79*
Shots Heard Round the World   *81*
Bunker, No, Breed's Hill   *84*
No More Middle Ground   *86*
On to Canada   *90*
Toward Independence   *92*
    A New British Strategy   *93*
Conclusions   *97*

CHAPTER **4**   **Maintaining Independence, 1777–1782**   *100*
Struggling Toward Independence   *101*
1777: The Year of Decision   *102*
    Saratoga Campaign   *102*
    Philadelphia Campaign   *107*
1778: Stalemate in the North   *109*
A Suffering Army   *109*
    Anger and Frustration   *111*

Struggle on the Periphery   *113*
  Continental Navy   *113*
  State Navies   *115*
Breaking the Iroquois Confederation   *116*
Spanish Conquests in the South   *117*
A New Southern Strategy   *118*
  Savannah and Charleston   *118*
  Embers of Defeat   *120*
Treason, Pensions, and Mutinies   *122*
The World Turned Upside Down   *123*
King's Mountain: Beginning of the End   *124*
Devil of a Whipping: War of Attrition in the Carolinas   *124*
Taking the War to Virginia   *126*
Yorktown   *129*
Winning the Peace   *131*
The Treaty of Paris   *131*
Conclusions   *132*

CHAPTER **5**   **Securing the Republic, 1782–1815**   *135*

Challenges for the New Nation   *136*
  Articles of Confederation   *136*
  A Peacetime Military   *137*
  The Tree of Liberty—Shays' Rebellion   *137*
  Constitutional Convention: "Experience Must Be Our Only Guide"   *139*
Federal Government   *140*
  Militia versus Standing Army   *140*
First War   *141*
Whiskey Rebellion   *145*
Quasi-War   *146*
Republican Ascendency   *148*
Barbary Pirates   *150*
Education and Exploration   *152*
War on the Horizon   *153*
  American Clouds   *153*
  Prelude to War   *154*
The War of 1812   *155*
  On to Canada: 1812   *156*
  War at Sea: 1812   *156*
  Visions of Defeat: 1813   *158*
  Victory on the Lakes: 1813   *160*
  To Montreal: 1813   *162*
  Triumph and Tragedy: 1814   *164*
  Niagara Stalemate: 1814   *164*
  Destruction in the Chesapeake: 1814   *166*
  Severing the Republic: Lake Champlain, 1814   *168*

War in the Southwest   *169*

Campaign for New Orleans   *170*

Conclusions   *172*

CHAPTER **6**   **Empire of Expansion, 1810–1849**   *175*

To Conquer Without War: The Gulf South   *176*

Reforming the Military   *178*

Following the Setting Sun   *181*

A Maritime Destiny   *182*

Trailing Tears: Indian Removal   *185*

Cherokees, Chickasaws, Choctaws, and Creeks   *185*

Black Hawk War   *187*

Second Seminole War   *189*

The Lone Star Republic   *193*

The War with Mexico   *196*

The Bear Flag Revolt   *199*

The Santa Fe Expedition   *200*

Taylor's Campaign   *201*

Scott's Invasion   *203*

Legacy of War and Expansion   *207*

Conclusions   *207*

CHAPTER **7**   **Disunion, 1849–1861**   *210*

The Military at Midcentury   *211*

The Indian Frontier   *215*

An Imperial Navy   *218*

The Sectional Crisis   *220*

War   *223*

First Fights   *228*

Troubled Waters   *230*

Turning Points   *233*

Conclusions   *236*

CHAPTER **8**   **Hard War, 1862–1865**   *239*

The Western Theater: 1862   *241*

The Eastern Theater: 1862   *245*

The Rise of Robert E. Lee   *246*

The Eastern Theater: 1863   *251*

Conscription   *255*

The Western Theater: 1863   *255*

Black Troops   *258*

Prisoners of War   *258*

Decisions   *259*

The Eastern Theater: 1864   *260*

The Western Theater: 1864   *263*

"Damn the Torpedoes": Naval Actions of 1864 *265*
The Final Acts: 1865 *267*
Conclusions *270*

CHAPTER **9** **Reconstruction and Conquest, 1865–1890** *273*
Unfinished Business *274*
Demobilization and the New Regular Army *275*
Reconstruction *277*
Expanded Role *279*
Technology *280*
The Last Indian Wars *281*
    Buffalo Soldiers *283*
    Frontier Constabulary *284*
    The Indians *284*
    Precursors *286*
    Bozeman Trail Setback *287*
    Southern Plains *288*
    Texas *290*
    Northern Plains *292*
    The Far West *296*
Professionalism *300*
Conclusions *302*

CHAPTER **10** **Empire and Intervention, 1890–1917** *305*
An Imperial Navy Again *306*
A Splendid Little War *308*
The Ugly War *315*
The Boxer Rebellion *319*
The Big Stick *320*
Punitive Expedition *323*
Technology *326*
Organization *327*
Separate but Not Equal *329*
Conclusions *330*

CHAPTER **11** **The Great War and Beyond, 1917–1940** *333*
The Great War *334*
    The Navy *337*
    American Expeditionary Forces *338*
The African American Experience *343*
Airpower *345*
Final Allied Offensives *345*
The Interwar Years *348*
The National Defense Act of 1920 *349*
Retreat from Intervention *351*

Billy Mitchell and the Pursuit of Airpower   *353*

Descent into War   *354*

Conclusions   *356*

CHAPTER 12   **Saving the World from Evil, 1939–1945**   *359*

The Road to War and American Unpreparedness, 1939–1941   *360*

The State of Military Unpreparedness   *360*

Shocked into Action   *361*

The Undeclared War   *362*

No Certain Victory: War in Europe, 1942   *362*

The Arsenal of Democracy   *363*

A Bloody War in the Atlantic   *363*

Into the Desert   *365*

Way up There in the Wild Blue Yonder   *367*

Europe From Above   *370*

Turning Point: May 1943–May 1944   *372*

Victory in the North Atlantic   *372*

Taking Control of the Skies   *372*

Flexing Newly Found Muscles   *373*

Everyone to the Front   *376*

The Double V   *376*

We Are Americans!   *378*

American Women at War   *379*

The Final Push   *380*

Operation Overlord   *380*

Two Tales   *382*

Light at the End of the Tunnel   *384*

The Slaughterhouse   *385*

Final Victory   *385*

Conclusions   *386*

CHAPTER 13   **War Without Mercy: Fighting in the Pacific, 1942–1945**   *388*

The State of Unpreparedness   *389*

The Perfect Disaster   *391*

The Allies on Their Heels   *392*

From Defeat to Victory: June 1942–October 1944   *393*

With Love from Shangri-la   *394*

The Invincible Laid Low   *394*

The Sleeping Giant Awakened   *397*

The First Step Toward Tokyo   *398*

Island Hopping   *401*

Death From Below   *403*

The War over Japan   *403*

The End of the Ground War   *406*
The Final Steps   *408*
 "I Am Become Death"   *410*
Conclusions   *412*

CHAPTER 14   **Different Kind of War: The Early Cold War
and the Forgotten War, 1945–1951**   *414*
From World War to Cold War   *415*
 The New War   *415*
 Preparing for the Peace   *417*
Toward a National Security State   *417*
 Off We Go into the Wild Blue Yonder   *419*
 Candy Bombers   *419*
A Brave New World   *420*
The Forgotten War: The Bloody War in Korea   *422*
 The Road to War   *423*
 Surprise and Retreat   *423*
 Standing their Ground   *424*
 The Immaculate Assault   *425*
**Snatching Defeat from the Jaws of Victory: November 1950–March
 1951**   *427*
 To the Yalu and the Long Retreat   *427*
 The Bloody Road   *428*
 Showdown Between Titans   *430*
The Air War   *432*
 Fighting While Negotiating   *435*
Conclusions   *437*

CHAPTER 15   **From the Top of the World to a Quagmire,
1953–1975**   *439*
Dwight Eisenhower and the New Look, 1953–1961   *440*
Dipping in Their Toe in Indochina   *441*
 A Good Stout Effort   *442*
Other Flashpoints   *444*
The Military-Industrial Complex   *445*
Pay Any Price, Bear Any Burden   *446*
Limited Partnership in South Vietnam   *449*
 Lovers, Not Fighters   *450*
 Jettisoning Diem   *450*
The Big Juicy Worm on the Hook: Major U.S. Involvement, 1963–1968   *452*
 Sliding into the Quagmire   *452*
 Hitting Them Hard from Above   *453*
 Boots on the Ground   *454*
 Bleeding them Dry in the Valley of Death   *455*

Blow for Blow   *456*

Rolling in from the Clouds   *459*

The Year of the Continuous Nightmare: 1968   *460*

The Road to Tet   *460*

The Big Surprise   *462*

A Crisis in Confidence   *462*

We've Gotta Get Out of This Place: Vietnamization and Withdrawal, 1969–1975   *463*

The War of Survival   *464*

The Racial Tinderbox   *464*

The Enemy Within   *465*

Adding A New Word to the Dictionary   *465*

The Baby Killer   *466*

Looking into the Mirror   *468*

The Lost Cause   *468*

Conclusions   *469*

CHAPTER **16**   **The Endless Wars: The Cold War and Beyond, 1975–Present**   *471*

Ghosts of Vietnam   *472*

The Carter Interregnum   *476*

The Iranian Morass   *476*

A New Day Dawning   *478*

Flexing Muscles   *478*

A New Day Dawning   *480*

Beyond the Cold War, 1989–2001   *481*

A Combat Pilot in the White House   *481*

Getting Public Enemy #1   *481*

Iraq 1.0   *482*

From Juggernaut to Peacekeeper   *484*

Wading Back into Deep Waters   *486*

Two Steps Forward, One Step Back   *487*

The Endless Wars, 2001–Present   *488*

Crashing Towers   *488*

Iraq 2.0   *490*

The Road to Baghdad   *492*

Insurgency   *492*

Fighting in the Rubble   *493*

To Contain an Insurgency   *495*

Back to Afghanistan   *499*

Conclusions   *499*

CREDITS   *501*

INDEX   *505*

LIST OF MAPS

Map 1.1 Jamestown, 1607–1612   8

Map 1.2 Settlement Patterns in New England   19

Map 1.3 Colonizing the Chesapeake, 1607–1700   23

Map 2.1 War, the Indian Slave Trade, and the Dispersal of Southeastern Indians, 1700–1730   57

Map 2.2 Major Campaigns of the French and Indian War   59

Map 3.1 North America after the Treaty of Paris, 1763   71

Map 3.2 The Siege of Boston and the Battles of Bunker Hill and Lexington and Concord   83

Map 3.3 Major Campaigns in New York and New Jersey, 1776–1777   95

Map 4.1 Major Campaigns in New York and Pennsylvania, 1777   105

Map 4.2 Major Campaigns in the South, 1778–1781   121

Map 4.3 Battle of Cowpens, 1781   125

Map 4.4 Yorktown, 1781   128

Map 5.1 Indian Wars, 1790–1814   142

Map 5.2 American Naval Battles, 1798–1815   147

Map 5.3 The Barbary Wars   151

Map 5.4 The War of 1812: The War in the North   158

Map 5.5 Battles and Campaigns of the War of 1812   163

Map 5.6 The War of 1812: Major Southern Campaigns   169

Map 6.1 The Gulf Coast, 1816–1818   177

Map 6.2 The United States Exploring Expedition, 1838–1842   184

Map 6.3 Indian Removal, 1820–1840   187

Map 6.4 The Seminole Wars, 1817–1858   190

Map 6.5 The Texas Revolution   194

Map 6.6 The Mexican War   199

Map 7.1 The West, 1850–1860   216

Map 7.2 Secession and the Civil War, December 1860–March 1862   224

Map 8.1 Principal Campaigns of the Civil War, 1862–1865   241

Map 8.2 The Battle of Shiloh, April 6–7, 1862   243

Map 8.3 Antietam, September 17, 1862   248

Map 8.4 Gettysburg, July 1–3, 1863   253

Map 8.5 The Appomattox Campaign   269

Map 9.1 Military Reconstruction   278

Map 9.2 The West, 1860–1890   288

Map 9.3 Battle of the Little Bighorn   294

Map 10.1 The Spanish-American War   310

Map 10.2 The Philippine-American War   316

Map 10.3 The United States in Central America and the Caribbean, 1898–1933   321

Map 11.1 The Western Front, 1918   342

Map 12.1 The African Campaign, 1942–1943   365

Map 12.2 The Italian Campaign, 1943–1945   374

Map 12.3 The Western Europe Campaign, June 1944–May 1945   380

Map 13.1 The Battle of Midway   393

Map 13.2 The Island-Hopping Campaign   400

Map 14.1 Military Blocs in Europe, 1948–1955   416

Map 14.2 The Korean War Through October 1950   422

Map 14.3 The Korean Peninsula in 1953   434

Map 15.1 The Cuban Missile Crisis   447

Map 15.2 Vietnam, 1965–1967   451

Map 15.3 Tet Offensive   461

Map 16.1 The First Gulf War   473

Map 16.2 UN Peacekeeping Missions in the 1990s   485

Map 16.3 The Invasion of Iraq   489

Map 16.4 Surge Efforts in Iraq, 2006–2007   496

Map 16.5 Afghanistan, 2001–2017   498

ISSUES IN MILITARY HISTORY

Chapter 1   The American Way of War   15
Chapter 2   Native Americans and the Middle Ground   40
Chapter 3   War for Independence or an American Revolution?   87
Chapter 4   George Washington and Civilian Rule   112
Chapter 5   Navalists Versus Antinavalists   149
Chapter 6   Race and the Mexican War   197
Chapter 7   Was the Civil War the First Modern War?   233
Chapter 8   Fallacies of the "Lost Cause"   266
Chapter 9   Was the Tragedy at Wounded Knee a Massacre?   301
Chapter 10 Unlearned Lessons of Small Wars   318
Chapter 11 Did America Provide the Decisive Force in World War I?   348
Chapter 12 The Effectiveness of the Strategic Bombing Campaign over Europe   369
Chapter 13 The Dropping of the Atomic Bomb   410
Chapter 14 President Truman and the Firing of Douglas MacArthur   428
Chapter 15 The Descent into Darkness: A Military Atrocity and the Vietnam War   467
Chapter 16 Women in the Military after Vietnam   475

PREFACE

Military history unavoidably is the story of violent human encounters through the use of arms. It is the story of political activity carried out to obtain political purposes, and it inevitably involves death and destruction. *In Harm's Way* focuses on the wars fought by this country, explains the reasons for conflicts, illustrates both the ironic and the dreadful realities of the battles, and, finally, explains the short-term impacts and long-lasting results of war. Each chapter builds to a crescendo, culminating with the peaceful end of a conflict.

This book depicts warfare as a human activity carried out within the context of a specific political/diplomatic, cultural, and technological milieu. It depicts the mechanisms of waging war (the strategies, tactics, and killing technologies), the costs of waging war, economic and otherwise, and the impact of war on individual humans.

This book endorses a Clausewitzian understanding that war is never legitimate unless it serves some sane, rational, and legitimate object of statecraft. Each chapter explains the significant developments that influenced changes in military thought during the period; the ways in which military operations were influenced by strategic design, tactical capability, and available technology; and the impact of the military on domestic and international society. Finally, the book shows how soldiers and statesmen throughout U.S. history have devised strategies to obtain their purposes and then employed tactics and technologies in pursuit of them.

The authors of this book strongly believe in the need for a fast-paced, highly readable synthesis of modern scholarship on the nation's experience in war in every era. Courses in American military history require a basic text that is comprehensive, accurate, and nuanced without being turgid, dry, or excessively long. This book provides a narrative synthesis and rolling analysis of America's wars and military policies from colonial times down to the twenty-first century and incorporates air-, land, and seapower. Instead of focusing exclusively on conflict, it embraces political and diplomatic challenges, social and economic changes, philosophical and ideological debates, and technological advances. In other words, it covers the practical development and working out of military thought in an account that is keyed to the experience of the American people at war, rather than drifting off into sterile analysis of the institutional military for its own sake. Perhaps most importantly, the authors want this book to be read, studied, and enjoyed.

ACKNOWLEDGEMENTS

The authors gratefully acknowledge the terrific team at Oxford University Press, led by our editor, Charles Cavaliere. Many thanks to editorial assistant Katie Tunkavige and the production staff at OUP. We also would like to thank the following professors who reviewed the manuscript:

Albert I. Berger, University of North Dakota
Gregory A. Daddis, Chapman University
Joseph G. Dawson, Texas A&M University
David Preston, The Citadel
Paul D. Lockhart, Wright State University
Thomas D. Mays, Humboldt State University
John C. McManus, Missouri University of Science and Technology
Ron Milam, Texas Tech University
Timothy B. Smith, University of Tennessee at Martin
Heathur Stur, University of Southern Mississippi
Samuel J. Watson, United States Military Academy

Professor Gene Allen Smith, author of chapters 1 through 6: I wish to acknowledge my colleagues at the United States Naval Academy, who helped me revise and conceptualize this project. These professionals, who are training the next generation of naval officers, helped me to understand how midshipmen internalized information and prepared for serving the nation. Some of my colleagues at Texas Christian University have also appreciated my fascination with naval and maritime topics and have encouraged me to continue my pursuit. I wish to thank Ken Stevens, Hanan Hammad, Bill Meier, Peter Szok, Alex Hidalgo, Todd Kerstetter, and Steve Woodworth for graciously encouraging my research. Alan Gallay, Larry Bartlett, and Gary Ohls, who recently retired from the Naval Postgraduate School in Monterey, California, read early chapters and offered constructive comments that improved my work. Many unnamed colleagues shared their expertise and in doing so helped shape this project. Perhaps no one offered more guidance and professional and life support than

James C. Bradford, formerly of Texas A&M University. I am the professional I am today because of his mentorship.

Professor David Coffey, author of chapters 7 through 11: First and foremost, I dedicate this effort to my wife and steadfast supporter Julie Hill, a vibrant soul and constant inspiration. I thank my colleagues at the University of Tennessee at Martin, especially administrative assistant Melanie Warmath, for their support and encouragement. I'm grateful to Professor Thomas Mays of Humboldt State and Dr. Tim Smith of the University of Tennessee at Martin for their excellent insights and useful recommendations. Special thanks also go to my friend and mentor Dr. Spencer Tucker for the numerous opportunities he has given me to expand my horizons in the field of military history. Finally, I extend my deep personal gratitude to Dr. David Jones, Dr. Walter Fletcher, and Dr. Nikhil Patel of Martin; Dr. Margaret Gore of Union City, Tennessee; Dr. James Wudel, Jr., of Wake Forrest Medical School; and Dr. Jonathan Cohen of Nashville, among many other health care professionals who have kept me going over the last ten years.

Professor Kyle Longley, author of chapters 12 through 16: I sincerely appreciate the support of a number of people who aided me in the process of writing this book. First and foremost, I acknowledge a huge intellectual debt to my doctoral mentor, George Herring, who molded and shaped me from graduate studies forward and remains a powerful force in my intellectual development today. I also note the aid of Dick and Dinky Snell, who have provided significant financial backing for my research endeavors. Their funding makes completing projects like this one much easier. I also want to thank my colleagues at Arizona State University, including Chouki El-Hamel, Andrew Barnes, Phil Vandermeer, Gayle Gullett, Ed Escobar, and Keith Miller, for their friendship during this process. Unfortunately, too many have retired and left a hole in the history department and university, but I appreciate their support. Finally, I must thank all my colleagues in the fields of military history and, by extension, diplomatic history for their support. There is a long list, and I cannot include everyone, but I especially thank Bill Allison (my brother from another mother), Greg Daddis, John McManus, Jaqueline Whitt, Jim Willbanks, Heather Stur, Mitch Lerner, Bob Brigham, Fred Logevall, Carol Reardon, Aaron O'Connell, Nick Sarantakes, and John Hall. As with all intellectual exercises, this project has taken many people to make it successful.

ABOUT THE AUTHORS

GENE ALLEN SMITH

Gene Allen Smith is Professor of History at Texas Christian University (TCU) in Fort Worth. During the 2013–2014 academic year he served as the Class of 1957 Distinguished Chair in Naval Heritage at the United States Naval Academy. He is author or editor of ten books, as well as numerous articles and reviews on the War of 1812, naval and maritime history, and territorial expansion along the Gulf of Mexico. One of his most recent books is *The Slaves' Gamble: Choosing Sides in the War of 1812* (2013). He is a prizewinning teacher, having twice received the AddRan College of TCU Distinguished Achievement as a Creative Teacher and Scholar. Since 2002 he has also served as the director of the Center for Texas Studies at TCU, and from 2007 to 2014 he was a history curator at a major Fort Worth museum.

DAVID COFFEY

Born in New Mexico and raised in Fort Worth, Texas, David Coffey holds a Ph.D. from Texas Christian University. He is Professor of History and chair of the Department of History and Philosophy at the University of Tennessee at Martin, where he offers classes in U.S., military, and Mexican history. His books include *John Bell Hood and the Struggle for Atlanta*; *Soldier Princess: The Life and Legend of Agnes Salm-Salm in North America, 1861–1867*; and *Sheridan's Lieutenants: Phil Sheridan, His Generals, and the Final Year of the Civil War*. He is a co-author of *Historic Abilene: An Illustrated History*. Additionally, he has contributed chapters to well-regarded anthologies on Civil War, Mexican, and Texas history. He has contributed to ten major historical reference works and served as an editor on three award-winning multivolume projects: the *Encyclopedia of the Vietnam War*; the *Encyclopedia of American Military History*; and the *Encyclopedia of the North American Indian Wars, 1607–1890*. Coffey is the assistant editor of the six-volume *American Civil War: The Definitive Encyclopedia and Document Collection*, to which he contributed more than forty entries.

KYLE LONGLEY

Kyle Longley was previously the Snell Family Dean's Distinguished Professor in the School of Historical, Philosophical, and Religious Studies and School of Politics and Global Studies at Arizona State University. He is currently the Director of the LBJ Presidential Library in Austin, Texas. He is the author of six books and the editor of two others, including *In the Eagle's Shadow: The United States and Latin America* (2nd ed., 2009); *Grunts: The American Combat Soldier in Vietnam* (2008); *The Morenci Marines: A Tale of a Small Town and the Vietnam War* (2013); *The Enduring Legacy: Leadership and National Security During the Presidency of Ronald Reagan* (2017); and *LBJ's 1968: Power, Politics, and the Presidency in America's Year of Upheaval* (2018). He is also a prizewinning teacher, having received the Centennial Professor Award from the Arizona State University Student Association and the Zebulon Pearce Prize for outstanding teaching in the Humanities at Arizona State University.

AN AMERICAN WAY OF WAR

The U.S. military has evolved from a small colonial force to the world's largest global military power in four centuries. In response to the changing geopolitical landscape, especially in the twentieth century, the United States went from maintaining a relatively small military to becoming a preponderant power, especially after World War II. Often, it has been a slow evolution, highlighted by rapid expansion during times of war, but increasingly it has become more prominent, always shaped largely by domestic and international considerations. Understanding these changes underscores the nature of the evolution and its importance for understanding modern America.

To better help people comprehend the nature of the evolution and its significance, we develop several major themes throughout the book, some of which are more pertinent in particular eras than others, but all of which nevertheless represent continuities in the American military experience. Each helps provide understanding of long-standing traditions within the U.S. military.

First, America's social, economic, cultural, and political institutions have played a significant role in the development and implementation of military policies. Few purely rational military considerations have existed outside the realm of these influences, which include Congress, special interest groups, and military contractors. At the same time, the American military and the accompanying national security state have been a force for social and cultural change in the United States as well as throughout the world, particularly during the colonial period and the early years of the republic. This has been especially evident in changing local conditions near military and industrial bases that are dependent on military spending, as well as in race and gender relations.

Second, the U.S. military imitates a pluralistic society that has blended professional and citizen soldiers, often reflecting democratic tensions between strong centralized organizations and decentralized ones as well as struggles over citizenship. Over time, the armed services have become more professionalized, leading to significant changes in command structures and the demographics of those serving. This has created an American military tradition, particularly in the modern era, of a professional officer corps that has remained stable even in periods of total war when the nation has mobilized fully and incorporated large numbers of nonprofessionals. The ebb and flow of national threats, particularly since the end of the Cold War and the end of the draft, have removed many of the military's nonprofessional elements, although this is a relatively new phenomenon in U.S. military history.

Third, there has been a fundamental commitment to civilian control of military policies that requires the development of relationships at the federal and state levels to create a series of checks and balances in terms of both manpower and material needs. Inherited from the British tradition of civil–military relations, this important trend has rarely been challenged since the foundation of the republic. Reorganizations of the military over the years have always reflected this tradition in command structures as well as constitutional mandates regarding the power of the commander-in-chief. With few exceptions, this tradition has been sustained.

Fourth, industrialization and its accompanying scientific and technological advances have shaped the way that wars are fought. The industrial revolution of the late nineteenth century fundamentally altered Americans and their role in the world. Impatience and a belief in the inherent superiority of the mechanized and industrial way of life fundamentally influenced the American way of war in the twentieth century and beyond. The advent of airpower and nuclear missiles changed Americans' perceptions of their global role even further.

This emphasis on technology has also shaped how Americans view war in other ways. Americans living in a democratic society abhor deaths among their troops, and the American military has engaged in a constant effort to decrease casualties by relying on technology. This trend also fits with the long-standing desire among Americans to keep military costs down. While that approach changed a great deal after World War II, the goal has continued to be to reduce potential enemy advantages in manpower by a reliance on technology.

Fifth, America's geographic positioning has played a fundamental role in shaping the U.S. military and its role in society. The U.S. military has evolved from a localized fighting force into a regional and ultimately global one. This has required an evolution in manpower and resource allocation and changes in perspectives on how to wage war, particularly as threats have multiplied because of technology and the closing of distances.

Sixth, changes in technology and geographical spaces have led to an evolution of military strategy and tactics over many years. A professional class of American military leaders, often shaped by European strategists, came to develop plans of action in diverse global arenas. They interacted with civilian leaders to fashion responses to major global nation-states in conflicts such as World War I and World War II, engaged in asymmetrical warfare against the Native Americans, and later took part in interventions in the nonindustrialized world. These actions were often carried out in tandem with civilian leaders.

While other trends exist in the evolution of the U.S. military, these six have been the most important, and they help provide some understanding of the traditions and continuities in this body as it has evolved from a colonial volunteer force to a global professionalized military, particularly after World War II. This ongoing process has adapted to changing geopolitical conditions and the rise of threats from both state and nonstate actors.

CHAPTER 1

SURVIVING IN A WILDERNESS
1585–1676

English Contact in North America • A Foothold in America • The Reality of Indian War
• The Militia Tradition and War • Praying for Peace and Providential Protection
• The Pequot War • A Rising Discontent

The English settlement of North America followed a proven and prescribed course of conquest initially developed during the occupation of Ireland in the early sixteenth century. In 1580, when Captain Walter Raleigh arrived in Cork, Ireland, he observed wild, filthy natives wrapped in enormous dirty yellow shirts and with long hair. Their barbaric appearance seemingly justified English attempts to bring Protestantism, order, and civilization to the region. Raleigh and his ninety-five men marched through a burned and ravaged landscape to Smerwick, where an invading papal force of 600 Spaniards and Italians had built and reinforced a fort called Castel de Oro on the Dingle Peninsula. The Catholics had waited there for months with supplies and weapons, hoping to be reinforced by the Irish. Despite these hopes, English soldiers under the Earl of Ormond and Baron Grey de Wilton cut them off from the mainland, launching a three-day siege of Smerwick. On November 11, the Catholic forces surrendered after being promised quarter. Instead, Grey de Wilton ordered that the fort's armaments and food be secured, and then Captain Raleigh's men slaughtered more than 500 men and women.

The execution, albeit a brutal massacre in a modern sense, reveals the violent nature of the colonial world, highlights the struggle between Catholics and Protestants that spread to and influenced the Western Hemisphere, and represented military practice for the age. It also provided the means by which an army in the midst of enemy territory could subdue its opponent. Such uses of violence and bloodshed also became common place for English soldiers traveling to North America.

ENGLISH CONTACT IN NORTH AMERICA

In 1583 Raleigh secured the Crown patent of his deceased half-brother Humphrey Gilbert and began recruiting influential courtiers and investors such as Francis Drake and Richard Grenville to colonize and develop North American lands. Raleigh sent Philip Amadas and Arthur Barlowe to explore the coast of North America, and by July 1583 they had made their way in two small vessels via the West Indies to the Outer Banks of present-day North Carolina, where they found a land teeming with vegetation, dense forests, and abundant wild game, fowl, and fish.

A party of armor-clad soldiers waded ashore and performed a ritualistic ceremony, claiming the land for Queen Elizabeth I. Just before sunset, three armed Indians appeared in a canoe. The menacing, tattooed natives came in peace, and later that evening fifty more Indians fished for the Englishmen and traded with them. This first meeting and exchange occurred without difficulties.

During the following month the Englishmen explored the coastline between Florida and the Chesapeake Bay, traded with the Indians, and considered suitable sites for a settlement and base that would be both defensible and accessible. Raleigh had wanted a site along the same latitude as the southern Mediterranean, which he believed would give English mariners a position from which they could raid Spain's commerce and treasure galleons. Convinced that Roanoke Island was an ideal location, the Englishmen departed, taking with them two Indians to provide information about the region and the native language.

The explorers' report, vividly substantiated by Indians, convinced Raleigh and his backers to establish a base on Roanoke Island. In the following spring of 1585, Raleigh organized an expedition commanded by Grenville, an experienced mariner, and recruited infantry captain Ralph Lane and 180 men for the venture. Arriving off the Outer Banks in July, the expedition's large vessels had too much draft to cross the sandbar to the inner sound, indicating that Roanoke Island would not be a suitable location for a permanent military base or settlement.

Soon other problems emerged. A silver cup disappeared while the Englishmen explored the interior, prompting them to burn an Indian village in retaliation. This act instilled in the Indians great suspicion about English intentions. That summer Grenville took his ships to raid Spanish trading posts and weaker commercial vessels in the Caribbean, leaving Lane and 107 men to construct a temporary fort and settlement on Roanoke Island. Most of the men spent their time looking for gold and silver rather than preparing for the winter. Fortunately, relations with Chief Wingina and the Roanoke Indians remained cordial until the English food supply ran low during late spring of 1586. When Lane demanded that the Indians provide corn for his men, Wingina offered seed corn and empty fields, which would have permitted the English to feed themselves. Lane instead viewed this gift suspiciously, especially when Wingina moved his tribe to the mainland to avoid future problems.

Believing the Indians planned to attack, Lane made a preemptive strike. Approaching the Roanokes' settlement under the pretense of peace, Lane and his men met privately with Wingina and his advisors. As the two groups parlayed, Lane suddenly shouted the password "Christ Our Victory," and the Englishmen turned on the Indians, killing Wingina and then decapitating him. This exceedingly violent approach to the growing food shortage exacerbated other problems, and thereafter, Indian communities refused to deal with the Englishmen. When Francis Drake arrived with ships fresh from a plundering expedition in the Caribbean, Lane and his men returned to England.

A few weeks later Grenville returned to Roanoke Island with supplies but found only an empty fort. He left fifteen men behind to hold the fort and resumed his raiding activities. Unknowingly, he had marooned this small group of Englishmen in the middle of hostile territory. A year passed before other English colonists arrived. In August 1587, eighty-eight men, seventeen women, and eleven children landed on Roanoke under the leadership of John White. The expedition had initially planned to settle on the Chesapeake Bay, but when they landed on Roanoke Island, they again found an empty fort. No one had planted crops for the arriving settlers, nor had anyone constructed the necessary accommodations, prompting White to leave immediately for England to secure supplies and assistance.

When White returned to England, he learned that war had erupted with Spain. The 1588 attack of the Spanish Armada forced White to remain in England until the summer of 1590, when the Spanish threat finally subsided. When he returned to Roanoke in August 1590, he found no one there and few signs of the settlers' previous existence: only the word "Croatoan" carved on a doorpost and the cryptic letters "C R O" carved on a tree. The fate of the settlers remains a mystery. This failed English attempt to carve a toehold on the North American continent illustrates the range of problems Englishmen faced during this period, including hostile Indians, an unforgiving environment, food shortages, unfamiliar diseases, and an intolerable climate. Englishmen needed to adapt before any successful settlement could be established.

TRADE, SHIPPING, AND COLONIES

During the Elizabethan Age, England competed against Catholic Spain and Portugal for wealth, status, and land. Because Portugal, Spain, and France refused to trade with the English, England was in need of new sources of timber, fish, sugar, and other goods. Subsequent English privateering hobbled Spain, draining its coffers of valuable precious metals, but these piratical activities did not provide a constant flow of income or the commodities needed to sustain the island nation. Trade and shipping, as the Dutch demonstrated during the sixteenth century, were means to secure the wealth and resources needed by a prosperous, growing nation. This realization convinced the English that colonies could be highly profitable endeavors.

In his 1584 tract *A Discourse on Western Planting*, Richard Hakluyt stressed the need to "plant Christian religion," "trafficke," and "conquer" or "doe all three" as reasons for colonization. Protestant colonies could convert the Indians, lessening the influence of Catholic missionaries. Colonies also offered a location where surplus English population could be sent, which in turn would stimulate the home economy, reduce poverty, and create a profitable colonial base in distant lands. As English colonies developed, Spain's hold on the New World would be weakened. More importantly, colonies would strengthen and advertise England's naval and military power. Dispossessing Spain of its territory and subduing the natives could

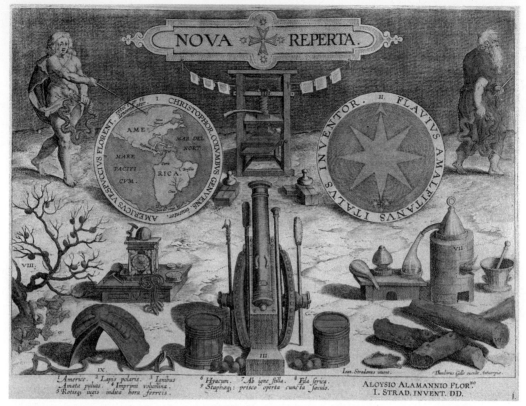

IMAGE 1.1 *Nova Reperta*   This image, from the book *Nova Reperta*, published in Antwerp in 1600, illustrates how Europeans discovered and conquered the New World. Military technology, such as the cannon at center flanked by gunpowder and shot, combined with other technologies, such as printing, as well as trade and shipping to provide Europeans an advantage over Native Americans.

be accomplished only by brute force, such as the English had used in Ireland. Finally, the establishment of North American colonies would provide England with the military training and experience necessary to preserve its detached and insular status within Europe.

The adoption of the compulsory militia, an Anglo-Saxon tradition brought from Elizabethan England to North America, resulted from the military insecurity of the mother country and colony. England was economically unable to maintain a professionally trained regular military force; short-term militia forces could be mustered for common defense in times of emergency. Citizen soldiers did not threaten Englishmen's perceived rights, as militiamen generally upheld societal mores and expectations. But in a dangerous land such as North America, the militia became crucial for defense and protection as long as the threat of Indian attack remained.

By the end of the sixteenth century the Spanish government had claimed the Caribbean and much of the Americas (Portugal controlled Brazil). Yet Spanish settlements and military outposts spanned too much territory for the state to control effectively. A limited Spanish military presence allowed English seadogs such as Francis Drake, John Hawkins, Richard Grenville, and others to prey on Spanish commerce by raiding poorly defended outposts and attacking the annual treasure fleet. These activities revealed Spanish weaknesses in the New World and also drove Spain and England to war.

Englishmen who traveled to North America came with preconceived and prejudiced views of the native inhabitants that they had learned from the Spanish. Although the Europeans believed that Indians had descended from Adam and Eve just like themselves, most Englishmen saw them as godless, wild savages. They worshiped idols and multiple gods, which the Christians abhorred. But English colonists soon learned they had to rely on these "savages" for food and supplies, and the degree of cooperation between the two groups ultimately determined English success or failure. If peaceful relations prevailed, English settlements might succeed, freeing colonists to focus on conquering the wilderness. If mistrust and prejudice triumphed, English settlements failed, as they did on Roanoke Island. As such, most Englishmen followed Hakluyt's prescription for establishing colonies by trying to win the Indians' hearts and souls for Christianity, control them economically through trade, and, if all else failed, conquer them with force. This formula generally served the English well during the seventeenth and eighteenth centuries.

A FOOTHOLD IN AMERICA

Twenty years passed before the English attempted to plant another outpost in North America. During the interlude sea captains scouted North American waters and reported on the raw natural bounty they found there. Yet the war with Spain, which ended in 1603, and Raleigh's commercial failure and imprisonment discouraged risky individual investments in a distant and hostile wilderness. By 1600 English merchants had decided to limit individual risk by creating opportunities for cooperative investments in colonial enterprises. Having many investors provide small amounts of capital greatly reduced the risk of individual financial failure. It also gave an enterprise monopoly rights while permitting the accumulation of sizable pools of capital. The key for these joint-stock endeavors was their ability to turn a profit for their investors and defend their holdings. North America offered a suitable climate, a source of indigenous labor, and raw materials, including potential reserves of precious metals.

Two merchant groups, one from London and the other from Plymouth and Bristol, invested funds in such an enterprise and convinced King James I to issue a charter and land patent for New World territory. Since these companies planned to develop commerce by peopling North American lands with English subjects, James I believed his Privy Council should supervise this venture. Once vested with this authority, the Privy Council created a seven-person Resident Council to oversee the investment in North America. While the king's charter did not permit settlers to trade with any other European nation, it provided them the same rights as all Englishmen—for example, like their brethren in England, they could possess land by paying a small annual fee or quitrent to the king. The charter also provided the settlers with broad powers, including the authority to develop all the lands within the territory, to mine for precious metals, and to defend their colony and expel foreign intruders.

JAMESTOWN

In December 1606 the London Company sent to North America three ships carrying 105 men under the leadership of Christopher Newport. The expedition had economic motivations, but its inclusion of forty soldiers reveals the danger the Englishmen perceived the Spaniards and natives to represent. Four months later the ships entered the Chesapeake Bay and sailed up the James River (named after King James) in search of a location for a town, stockade, and fields for cultivation. Seeking a place that had sea access and could be easily defended against attack, the settlers landed on a pear-shaped peninsula connected to the mainland by a very narrow neck. The men immediately built a stockade and settlement that they called James Fort. Located some sixty miles from the Bay, the peninsula had water access and natural defenses, as well as cleared ground for agriculture. The settlers did not know that high tide submerged one-third of the peninsula and that much of the remaining land was swampy and low-lying, making the area prone to disease. During the summer months this part of the river also became contaminated with seawater, and those who drank from it suffered salt poisoning.

JAMESTOWN, 1607–1612

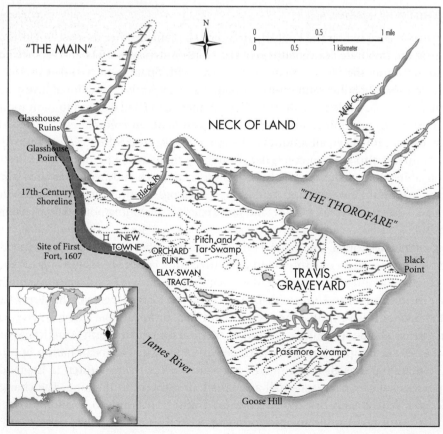

MAP 1.1   Jamestown, 1607–1612

IMAGE 1.2 Fort at Jamestown The Fort at Jamestown, as it may have appeared in 1607, had a palisade and faced the river to protect against passing ships.

Since most of the Englishmen had limited knowledge about fishing or surviving in a wilderness, they found themselves dependent on the Pamunkey Indians. Their chief, Powhatan, had forged a confederation of thirty-one tribes in the region, and early trade connections forged between the Pamunkey and the English reinforced his desire to absorb the white men and make them dependent on the confederation. This trade also further exacerbated the Englishmen's unwillingness to plant and tend crops. The Jamestown settlers had poor work habits and misunderstood their role in this perceived economic-military expedition. As soldiers, they would perform military service, but they were unwilling to do manual labor.

The company's directive to turn a profit reinforced the men's aversion to labor. After the settlers constructed crude huts and a stockade, Newport took the ships to the Caribbean to seek out a water route to the East. Those who remained at Jamestown searched for precious metals or an easily secured and exportable cash crop. Twenty-seven-year-old Captain John Smith led a party inland along the James River in search of these commodities but did not venture too deeply because of reports about hostile Indians beyond the fall line. During the following months Smith explored the region but never found a water route to the East or precious metals. By September 1607 half of the settlers had died from starvation or disease.

Smith became the colony's savior. The son of a farmer, he had studied to become a merchant before running away to a soldier's life. By age twenty he had fought with the Protestants in the Dutch revolt against Spain and with the Hapsburg army against the Ottoman Turks. The Ottomans had captured him in Hungary, marched him some 500 miles to Turkey, and imprisoned him as a slave. Smith reportedly escaped by seducing the mistress of his master and then killing his captor, stealing a horse, and riding hundreds of miles to Christian lines in southeastern Europe. Hired by the London Company as a mercenary, Smith possessed the military skills the colony needed to succeed.

In December 1607 Smith went up the Chickahominy River to obtain supplies and, according to his own account, was captured by Powhatan's warriors. Then, as Powhatan prepared to execute Smith with a club, the chief's favorite daughter, Pocahontas, threw herself on Smith, saving him. Smith maintained he had been on the verge of death, but modern theories suggest that the so-called clubbing represented an elaborate adoption ceremony in which Powhatan brought Smith into his chiefdom—much like the European tradition of knighting men to gain their fealty and support. As a result of the ceremony linking Smith and the Englishmen to him, Powhatan generously supplied the white men with food and permitted them to remain within his lands. The Englishmen did not realize to what extent they depended on the hospitality of Powhatan and the Indians.

In January 1608 Jamestown burned, leaving the Englishmen without protection. When new recruits arrived from England in the spring, only thirty-five of the original settlers remained. The arrival of supplies and people seemed providential, yet reality set in when the survivors realized rats from the ships had eaten or fouled much of the grain the vessels carried. Additional people also further strained the colony's already inadequate food supply. Had it not been for Smith's ability to secure food from the Indians, the Jamestown settlement would have collapsed. During the fall of 1608 Smith implemented a strict military regimen for the colony's survival—those who did not work would not eat. He had the settlers rebuild Jamestown's defenses, dig deeper wells to replace the colony's brackish water supply, plant subsistence crops for a dependable food supply, and harvest a shipment of timber for export to England.

Smith also launched a forceful policy of intimidation designed to realign the balance of power with the Indians. He demanded that the Indians provide the English food and agree to peace. When Powhatan or other Indians refused, the Englishmen burned Indian homes and fields. This aggressiveness reduced incidents of violence as well as the number of deaths from disease and hunger. It also established a precedent of increasing militarization, with the newly instituted Virginia Company sending soldiers and instructing Smith and his successors to occupy the region, subdue the Indians, and force them to contribute food and supplies. This new heavy-handed approach to dealing with the Indians increased tensions within the Chesapeake region, resulting in the First Anglo-Powhatan War (1609–1614).

THE REALITY OF INDIAN WAR

The Indians' traditional style of warfare sought revenge for perceived wrongs and resulted in few deaths. Prior to the European arrival, Indians tended to engage in short-term warfare because their logistical capabilities could not sustain continuous combat. However, the brief nature of these conflicts did not lessen their brutality. Native groups also engaged in formal battles, raids, and both small- and large-scale assaults, each of which served a particular ritualistic or symbolic function.

Small-scale ambushes and raids represented the most common form of Indian warfare. These activities focused on securing food, material goods, livestock, or human trophies to ensure a tribe's economic survival. These engagements usually did not provide the chance to acquire new territory or to assimilate rivals but rather permitted tribes to attack small outlying groups, killing only a few individuals at a time. Even so, these raids constituted a war of attrition against other tribes by devastating outlying communities and slaughtering a higher proportion of women than men.

Small-scale warfare frequently began because of personal or private conflicts yet often grew to a larger scale in an attempt to redirect self-destructive grief associated with the loss of tribal or family members. Mourning wars against other tribes, as practiced by Eastern Woodland Indians such as the Iroquois, attempted to fill the community's perceived spiritual void by capturing a number of enemy warriors equal to those who had been lost in prior conflicts; these warriors were either adopted into the community, tortured to death, or cannibalized in a ritualistic ceremony designed to appropriate the victim's spiritual power. These ceremonies were believed to rejuvenate the community's identity and spirituality while replenishing the number of fighting warriors. Despite a tribe's ability to completely annihilate or assimilate an enemy, these actions generally served to perpetuate a seemingly endless cycle of ambush, murder, and retaliation.

The First Anglo-Powhatan War hinted at the gruesomeness that lay ahead, as both sides tried to intimidate and terrorize the other. Indians painted and disguised themselves and used tactics of deception and surprise. Armed with bows and arrows, they made stealthy attacks on settlements, often fading back into the woods after striking. Indians saw no dishonor in fleeing the field or retreating. In some instances they attacked suddenly with shouts and whoops, frightening Englishmen. Their effective use of wooden and horn clubs and European iron hatchets combined with their knowledge of the woods made Indians extremely dangerous. Sometimes they also demonstrated cunning, using naked women to lure unsuspecting Englishmen into ambush or poisoning food and water that the white men needed to survive.

The English responded with equal brutality, employing violent practices perfected

IMAGE 1.3 John White's Watercolor of an Algonquian Village Much of our knowledge about the Algonquians during the early contact period comes from White's drawings. Here is a small Indian village surrounded and protect by tall wooden stakes.

during the conquest of Ireland. They raided and burned Indian villages and murdered non-combatants such as women and children. In one instance, Englishmen even threw Indian children into a river and shot them while forcing their mothers to watch before burning the mothers to death. Englishmen cruelly decapitated Indian prisoners, plundered much-needed stores of food, and desecrated Indian graves and holy sites in an attempt to demonstrate that Christianity held more power than native religions. For Englishmen, war represented a struggle for survival, and they engaged in total war to ensure their success.

The First Anglo-Powhatan War had a major impact on the Jamestown settlement. Occasionally, foraging parties vanished or returned with substantial casualties and little, if any, food. Although a group of 400 settlers arrived in the early fall of 1609, the increased population intensified the colony's hardships, as food again became scarce. Then, in October, Smith suffered a serious gunpowder burn, forcing him to return to England and leaving the settlement without effective leadership. Unable to feed themselves, the settlers turned to eating dogs, cats, snakes, and even the boiled leather of their shoes. John Smith wrote that one man killed "his wife, salted her, and had eaten part of her before it was knowne." These hardships almost destroyed the weakened English population, sapping morale and fortitude. By June 1610, the colony had only sixty people, and they wanted to return to England. The arrival of additional settlers and new governor Thomas West (better known as Lord De La Warr), who immediately implemented martial law, prevented Jamestown from failing.

The colony grew slowly and stabilized during the next four years. Deputy governor and marshal Thomas Dale forced the settlers to work and worship, and the colony became self-sufficient. By 1612 John Rolfe, who had arrived three years earlier, had crossbred a native tobacco strain with a West Indian variety to produce a sustainable and exportable crop. Rolfe's first shipment of tobacco in 1614 weighed 2,600 pounds; three years later the colony exported more than 20,000 pounds of the leaf. Tobacco placed the colony on a firm financial footing, but it further strained relations between the English and the Indians. The crop quickly depleted minerals from the soil, leaving Englishmen with one alternative—to move to another piece of fertile land. This characteristic of the crop brought the English desire to own or otherwise possess the land on which it grew into further conflict with the Indians' communal ideas about property.

The war subsided as prosperity arrived. In 1613 the English raided an Indian village, capturing Powhatan's favorite daughter Pocahontas and holding her for ransom. Pocahontas's capture, combined with a bold English attack against the large and influential Pamunkey tribe, convinced Powhatan to accept a humiliating peace settlement, ending the First Anglo-Powhatan War.

After the war, food became more plentiful, additional settlers arrived from England, and new settlements sprang up along the James River. The Virginia Company implemented a system of private landownership and relaxed the harsh laws that had governed the colony. The 1619 arrival of a new governor permitted a meeting between the six members of the governor's council and twenty-two burgesses elected by the freemen of the eleven "hundreds," or parishes. This first General Assembly of Virginia (then known as the House of Burgesses) introduced important representative institutions to North America. Unsurprisingly, the first law passed by the General Assembly prohibited Indians from being injured, lest the tenuous peace be broken and warfare resume. During 1619 the Virginia Company also sent ninety women to Jamestown to promote family settlements, and a Dutch ship dropped off twenty Africans, laying the foundation for English enslavement of Africans.

Pocahontas's 1614 marriage to John Rolfe eased tensions, yet relations worsened after her death in 1617 and Powhatan's death the following year. Opechancanough, Powhatan's brother and successor, disliked and distrusted Englishmen and wanted to drive them out of the region before they consumed Indian land, altered the native culture, and exterminated his people. Having experienced the English method of warfare, Opechancanough knew to wait for the appropriate time to strike. In early March 1622, a group of Englishmen murdered Chief Nemattanew, allegedly for killing a white settler and wearing his clothes. When the English refused to apologize or offer compensation for the death, Opechancanough planned coordinated assaults to destroy the colony.

On Good Friday, March 22, 1622, Indians entered English settlements along the James River as they had every day before. Maintaining a peaceful appearance of reverence, they visited white settlements to trade. Some entered family households and ate breakfast with their victims. Then, suddenly and unexpectedly, they attacked all white settlements simultaneously, hacking to death men, women, and children. They annihilated the seventy-five English settlers of Martin's Hundred, located only seven miles from Jamestown. Only a warning from an Indian servant boy saved Jamestown. By day's end, 347 Englishmen, or one-quarter of the settlers, had been killed.

The Second Anglo-Powhatan War (1622–1632), launched in retaliation for the massacre, brought more destruction. After planting the spring crops to ensure a fall harvest, the Englishmen launched a brutal war of attrition. The Virginia Company had sent over settlers and weaponry, and colonial officials dispersed arms to almost every inhabitant. These European weapons, which included armor, swords, pikes, and matchlock muskets, provided the settlers a technological advantage over their numerically superior foe. However, while the Englishmen possessed equipment that protected them, it did not serve them well in rugged terrain or against nimble enemies. Pikes were cumbersome and not useful against dispersed Indian raids or in dense woodlands. Matchlock muskets, which used a slow-burning string soaked in saltpeter to ignite priming powder, inflicted damage when they fired correctly, but roughly one in three shots misfired; they also took at least two minutes to load, and keeping matches lit in windy or wet conditions was difficult. As a result, Indian bows and arrows proved more accurate at a distance, while European swords and hatchets provided an advantage in close quarters.

Large armored parties of Englishmen, supported by their allies the Potomack Indians, destroyed fishing weirs, torched villages and crops, and looted food and valuables. The English waged total war, killing every hostile Indian they encountered. In one instance Captain William Tucker entered an Indian village under a white flag to talk about a peace settlement and exchange prisoners but attacked once the Indians had relaxed. Later, Tucker offered another village a cask of poisoned wine as a gift, which killed some 200 unsuspecting Indians. Tucker and his men decapitated fifty others.

Opechancanough escaped capture and continued fighting. In 1624 an intertribal group of 800 Indians—the largest native force assembled in the region—attacked sixty armored

Englishmen at Pamunkey. For two days, the Indians repeatedly assaulted the colonists before finally retreating in exhaustion. As they withdrew, they were forced to watch the English destroy their cornfields.

This engagement provides a brief snapshot of how the Anglo-Indian wars largely unfolded: a numerically superior Indian force encountered Englishmen with armor and advanced weapons that permitted the latter to survive. While both sides perpetrated unspeakable cruelties during the ten years of intermittent warfare that plagued the region, technology and the English "food fight" destroyed Indians' ability to produce the crops necessary for survival. As a result the region's Indian population fell precipitously from its pre-Jamestown levels.

THE MILITIA TRADITION AND WAR

The spring 1622 surprise attack reminded Englishmen of the danger they faced. The arrival of additional settlers placed the colony on a more stable economic foundation and also greatly reduced the danger. Once the English population surpassed 5,000, the Indians no longer represented a numerically superior foe. To protect further their position, during the 1630s the English built a system of fortifications stretching up the James River north to the York River, and also established a militia company for each of Virginia's eight counties. The militia became the primary form of defense for the isolated colony, with every able-bodied adult male having a compulsory military obligation.

Militia members participated in periodic musters at which attendance was mandatory; those who did not attend suffered heavy fines. Some militiamen received exemptions from service based on their occupations, but otherwise all men between the ages of eighteen and sixty were expected to provide and maintain their own weapons. Colonial laws required a well-armed populace to defend their territory. During times of peace, musters occurred only four times a year, but when threats increased, they occurred more frequently. In 1642, for example, Virginia's governor called for a threefold increase in militia training because of tense Indian relations. Once Englishmen subdued coastal areas and moved farther inland, the militia declined in importance in established areas, relegated to the status of a social and political organization. Though each English colony had its own militia, they bore little resemblance to each other, varying as much as the colonies themselves.

Militia leadership came from the upper class, and officers generally also held political appointments. This cross-institutional leadership integrated politics and the military and reinforced local society. The militia's primary obligation was to maintain security at home, and most legislatures forbid their operation outside of colonial boundaries. This restriction fragmented cross-colony military organization, but it ensured that no single ruler—king or governor—could control the military. It also marked a profound shift in the colonies' political paradigm. Governors originally had been granted executive and military power by the king, but gradually representative assemblies used the power of appropriations, including military expenditures, to check executive power. This trend laid the foundation for civilian control over the military, an arrangement that flowered during the period preceding the American War for Independence.

ISSUES IN MILITARY HISTORY

AN AMERICAN WAY OF WAR

Is there an American way of war? In the early seventeenth century, colonial Americans struggled with an environment and peoples they did not understand. Given the uncertainties of daily life, they took whatever action they deemed necessary to survive. In his classic study *The American Way of War*, Russell Weigley contends that Americans' style of war focused on achieving a crushing military victory over their opponents. The grinding strategy of attrition and sheer weight of numbers overwhelmed the need for tactical or strategic brilliance. Certainly, during the colonial era, the elimination of an opponent was far more important than strategic considerations. Moreover, Americans considered war an alternative to the bargaining process, and their concept of war focused on winning battles and campaigns. Generally, Americans did not try to transform their victories into strategic successes, a tendency that demonstrates that their concept of war focused on a way of battle rather than a way of war.

Max Boot's *Savage Wars of Peace* contends that Americans also practiced another sort of war that did not entail the complete overthrow of an opponent. American small wars—such as virtually all of the colonial wars, the Boxer Rebellion, the Philippine insurrection, and interventions in Bosnia and Kosovo—were more numerous than major conflicts and thus deserve inclusion in the definition of an American way of war. Rather than seeking to achieve decisive victory, these wars often sought to inflict punishment, ensure protection, achieve pacification, and/or benefit from profiteering. Boot builds his concept of the American way of war around modern characteristics such as speed, surprise, maneuverability, and flexibility. And while these characteristics are promoted by the Department of Defense today, they certainly were also significant during the colonial era, when they determined the outcome of almost all colonial encounters.

Both Weigley's and Boot's ideas, however, confuse winning campaigns or small-scale actions with winning wars—a problem that confronts the defense industry today. Plans focus primarily on winning battles, and planners move hardware, personnel, and weapons across a global battlefield trying to prepare for all contingencies. Certainly, before the Seven Years' War and the American War for Independence, operations focused on securing unrelated small-scale victories; strategic outcomes were seen as of little importance.

From the colonial era to the present, the American way of war has been little more than a way of battle. Early operations focused on destroying Indians and providing local protection rather than any larger strategic implications. Outnumbered and ill-prepared, colonists met the cruelties of Indian warfare with brutal tactics and a destructive, unlimited form of war—what John Grenier has termed the "first way" of war—that persisted and defined American warfare throughout the nineteenth century. Current and future asymmetrical warfare most likely will take Americans back to that first destructive way of war, which strives for battlefield victories rather than strategic success. It seems likely to remain an American way of battle.

Militia officers, who were generally elected by the men in their ranks, commanded companies, ranging from 50 to 200 men, which became the basic tactical unit. In the New England colonies, which were settled later than Virginia, compact towns formed their own companies, while the sparsely populated southern colonies often had countywide companies. Yet as each region grew in population, militia companies evolved from infantry-only outfits to units encompassing both cavalry and infantry, an expansion that increased their capabilities for fighting Indians on the frontier. Special units raised for frontier service reserved a position of importance in colonial society until the Indian threat had been completely eliminated.

By the early 1640s the English population of Virginia had increased to 8,000, and settlements had moved west of the fall line. New settlements had also sprung up on the Charles, Rappahannock, and Potomac rivers, further squeezing Indians from their traditional lands. Now almost 100 years old, an infirm and blind Opechancanough reiterated that the Indians must eliminate the English or lose forever their culture and way of life. Hearing that the English were engaged at home in a civil war, he planned a surprise attack, knowing that the Virginians would not receive support from abroad. As he had done in 1622, the old chief unleashed his warriors in March 1644 with exacting vengeance, killing more than 500 colonists in three days. While this attack resulted in more English deaths than had ever before occurred in the region and the complete elimination of several English outposts, Opechancanough's warriors only killed one-sixteenth of the Englishmen. Twenty years of growth, superior technology, and an organized militia and system of fortifications had created an English advantage.

The Third Anglo-Powhatan War (1644–1646) completely destroyed the Indians as an effective counter to English growth in Virginia. After initial Indian attacks, Governor William Berkeley rallied local Englishmen, who brutally retaliated, torching Indian towns and crops and killing or selling Indian men, women, and children into Caribbean slavery. The English attacks focused on driving Indians from the region, and by fall, most of the area had been subdued. Opechancanough, who had been captured and imprisoned in Jamestown, was stabbed by one of his guards. Afterward, the English sought out isolated pockets of Indian resistance, killing and enslaving their inhabitants to ensure that the Indians never rose again. By October 1646 Chief Necotowance had sued for peace, surrendering all the lands south of the York River and east of the fall line to the English. Future Anglo-Indian trade was limited to selected frontier forts, and neither group was permitted to enter the other's territory. This tenuous peace persisted for thirty years, lasting until 1676.

This conflict revealed a pattern that would be seen in other regions of North America as well. Initially, both Europeans and Indians valued trade and peace. But as the English population increased, the settlers needed and wanted more lands and viewed unused Indian lands as available. Violent Indian responses prompted equally brutal English counters, with conflict escalating as both sides resorted to untold viciousness. A growing English population armed with more potent weapons overcame surprise attacks and relegated Indians to subservient positions. Less than forty years after the founding of Jamestown, much of Virginia was dotted with English towns and villages. At the same time, surviving Indians were driven into the homelands of other tribes, initiating a domino effect whose impact would be felt during the following decades.

PRAYING FOR PEACE AND PROVIDENTIAL PROTECTION

Englishmen did not establish a permanent settlement along the shores of New England until thirteen years after the Jamestown settlement. In 1620 a group of forty-one Pilgrims and sixty-one other refugees fled from Holland and England aboard the *Mayflower*, seeking to escape religious persecution. The group had formed a joint-stock company and secured a land patent from the London branch of the Virginia Company, and it sought a location for a settlement where the Anglican Church could not dictate its members' beliefs. The Pilgrims, or Puritan Separatists, believed that the Anglican Church could not be redeemed from its corruption and unscriptural popish rituals and observances, and they called for the public severing of all ties with the Church of England and the establishment of an autonomous congregation. The Anglican Church and King James considered Pilgrim dissenters enemies of the state and held their ideas to be heretical. They declared that the Pilgrims must accept the divine right of the king and subservience of the church to the king and state or suffer the consequences. Economic and religious persecution had already driven many separatists from England to Holland. By 1620 many Pilgrims had realized that they had to travel to the uncertainty of America to find religious freedom and preserve their English heritage.

PILGRIM SEPARATISTS

On November 19, the *Mayflower* reached Cape Cod, and two days later the Pilgrims landed near present-day Provincetown. Before going ashore, the forty-one adult males entered into the formal Mayflower Compact, in which they agreed to abide by laws made by leaders of their choosing. Since they had landed outside the jurisdiction of any organized company or government, the drafters of the compact established a political corporation and structure that functioned as a democracy for stockholders but subjected them to royal authority. Five weeks later the Pilgrims landed at a place that John Smith had called Plymouth. The site had a deepwater harbor for ships, freshwater for drinking, and a nearby hill for a defensible fortress.

Most Pilgrims and Puritans who arrived in New England believed in *vacuum domicilium*, or the idea that they could appropriate vacant Indian property because the native inhabitants had not developed or used the land as God commanded. Indians had cleared the site for crops yet had not occupied the area, because two years earlier a European epidemic had wiped out most of their population. Their absence meant that the Pilgrims faced fewer obstacles than had the Virginians.

After building a crude fort and huts for shelter, the Pilgrims worked to develop cordial relations with local Indians. This proved difficult, because many tribes had previously experienced problems with Englishmen, who had kidnapped their boys and women, stolen their food, pillaged their valuables, cheated them in trade, and even killed them when transactions did not go as expected. Europeans had also introduced diseases such as smallpox, yellow fever, and typhoid fever for which the Indians had no immunity and that quickly spread with catastrophic results.

When the Pilgrims initially landed on Cape Cod in November, hostile Nauset Indians had tried to drive them and their lethal diseases away. Afterwards, the Pilgrims were surprised when the Wampanoag Indians of the Plymouth area treated them with respect and courtesy, partly because of effective communication between the two groups. Samoset and Squanto, the last surviving members of the Pawtuxet tribe, which had been decimated by disease, had been taken by a passing English ship years before, and they both spoke English.

The Pilgrims believed that the presence of English-speaking Indians in North America was the result of divine intervention. Samoset and Squanto taught the Pilgrims how to cultivate corn, how to fish, and how to tap maple trees for syrup, yet half of the Pilgrims still died during the winter.

By spring 1621 Massasoit, the sachem, or chief, of the Wampanoags, had chosen to ally with the Pilgrims rather than eliminate them. Massasoit saw the Pilgrims as a trading partner and ally against the more powerful Narragansetts to the west and the Massachusetts peoples to the north. Successfully playing on the Pilgrims' fears after Opechancanough's 1622 surprise attack in Virginia, Massasoit convinced them that the Massachusetts had planned a similar attack against Weymouth. Pilgrim soldier Miles Standish invited Wituwamat, the Massachusetts warrior who had reportedly planned the attack, to a feast at Weymouth. When the Indians appeared, Standish and his soldiers killed Wituwamat and several of his companions. Standish ordered that Wituwamat's severed head be taken to Plymouth as a warning to other Indians of what deceit might bring.

While this violent attack obviously worked to the benefit of the Pilgrims, it helped the Massachusetts as well. The preemptive strike, combined with an epidemic outbreak that further devastated the tribe, convinced them to pursue a policy of accommodation with the Englishmen, creating an environment of trust and permitting them to confront with English assistance their enemies the Tarrantines and Abenakis, who then inhabited present-day Maine and New Hampshire.

PURITAN CITY ON A HILL

A new wave of settlers called Puritans began arriving in New England in June 1630, greatly strengthening the English position in the region. These nonconformists were theological disciples of John Calvin who came to America to await the reform of the Church of England or the second coming of Christ. Wanting to protect themselves from church corruption, they fled England during 1630 to what Puritan governor John Winthrop called "a city upon a hill." By 1643 more than 16,000 Puritans had migrated, forming twenty towns throughout the region. This "Great Migration" greatly impacted the fate of the southern New England Indians.

In 1620 Massasoit had allied with the Pilgrims, and later the Massachusetts Indians decided to do likewise. It was into this region of stability that the Puritans flooded after 1630. But as additional Puritans arrived, they expanded even farther the boundaries of English settlement. New towns appeared at Boston, Medford, Watertown, Dorchester, Lynn, Roxbury, Salem, and elsewhere to the west and south. The absence of hostile Indians permitted the Puritans to concentrate on enforcing their own brand of religious orthodoxy, driving out perceived heretics such as Roger Williams and Anne Hutchinson.

The continued tide of Puritan settlement inevitably brought conflict, as English colonists pushed Massachusetts and Narragansetts from their lands. These tribes then spread into Pequot territory in southeastern Connecticut. By the mid-1630s the Dutch New Netherland colony, which had established a settlement at present-day Hartford on the Connecticut River, was also squeezing the Pequots from the west. Though newcomers to the area,

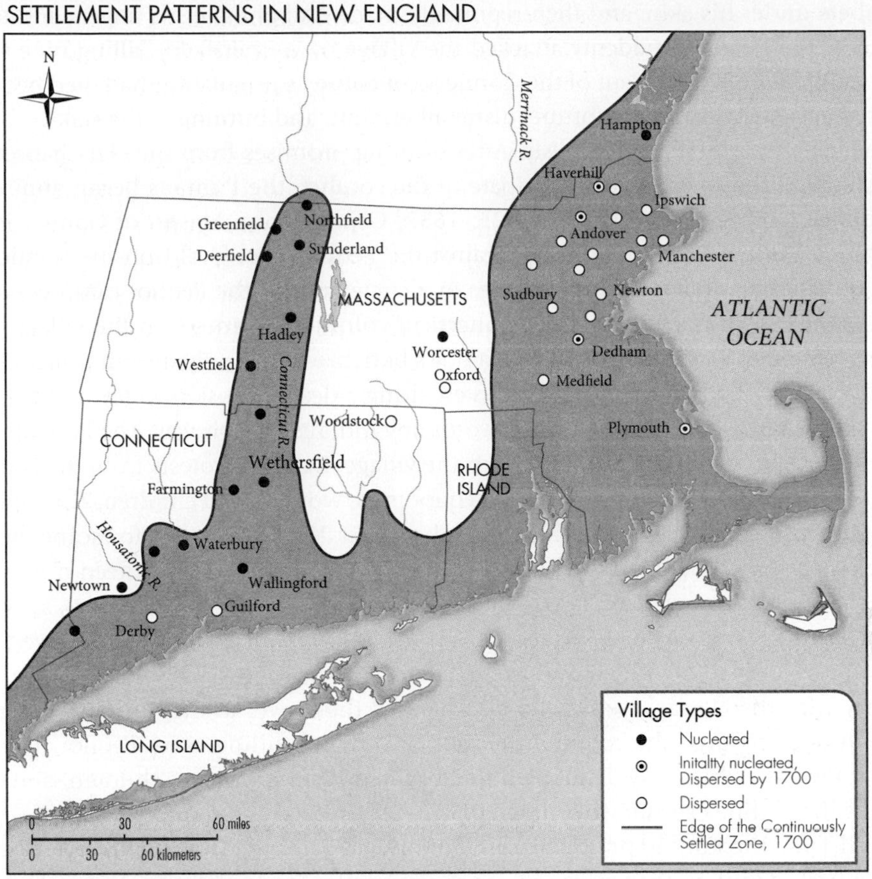

SETTLEMENT PATTERNS IN NEW ENGLAND

MAP 1.2 Settlement Patterns in New England

Pequots threatened to control the local production and trade of wampum (strings of white and purple shell beads), angering the Narragansetts and the region's other tribes.

THE PEQUOT WAR

The Pequot War (1636–1637) began with the 1634 murder of Virginian John Stone and eight English traders. The Pequots had promised to pay an indemnity of wampum and skins and to hand over the murderers, but they never did so. When the Pequots killed and mutilated John Oldham's body on Block Island in 1636, Puritan officials dispatched ninety armed volunteers under John Endicott to apprehend the killers.

The expeditionary force entered Pequot territory but found that the Indians had fled into the swamps and thickets. Endicott burned their villages and crops, hoping to lure them into an engagement. Instead, the Pequots attacked numerous settlements along the frontier and besieged the Puritan outpost of Saybrook at the mouth of the Connecticut River. During the Saybrook siege the Indians publicly tied to a stake one captured Puritan, flayed him, placed hot embers under his skin, and then reportedly made hatbands of his fingers and toes. In April 1637 the Pequots suddenly attacked the village of Wethersfield, killing nine settlers. By the spring of 1637 5 percent of the Connecticut colony's population had died because of Pequot attacks, most suffering torture, dismemberment, and burning at the stake.

The Puritans retaliated ferociously. After securing promises from the Narragansetts and Mohegans that they would not participate in the conflict, the Puritans began annihilating the Pequots. During the night of May 25, 1637, Captain John Mason of Connecticut led a combined Puritan and Indian force against the Pequot stronghold on the Mystic River. Mason quietly positioned his Indian allies in a circle around the Pequot camp while militiamen from the Massachusetts and Connecticut colonies advanced on the village. As the attackers nervously approached at dawn, a dog's bark broke the early morning silence, alerting the Pequots. The English quickly attacked, firing a deadly musket volley into the sleepy village. Other Englishmen hacked with swords any Indians in their way. The Pequots' determined resistance convinced Mason to burn the village. Despite protests from the Narragansetts, the Puritans burned alive some 500 Pequot men, women, and children. The Mohegans and Englishmen surrounding the village killed another 200 as they tried to escape the blaze.

The butchering of 700 hundred men, women, and children within fifteen minutes represented a new form of warfare. Two Englishmen perished (one by friendly fire), and twenty suffered wounds. Pequot chief Sassacus and some warriors escaped to country west of the Hudson River, only to be turned over to the English by the Mohawks. Some Pequots sought sanctuary with the Narragansetts, who also handed them over to the Puritans. English patrols with dogs scoured the countryside, rooting out and killing every Pequot they could find. The Puritans ultimately distributed the captured Pequot women, children, and elderly to other tribes, while executing warriors.

By fall 1637 the Puritan policy of annihilation had succeeded, as the Pequot tribe virtually disappeared (although they reappeared as a federally recognized tribe during the 1980s). Thereafter other tribes could not ignore the unrestrained barbarism exercised by Englishmen. Could this ruthlessness also be employed against them? Likewise, Puritans wondered if Indians would unexpectedly attack their settlements, as had occurred in Virginia in 1622. Believing that they were engaged in a violent life-and-death struggle with a savage enemy, the Puritans insisted that God expected no less than victory, regardless of the methods employed or consequences. Their victory over the Pequots brought peace to the region for the next forty years.

A RISING DISCONTENT

Englishmen traveled to North America during the seventeenth century for many reasons. Some pursued unrealistic economic opportunities, while others sought religious freedom they could not attain at home. Others still left England because of political uncertainty after the new Stuart monarchs attempted to increase their authority over local institutions, introducing different systems of taxation, new poor laws, and even modified regulations for militia service and leaving many excluded, marginalized, and unhappy with the newly established order. Yet these immigrants soon found that the new colonial order also limited their access to governmental decisions, economic opportunities, and social interactions. And like their fellow countrymen at home, they, too, demanded redress. Their claims had democratic implications.

THE ENGLISH CIVIL WAR

During the period from 1640 to 1690 the turmoil and uncertainty that characterized England filtered across the Atlantic to America, greatly influencing the development of the colonies. An uprising of Parliament and the Puritans against King Charles I's heavy-handed rule during the 1640s resulted in a bloody civil war in England and the king's execution in 1649. The overthrow of arbitrary rule and a focus on the preservation of law and order emphasized the importance of local authority, an agenda that resonated strongly with colonials. Oliver Cromwell's conservative and militaristic Commonwealth of the 1650s brought the Puritans to power within England and the colonies, and permitted colonials to redistribute power and privilege. However, the Restoration during the 1660s led to the reinstatement of the previous royal colonial administrations. Throughout these fluctuations, colonists protected their rights as Englishmen, even as bloodshed occurred in Maryland and during Bacon's Rebellion and Metacom's Uprising in 1676.

Maryland had been founded as a haven for persecuted English Catholics, but few ever moved to the colony. Instead, Puritans and other Protestants seized its fertile tobacco lands. Proprietor Lord Baltimore, Cecilius Calvert, insisting on religious coexistence, sent his younger brother Leonard to the colony in March 1634 with the first group of Catholic refugees. Leonard immediately built a fort, chapel, and storehouse and made alliances with the local Yaocomicos and Piscataways, both of whom saw the English as potential counterbalances to the neighboring Susquehannocks. Lord Baltimore's proprietary power allowed him to initiate all legislation, and he tried to promote cooperation between Catholics and Protestants. In 1638 he permitted a representative assembly, but conflict soon broke out. During the mid-1640s Virginian William Claiborne seized control of Maryland's Kent Island. Then, in 1644–1645, Protestant privateer Richard Ingle brought the English Civil War to Maryland when he attacked the colony's shipping and plundered St. Mary's.

By March 1655 Puritans in the northern portion of the colony were demanding a commonwealth from which both Catholics and Anglicans would be barred. Lord Baltimore responded by appointing Protestant governor William Stone, who marched north to oppose the Puritans with a religiously mixed proprietary army, only to be defeated at the Battle of Severn River— the only engagement of the English Civil War fought in North America. Afterwards, four of Stone's proprietary soldiers were executed, while the others fled or paid heavy fines. Political instability reappeared during the Restoration in 1660 and 1661, when Maryland's governor tried unsuccessfully to replace proprietary government with rule by the lower assembly.

BACON'S REBELLION

Throughout the English Civil War, Virginia remained a bastion of royal support. Governor William Berkeley assembled 1,000 armed men to challenge the Cromwellian fleet that arrived at Jamestown in 1652 to force the colony's submission. To avoid needless bloodshed, the colonists agreed to accept the supremacy of the General Assembly and the removal of the royal governor. Afterward, the colony suffered from the economic restrictions of the Navigation Act of 1651, which prohibited Dutch transport of Virginia tobacco. With the Stuart Restoration in 1660, Virginia resumed its status as a royal colony, and Berkeley returned as governor, remaining in power until 1677.

Berkeley's policies during the 1660s and early 1670s left the colony virtually defenseless. While enriching his supporters, his Indian trading policy encouraged marauding tribes from Pennsylvania and Maryland to encroach upon the defensive perimeter of forts that protected Virginia's Jamestown peninsula. Berkeley also levied a heavy tax on the population to build forts along Virginia's frontier, but the commonwealth was unable to protect the increasing number of English settlers who migrated west. Berkeley also failed to protect Jamestown from a seaborne invasion, and Dutch privateers sank eleven Virginia merchantmen in July 1673 during the third Anglo-Dutch War.

The 1660s and early 1670s also saw an increasing restlessness among Virginia's growing class of laborers, servants, slaves, and small farmers. Once Berkeley resumed his governorship, he implemented new licenses, duties, and taxes. He refused to offer tax breaks even after the tobacco market entered a depression, cattle plagues during the early 1670s killed off most the colony's herds, and a terrible 1675 drought destroyed most of its corn crop. Rumored servant uprisings in York and Gloucester counties illustrated the explosive social discontent that had spread throughout Virginia, prompting Berkeley to acknowledge that most of the colony's inhabitants were poor, indebted, and armed, and as such threatened the autocratic and entrenched governor.

In 1675 Indian-English conflict revealed the colony's defenselessness and exposed its social tensions. During the spring Doeg Indians from the Potomac River valley killed an overseer on Thomas Mathew's Maryland plantation when they tried to seize hogs as payment. Colonel George Mason, Captain George Brent, and Stafford County militia pursued the Doegs, killing a chief and ten others during a parley in September. Failing to distinguish Doegs from other Indians, Mason and his troops later killed friendly Susquehannocks. The Indians retaliated during the winter of 1675–1676, killing thirty-six colonists and forcing Virginia and Maryland to muster their militias to prevent the Indians from creating a confederacy that might join with Metacom (King Philip) in the north. Colonel John Washington (George's great-grandfather) and Major Isaac Allerton led nearly 1,000 militiamen to Matapoint Creek, where they besieged a Susquehannock and Doeg fort. When five chiefs emerged to parley, the colonists executed them. The Susquehannocks, now fully committed to war, ravaged the frontier, striking as far south as the falls of the James River and killing some 300 Virginians.

Berkeley did not want the conflict to escalate because it would bring economic hardship to the region. He instructed frontier settlers to relocate to fortified stronghouses, where they would be less vulnerable and ordered all shipments of arms to the Indians stopped and English vigilante activity curtailed. He also continued trading with friendly Indians, hoping to maintain their neutrality. Most controversially, he called for the construction of nine forts along the headwaters of Virginia's rivers, a proposal that infuriated critics, who argued that the forts were only intended to protect the governor's fur trade.

COLONIZING THE CHESAPEAKE, 1607–1700

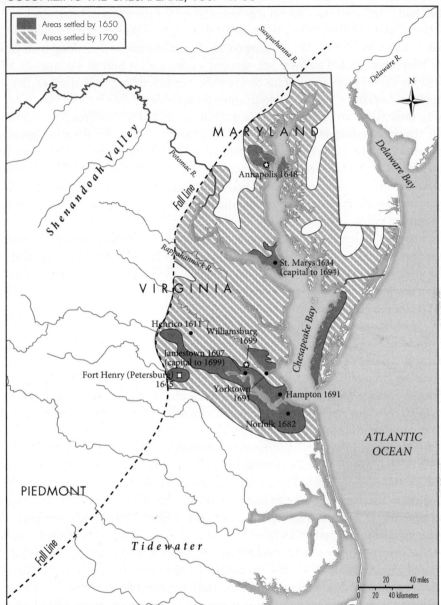

MAP 1.3 Colonizing the Chesapeake, 1607–1700

Frontiersmen believed Berkeley's plans did little to protect them from an attack and lusted for revenge. Rumors about a large number of Indians moving downriver toward Jamestown prompted militiamen to ask Governor Berkeley to send men to meet the enemy in an uninhabited area. When Berkeley refused, Nathaniel Bacon, Jr., a recently arrived planter whose overseer had been killed by Indians, led militiamen westward.

The troublesome twenty-seven-year-old Bacon had fled England rather than go to prison. His father had purchased the Cambridge-educated young man two plantations (an operating tobacco farm with slaves in the Tidewater region and another on the frontier), which established him as a gentleman. His wealthy cousin Nathaniel Bacon, Sr., along with Governor Berkeley, his second cousin by marriage, secured a position for him as a councilor. Even so, the ambitious Bacon spent most of his time on the frontier, where he and other planters felt increasingly excluded from power, opportunity, and privilege.

During their westward march, Bacon's militiamen joined with a group of friendly Ocaneechees, who tracked down and killed a group of Susquehannocks. After disagreeing over the division of spoils, a conflict that resulted in the death of several militiamen, Bacon's men butchered the Ocaneechee men, women, and children. Governor Berkeley angrily proclaimed Bacon a rebel because he had defied orders and was risking a full-scale Indian war. The governor also attempted to defuse the discontent by calling new elections for the first time in fourteen years.

With fifty men, Bacon marched for Jamestown, only to confront a small force sent out by Governor Berkeley. After a brief meeting Bacon agreed to disband his group, learned that he could not resume his previous position as a councilor, and then appeared before the Council to ask for a pardon for his offenses. In early June, he also learned he had been elected to the House of Burgesses to represent upland Henrico County. His populist support allowed him to resume his campaign on the frontier and call for renewed attacks against the Indians.

The newly seated House of Burgesses, trying to promote democratic government while undermining Berkeley's autocratic base of support, immediately voted for an aggressive Indian war and named Bacon commander of the expedition. Berkeley, though, denied Bacon his command. Meanwhile Bacon recruited some 400 men, who again marched on Jamestown to confront the governor. Facing an armed and hostile opposition, Berkeley acquiesced to the demands for war.

Now freed to take action, Bacon recruited more than 1,500 men and marched to Virginia's frontier. As he did, hostile Indians vanished into the woods, avoiding battle. The expedition did capture sixty warriors and kill two dozen women and children. Governor Berkeley, who had retreated to the Eastern Shore of the Chesapeake Bay, tried to raise troops and secure naval support and in July 1676 again declared Bacon a rebel. Rallying his recruits at Middle Plantation, located only a few miles from Jamestown, Bacon proclaimed Berkeley the traitor and marched triumphantly into the village as the governor and his supporters fled. There, Bacon issued a manifesto or "Declaration of the People" in which he decried Berkeley's cronyism, unfair taxation, monopolization of the Indian trade, and inadequate defense of the colony. He also demanded that councilors surrender or have their estates seized. Finally, he initiated a potential class war by calling for freemen (white property owners) to elect a new assembly to begin meeting in early September.

Bacon soon resumed his Indian war, marching into Dragon Swamp to attack friendly Pamunkeys. During his absence Berkeley returned to Jamestown to rally his supporters. On September 18, 1676, Bacon triumphantly marched into Jamestown, used the wives of Berkeley's supporters as human shields, and dared the governor's ships to use their artillery. The following day, his men burned the town, forcing the governor and his supporters to flee again. Bacon then offered freedom to all servants and slaves who agreed to take up arms and join his cause, and a considerable number seized advantage of the lawlessness to exact revenge. He had used his charisma to mobilize the lower classes against a common Indian foe and then turned their anger and distrust against the governor and his supporters.

In early September, Bacon learned that 2,000 troops from England would arrive shortly in the first deployment of English regular troops to America. If the rumors were true, it was possible that Virginians and other colonials would turn on the royal force, especially if the Crown did not guarantee or protect their rights. Bacon's plans remained vague. Most scholars agree that his actions likely represented a personal conflict with Berkeley rather than a commitment to a nascent movement for liberty and independence, even though he did produce a declaration that essentially fomented class warfare.

But before he could take action, Bacon died suddenly on October 26, 1676, and the movement he had led crumbled by mid-January of the following year. Prominent supporters switched their loyalty to Governor Berkeley, providing the support he needed to regain control. In January a sizable English fleet arrived with more than 1,100 troops and three commissioners, who planned to restore royal authority. King Charles II had also named Commissioner Herbert Jeffreys as Berkeley's replacement. Bacon's supporters received royal pardons, but Berkeley still rounded up and hanged twenty-three rebels and seized property from several others. The retribution continued until April, when Berkeley surrendered the governorship to Jeffreys. Berkeley returned to England, where the king refused to meet him; he died a few months later in disgrace.

In Virginia, Jeffreys ended the Indian wars, negotiating a treaty that restricted Indians to small tracts of land. He also destroyed their tribal identities, forcing them to work as tenant farmers and manual laborers. However, Charles II had not sent 1,100 soldiers to terminate the Indian war; rather, he sought to restore royal authority to the rebellious colony. The presence of royal troops and warships in Virginia made a vivid impression on the colony, which saw a far higher ratio of soldiers to the colonial population at the time of the rebellion than it did 100 years later during the turmoil leading to the War for American Independence. Thus the Crown made a forceful statement about its intentions in the colonies.

Bacon's Rebellion unleashed unanticipated political, social, and economic changes. It began as a campaign to make slaves out of the Indians but embodied demands by marginalized small planters and frontiersmen for broader rights. Berkeley's cronyism and favoritism had disregarded the growing rift between frontier and Tidewater society. By joining with Bacon, frontiersmen had voiced their concerns in a manner that the governor and the Crown could not ignore. After Bacon's death, his supporters subsequently lost many of the concessions that had been won with violence. Even so, small landholders represented the bulk of Virginia's population and thereafter assumed greater responsibilities within the colony, including expanded militia service to protect against Indian uprisings and slave insurrections. The factionalism that had been so prevalent before the rebellion blurred as great planters and small landholders alike realized they possessed more similarities than differences.

The rebellion also marked a major change in the development of Virginia society. Bacon had fomented a class struggle by enfranchising servants and slaves. Afterward, planters relied more exclusively on slaves, as they could be more easily controlled. The decline in the number of servants coming from England, combined with an abundant supply of inexpensive slaves from the Caribbean and Africa, profoundly changed the long-term demographic makeup of the colony. Before the 1680s most planters had intended to stay in Virginia only a brief time, relying on short-term indentured servants to make money quickly so they could return to England with their wealth. Servants often became competitors once their term of indenture ended, contributing to a growing frontier class. After the uprising, planters began to consider the colony's long-term prospects and invested in slaves as a source of stronger future dividends and profits. As indentured servants became less prevalent and slaves more important, Virginia started transforming from a society with slaves to a slave society. This reorientation wedded politics, society, and economics. Virginia ultimately became a permanent home that had to be protected from hostile Indians and foreign colonial threats, and the colonial militia increasingly became the means of maintaining order and stability.

METACOM'S (KING PHILIP'S) WAR

New England experienced relative peace after the Pequot War of the 1630s, yet the conflict revealed a sobering reality. Surrounded by Native Americans in a hostile land and facing an encroaching Dutch neighbor in the Hudson River Valley, Puritan leaders needed to unify. In May 1643 four Puritan colonies—Massachusetts Bay, Plymouth, Connecticut, and New Haven—formed the United Colonies of New England, or the New England Confederation, to provide collectively for the defense of the region and its inhabitants.

During its first decade of existence the Confederation successfully navigated several crises, including disruptions produced by the English Civil War, Indian threats, and Dutch encroachments. The civil war forced the colonies to protect themselves, and recurring Indian threats during the 1640s and 1650s provided an incentive for the colonies to unite and cooperate in military operations. The resulting Confederation acted as a regional security framework. In 1645 the Narragansetts asked the Confederation for permission to retaliate against an unprovoked Mohegan attack. When the colonists refused the request, the Narragansetts attacked anyway. The Confederation responded to the show of defiance by mobilizing 200 soldiers, who forced the Narragansetts to back down, pay heavy fines, and cede land near the Connecticut–Rhode Island border. A decade later, in 1654, and still against English wishes, the Narragansetts joined with the Eastern Niantics to again attack the Mohegans. This time the Confederation mobilized 300 men to force a quick settlement to the crisis. Both the Narragansetts and the Niantics surrendered lands to the English.

To face the threat of its expansive Dutch neighbor in 1650, the Confederation negotiated with Peter Stuyvesant to produce the Treaty of Hartford, which delineated the boundary between New England and New Netherland (New York). Acknowledging its weaknesses and limited resources when confronting a European power, the Confederation used diplomacy to preserve its position within the region. Without Anglo-Dutch conflict, Indian tribes could not play European competitors against one another or undermine the region's precarious balance of power. Nor could they capitalize on the English preoccupation with the Dutch. Local diplomacy in this instance provided the Confederation a more cost-effective solution than increasing, outfitting, and supplying its militias for operations against New Netherland.

During the next generation, few Dutch settlers immigrated to New Netherland. Meanwhile, the English population doubled from 1660 to 1675, and English settlers encroached on the ancestral homelands and hunting grounds of the Indians of southern Massachusetts and Rhode Island. The Puritans also felt compelled to bring Christianity to these tribes. In fact, missionaries concentrated on tribes that had already become economically dependent on the colonists. Thousands of "praying Indians" acquiesced to Christianity and relocated to villages where they adopted English ways of life. They prayed to the English God, cultivated crops in the European style, and adopted European dress and culture. Yet their assimilation into white culture and acceptance of the European economic system threatened the survival of the New England tribes. They faced a difficult choice: They could relinquish their lands and relegate themselves to positions of servility, or they could sell their lands and move west away from English settlements, placing themselves under the protection of the more powerful Iroquois tribes. Or they could unite and launch a unified pan-Indian attack against the English intruders. Most Wampanoags believed only armed resistance could secure their continued independence.

Metacom (sometimes spelled Metacomet), or King Philip, as the English called him, had witnessed the continued decline of the Wampanoags. His father, Massasoit, had befriended the Pilgrims when they arrived at Plymouth in 1620 and had fought with them afterwards. Massasoit had celebrated the Pilgrims' first harvest festival and shared in their good fortune. In fact, Anglo-Indian relations remained stable until his death in 1661. After he died, Wamsutta, Massasoit's oldest son, became sachem, and during his short-lived rule the influence of the tribe declined. In 1662 Pilgrim officials summoned Wamsutta to Plymouth to question him about a possible Indian uprising; shortly afterward, he mysteriously died. Puritans twice summoned Metacom, who replaced his older brother as sachem, to meetings. During the second meeting in Boston in 1671 the Puritans pressured Metacom into relinquishing the Wampanoags' large stock of weapons and forbid him from selling Wampanoag lands without permission. The sachem acquiesced to English demands only on the condition that the Pilgrims abandon plans to develop the new town of Swansea.

The murder of Christian Indian John Sassamon triggered the events that came to be called Metacom's War. Sassamon had straddled two worlds and two cultures, studying Christianity at Harvard and serving as Metacom's assistant. During the spring of 1675 he told Plymouth officials that the Wampanoags were planning for war against the English. Shortly thereafter he was killed. Pilgrim officials apprehended three Wampanoag warriors, tried them for Sassamon's death, and hanged them in June 1675.

The execution increased the possibility of a general Indian uprising. During the following weeks, young Wampanoag warriors, tired of submitting to the English invaders, retaliated by looting and burning several villages in the Plymouth colony. Their hit-and-run tactics and the English inability to defend against the raids emboldened other tribes to join the conflict, which quickly expanded from Plymouth to Massachusetts Bay, Rhode Island, and Connecticut. By the late summer the Pocomtucks, the Pocassets, the Narragansetts, and even the Nipmucs, whom the English had believed would remain friendly, had joined the movement. Several tribes from the upper Hudson River Valley also reportedly planned to join Metacom's alliance. Instead, the English governor of New York convinced the Mohawks to attack the northern tribes, ending the possibility of an alliance with the Wampanoags.

Puritan militia forces mustered to the frontier at the first sign of violence. During June and July more than 350 soldiers, joined by a number of Indian auxiliaries, moved across the Mount Hope peninsula and into the Pocasset swamp but found few hostile Indians. By fall 1675, almost every New England community had suffered the ravages of war, with Indians destroying 174 settlements stretching from the Merrimack River northeast of Boston south to Plymouth. Before the first snowfall, highly mobile Indian forces descended on the western Connecticut River settlements. These attacks convinced the Puritans to abandon eight communities in western Massachusetts. In the spring of 1676 Metacom and his allies launched coordinated attacks against Medfield and Weymouth, located only twenty miles from Boston and Providence, respectively.

The first successful English response occurred in November 1675, but the victory was only against the neutral Narragansetts, who had not yet decided to join Metacom's cause. Hearing that the Narragansetts had harbored the wives and children of Wampanoag warriors and that they planned to join Metacom early in 1677, the New England Confederation conscripted 1,000 men for a preemptive strike. Unlike the Virginia militia Bacon had commanded, New England law prohibited militia operations outside the colony, forcing community leaders to ask for volunteers and conscript young bachelors deemed not essential to the community's survival and well-being. Commanded by Plymouth governor Josiah Winslow, this army employed a uniquely American style of colonial warfare. Outfitting themselves in thick, close-fitting leather jackets and armed with muskets, the Puritans combined the stealth and ambush tactics of their Indian adversaries with traditional European methods of warfare. They prepared themselves mentally to strike against men, women, children, and the elderly and to burn villages, crops, and anything else Indians needed for the struggle.

After receiving information about a fortified Narragansett base in the middle of the Great Swamp, Winslow's army moved south into Rhode Island. More than 1,000 Indians lived behind the masonry walls of a five-acre city, which they believed was impregnable as a result of its location and fortifications. After a long, cold, and tiring march, the Puritans quietly approached the encampment during the afternoon of December 19, 1675, as the Indians inside prepared dinner. Choosing not to wait until the following morning, Winslow immediately attacked in a disorganized and haphazard fashion. A second assault discovered a gap in the city walls, through which Englishmen poured. Inside, the colonists indiscriminately shot inhabitants, torched wigwams, and destroyed everything in their path. The walls that had protected the Narragansetts now corralled them, preventing their escape. The bloody massacre, similar to the one that had occurred on the banks of the Mystic River forty years earlier, ended shortly before sunset. The Puritans had butchered 600 Narragansett men, women, and children, and many Wampanoags also lay among the dead. English losses numbered only eighty dead or wounded.

The savagery of the English soldiers during the Great Swamp Massacre heightened the war's intensity, as most Indians realized they were fighting not only for their lives, but also for their tribes' existence. In February 1676, the Nipmucks descended on the frontier community of Lancaster, killing every inhabitant except Mary Rowlandson and her three children, and a local minister's wife, who remained a prisoner for the next three months. During her captivity Rowlandson suffered from a lack of food, but the Indians treated her with respect.

Even so, a published account of her ordeal reveals the problems Indians faced during the struggle, recording how the Puritans' destructive war had destroyed winter food supplies, seeds for the spring planting, weapons, and stores.

Indian attacks against outlying frontier settlements and assaults on Providence and Plymouth underscored inherent problems in Puritan society. The Puritans' emphasis on local control and dependence on local militias prevented easy cooperation or unity, even in times of crisis. Many militiamen simply resisted the draft. Plymouth refused to provide soldiers, and Connecticut recalled its militia because of disagreements over the distribution and size of each colony's commitment. Furthermore, as westerners fled east to safety, communities increased taxes because of food shortages and higher prices. Throughout the winter of 1676 English morale waned as Puritans learned of more defeats than victories. Few positive results followed ministers' call for fasting and prayer, which greatly challenged Puritan concepts of identity and purpose. When Puritans did score victories, such as in the Great Swamp Massacre of December 1675, they perpetrated untold atrocities, disemboweling and decapitating their enemies and even exhibiting severed heads as trophies. The struggles of living in a dangerous land and facing deadly threats revealed the Puritans' barbaric tendencies, which contrasted with the hopes and expectations they had as a godly people undertaking a spiritual mission. The war's psychological impact lingered for years.

By the spring 1676 planting season the war had turned in favor of the English. Their destructive war of attrition had disrupted Indian society, leaving the people without food and shelter; women and children suffered particularly. The violent Puritan campaign had also divided tribes, with many Indians deciding to join the colonists as auxiliaries. English fortunes changed almost as soon as these Indian allies appeared. Massachusetts' militiamen slaughtered more than 100 Indians on the Fall River above Deerfield, while Connecticut forces won a similar victory two weeks later. Throughout the spring smaller groups of Indians surrendered without a fight. In early July Connecticut militias killed or captured some 230 Narragansetts without a single casualty.

The fighting slackened during the summer as hordes of hungry and sick stragglers surrendered to the Puritans. Many who chose not to surrender fled to the western tribes, including the Iroquois. By early August, the Puritans had learned of Metacom's location,

IMAGE 1.4 Medallion Presented to Christian Indians During King Philip's War, 1676 Christian Indians served as auxiliaries alongside New Englanders during King Philip's War. Massachusetts Bay officials gave this medallion to Indians for their service during the conflict.

and, disregarding the possibility of an ambush, Plymouth captain Benjamin Church led volunteers and Indian auxiliaries into the swamp near Mount Hope. As they neared Metacom's camp under cover of darkness on August 12, 1676, they found no trap. Metacom had fallen asleep without posting a sentry. Quietly creeping to the edge of the sanctuary, Church and his men stormed the unsuspecting camp. At the sound of gunfire the Indians scurried for safety, but Church's Indian allies slaughtered or captured most of them; only a few escaped. Metacom was shot and killed and, on Church's orders, decapitated and quartered. Church took Metacom's head to Plymouth, where it remained on display for several years.

While most of the fighting had ended, retaliatory violence against Indians continued for months. Militiamen rounded up Indian stragglers, executing most of them. Puritans sold many others, including Metacom's wife and son, into slavery in the West Indies and the Mediterranean and forced some Indian children to become bound servants in New England. Others still were interned on Deer Island near Boston or other reservations, where they suffered great hardships. Through battle, starvation, and disease, the Puritans had eliminated the region's Indian threat and forced the tribes to relinquish their lands. English supremacy had been guaranteed, but not by Puritan military superiority. Instead, exhaustion, starvation, and disease had resulted in thousands of Indian deaths and the loss of their independence.

Though victorious, the Puritans had suffered heavy losses as well. Fifty-two of ninety Puritan towns had been attacked and twelve frontier settlements completely destroyed. Even so, Connecticut escaped most of the ravages of the conflict because of deft use of Indian allies and fortifications inspired by the military revolution in Europe. General frontier development did not again reach its prewar levels until forty years later. More than 500 soldiers, or 1 out of every 15 men of military age, had been killed. Additionally, three times as many civilians died in the conflict as soldiers, with one out of every thirty-five Puritans perishing during the war. Measured proportionally, the death rate for Metacom's War was higher than that of the War for Independence, the American Civil War, or World War II. While limited in scope, this war represented one of the bloodiest and most costly conflicts in American history.

CONCLUSIONS

By the mid-1670s Englishmen had gained an unquestioned foothold on the North American continent and were well on their way to conquering all of the lands east of the Appalachian Mountains. Initially outnumbered and ill prepared, they survived because they met the cruelties of Indian warfare with their own brutal tactics and destructive form of colonial war. They also successfully used their technological advantages of armor, firearms, metal knives, and hatchets to overcome Indian supremacy. More importantly, English immigration during the 1630s and 1640s reshaped the coastal population balance in the Europeans' favor, and incoming Englishmen brought debilitating diseases that ravaged local tribes, with catastrophic results.

The colonial militia evolved to confront the Indian challenge. Assemblies permitted local militia to serve alongside other colonies' units and to pursue Indians across colonial boundaries. Initial defensive efforts fell short. Englishmen developed fortified blockhouses on the frontier to provide places of refuge during crises, but these sites did not offer security for property and homes. Militias also could not protect the frontier when colonists needed them during surprise attacks, thereby failing their theoretical local defense responsibility. Over time, militia companies developed a fighting style better suited to their environment. Instead of relying on the traditional European practice of fighting line abreast, which rarely worked in North American forests, they adopted Indian practices. Englishmen learned to lighten their loads and move quickly, spread their formations to avoid ambush, use the element of surprise, and embrace Indian auxiliaries as their scouts. They employed martial discipline when necessary and also used brutal tactics to survive in an unaccommodating wilderness.

The Indians initially had numerical superiority over the English, but that advantage deteriorated during the second half of the seventeenth century. The Indians' ability to live off the land also decreased as incoming Englishmen took their ancestral hunting grounds, depleted game reserves, and pushed Indians into areas claimed by other tribes. This shifting of tribes set in motion a domino effect that exacerbated intertribal hostilities and prevented Indian groups from unifying or allying. Indians also lacked manpower reserves to replace their losses, which led them to alter their tactics. Instead of concentrating on holding a piece of territory at the expense of numerous deaths, they moved quickly, traversed great distances, and struck their enemy with surprise and ferocity, attempting to discourage the Englishmen by their losses and suffering. However, they never secured the resources, developed the weapons, or produced the supplies that could sustain a successful, prolonged struggle against the Englishmen. In fact, the tribes' initial advantages soon withered, leaving them at the colonists' mercy and ultimately forcing them to assimilate or risk annihilation.

The encounters between Indians and Englishmen in the seventeenth century provided interesting lessons for both groups. More powerful interior tribes adapted to the presence of the European invaders and developed more effective methods to deal with them. By the end of the seventeenth century, Indians had learned to play competing European powers against one another within an intricate system of diplomacy, trade, and coexistence. In turn, the European powers tried to influence North American events by forming alliances with powerful tribes and confederations at the expense of their imperial competitors. The years from 1675 to 1763 witnessed a great and ongoing imperial struggle for dominance in North America, as well as a desperate Indian struggle for survival.

TIMELINE

1585	Establishment of English colony on Roanoke Island
1607	Establishment of English colony at Jamestown, Virginia
1609–1614	First Anglo-Powhatan War
1620	Establishment of Pilgrim colony at Plymouth
1622–1633	Second Anglo-Powhatan War
1636–1637	Pequot War
1640–1688	English Civil War
1644–1646	Third Anglo-Powhatan War
1675–1676	Metacom's War
1676	Bacon's Rebellion

SUGGESTED READINGS

Cave, Alfred A. *The Pequot War*. Amherst: University of Massachusetts Press, 1996.

Chet, Guy. *Conquering the American Wilderness: The Triumph of European Warfare in Colonial New England*. Amherst: University of Massachusetts Press, 2003.

Cress, Lawrence Delbert. *Citizens in Arms: The Army and the Militia in American Society to the War of 1812*. Chapel Hill: University of North Carolina Press, 1982.

Ferling, John. *Struggle for a Continent: The Wars of Early America*. New York: Wiley-Blackwell, 1992.

Gallay, Alan. *The Indian Slave Trade: The Rise of English Empire in the American South, 1670–1717*. New Haven, CT: Yale University Press, 2002.

Grenier, John. *The First Way of War: American War Making on the Frontier, 1607–1814*. New York: Cambridge University Press, 2005.

Jennings, Francis. *The Ambiguous Iroquois: The Covenant Chain Confederation of Indian Tribes with English Colonies from Its Beginnings to the Lancaster Treaty of 1744*. New York: W. W. Norton, 1984.

Lepore, Jill. *The Name of War: King Philip's War and the Origins of American Identity*. New York: Random House, 1998.

Malone, Patrick M. *The Skulking Way of War: Technology and Tactics among New England Indians*. Lanham, MD: Madison Books, 2000.

Shea, William. *The Virginia Militia in the Seventeenth Century*. Baton Rouge: Louisiana State University Press, 1983.

Silver, Peter. *Our Savage Neighbors: How Indian War Transformed Early America*. New York: W. W. Norton, 2008.

Steele, Ian. *Warpaths: Invasions of North America*. New York: Oxford University, 1994.

Warren, Jason W. *Connecticut Unscathed: Victory in the Great Narragansett War, 1675–1676*. Norman: University of Oklahoma Press, 2014.

Webb, Stephen Saunders. *The Governors-General: The English Army and the Definition of Empire, 1559–1681*. Chapel Hill: University of North Carolina Press, 1979.

CHAPTER 2

COMPETING FOR A CONTINENT
1565–1763

Prelude to Conflict • Anglo-Dutch Wars • Wars for North American Empire • King George's War • Great War for Empire • Global War • An Empire on Which the Sun Never Set

Imperial competition for North America began in 1493 when Pope Alexander VI penned the Treaty of Tordesillas, which divided all non-Christian lands in the so-called New World between Spain and Portugal. This settlement did not include provisions for England, France, or any other European nation, fueling jealousy and competition that grew in succeeding years. During the sixteenth century Spanish conquistadors conquered the rich Aztec and Inca empires and anticipated similar Indian wealth would be discovered farther north. Subsequent expeditions found little of value, convincing Spanish officials to concentrate their efforts on the ore-producing regions of Central and South America and use the northern regions as part of a defensive perimeter to protect the treasure galleons sailing to Spain.

In 1565 the Spanish king Philip II sent naval officer and entrepreneur Pedro Menéndez de Avilés to the Florida peninsula as an *adelantado*, or proprietor, to secure the region and convert its natives to Catholicism. A year earlier French Protestants—called Huguenots—had arrived in northeastern Florida under the leadership of Jean Ribaut to escape religious persecution then occurring in France. They established Fort Caroline near the mouth of the St. Johns River. During the summer of 1565, Menéndez founded the fortified town of St. Augustine forty miles south of Fort Caroline. In late September Menéndez's 1,500 soldiers descended on the French fort and butchered 300 Huguenots, who had surrendered believing they would be spared. They were not.

Menéndez constructed fortifications along the Atlantic and Gulf Coast to protect Spanish holdings against pirates. He built Fort Santa Elena at present-day Port Royal Sound, South Carolina, and established Jesuit missions throughout the region, including Ajacán near the mouth of the Chesapeake Bay, to win the hearts of the natives. Menéndez anticipated that the missions and fortifications would impress upon the natives Spain's spiritual and temporal power. Instead, Indians destroyed Ajacán, and the French burned Fort Caroline in retribution for the earlier massacre. By 1574 the Spanish presence along the Atlantic consisted of only St. Augustine and Santa Elena. When Englishman Sir Francis Drake captured the log fort at St. Augustine in 1586, Spanish officials evacuated Santa Elena, concentrating their resources on the northern end of the Florida Straits. The Spanish decision to withdraw inadvertently benefited the English, who located their 1607 Jamestown settlement near the ruins of the destroyed mission of Ajacán.

PRELUDE TO CONFLICT

North America became hotly contested during the seventeenth century, as Spain, England, and France, as well as the Netherlands and Sweden, all tried to carve out spheres of influence and control. The land offered a bounty of resources—minerals, timber, animals—and its economic possibilities provided the foundation for imperial development. Spain solidified its hold on the Florida peninsula and the American Southwest. English settlers carved settlements out of the wilderness of the Atlantic shoreline. French interests ultimately focused on Canadian lands watered by the St. Lawrence River, the Great Lakes region, and the Mississippi River Valley. This tricornered competition divided North America into three camps, with each group trying to winnow down enemy holdings. Yet territorial claims meant nothing in a practical sense, as Europeans' control rarely existed outside of their immediate settlements.

FROM THE SEA

When the English established their initial North American settlements during the late sixteenth and early seventeenth centuries, they feared Spanish attacks more than Indian threats. The first English fort at Roanoke Island had cannon aimed toward the sea rather than inland. In 1607 they located the Jamestown settlement sixty miles up the James River, well hidden from passing Spanish ships. The wide deepwater river provided an expansive English view of potential attacks. The anticipated Spanish assault never occurred, as English and Spanish officials signed in 1670 the Treaty of Madrid, in which Spain recognized England's colonies north of Florida. The two countries remained at peace until the end of the century.

While Anglo-Spanish tensions subsided, Anglo-French tensions heightened. Prior to the seventeenth century, France had provided little challenge to Spain's New World hegemony. Instead, the French developed a fishing and fur trading presence along the St. Lawrence River. French traders and Indians intermarried and developed a mutual dependency that bonded them together. The French also founded trading posts in Maine (1604), Nova Scotia (1605), and Québec (1608), where they consolidated their influence over the St. Lawrence River Valley, establishing important alliances with northern Indian tribes. Built by Samuel de Champlain on a high bluff overlooking the St. Lawrence River, Québec quickly became the center of French economic and political activity and an easily fortified point of entry into North America distant from the Atlantic Ocean. Most importantly, Québec's location near the seat of the powerful Huron tribe, which controlled the gateway to the western Great

Lakes, permitted French mastery over east–west trading networks connecting the Great Lakes to the Atlantic Ocean and Europe.

Champlain won Indian trust by demonstrating the power of French matchlock muskets. In June 1609 he and eight soldiers joined a Huron attack against the Five Nations (the Iroquois) near present-day Lake Champlain. Expecting a traditional Indian battle, the Iroquois advanced in mass, protected by wooden shields and breastplates. Suddenly, the Frenchmen jumped into full view, firing their muskets and killing three Iroquois chiefs. The remaining Iroquois quickly fled. The following year, in a bloodier attack, French muskets again proved the deciding factor. These defeats convinced the Iroquois to replace mass formations with hit-and-run tactics, and the superiority of muskets over traditional bow and arrows forced them to seek out a European ally.

Five weeks after Champlain helped the Hurons in their long-running struggle against the Iroquois, Henry Hudson, commanding a voyage for the Dutch East India Company, initiated trade with the Mohawks. Recognizing the economic potential of the region, Dutch agents in 1614 founded Fort Nassau, a fortified trading post on the Hudson River near present-day Albany that provided a shorter and generally ice-free outlet for the fur trade. This outpost also linked the Dutch to the easternmost tribe of the Iroquois Confederation, the Mohawks, who by the late 1620s dominated the fur trade. The Mohawks then used their newly acquired weapons and supplies to attack French trade north along the St. Lawrence. While the Dutch exploited the weapons-for-pelts trade, they could not deny the Mohawks weapons,

DEFEAT OF IROQUOIS AT LAKE CHAMPLAIN.

IMAGE 2.1 Samuel de Champlain's Fight With the Iroquois Engraving based on a drawing by Champlain of his 1609 voyage and depicts a battle between Iroquois and Algonquian tribes near Lake Champlain.

as they depended on Iroquois friendship for survival and economic prosperity. Ultimately, the Dutch became pawns of the Mohawks, who used Fort Orange, the replacement for Fort Nassau, as a base for expanding control over weaker and more poorly supplied enemies.

The fur trade permanently heightened the ferocity of Indian warfare in North America, giving rise to indiscriminate attacks by native peoples. But while much of the conflict resulted from Iroquois attempts to supplant Hurons in the fur trade, the Iroquois goal of obtaining captives to adopt into their family structures also played an important role. The Iroquois had suffered substantial losses from disease, and their "Mourning Wars"—conflicts in which they seized prisoners from opposing tribes to appease their grief and replace their dead—became a way to replenish their strength. By 1650 the Hurons had fled west beyond Lake Michigan or to Québec. Thereafter, Indian alliances shifted depending on marriage, kinship networks, and trade possibilities, permitting natives to pursue their own objectives while manipulating colonial allies.

The English feared the growing Dutch-Indian and French-Indian alliances. The May 1643 creation of the New England Confederation for mutual defense occurred in part because the English Civil War prevented the Crown from sending troops to protect its distant colonies. The negotiation of the 1650 Treaty of Hartford, which established a boundary between Dutch New Netherland and Puritan New England, offered a diplomatic solution to this tension, one that the Massachusetts Bay colony recognized even during the first Anglo-Dutch War (1652–1654).

ANGLO-DUTCH WARS

Dutch New Netherland faced Anglo-American encroachments from the east and south. Expansionist threats combined with an emerging mercantilist economic system, signaled by the passage of the 1651 Navigation Act, jeopardized the commercial viability of the Dutch colony. By attempting to exclude the Dutch from North American trade and simultaneously raising customs revenues, the Navigation Acts (others were passed in 1660, 1673, and 1696) contributed to three Anglo-Dutch wars in 1652–1654, 1664–1667, and 1672–1674.

Fought primarily at sea, these economic conflicts significantly altered colonial relationships in North America. The first war, which lasted from 1652 to 1654, witnessed Dutch and English attempts to martial Indians to their causes. And while the various tribes involved in this conflict devastated one another and raided outlying enemy settlements, their participation did not shift the balance of power in the northeast.

During the second war, fought from 1664 to 1667, Charles II sent a small English army to conquer New Netherland and eliminate illegal trade between the Dutch and English colonies. In mid-August 1664 English ships appeared off New Amsterdam, and John Winthrop, Jr.'s Connecticut militia surrounded the unfinished Dutch fort there. Dutch governor Peter Stuyvesant surrendered, and New Netherland became New York, named in honor of the king's brother, James, the Duke of York. When English commander Richard Nicholls sent soldiers to seize Dutch settlements that had formerly belonged to Sweden on the Delaware Bay, Dutch soldiers resisted, prompting the English to loot and plunder the settlements and sell Dutch captives into servitude in Virginia.

The third war, which lasted from 1672 to 1674, broke out after England and France signed the secret Treaty of Dover, in which Charles II pledged to support Louis XIV in France's conflict with the Dutch. During this unpopular war, Dutch forces briefly recaptured New Netherland, and Dutch ships raided the Chesapeake and Delaware bays. The Dutch returned New York to the English in 1674, strengthening the English hold on the Atlantic coast from Acadia to Florida.

WARS FOR NORTH AMERICAN EMPIRE

Prior to 1689 colonial wars were localized and left to locals to fight. European governments rarely sent ships or troops to North America to interfere. But between 1689 and 1763 conditions changed dramatically as Europeans began to understand the economic and strategic importance of the North American colonies. They soon realized that the conquest of enemy colonies removed resources from their competitors' coffers. Regardless, North America remained a secondary theater of action for the first half of the eighteenth century.

FIGHTING OVER FURS

Since the 1640s the French and Iroquois had struggled to control the fur trade in the North American interior. Soon after the British replaced the Dutch at Albany in 1664, they won control of the Iroquois fur trade. By the late 1680s British-armed Iroquois had extended their control across the Great Lakes region and along the Canadian frontier, forcing smaller tribes to assimilate into the Iroquois Confederation. Those that refused, such as France's trading partner the Illinois, suffered. The Iroquois also threatened French settlements that challenged their economic control in the region. In one surprise attack on the St. Lawrence island of LaChine, the Iroquois destroyed fifty-nine French farms and killed and captured most of the residents. To counter the Iroquois threat, French finance minister Jean Colbert sent twenty companies (1,000 men) of the Carignan-Salières Regiment to New France in 1665 to strengthen France's mercantilist position; they were later used against the Iroquois along the Hudson Bay and the coast of Maine. Just a few days after the raid on LaChine, French-supported Abenaki warriors attacked present-day Bristol.

EUROPEAN WARS FOR EMPIRE

WAR OF THE LEAGUE OF AUGSBURG, 1689–1697
Also called King William's War
England and Holland versus France
Ended by Treaty of Ryswick, 1697

WAR OF SPANISH SUCCESSION, 1701–1713
Also called Queen Anne's War
England, Austria, and Holland versus France
and Spain
Ended by Peace of Utrecht, 1713

WAR OF AUSTRIAN SUCCESSION, 1744–1748
Also called King George's War and the War of
Jenkins' Ear (1739)
England and Austria versus France and Prussia
Ended by Treaty of Aix-la-Chapelle, 1748

SEVEN YEARS' WAR, 1754–1763
Also called French and Indian War
England and Prussia versus France, Spain,
Austria, and Prussia
Ended by Peace of Paris, 1763

KING WILLIAM'S WAR

Frontier warfare would not have escalated into a larger war had it not been reinforced by international disagreements. Shortly before the Iroquois attack at LaChine, news arrived in North America of a war between England and France. The War of the League of Augsburg, better known as King William's War, began because of Louis XIV's attempts to expand French boundaries, including his invasion of the Spanish Netherlands (Belgium). The English king William III, who had come to power along with his wife Mary in the bloodless Revolution of 1688, wanted to preserve the balance of power in continental Europe while protecting the Netherlands, his homeland. The conflict was also exacerbated by Louis's unwillingness to recognize William and Mary as the legitimate monarchs of England; instead, he acknowledged the deposed Stuart king James II as sovereign. The European conflict so absorbed French and English energies that neither side committed resources to North America, leaving colonists and Indians to wage the struggle alone.

At the beginning of the war Louis XIV appointed Count Louis de Buade de Frontenac governor of New France. Frontenac sought to secure French power in North America by using Indian tribes and small Canadian militia contingents to attack English colonials, who were wracked by dissension, unwilling to cooperate, and distracted by the Glorious Revolution in England. Frontenac could have won a major victory over the English had he focused on capturing their post at Albany, which would have weakened the English-Iroquois alliance and perhaps even knocked the powerful confederation out of the war. Instead, Frontenac pursued a policy of terror and destruction in New York and New England. He believed this strategy would protect French settlements from English attacks and discourage Englishmen from fighting. The first raid occurred against Schenectady in February 1690. Frenchmen and Indians slogged through a semifrozen wilderness for almost two weeks before the weather turned cold again and snow started falling. Quietly approaching Schenectady at sunset, they watched English settlers finishing their daily chores. A few hours later, they quietly surrounded each structure; surprisingly, no dogs barked to reveal their presence. Suddenly, the attackers stormed the buildings, killing sixty people and capturing many men, women, and children before burning the town.

Frontenac's attacks spread terror across the northern English frontier but did not discourage the English from fighting. Instead, the colonists retaliated indiscriminately against French settlements. After French raids struck outposts in New York, New Hampshire, Massachusetts, and Maine, the English launched an operation against Port Royal in Acadia. Massachusetts Bay governor Simon Bradstreet assembled 750 men and seventeen ships under the command of Sir William Phipps, a native-born colonial who had been knighted by the Crown for his contributions to the English treasury. While wealthy and popular, Phipps lacked military experience, and the soldiers he commanded were an irregular force—not militiamen, but volunteers. Nevertheless, the force easily captured the poorly defended Port Royal in May 1690. Phipps's troops burned the fort, pillaged the settlement's Catholic church, and ransacked the town before returning to Boston.

Meanwhile, other English colonial leaders also joined the effort. Forces from New York and Connecticut commanded by Fitz-John Winthrop planned to attack Montreal by land while Phipps and others from Massachusetts and Plymouth assaulted Québec by sea.

If successful, these operations could destroy New France and give the English complete control over the fur trade.

Neither plan succeeded. Winthrop's overland assault from Albany failed because of disease and limited food supplies, while Phipps's attack failed because his soldiers were too inexperienced, ill equipped, and poorly supplied to undertake an operation in a distant and hostile enemy land. In both cases, English efforts were hampered by their inability to move, feed, supply, and equip soldiers. This reveals a fundamental truth about war in early America: logistics defined whether colonial units would be successful. Widespread English divisiveness also undermined the war effort, as colonies removed from danger saw little reason to commit resources to a conflict that would not provide them noticeable benefits and would leave local governments heavily indebted. Finally, the Iroquois-English alliance was weakened by the losses the Iroquois sustained. As a result of Frontenac's raids through Onondaga and Oneida territory, half of the confederation's warriors were killed, numerous prisoners were taken, and many villages were razed.

In September 1697 the European powers signed the Treaty of Ryswick, officially ending the war. While the European combatants traded continental possessions, the treaty settled nothing in North America, where it returned colonial conquests to their prewar status. The treaty also failed to settle discord along the English-Canadian frontier or alleviate the fear and anxiety Indian attacks had created. While the war had ended, warfare along the frontier continued as France and England vied for control over the valuable interior fur trade. Nevertheless, this struggle taught the English valuable lessons: prolonged European-style operations did not work in a frontier environment because they lacked the logistical ability to carry them out, they needed to present a united front against their French and Indian enemies, they had to regain the trust of the divided and factionalized Iroquois Confederation in order to eliminate the French threat and maintain control over the fur trade, and royal naval and military assistance were needed to eliminate the French presence.

QUEEN ANNE'S WAR

After the Treaty of Ryswick, France increased its presence in the Mississippi River Valley. Louisiana governor Antoine de la Cadillac authorized construction of a strategic fort and trading post at Detroit that would command the strait linking Lakes Huron and Erie. French Jesuit missionaries infiltrated the upper St. Lawrence Valley and Great Lakes region to convert Indians to the French cause. Meanwhile, Pierre Le Moyne, Sieur d'Iberville, created a short-lived French settlement on the Gulf Coast (present-day Biloxi), which later was relocated east to Mobile Bay. Thereafter France created an arc of trading posts and settlements that linked Canada to the Gulf Coast through the Mississippi River Valley. The French presence, along with Spanish control of the Florida peninsula, effectively limited the future expansion of the English colonies on the Atlantic.

European fighting resumed when the Spanish king Charles II died in 1700 and the throne passed to Philip of Anjou, grandson of French king Louis XIV. Most anticipated the French king would dominate his young grandson, uniting the thrones and resources of Spain and France and threatening the European balance of power. But the dynastic question alone did not drive Europe to war. When French soldiers again moved into the Spanish Netherlands

NATIVE AMERICANS AND THE MIDDLE GROUND

Traditional interpretations of Native Americans during the colonial period held that they were obstacles to white Western progress and civilization. Europeans manipulated the Indians, often pitting them against one another to achieve their own hegemonic imperial objectives. European courts frequently drew lines of demarcation in North America without regard for how their actions would play out on the ground. Moreover, Native Americans did not figure into negotiations between European imperial powers, which saw them as nothing more than pawns to be bartered and traded. The crux of this two-dimensional interpretation was that whites and Indians were pitted against one another—and the whites won.

In 1991 historian Richard White published *The Middle Ground: Indians, Empires, and Republics in the Great Lakes Region, 1650–1815*, which refocused our understanding of white–native interactions. White examines the *pays d'en haut* of the Great Lakes region between 1649 and 1815 as a place where the process of mutual accommodation between Algonquian-speaking Indians and French, British, and American colonists occurred. During this period the peoples of the region built a set of mutually un-derstandable practices—or a middle ground—that allowed them to bridge cultural differences without resorting to widespread destructive war. Since none of the actors could militarily dominate the other, this system forced them to live together in a harmonic balance that emphasized tolerance. The French maneuvered successfully in this "middle ground," obtaining trade agreements with the Indians and generally outwitting English/British officials, even after the French defeat in the Seven Years' War. Once the British won this conflict in 1763, they opted for a strategy of force over accommodation and ulti-mately lost control over the middle ground. The transition from a fluid system that allowed interactions between Indians and whites to the more rigid system of Anglo nation-states in North America left little room for Indians to maneuver.

White's prevailing thesis is built on the work of turn-of-the-century historians Frederick Jackson Turner and Herbert Eugene Bolton. Turner's important essay "The Significance of the Frontier in American History" suggests that the wilderness mastered the white man, forcing him to resort to Indian ways to survive. At the frontier, the environment was simply too strong for civilization, and this dynamic shaped the American experience and created unique American ways of war, survival, and government. Bolton's thesis, while ignoring the lives and significance of indigenous peoples, examines the Spanish-American borderlands as specific geographic places of cultural exchange.

The middle ground thesis has broadened our historical understanding of periods, places, and peoples. New Western historians have exposed faults in Turner's frontier thesis, while ethnohistorians have failed to place Indians within the larger American context. The North American wars of the seventeenth and eighteenth centuries show that the Indians were major players who helped decide the destiny of the continent. That both the English and the French attempted to coopt, persuade, or bully Indians into joining their cause reveals the ways in which the Indians occupied an important middle ground that determined the fate of European control over the continent.

(Belgium), they threatened the Dutch Netherlands. When Louis prohibited trade with the Spanish Empire, it threatened the economic prosperity of England and the Netherlands. Finally, when former Stuart king James II died, Louis recognized his son as the legitimate monarch of England, which aroused English indignation and prompted King William to declare war in 1701. This conflict came to be known as Queen Anne's War (Anne became monarch six months after the war began) or the War of Spanish Succession.

Again, a European imperial war provided North American belligerents the chance to settle old scores. This time the Iroquois saw no advantage in supporting their English ally, especially after they had suffered such heavy casualties during King William's War. Consequently they signed the 1701 Treaty of Montreal, in which the Five Nations pledged their neutrality in future Anglo-French wars (a policy that remained in place until the Seven Years' War). The middle English colonies also showed little interest in a conflict that did not impact them, leaving South Carolina and New England to suffer the brunt of the war.

When news of war arrived in North America in 1702, South Carolina governor James Moore planned to attack St. Augustine, because he thought eliminating the Spanish post would protect his colony. Equipped with a 500-man expeditionary force, 300 Yamasee, Tallapoosa, and Alabama Indians, and a fleet of fourteen ships, Moore easily captured the village of St. Augustine and in October laid siege to Fort Castillo de San Marcos. Even with a numerical advantage, Moore lacked the patience and proper equipment needed to carry out an effective siege against a masonry fort. His soldiers also lacked the discipline to move their lines slowly and methodically toward the Spanish bastion and the explosive artillery shells that could have been lobbed inside the fort to cause injury and damage. Two balmy months passed, and the siege accomplished little. In mid-December the sudden appearance of two Spanish ships off the coast of St. Augustine offered Moore a reason to end the ill-conceived and poorly conducted operation.

Moore returned to Florida in early 1704 with a more ambitious plan. Leading fifty Carolinians and some 1,000 Coweta Indians, he descended on the northeastern Gulf of Mexico frontier, terrorizing the Apalachee Indians who inhabited the region and disrupting French and Spanish trade with the southeastern tribes. His attack destroyed Apalachee villages, forced the Creek Indians to join with the English, and convinced the Alabama Indians to defect from the French. Otherwise, the raids did not alter the balance of power or alliance structure within the southeastern borderlands. The attacks did cause concern to both the French and the Spanish because of their potential to disrupt trade relationships with local Indians. This realization motivated a joint Franco-Spanish assault against Charleston in 1706, which the English easily beat back, killing more than 200 attackers and sinking one of the five enemy ships.

New England suffered far more than did the southern colonies. The French encouraged Abenaki warriors to seek retribution for English attacks, and in August 1703, they struck isolated farming and fishing settlements in Maine, killing or capturing more than 100 English settlers. The following March, the Abenakis surprised Deerfield in Massachusetts. In the early hours of March 1, 1703, Frenchmen and Abenakis used high snowdrifts to climb Deerfield's fortified walls and enter the palisade. Positioning themselves near each dwelling, they attacked on a gunshot signal, killing forty-seven and capturing more than a hundred others, whom they marched to Canada. One captive, Reverend John Williams, saw his wife and twenty others die during the frozen march. Only fifty-nine Englishmen returned home; twenty-eight children remained Abenaki captives.

Abenaki raids momentarily accomplished what the French governor-general of Canada, Philippe de Rigaud, Chevalier de Vaudreuil, sought: the postponement of any attack against Canada. Massachusetts offered a £40 reward for each Abenaki scalp, and conscripted soldiers vigorously defended the frontier looking for Indians.

Neither side gained a decisive advantage during the early stages of the war. The English failure to capture Port Royal in Acadia highlighted the lack of experienced leadership, the limited commitment of nonprofessional soldiers who wanted to return to the safety of their homes, the expense and logistical problems of supplying and outfitting a successful expedition, and the difficulty of coordinating a complicated joint operation with both land and naval forces. This failure greatly embarrassed Massachusetts officials and businessmen, many of whom were accused of profiting from the venture.

Several of these businessmen subsequently traveled to London to plead with the English government to rid Canada of French influence. Finally, in early 1709, the Privy Council agreed to send a fleet of six warships and 4,000 soldiers to supplement 2,700 men provided by the northern colonies. English plans called for a colonial land assault against Montreal and a combined land and naval attack against Port Royal and Québec. Colonial enthusiasm increased to a fever pitch as some colonies speedily enlisted far more than their troop quotas and recruited large numbers of Indian auxiliaries, reducing the number of New Englanders needed. Even middle colonies New Jersey and Pennsylvania committed money and troops.

Early that fall the colonials learned that the expected British expedition had instead been sent to Portugal. Although dispirited, Massachusetts and Connecticut continued to raise troops to capture Port Royal. The colonies offered tax breaks as well as generous bounties and salaries for those who enlisted, but they still had to rely on conscription to secure their full quotas. Even so, in early October 1710, some 3,500 colonials succeeded where two previous expeditions had failed. In doing so, the colonials achieved the only tangible English success during the war, capturing the poorly defended (manned by only 300 soldiers and militiamen) French fort at Port Royal. Acadia, renamed Nova Scotia, and Port Royal, renamed Annapolis Royal, joined the British Empire.

Such success emboldened English policymakers in London, who revived plans to conquer Canada. The Privy Council sent Rear Admiral Hovenden Walker to attack Québec with sixty-four ships, including eleven ships-of-the-line. The council also dispatched Brigadier General John Hill with 4,300 regulars, including seven veteran regiments from the Duke of Marlborough's Flanders army. This was the largest English military commitment during the war, and English authorities anticipated that they would succeed in their conquest.

Instead, there were problems from the onset. Admiral Walker arrived in Boston in late June 1711, but it took almost a month for him to secure supplies because of disagreements with colonial merchants over the exchange rate. Departing on July 30, Walker's flotilla suffered further delays at sea and did not enter the St. Lawrence River until mid-August, only two months before the onset of winter. Misfortune then became calamity when ten of Walker's ships—eight transport and two supply vessels—ran onto the rocks near Île aux Oeufs, killing 900 men. This setback proved too much. Walker halted the expedition before firing a shot.

Walker's failure galled New Englanders, who had by this time contributed to five failed expeditions into Canada. Their anger intensified when Walker claimed that colonial unwillingness to raise men and reluctance to supply his fleet had doomed the venture. Relations would have soured further had the war not ended. In April 1713 European diplomats signed the Treaty of Utrecht, which restored a balance of power. England gained control over Gibraltar, Minorca, and the Caribbean island of St. Kitts. More important for colonials, the English secured Hudson Bay, Nova Scotia, and Newfoundland, and claimed control over the Iroquois Confederation (although neither the French nor the Iroquois themselves agreed to such an arrangement). The English also gained the *asiento de negros*, a thirty-year monopoly to provide 4,800 slaves annually to the Spanish colonies.

Queen Anne's War revealed the importance of seapower to the survival of Britain—the political entity established by the 1707 Act of Union uniting England and Scotland—and the American colonies. As long as British merchant ships kept trade and communication routes open, everyone prospered. But blockages of or threats to sea routes undermined the mercantilist system upon which the imperial economy rested. By the end of the war, control of the sea-lanes had provided Britain with economic freedom and allowed it to move reinforcements and supplies to its colonies as needed, reducing the expense of garrisoning soldiers in distant lands. It also permitted the British to attack French trade and to harass the flow of wealth from the Spanish colonies in a more systematic way.

TUSCARORA AND YAMASEE WARS

King William's War and Queen Anne's War had delayed frontier settlement, resulting in greater population density in most American colonies. With peace, colonists moved west, encroaching on lands left to Indians by the Treaty of Utrecht. Violence intensified in 1723 when Massachusetts governor William Dummer led soldiers into northern and eastern Maine. Abenaki warriors responded to the intrusion by killing farmers, herders, and fishermen. The turning point in the conflict occurred in August 1724 when Captain Johnson Harmon raided the unsuspecting Abenaki village of Norridgewock on the Kennebec. Harmon's soldiers burned the town, killed most of the inhabitants, and brought their scalps to Boston, where they received £100 for each. Sporadic fighting continued for three more years, but its violence and intensity subsided after the bloody attack at Norridgewock.

The southern frontier also erupted in violence. The two Carolina colonies had grown beyond their coastal confines. They needed more land, wanted to expand their trade networks, and were pursuing native alliances in the southeast as counters to Spain. The Creek Confederation—a loose coalition of approximately 15,000 Indians of seven different ethnic groups living in sixty distinct villages—occupied the strategic territory between the Appalachian Mountains and the Gulf of Mexico. During the late seventeenth century Spanish missionaries had tried unsuccessfully to bring Christianity to the Creeks, hoping to create a buffer zone against English expansion. When these efforts failed, the Spanish attacked and burned Creek villages.

The Tuscaroras, an Iroquois people living in North Carolina, had suffered attacks by other tribes, which sold their children to white traders as slaves. Then German and Swiss immigrants had invaded their lands, building New Bern. The Tuscaroras' attempt to relocate to Pennsylvania rather than endure continued depredations at home failed when even the

Quakers refused to offer them refuge. With no other recourse, in September 1711 they sought retribution, killing about 150 settlers along the Neuse and Pamlico rivers. Furthermore, they introduced a racial element to the conflict by providing protection to runaway slaves who willingly fought against Carolinians.

Initially, North Carolina's provincial government lacked the ability to defend the colony's frontier. By the end of 1711 these lands had been devastated and Bath County almost completely abandoned. Only assistance from South Carolina and Virginia saved the colony. In January 1712 South Carolina slave traders sent thirty-three white soldiers and 500 allied Indians, who joined with a small contingent of Virginians, to destroy Tuscarora towns and a fort. Later that summer South Carolina sent another army—this time comprising thirty-three whites and almost 1,000 Indian allies commanded by Colonel James Moore—and Virginians provided the weapons and supplies that turned the tide. During March 1713 Moore's men burned alive several hundred Tuscaroras in the fortified village of Nooherooka and executed 160 males considered unsuitable for enslavement. Within eighteen months, more than 1,000 Tuscaroras had been killed or wounded and 700 had been sold into slavery, while almost every Tuscarora town had been destroyed. The southern band of the tribe never recovered, while the nonhostile northern band later joined the Iroquois Confederation.

The Yamasee Indians helped the colonists subdue the Tuscarora but soon regretted their alliance as South Carolina cattle raisers demanded more grazing lands and traders called in debts owed. After exchanging Tuscarora captives with the traders at a poor price, the Yamasees still found themselves more than 100,000 deerskins in debt, representing four to five years of successful hunting. Impatient Carolinians began seizing Yamasee women and children as payment.

In response, the Yamasees tried to create a pan-Indian alliance of the many fragmented coastal tribes and the powerful and populous Creeks, Cherokees, and Choctaws. Such an alliance could have united 30,000 Indians into a force and regained control over the southeast. But the last-minute decision by the Cherokees to join the colonists ultimately destined the Yamasees to the same fate as the Tuscaroras.

On Good Friday, April 15, 1715, Yamasee warriors joined by Creeks, who were resentful of British exploitation, attacked white traders on the southern frontier. Although hostilities initially concentrated on English traders, the war quickly spread as several smaller tribes such as the Catawbas used the conflict to settle their outstanding disputes with the colonists. Frontier trading posts suffered severe damage, with most of them being completely destroyed. The Indians also burned farms and plantations, killing their inhabitants indiscriminately. By the fall of 1715, the fighting had approached Charleston, leading many to believe that the Indians would accomplish what neither the Spanish nor the French had: the destruction of the English colonies south of Virginia. In this moment of crisis, South Carolina's leaders resorted to an army of 1,200 slaves and conscripted free blacks to avoid annihilation.

Initially the Cherokees had remained neutral, but their decision to support the British during the fall of 1715 determined the fate of the war. Carolina officials sent 300 soldiers, including a company of black slaves, into the mountainous Cherokee lands of southern Appalachia, while Creek emissaries tried to convince the Cherokees to join in a combined attack against the British invaders. When confronted with these extremes, the Cherokees chose war against the Creeks, believing the Carolinians would defeat the Yamasees; furthermore, the Cherokees needed English trade goods, and a successful Yamasee and Creek confederation threatened their continued prosperity. The Cherokees decided trade needs outweighed their support for the Yamasees or the Creeks.

When 4,000 Cherokee warriors joined the British in 1716, the Creeks were forced to abandon their eastern Carolina towns and move west to the Chattahoochee River region. The Yamasees, Catawbas, and smaller tribes suffered a far worse fate. Driven from the Carolinas, they fled south, seeking refuge in Spanish Florida under the lower Creek Confederation. During the following years Yamasees, Creeks, and runaway slaves continued raiding the English frontier, but South Carolina's survival no longer remained in doubt.

WAR OF JENKINS' EAR

In 1721 the British Board of Trade proposed strengthening the northern and southern extremes of the British Empire (Nova Scotia and the Carolinas), securing the western frontier with a string of fortifications, sending additional royal troops to the colonies, and appointing a captain-general to coordinate military activities in North America. Construction soon began on Fort Oswego on New York's western frontier and on Fort King George at the mouth of the Altamaha River in the southern borderlands, an area claimed by both Spain and England. Otherwise, the Board's strategic plans came to naught.

Continued trouble on the southern frontier convinced the British of the need for a buffer. General James Edward Oglethorpe's philanthropic campaign to ease the plight of debtors in Britain provided an opportunity for King George II to grant a charter to establish the colony of Georgia. Oglethorpe, a successful military officer who while in Parliament had promoted an aggressive policy toward Spain, became governor and in 1733 established the planned city of Savannah.

Anglo-Spanish competition intensified during the eighteenth century. The British conquest of Gibraltar during the War of Spanish Succession had disgraced Spain, while their violations of Spanish trade regulations in the Caribbean—namely, the terms of the *asiento*—challenged Spanish power. Spanish officials in the Caribbean addressed these insults by stopping British ships and punishing those involved in illegal trade. In 1731 Spanish officials cut off the ear of Robert Jenkins, a sea captain who had been captured off the coast of Florida. British imperialists used the outrage over this incident to create public support for a 1739 war to restore British predominance in the Caribbean.

In the War of Jenkins' Ear, so called because the Spanish mutilation of Jenkins helped fuel the parliamentary cry for war, the British focused on capturing Spanish treasure galleons, disrupting commerce, and seizing weakly held Spanish colonies. In November 1739 Vice Admiral Edward Vernon captured the valuable Caribbean seaport of Porto Bello on the Isthmus of Panama, reinforcing the belief that Spain's empire could be taken. The victory prompted an ambitious combined British–colonial operation against the well-defended South American port of Cartagena, which failed miserably in April 1741 because of disease among troops and poor execution of the attack; of the approximately 12,000 British regulars and American colonials sent to Cartagena, an estimated 8,400 died from yellow fever and combat. British officers unfairly blamed the colonials for the failure, accusing them of being untrained, inexperienced, and incapable of performing military service.

Meanwhile, tensions were growing on the English colonies' southern frontier. Carolinians had dealt with slave revolts in 1711 and 1714, the Yamasee War in 1715, and persistent rumors of slave conspiracies. One such conspiracy in 1720 saw participants flee to Spanish Florida, where they were incorporated by officials into a black militia. In 1726, fourteen slaves who had earlier fought with the Yamasees also fled to Florida, joined the militia, and participated in successful raids against their former masters, prompting an English attack on St. Augustine. During the resulting siege, the black militia proved to be some of the city's most capable defenders. In February 1739 Spanish governor Manuel de Montiano rewarded runaways by giving them a place to settle just north of St. Augustine called Gracia Real de Santa Teresa de Mosé. This military settlement, which included a stone and earthen fort, represented the first all-black community in North America.

Fort Mosé shielded St. Augustine and provided the Spanish with advance warning of British assaults. It also became an example of black resistance to English slavery and an

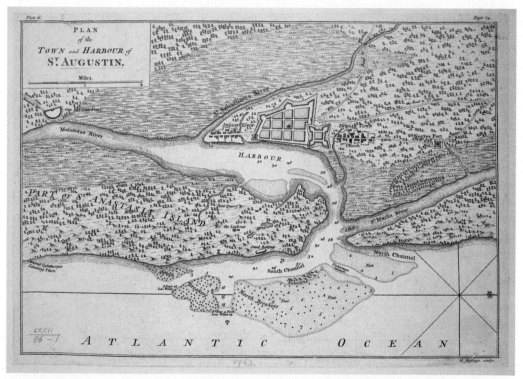

IMAGE 2.2 **"Negroe Fort"**   "Negroe Fort" or Gracia Real de Santa Teresa de Mosé, was approximately two miles north from St. Augustine and its fort. Fort Mose's strategic location, with its stone and earthen fort, represented the first all-black community in North America and a defiant threat to English slavery. Map by Thomas Jefferys, "Plan of the Town and Harbour of St. Augustin," in *A Description of the Spanish Islands and Settlements on the Coast of the West Indies* (London, 1762), plate 6.

entrepôt for slaves willing to risk their lives for freedom. In September 1739, only a few months after the settlement's founding, slaves along the Stono River in South Carolina rose up in a violent rebellion. During the uprising, armed slaves burned, looted property, and killed colonists as they tried to escape to Spanish Florida. White Carolinians brutally suppressed the rebellion and, believing it to be Spanish-influenced, planned retribution.

When Oglethorpe asked South Carolina to provide 2,000 men for an attack on St. Augustine in the war against the Spanish, the Carolinians, reluctant to participate because of slave unrest and Indian problems, provided only 900 men. The arrival of a Spanish flotilla at St. Augustine subsequently forced Oglethorpe to abandon his assault and instead lay siege to the city. This doomed the operation, because Oglethorpe could neither move his heavy cannon within range of the Spanish fortifications nor maintain the morale or health of his soldiers. In June 1740, Mosé's all-black militia mounted repeated bloody hand-to-hand attacks on the British, forcing them to evacuate. The defense of St. Augustine convinced Spanish officials to attack Saint Simon's Island, hoping the British would withdraw farther north. Yet the July 1742 Spanish assault proved as futile as earlier British operations had been. Two years of inconclusive fighting along the southern frontier had not altered the situation.

KING GEORGE'S WAR

The War of Jenkins' Ear (1739) merged with the larger and more significant King George's War (1744) when the French came to Spain's aid. The War of Austrian Succession had begun in October 1740 when Emperor Charles VI of Austria died and his daughter Maria Theresa succeeded him. In response, the Elector of Bavaria seized Austrian lands in Hungary, Spain made plans to take lands in Italy, and Frederick II of Prussia invaded Silesia. Maria Theresa pleaded for help from Britain and France to defend the Austrian Empire, and Britain responded with naval operations in the Mediterranean. In October 1743 France joined with Spain, and in early 1744 Britain and France declared war on one another.

Learning of the war, French troops in North America quickly captured the British outpost of Canso in northern Nova Scotia. In response, Massachusetts governor William Shirley raised a force for an expedition against Fort Louisbourg, the French bastion on Cape Breton Island that guarded the entrance to the St. Lawrence River. A masonry fort with cannon, a garrison of more than 1,500 regulars, and a supporting population of some 4,200 colonists, Louisbourg extended France's first line of defense to the Atlantic frontier. It was also the largest French settlement in North America and the most heavily defended position north of Havana, Cuba.

Shirley had convinced the British government to send Admiral Peter Warren and four warships from the Caribbean, and he offered Maine merchant William Pepperrell command of the expedition. The resulting operation against Louisbourg reeked of amateurism. Neither Pepperrell nor Shirley had ever led troops. Most subordinate officers had never seen war. And though the young militiamen displayed enthusiasm and energy, they had no experience fighting against trained regulars. Many were sickened by the sea voyage to Cape Breton Island, during which heavy seas caused the ships to roll and pitch violently, although fortunately the trip lasted only two days. Pepperrell's troops then easily forged their way ashore with little French opposition.

Before the end of May 1745 the colonial army had placed Louisbourg under siege. Initially many of the colonials spent their time drinking, gambling, and playing games. But as the campaign progressed, they found themselves dragging cannon, powder, and shot forward, digging trenches, and worrying about their own mortality. They encountered dysentery and pneumonia, horrible food, and almost intolerable living conditions and witnessed comrades dying from fatal wounds. The experience was not what they had envisioned.

Colonial morale waned dangerously until mid-June, when additional British warships appeared on the horizon. These vessels created a British naval blockade of Louisbourg, preventing the French from relieving or supplying the fort. In addition, the French had not fortified several nearby hills, and the Grand Battery, located two miles across the harbor from the fort, had its heavy guns facing the harbor entrance rather than land approaches to the fort. The blockade and colonial landing rendered these guns useless. British cannon slowly moved forward, bombarding the French position with 9,000 cannonballs and demoralizing the defenders. Without the prospect of relief, the French surrendered Louisbourg on June 17, 1745.

IMAGE 2.3 Newspaper of King George's War The 1745 siege and capture of the French Fort Louisbourg in Canada represented the most significant operation during King George's War. The *Pennsylvania Gazette* provided colonists with a map and account of this spectacular military victory.

Despite their ineptitude and inefficiency, the colonials achieved their greatest victory of the war, losing only 101 men. French and Indian raids against New York and the New England frontier proved devastating, and Massachusetts and the other northern colonies had to resort to conscription to garrison Louisbourg through the brutally cold Cape Breton winter, which resulted in the death of 1,000 soldiers before spring 1746.

News of the victory at Louisbourg convinced British officials to consider other operations in North America. Shirley and Warren planned a combined land–sea operation against Québec and Crown Point, but officials in London canceled the 1746 operations, instead sending troops north to suppress the Jacobite Rebellion in Scotland and ships to the English Channel to prevent French assistance to Bonnie Prince Charlie (Charles Edward Stuart). In this moment of crisis, colonial aspirations were relegated to secondary importance to preserving the power of George II and the Hanoverians.

Meanwhile, British diplomats met with other European representatives in the Rhineland town of Aix-la-Chapelle to negotiate the war's end. France controlled much of the European continent, while Britain dominated the seas. The two sides faced a stalemate, with neither side having an advantage. Late in 1748 British colonists angrily learned that British peace commissioners had returned Fort Louisbourg and Cape Breton Island to France in exchange for territory in Europe and India.

The capture of Louisbourg gave colonials great confidence in their military abilities. Citizen soldiers, supported by the Royal Navy, had conquered one of the most heavily fortified positions in the Western Hemisphere. But the peace settlement left them angry and frustrated. King George's War had not advanced colonial security or satisfied colonial ambitions. Instead, it had proved yet again that London viewed the colonial theater as secondary to grand European strategy, highlighting a growing difference that would become more acute in the following years.

GREAT WAR FOR EMPIRE

Previous eighteenth-century wars had settled very little in North America. The boundaries between Georgia and Spanish Florida and between New England and French Canada remained ill defined. France and Spain encouraged Native Americans to resist continued English expansion, and Spaniards along the British colonies' southern border also encouraged slaves to flee from their masters and then outfitted them as soldiers to defend their own extensive frontier. Throughout, the British government offered little support to the colonies. The Crown sent few troops to defend the numerous Atlantic seaports and extensive frontier settlements, and this salutary neglect forced the colonists to protect themselves.

THE OHIO RIVER VALLEY

After King George's War enterprising colonials extended the boundaries of the English colonies westward into the Ohio River Valley. Several prominent Virginian planters, including Lawrence Washington, formed land companies and appealed to the Crown for western territories; the Ohio Company received 500,000 acres for settling 100 families and building a fort at the headwaters of the Ohio River. Pennsylvanian and Virginian fur traders crossed the

Appalachians, negotiated a route through Iroquois country, and created trading posts in the Ohio Valley. Packhorses then carried furs back east across the Appalachians, undermining the French position.

The French worked to protect their Indian trade and land claims in the Ohio Valley. They constructed Fort Kaskaskia at the confluence of the Mississippi and Kaskaskia rivers. Admiral Roland-Michel Barrin, Comte de La Galisonnière and governor-general of Canada, wanted to confine British settlements along the Atlantic seaboard by connecting French settlements in the St. Lawrence and Mississippi valleys and along the Gulf of Mexico. In 1749 Galisonnière sent Captain Pierre-Joseph Céloron de Blainville to renew French claims to the Ohio Country, gather intelligence on English activities in the region, and demonstrate to the Indians France's ability to send soldiers deep into the backcountry. During five months Céloron traveled 3,000 miles, planting at intervals leaden plates with inscriptions asserting the French claim to the region.

As Céloron moved through the Ohio Valley he learned that the British Ohio Company had started building fortified trading houses on the upper Potomac River. Anglo-Americans used the waters of the Potomac, Youghiogheny, and Monongahela rivers to assert control over the eastern end of the Ohio Valley. By spring 1752 Ohio Company agents had secured permission from the Delawares, Shawnees, and Mingos to construct a fortified trading house at the confluence of the Ohio, Allegheny, and Monongahela rivers. The French lacked permanent trading stations in the Ohio Valley and trade goods that could compete with cheap British consumer products, so the Indians gravitated toward the British.

During the early 1750s the French tried to undermine British economic control of the region. In an attack on the trading post of Pickawillany, French raiders killed fifteen Indians and a British trader, but this assault did not discourage British commercial activity. The new governor-general of Canada, Ange de Menneville, Marquis Duquesne, intensified France's aggressive tactics. During the spring of 1753 the French built Fort Presque Isle on the southern shore of Lake Erie. A portage road connected it to Fort Le Boeuf on French Creek, a tributary of the Allegheny River. Later that fall the French established an encampment (named Fort Machault in 1756) at the Delaware village of Venango near the confluence of the Allegheny and French Creek. A fourth post, planned for 1754, would bear Duquesne's name and be located at the confluence of the Ohio, Allegheny, and Monongahela rivers—the same location that the British Ohio Company had chosen for the site of its fortified trading post.

British officials in London believed that France was seeking to isolate the American colonials along the Atlantic coast, block British northeastern expansion along the Nova Scotia frontier, and extend direct control over the Ohio River Valley. During summer 1753 the British Ministry instructed colonial governors to strengthen their defense of their lands. Virginia governor Robert Dinwiddie also received instructions to build two forts on the Ohio River to counter French expansion. Lacking resources to do so or to drive the French from the Ohio Country, Dinwiddie sent a twenty-one-year-old adjutant of the Virginia militia, George Washington, to demand that France stop building forts and withdraw from the disputed lands.

Washington traveled into the Ohio Country with the discerning eye of a surveyor, noting the best locations for forts and ideal lands for farming. He also learned that most Indians of the region sided with France rather than Britain. Arriving at Fort Le Boeuf on French Creek in mid-December 1753, Washington presented the French commander with Governor Dinwiddie's letter. While the commander drafted a reply, Washington counted 220 finished canoes and others under construction, convincing him the French planned to transport large numbers of troops via water, possibly during the spring. The French commander politely refused Dinwiddie's request to withdraw, asserting a French claim to the occupied territory.

With the French position seemingly clear, Governor Dinwiddie enlisted militiamen, who began moving under Washington's command toward the Forks of the Ohio River. Dinwiddie also directed Ohio Company agent William Trent to start building a fort at the Forks before the spring thaw. As Washington's forces approached, construction started in mid-February 1754 and was assisted by Seneca chief Half King and many Ohio Indians, who also brought information that the Frenchmen planned to move against the valley during the spring. Half King symbolically placed the fort's first log, insisting that this bastion belonged to the Indians and their British brothers; together, he declared, they would make war on France. On the morning of April 17, 1754, just after the British hung the gate, 600 French troops with eighteen cannon arrived in canoes and pirogues.

French captain Claude-Pierre Pécaudy de Contrecoeur demanded the Englishmen surrender. Outnumbered and overpowered, the Englishmen surrendered and departed the next day with their lives. Contrecoeur quickly began building a bigger fort—the planned Duquesne—which would soon join Forts Detroit and Niagara as the most impressive military establishments in the interior of the continent. These outposts provided France with unquestioned control over the Ohio Valley and momentarily restored trade with the Indians.

A WORLD WAR

Despite the surrender, Washington's expedition, which had only 160 men, continued toward the Ohio Forks. To permit the passage of wagons and cannon, the Englishmen had to widen the narrow forest track, which slowed them to only a couple miles of progress a day. Moreover, their noisy advance alerted everyone—Indians and Frenchmen alike—to their presence. Contrecoeur decided to send Joseph Coulon de Villiers de Jumonville as an emissary to determine if the Englishmen had reached French territory. If so, Jumonville was to demand their immediate withdrawal.

As his force neared the Forks, Washington split it, sending 75 men to intercept the French near the Monongahela River. But the French had encamped in a shadowy glen later known as Jumonville Glen that laid in the opposite direction as the river. When Washington learned of the French position, he marched his men through rain and darkness, arriving near the encampment by early morning. Giving his men time to eat and to dry their weapons, Washington and his Indian allies then quietly approached the French position.

What happened next on May 28, 1754, remains unclear. French reports claimed the Englishmen attacked without warning, firing from the heights above the glen. Washington contended that a Frenchman screamed upon seeing the English, warning his comrades, who immediately began firing. Regardless, Washington's men reportedly fired two concentrated volleys at the French in the hollow. The Frenchmen returned a few shots and tried to scurry to the trees and safety, but Half King's warriors had blocked their approach, forcing them back into the defenseless clearing. A French officer quickly called for quarter, and Washington directed his men to cease their fire. After only ten minutes, fourteen wounded Frenchmen lay on the ground, whereas only one British soldier was dead and three wounded.

Ensign Jumonville was one of the wounded Frenchmen. Through a translator he told the British that the detachment had come in peace and that he had been sent with a message calling for the English to withdraw from French possessions. An interpreter began reading the French letter to Washington, but the chaos of the scene, punctuated by the moans of suffering soldiers, made understanding difficult. The translation went poorly, and the letter had to be read again. Still Washington did not understand, so he grabbed the letter to give to his own translator. When he turned his back, an impatient Half King reportedly grabbed Jumonville, screaming at him, "Thou are not yet dead, my father." Raising his hatchet, Half King repeatedly struck Jumonville in the head until he had shattered the Frenchman's skull. In a dramatic gesture the chief removed a handful of bloody tissue and rubbed his hands in the brain matter. Then other Indians yelled out and began butchering the wounded Frenchmen. Shocked by the display, Washington instructed his men to protect the surviving French soldiers. As he whisked Frenchmen out of the glen to safety, the Indians scalped thirteen corpses, reportedly decapitating one and impaling its head on a stake. The first shots had been fired in a world war that would soon determine the fate of North America.

During the weeks following the massacre, Washington hastily constructed a stockade at Great Meadows Run, sixty miles from Fort Duquesne, near present-day Uniontown, Pennsylvania, naming it Fort Necessity. Washington planned to attack Duquesne, but he learned in late June that a large French force had arrived at the fort. He instead remained at Fort Necessity, where he would hold out until reinforcements arrived.

Captain Louis Coulon de Villiers, Jumonville's older brother, arrived at Fort Necessity on July 2, 1754, with 600 French regulars and Canadian militiamen, supported by 100 Indian allies. That night it began raining, and by the following morning Fort Necessity resembled a swamp surrounded by canals. During the day Frenchmen and Indians constantly fired from the protective woods surrounding the fort. After a demoralizing wet day, and seeing no possibilities of defense or escape, Washington surrendered. The Englishmen promised to leave the Ohio Territory and to not return for one year. In signing the terms of capitulation, which were written in French, Washington assumed responsibility for "assassinating" Ensign Jumonville. As the Englishmen departed the following day, July 4, 1754, Washington saw Shawnee, Delaware, and Mingo Indians, who were supposedly loyal to Britain, instead aiding the French.

ALBANY CONGRESS

Both England and France willingly risked war to prevent the other from gaining control of the Ohio Valley and its waterways. When news of Washington's surrender and the construction of Fort Duquesne reached London in September 1754, British officials devised a grand plan to eliminate French forts in the interior and secure control over the continent's waterways. One expedition would move against the forts of the Ohio Valley. Another would destroy Fort Niagara on Lake Ontario. A third would demolish Fort Saint Frédéric on Lake Champlain, while a fourth would eliminate French fortifications on the isthmus of Nova Scotia. The key to these plans would be early success in the Ohio Valley.

Regardless of British or French plans, Indians still controlled the North American interior. Natives defined the military balance of power, and their participation determined the outcome of any war. Although several autonomous tribes and villages often competed against one another, they exploited their strategic positions and commercial advantages by forcing Europeans to offer gifts and constantly seek their friendship and approval. During the spring of 1754 the British government instructed its colonies to establish a common fund for military defense and to secure the friendship of the Iroquois. In June seven colonies (from New Hampshire southward to Maryland) participated in an intercolonial congress at Albany, New York, with the Iroquois. Never before had the colonies demonstrated such unity.

Nevertheless, the ambitious Albany Congress accomplished little. The Iroquois chiefs, after being presented with gifts, indicated they were tired of fighting Britain's wars without support. Once they were convinced of the colonial commitment to war, the Iroquois maintained, they might join the struggle. Even this neutrality would have worked to British advantage had land agents from Pennsylvania and Connecticut not intrigued with lesser Iroquois chiefs to secure lands west of the Susquehanna River. The chiefs sold these lands knowing the Iroquois council would not approve the transaction. These land transactions undermined Benjamin Franklin's plan for a colonial union, which would have created a common war fund as well as a regular intercolonial congress with the power to tax, regulate trade, and exert control over military affairs and a president-general appointed by the Crown

IMAGE 2.4 Join or Die, *Pennsylvania Gazette*, May 9, 1754 Benjamin Franklin's cartoon of a snake appeared in the *Pennsylvania Gazette* on May 9, 1754, alongside an editorial about the perils of the disunited state of the British colonies. Encouraging a colonial union, Franklin's plan would be supported by neither the colonies nor the Crown.

with veto power. Franklin's plea to "unite or die" did not sway either the colonies or the Crown, because neither wanted to relinquish any authority. The inability to find consensus initially stifled the British war effort.

BRADDOCK'S CAMPAIGN

General Edward Braddock arrived in Virginia in February 1755 with two regiments (1,400 men), met with neighboring governors, and tried to secure colonial assistance for an attack against the French. Pennsylvania reluctantly offered money, but little else materialized. Franklin, in his capacity as postmaster-general, secured for Braddock the supplies, wagons, and horses needed for an expedition. Braddock also had authority to raise two regiments in the colonies and integrate these troops into a four-pronged British operation to attack Forts Duquesne, Crown Point, Beauséjour, and Niagara.

The veteran soldier Braddock, greatly frustrated by colonial indifference, underestimated his French and Indian opponents. He also lacked appreciation for the qualities and experiences of his colonial soldiers and failed to understand the geographical challenges of the North American landscape. His army began its campaign in mid-spring but moved slowly, carving a road through the wilderness as it proceeded. After one month, Braddock's force had advanced only thirty miles, reaching the Great Meadows. Continuing at this pace would permit the French to rush reinforcements to meet any British attack. As a result, Braddock divided his army in June, sending a "flying column" (advance units) ahead and supply trains to the rear. By early July the flying column had crossed the Monongahela River and was closing in on Fort Duquesne.

On the morning of July 9, 1755, thirty-four-year-old Lieutenant Colonel Thomas Gage's command cautiously crossed the twisting Monongahela. The stifling heat, steep terrain, and dense foliage greatly slowed the British advance. After crossing the river a second time before noon, the flying column moved ahead about four miles before it stumbled into French regulars, Canadians, and Indians. Once the firing began, French troops quickly seized a hill on the British troops' right and a ravine on their left.

Braddock and Washington, both in the rear when the firing began, rode forward to find British troops exposed and surrounded on three sides. Firing from the thick foliage, the Frenchmen and Indians had both cover and camouflage. Fear crept into the British ranks when whooping Indians suddenly appeared to scalp fallen soldiers. Within minutes the British vanguard had disintegrated, discipline had collapsed, and men had begun firing randomly. Some British soldiers fled to the rear after witnessing the horrors of Indian warfare. Meanwhile, Braddock tried to rally his troops. Even as the French shot five horses from beneath him, he continued to bark out orders until a musket ball passed through his right arm into his chest, lodging in his lungs. Braddock suddenly collapsed, and the British rout followed. Helping carry Braddock to the rear, Washington guided to safety the remains of the army.

It had been a costly defeat. Washington reported that only 30 of his 150 Virginians survived. No fewer than two-thirds of the British forces engaged in the battle had been killed (456) or wounded (421). Sixty-three of eighty-six officers, including Braddock, died. Soldiers buried Braddock in the road they had constructed so his body would not be desecrated.

Braddock had not effectively managed the campaign. He had not employed enough reconnaissance, he did not divide his force into manageable units, and he did not occupy defensive positions until the bulk of the army could come forward. He also failed to build blockhouses during the advance, which saved time but also left the frontier defenseless after the disaster. Braddock's defeat represented the worst setback British forces had suffered during the colonial period and presaged further disasters.

BRITISH COMMITMENT

The northern campaigns failed before they began. In August 1755 Massachusetts governor William Shirley arrived at Fort Oswego on Lake Ontario with a substantial army, but his inability to secure food, supplies, and boats doomed the operation. In fact, the British inability to provide its soldiers with adequate food and supplies, combined with the strategic mobility of the French and Indians, created challenges that neither the colonies nor the Crown could overcome. The British–colonial army spent the remainder of the year in the dilapidated fort without securing the Niagara frontier. Shirley ultimately blamed his inactivity on Braddock's failure, which had left a sizable French defensive force across the lake at Fort Frontenac.

Meanwhile, Indian agent William Johnson led British troops north from Albany, constructing a road through the woods and building Fort Edward fifty miles up the Hudson River and Fort William Henry at the southern end of Lake George. The British planned to eliminate the French presence at Fort Saint Frédéric, forty miles north of Fort William Henry. In turn, French general Jean Armand, Baron de Dieskau, who occupied Fort Saint Frédéric, planned to advance against Fort Edward to the south, sever the supply lines, isolate Fort William Henry, and then destroy both forts. But in early September 1755 he could not convince his Indian allies to attack the unfinished Fort Edward, so instead he moved against Fort William Henry. His Iroquois allies—Kahnawake Mohawks—warned the Mohawks allied with the British of the impending attack because they did not want to shed one another's blood. When Johnson learned from Indian scouts that French forces were advancing en masse toward Fort Edward, he sent 1,200 colonials to reinforce the southern fort.

On September 8, English and French forces unknowingly advanced toward one another. Dieskau learned first of the English location and ambushed unsuspecting colonials in a ravine about four miles south of Lake George in a clash that came to be known as the Bloody Morning Scout. The British suffered devastating losses within minutes. Survivors fled south to Fort Edward, with Dieskau's army in pursuit. Later that day, in the Battle of Lake George, French forces brazenly attacked Fort Edward but found it manned and heavily defended with cannon; this time, British and colonial forces repulsed the French. Wounded and captured during the engagement, Dieskau later commented that the Englishmen had first fought like little boys, then like grown men, and finally like uncontrollable devils who could have crushed the French and Indian attackers had they followed their retreat. The battle became an example of the prowess of colonial American woodland fighters, who had succeeded in defeating a regular French army and its Indian allies. Johnson later completed the two unfinished English forts to prevent further French incursions into northern New York.

Of the four British campaigns of 1755, only Colonel Robert Monckton's attack against French installations on the isthmus of Nova Scotia had any success. Fort Beauséjour, defended by only 160 Frenchmen, fell to Monckton's 2,000 New Englanders after a four-day siege, and Fort Gaspereau surrendered the following day. Fearing a French counterattack from Louisbourg, the British government in Nova Scotia ordered the removal of all Acadian inhabitants who refused to take oaths of allegiance to Great Britain. The British scattered as many as 5,400 Acadians from Maine to Georgia with only a few possessions. Some 10,000 more Acadians fled to the mainland, where they joined with Indians and fought to regain their homeland. Many more, impoverished and homeless, desperately found their way to French Louisiana, where they came to be known as Cajuns—a corruption of the word "Acadians."

The British possessed a profound advantage in North America. With a colonial population of about 1.5 million and territory stretching north from the Savannah River to Passamaquoddy Bay and Nova Scotia, Britain could mobilize an estimated 45,000 men. New France had always been an afterthought of the French Empire, which sent few settlers (27,000, of whom only 10,000 stayed) and even fewer resources across the Atlantic. By the mid-1750s the French government's inattention had become evident: the colony had only 55,000 settlers, and the government could muster fewer than 10,000 regulars and provincials throughout Canada. France's Indian allies could potentially offset the British population advantage, and Governor-General Pierre de Rigaud de Vaudreuil and General Louis-Joseph Montcalm mobilized them. In August 1756 Montcalm's Indian allies captured Fort Oswego on Lake Ontario after a three-day siege; promised the honors of war, the Indians instead butchered 50 of the 1,600 English prisoners. Montcalm's efforts to prevent the atrocity ultimately alienated the Indians. Afterward, Montcalm minimized Indian participation in war efforts, which sparked a dispute with the governor and weakened the French war effort. During the following March, Vaudreuil's brother commanded troops who quietly crossed the snowy terrain and surprised the English defenders of Fort William Henry. After four days of bloody fighting, which inflicted severe British casualties and destroyed much of the fort's interior, the French and Indians quietly departed. The French had not captured the fort, but their attack delayed British offensive plans in the region for a year.

Braddock's replacement, John Campbell, Earl of Loudoun, initially appeared well suited to North American command. The fifty-two-year-old Scotsman had a distinguished record and the energy needed to forge a collective army made up of soldiers from disparate colonies. After arriving in New York during the summer of 1756, he soon learned the reality of colonial war when French and Indian forces struck along the frontier, attacking settlements in Virginia, Pennsylvania, Maryland, and the Ohio Valley. These attacks left Loudoun without the colonial cooperation and support he needed and allowed the French to move against Forts Oswego and William Henry. Loudoun then challenged colonial sensibilities in Albany during the winter of 1756–1757 by quartering British troops in private homes, an act that virtually all colonists believed violated the English Bill of Rights of 1689 and other parliamentary decrees, including the Mutiny Act. The New York assembly responded with appropriations for the construction of army barracks.

Having fought the clans in the rough terrain of the Scottish Highlands, Loudoun understood partisan warfare. He used British ranger units to gather intelligence and engage in guerrilla operations. New Hampshire's Robert Rogers, as well as New Englanders John Stark and Israel Putnam, commanded units that interrupted French communications, disrupted enemy reconnaissance, captured and interrogated prisoners, and conducted diversionary raids. Loudoun appreciated irregular warfare, but he doubted whether undisciplined frontiersmen could conduct long-term operations. During the early months of 1758 he created detachments of lightly armed mobile colonial units commanded by British officers skilled in the art of bush fighting.

French attacks at Oswego and Fort William Henry soon forced Loudoun to focus on Fort Louisbourg. Still the most heavily defended French position in North America, its capture would sever New France's communication, transportation, and resupply lines. But by year's end, Loudoun had obtained no victories in North America, and the character of the war had changed.

GLOBAL WAR

For two years the war in North America had raged without a European response. But in 1756 the colonial conflict merged with European affairs when Austrian Empress Maria Theresa orchestrated a French and Russian alliance against Frederick the Great of Prussia. Great Britain, ever mindful of the European balance of power, deserted Austria and joined with Prussia. King George II claimed Britain entered the war because France invaded Minorca.

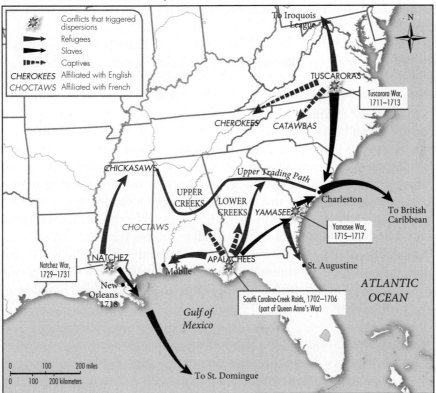

MAP 2.1 War, the Indian Slave Trade, and the Dispersal of Southeastern Indians, 1700–1730

At the same time, both Britain and France had deep-rooted interests in North America, and both saw the conflict as a way to determine who would control the continental interior and its profitable Indian trade. Though the Seven Years' War—also known as the French and Indian War and as the Great War for Empire—had American origins, it soon exploded into an international conflict.

LOCAL YET IMPERIAL DIMENSIONS

By the time the Seven Years' War began, warfare in the colonies had changed drastically. Originally colonists had protected themselves from Indians by constructing small, crude wooden bastions and using trade to pit one tribe against another. When isolation and trade failed to secure peace, colonists launched destructive campaigns aimed at eliminating the Indian presence. As war evolved to include European opponents, diplomacy and securing peace became more complex. The colonists realized that their styles of defense and fighting were inadequate; their methods had worked against Indians but seemed ruthless in the eyes of other Europeans. Moreover, their traditions, customs, and preference for militias rather than standing armies were suited only to local concerns and were unable to satisfy imperial ambitions. Poorly trained and outfitted, colonial militias refused to participate in campaigns outside their region for people who practiced a different religion or had a different ethnic origin. Instead, colonials had local concerns at heart. They wanted to protect their homes and families. Even the colonial alternative of calling up volunteers proved inadequate to meet imperial objectives, because most units served for only one campaign and disbanded when it concluded or failed. British officers also frequently complained that colonial soldiers lacked discipline and often retreated during battle. Given these perceptions, the British believed only Redcoats could wrest control of the North American interior from France.

As the global war intensified—with battles in Europe, North America, the Indies, and the Far East—British sea control became increasingly important. In April 1756 French forces landed on the British-held Mediterranean island of Minorca. In response, British admiral Sir John Byng moved to relieve British forces on the island, but in mid-May he instead attacked the blockading fleet of French admiral Roland-Michel Barrin, Comte de La Galisonnière. During the battle Byng maintained the standard British column-ahead formation rather than employing a general melee that might have secured a victory. Byng believed a melee with the French fleet could compromise the British position in the Mediterranean, including its hold on Gibraltar. Ultimately, Britain lost Minorca to the French, and a court of inquiry found Byng guilty of failing to "do his utmost" to defeat the enemy; he was executed by a firing squad. The trial and execution refocused British attention on naval operations and ship tactics and taught British officers to seek victory and honor instead of following inflexible rules of engagement.

WILLIAM PITT TAKES CHARGE

News of Braddock's and Byng's failures arrived in London at about the same time, precipitating the collapse of the Duke of Newcastle's government. The August 1756 emergence of William Pitt—known as the "Great Commoner"—as secretary of state and prime minister,

a role in which he wielded dictatorial power over ship and troop movements, reinvigorated the war effort. Pitt acknowledged that Britain lived by trade and that commerce
created wealth, which in turn enhanced military strength and naval supremacy. Britain's
small army could not sway the European balance of power, but the Royal Navy could win
any war with a maritime component, whether it was fought in Europe, the Far East, the
Caribbean, or North America. Pitt therefore directed the navy to blockade the French fleet
in port, preventing French reinforcements and supplies from reaching the New World.
Royal naval operations raided French seaports (destroying privateers, fortifications, and
shipping at St. Malo and Cherbourg in June and August of 1758, respectively), closed the
Strait of Gibraltar to French commerce, sealed French fleets in the Mediterranean, and
transported British troops to all regions of the globe. During the war France lost five times
more ships-of-war than did Britain, six times the number of privateers, and three times as
many commercial vessels, all of which decisively shaped the outcome of the North American struggle.

William Pitt also appointed younger, more aggressive officers to reinvigorate the war
effort abroad. Though Loudoun had laid important logistical foundations in North America
that assisted future operations, when his campaign failed, Pitt replaced him with James
Abercromby and appointed Jeffrey Amherst and John Forbes to subordinate commands. In
fall 1757 the Pitt ministry promoted John (Jean Louis) Ligonier to commander-in-chief of
British forces, and afterward he worked closely to craft a policy that would bring victory in

MAJOR CAMPAIGNS OF THE FRENCH AND INDIAN WARS

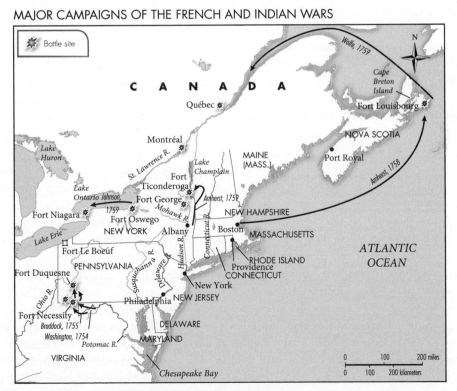

MAP 2.2 Major Campaigns of the French and Indian War

America. Pitt also provided financial subsidies to Frederick the Great, because his success on the European continent would force France to focus its attentions there. Finally, Pitt sent overseas the largest British armies ever committed to North America and introduced an "America-first" policy that provided cash reimbursements for colonial cooperation. While these unprecedented commitments helped Britain secure victory, they also burdened the nation with future debt and wrecked the empire.

1758: THE YEAR OF DECISION

In 1758 the British ministry adopted a three-pronged strategy to break French control in North America. General Amherst, supported by the Royal Navy, would move against Fort Louisbourg and then Québec. Abercromby would advance north through the Lake Champlain corridor into Canada, while John "Iron Head" Forbes moved against Fort Duquesne on the Ohio River. Although this approach resembled Loudoun's previous plan, Pitt opted to carry it out using British regulars rather than colonials.

Amherst had gained a reputation as a capable and steady officer. The forty-three-year-old soldier had never experienced an independent command, but he had gained the attention of Pitt and King George II, both of whom agreed he should be given a chance. By the time Amherst arrived in North America events were already in motion, with troops and ships awaiting direction. A naval blockade had given the British an incalculable advantage, preventing French reinforcements from reaching Louisbourg. Amherst and Admiral Edward Boscawen knew that the British fleet's long guns could pound the fort into submission, but a landing force needed to seize the bastion. Another rising officer, the thirty-one-year-old general James Wolfe, commanded the landing.

Since the end of King George's War the French had strengthened Louisbourg, building outlying entrenchments and fortifications. In the early morning hours of June 8, the weather and seas improved enough for Wolfe to land. Still, heavy surf smashed the landing boats against the rocks. French artillery and muskets picked off many of those British soldiers who did not drown in the swirling waters, and within a few minutes more than 100 had perished. Wolfe, convinced that the operation had failed, signaled for the boats to return to the fleet. But some of the boats either misunderstood the signal or completely disregarded it. Instead, they pushed ahead to a cluster of rocks west of Flat Point that the French had left undefended. Once these men had made it ashore, others quickly established a beachhead. The Frenchmen offered only token resistance before falling back four miles to the safety of Fort Louisbourg. During the next two weeks Boscawen's ships tightened their blockade of the island, while Wolfe's artillery inched ever closer to the fort. British artillery destroyed a French ship in the harbor and the fortress's headquarters, the largest building in North America. On July 25, Boscawen's ships eliminated the last two French ships-of-the-line in the harbor. The following day, July 26, 1758, Louisbourg surrendered to Wolfe. Certainly, the French could have withstood the British assault longer, but French governor Chevalier de Drucor chose not to risk more civilian lives. Unfortunately, the British victory occurred too late in the summer for the forces to continue operations against Québec. The victory did cut off supplies and communications to and from the interior, leaving French forces isolated and frozen in Canada.

Unaware of the British fortunes at Louisbourg, in July 1758 General Abercromby moved north with 28,000 regulars and provincials through the Champlain Valley. He arrived in early July at Fort Ticonderoga, where he found the French commander Louis Joseph, Marquis Montcalm, had only 6,000 men. Montcalm had moved his forces west of the fort to high ground and had erected a breastwork of trees lined with sharpened stakes. He also anticipated the arrival of reinforcements, forcing the unimaginative Abercromby to attack once reconnaissance indicated the earthworks could be taken. Abercromby chose not to use his artillery to destroy the wooden abatis but instead ordered his men to charge ahead, with devastating results. More than 1,500 regulars and 300 colonials were killed or wounded in the bloodiest single battle fought in North America before the Revolution. Dispirited and disorganized, Abercromby's force retreated south, with the general cursing and blaming the failure on his colonials. Some British officers, including Charles Lee, suggested the disaster had occurred because of Abercromby's incompetence. Whatever the reason, the setback delayed British operations against Canada.

Meanwhile, Forbes had organized some 7,000 men and in July began his advance on Fort Duquesne. Ignoring the road that Braddock and Washington had cut three years earlier, Forbes laboriously cut a new path through the Pennsylvania forest. Unlike Braddock, he built supply forts along the way for protection from the Indians who constantly harassed him, raided his baggage train, and drove off herds of livestock. It was a slow process. At the first frost some troops considered abandoning the campaign until the following spring. But in November Forbes learned that Fort Duquesne lacked food and supplies and that the Indians there were deserting the French, so he moved to attack quickly. Sending three brigades to the Ohio River on parallel routes to prevent a repeat of the Braddock ambush, Forbes's troops arrived at Three Rivers on November 26, 1758. They found that the French had evacuated the fort, leaving only smoking ruins.

In August 1758 Abercromby sent Colonel John Bradstreet to attack Fort Frontenac with 3,000 colonials. Knowing that colonial soldiers often deserted during long campaigns, Bradstreet believed he had a narrow window for success. By month's end he had arrived at Frontenac, where he positioned his guns and began siege operations. On the second morning of the attack Bradstreet moved his guns closer, greatly increasing their effectiveness. Within a few hours the French commander had surrendered the fort, with the British suffering no losses.

British victories in 1758 represented a turning point in the North American war. British naval forces prevented France from reinforcing and resupplying its positions. Military operations against Louisbourg, Duquesne, and Frontenac tightened the noose around Québec and other French settlements along the St. Lawrence River. Even the British defeat at Ticonderoga demonstrated that in time the French would have to withdraw north. Furthermore, Pitt's decision to pour additional money and troops into North America exhausted France's resources as it struggled to compete at the same level. In 1755 only 15 percent of Britons fighting in North America had been regulars, whereas by 1758 more than half were. Colonials drew their manpower from young men, who saw military service as a way for advancement; in both Virginia and Massachusetts the army reflected the social structure of the colony. Young men, seeing the financial benefits of land grants and bounties, enlisted in increasing numbers, further strengthening the British war effort. Britain was able to muster more than 45,000 men (regulars and colonials) in 1758, while France could count fewer than 10,000 men in its North American force.

QUEBEC

By 1759 New France was teetering on the brink of collapse. Poor harvests in 1757 and 1758 had driven food prices skyward, bankrupting the Canadian economy. French troops were forced to survive on partial rations, demoralizing the soldiers, who felt abandoned. The scarcity of French trade goods also drove Indians to British traders, who provided them the weapons, powder, and shot needed for hunting and war. In April 1759 the Iroquois acknowledged the power shift by renouncing their neutrality and joining with the British; led by Indian agent Sir William Johnson, they helped the British capture Fort Niagara in July 1759. The Canadians felt abandoned by their Indian allies and forgotten by their government.

Amherst received instructions in 1759 to advance north through the Lake Champlain Valley to join General Wolfe in an attack against Québec. To avoid the same fate Abercromby had suffered, he needed to eliminate French forts Ticonderoga and Crown Point. He spent weeks gathering men, equipment, and artillery, delaying his campaign until late July. By the time he brought forward his artillery to lay siege to Fort Ticonderoga, the French had destroyed it and retreated. The French also destroyed Crown Point when reinforcements failed to arrive. Despite these retreats, France maintained a presence on Lake Champlain, forcing Amherst to spend weeks building a brig and sloop to join his fleet of transport vessels.

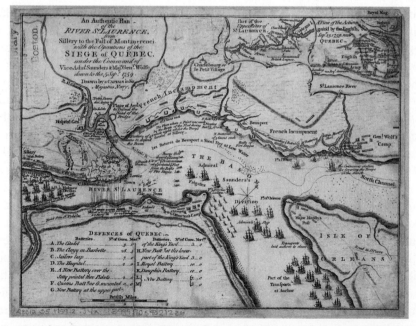

IMAGE 2.5   Map of Operations around Québec, 1759, drawn by Thomas Jeffreys. Map reproduction courtesy of the Norman B. Leventhal Map Center at the Boston Public Library.

By mid-October the newly constructed British fleet had seized control of the lake, but it was too late in the year to continue operations north to Québec.

Québec represented the linchpin of France's North American empire. Situated on the St. Lawrence River where it broadened into a great tidal estuary, the city commanded trade and communication routes into the North American interior. Located on a peninsula bounded by the St. Charles River to the east and the upper river of the St. Lawrence to the south and west, Québec's fort sat upon a rugged bluff that rose 250 feet above the river, seemingly virtually impregnable.

By the spring of 1759, Wolfe had assembled a naval flotilla of twenty-two capital ships; a dozen frigates; a host of sloops, bomb-ketches, and fireships; 119 transport craft; and 9,000 troops. Commanded by Admiral Charles Saunders, the massive naval fleet demonstrated Britain's resolve to conquer Canada. When Montcalm had learned of British plans for 1759, he had immediately shifted men from Montreal to Québec, a move that gave him more than 16,000 regulars, militiamen, and Indian allies. But despite having a numerical advantage in troops, Montcalm could not prevent the British approach, and the expedition moved slowly up the St. Lawrence; sailing master James Cook, who later explored the Pacific Ocean, sounded the river for passes and guided the amphibious operation though the treacherous Traverse Channel off the Île d'Orléans. After landing on the long and wide island in late June, British soldiers immediately began siege operations within sight of the city, four miles across the estuary from Québec.

Governor Vaudreuil and General Montcalm were astonished by the size of the British flotilla. Never had Britain devoted so many resources to operations in North America. The sight of British ships blockading the river and Redcoats digging in for a siege worried the French commanders. On the evening of June 28, Montcalm tried to break the naval blockade by setting adrift seven burning merchant ships loaded with explosives. He hoped these fireships would destroy the British fleet. Instead, British sailors towed the blazing hulks ashore before they did any damage. A few nights later Montcalm chained together fireships and set them adrift, but they too did no damage. Wolfe ultimately stopped the inferno by warning Montcalm that future fireships would be permitted to ram transports carrying French prisoners.

Wolfe understood that winter would arrive early and that his combined force needed to secure a quick victory, withdraw, or be frozen in place. During late July he tried to establish a beachhead below the city. He anticipated that the French could be lured from behind their defenses to fight a European-style battle, but two attacks failed to draw them out. Drawing on his experience in the brutal suppression of the Scottish Highlanders after the defeat of the Jacobite Rebellion, Wolfe then sent rangers and light infantry into the surrounding countryside to destroy all supplies and retaliate for partisan attacks against his army, seeking to demoralize the enemy by taking the war into their homes. British forces destroyed more than 1,400 farms as well as many small villages, but the French still did not leave their fortifications.

In late August Wolfe discovered that British ships could pass Québec's guns at night with the incoming tide. This convinced British officers that they could make a landing upriver from Québec, cut off Montcalm's supplies from the interior, and drive the French out of their defenses. Throughout early September, Wolfe steadily bombarded the city's Beauport defenses, prompting Montcalm to believe the British would land there.

Instead, during the early hours of September 12, 1759, Wolfe sent thirty flatboats with 1,800 men accompanied by frigates and sloops upriver with the tide. The moonlit night revealed these British operations to the French, permitting Louis-Antoine de Bougainville to march his French soldiers parallel to the British course on the bluffs along the river. When the tide turned, the sailors aboard the flatboats rowed vigorously downriver, quickly outdistancing Bougainville's exhausted men. Shortly after four in the morning British landing craft went ashore at their intended landing site—L'Anse au Foulon, only six miles from Québec.

British soldiers had strict instructions not to talk, smoke, or even cough, lest they lose the element of surprise and doom the expedition. Working against time, British officers unloaded the craft and sent vessels across the river to pick up additional men. Light infantry overwhelmed isolated French pickets near the river and then began climbing the steep cliffs. But as more British soldiers landed, the sound of their equipment clanging on the steep rocks alerted French outposts atop the cliff. When a French sentry shouted a challenge, a British officer responded in French that the noise was due to boats that had arrived from Cap-Rouge loaded with flour. Then British forces rushed the unsuspecting Frenchmen, who began running through cornfields to warn Québec. By sunrise, almost 5,000 British troops stood on the heights above the river. Sailors even dragged two six-pounders up the cliff, creating a small British artillery presence.

With the landing site and the path up the cliff secured, British forces took a defensive position on the Plains of Abraham, west of Québec. Wolfe cleared the area of enemy snipers and established a defensive line to the rear of his position to protect against Bougainville, whose riverside force could appear at any moment. Initially Montcalm refused to believe the British could scale the steep cliffs, viewing the British presence as a ruse to distract from a main attack that would occur below the city. Finally he received news that the entire British army stood west of the city. Even so, Montcalm could have withdrawn behind the city walls and waited for winter—although if he did, the British could also bring forward artillery to pound Québec's weaker western walls. Ultimately, Montcalm decided to give up his position on high ground and drive the British back down the cliffs.

Montcalm assembled 4,500 regulars, marines, and Indians, calculating that if Bougainville arrived with his 2,000 men at the rear of the British army, the British could be crushed in a vise. Unfortunately Bougainville never arrived. Shortly after eight in the morning, Montcalm's army began its advance toward Wolfe's position. Initially, British soldiers relaxed to avoid French fire and to rest. When the Frenchmen came within 350 yards, Wolfe instructed his men to rise, load their muskets with double shot, fix their bayonets, and hold their positions. Montcalm's advance seemed disorganized, and haphazard French shots had little effect. As Montcalm's army drew within 130 yards, the soldiers again fired, with shots hitting their targets. One shot struck Wolfe's wrist, which he wrapped with a handkerchief. After reloading, the Frenchmen resumed their approach, firing again from 100 yards. This time a half-spent shot struck Wolfe in the groin, momentarily doubling him over. Regaining his composure, Wolfe remained in front of the British battle line, still instructing his men to hold their fire. The British soldiers remained eerily quiet.

Reloading a third time, the French advanced to within 70 yards before firing again. At this range Redcoats began falling. Nonetheless, the British soldiers closed their ranks and remained steady. Montcalm advanced to within 40 yards. Then, just as the Frenchmen prepared to fire again, British officers preempted the moment, screaming for their men to fire. A sudden explosion of musket fire and artillery shot swept through French ranks. Then the Redcoats pressed their advantage, immediately firing again into the rattled Frenchmen. Montcalm's right wing immediately collapsed, and soon his left and center broke as well. The engagement devolved into a melee, with bagpipers playing a Highland tune in the background while British bayonets and Scottish broadswords exacted revenge on the fleeing French soldiers.

Wolfe suffered a third wound when a musket ball struck his chest. Soldiers carried him to the rear bleeding from his chest and groin. Knowing he was dying, Wolfe declined medical attention and then instructed that the French retreat be cut off immediately. Finally, he whispered, "I will die in peace."

His counterpart suffered a similar fate. Sitting astride a black charger, Montcalm had directed his Roussillon Regiment to hold its ground while other French units fled. Shortly before the regiment was overrun, a musket ball struck Montcalm's midsection. French soldiers kept him atop his horse and escorted Montcalm back into the city, where he died the following morning.

The fighting on the Plains of Abraham lasted only fifteen minutes, but it determined the outcome of the North American war. French troops surrendered the city six days later—September 18, 1759—while most French forces retreated toward Montreal. Six months later, in April 1760, General François-Gaston de Lévis tried unsuccessfully to

IMAGE 2.6 Benjamin West's *The Death of General Wolfe*, 1770   Pennsylvania artist Benjamin West painted this some 11 years after the British captured Québec. Creating a highly fictionalized portrayal of Wolfe's demise, colonists purchased thousands of copies of West's work, revealing their desire to identify as citizens of the British Empire.

retake Québec. By September, General Amherst had brilliantly overseen the convergence near Montreal of 15,000 British troops from three armies traveling from the west, south, and east. In the face of this force, Governor Vaudreuil's French irregulars deserted, and his Indian allies melted away, leaving him with only 2,000 defenders. On the morning of September 8, 1760, Vaudreuil surrendered Montreal, suspended resistance throughout Canada, and relinquished all remaining French posts to Britain. The war in North America had ended.

AN EMPIRE ON WHICH THE SUN NEVER SET

While Britain had conquered North America, the war continued elsewhere. Spain entered the conflict in 1761 in a futile attempt to maintain the European balance of power. During the next year British forces seized Manila in the Philippines and Havana in Cuba, and held Gibraltar. Britain also scored impressive victories in India, where Redcoats and sepoys reduced French outposts, establishing British control over the subcontinent. The year 1759 became the *annus mirabilis* (the miraculous year) during which Britain secured an empire on which the sun never set.

In the 1763 Peace of Paris concluding the war France ceded Nova Scotia, Cape Breton Island, and Canada to England. Spain relinquished both East and West Florida to England and in return received Cuba and the Philippines. France also gave Spain the colony of Louisiana west of the Mississippi River and the city of New Orleans and transferred the West Indian islands of Tobago, Dominica, Grenada, and St. Vincent, as well as the Indian subcontinent to Britain. With British conquests in North America, in the West Indies, the Philippines and India, and against the French West African slave-trading bases of Gorée and Senegal, the Royal Navy had demonstrated the international nature of future conflicts, as well as the importance of securing dominance and control over the oceans, seas, major rivers, and resources of several continents. Colonies, it was clear, existed for the benefit of the imperial power.

CONCLUSIONS

During the eighteenth century wars for empire, Great Britain emerged as a superpower, with domains spanning from Asia to Africa through the Mediterranean and the Caribbean to North America. Local-minded American colonials believed that they had defeated the French in North America and wanted to revel in their victory. The American mood was optimistic: new western lands and bountiful Indian trade lay just across the horizon, and colonists believed they could capitalize on the Indian fur trade, which was now dependent on consumer items, weapons, and powder. Instead, the British government began regulating the colonies in ways the people had not experienced or expected. While Britain acknowledged the strategic and economic value of its North American territories, the Crown expected the colonies to integrate more fully into the empire and help pay the debt incurred in their defense. Royal and colonial expectations and reactions ultimately put the two sides on the path to conflict.

British perceptions of the colonies evolved drastically between the beginning and end of the eighteenth century. Initially the Crown left the colonies alone. The colonists protected themselves, made their contribution to the royal coffers, and showed allegiance and obedience to the monarch. This permitted the imperial government to focus on the larger concerns of strengthening the empire and weakening its competitors. For most British leaders the colonies represented only locations on maps that signified imperial loss or gain. For locals those map points represented the nexus of their lives and survival.

The wars of the early eighteenth century were localized af-

TIMELINE

1609	Samuel de Champlain joins Huron attack against Iroquois
1652–1674	Anglo-Dutch Wars
1689–1697	King William's War
1701–1713	Queen Anne's War
1711–1715	Tuscarora War
1715–1717	Yamasee War
1739–1748	War of Jenkins' Ear
1744–1748	King George's War
1754–1763	Seven Years' War

fairs. Colonists fought against Frenchmen, Indians, and Spaniards, and each side tried to control geography—the St. Lawrence River, the Great Lakes, the Hudson River and Lake Champlain, and the Ohio–Mississippi watershed. By the early 1750s England and France were each focusing on the Ohio River Valley as the key to their colonial development because of the importance of the region's water routes to the continent's transportation and communication networks. The French believed that the Ohio River and its northern tributaries represented a strategic lynchpin connecting the Gulf of St. Lawrence to the Gulf of Mexico via the Mississippi River. This arc of settlement would produce the food and raw materials necessary to sustain France's North American colonial ventures, and the waterways would make these vibrant colonies accessible. But the British also needed the Ohio River Valley to relieve their colonies' growing population pressure, and the western waterways remained essential for communication and transportation. Ultimately the Seven Years' War was as much about controlling the continent's water avenues as it was about controlling the continent itself.

The eighteenth-century wars changed economic, political, governmental, and social relations between Britain, France, and Spain, their colonies and colonists, and the natives who inhabited these territories. By 1763 France had lost its North American holdings and Britain had gained control over the eastern portion of the continent. Both empires, however, suffered financially because of the war. American colonists believed that they had suffered more.

SUGGESTED READINGS

Anderson, Fred. *Crucible of War: The Seven Years' War and the Fate of Empire in British North America, 1754–1766.* New York: Oxford University Press, 2000.

Braund, Kathryn E. Holland. *Deerskins and Duffels: Creek Indian Trade with Anglo-America, 1685–1815.* Lincoln: University of Nebraska Press, 1996.

Brewer, John. *The Sinews of Power: War, Money, and the English State, 1688–1783.* Cambridge, MA: Harvard University Press, 1990.

Brumwell, Stephen. *Redcoats: The British Soldier and War in the Americas, 1755–1763*. New York: Cambridge University Press, 2002.

Dowd, Gregory Evans. *War under Heaven: Pontiac, the Indian Nations, and the British Empire*. Baltimore: Johns Hopkins University Press, 2002.

Harding, Richard. *Amphibious Warfare in the Eighteenth Century: The British Expeditions to the West Indies, 1740–42*. Suffolk, UK: Boydell and Brewer, 1991.

Hatley, Tom. *The Dividing Paths: Cherokees and South Carolinians Through the Revolutionary Era*. New York: Oxford University Press, 1995.

Jennings, Francis. *Empire of Fortune: Crown, Colonies, and Tribes in the Seven Years War in America*. New York: W. W. Norton, 1988.

Leach, Douglas Edward. *Roots of Conflict: British Armed Forces and Colonial Americans, 1677–1763*. Chapel Hill: University of North Carolina Press, 1986.

Mays, Thomas D. *American Guerrillas: From the French and Indian Wars to Iraq and Afghanistan—How Americans Fight Unconventional Wars*. Guilford, CT: Lyon Press, 2017.

Peckham, Howard H. *The Colonial Wars, 1689–1762*. Chicago: University of Chicago Press, 1964.

Starkey, Armstrong. *Europeans and Native American Warfare, 1675–1815*. Norman: University of Oklahoma Press, 1998.

Steele, Ian. *Betrayals: Fort William Henry and the "Massacre."* New York: Oxford University Press, 1990.

Swanson, Carl E. *Predators and Prizes: American Privateering and Imperial Warfare, 1739–1748*. Columbia: University of South Carolina Press, 1991.

White, Richard. *The Middle Ground: Indians, Empires, and Republics in the Great Lakes Region, 1650–1815*. Cambridge, UK: Cambridge University Press, 1991.

CHAPTER 3

'TIS TIME TO PART

1763–1776

A Changing Relationship • Revenue Acts • The Boston Massacre • Troubles over Tea
• Shots Heard Round the World • Bunker, No, Breed's Hill • No More Middle Ground
• On to Canada • Toward Independence

Following the Seven Years' War, successive British ministries tried to implement reforms that would cut administrative costs and raise more revenue in the North American colonies. These reforms aimed to strengthen Britain's military position within the colonies, provide defense against foreign enemies, and help extinguish the burdensome debt incurred during the Seven Years' War. Among them were orders that the Royal Navy help enforce customs laws in American ports.

Lieutenant William Dudingston had arrived in Narragansett Bay in the colony of Rhode Island in late March 1772 as commander of the customs schooner HMS *Gaspee*. Rhode Islanders had overtly flaunted British maritime restrictions, smuggled, and even traded with the enemy during the Seven Years' War. Dudingston and his officers immediately began enforcing British laws, overzealously boarding and detaining ships and indiscriminately condemning and seizing cargoes, all of which greatly angered colonials.

On June 9, 1772, *Gaspee* began chasing the packet boat *Hannah*, which was en route from Newport to Providence. While in pursuit that afternoon, *Gaspee* ran aground on the shallow northwestern side of Narragansett Bay, near present-day Warwick. Unable to refloat his schooner, Dudingston anticipated that a rising morning tide would dislodge the vessel. But before the tide came in, a group of Providence-based "Sons of Liberty" rowed out and forcibly boarded the British ship; in the process, Lieutenant Dudingston was shot in the groin. Without trying to disguise their identities, the colonials—including prominent Providence merchant John Brown—removed Dudingston and his crew to safety, looted the schooner, and then torched it. This deliberate destruction of a British ship was interpreted by authorities as a treasonous act.

British admiral John Montagu was placed in charge of determining who had been responsible. Dudingston and his crew offered to identify those involved, but local courts hostile to heavy-handed British authority would not condemn colonials to a certain death penalty. The British Ministry appointed a commission of inquiry to investigate the affair, which concluded in January 1773 that no one, including civil officials in Rhode Island, was guilty. Nevertheless, alarm spread throughout the colonies over the many powers granted to the commission, including the authority to send the accused, witnesses, and evidence to England for trial, which directly violated the ancient English right of trial by a jury of one's peers. Newspapers speculated as to what the next assault on colonial rights would be. In Virginia, an alarmed House of Burgesses quickly instructed its correspondence committee to communicate with other colonies about British threats. Within twelve months all of the colonies, except Pennsylvania, had created correspondence committees that would serve as an intercolonial information network. In the face of a changing relationship, colonials were developing a common awareness.

A CHANGING RELATIONSHIP

The end of the Seven Years' War changed the North American environment. France lost its colonial possessions in North America. Spain relinquished the Florida peninsula to Great Britain but assumed control over France's Louisiana colony and lands west of the Mississippi River. Great Britain gained France's territorial claims to all lands east of the Mississippi River, which permitted it to strengthen and consolidate its empire. American colonials assumed they would have greater access to the recently gained spoils.

British policymakers had also learned that the American colonies possessed strategic as well as economic importance. A burgeoning population corralled and isolated along the Atlantic coastline would create markets for trade and permit officials to extract more revenue from the colonies for imperial operations. British merchants could also profit from the native fur trade. In this view, natives and colonials would coexist in a system that kept each in their respective domains and permitted the mercantilist system to maximize profits for the Crown. Unfortunately, this system was challenged immediately by the Indians and then by colonials, who felt that their rights were being threatened as the policy of "benign neglect" gave way to active imperial intervention.

PONTIAC'S REBELLION

For generations Native American tribes had played the European powers against one another for their own benefit. With the end of the Seven Years' War, Indians expected changes in their relationships, but not to the extent they experienced. Without French competition, there were fewer trading centers, and the victorious British frequently played the tribes against one another. The British army occupied Indian country, officers stopped gifting items to the tribes, and English traders increasingly defrauded Indians during exchanges.

Inspired by a religious vision, Delaware prophet Neolin insisted that Native Americans reject European ways and return to a traditional lifestyle. Ottawa chief Pontiac and other

Great Lakes tribes embraced Neolin's call to drive out British soldiers and settlers. Beginning in May 1763 Pontiac's warriors attacked Fort Detroit and sacked eight other western British forts; hostile tribes then targeted frontier settlements in Pennsylvania, Maryland, and Virginia. By July the Indians had destroyed all western British posts, except for Forts Pitt, Detroit, and Niagara. During one bitter attack against Fort Pitt, British troops reportedly distributed smallpox-infested blankets and handkerchiefs to the Indians in order to infect the attackers and break the siege. By the end of the year, Pontiac's allies had killed or captured 600 colonials.

In December 1763, some fifty colonial vigilantes from the Paxton area of Pennsylvania descended on a peaceful Susquehannock village and slaughtered six Christian Indians. Local officials quickly placed sixteen other Susquehannocks in custody in Lancaster for their

NORTH AMERICA AFTER THE TREATY OF PARIS, 1763

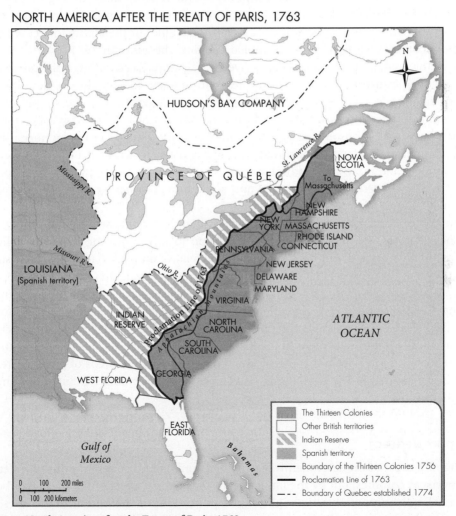

MAP 3.1 **North America after the Treaty of Paris, 1763**

safety, but the Scotch-Irish Presbyterian Paxton mob, angry about the frequent Indian raids as well as the Pennsylvania government's unwillingness to protect its citizens, broke into the jail and brutally butchered them too. The vigilantes then turned east toward Philadelphia with the intention of killing every Indian within the colony. Only the presence of Pennsylvania's militia and British soldiers, along with negotiations by Benjamin Franklin and Governor John Penn, prevented the further massacre of peaceful Indians who had gathered in Philadelphia.

The spring and summer of 1764 witnessed increased native raids throughout western Virginia and Pennsylvania. Colonels John Bradstreet and Henry Bouquet responded with armed incursions into the Ohio Country, in which they burned native villages and destroyed food supplies to punish Indians for the attacks. Meanwhile, William Johnson convinced the Iroquois to remain neutral and the Senecas to renounce their support for Pontiac, and Indian agent John Stuart kept the southern tribes from joining Pontiac's coalition. These agreements kept more than 2,000 Indians from descending on other white settlements. Without the support of additional Indian allies or the ability to secure French supplies, Pontiac's struggle soon crumbled. During the autumn of 1764 the Seneca-Cayugas, the Shawnees, and the Lenapes (Delawares) acquiesced within quick succession, returning their captives and ceasing hostilities. Within weeks most of the smaller tribes had stopped fighting as well. Pontiac himself never surrendered. Instead, he simply became less strident and defiant, even traveling during the summer of 1766 to New York, where he signed a treaty with Johnson. The agreement neither acknowledged surrender nor called for Pontiac to relinquish land or prisoners. Ostensibly, Pontiac accepted British sovereignty, while younger and more strident Indian leaders crossed the Mississippi River into Spanish (formerly French) territory. Negotiation and accommodation rather than military victory brought an end to the war.

The end of Pontiac's Rebellion opened western lands to white settlers and farmers. But even before peace was restored, settlers had begun to move into the Kanawha Valley of western Virginia at an alarming pace. George Grenville's ministry had anticipated such a possibility and the prospect that it would rekindle an Indian war. On October 7, 1763, King George III issued a royal proclamation closing the west between the Appalachian Mountains and the Mississippi River to white settlement and creating three new colonies out of former Catholic (French and Spanish) lands: Québec, East Florida, and West Florida. The proclamation specifically forbid settlement in the Kanawha Valley and Ohio Country, and instructed soldiers to evict settlers from these territories. Within months hundreds of pioneers, resentful of heavy-handed British regulations, had crossed the mountains, blatantly ignoring the Crown's directives.

SALUTARY NEGLECT

Throughout most of the seventeenth century, England had no coherent policy for dealing with overseas colonies, but by the latter part of the century mercantilist ideas had begun to shape English imperial thought about and policy toward the American colonies. The passage of the first of the Navigation Acts in 1651, which forbade the use of foreign ships for trade between England and its colonies, had sought to keep the benefits of trade within the empire while minimizing the loss of gold and silver to competitors; successive renewals of this act had occurred in 1660, 1663, 1670, and 1673, all aimed at tightening restrictions. The 1696 Navigation Act had closed an earlier loophole, further strengthened enforcement after the Anglo-Dutch Wars, and provided for additional oversight of colonial trade.

The consolidation of Scotland and England into Great Britain with the Act of Union in 1707 had permitted the Scots to operate within English trade and financial networks. British commerce also flourished. Robert Walpole, who acted as prime minister from 1721 to 1742, came to power in the aftermath of the so-called South Sea Bubble and solved this financial mess that had almost destroyed Britain's economy. Under his guidance, the government enacted legislation such as the Hat Act of 1732 (which placed strict limits on the manufacture, sale, and export of American-made hats) and the Molasses Act of 1733 (which heavily taxed non-English molasses and sugar) aimed at regulating commerce and raising revenues. His successor, Henry Pelham, ushered in the Iron Act of 1750, which attempted to restrict manufacturing in the American colonies. These measures all attempted to control American trade and produce positive income streams for the British government. Despite the economic shift produced by the Old Colonial System—or mercantilism—American colonials still held to the idea that they governed themselves and controlled their own economic destiny. After 1763, neither would be the case as successive British governments passed acts designated to regulate—not oppress—the American colonies.

The British policy of salutary neglect, which gave rise to decades of imperial indifference toward the empire's North American holdings, permitted the American colonies to conduct their own affairs as long as those actions did not contradict or challenge British policy. Under the economic theory of mercantilism, colonies developed economic activities and prospered with little oversight; they governed themselves and for the most part protected themselves as well. Colonials accepted taxation as long as the taxes regulated trade and benefited the empire as a whole—considering themselves full citizens of the empire, they were willing to shoulder their load. They would also accept higher prices for certain imported products from other British colonies as long as the system also supported a market for the items they produced. Under this economic system—often described as triangular trade—all benefited, although some more than others, and the empire generally prospered. Settlers willingly accepted less economic profit for the benefits of being included within this closed economic system and being part of the British Empire.

The British Constitution guaranteed that subjects would not be taxed without their consent. Only a representative Parliament could pass taxation measures to raise revenue. Since the colonists had no elected members in Parliament, they believed that this body could not impose revenue taxes without their explicit consent, as such action would represent a violation of their rights under the British Constitution. Nevertheless, Parliament could and would pass legislation that adversely regulated economic development within individual colonies, and royal governors—who were very often also military officers—would see that the colonies abided by parliamentary decrees that purportedly benefited Britain as a whole.

SUGAR AND STAMPS

After 1763 successive ministries tried to tighten economic controls over the colonies while increasing revenue to reduce British debts that by January 1764 totaled about £130 million. In September 1764 the Grenville ministry replaced the Molasses Act with the Sugar Act (also called the American Revenue Act), which permitted the importation of molasses and sugar from non-English colonies while lowering the tax rate on these products and working to enforce collection of the duty. The language of the bill made it abundantly clear that the British government was taxing American colonials to raise revenue rather than regulate commerce. This indirect tax would help reduce the burdensome debt. Parliament also passed the Currency Act, which restricted the supply of colonial paper money and required that British merchants be paid in specie. These measures aimed to increase the flow of revenue and specie from the colonies to Britain. Caught in a postwar economic depression, the colonials protested the acts not because of constitutional concerns about taxation and representation, but because of these measures' impact on daily colonial life.

The Grenville ministry authorized the presence of a small fleet (eight warships and twelve sloops) in American waters to protect the colonies and enforce customs regulations. Additionally, it approved the stationing of seventeen regiments of soldiers (some 8,500 men) in America under the command of General Thomas Gage. This was more than twice the number of British Redcoats who had been stationed in America before the war with France. In May 1765 Parliament passed the Quartering Act requiring the colonies to provide accommodations for these troops in public barracks, vacant buildings, or taverns; the colonies also had to contribute cider or beer, firewood, candles, and other supplies for the soldiers, as well as military transport at fixed prices. Colonists viewed this measure as a direct violation of their individual liberties and of the British Mutiny Act, legislation passed annually by Parliament that forbade the quartering of troops in private residences. The forced quartering of a standing army and the presence of ships along the coast convinced many colonials that these military instruments would be used to suppress further their rights.

By 1765 Grenville had concluded that a stamp tax could be a successful method of raising revenue from the American colonies. Britain had a successful stamp tax for decades that had worked with little effort. Since the American colonies did not suffer as heavy a tax burden as did England, Grenville believed it was time for the colonies to take on their share of the imperial burden. The direct revenue stamp tax—which required that a Crown stamp be placed upon newspapers, magazines, almanacs, pamphlets, all legal documents (including birth and death certificates), insurance policies, ships' papers, licenses, and even dice and playing cards—had to be paid in specie rather than colonial paper money, with the revenue used to maintain troops in North America. The legislation revealed London's belief in the sovereignty of Parliament, and the revenue it generated freed royal officials in the colonies from being held hostage by recalcitrant colonial assemblies.

The *Maryland Gazette* revealed during the spring of 1765 that colonists were "THUNDER-STRUCK" by the pattern of tyranny emerging: they had to support an army they did not want or need, they had been forbidden to expand into the interior of the continent, their maritime commerce had been crippled by rigid rules, their supply of currency had been severely restricted, and they had been forced to pay a heavy stamp tax that violated their rights as

MINISTERIAL TURNOVER IN BRITAIN

LEADING MINISTER	DATES	AMERICAN POLICY
Lord Bute	1760–1763	Mildly reformist
George Grenville	1763–1765	Ardently reformist
Lord Rockingham	1765–1766	Accommodationist
William Pitt/Charles Townsend	1766–1770	Ardently reformist
Lord North	1770–1782	Coercive

Englishmen. The slogan "no taxation without representation" emerged as a popular colonial refrain. Local protests and demonstrations, led by the Sons of Liberty, mobilized people, often in violent and destructive ways, giving rise to threats against Crown officials and tax distributors of tarring and feathering or other physical punishment.

Colonial committees of correspondence transmitted information between colonies, and were responsible for convening the first meeting of officials to present a unified voice against British taxation. Held in New York City in October 1765, the body, which came to be known as the Stamp Act Congress, drafted a Declaration of Rights and Grievances for King George III in which delegates from nine colonies proclaimed their loyalty to the Crown while insisting that Parliament had no authority to tax them because it contained no members from the American colonies. This legalistic approach—insisting that the colonists were loyal to the Crown, contending that they had rights that were being abused, and asking for their grievances to be redressed—became characteristic of colonial complaints. The delegates acknowledged that the Crown could levy external taxes (duties on external trade) but did not believe that Parliament could levy internal taxes (derived from internal colonial transactions) unless the colonies were represented there. Upon learning of this argument, Grenville blustered that all colonies were represented virtually—no individual Member of Parliament represented a district but rather acted for the empire as a whole. George III never addressed colonial concerns, but Parliament buckled to the growing commercial pressure, soon agreeing to repeal the despised act.

The Stamp Act was in fact broadly unpopular. British merchants and industrialists opposed it because it threatened their trade with the Americans. Colonials hated it because it attempted to generate revenue without their approval. Grenville did not have to endure the protest long, because he soon fell out of favor with the king, who replaced him with Charles Watson-Wentworth. This reflected another problem: the colonies faced a revolving door of ministers, each more insistent on forcefully solving the American crisis. King George III was continually reshaping British politics by installing like-minded ministers who would enforce his policies. And even though many British merchants and Whig opponents had favored repealing the Stamp Act, most colonial sympathizers urged that Britain's authority over the colonies be strongly asserted. On March 18, 1766, Parliament repealed the Stamp Act and in the same breath passed the Declaratory Act, a far more dangerous measure because it proclaimed that Parliament had the full power and authority to bind the colonies and their people "in all cases whatsoever." In other words, Parliament maintained that it had complete and absolute power to govern the colonies even though colonials had no representation in Parliament. Colonials, overjoyed at the repeal of the Stamp Act, took little notice of the Declaratory Act.

REVENUE ACTS

Charles Townshend, the British chancellor of the exchequer (treasury minister) under William Pitt, believed the contemptuous colonials had to pay for their disobedience. Taking advantage of a brief absence of Pitt due to illness, Townshend proposed the Revenue Act of 1767 (also called the Townshend Revenue Act), an external duty that taxed tea, paints, paper, lead, glass, and other items imported by the colonists. He sought the imposition of these taxes to buttress British authority as well as to meet the expenses of maintaining an army in the colonies. Money raised would maintain troops and ships in America that could enforce the legislation. Townshend died unexpectedly during the summer of 1767, but before his death he convinced Parliament to create four new admiralty courts in North America (at Halifax, Boston, Philadelphia, and Charleston), which allowed more vigorous enforcement of the Townshend Taxes. Townshend's successor, Lord Frederick North, fearing growing colonial protest, sent regiments of Redcoats to New York, New Jersey, and Pennsylvania and at the same time permitted white settlement beyond the Appalachian Mountains in an attempt to pacify rising anger. Nevertheless, the Townshend duties, along with the reallocation of troops, dared colonials to resist.

Most colonists found that they could simply avoid consuming the taxed items, except for tea, which had become almost as popular as coffee. They could avoid paying taxes on that product by smuggling cheaper Dutch teas into American harbors. The return of economic prosperity in Britain further prompted colonials to clamor against growing British control. Some colonists began demanding that the Townshend taxes be repealed, while others simply boycotted British goods—a type of economic warfare that permitted the colonists to show their anger without violence or disorder. John Dickinson's response to the Townshend Acts, "Letters from a Farmer in Pennsylvania," argued that no difference existed between internal and external taxes, and that any duty that raised revenue was therefore unconstitutional. The Massachusetts House of Representatives officially echoed Dickinson's argument in a petition to King George III that pleaded for the repeal of the Revenue Act. Virginia and Pennsylvania sent similar petitions to Parliament. Instead of acceding to colonial demands, British colonial secretary Lord Hillsborough instructed royal governors to dissolve legislatures that refused to rescind their petitions.

Boston soon became the epicenter of protest against the Townshend Acts. Royal customs collectors, trying to do their jobs, suffered verbal and physical abuse. Mobs threatened collectors and burned them in effigy on "Liberty Trees." The escalation of violence forced General Gage to send four regiments of troops to Boston early in 1768, which brought a momentary calm to the city. In early June 1768 the fifty-gun frigate *Romney*, which had been sent to enforce customs restrictions, assisted with the capture of the merchant ship *Liberty*, owned by John Hancock. The ship had supposedly landed a cargo of Madeira wine without paying customs duties, prompting its seizure. Bostonians, already angry because the frigate's captain had been impressing locals to fill the ship's complement of crew, threatened customs' collectors, heckled and ridiculed troops, and rioted. Lord Hillsborough instructed Massachusetts governor Francis Bernard to find evidence of treason in Boston. Because the Treason Act of 1543 was still in effect, anyone accused of that crime would be transported to England to stand trial. Bernard could find no one willing to provide reliable evidence, and the possibility that colonials would be arrested and sent to England for trial created further outrage and made the colonists even more suspicious of Crown intentions.

THE BOSTON MASSACRE

Even with four regiments of troops in Boston, General Gage could not prevent trouble in the city. Violence was common, and cultural differences exacerbated the situation. There was also the problem of economic competition, as soldiers worked part-time jobs to supplement their pay, which limited the number of jobs for colonials. Tensions mounted as violent mobs assaulted customs officials, attacked newspaper printers, and in one instance tarred and feathered a customs informer. In October 1769 a crowd attacked a soldier as he went off duty, forcing other troops to mount their bayonets to defend themselves.

The first death of the struggle occurred on February 22, 1770, when a mob gathered around the house of Ebenezer Richardson, an infamous customs informer. Richardson came out of his house with a musket, demanding that the mob leave. The crowd refused, and Richardson fired a shot, which accidently struck and killed eleven-year-old Christopher Snyder, a boy who was there to watch the commotion. The mob dragged Richardson to jail, but the General Court later acquitted him. Afterward mobs paraded through the streets seeking British officials, soldiers, and trouble.

Two weeks later, on March 5, 1770, a crowd surrounded a sentinel standing guard in front of the customs house on King Street. Feeling overwhelmed and threatened, the guard called loudly for help. Responding to his call, Captain Thomas Preston and seven soldiers quickly ran through the city with mounted bayonets, followed by throngs of people. Church bells rang, and within minutes the soldiers faced a crowd of almost 400. As the gathering became more unruly, the crowd backed the soldiers up against the customs house, belaboring them with epithets, taunting them, and then throwing frozen vegetables, icy snowballs, and rocks at them. Preston formed his Redcoats into a semicircle, yelling for the mob to disperse. Suddenly, a soldier was knocked down, and he dropped his weapon. When he rose from retrieving it, he angrily shouted, "Fire," and discharged his musket into the crowd. Preston had given no such command, and a pregnant pause of several seconds followed. Then the colonials fiercely swung clubs and threw objects at the soldiers, who responded with a ragged series of six shots that struck eleven men, killing five civilians and wounding six others in what came to be termed the "Boston Massacre." Crispus Attucks, a runaway mulatto slave and a ringleader of the mob, was one of the first to die for American liberty, even though he himself lacked freedom.

On the same day as the Boston Massacre, Lord North introduced provisions to repeal the Townshend duties—but he insisted that the tea tax remain in place, inasmuch as it offered

IMAGE 3.1 Boston Massacre   Paul Revere published this sensationalized engraving of the Boston Massacre in March 1770. It reveals the massacre of unarmed citizens in front of the Boston Custom House, which Revere labeled "Butcher's Hall" and colorized with red to symbolize the blood and Redcoat troops.

proof that the Crown had the power to tax the colonies. Since the royal government did not rigidly maintain or enforce this tax, colonial passions quickly subsided. Colonists could, if they wanted, secure smuggled leaves far more cheaply. Even with British warships off shore, smugglers had little difficulty entering the city. In some instances, royal agents did thwart smugglers, but in others colonials boldly challenged British authority. In June 1772, the captain and crew of HMS *Gaspee* learned how brazen colonials could become when the latter seized a British customs ship and burned it. Trials began in January 1773 to find those responsible, but colonials refused to send their own to trial in England, which undoubtedly would result in a death sentence.

In early 1773 Lord North also decided that colonial judges and the Massachusetts governor should be paid by receipts from customs duties, which now necessitated vigorous enforcement of restrictions. For colonials, it appeared that the British government had created a system in which they would be under the control of an executive and judicial power controlled by London and maintained by military force.

TROUBLES OVER TEA

By 1773 the British "John Company," or East India Company, was facing financial trouble as its stock prices dropped precipitously from £280 to £160. The company's stockholders included Members of Parliament and ministers, and it also served as the instrument of government in India. Should the company fail, British authority over the subcontinent could collapse. While the company suffered, it did have assets that could be liquidated into cash, including 17 million pounds of tea in warehouses and more en route to the United Kingdom. If the company sent its tea directly to America without paying duties, then it could undercut Dutch smugglers and solve two problems—the company's financial crisis and the royal government's problem with revenue collection. Lord North secured passage of the Tea Act in May 1774, which authorized the East India Company to ship tea directly to America without paying tax. Additionally, the company would sell its tea in the colonies only through a select group of merchants. Even burdened with the Townshend tax, the resulting price of the company's tea surprisingly undercut that of smuggled Dutch tea.

Before the end of 1773 East India Company ships began arriving in American port cities. Local committees of correspondence had alerted colonials to the coming troubles. In Boston, thousands of locals interpreted the company's actions through the lens of patriotism. Marching down to the waterside on the evening of December 16, 1773, men barely disguised as Mohawk Indians boarded three ships and threw overboard some 342 chests of tea representing a monetary loss of £9,000. In Charleston, South Carolina, a cargo of tea landed by a ship captain despite threats was locked up by colonists, who ultimately sold it to support the Patriot cause. On Christmas Day, a tea ship arrived off Philadelphia, and locals told the captain he should return to England. He did so. In April 1774 Sons of Liberty threw overboard the cargo of one tea ship in New York City, while another opted to return to England. The last tea party occurred in Annapolis, Maryland, during the fall of 1774, when a merchant tried to bring ashore some 2,000 pounds of tea. Ultimately the tea and the ship carrying it were destroyed with the coerced consent of the owners. This type of vigilante action harkened back to the *Gaspee* affair, prompting some, such as Benjamin Franklin, to argue that Americans had gone too far and should reimburse the company for the destruction of private property.

British indignation soared when news of the tea parties reached London. The colonists had not only resisted the British government but also destroyed private property. British

THE DESTRUCTION OF TEA AT BOSTON HARBOR.

IMAGE 3.2   Boston Tea Party   This engraving of the Boston Tea Party shows fanciful disguised colonists resembling Mohawk Indians boarding East India Company ships and destroying 342 chests of tea. The colonists had resisted the British government and destroyed private property, prompting King George III to decry that the "colonists must either submit or triumph." Colonists saw this through the lens of patriotism.

officials believed the fate of the empire was at stake. Angrily, George III thundered that the "colonists must either submit or triumph," forcing Lord North to make an example of Boston. Previously the British government had forced certain cities to pay for damage inflicted by riotous citizens, and North decided to exact that punishment on Boston. On the last day of March 1774, the king signed the Boston Port Bill, which closed the harbor to commerce until peace and law and order were restored in the city and required Boston to pay for the lost tea. Parliament also passed the Massachusetts Government Act, which restructured the colonial government under a royally chosen council and permitted each community only one town meeting per year; the Administration of Justice Act, which allowed trials to be moved from Massachusetts to Britain; and a new Quartering Act, which compelled locals to provide lodging for British soldiers. These measures, known as the Coercive Acts, aimed to isolate Boston and make an example of the colony. Colonials saw them as "Intolerable Acts" that should be resisted, lest other colonies suffer likewise. General Thomas Gage now became governor of Massachusetts, and with his 4,000 soldiers he implemented martial law.

Gage had been in the army since 1741 and had participated in the War of Austrian Succession as well as the defeat of Bonnie Prince Charlie at the 1746 Battle of Culloden. Having arrived in America as a part of Braddock's expedition, in early 1758 he created the British army's first light infantry units, which were better suited for woodland warfare. After General Jeffrey Amherst's return to England in 1763, Gage became the highest-ranking military officer in North America and administered the widespread colonial holdings. Coming to believe that democracy was too prevalent in America and that town meetings were dangerous to British rule, on June 1, 1774, he closed the port of Boston. Gage thought that his magnanimous gesture of permitting the legislature to meet would convince that body to pay for the tea. Instead, the Massachusetts Committee of Correspondence issued an invitation for colonies to send delegates to a congress that would convene in Philadelphia on September 5, 1774. Gage immediately dismissed the recalcitrant legislature and asked for more troops, which began arriving during the summer. In early August Gage announced he would implement the new royal government for Massachusetts, consisting of a twenty-four-member royal council of men loyal to the king, and issued writs for elections for the new colonial legislature. Outside of Boston, farmers, merchants, and villagers asserted that they would not allow the new government to operate. They began gathering arms and indicated that they would use them if soldiers left the city.

On September 1, Gage sent out a detachment of 250 men from Boston to Cambridge to seize 125 barrels of gunpowder. The mission occurred without incident, although the march aroused the whole countryside. The following day thousands of armed men converged on Boston. After the crowd peacefully disbanded, Gage fortified the city and requested additional troops and ships to bolster his position.

Meanwhile, fifty-six delegates from twelve colonies arrived at Philadelphia's Carpenters' Hall for the First Continental Congress to respond to British aggression. Represented by the likes of John and Samuel Adams, Patrick Henry, Richard Henry Lee, John Jay, and George Washington, the group was a deliberative rather than a legislative body. After considerable discussion they proclaimed the Coercive Acts null and void, urged Massachusetts to defend itself, and called for economic sanctions against Britain. Likewise, they adopted the terms of the Continental Association, which encouraged colonies and communities to form committees that would enforce economic restrictions against Britain. Finally, they drafted a Declaration of Rights in which they proclaimed first and foremost their loyalty to the king but also insisted that their liberties were based on the laws of nature, several colonial charters, and the principles of the English Constitution. The Congress sent a signed copy of this declaration to King George III, and the members agreed to reconvene in six months if their complaints had not been addressed.

SHOTS HEARD ROUND THE WORLD

When George III learned of the colonial meeting in late December he exploded in anger. The colonies were in a state of rebellion, he bellowed, and he would not negotiate with them. Neither would Parliament. Military force provided the only option for dealing with this uprising. The government agreed to send General Gage additional troops and three generals—William Howe, John Burgoyne, and Henry Clinton. By mid-April Gage had also received orders to move swiftly and aggressively against the Massachusetts rebels, which meant that the British army would have the responsibility for suppressing any rebellion.

During the early months of 1775 Gage took steps to show British power in the Massachusetts countryside and to get his men ready for action. Week after week he sent expeditions into the countryside simply to make the colonials aware of the army's presence, and in no instance did violence occur. He sent 100 soldiers to Marshfield to protect Loyalists without any trouble. When he learned that rebels had landed cannon in Salem, he sent 200 soldiers to seize the weapons; as the troops approached town, colonists told them they had been misinformed, and the soldiers returned to Boston without a clash. Gage also instructed British Indian agents John Stuart and Colonel Guy Johnson to prepare the natives to secure the frontier. Finally, in mid-April the general received instructions to settle the trouble in Massachusetts.

Gage had been keeping an eye on the rebellious Massachusetts legislature, which had relocated to Concord. That body had called upon the people to defend themselves through the militia, consisting of all free male inhabitants between sixteen and sixty years old. Certain local militia units known as Minutemen had been trained and paid extra by their towns to go into swift action in the event British troops left Boston on offensive operations. Through informers, Gage also learned that rebels at Worcester and Concord had gathered military supplies, including some light artillery, muskets, and gunpowder. Hearing that the renegade legislature would adjourn on April 15, Gage made plans to act decisively by arresting the rebel leaders and seizing the military supplies but he failed to keep his plans secret.

Setting aside several companies of light infantry and grenadiers for special maneuvers, late on the evening of April 18, 1775, Gage used boats to transport about 700 marines and soldiers across Boston Harbor. But the Patriots had learned of Gage's intentions and hung two lanterns in Boston's Old North Church to alert Paul Revere and William Dawes, who departed on their famous rides along separate routes to spread the alarm. At about 3 a.m., the British soldiers, under Lieutenant-Colonel Francis Smith and Major John Pitcairn, began a silent march toward Concord. As alarm spread, gunshot warnings were heard throughout town—the colonials knew British soldiers were on the march.

By 4:30 a.m., the British force had covered eight miles and marched into Lexington, where they saw some seventy militiamen on the village green. These colonials had assembled to support their king, their charter rights, and their constitutional liberties against a regular army that they believed enforced the wishes of a corrupt Parliament. Pitcairn rode to within 100 feet of the militiamen and screamed for the "damned rebels" to lay down their arms and disperse. Militia captain John Parker intended his force of dairy farmers and artisans would make only a silent protest, so he instructed his men to withdraw. This did not satisfy Pitcairn, and he yelled again for the militia to lay down their weapons. As the militiamen backed away, someone fired a shot, and then a British officer ordered the Redcoats to fire. After discharging a volley, the British soldiers, with their bayonets mounted, then made an orderly advance toward the retreating militiamen. Within two minutes they had killed eight militiamen and wounded ten others.

THE SIEGE OF BOSTON AND THE BATTLES OF BUNKER HILL AND LEXINGTON AND CONCORD

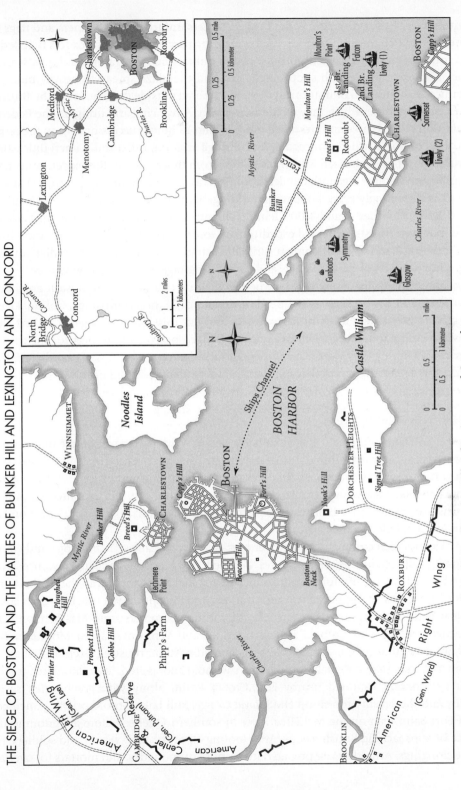

MAP 3.2   The Siege of Boston and the Battles of Bunker Hill and Lexington and Concord

With all hope of surprise gone, the British soldiers unfurled their banners and flags and resumed the march toward Concord. But by the time they arrived, rebel leaders had fled the town, and colonials had carried off most of the military supplies. While soldiers searched for the supplies, a blacksmith shop caught fire, and the blaze spread to nearby buildings. Militiamen from nearby communities who had gathered outside town believed the British to be burning the village, which they would not permit. Advancing and firing on the Redcoats, Patriot militia killed three and wounded nine soldiers in quick succession. When the retreating British column reached Concord's North Bridge at noon, other militiamen unleashed a volley that resulted in fourteen British casualties. From this moment, the sixteen-mile march back to Boston became a gauntlet of death for British soldiers, as militiamen sniped at them from behind seemingly every stone wall, building, barn, and tree. When the British soldiers reached Lexington they found 1,000 reinforcements had arrived to escort them back into Boston, but even this strengthened expeditionary force encountered tough resistance, sometimes enduring hand-to-hand combat. British frustration mounted, with soldiers burning and looting property to exact revenge, and colonial outrage escalated the violence.

By sunset, the British army had returned to the safe confines of the Boston area, but it had suffered 273 total casualties (73 dead, 174 wounded, and 26 missing). Colonial losses amounted to fifty killed, thirty-nine wounded, and five missing. British general Lord Hugh Percy, who commanded the relief force, acknowledged begrudging respect for his colonial adversaries, claiming they were not an irregular mob but rather an armed population. Gage sent London a sobering report that militiamen had gathered beyond his lines.

BUNKER, NO, BREED'S HILL

Lexington and Concord taught Gage a valuable lesson. With such a weak force in Boston, he could not risk another expedition outside the city. Instead, he chose to concentrate on defending Boston and to hope troops would quickly arrive from England or Ireland. Gage agreed to allow Patriots to leave town and Loyalists to enter. For two months he waited, hoping for good news, but none arrived. Instead, he learned in mid-May that Fort Ticonderoga on Lake Champlain had fallen to the Patriots.

Fort Ticonderoga commanded the river portage between Lakes Ticonderoga and George and strategically controlled trade routes between the Hudson and St. Lawrence rivers. Although in disrepair, the forty-eight-soldier-garrisoned fort, known as the "Gibraltar of America," served as an important communications and transportation link between Canada and New York. Shortly after dawn on May 10, militia volunteers from Massachusetts and Connecticut, along with Colonel Benedict Arnold and Vermont's Green Mountain Boys under Colonel Ethan Allen, stormed the undefended bastion, rousting sleeping British soldiers and officers. The colonials took the fort without bloodshed. Two days later, a small Patriot detachment captured nearby Fort Crown Point, along with a schooner, several bateaux, and the seventy-ton sloop HMS *Royal George*. Still later, Arnold briefly gained control of Fort Saint-Jean on the Richelieu River in southern Québec before abandoning it in the face of approaching British troops. After looting all of the fort's liquor and soldiers' personal belongings, Arnold's force prepared its cannon, cannonades, and mortars for overland transport. During six weeks of the winter of 1775–1776 Colonel Henry Knox hauled the heavy cannon and armaments by ox-drawn sled across some 300 miles of ice-covered rivers and the snow-draped Berkshire Mountains to Boston, arriving in late January 1776. The big guns would soon be deployed to Dorchester Heights, overlooking Boston Harbor.

Meanwhile, Gage also learned that the colonies had been seizing powder and shot from everywhere; in New York City the Sons of Liberty had captured 500 muskets and gunpowder from City Hall. Patriots had also expelled or simply ignored governors. Amid this bleak news, reinforcements arrived from England, giving Gage 6,000 men in Boston and Generals Howe, Burgoyne, and Clinton. While he would have preferred 3,000 additional men to the three new generals, Gage knew that British manpower reserves were strained and that any loss of men could be catastrophic. He immediately ordered regiments from New York to Boston. On June 12, 1775, Gage proclaimed martial law, offering pardons to all Patriots who laid down their arms.

During June 1775 the Patriots occupied high ground on the Charlestown peninsula. Though they had no artillery, they were able to marshal 15,000 militiamen. A British doctor described the untrained and poorly organized soldiers as a group that "would fall to pieces of itself." On June 16 colonial colonels Israel Putnam and William Prescott took 1,600 men to fortify Bunker Hill, the tallest point on the peninsula. After surveying the position Putnam moved his men forward to Breed's Hill, which stood nearer to the bay. During the night they dug a redoubt that by morning had ramparts six feet high.

Daylight made it easier for the Patriots to complete their digging, but it also made them visible to British ships at anchor in the harbor. Naval gunfire temporarily stopped the digging, even though the shots did nothing but unnerve the inexperienced Patriots. With his men quietly slipping away, Putnam stood on the top of the ramparts to win his troops' confidence and inspire them to keep working. Naval guns, he demonstrated, could not send shot high enough to damage the Patriots' ramparts.

British forces did not land until early afternoon. By this time the Patriots had realized that their left flank was vulnerable and had begun defending it. When General Howe positioned his 1,500-man landing force at about 1 p.m., its positioning vividly illustrated the Patriots' weaknesses. Conditions were hot, loud, smoky (British ships had fired incendiary shots into Charlestown), and terrifying for those unaccustomed to war. Howe ignored the military doctrine that units should advance in columns and instead chose to use lines to make a statement to his opponent. Had he used columns, presumably the Patriot entrenchments could have been quickly overpowered, but the line formation permitted the Patriots to inflict serious casualties on the British even before they reached the colonial entrenchments. Howe's plan was also complicated, entailing precision, timing, and coordination, and it did not include reserves and made no provisions for the wounded—perhaps because Howe anticipated that he would achieve victory without trouble.

Supported by light infantry, Howe's Royal Welch Fusiliers led the uphill attack with bayonets fixed. They did not load their muskets, as the hardened and disciplined troops planned to overrun the Patriots and make quick business of the affair. The four British lines waded through high grass and crossed sturdy fence rails. They slowly and steadily advanced until they were within fifty yards of the entrenched colonials. Colonel Prescott had instructed his men to aim low and conserve their ammunition: "Don't fire until you see the whites of their eyes," he reportedly barked. Putnam and other commanders repeated the order down the Patriot line. When the colonials finally opened fire, Redcoats fell in alarming numbers. But as each soldier collapsed, another trained Redcoat stepped into the gap. British troops kept advancing for a few minutes, but suddenly the attack stalled, and Redcoats began falling back.

Howe's dispirited men reformed at the bottom of the hill and then launched another attack. Again, they were pummeled by heavy fire, resulting in a terrible slaughter. Howe later recounted the experience as a "moment that I never felt before"—horror and fear that his command was about to collapse. But the colonials were running low on shot and powder and had begun evacuating Breed's Hill. Thirty minutes later Howe, reinforced by General Clinton and additional troops from Boston, ordered a bayonet charge. Advancing initially in columns, the Redcoats soon moved into lines to overwhelm the enemy. This time everything worked for Howe. His men ran uphill with bayonets readied, his artillery moved forward to enfilade the colonial breastworks, and the Patriots ran out of ammunition. A final American volley stunned the British advance, killing Major John Pitcairn of Lexington infamy, before the Redcoats breached the colonial lines. Fighting became hand-to-hand as Putnam's men made a disorderly retreat. By the time General Clinton had reorganized the assault, the colonials had evacuated the peninsula.

People had climbed to their roofs to watch the battle, and it had been appalling. By nightfall the British had secured the battlefield, but it had been a costly victory. The British claimed 40 percent casualties, with 226 dead and 828 wounded, while the Patriots suffered approximately 450 casualties (140 killed, 271 wounded, and 30 captured). A French emissary watching from a nearby rooftop wrote to Paris that two more such victories and Britain would have no army in North America—not exactly true, but close enough that Gage decided against trying to occupy Dorchester Heights south of Boston Harbor. Even though four regiments arrived from New York, Gage remained quietly within Boston until his superiors decided what action he should take. Meanwhile, he advised the British government to commit earnestly to the conflict or to give up the business, because it was apparent that the New Englanders were organized and determined.

NO MORE MIDDLE GROUND

Some 2.5 million colonists—including a half-million slaves—without an army, a navy, a government, or adequate financial resources were foolishly confronting an established nation of 8 million people with a professional army and navy, a sound government, and abundant financial resources. Nonetheless, the colonists were angry, wanted to defend their perceived rights, and believed that God would assist them in protecting their and their progeny's freedom. To achieve victory, Britain would have to control a decentralized land and population without a strategic heart; repeatedly send troops, equipment, and supplies across 3,000 miles of ocean; and unite a British populace to support and fight a war it did not want. Without adequate numbers of troops, the British had to hire almost 32,000 mercenaries from six German principalities, mobilize Loyalists and Indians, and enlist slaves, an action that further angered the colonists. Britain also lacked an early policy for conducting the war, instead vacillating between coercion and conciliation, which neither instilled fear nor inspired affection among colonists. The colonials had only to fight a defensive war and not lose.

ISSUES IN MILITARY HISTORY

WAR FOR INDEPENDENCE OR AN AMERICAN REVOLUTION?

A revolution is a forcible overthrow of an established government or a complete change in something made especially quickly. These definitions of the word do not necessarily describe the events that produced a free and independent American nation. American colonials neither sought a radical restructuring of society nor the immediate destruction of the old order, but instead wanted to preserve traditional rights.

Shaped by the writings of John Locke, Baron Montesquieu, and John Calvin, as well as the Magna Carta, the English Bill of Rights, and individual colonial charters, American colonists believed in a contractual view of government that they thought England had violated. In this view, King George III and his Parliament were encroaching upon the colonials' ancient chartered rights and imposing taxes and laws that were unlawful in England. The Americans were not benefiting from the peace of the Seven Years' War but instead were being heavily taxed to cover government and war costs. The colonists wanted to reform the English government so that the colonies could be governed constitutionally. They followed a prescribed legal format when lodging protests to the Crown: first, they pledged their loyalty to the king; then, they expressed their grievances through petitions; and finally, they requested that the Crown redress their grievances and restore their rights. But from the Stamp Act Congress in 1765 to the Declaration of Independence in 1776, the colonists' petitions for redress were answered only by repeated injury.

Covenant-minded colonists exhausted every remedy to their grievances before breaking the "contract" and resorting to war. They had protested the unconstitutional taxes they believed to be paving the road to tyrannical British rule and in response were labeled rebels—a title they insisted ought to be given to the king, who had undermined the colonial governments and become a tyrant. When the colonists ultimately chose war, they did so to reform England's government so that the colonies would be governed constitutionally. They had no desire or intention to create a new government but rather wanted to restore their previous just rights, which they believed had been denied by a revolutionary king seeking to change the established relationship.

The struggle that produced the American nation was thus not so much a revolution as a war for independence or even an American reformation. Colonials went to war to defend their rights; they threw off British authority in order to restore their liberties and self-government. Their struggle to preserve traditional rights was, in effect, an attempt to reform the British government. Yet what was revolutionary was the American statement of men's rights: "We hold these truths to be self-evident, that all men are created equal, that they are endowed by their Creator with certain unalienable Rights, that among these are Life, Liberty and the pursuit of Happiness." The American government and the Constitution it created thereafter has defended those rights by restraining people who would destroy life and liberty. It is this tradition that makes the struggle's results revolutionary.

The British army numbered some 48,000 men, with twenty regiments of infantry stationed in England, twenty-one in Ireland, eighteen in the Americas, and seven in Gibraltar. Britain could also count sixteen regiments of cavalry and 2,712 artillerymen. The British navy, which was second to none, could insert and extract soldiers where and when needed, meaning that the army needed fewer soldiers for operations. Even counting German mercenaries, Britain had too few soldiers to fight a war in America and defend the empire. Between

1775 and 1781 Britain increased the size of its regular army to 121,000—watering down the quality and effectiveness of the units serving—and shifted its strategy from containing the rebellion in New England to luring the Americans into a pitched battle that would destroy the rebellion. Throughout the conflict colonial commander George Washington would refuse to permit his forces to be destroyed.

Initially colonies relied on local militias who understood their environs, as they trained irregularly in their own neighborhoods. Previously, the primary functions of the militia had been to maintain security by patrolling the frontier and protecting the community against slave insurrections and to participate in limited small-scale warfare. Prior to Lexington and Concord, colonial assemblies began reforming their militias, increasing the number of mandatory training days; stockpiling powder, shot, and muskets; and tightening punishments for missing musters and rules for exemptions. When war began, despite their training, militia units generally performed poorly. Depending on their officers, they often formed quickly in response to danger, engaged their opponent with varying degrees of success, and then quickly vanished. They were a people's army responsible only to one another and their communities and would not act beyond their boundaries or contractual obligations. The Continental Congress, understanding the parochial nature of the militia, created a national army—the Continental Army—that could cross boundaries and fight large-scale engagements.

The weaponry used by the militias and the Continentals had changed little over time. The standard American weapon was the .70-caliber smoothbore musket, which had an effective range of only about 100 yards and misfired about 15 percent of the time. Frontiersmen often carried rifles, generally .40-caliber with grooved bores, that had an effective range of about 300 yards. Powder and shot were also in short supply, as there were only a few hundred powder mills across the country. British soldiers carried the Brown Bess, a .75-caliber flintlock smoothbore musket with an effective range of no more than seventy-five yards. These weapons were designed for mass volleys and bayonet charges, and well-trained Redcoats often used only their discipline and precision to overwhelm American units. The most important weapons Britain possessed were ships, which allowed the supply and transport of troops to any part of the American coast. Superior British seapower permitted the war to be conducted where and when British army commanders wanted.

On June 10, 1775, the Second Continental Congress convened in Philadelphia and immediately took control of the war effort. Congress rejected Lord North's Conciliatory Resolution, which promised Parliament would not impose regulatory taxes on colonies that taxed themselves. Instead they offered George III the Olive Branch Petition asking him to negotiate with his loyal subjects. When the petition reached London in August, George III refused to look at it, instead declaring the colonists to be in rebellion. Congress also drafted the Declaration of the Causes and Necessities of Taking Up Arms, which rejected independence but claimed that the colonists would rather die than be enslaved. Later that fall Congress authorized the formation of a navy (for which it purchased two ships, two schooners, two sloops, and two brigs), appointed Esek Hopkins commander-in-chief of the fleet, and authorized two battalions of marines to serve with the navy. Before the end of the year the Americans began to seek European assistance, learning in late December that France might offer aid. George III's decision to hire German mercenaries to crush the rebellion absolutely shocked

Americans, who had heard of these soldiers' reputation for butchery, barbarity, and looting. Why would their king inflict such monsters on them?

Perhaps most important, Congress appointed Virginia's George Washington as commander-in-chief of the Continental Army. Washington had been born into a moderately prosperous family of the provincial gentry. After beginning his adult career as a surveyor, he inherited tobacco plantations and slaves with the 1752 death of his half-brother Lawrence. A major in the Virginia militia, in 1753 Lieutenant Governor Robert Dinwiddie sent him on a mission to the Ohio Valley—one that ultimately resulted in the beginning of the French and Indian War. During that conflict, Washington served as the senior American on General Edward Braddock's ill-fated expedition and later participated in the Forbes conquest of Fort Duquesne. Yet Washington's dream of receiving an officer's commission in the British army died with Braddock. Even so, he gained a reputation as a courageous, resourceful, and confident leader. After the war, he married wealthy widow Martha Dandridge Custis and secured control over additional lands, becoming one of the wealthiest men in British America. After winning election during the late 1750s to

IMAGE 3.3   George III   King George III assumed the throne of Britain in 1760 during the French and Indian War. During his sixty-year reign, he expanded the boundaries of the first British Empire but his insistence on royal privilege contributed to the loss of the 13 North American colonies. His decision to employ German mercenaries drove the colonies further into revolt.

the Virginia legislature, Washington evolved into a critic of British taxation and mercantilist policies. He participated in the first two Continental Congresses as a Virginia delegate, and his appearance in military uniform during the second signaled his readiness for war. When Congress created the Continental Army in June 1775, New Englander John Adams nominated Washington to be its commander.

Chosen by unanimous vote, Washington wanted the position but announced that he would not accept pay for his service (he would be reappointed annually to command until the war concluded); a noble gesture that contributed to his reputation as a commander not interested in the financial benefits of leadership. Washington would defer to civilian leadership—the Continental Congress—throughout the war, even when that body could not pay, feed, or support the army. His deference to civilian control established an all-important principle that has defined the relationship between the American people and the American military to this day. Even during the later crises of the Conway Affair and the Newburgh Conspiracy, Washington did not waver in his commitment to civilian control, and his officers adopted this stance out of loyalty to him. It is this principled stand that unquestionably makes him the greatest figure in American military history.

After his appointment, Washington immediately proceeded to Boston, took command without ceremony, organized his troops, and began considering a course of action. He could not attack Boston without heavy cannon, so weeks and months passed with only minor skirmishes. With the arrival of winter at the end of 1775, Washington faced a crisis: the term of service for the militia was about to expire. Militiamen could not find wood to burn, and most simply wanted to go home. Convincing 1,000 to remain, Washington secured gunpowder, fuel, and food, winning momentary confidence in his command.

In late January Colonel Knox arrived from Ticonderoga with cannon, which by early March had been emplaced on Dorchester Heights overlooking Boston. This strategic position permitted the Patriots to throw shot down on the city, on Redcoat troops, and on Royal Navy ships in the harbor. Gage had returned to England to discuss plans, leaving General William Howe in a predicament. Rather than risk another Bunker Hill, Howe evacuated the city, agreeing to leave without destroying it if Washington did not fire upon him. On March 17, 1776, British soldiers and Loyalists departed for Halifax.

ON TO CANADA

The Continental Congress had decided in July 1775 to authorize a two-pronged attack against Canada. Many Patriots believed an invasion of Canada might encourage the conquered French to join their struggle. It would also add a fourteenth colony to the Patriot cause while eliminating a British base of operations. Governor-General of Canada Sir Guy Carleton had taken care to prevent the widespread circulation of these plans and had also sent troops to protect Fort Ticonderoga—although they arrived only in time to prevent the Patriots from holding onto Fort Saint-Jean on the Richelieu River. After the engagement at Bunker Hill, Congress voted to send the cautious and timid Philip Schuyler to invade Canada. Unfortunately Schuyler spent too much time at Fort Ticonderoga planning the attack, and his second-in-command, Richard Montgomery, began marching north with 1,200 men. By early September Montgomery's troops had begun the siege of Fort Saint-Jean, which fell to the Patriots in early November. Two weeks later these American forces marched into and took Montreal. Governor Carleton barely escaped, ultimately making his way to Québec. Meanwhile a second invasion force of some 1,050 men under the command of Benedict Arnold hacked its way north though the Maine woods toward Québec. The march was slow and riddled with hardship, and Arnold lost 400 men to disease and cold. By the time he arrived on the Plains of Abraham in mid-November his army had dwindled to about 600 soldiers, and they faced a strong and well-armed masonry fort with more than 1,000 defenders. By early December Montgomery had arrived to reinforce Arnold, and together they began the siege.

Carleton and both his American opponents knew that the British only needed to hold out until the spring thaw, when reinforcements would arrive to relieve the defenders. In the

early morning hours of December 31, 1775, Arnold and Montgomery launched a complicated two-pronged attack against the lower part of the city, but Carleton had learned of the
American plans and had heavily defended it. When Montgomery's forces entered they found
a fortified house with four artillery pieces that slaughtered the attacking Americans. Montgomery was instantly killed. Arnold's forces, meanwhile, fought to the rendezvous point, but
instead of meeting Montgomery, they found Carleton with fresh bayonet-mounted regulars.
The Patriots were killed or forced to surrender. Arnold suffered a severe wound to his left
leg during the attack but escaped. The failed invasion resulted in more than 100 Americans
killed and another 400 taken prisoner, while British losses were negligible.

Despite the failure, Arnold resumed the siege until the late spring of 1776, when Carleton attacked the smallpox-ravaged Patriot force and drove it back into New York and New
England. The first American offensive had failed for a variety of reasons, but it did force the
British to be more cautious and also made them aware of the American intent to fight. As
the surviving American Continentals returned home, they recounted the catastrophic story,
the squalid camp conditions, and the horrors of the smallpox that had swept through their
ranks, making long-term recruitment of new soldiers difficult at best. Unbeknownst to them,
many of these soldiers also carried the smallpox virus back into their home communities,
and the disease soon spread throughout the population.

By the end of 1775 the war had spread south from New England. In Virginia governor
Dunmore mobilized Loyalists, a handful of soldiers, marines from British ships in the
Chesapeake Bay, and 300 slaves—to whom he promised freedom—to ravage the coastline. On December 9, 1775, the Patriots confronted Dunmore at the Battle of Great Bridge
south of Norfolk and scored a victory. The defeated Dunmore retaliated by using ship
cannon to bombard Patriot houses in Norfolk; in turn, Patriots burned Loyalists' homes.
While the battle was of little military consequence, Dunmore had opened Pandora's box
by enlisting slaves and introducing a racial component to the struggle. In North Carolina,
Royal Governor Josiah Martin rallied Tories (loyal colonials or Loyalists who supported
the king and opposed American secession) to confront the Patriots, and in early February
1776 some 1,700 Loyalists began marching toward Wilmington to meet the anticipated
arrival of a British fleet and its accompanying soldiers. On February 27, the Loyalists
arrived at Moore's Creek Bridge, where Patriots had ripped boards from the overpass.
Precariously crossing the bridge struts, the Tories attacked a well-entrenched Patriot force
that drove them back across the creek. During the next few days, Patriots rounded up
850 Tories and held them captive, a move that kept Loyalists in North Carolina quiet for
several years afterward. Meanwhile, in South Carolina General Henry Clinton's expeditionary force attempted to capture Charleston. British naval forces leveled a devastating
bombardment at an unfinished fort on Sullivan's Island that commanded the opening to
Charleston Bay, but because Patriot general Charles Lee had created makeshift fort walls
from extremely soft palmetto logs, the shot became embedded in the wood and did no
damage. At the same time, the Patriots drove two smaller British vessels aground and
damaged a frigate and the fifty-gun British flagship. Clinton gave up his attack. British
attempts to mobilize southern Loyalists had failed, as civilians themselves decided which
side they would support.

TOWARD INDEPENDENCE

George Washington understood the reason for the Québec failure: the involvement of short-term soldiers who had little if anything invested in the cause had forced Montgomery and Arnold to attack before they were ready. Short-term enlistees did not possess the discipline, the training, or the commitment to the cause needed to achieve victory. How could Patriot leaders expect to win a war against a professional army when they only had part-time soldiers? Washington knew it would not happen, so he began lobbying Congress to remodel the Continental Army. The core of the army needed soldiers who would serve until the end of the conflict and in return would be well paid with money and land bounties. These enlistees should be inured to camp life and combat, and have pride in the service that they rendered. Officers and soldiers both needed to be given incentives to remain in the army.

The possibility of a permanent standing army offended republican-minded Patriots who embraced the concept of virtuous citizen-soldiers. Permanent troops were expensive, these Americans argued, they posed a threat to republican liberties, and they defined themselves as a class or body outside the limits of society. Finally, a despotic commander could use his loyal troops to overthrow civilian government or support a regime that embraced only the wishes of officers and soldiers. In response, supporters of Washington's proposal argued that the lack of a permanent, professional military force undermined the balance between security and liberty. As more part-time soldiers deserted or fulfilled their contractual obligations, the Continental government became weaker. Increasing and lengthening terms of military service would create a stronger army and government. The Continental Congress would have to reconcile these competing views in its consideration of Washington's request for a new kind of army.

For more than fourteen months after the Battle of Lexington and Concord, Patriots fought for what they claimed were their rights within the British Empire. They proclaimed their loyalty to King George III even as they fired on his troops. However, the appearance of a civilian manifesto in January 1776 forced Patriots to reconsider their relationship with Britain. This anonymous pamphlet from Philadelphia, entitled *Common Sense*, called for the Patriots to divorce themselves from Britain and stand forth as champions not only of American liberty but of the rights of all mankind. Thousands of copies of the work circulated throughout the colonies, creating a furor in response to its "irrefutable" arguments. The unknown English author, Thomas Paine, attacked the principle of monarchy, the English kings in general, and George III in particular. Americans, he argued, owed neither King George III nor the English people anything, and so, Paine concluded, "'Tis Time to Part." The Americans must form an independent republic without delay. His writing gave voice—fluently, vividly, and fervidly— to opinions and feelings that colonials had been unable to express.

Throughout the spring of 1776 individual colonial governments in Massachusetts, South Carolina, Georgia, North Carolina, and Virginia issued instructions for their Philadelphia delegates to pursue separation from Britain. In early June, Virginian Richard Henry Lee introduced resolutions to the Continental Congress, insisting that "these United Colonies are, and of right ought to be, free and independent states." While Congress bitterly debated the resolutions until early July, a committee composed of Benjamin Franklin, John Adams, Robert Livingston, Roger Sherman, and Thomas Jefferson prepared a separation statement.

Principally drafted by Jefferson and revised by the committee, the statement, based on commonly accepted ideas, provided a public explanation for colonial discontent and a reason for independence. Approved on July 4, 1776, the Declaration of Independence changed the aims of the war: colonial soldiers were no longer fighting for a redress of grievances but instead for freedom and independence. Still, even though the colonies had declared themselves independent, not all colonists agreed—roughly a quarter of the population remained loyal to the Crown, including some 50,000 men who fought for the British. A third of the population also remained unaligned or indifferent. Because only a minority of the colonial population supported the American struggle for independence, gaining the support of the unaligned would sway the balance of the war.

A NEW BRITISH STRATEGY

On July 9 General Washington had the Declaration of Independence read to his troops in New York City. As long as the general could preserve his force and prolong the struggle, each passing day brought the possibility of Patriot victory. In New York

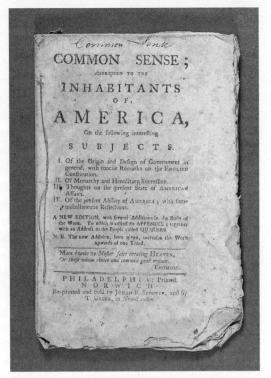

IMAGE 3.4 Thomas Paine's *Common Sense*
Thomas Paine's eye-opening pamphlet *Common Sense* shook American colonials to their core. Calling for colonials to "part" themselves from Great Britain, he offered commonsensical reasons why the American colonies could survive on their own. The radical Paine, who had arrived in America in 1774, became a spokesman for the revolutionary movement.

Harbor British ships carrying thousands of Redcoat troops sat poised for an invasion. Until the spring of 1776 the basic British strategy had been to contain the Patriot uprising to the Boston area, but the March evacuation forced the British to adopt a new approach. The summer campaign against New York marked a new British objective of luring Americans into a traditional battle in which the Patriot army could be destroyed. Such a decisive victory could certainly end the American rebellion, but if the British were drawn too deeply into the interior in search of victory, their logistical weaknesses and long supply lines could bring them defeat. As long as the British used naval vessels to insert troops and provide immediate logistical support, operations could take place when and where commanders chose without the fear of becoming bogged down in the American interior.

British general William Howe and his brother, Admiral Richard Howe, had planned a combined army–navy expedition against New York that aimed to destroy Washington's army while subduing New England. With 32,000 soldiers—the largest single army assembled by the British during the eighteenth century—landing in New York, General Howe could push north and east toward Boston. Meanwhile, another British command under Sir Guy Carleton would proceed south from Québec, and Admiral Howe's 400 ships would harass the New England coastline. Once New England had been subdued and severed from the other colonies, British forces could move south and sweep up the remaining opposition.

Washington had been trying to erect defenses for New York since the spring of 1776, as the superior British naval power left the area greatly exposed. But with only 19,000 poorly trained and inadequately provisioned militiamen, Washington could only hope to delay any British movements. On August 22, 1776, General Howe orchestrated the largest amphibious operation to that point in world history, putting his army ashore at Gravesend Bay on Long Island. Exploiting a weakness in Washington's defensive line, Howe's right wing destroyed the Patriots' left flank with a brutal bayonet attack. As the American flank collapsed, British soldiers attacked elsewhere along the Patriot line until it broke and the Americans retreated. Washington's humiliated army fled to defensive positions on Brooklyn Heights. But General Howe then hesitated for almost a week instead of following up on his initial victory. British ships also failed to cut off Washington's route of escape, another costly mistake. On the rainy, foggy, and windy evening of August 28–29, Washington used the cover of bad weather to evacuate 9,000 men, artillery, and supplies in Colonel John Glover's small boats to Manhattan Island. The Battle for Brooklyn Heights had ultimately resulted in more than 1,000 Americans captured (including General John Sullivan), hundreds of casualties, and a devastating blow to Patriot morale; British casualties numbered fewer than 400 men killed, wounded, or captured.

Howe used the captured General Sullivan to send a message to the Continental Congress, which responded with a commission to meet with the Howe brothers. Yet the summit only strengthened American resolve for independence. Meanwhile, Washington realized his tenuous position on Manhattan Island, so on September 12 he moved his army north, where he could cross the river if necessary. Three days later 4,000 British and Hessian troops landed on the eastern shore of Manhattan Island and immediately engaged the rear of Washington's army. After landing an additional 9,000 soldiers, Howe marched his army north toward the Patriot position on Harlem Heights. On the morning of September 16 advance American scouts encountered British pickets, and fighting began. British regulars immediately moved forward in support of the pickets, and the Americans retreated with confidence toward their earthen defenses. The day's fighting revived American morale, although it was not technically an American victory. Washington recognized that if he stayed on Harlem Heights the British could surround his army. But again, Howe hesitated nor did he use his brother's naval forces to follow up on his advantage.

For twenty-six days Washington prepared his defenses, but he did not receive reinforcements or additional supplies. Troop morale plummeted, and soldiers began to desert in increasing numbers. Washington's situation grew desperate. Howe, having learned that he would receive additional Hessian reinforcements, on October 12 finally resumed his offensive with an encircling maneuver, trying to cut off Washington's escape. Unfortunately, his selected landing site at Throg's Neck provided limited options for advancement and was also heavily defended by colonials. Giving up that attempt, British forces landed at Pell's Point six days later.

After observing British offensive operations, Washington decided to retreat from Manhattan Island. On the same day that Howe's army went ashore at Pell's Point, Washington's

MAJOR CAMPAIGNS IN NEW YORK AND NEW JERSEY, 1776–1777

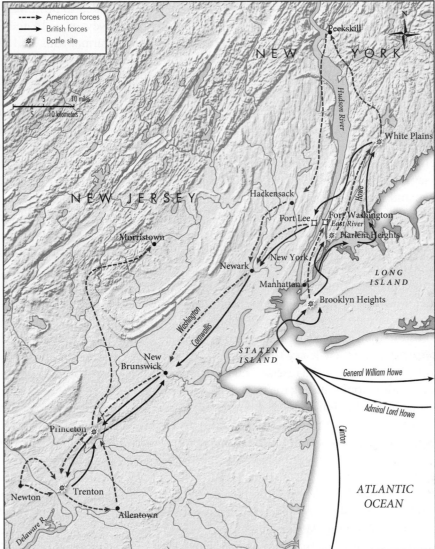

MAP 3.3 Major Campaigns in New York and New Jersey, 1776–1777

troops began a slow march north toward White Plains. Again Howe might have been able to cut off the American retreat, but John Glover's 750 Marblehead Massachusetts men kept the British engaged for most of the day. Howe had lost his chance, so he began a slow, steady, and deliberate advance north toward White Plains.

As Washington's army received sustenance and rest, their morale improved, and on October 28 Washington attempted to take the offensive, but Howe forcefully responded, driving the Patriots northward. And again, Howe hesitated. When he finally decided to make an attack on the morning of November 1, Washington's army had moved to a hilly position where the Americans could not be outflanked. Instead, Howe decided to push west toward the Hudson River, where his forces captured Fort Washington on November 14 and Fort Lee five days later. The loss of these forts, with their valuable garrisons, armaments, and supplies, represented a major setback for the American war effort.

Washington's army continued to dwindle. Troop morale dropped lower than ever, and the expiration of many of his troops' enlistments on December 31, 1776, was rapidly approaching, threatening to decimate the army overnight. By the time Fort Lee fell, Washington had crossed the Hudson River, making a harrowing retreat south with the bold thirty-seven-year-old General Charles Cornwallis in aggressive pursuit. Cornwallis harassed Washington's dwindling army across New Jersey. Although he pleaded for help from the Pennsylvania and New Jersey militias, Washington got little assistance as he retreated through New Brunswick, Princeton, and ultimately across the Delaware River into Pennsylvania. By early December, Washington's army numbered fewer than 2,000 dispirited soldiers. The American army had wilted in the face of aggressive British bayonets, popular support for the cause was wavering, the Continental Congress abandoned Philadelphia for Baltimore, and the revolutionary movement appeared in jeopardy.

After taking possession of Trenton on December 8, 1776, Howe suspended activities for the winter. Meanwhile, he sent General Clinton with 6,000 men to take Newport, Rhode Island, to provide a deepwater anchorage for the Royal Navy and a base for future operations against Boston and Connecticut. Howe also established a chain of outposts that stretched across New York and New Jersey to the Delaware River. From Trenton, the British were in position to invest Pennsylvania, seize Philadelphia, and strengthen Loyalist control across the mid-Atlantic colonies during the next campaign season.

The American rebellion seemed about to collapse. Overconfident in British prospects, Howe believed the Patriots were too disorganized for any operations and he spread his army across New Jersey and New York for the winter without regard for his units' inability to reinforce one another. On the southern frontier at the Delaware River outpost, he positioned Colonel Johann Rall and three regiments (1,500 soldiers) of Hessians. Rall chose not to dig fortifications because he believed himself to be completely isolated, instead quartering his men in available buildings. At nearby Bordentown, New Jersey, Colonel Karl von Donop commanded 2,000 additional Hessians.

During the New York campaign, Washington had learned the consequences of an American dispersion of troops and the British concentration of forces. Working from a position of weakness, he decided to concentrate his army and focus on a small part of the dispersed enemy force—the Hessians at Trenton and Bordentown. Knowing that many of his soldiers' enlistments would expire soon, Washington took aggressive action. After General Charles Lee's capture, General John Sullivan's arrival with troops permitted Washington to cobble together an army of about 6,000 soldiers and militiamen. With these forces, he would cross the ice-laden Delaware River and attack the Hessians at Trenton and Bordentown before his men's enlistments expired.

On the snowy night of Christmas 1776, John Glover's mariners rowed 2,400 American soldiers across the icy floes of the Delaware River. Only one of three intended columns made it across the river, but Washington still had enough men. Colonel Rall had anticipated something might happen, so he had taken precautions. While belief persists that the Hessians were drunk, most were not, but a terrible snowstorm had greatly reduced visibility, permitting the Patriots to enter town at dawn almost undetected. They quickly and easily overwhelm the Hessians. The Patriots captured some 900 and killed another 100, including Colonel Rall, while about 500 managed to escape. Six of Washington's men suffered wounds, including a young Lieutenant James Monroe.

The victory at Trenton not only boosted the morale of the Continental Army but also brought General Cornwallis out of New York with 6,000 Redcoats. Marching immediately toward Trenton, Cornwallis engaged Washington's army on the afternoon of January 2, 1777. That night Washington kept his campfires burning to give the appearance of being in camp, but he moved most of his men against a portion of Cornwallis's army at nearby Princeton. On the following morning Washington's troops successfully endured three frontal bayonet assaults at Princeton during which Washington rode forward to rally his troops and then personally led them in an attack, forcing the British to retreat. After this victory, Washington evacuated his small but emboldened army to winter quarters in Morristown, in the hills of northern New Jersey. These daring tactical victories bought the Patriots a winter of relative calm. The British had lost a quarter of their force in the engagements, and the loss of so many Hessians greatly angered Frederick II, Landgrave of Hesse-Kassel, who would be reluctant to rent more soldiers to the British.

CONCLUSIONS

American colonists had reluctantly decided to rebel against the British Crown after years of trying to assert their constitutional rights. Since 1763 they had followed a legal formula of proclaiming their loyalty to the Crown, asking for redress of their grievances, and protesting only after their concerns had not been addressed. The escalation of parliamentary attacks against their perceived rights as Englishmen forced them to beg protection from their king, but with no protection forthcoming, they chose to defend their own rights.

Colonists forcefully reacted to heavy-handed British policies in such incidents as the brazen attack on HMS *Gaspee* in 1772. This perceived act of treason, combined with Bostonians' 1774 destruction of East India tea, convinced George III that the colonies were in open rebellion and should be brought back into the imperial orbit. The "Intolerable Acts" and the subsequent British march against Lexington and Concord convinced colonials that they had to protect their rights with force of arms. With only a militia, they stood up to British tyranny at Lexington, Concord, and Bunker (Breed's) Hill. As the scope of the conflict grew, the democratized and localized nature of limited warfare gave way to nationalized military authority supported by localized militias. During this uneasy transition British commanders and policymakers grappled with the decision of whether to subdue or crush the rebellion. William Howe's indecision gave Washington and the American movement for independence the opportunity to survive and learn from its mistakes.

TIMELINE

1763–1764	Pontiac's Rebellion
1765	Stamp Act
March 1770	Boston Massacre
December 1773	Boston Tea Party
April 1775	Battles of Lexington and Concord
June 1775	Battle of Bunker (Breed's) Hill
July 1776	Declaration of Independence
August–December 1776	British New York campaign
December 1776	Battle of Trenton
January 1777	Battle of Princeton

Despite American missteps during the fall of 1776, Washington and the American cause endured. During these "times that try men's souls," as Thomas Paine proclaimed in *The American Crisis*, American morale appeared to be shattered and the movement lost. Washington's daring attacks at Trenton and Princeton restored American faith in the struggle, although the British continued to hold New York City and its harbor, Long Island, and the surrounding agricultural areas, as it would for the remainder of the war.

General Howe minimized his defeats, but some British ministers saw exactly what had happened. Howe maintained that his failures had resulted from a lack of soldiers, and he requested more. General Washington was also under attack by some in Congress, who called him incompetent and called for his removal. Washington, ever subservient to the civilian government, responded that the setbacks had occurred because Congress had not provided for the army. Despite his troubles, Washington had orchestrated a tactical masterpiece, outmaneuvering and outfighting the pride of the British army. He had proved that the British army was not invincible, and his boldness had saved the American republic when all seemed lost. Never again would the struggle be so close to failing.

SUGGESTED READINGS

Bailyn, Bernard. *The Ideological Origins of the American Revolution*. Cambridge, MA: Belknap Press, 1967.

Breen, T. H. *The Marketplace of Revolution: How Consumer Politics Shaped American Independence*. New York: Oxford University Press, 2004.

Christie, Ian R. *Crisis of Empire: Great Britain and the American Colonies, 1754–1783*. New York: W. W. Norton, 1966.

Countryman, Edward. *A People in Revolution: The American Revolution and Political Society in New York, 1760–1790*. Baltimore: Johns Hopkins University Press, 1981.

Fenn, Elizabeth A. *Pox Americana: The Great Smallpox Epidemic of 1775–1782*. New York: Hill and Wang, 2001.

Ferling, John. *A Leap in the Dark: The Struggle to Create the American Republic*. New York: Oxford University Press, 2004.

Fisher, David Hackett. *Washington's Crossing*. New York: Oxford University Press, 2004.

Gruber, Ira D. *The Howe Brothers*. Chapel Hill: University of North Carolina Press, 1972.

Kammen, Michael. *Empire and Interest: The American Colonies and the Politics of Mercantilism.* Philadelphia: J. B. Lippincott, 1970.

Lemisch, Jesse. *Jack Tar vs. John Bull: The Role of New York's Seamen in Precipitating the Revolution.* New York: Routledge, 1997.

Maier, Pauline. *From Resistance to Revolution: Colonial Radicals and the Development of American Opposition to Britain, 1765–1776.* New York: Vintage, 1973.

McCullough, David. *1776.* New York: Simon and Schuster, 2005.

Shy, John. *A People Numerous and Armed: Reflections on the Military Struggle for American Independence.* Ann Arbor: University of Michigan Press, 1990.

————. *Toward Lexington: The Role of the British Army in the Coming of the Revolution.* Princeton, NJ: Princeton University Press, 1975.

Tucker, Robert W., and David C. Hendrickson. *The Fall of the First British Empire: Origins of the War of American Independence.* Baltimore: Johns Hopkins University Press, 1982.

CHAPTER 4

MAINTAINING INDEPENDENCE
1777–1782

*Struggling Toward Independence • 1777: The Year of Decision • 1778: Stalemate
in the North • A Suffering Army • Struggle on the Periphery • Breaking the Iroquois
Confederation • Spanish Conquests in the South • A New Southern Strategy • Treason,
Pensions, and Mutinies • The World Turned Upside Down • King's Mountain: Beginning
of the End • Devil of a Whipping: War of Attrition in the Carolinas • Taking the War to
Virginia • Yorktown • Winning the Peace • The Treaty of Paris*

General George Washington appeared before the Continental Congress at the Maryland State House in Annapolis at noon on Tuesday, December 23, 1783. Inside, the crowded gallery anxiously murmured as Washington entered the room and took his seat across from President Thomas Mifflin. After a few moments Washington rose and read a speech revealing the emotion and loyalty he had felt toward his country and his fellow officers. His final sentence begged leave to resign his commission and retire from "all the employments of public life." Then Washington offered the Congress his signed commission, relinquishing his command. President Mifflin read a speech drafted by Thomas Jefferson, and one sentence resonated like thunder: "You have conducted the great military contest with wisdom and fortitude invariably regarding the rights of the civil power through all disasters and changes." Washington then bowed to the congressmen and departed, intent on being at Mount Vernon for Christmas.

General Washington's conduct during the war and resignation underscore his importance to the revolutionary struggle and the formation of the United States. They established a tradition of civilian rule over the military that has prevailed for more than 200 years. In fact, when King George III heard of Washington's intention to give up power, the monarch reportedly uttered, "If he does that, he will be the greatest man in the world." To a country that had struggled through a bitter, divisive war with Great Britain, Washington was exactly that.

Washington navigated the country through the conflict by preserving his army and not being annihilated. While Great Britain had a large professional army, the Americans relied on citizen militias and a very small group of Continental Army soldiers. After the New York campaign, in which the ill-trained and unprofessional American force was beaten, battered, and bruised, Washington understood that for a national movement to survive, he needed a national army. The military body that eventually emerged survived the British occupation of Philadelphia, stood toe to toe with the British during the Battle of Monmouth, and after 1778 limited the British to smaller operations around New York City. Training, discipline, and commitment transformed Washington's farmers and mechanics into a European-style army infused with a devotion to their cause.

Similarly, the British had the largest navy in the world, while the Americans had only a hodgepodge collection of sailing ships. That Royal Navy played a key role in the Revolution by supplying and reinforcing the British army in North America and after December 1778 permitted General Clinton to expand British operations to the southern colonies. Naval superiority permitted the British to successfully conduct operations 3,000 miles from England. But once the war became an international conflict with the involvement of France, Spain, and the Netherlands, Britain could commit fewer naval resources to the North American struggle, and this left General Charles Cornwallis isolated on the Jamestown peninsula. Cornwallis's fate was determined as much by British naval overcommitment as by the actions of Washington's army at Yorktown.

STRUGGLING TOWARD INDEPENDENCE

The Howe brothers had hoped that aggressive British military operations during 1776 would convince the Americans to surrender. Instead, they prompted them to declare independence. This understanding of the aims of the conflict partially explains William Howe's reluctance to engage aggressively Washington's crumbling army. Howe wanted to inflict defeat and then offer the olive branch to bring Americans back into the fold. But time and again, he learned that the Patriots would not return to the empire as dependents. By the time he realized diplomacy had failed, the fighting season had ended. Then Washington's brilliant tactics at Trenton and Princeton undid much of the progress the British had made during fall fighting.

During the winter plans crystallized for two British spring operations. Howe sent operational plans to London calling for the concentration of the British armies and the elimination of American opposition by overwhelming action. Generals John Burgoyne and Henry Clinton both returned to London to plead personally their case for command. British colonial secretary Lord George Germain prepared to make a recommendation to the government and to King George III.

Washington understood that given American weaknesses—limited enlistments, few supplies, inadequate weapons, and an expansive area to protect—the preferred American strategy should focus on defending posts. Britain's control of the seas permitted rapid movements and the concentration of troops. Washington responded by positioning his troops in posts chosen not for tactical or strategic reasons, but because they stood in locations that would persuade free volunteer soldiers to do their duty.

Congress had authorized Washington to enlist sixteen additional battalions, 3,000 cavalrymen, and corps of artillery and engineers, which would have given him 75,000 troops.

IMAGE 4.1 George Washington Charles Wilson Peale's portrait of General George Washington depicts the commanding presence and physical confidence he possessed after the December 1776 victory at Trenton—a major turning point in the war. Washington's cool determination kept the army loyal to the nation despite congressional indifference.

But in reality Washington could neither obtain that many soldiers nor sustain them. While Congress offered cash and land bounties to those willing to endure cold and hardship, few troops enlisted because of a smallpox outbreak and the army's perpetual shortage of food. Washington's force shrank to fewer than 9,000 effective men, but those who stayed gained experience and became hardened by battle and camp life. Indeed, though supplies remained scarce, by March 1777 secret aid had started arriving from France and Spain. During winter 1777 two French ships landed muskets, tents, cannons, uniforms, and other military gear in New Hampshire. News reported that more supplies would arrive soon, which renewed the Patriots' spirits.

1777: THE YEAR OF DECISION

After meeting with Generals Burgoyne and Clinton and considering Howe's plans for the 1777 campaign season, Lord Germain decided that Burgoyne would lead one army south from Canada down the Lake Champlain–Hudson River corridor through New York, which would sever and isolate New England from the other colonies. Meanwhile Howe would take Philadelphia. Enthusiasm for the conflict had not risen in Britain, and foreign manpower sources had already been exhausted, meaning that England could not send additional troops, so the two plans needed extensive coordination and cooperation.

SARATOGA CAMPAIGN

The opportunity to win great glory finally came to General John Burgoyne. Despite being the junior general sent to North America, Burgoyne, at age fifty-five, was older than Clinton, Carleton, or Howe. He had lived the colorful life of a gentleman about London, preferring gambling and drinking to studying tactics and strategy, and had eloped with the daughter of the Earl of Derby. While he had been a successful cavalry officer in Portugal in the Seven Years' War, during the Saratoga campaign he would have no cavalry—only infantry and Indian allies.

In June 1777 "Gentleman" Johnny marched his handsomely equipped army—8,000 Redcoats and Hessians, 150 French Canadians, 100 Tories, and some 400 Indians—south from Canada. Landing toward the southern end of Lake Champlain on July 1, he prepared to attack Fort Ticonderoga. Among his supplies, Burgoyne carried not only heavy artillery but also some thirty carts of personal items that included champagne and wine, fine foods, and clothing for his mistress. As many as 1,000 women accompanied the British army, including the Baroness von Riedesel, who brought her three children. This baggage and the noncombatants greatly slowed Burgoyne's advance, giving the Patriots time to react.

Meanwhile, British lieutenant-colonel Barry St. Leger assembled a second force of 900 soldiers and 1,000 Iroquois warriors that advanced east from Fort Oswego toward Albany in late July. Burgoyne anticipated that General Howe would send a contingent of soldiers north from New York along the Hudson River to unite with his other forces. Bringing together three armies along the Lake Champlain–Hudson River corridor would permit the British to sever the troublesome New England from the remainder of the colonies and potentially end the conflict.

Fort Ticonderoga held fewer than 2,500 Patriots under the command of Arthur St. Clair. While rebuilding and reinforcing Ticonderoga, the Patriots had also linked it with a strengthened Mount Independence nearby. Expecting a challenge, on July 2 Burgoyne's soldiers drove the Americans' outer positions back to the cover of the fort. Suddenly Burgoyne recognized that the Americans had neglected to fortify a lofty nearby perch known as Rattlesnake Mountain or Mount Defiance, from which shot could be thrown down into both American forts. In fact, the Americans had not neglected the high spot but rather believed that cannon could not be dragged to the top of the hill. Burgoyne's engineers soon learned that they could. By July 5 two British heavy guns sat high on the hill, and others were on their way up. That night St. Clair and the Patriots knew that they could no longer defend Ticonderoga. By the following morning, all the Patriots were gone.

The easy British capture of Fort Ticonderoga was a shattering blow to the Patriots, and it prompted Burgoyne to advance immediately the seventy miles to Albany, leaving 900 men to garrison Ticonderoga and another 400 to occupy Crown Point. Unfortunately, the winding and muddy roads to Albany pierced through thick forests and crossed several streams. As before, the artillery and baggage greatly impeded British progress. Furthermore, American general Philip Schuyler had ordered his soldiers to cut down trees over roads, block roads with stones, divert streams, and harass British units at every opportunity. Even Baroness von Riedesel noticed that the roads were horrible, the horses exhausted, and food was in short supply. Ultimately, the march led to some 200 casualties. After resting for a few days at Skenesboro, Burgoyne decided to proceed south to Fort Miller, where he would wait for the remainder of his cannon and supplies. Gentleman Johnny anticipated that he would arrive in Albany long before winter.

Since General Schuyler had lost Ticonderoga and had done little to check the British advance, the Continental Congress replaced him in August with General Horatio Gates. Gates soon found that Schuyler's reports were not as gloomy as they seemed. Militia from New York and New England had mustered in overwhelming numbers. The prospect of British soldiers approaching and plundering their homes, combined with the brutal Indian murder of attractive Loyalist Jane McCrea and Burgoyne's unwillingness to punish the perpetrators, had stiffened militia resolve. The Patriots had also successfully rounded up local livestock and supplies, which prevented the British invaders from securing needed provisions.

While Burgoyne slogged through the New York wilderness, St. Leger advanced from Oswego toward the American position at Fort Stanwix on the Mohawk River. After beginning his siege of the fort on August 2, St. Leger learned of the impending arrival of the Tryon County militia. Four days later a force of British regulars and Indians ambushed the militia at the bloody Battle of Oriskany, in which the Americans held the field but ultimately retreated because of high casualties. During the battle, the Americans conducted a sortie (deployment of one unit)to raid the almost empty Indian camp, an attack that demoralized St. Leger's Indians.

Meanwhile, American general Benedict Arnold was moving toward the nearby Fort Dayton, where he anticipated recruiting the Tryon County militia. After taking such high casualties at Oriskany, however, only 100 militiamen joined with Arnold when he arrived on August 21, certainly not enough for his plan to prevent Leger from reaching Albany. Resorting instead to subterfuge, Arnold orchestrated the escape of a half-witted Loyalist captive, who immediately fled to St. Leger with erroneous information that Arnold had a large force sweeping toward Fort Stanwix. This news panicked Mohawk chief Joseph Brant and his Indian allies, who decided to leave with most of the British supplies. Without his Indian contingent or supplies, St. Leger had to break off the siege, withdraw, and hastily return to Fort Oswego. Arnold turned his contingent toward Saratoga.

Burgoyne's troops desperately needed food, draft animals, and supplies. Hessian general Friedrich Adolphus Baron von Riedesel had suggested to Burgoyne that they make a raid into Vermont, where they could acquire these items. Consequently, Burgoyne sent Lieutenant Colonel Friedrich Baum and 700 troops, mostly Hessians, toward Bennington, incorrectly believing it to be undefended. In actuality, the Patriots had 2,000 New Hampshire, Vermont, and Massachusetts militiamen in the area under the command of General John Stark, who had served under Robert Rogers as a ranger during the French and Indian War. As Baum's troops moved toward Bennington, they quickly realized the presence of a much larger American force than anticipated. Being outnumbered, the British retreated to a hill overlooking the Wallomsac River to await reinforcements from Burgoyne. Early on the morning of August 16, the Patriots suddenly attacked the British from all sides. Baum's Canadians and Indians fled immediately, and his Tories retreated soon after. His remaining Hessians and Redcoats fought bravely, twice using cavalry to try and break the American lines, but to no avail. Having exhausted their ammunition, and with Baum mortally wounded, the remaining troops fled or surrendered.

As the Americans mopped up the battlefield, two groups of reinforcements arrived almost simultaneously: 650 British and Hessian troops under the command of Lieutenant Colonel Heinrich von Breymann and 350 Green Mountain Boys commanded by Continental colonel Seth Warner. The appearance of these two groups renewed the battle, which was fought fiercely until the late afternoon, when British troops again ran out of ammunition and fled. By sunset the Americans could count two victories at Bennington, in which they had killed 200 and captured 700 Hessian and British soldiers, about 10 percent of Burgoyne's invasion force.

MAJOR CAMPAIGNS IN NEW YORK AND PENNSYLVANIA, 1777

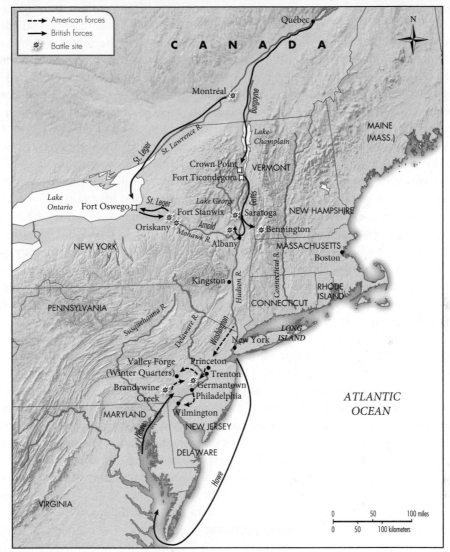

MAP 4.1 Major Campaigns in New York and Pennsylvania, 1777

In mid-September, Horatio Gates moved north to confront the British invasion. Although Gates was not a great commander, he had great luck, and by this time his army had grown to more than 7,000 battle-tested Continentals and several thousand militiamen. Gates ultimately chose to dig in at Bemis Heights, where the only road to Albany passed through a defile between the woody heights and the Hudson River. This defensible position had a commanding view of the area and permitted Polish engineer Tadeusz Kościuszko to construct entrenchments that would protect artillery and riflemen from bayonet attacks.

On September 18, 1777, the vanguard of Burgoyne's army arrived about four miles north of Saratoga. After sending out scouts to reconnoiter the American position, Burgoyne chose to attack with three columns the following morning. The British left column would advance along the river with artillery support from field guns and boats. The center column would attack the heights, while the right column would sweep through the heavy woods north and west of the heights and turn the American left flank. Though Gates and Arnold had been feuding since the latter's arrival from Fort Stanwix, Arnold nonetheless convinced Gates to send reinforcements—Daniel Morgan and his riflemen—to the American left, where their marksmanship could prove useful in the dense woods.

Although he preferred a strategy of waiting for the enemy to attack his defensive works, Gates also begrudgingly permitted Arnold to reconnoiter in force toward the farm of John Freeman, where he found British advance troops. Morgan's riflemen picked off virtually every British officer in the advance force. Burgoyne then pushed his main column toward Freeman's farm, and Gates responded by sending reinforcements. Throughout the day each side gained a momentary advantage. Morgan's riflemen were so successful in targeting artillerymen that the Americans won control over British field guns time and again, only to lose their edge in successive British bayonet charges. Had darkness not set in and allowed the Americans to withdraw into their entrenchments, Arnold might have lost the left. Burgoyne and the British had won the field, but it had been a costly victory: the Redcoats had suffered some 600 casualties, including three-quarters of their artillerymen, which represented staggering losses.

Believing General Clinton would advance north from New York City and arrive in the area of Saratoga by the end of September, Burgoyne chose to wait and remained quiet for the next eighteen days. But Clinton did not leave the city until early October, and while he did capture Forts Montgomery and Clinton, he never came close to Saratoga. Then Burgoyne received news that the Patriots had captured outposts between Ticonderoga and Fort George, effectively cutting off his supply line and route of evacuation. Burgoyne did not know that Patriot troop numbers had also grown, as militiamen swarmed into Gates's camp. During a British war council, German general Riedesel suggested a retreat. Unwilling to accept this dishonorable option, Burgoyne chose to attack the American left flank with 2,000 men, including 1,500 regulars and 600 Tories—more than one-third of his army.

On October 7, Burgoyne personally positioned his soldiers on the American left flank and set his artillery on a rise overlooking an open field. In reality the British guns sat too close to the woods. Gates's 8,000 troops quietly responded to Burgoyne's movement and prepared for the attack. British grenadiers briskly moved forward with bayonets mounted, and the Americans held their fire until the Redcoats came within close range. Then suddenly Burgoyne found himself overwhelmed from three sides as Patriot shots struck his horse, hat, and waistcoat. As British units fell back to their entrenchments, six of Burgoyne's ten cannons fell to the Americans. The British suffered 400 casualties.

Arnold, whom Gates had relieved of command because of ongoing disagreements, mounted a horse and took off for the front of the American lines. Gates sent an officer in chase, but Arnold arrived in time to lead the Americans in an assault on the gap between two entrenchments on the British right, exposing the British rear and right flank. As Continentals and militiamen overwhelmed the two redoubts, British fire struck Arnold and his horse, and his leg was shattered. Gates's emissary finally caught up to Arnold and made sure the wounded general was taken back to camp on a litter. Even so, Arnold had again led the Americans to a victory, again with only darkness preventing the complete destruction of Burgoyne's army.

Realizing he could not take Albany, Burgoyne retreated north toward Saratoga in a driving rain. As Americans harassed his column and his soldiers suffered from a lack of food and supplies, Burgoyne's officers suggested that the army flee to Canada. But such an evacuation proved impossible, because Burgoyne learned on the morning of October 13 that an estimated 20,000 Patriots surrounded his army. Dejectedly he informed Gates that he would surrender, and the two sides agreed to terms. On October 17, 1777, in a solemn affair, Burgoyne offered his sword to Gates, who returned it to the British general. Then some 5,000 British soldiers marched through hordes of Patriots to lay down their arms. Burgoyne finally made it to Albany, but as a prisoner.

Saratoga, in which Britain lost a major army to the upstart Americans, represented a major turning point in the war. News of the defeat and British difficulties in Pennsylvania finally convinced French officials to offer assistance to and ally with the American colonies in the war.

PHILADELPHIA CAMPAIGN

Even before General Howe learned that Lord Germain had endorsed his plan to subdue the American heartland, he had begun making arrangements to attack Philadelphia via the Delaware River. His operational plan called for leading 11,000 troops against Philadelphia, keeping 4,700 in New York City and 2,400 in Newport, and sending 3,000 Tories under General William Tryon to the lower Hudson River. However, this plan had a major flaw: it left too much distance between Howe's forces at sea and Burgoyne's army advancing south from Canada. Moreover, Howe did not take precautions to provide for the safety of Burgoyne's army. Germain approved of Howe's plan but assumed he would assist Burgoyne after the conquest of Philadelphia. Instead, Howe found that preparations took far too much time.

In late May, Howe tried to entice Washington's army from its winter camp in Middlebrook, New Jersey. Giving the appearance of retreating toward New York, Howe lured part of Washington's army into the open, and Cornwallis suddenly attacked the Patriot left flank. Washington prudently withdrew back to Middlebrook and patiently watched as the British concentrated again in New York City. Thereafter, as weeks of good weather passed, Washington could only guess at Howe's intentions. Would he move north to help Burgoyne, attack Philadelphia, or proceed farther south? Howe did not tip his hand until July 23, 1777, when 19,000 soldiers embarked aboard 250 vessels. Still, Washington could only speculate about the British destination, so he had to wait until intelligence confirmed that the British fleet had sailed south and entered the Chesapeake Bay. Only then did Washington move troops to Philadelphia.

Howe's army, which landed on August 25 at the northern end of the Chesapeake Bay some fifty-five miles southwest of Philadelphia, had been sickened and weakened by the long sea voyage. Washington had proceeded south cautiously, entrenching 11,000 soldiers on the northern side of Brandywine Creek. On September 11 Howe gave the appearance that he would cross the creek and engage Washington directly, skirmishing with American troops as he marched north, but in fact, he quietly moved most of his army to the west, far beyond Washington's right flank. American scouts did not detect the British movements until Redcoats had gained the rear of Washington's defense. Nevertheless, when British troops suddenly attacked both of Washington's flanks, the Americans initially offered stiff resistance. But once Washington's right flank collapsed, his left flank crumbled too, forcing the Americans to retreat hastily to the northeast. Washington had made a mistake by leaving his right flank inadequately protected, an oversight that resulted in a near annihilation. With Washington's retreat, Howe and the British army marched into the city unopposed on September 25, 1777.

Once in Philadelphia, General Howe immediately opened the lower Delaware River so his army had access to communication and supplies. Garrisoning the city with 3,000 of his best soldiers, he sent 9,000 troops to Germantown to protect against any counterattack Washington might consider. But these British troops did not dig entrenchments, and their carelessness convinced Washington to attempt a bold move. On the night of October 3, Washington advanced on Germantown with 11,000 men in four columns. Two columns would make a frontal assault on the following morning, while the other two columns would try to flank the British positions; later, all four columns would converge near Germantown.

Moving slowly and hesitantly through the darkness, the four columns could not maintain contact with one another. By dawn, three of the four were not in position to attack. Eventually, a flanking column composed primarily of militia reached the British camp and fired a few rounds of artillery before retreating in the face of approaching Redcoats. Another column, slated for the frontal attack, initially forced British pickets to withdraw before encountering six Redcoat companies (about 140 men) occupying a strongly built stone house called the Chew House about two miles from the British army. The Americans tried several times to dislodge the smaller force from the house, but every time they were repelled. Meanwhile, the other two columns moved about 200 yards ahead of the Chew House, but their vision was obscured by smoke and fog. When they found Howe's contingent of Redcoats and Hessians, they initially repulsed them while suffering heavy casualties. Then suddenly the American attack crumbled, and soldiers began retreating as the British restored their line. Lord Cornwallis, who had ridden from Philadelphia, pursued the retreating Patriots for about nine miles before disengaging because of impending darkness. The day, which had begun with bold American optimism, had been costly, with some 670 Americans killed or wounded. A Hessian staff officer claimed that the British had also captured 438 Americans. Meanwhile, British losses numbered 525 killed, wounded, and missing.

The Patriots derived renewed strength from the attack despite it being a defeat. Only three weeks earlier Washington had been almost annihilated at Brandywine Creek. Germantown proved that recent disasters notwithstanding, the new Continental force could stand up to the British army. In its aftermath Washington did not retreat but instead established a defensive line at Whitemarsh, daring the British to attack. Howe chose not to engage but instead to take up winter quarters in Philadelphia. Washington encamped in the hills of Valley Forge, some twenty miles northwest of Philadelphia.

1778: STALEMATE IN THE NORTH

The news that Burgoyne had surrendered at Saratoga shook the British nation and the North ministry. When it reached Paris, along with information that General Washington had survived a British thrust into Pennsylvania, French foreign minister Comte de Vergennes, an advisor to King Louis XVI, saw that the Americans would make worthy allies and that this struggle was more than a feeble insurrection—it was a full-fledged rebellion. Vergennes argued that the time had come for France to aid publicly the Americans and strike back at Great Britain. Consequently France recognized the independence of the United States of America and on February 6, 1778, signed a formal alliance with the new nation. Spain later agreed to ally with France—not the United States—in April 1779. Great Britain declared war on the Dutch Republic in 1780 because it had continued to trade with France and the Americans during the conflict. The joining together of the three European powers against Great Britain transformed the North American struggle into a world war, as fighting soon spread to India, Africa, the Mediterranean, the West Indies, and the high seas. Even so, General Clinton believed that opening the Hudson River, as Burgoyne had planned, would sever New England, protect New York, and determine the outcome of the war.

A SUFFERING ARMY

Despite news of the Franco-American alliance, the winter of 1777–1778 was one of great hardship for Washington and his men. The area around Valley Forge had been swept of cattle. Washington's soldiers had difficulty securing food and supplies because civilians chose to sell to the British for hard cash rather than to Americans for depreciated paper money. Those with Loyalist sympathies who refused to sell often found their goods confiscated, and since women's assets were automatically transferred to their husbands, once Congress passed confiscation laws a woman could lose her home and property because of her husband's politics. Soldiers also had inadequate clothing, few shoes, and hardly enough blankets. Their only shelters were crude wooden structures that provided little protection as winter temperatures dropped precipitously during what old-timers remembered as the coldest winter on record. With such suffering, American soldiers began deserting in greater numbers, and it was said that one could track them by their blood on the rough frozen ground. Could winter defeat Washington where Howe could not?

In response to the crisis, Washington reorganized the army, appointing General Nathanael Greene to command the Quartermaster Department and giving him the power to appoint forage and wagon masters. Greene brought a boundless energy to logistics and a cunning ability to the search for food, sending foragers far and wide. He sent Anthony Wayne and Henry Lee into Delaware, New Jersey, and eastern Maryland, where they found abundant food, horses and livestock, and hay and grain. Though unable to get it all back to Valley Forge, Greene ordered the surplus burned so the British could not use it. By early March 1778, Washington's skeletal force had begun to flesh out.

The 10,000 men at Valley Forge soon learned the essentials of military drill, tactics, and discipline from Friedrich Wilhelm August Ferdinand, Baron von Steuben. The fiery German-speaking Steuben, who claimed to have served under Frederick the Great, composed a French-language manual to teach soldiers how to drill and handle their weapons and personally taught a 100-man model company close-order drill. He believed the Americans had a special character, telling an old European comrade that he had to explain to these Republican soldiers the reason for doing things rather than simply using threats, but by doing so he gained their loyalty and commitment to the cause. Steuben's repetitive instruction—what Joseph Plumb Martin called "continual drill"—taught the soldiers the precision and close-order movements they needed when under fire. Their ability to perform well-executed movements and drill on the parade field gave the soldiers the confidence to move effectively in battle. Having suffered through common hardships that built a bond of endurance, by spring 1778 the Continental soldiers had been transformed into a professional fighting force that looked like a band of scarecrows but drilled like a traditional European army.

Washington also faced adversity because of his failure to win any victories in 1777. Many members of Congress attacked him personally, demanding he be replaced, but no official motion was ever offered. Even so, doubt trickled from the halls of Congress through the officer corps to the rank and file. General Howe faced problems as well. Philadelphia Loyalists had not swelled British ranks—only 300 had enlisted—as he had anticipated. He had also not defeated Washington. So when Howe asked to resign, Lord North refused unless General Jeffrey Amherst consented to replace him. Amherst flatly declined. Lord Germain finally agreed to accept Howe's resignation and in early February 1778 gave command to Henry Clinton, who would face a reinvigorated enemy outfitted and supplied by the French. Rather than stay in Philadelphia, Clinton departed on June 18, 1778, marching overland across New Jersey with the bulk of his forces toward New York, where he planned to consolidate and reorganize the army.

After querying his officers, Washington was torn between letting the British evacuate without attacking and engaging the Redcoats as they retreated. He decided on a middle course—striking a partial blow at Clinton's retreating army but avoiding a general engagement. On the terribly hot morning of June 28, 1778, Washington sent General Charles Lee's 4,000 troops against the British rear guard at Monmouth Court House in New Jersey. Lee, who had advocated letting the British evacuate without an attack, hesitated. Once he did attack he recognized that his soldiers had engaged the main British army rather than the rear guard. Lord Cornwallis responded forcefully and aggressively. Not wanting his command to be destroyed, Lee quickly withdrew across three small ravines, taking a defensive position on a small hill. Washington rode forward, publicly criticized Lee for not attacking, angrily dismissed the general, and assumed personal command. Under his leadership, the Patriots repulsed several British counterattacks, including a cavalry charge led by Clinton himself. During the intense fighting, an American artilleryman's wife named Mary Hays reportedly brought water to thirsty soldiers in the intense June heat and even took her husband's place in a gun crew when he fell injured, becoming one of several women associated with the legend of Molly Pitcher. By now the temperature had spiked above 100 degrees, and heatstroke claimed as many lives as did musket fire. By sunset Washington's artillery had enfiladed the British ranks and forced the exhausted Redcoats to retreat. During the night Clinton quietly marched off toward New York, with Cornwallis protecting his rear.

Technically, the battle had ended in a draw—the Americans had held the field, while the British had won a tactical victory in Clinton's successful march to New York—but the newly trained Continental Army had also demonstrated the growing effectiveness of Steuben's professional training. Thereafter the northern theater devolved into a long stalemate, with the British occupying New York City and Washington harassing Redcoats on the outskirts of the city whenever the opportunity presented itself.

ANGER AND FRUSTRATION

As the war dragged on, American officers and soldiers alike began questioning their commitment to the cause. Gentleman officers focused on questions of rank and economic survival. They worried about any slight to their honor and dignity, which they interpreted as an assault on their rights as gentlemen. Although the officer corps received payment for their duty, Congress remained insensitive to their feelings, which predictably created suspicion and mistrust among those members of the military from the wealthiest ranks of American society.

Officers believed that service had deprived them of income and general prosperity. Inflation undermined their limited salary, and the cost of purchasing uniforms and supplies—to uphold the standards of an officer—further strained them. Officers even suggested that Congress provide them with half-pay pensions for life, as Britain did for its officers, but Congress concluded that pensions were contrary to republicanism and that half-pay for former officers would give the appearance of a peacetime standing army. Overall, Congress treated American officers like professional mercenaries rather than propertied citizens of high military rank who were making sacrifices for civilian freedom. By the late spring of 1778 many officers had resigned, and the army appeared on the brink of collapse. Congress succumbed to pressure, agreeing to increase salaries and provide half-pay pensions for seven years. A standoff between greedy officers who were fighting for financial gain and civilians who would permit the army to perish rather than incur additional obligations had been avoided, but the issue was not settled.

Washington also battled with bureaucratic inefficiencies as he tried to feed and clothe the soldiers in the ranks. Congress's repeated unwillingness to correct glaring commissary problems left soldiers exposed to cold weather and without food and clothing. Food that did arrive was often spoiled and rancid, making it virtually inedible. Poorly constructed clothing frequently arrived filled with moths. Draft animals suffered as well, with many dying because Congress did not provide funding for forage. Hungry and exposed soldiers remained in camps filled with the stench of putrid food and decaying horses, and they began to wonder why they were suffering for indifferent and uncaring civilians. Since the ranks consisted of lower-class Americans, most civilians truly did not care about soldiers' conditions and would not sell goods for depreciated Patriot currency. This intransigence forced Washington at times to confiscate foodstuffs and supplies to prevent starvation, which strained the relationship between the army and the populace. Sometimes soldiers also requisitioned goods such as dining tables, chairs, and dishes. Many people thought they would fare better should the Continental Army be destroyed.

ISSUES IN MILITARY HISTORY

GEORGE WASHINGTON AND CIVILIAN RULE

Americans distrusted the standing army, preferring instead a militia of citizen-soldiers to provide defense. Once any crisis ended, these citizen militiamen generally returned home without abusing their power. Militiamen were first and foremost citizens who sought to protect their homes and families and serve their local communities. Unlike professional soldiers, they did not expect to be paid for their services.

When George Washington assumed command of the Continental Army, he served the Continental Congress rather than the people. Congressional delegates received their authority and instructions from elected representatives of the individual colonies. Congress placed limits on Washington's authority and freedom to act. The subordination of the commander and his army to civil officials was, in effect, subordination to the law. During the conflict Washington constantly deferred to provincial leaders (who provided personnel and supplies) and Congress (who provided authority and guidance), strengthening civil authority rather than enhancing military power. He informed leaders about military affairs, consulted them on strategy, did not make public statements about congressional decisions, and always requested rather than demanded support. Even when Congress made decisions contrary to his preferences, Washington respected those choices, maintaining a subordinate position to the civil authorities. Through his deference to Congress, Washington established firm precedents of military subordination to law and to the citizenry.

As the end of the Revolution approached, this principle of civilian control was momentarily undermined. Congressional control over the military weakened, and officers and soldiers became convinced that they would not be compensated for their services. During 1781 Continental soldiers from Pennsylvania and New Jersey marched on Philadelphia to express their displeasure with the indifferent civilian rule, but Washington and cool-headed civilian leaders defused the crisis. During March 1783 a group of Continental army officers hatched the "Newburgh Conspiracy" with the intention of using the military to overthrow the civilian government and then crown George Washington as king. Washington confronted the discontented officers and placated them, winning their loyalty to the civilian republican government. A few months later army officers established the Society of Cincinnati, which appeared to create a hereditary ruling class of former military officers. Many civilian leaders boasted membership in the Society, with Washington even being named its first president. But Washington settled the question of the proper relationship between the government and the military when in December 1783, he traveled to Annapolis, Maryland, to surrender his sword to the civilian government and beg leave to go home as a private citizen.

The principle of civilian control over the military continues to evolve. A definitive split has developed between the civilian and military spheres of influence, with the civilian sphere directing policy regarding the use of force and the military sphere implementing that policy. Modern assertions of the civil–military relationship all rest on the same foundation: civilian control of the military is a good thing. Washington's relationship with the states and Congress was not perfect, but his actions established a functional model for civil–military affairs that survives today.

The *rage militaire* of the soldiers and officers had greatly subsided by the late 1770s. They still believed in the cause for which they fought, but they had come to despise the civilians who profited from their discomfort. Contemptuous of their lower-class origins, most civilians ridiculed soldiers as drunks, troublemakers, and hirelings. Even the threat of 100 lashes did not prevent hungry and angry soldiers from looting and plundering the countryside, especially when civilians did not live up to their obligations. Soldiers protested their treatment daily through cursing, drinking, looting, bounty jumping, and desertion. When they believed their personal freedom was threatened, officers and soldiers alike were prepared to mutiny. During the winter of 1781 the Pennsylvania and New Jersey lines both mutinied over the issues of payment and enlistments. Congressional intransigence and civilian distrust rather than Great Britain threatened to bring about the defeat of the army.

STRUGGLE ON THE PERIPHERY

While the U.S. Navy dates its birthday to October 13, 1775, it is difficult to determine precisely the beginnings of the sea service or who was responsible for its creation. On that day, the Continental Congress authorized the purchase of two ships, two brigs, two sloops, and two schooners and voted to build thirteen more ships, although only six got to sea, and they accomplished very little. On November 10, Congress also established the Marine Corps, authorizing two battalions of marines. During the conflict the American navy and marines emerged as products of military necessity and political circumstances. The small sailing force demonstrated persistence and a willingness to improvise rather than any sense of strategic insight or applied doctrine as it faced a Royal Navy built around seventy-four-gun ships-of-the-line. Without armed Continental warships or the resources to construct naval forces that could confront the Royal Navy, eleven of the thirteen colonies commissioned smaller armed vessels to protect local waters, and individuals outfitted privateers to harass British shipping.

Britain possessed 131 ships and innumerable smaller craft when the war began, but many of those vessels had suffered from neglect and were no longer seaworthy. As a result, British strategy initially used its navy to reinforce the army by supporting land operations, providing naval brigades for land service, and transporting supplies for the armies in the field. As the war progressed, the Royal Navy expanded its role and engaged in punitive expeditions against American coastal towns (such as Portland, Maine, in October 1775), aggressively pursued American commerce raiders, and tried to blockade ports from which American privateers operated.

While in Boston during 1775 George Washington laid the foundations of his navy when he chartered Colonel John Glover's fishing schooner *Hannah* to raid British shipping. While foraging for the army, *Hannah* captured only one vessel before being run aground by a British warship. Other chartered craft—ultimately numbering eleven—later captured more than fifty prizes, including the supply brig *Nancy*, carrying 2,500 muskets, several cannon, and more than thirty tons of shot. Washington's makeshift fleet helped supply his army during the winter of 1775–1776 and encouraged Congress to create the Continental Navy.

CONTINENTAL NAVY

After creating the navy, the Continental Congress appointed Esek Hopkins as commander-in-chief of the fleet. The younger brother of an influential member of Congress, Hopkins had orders to drive Lord Dunmore's squadron out of Virginia waters and to then cruise off the Carolina Capes to protect Patriot property. Departing with eight ships in January 1776, Hopkins instead sailed directly to the Bahamas to capture booty. Arriving at the islands with only six ships in early March 1776, Hopkins sent Captain Samuel Nicholas and marines ashore at New Providence, where they captured two forts guarding Nassau and then spent two weeks loading fifty-eight captured cannon and some munitions, and drinking captured spirits. Marines maintain that this was the service's first engagement and first amphibious landing. While Hopkins did deliver some ordnance to the Patriots, he had not protected the southern states as instructed. As a result Congress censured Hopkins and in 1778 dismissed him because he also refused to attack the Newfoundland fisheries.

Commerce raiding of the British merchant fleet, the largest in the world, became the most successful naval effort undertaken by Patriots during the war. Privateers operating from French and Spanish ports precipitated the breakdown of Anglo-French diplomatic relations, contributing to the outbreak of war between the two nations. These privately owned ships, which carried commissions called "letters of marque," joined with armed merchant ships to harass British shipping, taking legal prizes whenever possible. Called *guerre de course*, or "war on commerce," privateering threatened Britain's transatlantic supply line and eventually brought the war to British waters. As British maritime insurance rates doubled, London merchants lost their zeal for the struggle. Soon the British public's hunger for the fight also abated, and the government lost its mandate for war.

Among the most successful Continental privateers were Lambert Wickes, Gustavus Conyngham, and John Paul Jones. In June 1777 Jones gained command of the eighteen-gun *Ranger* and took the war to the Irish Sea. Landing a small force on Whitehaven Bay on central England's western coast, he tried to kidnap the Earl of Selkirk, but the earl was not home at the time. While circumnavigating Ireland, Jones defeated the twenty-gun British sloop *Drake* in the North Channel before returning to France, where he gained command of an old French East Indiaman that had been rechristened *Bonhomme Richard*. Sailing with a small squadron of ships, Jones again attacked English shores, capturing a dozen prizes in the British Isles' western waters before encountering HMS *Serapis* in the North Sea on September 23, 1779. During the engagement Jones lashed *Bonhomme Richard* to the *Serapis* to fight in close quarters. Throughout the night the two ships, lashed together bow to stern a few feet apart, battered one another with their eighteen-pound guns while sailors fought to gain control over their enemy's ship. After *Bonhomme Richard* began taking on water, the *Serapis*'s captain asked Jones if he had struck his colors. Jones barked: "I have not yet begun to fight!" Shortly after, a fire aboard *Serapis* threatened the ship's magazine, prompting the British captain to surrender instead. Thereafter British and American sailors worked together to extinguish the fire and save *Serapis* before *Bonhomme Richard* sank two days later. These daring exploits, carried out within eyesight of the British coast, brought the war to England in a dramatic way that further melted public support for the American struggle.

IMAGE 4.2 *Bonhomme Richard* Named in honor of Benjamin Franklin's "Poor Richard Almanac," John Paul Jones's rechristened ship *Bonhomme Richard* took the war to the coast of England, threatening British merchant shipping, driving up shipping insurance, and crippling Britain's transatlantic supply lines. When Jones captured HMS *Serapis* off the coast of Yorkshire in September 1779, it disproved the invincibility of the British navy and also convinced the French to increase their support of the naval war against Britain.

STATE NAVIES

Massachusetts and Rhode Island were the first states to commission ships, and ultimately eleven of the thirteen states followed suit (only Delaware and New Jersey did not). In most instances states created sailing forces to provide coastal defense against the British navy, Loyalist smugglers, privateers, and pirates. But the states did not have the resources to construct a fleet that could stand up to the Royal Navy. Their ships rarely operated outside state waters, and they seldom cooperated with one another. In one instance Massachusetts and New Hampshire ships participated with the Continental fleet in an operation in Penobscot Bay (Maine) during the summer of 1779. Massachusetts committed two brigantines and convinced sixteen state privateers to join with New Hampshire's only state vessel, three Continental warships, and eighteen Continental transports. The combined fleet of forty vessels, which lacked a unified command, could not agree on objectives, and the indecision resulted in catastrophic failure when a British ship-of-the-line, three frigates, and three sloops entered the harbor in August 1779 to relieve the siege. The forty American ships fled up the Penobscot River until they ran aground, demonstrating the lack of unity between states, between states and the Continental Navy, and between naval forces and privateers.

BREAKING THE IROQUOIS CONFEDERATION

With Clinton's army controlling New York and Washington's forces remaining along the Hudson River and in New Jersey, the focus of the war moved momentarily to the west. There, British colonel William Hamilton's soldiers at Forts Niagara and Detroit encouraged frontier Tories and friendly Indians to attack western American settlements; Hamilton even offered bounties for white scalps. As Hamilton tried to enlist the Iroquois in the British effort, the confederation split. The Senecas sided with the British and attacked pro-American Oneidas, the Oneidas destroyed Mohawk towns and corn supplies, and neutral Onondaga chiefs traveled to Québec to negotiate. When Washington learned of the Onondagas' intentions he sent General John Sullivan to destroy the tribe's ability to make war. Sullivan leveled forty Seneca and Cayuga villages and eliminated the Onondagas' corn supply, forcing them to side with the British and compelling the Oneidas to seek American protection. As a result the Iroquois Confederation, which had been founded before Europeans arrived in America, was divided and weakened.

In early 1778 George Rogers Clark and 175 militiamen proceeded down the Ohio River on flatboats and captured Kaskaskia (in present-day Illinois) on July 4, much to the surprise and excitement of the village's French settlers. Moving overland with French volunteers, Clark also captured Vincennes (in present-day Indiana) from the French without firing a shot. Leaving only four men at Vincennes, Clark and his French allies then moved on Cahokia (opposite of present-day St. Louis) and Prairie du Roche, spreading news of the Franco-American alliance. These victories supposedly opened the Mississippi River for safe passage and ensured that Patriots could receive supplies from Spanish New Orleans. In response, Colonel Hamilton immediately sent a relief force from Detroit of 500 soldiers, Tories, and Indians that reached Vincennes in mid December 1778; the four Americans garrisoning the town obviously surrendered. Hamilton, believing no one would attack during the winter, permitted his Tory militiamen and Indians to return home, leaving only thirty-five soldiers garrisoning Vincennes.

Learning that Vincennes had been retaken, Clark believed that the British had planned a spring campaign that would sweep through the Kentucky territory and gain unquestioned control over the Ohio River Valley. Clark's 170 French and American troops marched through cold mud and swollen creeks on a 180-mile trek to Vincennes. By the time they arrived in late February, Clark had realized the need for deception. Using the undulating terrain to his advantage, he marched his men in circles across a small clearing, giving townspeople the impression he had as many as 1,000 men. Locals decided to remain silent rather than alert British troops to the "overwhelming" American presence. Once Clark's troops occupied town, he sent men to surround the fort, with orders to fire upon his signal. When the Americans fired,

Colonel Hamilton thought he was surrounded. Even British officers who had just returned to the fort reported that a sizable American army had taken the town. Clark then had eight Indians brutally executed in full view of the British garrison while American sharpshooters targeted his gun crews. Surrounded and without the use of his cannon, Hamilton surrendered. Only then did he realize how small the American army was. Clark had prevented the British and Indians from opening a second front in the west, opened channels of trade from Spanish New Orleans, and discouraged further Indian participation.

During 1776 British-sponsored delegations of Shawnees, Delawares, and Mohawks had traveled south and convinced the Cherokees to attack frontier settlements in Virginia and the Carolinas. Soon violence had also erupted along the Watauga, Holsten, Nolichucky, and Doe rivers in eastern Tennessee. Cherokee raiding parties expanded their attacks, ravaging the southern backcountry of Kentucky, Virginia, North and South Carolina, and Georgia. During the first phase of this conflict, which lasted from summer 1776 to summer 1777, a united Cherokee nation led by several chiefs, including the charismatic Dragging Canoe, fought against territorial encroachment. Patriot militias swiftly retaliated throughout Cherokee country, burning more than fifty villages, destroying crops and orchards, slaughtering livestock, and selling captives into Caribbean slavery. By spring 1777 many Cherokee towns, seeking to escape American retribution, had betrayed war chiefs such as Dragging Canoe. Through treaties with Virginia, North and South Carolina, and Georgia, the peace factions also ceded land to the colonies. Dragging Canoe continued his war against the Americans, joining with British-sponsored Choctaws and Chickasaws farther west to prevent American incursion along the western Tennessee and Mississippi rivers, but ultimately the Cherokee split determined this faction's defeat.

SPANISH CONQUESTS IN THE SOUTH

After declaring war on Britain in early May 1779, King Charles III of Spain directed his colonial subjects to take action. Bernardo de Gálvez, the colonial governor of Spanish Louisiana, immediately attacked British positions. Braving a mid-August hurricane, Gálvez's multiethnic force of free blacks, Spanish creoles, Acadians, Indians, and Anglo-Americans captured Fort Bute on Bayou Manchac, Baton Rouge, and Fort Panmure (present-day Natchez). These victories cleared the lower Mississippi Valley of the Redcoat presence, leaving Mobile and Pensacola as the only British establishments in West Florida.

In early March 1780, Gálvez laid siege to Mobile's Fort Charlotte with 750 New Orleans soldiers and 450 reinforcements from Havana. The fort's walls crumbled after only two weeks, forcing British captain Elias Durnford to surrender. Although Choctaw and Creek Indians defected from the British and strengthened Gálvez's coalition, a fall 1780 hurricane slammed the Gulf Coast, delaying the planned expedition to take Pensacola.

Spanish ships finally entered Pensacola Bay in mid-March 1781, with troops landing by the end of the month. Fighting pro-British Creeks and Choctaws, Gálvez's troops advanced against the city's outer defenses, taking three redoubts. The Spaniards constructed trenches and covered roadways between their redoubts and bunkers to bring in armaments and supplies to advance the siege, but periodic Choctaw and Creek attacks slowed the digging.

Then, in mid-April, a large fleet from Havana appeared off the bay, carrying 3,000 additional Spanish soldiers and sailors and giving Gálvez 8,000 troops at his disposal. Suddenly, in early May a tempestuous hurricane swept through the region, delaying land operations and forcing Spanish ships to leave the harbor. For two days—May 5–6, 1781—storms battered the Spanish soldiers, who hunkered down in trenches that became rushing creeks and rivers. Finally, on May 8, a Spanish howitzer blast struck the powder magazine of Fort Crescent, one of British Pensacola's three fortifications. The resultant explosion permitted Spanish infantry to seize the fort, reposition their guns, and begin bombarding the two other forts. Recognizing he could not hold Pensacola, on May 10, 1781, General John Campbell surrendered more than 1,100 men. Spanish forces had seized the Gulf Coast and the lower Mississippi Valley, greatly assisting the Patriot cause.

A NEW SOUTHERN STRATEGY

In New York General Clinton found problems similar to those his predecessors had encountered. He needed troops to continue sustained operations against the Patriots. Throughout 1778 and 1779 his forces remained in the city and suffered death by a thousand cuts as Washington continually nibbled at British outposts. Occasionally Clinton's forces fought limited engagements in New Jersey and the Hudson Highlands, trying to weaken Washington's defensive position or draw him into a general engagement. During one operation against Middlebrook, Connecticut, in early June 1779, Clinton took a complement of troops from Stony Point, greatly reducing the British presence at the earthen bulwark. Noting the reduction, in mid-July 1779 General Anthony Wayne led a daring nighttime infantry bayonet attack on the post, quickly sweeping into the defensive works and capturing 500 Redcoats. Wayne abandoned the fort the following day, but the engagement emboldened the Patriots. A year later, Clinton tried to expand the war into New Jersey but in June was driven back at Connecticut Farms and Springfield. These repeated setbacks finally convinced Clinton to abandon northern operations and embrace a southern strategy.

SAVANNAH AND CHARLESTON

Clinton and British leaders believed that a sleeping Tory ally resided in the American South, and that a British presence there would awaken these slumbering Loyalists. In fall 1778 Clinton dispatched Lieutenant-Colonel Archibald Campbell and 3,100 soldiers from New York to Georgia, supplementing this force with additional troops from St. Augustine. Arriving in Georgia in late December 1778, Campbell surmised the weakness of American defenses and decided to attack before the troops arrived from St. Augustine. Taking advantage of local assistance, he seized Savannah and forced the Patriots to flee into South Carolina. When Redcoats arrived from St. Augustine in mid-January 1779, they moved immediately inland against Augusta, occupying it after minimal resistance. The British held Augusta for only a month before they evacuated and returned to Savannah. Campbell proclaimed to his superiors that he had removed a star and stripe from the American flag, but he failed to admit that the Patriots still held the backcountry.

During the early fall of 1779, Continental general Benjamin Lincoln led a joint Franco-American attempt to reclaim Savannah. With the participation of Admiral Charles Hector, Comte d'Estaing, who brought more than 500 French recruits from Saint-Dominigue, several hundred French soldiers of color, and some slaves, along with a French fleet from the Caribbean, the combined force represented the most significant foreign contribution to the American war effort to that point. As French ships bombarded the town, the combined land force assaulted the outer redoubts, initially making progress but soon encountering fierce resistance. Admiral d'Estaing suffered two wounds, and Polish cavalry officer Count Casimir Pulaski was killed while leading an assault. After more than an hour of bloody fighting, Lincoln and d'Estaing reluctantly abandoned the attempt to reclaim Savannah. The brief attack proved one of the bloodiest battles of the war, with Franco-American losses totaling 244 killed, 600 wounded, and 120 men captured; British casualties numbered barely 150. The British held Savannah until July 1782. The Americans retreated into South Carolina, while French forces returned to the Caribbean.

Emboldened by the defense of Savannah, General Clinton renewed his efforts in the South. In October he evacuated Rhode Island, sending the troops there to Savannah. The day after Christmas 1779 he departed New York for Charleston with 8,500 men. When Lord Francis Edward Rawdon joined him with additional troops, the size of the expedition swelled to almost 14,000 men and 90 ships. Clinton's voyage south proved troubling, as the ships carrying his heavy artillery sank, the horses for his cavalry died or were lost at sea, and Patriot privateers captured many of his supplies. Clinton then found that Patriot commodore Abraham Whipple had scuttled five American frigates near the mouth of the Cooper River to prevent British ships from coming too close. After landing troops in mid-February on Simmons Island, thirty miles south of Charleston, Clinton maneuvered closer to the city, crossing the Ashley River on March 29, 1780. Cutting the city and General Lincoln off from relief, Clinton opened the siege of Charleston on April 1, 1780.

Inside the city, General Lincoln mustered 2,650 Continentals and about 2,500 militia defenders. He told city leaders he would hold out and evacuate only if it looked as if the city would fall. By April 10, Clinton's artillery was in place and had begun bombarding the town. As the city burned, Lincoln's officers urged him to evacuate, but local leaders and citizens panicked, pleading for the army to protect them. Lincoln's decision was ultimately made for him when in mid-April British cavalry lieutenant-colonel Banastre Tarleton routed Virginia cavalry and a supply train at the Battle of Moncks Corner, eliminating an escape route for the Patriot army. In early May, Tarleton again routed Patriot cavalry at Lenud's Ferry, a crossing point on the Santee River and another escape route. Thereafter Lincoln's troops had to stay in the city as British artillery attacks intensified. When city leaders finally decided to surrender, Lincoln had no options. On May 12, 1780, Lincoln and his American Continentals became prisoners, while the militiamen returned home on a pledge that they would not take up arms again. The loss of Charleston—with 5,500 soldiers, a large number of arms and artillery, and 376 barrels of gunpowder—represented the worst American defeat of the war and the largest surrender of U.S. troops before the American Civil War. With very few casualties, General Clinton had seized the South's largest city and most important seaport. He had won the greatest British victory of the war, and the subsequent occupation of South Carolina and

Georgia represented the first time during the conflict that the British had attempted to pacify so large a geographical area. Jubilant, Clinton returned to New York, leaving 8,000 men in South Carolina under the command of Lord Cornwallis, who was instructed to make sure the conquests were not lost. The offensive-minded Cornwallis was the wrong man for this defensive assignment.

EMBERS OF DEFEAT

The defeat at Charleston reshaped the Patriot war effort in the South. The remnants of the southern Patriot forces retreated toward North Carolina, with Tarleton intently following. Reportedly, a group of Virginians surrendered—dropping their arms and hoisting white flags—to Tarleton's cavalry at the Battle of Waxhaws on May 29, but British dragoons continued their campaign of killing, showing no mercy. This unconfirmed story of "Tarleton's quarter" quickly spread throughout the region, becoming a rallying cry for Patriots, and "Bloody Tarleton" became the most hated man in the South.

After suffering at the hands of Loyalists and British troops, several American militiamen—most importantly those commanded by "Swamp Fox" Francis Marion, Thomas Sumter, and Andrew Pickens—chose to become partisans who participated in guerrilla warfare, engaging in fighting and then fading into the swamps and woods. These shadowy fighting units, which chipped away at isolated British units and poorly protected supply depots, threatened retribution for each British or Loyalist transgression, and their clandestine activities scared Loyalists far more than did Continental troops or Patriot militias. Cornwallis became increasingly incensed and dealt harshly with Patriots he captured, which further alienated the unaligned population. The British general also required Carolinians to swear allegiance to the Crown. Those who did received thanks and rewards from the newly restored royal government, while those who did not suffered further. Loyalists also sought personal revenge for grievances, expropriating the property and slaves of Patriots. Vengeful Loyalist militias sacked the homes of both Patriot noncombatants and those on parole as they subdued the backcountry. This asymmetrical pattern of warfare created a southern frontier awash in personal violence that was exacerbated by Loyalist, Patriot, and British viciousness.

Many locals thought that South Carolina had been deserted by the American war effort. Instead, Washington sent Baron de Kalb from New Jersey to North Carolina with 1,400 of the best Continental soldiers. Meanwhile, the Continental Congress squelched rumors of a proposed British peace treaty and sent Horatio Gates to replace Benjamin Lincoln as southern commander. While Washington believed others more suited to such a task, Gates nonetheless arrived in North Carolina in late July and began assembling his army of 4,000 hungry Continentals and militiamen, many of whom suffered from dysentery and the oppressive heat. Even so, Gates marched his troops through the barren landscape into South Carolina, toward the crossroads community of Camden, which reportedly had a British supply depot. As Gates's debilitated and hungry men neared Camden on the evening of August 13, they gorged on the abundant green corn that grew in the countryside and was known for causing human bowel movements. Having learned of Gates's maneuvers, Cornwallis had moved 2,100 troops from Charleston, who arrived at Camden on the same day.

MAJOR CAMPAIGNS IN THE SOUTH, 1778–1780

MAJOR CAMPAIGNS IN THE SOUTH, 1781

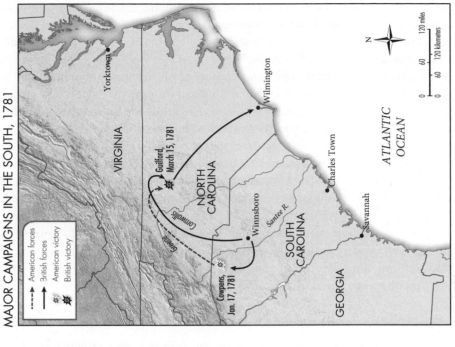

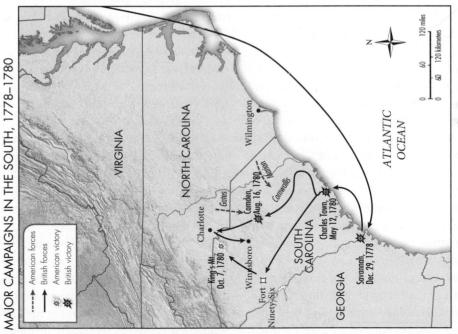

MAP 4.2 Major Campaigns in the South, 1778–1781

The two opposing armies had scouted one another for two days, and each thought it had an advantage. Gates did not know that Cornwallis had brought additional troops from Charleston, while Cornwallis did not know of the debilitated condition of Gates's army. Just after dawn on August 16, 1780, Cornwallis attacked Gates's entrenched left flank with a bayonet charge. The American defense, composed of North Carolina and Virginia militiamen, crumbled immediately and fled in the face of the advancing Redcoats. Within minutes, Gates had also fled. The American right flank, composed of Continentals commanded by de Kalb, tried to hold their line by advancing and breaking through the British left. The counterattack surprised and weakened the Redcoats, and it suddenly appeared that the British left might collapse. Then the British soldiers who had broken through on the American left wheeled around and struck de Kalb's left flank; while trying to rally his men, the baron was shot eleven times. Tarleton's cavalry then attacked the American rear, and within minutes the entire Patriot line had been shattered. Minutemen and Continentals alike fled in panic, with Tarleton pursuing and harassing the bedraggled Americans for twenty miles. Gates did not stop riding until late that evening, when he reached Charlotte, some sixty miles away. Within only a few hours, the Americans had lost 2,000 men, including almost 1,000 prisoners, surrendered seven guns and an entire baggage train, and experienced the complete destruction of a second southern army during one campaign season. Despite the activities of partisans, the southern war had become an American disaster.

TREASON, PENSIONS, AND MUTINIES

During the summer of 1780 General Washington had agreed to give Benedict Arnold command at West Point, New York. Unhappy with his personal situation and pessimistic about the country's future, the cantankerous Arnold had months earlier made contact with British spymaster Major John André, with whom he often communicated using his young wife Peggy Shippen as an intermediary. By late August 1780 Arnold was in command at West Point, and he had agreed to surrender the position and General Washington to the British in return for handsome payment. In the meantime, he provided the British with information regarding Washington's movements and the arrival of French troops and also weakened West Point's defenses. While visiting West Point during mid-September 1780 to check on fortifications, Washington discovered Arnold's plans, which unraveled. Had they succeeded, Washington would have been taken prisoner, a major prize. Instead, André was apprehended and later hanged; Arnold fled to New York as the most infamous traitor in American history. While it did not succeed, Arnold's betrayal revealed growing cracks in the revolutionary movement—fissures that could ultimately defeat the war effort in ways the British could not.

The struggle for American independence touched every sector of the country as families lost sons, fathers, and husbands. Soldiers who came home returned maimed or sick, with many never regaining their health or recovering from their psychological scars. Farmers were deprived of their crops and livestock. Shops were destroyed. Local economies were severely disrupted. Even the instruction of the young was interrupted. Many were simply tired of the deprivation, especially when a parsimonious Continental Congress seemingly feathered its own nests with the sacrifice of those in the ranks. Arnold's treason finally convinced some in Congress of the need to provide for those in the field, despite political fears that such measures would create a privileged military caste. While Congress promised the officer corps half-pay for life once the war ended, the body never delivered on its pledge. Congress also refused to provide pensions for common soldiers.

As soldiers started to see themselves as part of a larger group, they became emboldened. They voiced their frustration about lack of pay, their unsettled existence, and nonexistent supplies. When disease swept through the ranks, it spurred isolated incidents of protest among the Continental lines. Rhode Island and Connecticut regiments saw full-scale riots in 1779, and in January 1781, 1,500 troops of the Pennsylvania line seized artillery and began marching from their winter encampment at Morristown toward Philadelphia, where they planned to present their demands to the Continental Congress. When the mutinous soldiers reached Trenton, Pennsylvania, Continental officials met with them to address their concerns, ultimately offering soldiers back pay, new uniforms, immunity for the crime of deserting the field, and even discharges for those who reportedly had completed their three-year enlistment. By the end of January, order had returned to the Pennsylvania line, when suddenly the New Jersey line rose in mutiny. In this instance Washington used brutal force to bring the uprising under control, executing two mutineers. While he believed that his actions preserved the republican cause, the mutinous militiamen believed their protest was an attempt to preserve their rights. By the early part of 1781, hardened and battle-worn soldiers had begun questioning their devotion to a cause that seemed to have no sympathy or compassion for them. Fortunately for Washington and the country, the course of the war had by this time turned in favor of the Patriots.

THE WORLD TURNED UPSIDE DOWN

While affairs in the South had been disastrous, Washington received some good news during the summer of 1780. The French aristocrat Marquis de Lafayette, who had paid his own way to join the American cause because he believed in the American struggle for liberty, arrived in South Carolina in June 1777. He volunteered to serve the cause without pay and the Continental Congress commissioned him a major general in late July. Lafayette was wounded in the leg at the Battle of Brandywine, shared the hardship of his troops at Valley Forge, sent Washington a note that prompted the general to ride to the front at the Battle of Monmouth, and decided to return to France during the winter of 1779–1780 to convince King Louis XVI to send an army to America to serve under General Washington. Afterwards the king sent Jean-Baptiste Donatien de Vimeur, Comte de Rochambeau, who arrived in Newport, Rhode Island, with 5,000 French soldiers in July 1780. Admiral François-Joseph Paul, Comte de Grasse and commander of France's West Indies fleet, made arrangements to coordinate with Washington's army along the coast of North America. In May 1781, Washington met with Rochambeau in Wethersfield, Connecticut, to discuss options; he preferred to drive the British from New York, while Rochambeau had sent de Grasse a note urging him to bring the French fleet to the Chesapeake Bay.

Lord Cornwallis's easy victory at Camden had emboldened him. He had orders to maintain what Clinton had secured, but he also had authority to advance if he did not risk losing what had already been won. Broadly interpreting these orders permitted Cornwallis to push into North Carolina and Virginia in pursuit of the enemy. Cornwallis also believed, even before his victory at Camden, that he must conquer North Carolina so Patriots could not use it as a supply base. He would not fight a guerrilla war but rather destroy his distant enemy and deprive southern Patriots of all hope of help.

KING'S MOUNTAIN: BEGINNING OF THE END

Advancing toward Hillsborough, North Carolina, Cornwallis stopped near Charlotte in late September 1780 to reform his invasion force. As Major Patrick Ferguson—protecting Cornwallis's left flank with 1,200 Loyalists—marched from Ninety Six, South Carolina, toward Hillsborough, he found himself stalked by a growing number of frontiersmen, or "overmountain men." Ferguson pled with Cornwallis for assistance and then ascended a promontory summit he named King's Mountain to await relief, boasting that he was king of the mountain and that God himself could not drive him off of it. He was so very wrong.

With no reinforcements arriving, on the morning of October 7, 1780, Ferguson sent 200 men to forage. Almost as soon as they departed, 900 mounted Patriots began slowly moving up the hill, advancing even before the American infantry could join them. Scaling the summit from three sides, Patriots hid behind trees as they advanced, firing indiscriminately at Loyalists. Ferguson would not let his men hoist a white flag, so the Patriots exacted a horrendous revenge for the brutal treatment they had received from Loyalists. Hacking to death wounded Loyalists and even firing on Tories who tried to surrender, the frontier irregulars killed 157, wounded 163 others, and took 698 as prisoners. During the following days, they hanged nine of the most infamous Loyalists for the crimes they had committed during Tarleton's raids. By comparison, among frontier Patriots only twenty-eight were killed and sixty-two wounded. This American victory represented a turning point of the war in the South. It not only proved that the British were not invincible, it demonstrated to Loyalists that Britain could not and would not protect them, and as a result fewer chose to join their cause. Conversely, the American victory convinced southern farmers to join guerrilla units, further strengthening the Patriot war effort.

DEVIL OF A WHIPPING: WAR OF ATTRITION IN THE CAROLINAS

Realizing he was being surrounded by Patriot militias, Cornwallis retreated to Winnsboro, South Carolina, for winter quarters. His left flank had disintegrated, and he understood that southern loyalty to the Crown had evaporated. Without reinforcements from New York or abroad, Cornwallis knew he would have to pursue Continental forces through North Carolina and into Virginia, destroying crops and food supplies as he could.

The Continental Congress had chosen the fighting Rhode Island Quaker Nathanael Greene to replace the disgraced Horatio Gates. Greene immediately proceeded to Charlotte, where he arrived in December 1780 to find a small, thirsty, and hungry army. Eschewing a traditional strategy of concentrating his troops, Greene split his army. He sent General Daniel Morgan with some 600 men west of the Catawba River to defend and rally locals to the Patriot cause while he himself advanced with 1,100 men toward Cheraw Hill, South Carolina, where he planned to blunt Cornwallis's northern advance.

Morgan's western force threatened Cornwallis's flank, so the British commander sent Tarleton and his legion to remove the threat. When Tarleton arrived at Ninety Six, South Carolina, with 1,150 men he learned that Morgan's army was nearby. Choosing to pursue the Americans aggressively, on the afternoon of January 16, 1781, Tarleton approached Morgan's force near the rain-swollen Broad River. Morgan had selected a cattle pasture called Cowpens to set up his defense. He placed his army between the Broad and Pacolet rivers, limiting the opportunity for militias to retreat. The geographic landscape also provided Morgan the chance to deceive his opponent and to use his combination of Continentals and militiamen effectively.

Devising a plan that played on traditional expectations of American and British fighting units, Morgan instructed his Continental troops to stand firm and his militias to break before British bayonets. As such, he placed his Maryland and Delaware Continentals in a line across a low hill. Behind the hill, he positioned Colonel William Washington (George's cousin) with two small cavalry units. Putting his militia in the very front line, Morgan carefully instructed his men on their manner of retreat—they should fire two shots, aiming for officers, and then fall back around the American left flank.

Morgan also knew that British arrogance would tempt Tarleton to make a frontal assault. After a five-hour forced march on the morning of January 17, Tarleton saw militiamen at the front of the American line. Slyly smiling, he quickly ordered his soldiers ahead, expecting

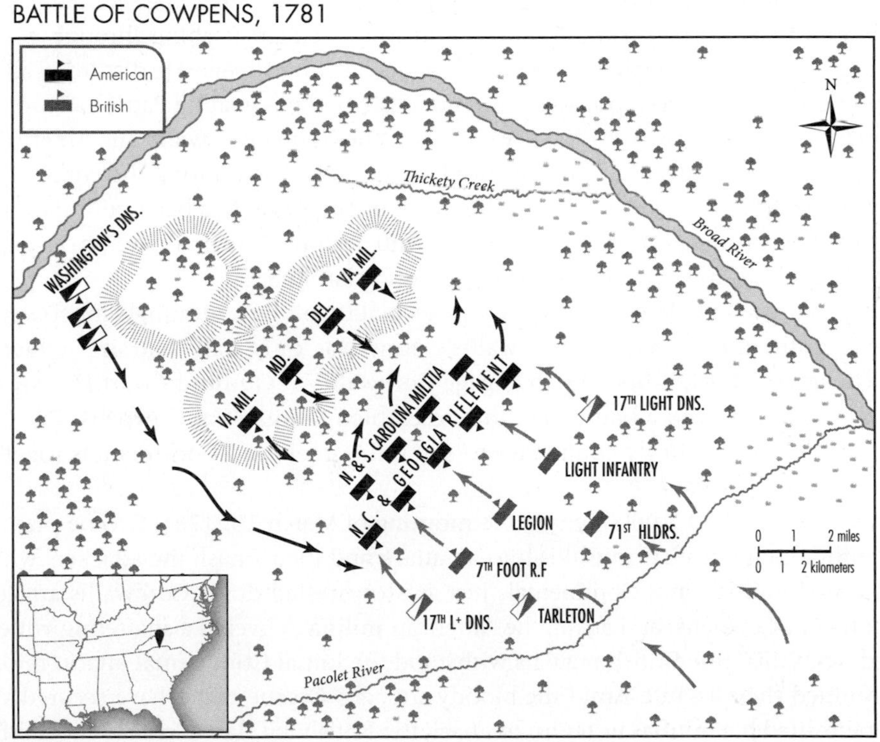

BATTLE OF COWPENS, 1781

MAP 4.3 Battle of Cowpens, 1781

an easy victory. As Morgan planned, the American militiamen fired two devastating volleys before beginning what appeared to be a disorganized retreat. Sensing a rout and a victory, Tarleton ordered his cavalry in hot pursuit. Suddenly William Washington's cavalry units appeared just in time to protect the retreating militiamen. Once they had driven off Tarleton's cavalry, Washington's horsemen slammed into the British right flank. The retreating militiamen reformed behind the hill and circled around to attack the British left flank. Meanwhile Morgan's Continental regulars calmly held against two British frontal assaults before driving the Redcoats back. The shocked British units, assaulted on three sides with deadly fire and bayonet attacks, collapsed in retreat. Only Tarleton and some 140 horsemen escaped, as the British suffered 329 killed and 600 captured. Among Morgan's forces only twelve were killed and sixty wounded. This impressive engagement at Cowpens—described by Morgan as "a devil of a whipping"—represented more than just an American tactical victory. It also demonstrated how competent commanders could use militiamen and Continentals effectively and play on the enemy's perceptions. Finally, it served as another staggering blow to Cornwallis's southern offensive, as each defeat further diminished British capabilities while bolstering American confidence.

TAKING THE WAR TO VIRGINIA

An angry Cornwallis wanted to punish Morgan. With 3,000 Redcoats, the general aggressively pursued Morgan's retreating force into North Carolina, where they joined Greene at Cheraw, South Carolina, to continue their northward retreat. Pushing through cold, wet conditions, Cornwallis thought he was ever closer to catching Greene. He discarded all heavy baggage to increase his speed but still could not ensnare the retreating Patriots. Throughout late January and early February 1781, several skirmishes erupted between the American rear guard and the British advance, with Cornwallis losing 250 men during the chase. By mid-February, Greene's army had crossed the Dan River in boats that had been built months earlier. Unable to cross the same swollen river and with a supply line on the verge of snapping, Cornwallis retraced his steps to Hillsborough, North Carolina.

Greene's army had slowly grown to almost 4,500 soldiers, although most were still unreliable militiamen. Even so, Cornwallis's army was only half that size, which convinced Greene to attack. Choosing to engage Cornwallis at Guilford Court House, North Carolina, Greene devised a battle plan that resembled Morgan's at Cowpens. But Greene did not have the same steely confidence to use militiamen and Continentals together as Morgan had.

Cornwallis only had 2,000 men on the morning of March 15, 1781. Greene planned to use his militiamen to lure Cornwallis into an attack and then smash the attackers with cavalry, reformed militias, and Continentals just as Morgan had done. Cornwallis attacked as Tarleton had at Cowpens, and again, the American militia delivered a shattering volley and retreated—but this time British regulars withstood the initial Continental attack, reformed, and continued their assault. Amid the bloody struggle, Greene could have secured victory had he permitted his militias to return to attack the British left flank. Instead, he held them in reserve because he was not ready to risk everything. During ninety minutes of fighting neither side gained an advantage, so Greene slowly retreated, leaving the British controlling the battlefield. It had been a costly British victory, with 532 casualties (93 dead, 416 wounded, and 26 missing or captured) compared to only 264 on the American side. Having lost approximately 25 percent of his army, Cornwallis knew he was much too weak to remain safely in the North Carolina interior, and so he fled 175 miles east to Wilmington to gain assistance, supplies, and reinforcements. Greene had greatly weakened Cornwallis, and the course of the war in the South had reversed. After the disastrous losses of Savannah and Charleston, the southern campaign had revived the Patriot cause, stifled Tory support, and altered the course of the conflict.

Cornwallis remained in Wilmington only a short time before deciding that he needed to confront and defeat the Americans in Virginia in order to hold onto the southern colonies. Against General Clinton's wishes, he marched into southern Virginia to cut the supply lines that made the Patriot's southern campaign possible. Without the luxury of supplies and allies, Cornwallis raided every farm or plantation he crossed and allowed his Loyalists to plunder anything they desired, driving locals into American arms. Cornwallis also freed 12,000 slaves, thinking it would undermine the southern economy, but this served to alienate even more southerners. Finally, Cornwallis did not completely pacify the areas through which he passed, which permitted the Patriots to regain the allegiance of those civilians.

In December 1780 Clinton had sent General Benedict Arnold with 2,000 Redcoats to Portsmouth to ravage the Virginia coast. Arnold's soldiers proceeded as far inland as Richmond, where they destroyed military targets and much of the city. Learning of increasing American opposition in Virginia—twice Arnold's force was almost surrounded—Clinton sent 2,000 more troops and General William Phillips to take command. Clinton had not wanted to make Virginia a major battleground, but as Cornwallis arrived in Petersburg with his 1,500 soldiers on May 20, 1781, bringing the total number of Redcoats in the Old Dominion to 7,500 men, it became one.

Cornwallis sent Tarleton to raid the Virginia countryside, where he burned tobacco plantations and warehouses indiscriminately. In early June, Tarleton's cavalry dashed toward Charlottesville in an attempt to capture Virginia governor and Declaration of Independence author Thomas Jefferson, who escaped shortly before troops descended on his Monticello home. Having learned that a powerful French fleet had departed Brest and would soon arrive in American waters, Clinton decided to reconcentrate his forces in New York. He ordered Cornwallis to find a base on the Chesapeake Bay, fortify it, and then lead the bulk of his army north to New York. Cornwallis rejected these orders, telling Clinton that he needed all of his men to establish a base on the Chesapeake. Tired of the power struggle in which Lord Germain favored Cornwallis, Clinton instructed Cornwallis to proceed to Old Point Comfort at the mouth of the James River. Instead, Cornwallis talked with engineers before concluding that Yorktown, on the southern shore of the York River, would be more easily defended. After three weeks of raiding, in early August Cornwallis started building fortifications at a site where his army could have deepwater access to the sea.

George Washington had sent troops to Virginia each time the British escalated operations there. This time he sent the Marquis de Lafayette with Continentals, Anthony Wayne

YORKTOWN, 1781

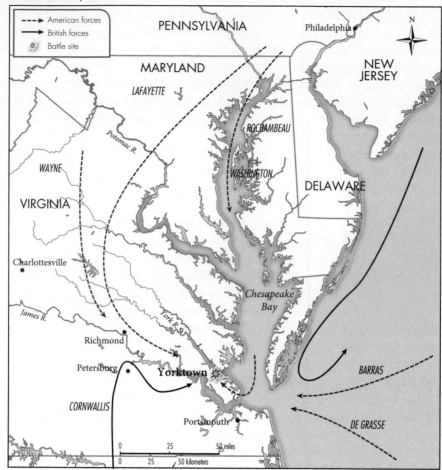

MAP 4.4 Yorktown, 1781

with Virginia militias, and Baron von Steuben, and by late May the American force in the commonwealth totaled 4,500 troops. Still facing some 7,200 British soldiers, Washington tried to tighten the noose around Cornwallis's army. After meeting with Rochambeau in May 1781, Washington initially decided to move against New York. But the arrival of Hessian reinforcements during the summer increased Clinton's occupation force there to more than 15,000—far too large of an army to attack. Then, in mid-August, Washington learned that Admiral François Joseph Paul de Grasse's fleet of thirty ships and 3,000 soldiers would soon arrive in the Chesapeake Bay. Prodded by Rochambeau and French officers, Washington finally decided to send 3,000 more American and 4,000 French soldiers to Virginia. To maintain secrecy about their destination, Washington sent out fake dispatches indicating that the troop movements were for an attack against New York. Clinton received copies of Washington's phony orders, which convinced him of Cornwallis's safety.

YORKTOWN

In late August the French fleet landed troops in the Chesapeake Bay to bolster Lafayette. All of a sudden Cornwallis recognized that his army faced great danger. Even so, he believed that the Royal Navy could fight through the French fleet and evacuate his troops. This would certainly be easier than slogging through enemy territory for hundreds of miles under constant attack. However, Cornwallis did not know that Britain no longer exercised naval superiority along the American coast. When British admiral George Rodney received news that de Grasse was sailing from the Caribbean, he only sent a few ships north under Admiral Samuel Hood because he did not think that the French would send their entire West Indian fleet to the coast of America. Hood had mirrored the French journey north from the Caribbean, arriving at the mouth of the Chesapeake a few days before the French fleet arrived. Seeing no French ships, he sailed on to New York. As a result, the British naval commander at New York, Admiral Thomas Graves, only had nineteen ships available to send south to rescue Cornwallis.

On September 5, 1781, Graves's and de Grasse's fleets met just outside the Chesapeake Bay in what came to be known as the Battle of the Virginia Capes. For about six hours the two sides maneuvered for advantageous wind. When the fleets finally met in line-ahead formation, only their van and center portions actually encountered one another. Although the sides were fairly equally matched, the French fleet severely damaged five British ships. When the battle concluded at sunset, after only about two hours of fighting, the two fleets broke off to assess their damages. For the next two days each tried again to gain the wind as they skirmished with one another. On September 10, additional French ships from Newport arrived under the command of Comte de Barras, making the French naval force too powerful to attack and giving it control of the Chesapeake. Admiral Graves chose to return to New York, leaving Cornwallis completely encircled.

Meanwhile, American and French land forces had prevented a British escape. By the time that Washington and Rochambeau arrived at Yorktown on September 24, the allied Patriot army numbered 16,000 battle-tested veterans. Cornwallis finally knew he could not hold out. While he pleaded for help from New York, he sent out raids to discourage the Patriots. On the stormy and overcast night of October 6, 1781, Franco-American forces started digging parallel trenches only 600 yards away from Cornwallis's army. Despite constant artillery fire during the next two days, the allies pulled their heavy guns into position. On October 9, fourteen big guns began firing, disabling British land guns and driving a British frigate across the York River, where it had to be scuttled. For the next two days French and American cannon harassed and demoralized the British troops as food became increasingly scarce and smallpox swept through their ranks. Over the following four nights the allied trench moved to within 300 yards and then 150 yards of Cornwallis's outer defenses. Then, on October 14, two separate French and American assaults overran the British Redoubts 9 and 10, giving the allies a position from which to fire into Redcoat ranks at close range; Alexander Hamilton led the assault on Redoubt 10. Cornwallis tried unsuccessfully to reclaim the trench before attempting to escape across the York River, but stormy weather prevented his flight. With his cannon silent, his defenses crumbling about him, and no options for retreat, Cornwallis on the morning of October 17, 1781, sent a lone drummer and officer with a white handkerchief to the American line with a message suggesting terms of surrender.

Cornwallis offered to lay down his arms with the stipulation that his troops be permitted to return to England. Washington refused, instead demanding complete and unconditional surrender. Cornwallis had to accept. At 2 p.m. on the afternoon of October 19, 1781, 8,000 British soldiers and sailors marched between American and French ranks to lay down their arms. The British soldiers turned their eyes to the French rather than acknowledge the Americans. As they did so, a British band played a German or British march. An American band responded loudly with "Yankee Doodle," further aggravating the Redcoats. Despite the tension, it was a solemn and emotional occasion punctuated with moments of humor: Admiral Barras, who represented Admiral de Grasse, attended on horseback; when the animal stretched to vent itself, de Grasse cried out, "Good Heavens! I believe my horse is sinking!" The French and British soldiers looked splendid in their uniforms, while the shabbily dressed Americans beamed with pride. Claiming illness, General Cornwallis refused to appear at the surrender. Instead, he sent General Charles O'Hara, who tried to hand the absent general's sword to Rochambeau. The French general directed him to Washington, who refused based on protocol, instead allowing General Benjamin Lincoln, who had been captured and humiliated at Charleston, to receive it, but Lincoln too refused to accept it. Some five days later Admiral Graves's reinvigorated fleet arrived from New York to evacuate Cornwallis, but it was too late. When British prime minister Lord North learned of the defeat

IMAGE 4.3 Yorktown Surrender This depiction of the British surrender at Yorktown, 19 October 1781, shows General Benjamin Lincoln receiving Cornwallis's sword from British General Charles O'Hara. In the background British troops march forward between lines of French and American troops to surrender their weapons and become prisoners.

in late November 1781, he moaned, "Oh God, it's all over." One month later Parliament voted against continuing the war, and Lord North resigned. It was all over.

WINNING THE PEACE

The victory at Yorktown did not completely end the war. British troops marched to prison camps, and Washington proceeded north to New York to lay siege to that city. Both Washington in the North and Greene in the South found it increasingly difficult to keep soldiers in the field. Those who remained began to fester with dissatisfaction about what they had been promised and what they had actually received. Schemes emerged that threatened to undermine the American army. During 1782 a group of disgruntled Continental officers in South Carolina devised a plan to capture and hand over General Greene to the British for ransom payments. The plot never materialized, and the plotters fled to the British. In March 1783 Washington faced a full-scale defection of officers at the Newburgh cantonment in New York. Meeting the defectors in person and appealing to their sense of loyalty, Washington revealed his own frailties to keep the men from turning; he pulled out a pair of reading glasses and commented on his own personal sacrifices during the struggle, humbling the battle-hardened officers and spurring them to remain loyal to the republican government. Washington's personal intervention, which stopped his officers from potentially carrying out a military coup, is perhaps one of the most important events in American history. Finally, though Yorktown had all but ended the war, there were still some 30,000 British troops in America, and during the next eighteen months skirmishes occurred in New York, New Jersey, the Carolinas, Georgia, and the Ohio River Valley. Peace remained elusive.

THE TREATY OF PARIS

The Continental Congress appointed Benjamin Franklin, John Jay, John Adams, and Henry Laurens to negotiate peace with the British in Paris. There, the Americans learned very quickly that France would not back them up in arguments with Spain. France had allied with the United States, while Spain had allied with France and entered the war for its own purposes. Both sides had fought the British and continued doing so even after Yorktown. France had made a promise to Spain to recapture Gibraltar from England and had also promised to constrict the American republic to ensure that it did not threaten Spain's New World possessions. When France could not deliver Gibraltar, the American diplomats feared the French might offer American concessions instead. French minister Count Vergennes, who had focused on dismembering the British Empire, believed Spanish expectations in America ultimately coincided with French objectives. France and Spain would emerge as monarchical victors after peace, while Britain and the thirteen states would be the losers—the balance of European power would shift toward the Bourbons.

The spokesman for the Americans, Benjamin Franklin, had served as the ambassador to France since 1777 and had learned the wily tricks of European diplomacy. He recognized France's deception, as well as British attempts since the spring of 1782 to negotiate a separate peace with only the United States. Franklin initially refused to let the United States be separated from its French ally. But in the summer of 1782, John Jay, who had been negotiating with Spanish officials, learned of a Franco-Spanish plan to limit the United States to the lands east of the Appalachian Mountains and north of the 31st parallel; according to the rumors, Great Britain and Spain would share the trans-Appalachian west, and Spain would keep the Florida peninsula. Such machinations finally convinced Franklin to pursue a separate peace with Great Britain.

In September 1782 a new British diplomat, Scotsman Richard Oswald, arrived in Paris and he agreed to negotiate with the "13 United States." During the following month discussions moved quickly. Britain would recognize the independence of the United States, with a western boundary of the Mississippi River; grant Americans fishing rights off Newfoundland; and remove all British troops from American soil. While the United States did not secure Canada, the Americans promised to encourage the states to indemnify Tories whose property had been confiscated and not to hinder British merchants in their attempt to collect prewar debts. These concessions sealed the deal. Franklin then informed Count Vergennes of the peace treaty, one day before the United States signed it. During that same conversation Franklin also asked France for a guaranteed loan of 6 million *livres*, a matter that had been under negotiation. Although angry, Vergennes approved the American loan. The Franco-Spanish attempt to win Gibraltar failed in early January 1783, and the European powers soon agreed to an armistice. The final peace treaties were signed on September 3, 1783. The United States had finally secured its independence.

CONCLUSIONS

During the twenty years from 1763 to 1783 a single United States was forged from thirteen American colonies. But while the country had secured its independence, few believed the republic could survive. Most anticipated that the new country would descend into anarchy and ultimately would evolve into a dictatorship or even a monarchy. The Articles of Confederation government failed to secure a quorum in 1784 to even ratify the peace treaty. Moreover, Washington's soldiers were restless because their pay was in arrears, and most believed they would be sent home without payment. A commission of army officers approached Congress during the winter of 1782–1783, asking that provisions be made for the Continental soldiers, but Congress ignored them. Some officers suggested the army take justice into its own hands. Others wanted George Washington to accept an American crown and become King George I of America. This potential threat scared congressmen, who agreed to provide Continental officers full compensation for five years in lieu of the half-pay that most expected. Finance minister Robert Morris even found enough money to offer noncommissioned officers three months of pay. Not surprisingly, cash momentarily muted the uproar from the army.

The debate over the nature of the American military continued until after the War of 1812. Washington acknowledged that the professionalized Continental army had provided the basis for the military victory, but he also understood the public's fascination with the militias. Citizen-soldiers were members of the public, and their successes permitted everyone to take credit for victory. But as the years passed, Americans embellished the successes of the militiamen, believing that they alone had won the war and they alone could provide defense for the country; using militia would also save money and avoid creating an elite military class that might seize the government and elevate themselves above the citizenry. Republics did not need professional soldiers, only citizens willing to defend American shores.

George Washington refused to accept a crown. He claimed that he had been fighting to create a republic. His steadfast devotion to the cause and loyalty to the civilian government swayed many officers and men who might have otherwise shown support for a monarchy. During August 1783 some 29,000 Loyalists departed from New York, increasing the total number of Tory departures to more than 100,000. Sir Guy Carleton, the last commander of British North America, reported

TIMELINE

June–October 1777	Saratoga campaign
August–October 1777	Philadelphia campaign
Winter 1777–78	Washington's army encamped at Valley Forge
February 1778	French-American alliance
June 1778	Battle of Monmouth Courthouse
December 1778	British capture of Savannah
September 1779	Battle between *Bonhomme Richard* and *Serapis*
May 1780	British capture of Charleston
October 1780	Battle of King's Mountain
January 1781	Battle of Cowpens
August–October 1781	Battle of Yorktown
September 1783	Treaty of Paris

to the Continental Congress that he was preparing for the withdrawal of refugees, liberated slaves, and soldiers. At noon on November 25, 1783, the last British troops sailed out of New York Harbor. Nine days later Washington bid a tearful and heartfelt farewell to his officers and departed for Annapolis to surrender his sword and command. The Revolution had ended.

SUGGESTED READINGS

Buchanan, John. *The Road to Valley Forge: How Washington Build the Army that Won the Revolution.* New York: Wiley, 2004.

Buell, Richard, Jr. *In Irons: Britain's Naval Supremacy and the American Revolutionary Economy.* New Haven, CT: Yale University Press, 1998.

Carp, E. Wayne. *To Starve the Army at Pleasure: Continental Army Administration and American Political Culture, 1775–1783.* Chapel Hill: University of North Carolina Press, 1984.

Fowler, William M. *Rebels under Sail: The American Navy in Revolution.* New York: Scribner's, 1976.

Frey, Sylvia R. *The British Solider in America: A Social History of Military Life in the Revolutionary Period.* Austin: University of Texas Press, 1981.

Galloway, Colin G. *The American Revolution in Indian Country: Crisis and Diversity in Native American Communities.* Cambridge, UK: Cambridge University Press, 1995.

Higginbotham, Don. *The War of American Independence: Military Attitudes, Policies, and Practices, 1763–1789.* New York: Macmillan, 1971.

Mackesy, Piers. *The War for America, 1775–1783.* Cambridge: Harvard University Press, 1964.

Martin, James Kirby. *Ordinary Courage: The Revolutionary War Adventures of Joseph Plumb Martin.* New York: Wiley-Blackwell, 2012.

Mayer, Holly A. *Belonging to the Army: Camp Followers and Community During the American Revolution.* Columbia: University of South Carolina Press, 1999.

Neimeyer, Charles Patrick. *America Goes to War: A Social History of the Continental Army.* New York: New York University Press, 1995.

Pancake, John S. *This Destructive War: The British Campaign in the Carolinas, 1780–1782.* Tuscaloosa: University of Alabama Press, 1985.

Royster, Charles. *A Revolutionary People at War: The Continental Army and American Character, 1775–1783.* New York: Norton, 1975.

Spring, Matthew H. *With Zeal and with Bayonets Only: The British Army on Campaign in North America, 1775–1783.* Norman: University of Oklahoma Press, 2010.

Weigley, Russell F. *The American Way of War: A History of United States Strategy and Policy.* New York: Macmillan, 1973.

CHAPTER 5

SECURING THE REPUBLIC
1782–1815

*Challenges for the New Nation • Federal Government • First War • Whiskey Rebellion
• Quasi-War • Republican Ascendency • Barbary Pirates • Education and Exploration
• War on the Horizon • The War of 1812*

Disaster struck for Captain William Bainbridge and the frigate *Philadelphia* on October 31, 1803, as the ship carried out blockade duty off Tripoli. While chasing a corsair trying to enter into harbor, the *Philadelphia* ran aground on an uncharted reef. The American ship could not defend itself from Tripolitan gunboats that soon swarmed in. After four hours of unsuccessful attempts to refloat the ship, Bainbridge tried to scuttle it before striking his colors and surrendering. That evening the Tripolitans paraded Bainbridge and his 300 crewmen through the city, signifying a humiliating American defeat.

Three months later, on February 16, 1804, Lieutenant Stephen Decatur sailed a captured Turkish vessel, renamed *Intrepid* and disguised as a Maltese merchant ship flying British colors, into the harbor under cover of darkness. With sixty men (mostly marines) dressed as Maltese and Arab sailors, Decatur brought *Intrepid* alongside *Philadelphia*, claiming his ship had lost its anchors. Then Americans quickly boarded the frigate. Armed with cutlasses and pikes, they won control of *Philadelphia* within ten minutes. But being unable to sail the ship or to tow it out of the harbor, Decatur set fire to the vessel to prevent the Tripolitans from using it. As fire engulfed *Philadelphia*, *Intrepid* sailed out of the harbor without injury. British admiral Horatio Nelson called Decatur's destruction of *Philadelphia* "the most bold and daring act of the Age." And while Decatur became an immediate national hero and won instant promotion to captain, the raid did not end the Barbary Wars.

The capture of *Philadelphia* was one of the most embarrassing episodes for the neutral United States during the period of 1783 to 1815. It revealed both American military weakness and the precariousness of U.S. independence. Barbary pirates threatened American sovereignty, imprisoned U.S. citizen-sailors, and offered no apology for their actions.

President Thomas Jefferson and the United States could offer only a limited response to these provocations, having chosen to have a citizen-based military rather than a professional fighting force.

CHALLENGES FOR THE NEW NATION

Americans had won their independence from Great Britain through a prolonged and violent military struggle, and during the 1780s the new nation sought peace. The army was reduced to a bare minimum, and the navy was dismantled completely. The desire to reduce financial obligations and extinguish outstanding debts prompted American leaders to rely primarily on diplomacy for national security. Because of the nation's geographic isolation, most leaders believed the United States did not require a permanent military establishment but rather could depend on citizen-soldiers to preserve its freedom and independence. But the new country soon encountered threatening European and African nations, hostile Native Americans, and divisive internal plots that imperiled the country in ways that Britain had not.

Overseas, the Barbary States of North Africa declared war on the United States and began seizing American merchant ships. Then the great powers of Europe began a quarter century of wars during which they also violated the maritime rights of Americans. Hopeful that the republican experiment would fail, European agents sabotaged American trading plans and plotted to dismantle the nation's western, southern, and northeastern territories. European operatives also armed, supplied, and encouraged Indians to resist American expansion. When diplomacy failed, the United States found itself fighting French marauders in the Caribbean during the Quasi-War (1798–1801), North African corsairs during the early years of the nineteenth century (1801–1805), and Great Britain, its Canadian subjects, and its Indian allies during the War of 1812.

ARTICLES OF CONFEDERATION

Under its adopted governing principles, the Articles of Confederation, the U.S. government did not have the power to tax, could not regulate domestic or foreign commerce, and could not enforce its laws. Americans were extremely distrustful of government. Most states did not permit governors to serve more than a one-year term, several states forbid governors to have veto power, and most states had drafted revolutionary constitutions broadening individual political rights. Each state cast only one vote in the Articles Congress, regardless of size. This decentralized system aimed at eliminating the abuse of power, but the checks the founders built into it also prevented the government from working in an organized or efficient manner.

The Articles government's greatest success came in the areas of land policy and territorial governance. Otherwise, it succeeded in passing few laws, and by summer 1786 the country's financial situation had become desperate. Imports from and exports to Britain had dropped. Farm wages had declined as much as 20 percent from 1780 levels. The combination of money shortages, high taxes, and insistent creditors brought demands for economic relief through state issuance of paper money. By the end of the summer six states had begun printing paper money, creating financial anarchy.

A PEACETIME MILITARY

The country's debilitating economic depression of the 1780s forced Superintendent of Finance Robert Morris and Congress to dismiss the officers and sailors of the Continental Navy, and in 1785 the government auctioned off its eleven surviving ships. But while the navy no longer existed, the American merchant service had continued to grow and reshape its trading routes. Almost as soon as the last Continental warship was sold, two American merchant ships with twenty-one crewmen were captured by pirates sailing for the dey of Algiers. Motivated by greed rather than religion or ideology, the Barbary pirates had been seizing ships and enslaving Christian crews for centuries, and most European states either placed a naval force in the Mediterranean to protect their merchant fleets or paid the pirates ransoms or tribute to free their citizens. The United States was too poor to ransom its citizens and had no fleet to protect its merchant ships; most Americans could not comprehend how an unseen navy in distant waters could actually protect the country.

To further reduce governmental expenditures, Robert Morris also furloughed army officers and soldiers before discharging them. In this task, Congress turned to Washington, who consulted with his staff officers about how to reorganize and downsize the peacetime army. Ultimately Washington suggested that the U.S. military be made up of four components: a small regular army to garrison the western frontier, a uniformly trained and organized citizen militia, a system of coastal fortifications and arsenals, and a military academy to train the army's artillery and engineer officers. Although Washington's proposed regimental organizations mimicked Continental Army patterns, his plan also included provisions for increased strength when needed and for the militia to serve as the first line of defense until the regular army could expand, as had occurred during the Revolution. After considering Washington's report on June 2, 1784, Congress discharged all remaining soldiers except twenty-five caretakers at Fort Pitt and fifty-five at West Point. Fiscal concerns trumped all, and reliance on the citizen-soldiers who purportedly had defeated Britain cost little.

Lawmakers also had philosophical objections to a permanent standing army, which many believed would create an elite military class at the expense of American taxpayers. This belief hearkened to before the Revolution, when the British required colonials to quarter troops in their residences. Some critics also feared that a standing military would be used by the national government against states and individuals or as an instrument of capricious power. But whether or not these fears were legitimate, the Articles government did not have the financial means to create a standing military force. Instead, Congress raised a temporary one-year contingent of 700 state militiamen to protect the frontier against Indian attack and divided the force into eight infantry and two artillery companies, commanded by Pennsylvanian Josiah Harmar. The following year Congress transformed this haphazard organization into a permanent unit—the 1st American Regiment (to which the modern 3rd U.S. Army Infantry Regiment traces its lineage).

THE TREE OF LIBERTY—SHAYS' REBELLION

The Massachusetts state legislature adjourned in mid-July 1786 without dealing with a growing problem. Representatives had not heeded petitions from debt-ridden farmers for more paper money or for laws to prevent foreclosures. After adjournment, several communities conducted town meetings, at which they condemned the legislature's inaction. During the summer armed mobs prohibited judges from ruling on foreclosures, prevented tax collectors from doing their jobs, and seized property that had been confiscated by local constables. Governor James Bowdoin instructed officials to collect back taxes. The legislature levied additional property taxes to fund the state's portion of the federal foreign debt. But the debt burden had grown too large, with conservative statesmen like John Adams acknowledging that taxes were heavier than people could bear.

Revolutionary war captain and farmer Daniel Shays had not been paid for his military service, and the court had ruled against him because he had unpaid debts. Supporting the cause of his fellow farmers, he participated in a protest at Northampton and later organized resistance in Hampshire County, while Luke Day did likewise in Hampden County. In late September, the two planned to prevent the Springfield court from meeting, and a nearby protest convinced judges to adjourn without hearing cases.

Without a federal standing army to turn to, Governor Bowdoin and Boston businessmen privately raised a militia force. Former Continental Army general Benjamin Lincoln mustered 3,000 militiamen from the eastern counties of Massachusetts, and on January 19, 1787, they marched to Worcester. In the western counties, Shays, Day, and other leaders organized their forces, elected officers, and decided that with militia approaching, their first objective should be to capture the federal armory in Springfield. Once they had secured weapons, they planned to march on Boston. Fearing that this armed force would try to reorganize society and confiscate property, Bowdoin instructed local militia general William Shepard to seize the armory; Shepard subsequently used the weapons to arm 1,200 militiamen, even though the armory was federal, not state, property.

At about 4 p.m. on January 25, 1787, Shays' 1,500 haphazardly armed farmers moved against the armory. Shepard instructed his waiting militiamen to fire warning shots over the attackers' heads, but Shays' forces continued advancing. Then Shepard ordered two cannon to fire grapeshot. The single volley from the two guns killed four and wounded twenty others. Immediately Shays' force disintegrated, fleeing north; they later regrouped near Amherst. General Lincoln, learning of the encounter, departed Worcester and on February 3 pushed his 3,000 militiamen on a punishing thirty-mile overnight march to Petersham in subzero temperatures and falling snow. The following morning Lincoln's militiamen surprised Shays' camp, capturing 150 of the protestors. Shays and other leaders escaped, fleeing north to New Hampshire and Vermont. The revolt was over.

Afterwards 4,000 people signed confessions that they had participated in the event, and most received amnesty. Eighteen ringleaders were tried, convicted, and sentenced to death. Only two men suffered execution; Shays and Day received pardons. The event sent shockwaves through conservative communities, which feared the reorganization of society, property, and wealth. Elites could not deny the need for a stronger central government, but Shays' Rebellion served as a harbinger of greater evils. When Thomas Jefferson, then serving as an ambassador to France, learned of the rebellion, he remarked, "The tree of liberty must be refreshed from time to time with the blood of patriots & tyrants." Ultimately, the rebellion drew George Washington back to public life and revealed both Patriot desperation and the

Articles' impotency, convincing many that a Philadelphia meeting scheduled for May 1787 needed to produce results.

CONSTITUTIONAL CONVENTION: "EXPERIENCE MUST BE OUR ONLY GUIDE"

Because the Articles government had proven that it could not deal with the problems of the new republic, states had attempted to fill the void. Delegates from Virginia and Maryland had met at Mount Vernon during March 1785 to discuss economic issues. In September 1786 delegates from five states convened at Annapolis to discuss the Articles' inadequacies, adjourning without taking action but agreeing a future meeting should occur. In February 1787 even the Articles legislature called for a convention to revise the system of government.

Fifty-five delegates from twelve states (Rhode Island did not attend) participated in the Philadelphia meeting, which began on May 25, 1787. Widely read in political philosophy, the delegates knew that "experience must be our only guide" since "reason may mislead us." Agreeing that government derived its power from the consent of the governed, they believed the people should have a voice in their own governance. Virginia delegate James Madison designed a new governmental structure based upon checks and balances and the separation of powers that was introduced to the convention. Thereafter the delegates hammered out compromises over political structure, taxation and trade, and slavery and the slave trade, and ultimately agreed to a document that permitted amendments and could evolve over time.

General Washington agreed to serve as the convention's president. His presence demonstrated the importance of public virtue and civilian government. Opponents of a strong centralized government frequently warned that monarchs often used military forces to uphold their abusive regimes, maintaining control through the threat of military retribution. That overwhelming fear, born out of knowledge of history and the recent conflict against Great Britain, pushed the delegates to create a system that divided power between the states and the national government and spread national powers between the executive, legislative, and judicial branches. It also made the military subservient to the elected civilian government. Article I of the new Constitution authorized Congress to declare war, to collect taxes, and to appropriate funds for the maintenance of an army and navy. Congress could regulate—organize, arm, and discipline—and provide for a militia as well as employ the militia against insurrections, rebellions, and invasions that threatened domestic tranquility. Article II named the president as commander-in-chief of the army, navy, and militia while also giving the position authority to commission officers with the consent of the Senate. Shared power between the executive and legislative branches would prevent the despotic use of the military.

Throughout the summer of 1787 the closed, secretive convention hammered out its compromises. Individuals, states, and the federal entity would exercise power in separate domains, with built-in mechanisms preventing one branch from becoming too powerful. Once the convention concluded, ratification of the Constitution, which outlined the new government and its structure, was passed to state conventions, which met throughout late 1787 until mid-1788. During contentious debates over the proposed system, Antifeder-als vociferously argued that a centralized government and a standing military threatened people's rights. Federalists countered that checks and balances and the separation of powers would prevent abuses. By the summer of 1788, enough states had ratified the Constitution, and on October 10, 1788, the Articles government transacted its last business.

During the early spring of 1789 federal electors unanimously chose George Washington to be the first president of the United States. While Washington had willingly surrendered power before, many still feared the new government. States reserved the right to maintain their own militias, but the Constitution forbid them from declaring war, entering into alliances, or maintaining their own standing army or navy. Through the Second Amendment (ratified in December 1791), individuals retained the right to keep and bear arms to ensure the security of a free state and to maintain a well-regulated militia. Although much debated today, the Second Amendment rested on the founders' belief that a citizen militia provided a counter to a state-controlled army. Also in reaction to fears of government tyranny, the Constitution's Third Amendment prohibited the quartering of troops in peoples' homes. Even with these amendments added to the federal Constitution, Americans viewed the government's legislative attempts with suspicion, worrying that it would seek to reduce further the people's power.

FEDERAL GOVERNMENT

The new federal government took office in April 1789 and began to solve problems the Articles had deferred. With the power to tax, regulate trade, and enforce laws, President Washington, Secretary of the Treasury Alexander Hamilton, and Federalist leaders centralized the new government and its power. They crafted a viable financial plan that provided for funding and assumption of debt, established a national bank, and a federal mint, conducted diplomatic relations that supported and enhanced their commercial aspirations, and created procedures to enforce federal law, including tax collection. A small professional army, supplemented by state militias, provided the means to enforce compliance with federal directives. The establishment of this system gave rise to a divisive ideological debate, which ultimately drove the Federalists from power and destroyed the party.

MILITIA VERSUS STANDING ARMY

In 1783 Washington, Hamilton, and other politicians and soldiers had advanced an ambitious plan for a national standing army and an extensive military establishment, but the Continental Congress had rejected the proposal. By the time the Federalists left office in 1801, the United States had embraced a small professional army and military establishment as necessary instruments for peace and survival.

The debate over the proper nature of the military became entwined with questions about the essence of government itself. Hamilton's financial plan of the 1790s, according to the emergent opposition party, the Jeffersonian Republicans, created dependency. It forced the government to raise money to implement programs and to pay the national debt and government employees. It also used the army to uphold taxation that supported governmental policy and maintained order and peace. The Republicans feared standing armies because they believed that centralized control threatened individual liberties and destroyed republican government. A permanent standing army would drain money from public coffers, leaving citizens perpetually indebted to a system that oppressed them. Conversely, employing citizen-soldiers who swore to execute federal law, suppress insurrections, and repel invasions would reduce the need for high taxes, remove the need for centralized programs to raise monies, and eliminate the need for a professional military. Furthermore, citizen-soldiers had a vested interest in the American experiment and would defend their country when needed.

In response, Federalists maintained, and events repeatedly proved, that militias were untrained, undisciplined, and ill equipped. Though willing to fight, militias frequently lacked fighting ability. The federal government, which was empowered to organize, arm, and discipline militias, often refused to permit militia training because of the expense. State governments, which had the power to appoint officers and train them, often refused to place their units under federal control, claiming that the federal government had not met constitutional requirements. The division of responsibilities also broke down when militiamen appeared for muster lacking weapons, clothing, and equipment needed for a campaign. Only rarely did militiamen have the necessary training to perform basic military duties, and as a result they frequently retreated when engaging the enemy. In strategically important frontier areas such as Ohio, a small population and tax base also doomed the militia to failure. By the end of the War of 1812, leaders of both parties had acknowledged the militias' inability to defend the nation. Still, society harbored republican prejudice toward a standing army despite the need for such an institution.

FIRST WAR

The 1783 Treaty of Paris gave the United States control over the Northwest Territory and its natives. This shift ushered in a new trading policy—the U.S. Land Ordinance of 1785 and the Northwest Ordinance of 1787, which systematically surveyed, organized, and made available lands of the Old Northwest for white settlement—that alienated Indians. Since Americans still owed debts to British merchants, British policymakers retained control over forts in this area, from which they supplied the Indians and encouraged them to continue resisting U.S. expansion. Delaware, Miami, Ottawa, Shawnee, and Chippewa warriors raided American settlements, killing white trespassers.

President Washington had written to Northwest Territory governor Arthur St. Clair, questioning the intentions of Indians living along the Wabash and Illinois rivers. Reporting that the Indians wanted war, St. Clair gathered the territorial militia at Cincinnati and Vincennes. Washington and Secretary of War Henry Knox directed General Josiah Harmar to use these men against Miami and Shawnee raids.

Gathering 320 regulars from the 1st American Regiment, more than 1,100 militiamen, and three six-pound cannon, Harmar moved against the large Miami village of Kekionga (present-day Fort Wayne, Indiana), where the Joseph and St. Mary's rivers formed the Maumee River. Harmar's expeditionary force lacked experienced militiamen or frontiersmen and departed in early October before training could take place. Moving within 25 miles of Kekionga, Harmar learned the Indians planned to attack. Striking out before dawn on October 15, 1790, Harmar's soldiers swept and burned Kekionga, which in the meantime

INDIAN WARS, 1790–1814

MAP 5.1   Indian Wars, 1790–1814

had been abandoned. Two days later Harmar found other nearby villages that were also abandoned and swept them as well.

Harmar then split his force, sending 180 militiamen, regulars, and cavalry under Colonel John Hardin to attack the village of Chief Le Gris. When they were only a few miles from their destination, troops saw an Indian fleeing on horseback, which drew Hardin's pursuing column into the swampy lowland near the Eel River. Suddenly Chief Little Turtle and his men attacked from three sides. Most militiamen fled immediately, and within minutes twenty-two regulars and forty militiamen had been killed. Harmar then sent 300 men north, scouting for Indian movements, and twenty more were killed during another ambush.

On October 22, Hardin, with 300 militiamen and 60 regulars, found almost 1,000 Indians encamped at Kekionga. When he requested help from Harmar, he learned none would be forthcoming. Instead, Harmar had formed his remaining 800 men into a defensive square. Without aid, Hardin divided his command into four units to attack the Indians on all flanks. But before he could take action, Little Turtle sent Indian parties to bait the militia by firing and then retreating. In response, undisciplined militiamen pursued the Indians, leaving the regulars isolated. Then the Indians attacked the divided Americans from all sides. Hardin's men fought bravely for three hours before falling back to Harmar's army, having suffered 180 men killed or wounded; Indian casualties numbered 120 to 150. Ultimately Harmar's decision to divide his army and his officers' decision to divide the force further permitted Little Turtle to attack smaller contingents successfully.

Little Turtle's victory encouraged Indians in the Northwest Territory to attack settlements throughout the region. Frustrated by news of the defeat, Washington instructed Governor St. Clair to launch another campaign by summer 1791. Congress raised a second regiment of regulars for six months, but with reduced pay. As a result the regiment only secured half its troop allotments. When combined with the demoralized remaining 299 soldiers of the 1st American Regiment, St. Clair's army mustered only 600 regulars. He augmented this command with Kentucky militia and two regiments of six-month levies (state-paid volunteers under federal control).

Washington wanted action, but logistical problems plagued the governor's efforts. With limited food of poor quality, not enough horses, and inadequately trained and undisciplined men, St. Clair did not depart Fort Washington (present-day Cincinnati) until October 1791. As he marched northward toward Kekionga, sickness and desertion decimated his army, with his numbers dwindling from 2,000 to slightly more than 1,100 by November. Indians also shadowed his march, attacking stragglers, raiding supplies whenever possible, and further demoralizing the Americans. On the afternoon of November 3, St. Clair encamped on an elevated meadow near the headwaters of the Wabash River without constructing defensive works.

During the night Indians gathered in the woods. Miami chiefs Little Turtle and Blue Jacket were joined by Lenape Delawares and a large number of Potawatomis from eastern Michigan to form a force of 1,000 warriors. Waiting in the woods until dawn when the soldiers stacked their weapons to have breakfast, the Indians struck suddenly and overran the camp. The militiamen fled without their weapons, while the regulars tried to form battle lines and return fire. Little Turtle's warriors then flanked the regulars, inflicting serious casualties, and killed artillerymen before they could fire. In response, regulars fixed their bayonets and charged the Indians' position, attempting to drive them into the woods. As each American charge drove deeper into the forest, the soldiers were surrounded by Indians and attacked on all sides, suffering terrible casualties.

Finally the Americans mounted one last bayonet charge to break through Indian lines, lest they face complete annihilation. Leaving supplies and their wounded behind, they charged through Little Turtle's attack, just as the Indians had permitted before, but this time continued running on toward Fort Jefferson with the Indians in pursuit for a few miles. Finally giving up, the Indians returned to loot the camp and kill the wounded. St. Clair's expedition had been destroyed; his command suffered the highest casualty rate (97.4 percent) ever recorded by a U.S. Army field force. Only 24 of the 940 Americans engaged emerged unscathed. Moreover, nearly all 200 camp followers were slaughtered as well. The disaster produced the first congressional investigation, which blamed contractors, the War Department, and Secretary of War Knox rather than St. Clair. Outraged, President Washington forced St. Clair to resign.

The catastrophe also left the country virtually unprotected, prompting Washington to ask Congress to raise another army to move against the Indians. During spring 1792 Congress authorized the Calling Forth Act, which gave the president the power to call out state militias to enforce laws or suppress rebellion, and the Uniform Militia Act, which required all able-bodied men between the ages of eighteen and forty-five to enroll in local militias and to provide their own weapons and equipment. Congress did not provide the well-trained and well-equipped militia Washington wanted. Furthermore, states ignored the law and continued training and organizing men as they always had; militiamen continued electing officers, training remained inconsistent, and politics permeated the entire structure. Even so, these acts provided the groundwork for the American militia system (which was reformed in the aftermath of the Whiskey Rebellion in 1795, in 1862 to permit African Americans to serve, and in 1903 to establish the U.S. National Guard as the country's formal organized body of military reserves).

Congress also enhanced the regular army, creating the Legion of the United States, a name that appealed to Congress because it hearkened back to Republican Rome, and mitigated fears of a standing army. Washington selected General "Mad" Anthony Wayne to command the combined force of cavalry, heavy and light infantry, and artillery, which was divided into four sub-legions. During the summer of 1792 Wayne recruited, organized, and trained his legion to deal with Indian woodlands warfare. Each subdivision had its own organization and allotment of artillery, dragoons, and infantry, and could fight in small units on its own. Wayne taught his men to move quickly against the Indians so they could not regroup. His campaign would be aggressive and continuous.

By the fall of 1793 Wayne had crossed the Ohio River, advancing into Indian country. He moved slowly and methodically, building forts and protecting them with troops to ensure a reliable supply line. By March 1794 Wayne's men had built Fort Recovery on the banks of the Maumee, where St. Clair's army had been defeated. In late June 1794, Chief Blue Jacket, accompanied by a youthful Tecumseh and 2,000 warriors, attacked a wagon train departing the fort. Driving the soldiers back behind the walls, the Indians continued attacking for two days, apparently in an effort to take the cannon that St. Clair had buried. Instead, the Americans dug up and used the guns to repel the attack.

During this time British agents had been supplying the Indians and also paying them to attack American settlements. The British government envisioned the Ohio Valley as an Indian buffer state that could protect Canada. But when war erupted between Great Britain and France in 1793, the British acknowledged the need to repair relations with the United States. They backed off their support for the Indians, and in November 1794 a new British ministry signed Jay's Treaty with the United States, substantially improving Anglo-American relations.

On August 20, 1794, Wayne's legion approached Blue Jacket's 1,500-man allied force—made up of Shawnees, Delawares, Miamis, Wyandots, Ojibwas, Potawatomis, and Mingos, as well as a company of British Canadian militiamen—along the Maumee River (near present-day Toledo) near the British supply outpost of Fort Miami and a stand of trees that had been felled by a recent storm. Believing the downed trees would slow the American advance, Blue Jacket was stunned at how quickly Wayne's men advanced. Wielding bayonets, the infantry charged ahead, while cavalry outflanked Blue Jacket's position. The Indians retreated toward Fort Miami, anticipating British protection. But Major William Campbell, the fort's commander, refused to open the gates because he did not want to provoke a war with the United States. The Battle of Fallen Timbers quickly devolved into a massacre of Indians, and afterward Wayne's army destroyed tribal villages and crops in the area.

The British soon abandoned their Indian allies, resulting in the complete defeat of the pan-Indian alliance. With Jay's Treaty the British withdrew from the Ohio Valley. By the following summer, Wayne had coaxed the surviving Indians to sign the Treaty of Fort Greenville, in which they surrendered two-thirds of present-day Ohio, opening the area to white settlers. Wayne's campaign reversed four years of futile military and political policies, bringing a temporary end to the Indian Wars.

WHISKEY REBELLION

In 1791 Congress had passed an excise tax upon distilled spirits because the federal assumption of state debts necessitated increased revenue. As early as 1792 the high tax—25 percent of the net price of a gallon of whiskey—created discontent among producers from Georgia to Pennsylvania. Backwoodsmen and farmers attacked tax collectors, threatened government officials, and destroyed whiskey stills belonging to those who paid the tax. By early 1794 the government had stopped functioning in four southwestern counties of Pennsylvania, prompting Washington to declare the area in a state of emergency.

Washington feared that if he deployed the standing army, he would open the door to Republican claims of tyranny. Instead, he asked Virginia, Pennsylvania, Maryland, and New Jersey to provide 12,950 militiamen to suppress the rebellion. This federalized militia represented the largest army Washington had commanded since the early years of the Revolution.

During early September 1794 General Henry "Lighthorse Harry" Lee assembled troops in Harrisburg, Pennsylvania, where both President Washington and Secretary Alexander Hamilton soon joined him. Washington remained with the army for a few weeks and by doing so became the only sitting president to command an army in the field. Hamilton remained with the army throughout the campaign. When the army marched across the Alleghenies, the insurrection evaporated. Rebels could not be found, and most of their leaders had fled to Ohio. The army rounded up twenty prisoners and marched them through Philadelphia. Ultimately two were found guilty of treason in federal court and sentenced to death but were pardoned by Washington before their execution.

The Whiskey Rebellion was the first instance of domestic opposition to the new government, but the latter's forceful suppression of the unrest with the militia won popular support. The government gained a reputation for not only strength and resolve, but also compassion and fairness that endured. The rebellion and its suppression also drove a deeper divide between the ruling Federalist Party and the opposition Republicans. Both argued that the episode had revealed the true nature of federal military power. Federalists insisted that the militia had allowed the government to maintain order and stability, while Republicans contended that the military had permitted the government to enforce arbitrary policies.

With the Indians defeated and rebellion quashed, many questioned whether there was any need for a standing army. In 1796 Congress disbanded the Legion of the United States, leaving a standing army of only four regiments and a complement of dragoons. Evidently, Americans still viewed the army with distrust. Thereafter, the small American army was expanded when needed to meet threats and reduced once trouble subsided—a model that served the country for the next 100 years.

QUASI-WAR

Washington's government had defeated the Indians, crushed rebels, and found common ground with Great Britain and Spain. In doing so, Franco-American relations had suffered. Successive French revolutionary governments believed the United States had reneged on its treaty obligations. Moreover, Jay's Treaty, in which Anglo-American diplomats agreed that food, naval supplies, and war materials were contraband of war and could be seized, suggested to France that the United States was not neutral. During 1795 and 1796 French corsairs operating in the West Indies captured more than 300 American ships.

Newly elected President John Adams tried to repair this fractured relationship. Shortly after his 1797 inauguration, Adams sent a three-member commission made up of Charles Cotesworth Pinckney, John Marshall, and Elbridge Gerry to France to restore relations between the two countries. Once in Paris the commission encountered demands from four French agents (called W, X, Y, and Z) that the United States pay a bribe, provide a loan to the French government, and apologize for President Adams's anti-French remarks. Once these demands were fulfilled, the agents declared, negotiations could begin with Foreign Minister Maurice de Talleyrand. While bribes were part of international diplomacy during this period, these demands seemed excessive for a simple promise to negotiate. The committee angrily refused and returned home. In April 1798 Adams revealed to Congress the so-called XYZ Affair and Americans demanded war.

As the slogan "Millions for defense but not one cent for tribute!" resonated across the country, President Adams sought a peaceful alternative to war because the country was not prepared for such a conflict. Increased French depredations convinced the parsimonious Congress to create the Navy Department under Secretary Benjamin Stoddert, to re-create the U.S. Marine Corps, and to complete the construction of ships begun during Washington's presidency. The Joshua Humphreys–designed frigates—*Constitution, Constellation, United States, President, Congress,* and *Chesapeake*—were hybrids of a ship-of-the-line and a frigate. Longer and narrower than traditional frigates, they were supported by diagonal ribs to prevent the long hull from hogging (bending upward because of stress) and constructed with dense live oak. They were also faster and more heavily armed than their predecessors and consequently formed the navy's core until the emergence of iron and steam technology.

AMERICAN NAVAL BATTLES, 1798–1815

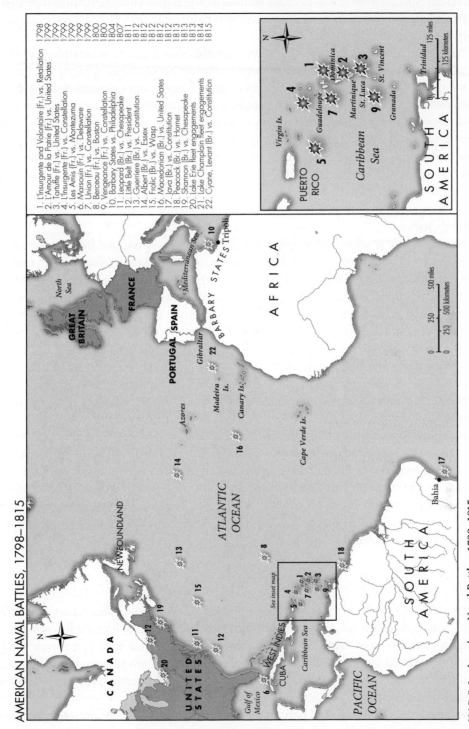

1. L'Insurgente and Volontaire (Fr.) vs. Retaliation — 1798
2. L'Amour de la Patrie (Fr.) vs. United States — 1799
3. Tartuffe (Fr.) vs. Constellation — 1799
4. L'Insurgente (Fr.) vs. Constellation — 1799
5. Les Amis (Fr.) vs. Montezuma — 1799
6. Marsouin (Fr.) vs. Delaware — 1799
7. Union (Fr.) vs. Constellation — 1800
8. Berceau (Fr.) vs. Boston — 1800
9. Vengeance (Fr.) vs. Constellation — 1800
10. Barbary States vs. Philadelphia — 1804
11. Leopard (Br.) vs. Chesapeake — 1807
12. Little Belt (Br.) vs. President — 1811
13. Guerriere (Br.) vs. Constitution — 1812
14. Albert (Br.) vs. Essex — 1812
15. Frolic (Br.) vs. Wasp — 1812
16. Macedonian (Br.) vs. United States — 1812
17. Java (Br.) vs. Constitution — 1813
18. Peacock (Br.) vs. Hornet — 1813
19. Shannon (Br.) vs. Chesapeake — 1813
20. Lake Erie fleet engagements — 1813
21. Lake Champlain fleet engagements — 1814
22. Cyane, Levant (Br.) vs. Constitution — 1815

MAP 5.2 American Naval Battles, 1798–1815

Coastal cities also raised funds to build additional warships, while merchants outfitted privateers. Before the end of the year the country was fighting an undeclared naval "Quasi-War" against France in the Caribbean.

During the conflict the reborn U.S. Navy captured or sank ninety-nine armed French vessels while losing only one warship. Although such numbers indicate a staggering American victory, most of the French vessels were small, lightly armed, and operated by inexperienced commanders and crews—the smallest captured craft had only six crewmen. These vessels could not oppose an armed sloop or frigate, and they were easily captured when engaged by more powerful ships. Only seven of the American victories occurred against vessels with crews larger than 100 men. Regardless, Americans reveled in the victories, including the most famous one on February 9, 1799, when Captain Thomas Truxtun's frigate *Constellation* defeated the French frigate *L'Insurgente* in ninety minutes. The following January 31, 1800, *Constellation* severely damaged but did not sink the French frigate *Vengeance*—still an outstanding victory.

As Franco-American tensions escalated in 1798, Congress ordered the expansion of the army by 10,000 additional men and the creation of a 15,000-man provisional three-year army. Adams convinced Washington to come out of retirement to command the force, but the former president would only agree if Hamilton served as his second-in-command. Adams bristled at the request but acquiesced, creating rifts in the military and the Federalist Party, as many refused to serve under Hamilton. However, the army never took the field, and Adams disbanded the provisional army. Federalists also passed the Alien and Sedition Acts, giving the government authority to deport or jail those who threatened the United States. Had a full-scale war begun, Americans might have tolerated these restrictions. Since it did not, Republicans painted Federalists as curbing American liberty at the point of a bayonet.

Peace overtures began before the fighting started. President Adams sent emissaries to negotiate with a new French government headed by First Consul Napoleon Bonaparte. Since neither side wanted war, the countries agreed on the Treaty of Mortefontaine, or Convention of 1800, in which the United States gave up its claims to French ship seizures and in return the French suspended the 1778 treaty of alliance and ended the Quasi-War. The United States did not sign another such treaty for almost 150 years, as George Washington's warning in his 1797 Farewell Address against entangling alliances reverberated strongly.

REPUBLICAN ASCENDENCY

The presidential election of 1800 between Federalist incumbent John Adams and Republican Thomas Jefferson marked the first time an opposition party had gained power in the United States. Jefferson's rule also marked the emergence of a new democratic political system highlighted by wider public participation. The orderly transfer of power from Federalists to Republicans, which was effected without military involvement, revealed the political maturity of the country.

As president, Jefferson found himself caught between the desire for national security and the need to reduce governmental spending. These were conflicting goals, especially since

Republicans inherited an $82 million debt from outgoing Federalists. Simply put, Jefferson wanted to cut expenses by reducing the military. His proposal called for the standing army to be kept to a minimum and for the country to rely on citizen-soldiers. Fearing even harsher Republican measures, the outgoing Federalists had made sure to preserve the navy on the statute books while discharging all but forty-five officers. They had also sold more than twenty frigates, keeping only thirteen ships, which Jefferson planned to use in conjunction with land-based fortifications, militiamen, and a fleet of gunboats to protect the country. Jefferson preferred small shallow-draft coastal gunboats to capital ships because these defensive craft were unlikely to provoke incidents at sea.

The rebirth of the U.S. Navy occurred as a direct result of the war between Great Britain and revolutionary France and the depredations of North African pirates who seized American ships and imprisoned their sailors. The construction and use of seagoing frigates had raised new questions about the country's role in world affairs. The debate over the type and number of ships the United States should support ultimately determined the force structure of the navy and defined the nation's role in world affairs. Navalists, who were generally Federalists, wanted to build a seagoing fleet capable of influencing the European powers, protecting American commerce, and enhancing American prestige abroad. Antinavalists, who were mostly Republicans, preferred a coastal naval force designed to defend the country's shoreline.

ISSUES IN MILITARY HISTORY

NAVALISTS VERSUS ANTINAVALISTS

One of the most significant debates of the early republic regarded the composition and philosophy of the newly reconstituted American navy. Should the United States have seagoing ships that could protect American commerce away from the American coast? Or should the country possess a defensive fleet of smaller and less expensive vessels designed to protect the American coastline from enemy invasion?

Thomas Jefferson's administration inherited the newly re-created navy in 1801, as well as staggering and crippling debt. In an attempt to rein in spending, his administration downsized the army and navy. One thesis maintains that the resultant gunboat program represented an "antinavalist" approach to naval power and national defense in which geography and small boats, manned by a naval militia, acted as the primary defenders against foreign invasion.

While Jefferson's most famous naval-related quote refers to "the ruinous folly of a navy," his economy-minded naval plan called for shallow-water defensive gunboats—which were generally forty to eighty feet long, fifteen to twenty feet across the beam, and four to seven feet in the hold, and were armed with either one or two long twenty-four- or thirty-two-pound cannon plus assorted smaller guns—to work in conjunction with seagoing ships, coastal and harbor fortifications, the army, and the national militia. This sophisticated multifaceted defense program was never implemented in whole because parsimonious Republican congressmen would not appropriate enough monies for gunboats, ships, forts, and an increased army. Ultimately, antinaval congressmen chose gunboats as an economical alternative to seagoing ships, authorizing construction of 177 vessels, and the brown-water defensive craft became stereotyped as the Jeffersonian alternative to a blue-water navy. Congress's failure to

continued

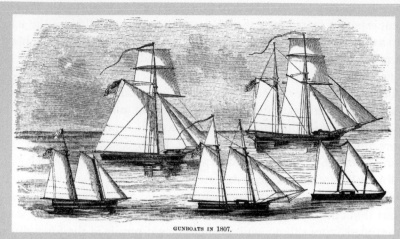

GUNBOATS IN 1807.

IMAGE 5.1 Gunboats Gunboats such as these, depicted in Benson J. Lossing's *Pictorial Field Book of the War of 1812* (New York: Harper and Brothers, 1869), were to be a primary component of President Thomas Jefferson's defense system. Image courtesy of the Naval History and Heritage Command.

defend the United States against British seagoing ships during the War of 1812 represents congressional myopia rather than the inadequacy of Jefferson or his naval policy.

Jefferson's gunboat program attempted to provide the country with a pluralistic defensive policy. But this plan soon became part of a much larger political argument. Rather than simply representing a naval program or serving as an instrument that pitted navalists against antinavalists, Federalists against Republicans, and East against West, gunboats were part of Jeffersonian Republican philosophy, and the vessels reflected the political and diplomatic course the country followed during the early nineteenth century.

Gunboats and Jeffersonian naval policy have typically been measured against the great expansion of the American fleet during the late nineteenth and early twentieth centuries. Once the War of 1812 ended, the gunboats' demise came quickly. The remaining boats were sold, creating a legacy of opposition to small vessels and a prejudicial view of Jeffersonian military policies that lasted well into our own century. While historians like Alfred Thayer Mahan may look to battleships (chapter 10) as the primary indicator of broad control of the seas, light shallow-draft craft able to work close to the shore remain essential for gaining complete command of the seas. Mahan's late-nineteenth-century ideas regarding seapower have relegated Jefferson's gunboats and ideas for a flexible, pluralistic military policy to the shadows of American naval history.

BARBARY PIRATES

The conflict between the United States and the Barbary nations (Tripolitan War, 1801–1805; Algerine War 1815–1816) broke out after North African pirates waged a commercial war on U.S. ships motivated by the lure of money rather than religion. After independence, the United States had hoped to engage in free trade, but in 1784 the Barbary states began capturing American ships and enslaving U.S. citizens. Successive American governments paid monetary tribute to protect ships and men from seizures by the North African states, resulting in more than $1 million in American payments by 1800. All countries with Mediterranean commercial interests, whether weak or strong, suffered likewise.

A September 1800 incident involving Captain William Bainbridge and the frigate *George Washington* revealed U.S. standing in the region. A three-year-overdue American tribute to Algiers infuriated the dey, who ordered Bainbridge to transport passengers and cargo to the sultan at Constantinople. Bainbridge, realizing that his failure to comply meant war, made the trip. News of this embarrassment forced President Jefferson to choose between using the navy in the Mediterranean and buying peace. Jefferson estimated that sending a small fleet to the Mediterranean cost little more than maintaining it in American waters. Additionally, American officers and men would acquire training. Consequently, he pursued a limited offensive action in the Mediterranean, dictated by budgetary constraints.

Jefferson sent four consecutive squadrons to the Mediterranean. Neither Richard Dale (1801–1802) nor Richard Morris (1802–1803) achieved any appreciable results in suppressing piratical activities or blockading Tripoli. When replacement Captain Edward Preble arrived in the Mediterranean in September 1803, he gathered smaller shallow-draft ships and instituted a vigorous blockade. On October 31, 1803, hard-luck Captain William Bainbridge's *Philadelphia* ran aground near Tripoli Harbor and had to surrender. Decatur's decision to set fire to the frigate in mid-February 1804 under the walls and guns of the harbor denied Tripolitans the use of the ship while restoring American honor.

During the summer of 1804 Preble aggressively attacked Tripoli in a series of inconclusive battles while also making diplomatic overtures to end the conflict. His replacement, Samuel Barron, who arrived in September 1804, continued the blockade while trying to undermine the pasha of Tripoli's authority. The turning point came when ex-consul William Eaton led a combined force of American marines ("to the shores of Tripoli . . .") and Arab, Greek, and Berber mercenaries in a 500-mile overland trek to attack the city of

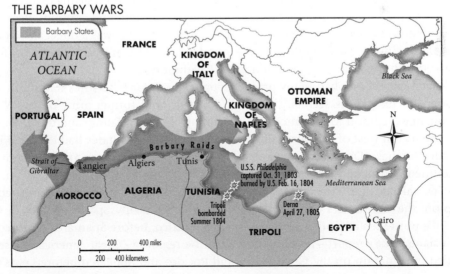

MAP 5.3 The Barbary Wars

Derna. Eaton's campaign to overthrow the government of Tripoli and place the pasha's older brother on the throne ended the conflict. Eaton captured and held Derna, but his attempt to create a new American-friendly government failed because the pasha, fearing his overthrow, negotiated the war's conclusion. In June 1805 the United States ended the First Barbary War, paying a $60,000 ransom for American prisoners but not offering any additional tribute. The U.S. Navy and its officers had gained wartime experience in single-ship and fleet actions, which paid off later when U.S. forces were pitted against the world's largest navy.

EDUCATION AND EXPLORATION

Washington and Hamilton had suggested the creation of a military academy to train soldiers in the art of war, engineering, and artillery, but congressmen feared the prospect of an elite officer class. After the Adams presidency ended, military engineers and artillerists received training at Carlisle, Pennsylvania; Springfield, Massachusetts; and West Point, New York, but no centralized training institution existed. Jefferson wanted the military to support civil society rather than threaten it, so he coopted the military, replacing outspoken Federalist officers with Republicans. Then, to further Republicanize the military, Jefferson created a Hamiltonian-style national military academy that focused on training soldiers in engineering and practical matters. His Peace Establishment Act of 1802 created the U.S. Military Academy and selected as its site the well-established post at West Point along the Hudson River.

Jefferson's academy provided practical educational and institutional training to politically acceptable Republicans, permitting the continued transformation of the military. As president, he enlarged the army while reducing the influence of Federalists. After 1808 Republican-trained West Point graduates began forming the new officer corps of the enlarged army. In doing so, Jefferson turned the army over to the people, giving rise to appointments from across the country and from every segment of society, and creating a Republican army of volunteer enlisted soldiers and professional officers. This was a direct affront to the Society of Cincinnati, the hereditary society founded in 1783 that was composed of former Continental officers who had served during the Revolution.

Military engineering had many practical applications for Jefferson's nation. In 1804, Jefferson sent his private secretary, Meriwether Lewis, and former army officer William Clark on an expedition to document the geography, flora and fauna, and trade possibilities of the region west of the Mississippi River that the United States had acquired in the Louisiana Purchase. During the two-and-a-half-year expedition, Lewis and Clark traversed the continent, ultimately staking an American claim to the Pacific coast of Oregon. Likewise, General James Wilkinson sent army officer Zebulon Pike on an 1807 expedition to explore the headwaters of the Arkansas River. Captured by Spanish forces in Colorado, Pike was taken as a prisoner to Chihuahua, Mexico, before Spaniards returned him to Louisiana. Pike's report—in which he called the region a "Great American Desert"— provided information on the Great Plains and Rockies and appeared before Lewis's and Clark's reports.

Jefferson sent other civilian missions into the West to acquire geographical and scientific knowledge and to strengthen the U.S. presence in the region without the threat of war. Shortly thereafter U.S. army units would create constabulary posts (forts designed to police an area and maintain control over it) to ensure American possession.

WAR ON THE HORIZON

The most severe threat to American independence emerged beginning in 1793 with the wars between Great Britain and revolutionary France. Initially, American merchants and ship owners prospered by trading with both countries, but Britain and France soon started to seize ships trading with their enemy. The enforcement of British admiralty laws—especially the "Rule of 1756," which maintained that any trade illegal in peacetime was also illegal during war—led neutral states to evade such restrictions. Americans posited that stopping a vessel in an American port converted its cargo to neutral American goods, and during the Quasi-War a British admiralty court upheld the legality of this "doctrine of the broken voyage" in the *Polly* decision. Four years later, in 1804, with the United States and France at peace, an admiralty court ruled in the "Essex Case" that the point of origin determined the nationality of goods, upholding the "doctrine of the continuous voyage." During the same period British Orders in Council—regulations issued by the monarch with approval of the Privy Council—also limited trade by expanding the list of goods illegal to sell a belligerent. Absolute contraband included arms, ammunition, naval stores, and other military items, while conditional contraband consisted of food or any item that could be used to support military operations.

On October 21, 1805, Admiral Horatio Nelson defeated a combined Franco-Spanish fleet off Cape Trafalgar, capturing or destroying twenty-two enemy ships without the loss of a single British vessel. The victory gave the Royal Navy control of the seas for the remainder of the war. Six weeks later, on December 5, Napoleon's victory at Austerlitz made France the master of the European continent. Thereafter the war devolved into a conflict between the "Tiger" and the "Shark," with the United States caught in the middle.

AMERICAN CLOUDS

Unable to engage one another directly, Britain and France waged economic warfare. Orders in Council issued in mid-May 1806 required any ship bound for French-controlled ports to stop first at a British port to allow itself to be searched for contraband. Napoleon responded with his "Continental System," which tried to paralyze British commerce; his Berlin Decree (November 1806), which forbade British ships to enter European ports; and his Milan Decree (December 1807), which permitted the French seizure and confiscation of any neutral ships complying with British rules before landing in Europe. American ships obeying British regulations risked seizure by the French, while those that ignored British rules could be seized by the Royal Navy.

To man its ships, the Royal Navy also resorted to impressments—forcing sailors into service. In theory, only British citizens could be impressed, but in practice naval officers put their need for seamen above legal distinctions. Americans maintained that a person could change citizenship and that a neutral nation's flag protected its sailors, views rejected by Britons, who maintained that British sailors remained subject to British law, including impressment, wherever they were. The British reportedly impressed as many as 10,000 American mariners during their wars with France. When HMS *Leopard* fired on the USS *Chesapeake* in June 1807 and impressed its sailors, outraged Americans demanded war. President Jefferson instead called Congress into session. Meanwhile, he instructed state governors to make preparations for defense, and he quietly enlarged the army and navy, trained militia, and repaired fortifications.

When Congress convened, Republicans passed the Embargo Act forbidding all foreign trade. Republicans hoped that the loss of American trade would convince the British and the French to respect American neutral rights. Instead, from December 1807 to March 1809 American ships sat at wharves, agricultural harvests went unsold, and government revenues declined by $9 million. Many Americans violated the embargo and engaged in illegal trade, especially with Canada and Spanish Florida. Neither the navy nor the Revenue Service could effectively enforce the embargo, and the policy revived the Federalist Party.

Congressional Republicans repealed the Embargo Act during Jefferson's final days as president, replacing it with the Non-Intercourse Act of March 1809, which lifted all embargoes on American shipping except for those vessels bound for British or French ports. This restrictive measure also failed, because once ships departed there was no way to control where they went. In May 1810 Congress replaced the Non-Intercourse Act with Macon's Bill Number 2, which forbade British and French warships from entering American waters and declared that if either Britain or France ceased its attacks upon American shipping, the United States would end trade with the other. Napoleon announced that France would respect American neutral rights, but he did not intend to follow through on his promise. President Madison, who succeeded Jefferson, nonetheless accepted Napoleon's offer and threatened to stop trade with Britain.

PRELUDE TO WAR

Relations between the United States and Britain deteriorated throughout the spring of 1811. In early May, the thirty-eight-gun HMS *Guerrière* stopped the merchant brig *Spitfire* off New York Harbor and impressed an American passenger. After learning of the outrage, Captain John Rodgers departed from Annapolis with the forty-four-gun *President*, hoping to recover the American. On May 16, Rodgers spotted a ship he believed to be *Guerrière*; in fact, it was the twenty-two-gun HMS *Little Belt*, captained by Arthur Bingham. As darkness and fog enveloped the two ships, both Rodgers and Bingham loudly demanded the other ship identity itself; neither captain responded. Shortly after 10 p.m. both ships began firing, and within fifteen minutes British guns fell silent. Badly damaged in the exchange, *Little Belt* suffered thirteen killed and nineteen wounded. *President* had one man wounded. Americans believed this action was just retribution for what had happened to *Chesapeake* four years before.

On the northwest frontier, Shawnee chieftain Tecumseh along with his shaman brother Tenskwatawa (known as the Prophet) had formed a coalition of Indian tribes to resist white expansion, and Tecumseh had traveled south to recruit members. In early November 1811, Indiana Territory governor William Henry Harrison advanced with 1,000 regulars and volunteer militiamen to confront the Indians. Although he had been encouraged to negotiate a diplomatic settlement, Harrison anticipated a battle. Making camp in an elevated defensive position close to Prophet's Town (near present-day Lafayette, Indiana), he instructed his men to sleep with their guns. But Harrison did not create fortifications, which encouraged the Prophet's warriors to attack during the predawn hours of November 7, 1811. Despite suffering almost 200 casualties, the Americans held their position, drove the attackers back, and forced the Indians to retreat. Following this conflict, which became known as the Battle of Tippecanoe, Harrison's men found British weapons in the area and burned Prophet's Town, believing Britons responsible for the violence in the Northwest.

THE WAR OF 1812

President James Madison's 1811 annual address asked Congress to bolster the country's defenses. Congress increased the army by 25,000 recruits, added 50,000 militiamen, and appropriated $2 million for ordnance but did not expand the navy, because many Republicans believed the resources would be wasted given the size of Britain's navy. War Hawks—predominantly southern and western Republican congressmen who supported territorial expansion and resented British economic policies and impressments—noted the Royal Navy's Halifax Squadron had 111 ships, including 7 ships-of-the-line and 31 frigates, while the U.S. Navy had only 17 frigates, sloops, and brigs, plus 170 gunboats. Antinavy Republicans repeatedly defeated proposals to build ships, believing American troops could easily capture Canada and force Britain to the peace table without a naval campaign.

In May 1812, news reached America that the British government had not softened on neutral trade or impressment. Madison responded by sending a message to Congress on June 1 citing four reasons for declaring war against Great Britain: (1) impressment, (2) illegal blockades, (3) the Orders in Council, and (4) British support for the Indians of the Northwest Territory. War Hawks pushed the vote through the House (79–49), while the measure passed the Senate by only three votes (19–13). Britain's foreign secretary suspended the Orders in Council on June 16, but that decision did not change American attitudes.

British Canada has often been compared to a tree, and in the early nineteenth century, its taproots were the sea-lanes connecting it with England; its trunk was the St. Lawrence River, dominated by Québec and Montreal; and its branches were the Great Lakes. As such, the key to conquering Canada was controlling the St. Lawrence River, and so American strategy fixated on severing the trunk throughout the war. Most Americans anticipated the conflict would be a quick affair; Jefferson boldly predicted the conquest of Canada would be "a mere matter of marching." Unfortunately this confidence was greatly misplaced, given the state of the U.S. military. As American forces tried repeatedly to control the St. Lawrence, British leaders protected Canada and maintained open sea-lanes to supply it. The Napoleonic threat initially forced Britain to keep only a modest naval presence in American waters, but by early 1813 Britain had increased its naval force in the region, providing enough ships to blockade the entire American coast south from New England, which stymied the American economy to the point of collapse. With the defeat of Napoleon in 1814, a new British policy aimed at destroying the American will to fight.

ON TO CANADA: 1812

American hopes for conquering Canada proved unrealistic. During the fall of 1812, the army failed in three successive invasions. In mid-July General William Hull crossed from Detroit into Canada with plans to advance on the city of York. As he marched toward Fort Malden, Hull learned that Fort Michilimackinac at the head of Lake Huron had fallen to British and Indian forces. This loss and increased attacks by Tecumseh's Indian allies convinced Hull to retreat to Detroit.

When British general Isaac Brock discovered Hull had retreated to Detroit, he was convinced the American had lost his nerve. Sensing an advantage, Brock moved quickly against Detroit, using his small contingent of British soldiers and Indians to surround the fort, a stratagem giving the appearance that he had more men than he actually did. Brock then fired his artillery into the fort while his Indians screamed simultaneously, which demoralized Hull because he feared for the safety of his daughters. On August 16, 1812, Hull surrendered Detroit without a fight, giving the British control of the western Great Lakes.

In mid-October General Stephen Van Rensselaer launched a second invasion against Canada. Intending to join with Hull in Upper Canada, Van Rensselaer gathered militiamen and soldiers, supplies, and weapons but found General Alexander Smyth unwilling to cooperate. The plan was to cross the Niagara River and capture Queenston before winter began, creating a Canadian foothold.

The Americans crossed the river early on October 13, 1812. But most of Van Rensselaer's New York militiamen refused to advance into Canada, arguing that their contractual obligation was limited to the defense of their state, not offensive operations in another country. Without the militiamen, Van Rensselaer's 600 regulars found themselves confronting General Brock's regulars, who had recently returned from Detroit. British cannon commanding the heights drove many American boats back across the river and pinned down those who landed. After locating an obscure fisherman's path, Lieutenant Colonel Winfield Scott and three companies of American soldiers climbed the steep path to the top of the plateau unobserved. From there, they suddenly spilled downhill, mortally wounding Brock as they attacked and driving the British from the heights. Soon British black, white, and Indian reinforcements from nearby Fort George counterattacked uphill, overwhelming the Americans. Scott and many of his soldiers surrendered, while others fled across the river. This invasion had failed too.

Before the end of the year a third operation against Canada had failed before it even began. General Henry Dearborn, wanting to sever British supply and communication routes farther down the St. Lawrence River, gathered militia for an attack against Montreal through the Lake Champlain corridor. As his army marched north, Dearborn learned that the militiamen were refusing to enter Canada, and the campaign stalled. By the end of 1812, the U.S. Army had lost every major engagement in which it fought, and Canada remained in British hands.

WAR AT SEA: 1812

Upon learning of war, Captain John Rodgers's four-ship squadron hoped to catch a British Jamaica convoy that had recently departed the Caribbean. While engaging the slower and weaker thirty-two-gun British frigate *Belvidera* in late June 1812, a terrifying explosion ripped through Rodgers's forty-four-gun *President*. A gun had exploded, setting off nearby powder and spewing fire through the bow. Sixteen lay dead or wounded, and nearby cannon were badly damaged. Before the explosion *Belvidera* had appeared on the verge of defeat, but now it slipped away. The first shots of the War of 1812 at sea had been inglorious.

On August 19, 1812, Captain Isaac Hull's forty-four-gun *Constitution* encountered the thirty-eight-gun HMS *Guerrière* 700 miles east of Boston. British captain James Dacres initiated battle by twice crossing the bow of *Constitution* while firing broadsides. During both passes American sailors could read "NOT THE LITTLE BELT" painted across the fore-topsail of *Guerrière*. After the second British pass and broadside, Hull closed quickly on the *Guerrière*'s port quarter. For twenty minutes the two ships exchanged fire. Then suddenly the British frigate's mizzenmast snapped, crashing across the deck. This proved the turning point in the engagement, because the mast acted as an anchor, impacting *Guerrière*'s sailing ability. When the riggings of the two ships became entangled, *Guerrière*'s foremast and main mast also collapsed, forcing the British ship to surrender.

Six weeks later, on October 25, Stephen Decatur's forty-four-gun *United States* engaged the thirty-eight-gun HMS *Macedonian*. As Decatur and British captain John Carden maneuvered against one other, Decatur maintained the windward advantage, preventing the British ship from bringing its carronades (short-range large-caliber smoothbore cannon used to repel boarders and damage a ship's upper decks and rigging). Forced to rely on its eighteen-pound main deck guns, *Macedonian* could inflict little damage on the *United States*, while broadsides from the American frigate's long-range twenty-four-pound cannon ripped into the *Macedonian*'s hull, masts, sails, and rigging. Once the British frigate's mizzenmast broke, Carden surrendered rather than suffer certain death.

Captain William Bainbridge, who took command of the frigate *Constitution* in late October 1812, found two British ships off Rio de Janeiro in late December. The larger British frigate, the thirty-eight-gun HMS *Java*, commanded by Captain Henry Lambert, closed in on *Constitution*. Bainbridge fired two broadsides, damaging the British frigate's riggings and sails. *Java* then crossed astern of *Constitution*, delivering a raking broadside that wounded Bainbridge, destroyed the ship's wheel, and killed several sailors. "Old Ironsides" started to drift before the suffering Bainbridge instructed his sailors to steer using the ship's tiller. Within minutes *Constitution* had regained a windward position and heavy American guns had ripped through *Java*. Lambert had wanted to board the American frigate, but the two ships suddenly collided, and *Java*'s foremast crashed into the sea. *Constitution*'s heavy guns hammered *Java* into submission, giving the Americans a third frigate victory in what was perhaps the bloodiest battle of the naval war—9 Americans were killed and 27 wounded, while the British suffered 22 killed and 102 wounded.

American naval victories during 1812 convinced Secretary Paul Hamilton of the merit of single-ship or tandem cruises rather than sailing in squadrons. They also forced the British to alter their strategic plan for North American waters. By the end of 1812 the Royal Navy had lost five ship-to-ship engagements. To prevent additional losses the British Admiralty ordered frigate captains to avoid single-ship engagements with the heavily armed American frigates and to tighten their blockade to prevent American warships from getting to sea.

VISIONS OF DEFEAT: 1813

The war had gone poorly in 1812, prompting President Madison to replace Secretary of War William Eustis with John Armstrong and Navy Secretary Hamilton with Philadelphia merchant William Jones. Eustis focused the war on Canada, while Jones stressed a new shipbuilding program on the northern lakes and sent additional resources to upstate New York and western Pennsylvania.

Canada represented the only place where the United States could strike at Britain. Wanting to push the war aggressively, Armstrong planned to deploy army and naval forces on Lake Ontario to attack the royal shipyard at Kingston, then move against the capital of York, and finally advance against Fort George on the Niagara River. But by the time the spring ice

THE WAR OF 1812: THE WAR IN THE NORTH

MAP 5.4 The War of 1812: The War in the North

had thawed, Major General Henry Dearborn and Captain Isaac Chauncey had decided to attack York first because of the strong contingent of British troops reportedly at Kingston.

During late April Chauncey's corvette, brig, and twelve schooners supported a raid led by General Zebulon Pike. Landing to the west of York, Pike's regular infantry met little resistance as they advanced into town. British general Roger Sheaffe, the lieutenant governor of Upper Canada, had regulars, militiamen, and Indian allies, but the town had few defenses otherwise. While Pike's men fought their way into York, Sheaffe ordered one of the ships at the dockyard torched, the fort's magazine detonated, and a wooden bridge over the River Don destroyed after his troops crossed it. With militiamen and townspeople still in the streets and the Union Jack flying above the fort, the magazine exploded, throwing debris that killed Pike and 37 American soldiers and wounded 200 others. Already angry, American soldiers subsequently set fire to public buildings and looted unattended homes, acts that ultimately hardened Canadian attitudes toward the Americans.

Chauncey then sailed westward to support Colonel Winfield Scott's late May attack against Fort George at the mouth of the Niagara River. Landing on the shores of Lake Ontario, Scott's 4,000 regular infantry quickly advanced toward the fort. British general John Vincent had only 1,000 men, so he retreated before being surrounded. Vincent had ordered the guns spiked and the magazines detonated, but his men did not complete their task. Scott's soldiers captured the fort intact and also momentarily pursued Vincent's retreating army. The Americans held Fort George until December 1813, when they evacuated the position and burned the village of Newark. On December 19, 1813, British troops used deception to seize Fort Niagara, located near the meeting point of the Niagara River and Lake Ontario. Afterward British troops responded by burning almost every village on the American side of the river, including Buffalo and Lewiston. The British held Fort Niagara for the rest of the war.

British commodore Sir James Yeo took advantage of Chauncey's absence to attack the American naval base at Sacket's Harbor on May 28, 1813. There he burned two vessels and destroyed stores valued at $500,000. Convinced that the British would not have attacked had his squadron been present, Chauncey vowed not to leave Sacket's Harbor again until he had gained unquestioned naval control over the lake. As a result, the struggle on Lake Ontario devolved into a war of the adze, axe, and hammer—a naval building race in which neither side gained an advantage. Before the war ended, the British had launched a 102-gun ship on the lake, and the Americans had two 120-gun ships under construction.

In the Northwest Territory, General William Henry Harrison replaced General James Winchester and ordered him to Maumee. When Winchester arrived, he found his troops underfed, poorly clothed, and with bad morale. The malcontented officers of his command convinced Winchester to rescue Americans trapped thirty miles away in Frenchtown on the River Raisin. On January 18, 1813, against Harrison's wishes, 800 Kentuckians and French-speaking Michigan militiamen advanced along the ice-bound Lake Erie to the frozen River Raisin and Frenchtown, which was held by 63 Essex Canadian militiamen and 200 Potawatomis. The Americans attacked the town, fighting from building to building. The outnumbered Canadians and Indians determinedly held their ground for hours before slowly retreating north toward Detroit. Winchester's men celebrated their victory by drinking all of the local liquor and failing to strengthen the town's defenses. Despite Harrison's warning of a potential British counterattack, Winchester did not bring forward supplies or ammunition from Maumee. Locals also reported that a large British army was approaching, but Winchester believed it would not arrive for days.

Before sunrise on January 22, 1813, British general Henry Procter attacked Frenchtown on three sides with 600 regulars and 800 Indians. Shocked American regulars held their ground for only twenty minutes before most fled. Winchester was captured, and more than 200 Americans were killed, with Indians scalping many of them; several dozen Americans surrendered, laying down their arms, only to be slaughtered by Indians. Still, several volunteers and Kentucky regiments continued fighting, inflicting severe casualties on British artillery units. Refusing to surrender even when Winchester ordered them to, they fought for three hours because they believed the Indians would kill them too. Ultimately 547 Americans surrendered. The uninjured were taken as prisoners into Canada, while all wounded remained behind. The following morning Indians slaughtered the wounded and burned the town. Word of the River Raisin Massacre—in which an estimated 30 to 100 wounded Americans were killed—instantly became a rallying cry for Kentuckians and Americans to enlist for the war.

The River Raisin disaster forced Harrison to cancel his plans to attack Detroit. Instead, in February his men began building Fort Meigs on the Maumee River. During the unforgiving winter soldiers felled trees, partially buried them in the frozen ground, and threw up an earthen parapet in the interior, making Meigs the largest wooden fort in North America. General Procter and his Shawnee ally Tecumseh besieged the fort for nine days in early May before realizing that artillery had little effect on the internal earthen embankments, which absorbed the shock from incoming rounds. Later, Procter tried again to capture Fort Meigs for a week during late July before moving against Fort Stephenson, which protected American shipbuilding facilities at Presque Isle (present-day Erie, Pennsylvania). Procter, needing to eliminate Stephenson at the head of the Sandusky River to gain control over Lake Erie, launched a naval and land attack on August 2, 1813, but the siege failed, forcing the British general to withdraw into Canada.

VICTORY ON THE LAKES: 1813

During 1813 the Royal Navy extended its blockade. By mid-year, *Constellation* had been bottled up in Norfolk, and *United States* and *Macedonian* were in New London. For the remainder of the war most American ships remained in ports from New England to Virginia, permitting the Navy Department to send sailors and junior officers to the struggle on the inland lakes.

American captain James Lawrence, commanding *Chesapeake*, had been waiting in Boston for the chance to sail. British captain Philip Broke, commander of the thirty-eight-gun HMS *Shannon*, was confident that he could defeat the Americans, even ordering his cruising companion to leave the area so he could challenge Lawrence to a ship-to-ship duel. Despite his untrained crew and *Shannon*'s reputation for having the most skilled crew in the British fleet, Lawrence foolishly accepted Broke's challenge. Lawrence knew British long guns created an advantage, but he planned to fight at close range, where his cannonades could prevail.

Raising a flag that bore the slogan "Free Trade and Sailors' Rights," Lawrence encountered the British frigate on June 1, 1813. A sustained, disciplined, and precise British cannon barrage broke Lawrence's untrained crew. Soon *Chesapeake* floundered, drifting uncontrollably into the range of British snipers, who began killing American officers. When *Shannon* closed to boarding distance, a sniper's bullet struck Lawrence, and he was carried below, repeatedly uttering, "Don't give up the ship." Nevertheless, within minutes British sailors had raised the Union Jack, signifying Lawrence's ship had been taken. The brutal hand-to-hand engagement had resulted in 70 Americans killed, 100 wounded, and the loss of the frigate. This defeat convinced other American officers to remain in port rather than try to run the British blockade.

On Lake Erie, Lawrence's friend Oliver Hazard Perry succeeded Jesse Elliot in command at Presque Isle during the spring of 1813. When Perry arrived he found eleven vessels in varying stages of completion. He overcame shortages in cannon, construction materials, and equipment to complete most of the ships by August. Then, taking advantage of a storm that drove a blockading British squadron from its station, Perry redeployed his ships to Put-in-Bay at South Bass Island, a position from which he could threaten the British-Canadian line of communication through Lake Erie.

Perry's bold move forced British captain Robert H. Barclay to engage the American fleet early on the morning of September 10, 1813. Above Perry's twenty-gun flagship *Lawrence* flew a banner emblazoned with "Don't Give Up the Ship," the dying words of his friend. Perry's fleet—led by *Lawrence* and the twenty-gun *Niagara*—carried short-range carronades, meaning Perry needed to close on his opponent. The British ships *Queen Charlotte* (armed with sixteen guns) and *Detroit* (twelve guns) could fight at longer range. Perry planned to pair his larger ships with those of the British, leaving commanders of his smaller ships to fire on any target. He advanced on the British fleet at an acute angle, minimizing the damage of British long-range raking fire. During the attack, Perry's *Lawrence* became separated from the rest of the American fleet, and Jesse Elliot's *Niagara* lagged behind. For two hours, *Lawrence* endured the brunt of attacks from three British ships while fighting alone. When some 80 percent of the crew had been killed or wounded and *Lawrence* could no longer fight, Perry left the national ensign on the mast, lowered his commodore's pennant and battle flag, boarded a small rowboat, and departed for the *Niagara*.

With a fresh flagship, Perry sailed the *Niagara* across the bow of the *Detroit*, delivering a damaging broadside. When the *Detroit* swung around to bring a fresh broadside into action, it collided with the *Queen Charlotte*, leaving both ships immobile. Perry cautiously positioned *Niagara* so he could fire on both British vessels, and within minutes both had surrendered. Taking an old letter from his jacket, Perry quickly scribbled a note to General William Henry Harrison: "We have met the enemy and they are ours: Two Ships, two Brigs, one Schooner, & one Sloop."

Perry's victory on Lake Erie profoundly altered the war in the Northwest, severing British waterborne supply and communication lines; the tree limbs had been severed from the trunk. By month's end, Perry had transported Harrison's army across Lake Erie, forcing the British to evacuate Detroit and Malden. Tecumseh had tried to convince Procter to remain at Detroit to protect his Indian allies and their lands, but the British general hadn't heeded his warning. Without guns, and with food and supplies running low, British forces crossed into Canada on September 27, joined by Tecumseh's Indian allies. Harrison followed, catching British stragglers and Indians near Moraviantown on the evening of October 4, 1813. The next morning Harrison's men impetuously attacked a group of well-aligned but dispirited and hungry British regulars who had positioned their artillery on a road running between the Thames River and a small swamp, in which Indians hid on the British right flank. Mounted Kentuckians angrily rushed the British line, which collapsed immediately. Procter and his regulars ran, while the Indians continued fighting in the swamp. Reportedly, during the struggle Kentucky colonel Richard Mentor Johnson killed Tecumseh during a cavalry charge, and the body was later mutilated. With Tecumseh's death, the Indian confederation collapsed, and the American victory at the Thames restored the Northwest Territory to the United States.

TO MONTREAL: 1813

Under Secretary of War Armstrong's 1813 plan for the invasion of Canada, General James Wilkinson's 8,000 men at Sacket's Harbor on Lake Ontario would move down the St. Lawrence River and rendezvous with General Wade Hampton's 4,000 troops advancing north from Plattsburgh. Armstrong wanted the two armies to move together against Montreal, but his plan had several flaws. The two generals, who despised and mistrusted each other, could not agree on the objective: Wilkinson wanted to attack Montreal, while Hampton wanted to attack Kingston. Bad weather, lack of supplies, and ill-trained troops compounded their troubles.

Hampton had moved his forces to Plattsburgh in mid-September, and that fall he marched 4,000 men to Four Corners on the Chateauguay River and waited for Wilkinson. There, he complained that Wilkinson's delay was further draining his supplies and giving the British the opportunity to concentrate against him. Discovering by mid-October that Wilkinson still had not departed, Hampton moved down the Chateauguay River. When he arrived at the Canadian border, 1,400 of his New York militiamen refused to cross into Canada, leaving the invasion force with 2,600 regulars. By this time, responding to the American movements, British general Louis de Watteville had felled trees across the roads, destroyed bridges, and gathered a small force of regulars and reserves to defend Canada. British lieutenant colonel Charles de Salaberry had used fallen trees to fortify a strategic ford across the Chateauguay River, and he also sent several buglers into the surrounding woods. On October 26, 1813, Hampton's troops tried for two hours to take the ford, but the hastily created Canadian defenses held. Then de Salaberry's buglers sounded the "advance," giving unnerved Americans the impression that they were outnumbered and about to be attacked on their flanks. Hampton's dispirited army fled, retreating temporarily to Four Corners before taking winter quarters in Plattsburgh.

The nefarious James Wilkinson, suffering from illness, did not begin his campaign until mid-October. Sleet and driving rain pounded his small boats on the St. Lawrence River, and rough water sank fifty of his craft, losing men and supplies. By the beginning of November, Wilkinson's troops had landed and taken the village of Cornwall. Learning that British forces were encamped nearby at Crysler's Farm, on a cold and rainy November 11, 1813, Wilkinson's troops attacked. Unable to bring up artillery, General John Boyd for two hours repeatedly attacked entrenched Canadian regulars, who held their ground. By sunset, American troops were slowly retreating back to the river and to the protection of their boats. The following day, the American boats ran the treacherous waters of Long Sault Rapids only to learn that Hampton had retreated south. Without Hampton's troops and supplies, Wilkinson abandoned the campaign for Montreal.

American operations during 1813 highlighted the United States' lack of military planning and the disconnect between political and military objectives. Political posturing and disagreements between Republicans and Federalists derailed military success and infected the officer corps at the highest level. Reliance on older generals and on the militia resulted in poor command decisions and the inability to carry out even poor ones. The naval war on the high seas had reversed the country's 1812 fortunes, and the defeat of several American ships dispelled the belief in the invincibility of American frigates. The tightening of the British blockade also severely disrupted the American economy. Surprisingly, the year revealed the promise of joint army-navy operations and the emergence of a promising cadre of younger army and naval officers.

BATTLES AND CAMPAIGNS OF THE WAR OF 1812

MAP 5.5 Battles and Campaigns of the War of 1812

TRIUMPH AND TRAGEDY: 1814

A gloom hung over the United States. On March 31, 1814, the European Allied coalition armies had entered Paris, and four days later the French army had surrendered, forcing Napoleon to abdicate. With France subdued, Britain turned the full force of its military against the United States for the first time during the war. Canadian forces had prevented the Americans from gaining control over the Niagara frontier, and now the British government devised a four-pronged strategy to break the American will to fight. The British intended to (1) tighten the blockade and extend it to include New England, (2) increase military operations in the Chesapeake Bay to prevent American troops from being transferred northward to Canada, (3) launch an invasion southward from Canada along the Lake Champlain corridor to sever New England from the remainder of the Union and force the Americans to accept peace, and (4) attack New Orleans to close the Mississippi River to American exports and obtain a bargaining chip for negotiations. British leaders believed these operations would bring about the collapse of the United States.

NIAGARA STALEMATE: 1814

Despite a numerical advantage, the American conquest of Canada had failed during 1813. James Wilkinson was relieved of command, and Wade Hampton resigned. President Madison named Jacob Brown commander of the Left Division of the North (which was focused along the Niagara frontier), with Winfield Scott as one of his two brigadier generals. General George Izard assumed command of the Right Division (focused in the Lake Champlain–Plattsburg area) and selected General Alexander Macomb as his subordinate. With these aggressive and talented commanders in place, Secretary of War Armstrong planned to seize Lake Ontario and then move against Montreal.

American plans could not be carried out by the army alone. Commodore Isaac Chauncey, commanding naval forces at Sacket's Harbor, refused to participate in operations until the completion of his new ships in the summer. Unwilling to waste so much operational time, Brown focused on the Niagara region while Scott transformed his troops, drilling the Left Division ten hours a day using the 1791 French Revolutionary Army manual. Through drill and obedience, Scott instilled discipline and motivation among the forces. When blue cloth was unavailable for army uniforms, he commandeered gray and white cloth. By summer, Brown's gray-clad men were healthy, trained, clothed, and ready to advance into Canada.

In early July Brown's 2,800 troops crossed the Niagara River, capturing Fort Erie without losses. Supplemented by 750 New York militiamen and 600 Iroquois, they marched north along the river road toward Queenston. British troops could not destroy bridges fast enough or cut down enough trees over the road, and Scott's army quickly moved to Chippawa Creek, where British soldiers dug in on the east side. British general Phineas Riall, believing that Fort Erie remained in British hands and that the Americans were inexperienced militiamen, decided to cross the creek, mount an attack, and drive the Americans across the Niagara.

Early on the morning of July 5, 1814, British light infantry, militia, and Indians crossed the Chippawa ahead of Riall's main body of troops. General Brown responded by sending militiamen and Indians to clear the woods, but they encountered Riall's advancing army of 2,100 instead. Scott's 1,500 regulars stepped forward, stalling the British advance. Riall, believing the troops in gray were militiamen, expected the American line to collapse at any moment. Instead, Scott's troops held steady, prompting Riall to utter, "Those are regulars, by God!" Scott then pushed his flanks ahead very quickly, forming his line into a U-shape, and caught Riall's advancing army in a three-sided crossfire. For twenty-five minutes both sides repeatedly fired into one another's ranks before Riall withdrew across the Chippawa.

Scott's "Grays" had saved the day, and in honor of the victory West Point later adopted the gray tunic as its official uniform. And while the casualties on both sides were commensurate (500 British killed, wounded, and missing to 325 Americans), the victory boosted American morale. Two days later, Brown's army crossed the Chippawa, driving British forces back to Fort George. The American advance halted only because Isaac Chauncey's ships had not been completed, and the army needed naval support to continue. Brown's army occupied Queenston for most of July, waiting for Chauncey.

A few weeks later General Riall's light infantry and militia moved in strength to Lundy's Lane, four miles north of the Chippawa. On July 25, Scott advanced north, believing the British would recall troops coming south from Fort Niagara toward Fort George. But although Riall had wanted to retreat to Fort George, General Gordon Drummond, the lieutenant governor of Canada, had forced-marched reinforcements toward the lane, where they arrived shortly before the 6 p.m. appearance of the Americans.

British artillery on the high ground at Lundy's Lane ravaged Scott's regulars as they emerged from the woods into an open field. Reforming his line, Scott sent the 25th U.S. Infantry to outflank the British left. The soldiers found an unused path that led to the river and then completely around British lines. When they emerged, they surprised British regulars and Canadian militiamen from behind, driving them off the road and capturing Riall himself. Meanwhile, Scott's steady and disciplined line persuaded Drummond to withdraw the center of his line, leaving British artillery in front of the infantry. By nightfall, Brown had arrived with American reinforcements, and they moved quickly toward the British guns; a subsequent bayonet charge overran the high ground and captured the artillery. Three bloody British counterassaults, the last of which occurred shortly before midnight, tried unsuccessfully to retake the guns. After midnight on July 26, Brown withdrew his exhausted men, but without much of the captured artillery. At daylight he sent troops to reclaim the guns, but Drummond had already reoccupied the field. Casualties numbered more than 800 on each side, with survivors describing the engagement as the fiercest fighting of the Niagara campaign and perhaps the bloodiest battle of the war. With the military power along the Niagara shifted from attacker to defender, Brown had no choice but to retreat to Fort Erie.

Drummond had secured a strategic advantage, and he tried to use it to push the Americans across the river. From August 4 to September 21, 1814, Drummond besieged Fort Erie. On the night of August 15 he attacked the fort with bayonets during a pelting rainstorm. For two hours the British engaged in hand-to-hand combat with Americans to gain the fort's outer defenses, but an exploding American magazine doomed the attack, killing and wounding some 500 British soldiers. Afterward, Drummond positioned three artillery batteries about 500 yards from the fort and began a systematic bombardment while sending parties across the Niagara River to raid Buffalo and Black Rock. However, during mid-September an

American sortie overran two of the artillery positions, destroying guns. Thereafter, the British withdrew across the Chippawa. The British leadership refused to commit additional troops to the Niagara because of an impending invasion south along the Lake Champlain–Hudson River corridor. On November 5, 1814, Brown destroyed Fort Erie, withdrawing his army across the Niagara River into the United States. The 1814 campaign, which had begun with such optimism, ended with neither side gaining momentum. But American soldiers had proven that they could stand toe-to-toe with Redcoats.

DESTRUCTION IN THE CHESAPEAKE: 1814

British admiral George Cockburn had spent much of 1813 reconnoitering and raiding the Chesapeake Bay. British troops plundered Frenchtown on the Eastern Shore in late April, and a few days later, in early May, they ransacked and burned forty of the sixty houses at Havre de Grace, Maryland. In early June, Cockburn's forces neutralized Commodore Joshua Barney's Chesapeake Bay Flotilla by driving American gunboats and barges into St. Leonard's Creek off the Patuxent River. Leaving a few vessels to blockade Barney, Cockburn's army and naval forces unsuccessfully attacked Craney Island, hoping to destroy the U.S. Gosport Shipyard in Portsmouth and capture the USS *Constellation* at anchor in Norfolk. Failing there, Cockburn sacked the nearby town of Hampton, where British-led French troops perpetrated untold atrocities. Nonetheless, the British encountered so little opposition in the Chesapeake Bay that they seized Tangier Island in early 1814, built Fort Albion, and began daily raids that by war's end had destroyed the coastal Virginia and Maryland economies. British raiding parties looted tobacco and burned plantations. They also liberated slaves, relocating refugees to British colonies and outfitting 600 as colonial marines to fight against the Americans. This war of attrition demoralized American slaveholders: should militiamen muster to meet a British invasion, slaves would flee to the British; should slaveholding militiamen keep their "property" in check, the coastline would remain undefended. Britain's seapower provided it the ability to attack and raid anywhere.

After British admiral Alexander Cochrane assumed command in the Chesapeake Bay in early 1814, Cockburn intensified his operations, destroying trade, raiding farms, and liberating slaves. With the summer 1814 arrival of General Robert Ross and 2,500 veteran troops fresh from Europe, Cochrane suggested an attack against Baltimore. Instead, Cockburn recommended Washington, D.C., because it would be easier to attack and was the American capital. By mid-August, British forces were moving easily up the Patuxent River. They landed troops at Benedict and marched north along the river while barges closed in on Barney's gunboat flotilla. Barney scuttled his vessels on August 23 and retreated with his sailors and marines to Washington. When informed that the capital was in peril, Barney's troops pulled artillery to the western side of the Anacostia River at Bladensburg. There they joined General William Winder's 7,000 militiamen and regular troops as the only defenders of Washington.

On August 24, 1814, British forces faced withering fire from Barney's artillery as they crossed the Anacostia River at Bladensburg. As British soldiers determinedly pushed across the river, American militia broke and ran, most fleeing west to Georgetown. Barney's men held their ground, but when their commander fell wounded, they too retreated.

That evening British troops marched easily into Washington and burned public buildings, including the Capitol and the Executive Mansion. American captain Thomas Tingey had earlier set fire to the Washington Navy Yard and two warships then under construction to keep them from falling into British hands. Early on August 26 British forces quietly evacuated the city, returning to their fleet in the Chesapeake. Meanwhile, two British frigates sailed up the Potomac, reaching Alexandria three days later and the city surrendered without a fight.

After the easy victory at Washington, the British attacked Baltimore. On September 12, General Ross and his troops landed at North Point to assault the city from the east. Almost immediately Ross was mortally wounded by sniper fire. His successor, Colonel Arthur Brooke, pushed British troops on toward Baltimore but retreated the following morning when entrenched defenders blocked their advance. That same morning, September 13, British ships in the harbor began shelling Fort McHenry; for twenty-seven hours cannon and Congreve rockets battered the fort. When the British withdrew, an American flag still flew above the fort, symbolizing that Baltimore remained in American hands.

A VIEW of the BOMBARDMENT of Fort M.Henry, near Baltimore, by the British fleet taken from the Observatory under the Command of Admirals Cochrane & Cockburn on the morning of the 13th of Sep.r 1814 which lasted 24 hours, & thrown from 1500 to 1800 shells in the Night attempted to land by forcing a passage up the ferry branch but were repulsed with great loss.

IMAGE 5.2 Battle of Baltimore The bombardment of Fort McHenry on September 13–14, 1814 resulted in the British firing more than 1,500 mortar shells and Congreve rockets during the twenty-seven-hour engagement. Suffering little damage, by morning the Americans in Fort McHenry raised an oversized American flag. Annapolis lawyer Francis Scott Key, who had been forced to watch the bombardment from a British ship, commemorated the event in a poem, which later became known as the "Star Spangled Banner."

British operations in the Chesapeake during 1814 had devastated the American economy and morale. British forces had raided the region with impunity and captured the American capital, but the United States had not collapsed. In fact, spring and summer setbacks simply set the stage for fall and winter successes.

SEVERING THE REPUBLIC: LAKE CHAMPLAIN, 1814

In the north British governor general Sir George Prevost and 8,000 men launched an invasion of New York that they anticipated would allow the British to win the war. As in the American Revolution, gaining control of Lake Champlain was critical for success. American master-commandant Thomas Macdonough had spent months carving a fleet from the wilderness of New York and Vermont to counter the flotilla being constructed by British captain George Downie. Macdonough's program represented a remarkable achievement, as American carpenters completed the twenty-six-gun *Saratoga* in thirty-five days and the twenty-gun *Eagle* in only nineteen, forming a squadron of four ships, six row galleys, and four gunboats.

When news arrived that the British were advancing south, Macdonough, who was short of men, begged the army for anyone with naval or artillery experience. He also realized that with short-range guns and inexperienced crewmen, he could only defeat Downie by fighting in close. Macdonough deployed his ships in a line off Plattsburgh and skilfully prepared for battle by running lines fore and aft to kedge anchors, which would permit him to wind his ships (turn each one around) to bring a fresh broadside to bear on the enemy should that be necessary. Macdonough knew that should Prevost's army take the town, British artillery could drive his ships into open waters, where British long guns would dictate the battle. Instead, New York and Vermont militiamen and regulars poured into General Alexander Macomb's defensive works north of the city, stalling the British advance.

Captain Downie also lacked confidence in his sailors but believed the long guns of his four ships and twelve gunboats could prevail. Prevost had prodded Downie to move quickly against the Americans in a joint attack, even though the thirty-seven-gun *Confiance* was not fitted out or fully manned. On September 11, Downie acquiesced. As he rounded Cumberland Head, the peninsula blocked the wind, and Downie's ships drifted slowly toward the American line. Just as Macdonough had wanted, the battle would be determined by close gunfire rather than by sailing ability.

Anchoring some 300 yards apart, Macdonough's *Saratoga* and Downie's *Confiance* pounded one another for what seemed like hours. Then, Macdonough ordered his anchor lines cut, and his crew hauled in his kedge anchors, which wound his ship around and presented a fresh battery of guns. The lieutenant who had taken charge of the British ship after Downie was killed at the start of the engagement tried to duplicate Macdonough's maneuver, but without having prepared kedge anchors, the *Confiance* turned only halfway, leaving its vulnerable bow facing the fresh guns of *Saratoga*. American cannon raked the British ship, and within minutes *Confiance* had surrendered. The other British ships followed suit as two gunboats withdrew unmolested. Seeing the naval disaster, Prevost stopped his land attack, retreating to Canada.

Occurring immediately after the British burning of Washington, the victories at Baltimore and Lake Champlain boosted American morale while weakening British resolve to fight. In early October British negotiators in Belgium softened their demands. By late November diplomats had agreed to a *status quo ante bellum* treaty, a return to the state of affairs that had existed before the war. Although several controversial issues—including the maritime concerns that had helped cause the war—remained unresolved, both sides acknowledged that the Treaty of Ghent ended the war without sacrificing honor, territory, or rights. News of the treaty, signed on December 24, 1814, did not reach America until several weeks later, and the war did not end until mid-February 1815.

WAR IN THE SOUTHWEST

Never a major theater of operations, the Gulf of Mexico assumed a new and more important character in 1813. In April General James Wilkinson had led a joint army-navy attack against Spanish Fort Charlotte in Mobile, even though the two countries were not officially at war. Spanish forces surrendered and retreated to Pensacola, and the Americans deprived the British of a potential base for a Gulf campaign. Later that summer, the Anglo-American

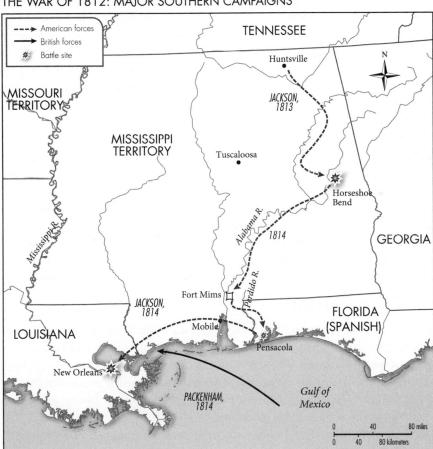

THE WAR OF 1812: MAJOR SOUTHERN CAMPAIGNS

MAP 5.6 The War of 1812: Major Southern Campaigns

war along the Gulf merged with a Native American civil war between pro-American National Creek Indians and pro-British Red Stick Creeks. In August 1813 Red Sticks massacred 250 American and Indian allies at the isolated Fort Mims, bringing intense war to the Gulf.

During the summer of 1814, as Admiral Cochrane planned a southern campaign, he learned the Creek Indians were fighting a civil war and that General Andrew Jackson had marched Tennessee militiamen into Creek country, inflicting a devastating defeat on the pro-British Red Sticks on March 27, 1814, at the Battle of Horseshoe Bend. Cochrane did not know that the other major southern tribes—the Cherokees and Choctaws—had also sided with the Americans.

With little information about the Creek War, Cochrane sent agents to the Gulf during the spring of 1814 with arms and supplies for Britain's black and Indian allies, establishing a base on the Apalachicola River for training and supplying Indians and runaway slaves. By mid-August 1814 British forces had taken Spanish Pensacola and were poised for a campaign against New Orleans. In early September 1814 Cochrane sent army and naval forces to attack the earthen and timber Fort Bowyer, which commanded the entrance to Mobile Bay. During the attack American artillery luckily sunk a British frigate, while the land attack against Bowyer failed, forcing Cochrane to alter his plans. Then Jackson, wanting to deny the British bases along the Gulf Coast, attacked Pensacola on November 7, 1814, with 4,000 men. When Jackson's soldiers descended on the Spanish city, British troops retreated into coastal forts that they quickly evacuated and destroyed. By early December Cochrane had realized that one of his few options was to attack New Orleans via Lake Borgne, proceeding along the Bayou Bienvenue to the Mississippi River—a seventy-mile water supply and communication lane defended only by Lieutenant Thomas ap Catesby Jones and five American gunboats. Overwhelming British numbers easily captured Jones's gunboats in mid-December 1814, resulting in a costly U.S. tactical defeat.

Americans had previously constructed forts and positioned smaller seagoing vessels, as well as stationary, movable, and floating artillery, along the Mississippi River to guard the most obvious avenues of attack. Jackson was unsure whether the British would test the river defenses, march overland and attack the city from the north, or advance across Lake Borgne or Pontchartrain. The British capture of the gunboats alerted Jackson to their direction of attack and gave him time to position additional defenses before Redcoats could reach the city. It took British forces a week to cross Lake Borgne and land on the levee of the Mississippi River. They then launched the two-week land campaign for New Orleans.

CAMPAIGN FOR NEW ORLEANS

Throughout the fall of 1814 Cochrane had continued operations along the Atlantic coast, intensified the blockade of New England, captured ports in Maine, and expanded the war to Georgia and South Carolina. The New Orleans campaign, which would relieve pressure on Canada, represented another way to force Americans to sue for peace. New Orleans also offered an opportunity to secure prize money and to seize territory that might improve Britain's bargaining position in peace negotiations.

During the British campaign—a series of engagements lasting from December 23, 1814, until January 8, 1815—Jackson, who was short of men, weapons, and supplies and facing a potentially disloyal citizenry, cobbled together a multiracial, heterogeneous army consisting of regulars, Spanish and French Louisiana Creoles, Tennessee and Kentucky frontiersmen, Baratarian pirates, free men of color, slaves, and Choctaw Indians. He also secured artillery, flint, and powder from pirate Jean Lafitte's lawless associates.

The 1,800-strong British vanguard arrived on the Mississippi River banks during the morning of December 23. Instead of marching the nine miles directly to the city, the Britons awaited reinforcements. This delay permitted Jackson to launch a nighttime attack against the British camp with French Creole soldiers, regular infantry, and free men of color. Major Jean Plauché ordered his men in French, *"En Main! En Main!"* ("Charge! Charge!"), shocking British soldiers fresh from Europe. After a two-hour hand-to-hand struggle, Jackson withdrew four miles upriver to a defensive position at the Laronde plantation. He had suffered 10 percent casualties, but the battle was arguably the turning point in the New Orleans campaign, because it forced the British to delay, giving Jackson time to strengthen his defenses.

On Christmas Day, British general Edward Michael Pakenham arrived with a force of Napoleonic War veterans. To determine American strength, he ordered a reconnaissance-in-force against the American lines at Chalmette three days later. As British artillery fired on Jackson's defenses and infantry probed the American line for weaknesses, Jackson's defenses held firm. Supported by the sloop *Louisiana* in the river, whose cannon enfiladed British flanks, Jackson's line stifled the attacking columns and then silenced British artillery.

Jackson strengthened his defensive line at Chalmette with eight artillery batteries to protect the earthworks, which stretched some 500 yards from the Mississippi River to an impenetrable cypress swamp in the east. He also sent troops across the river to the west bank with four field artillery pieces. By January 1, 1815, 8,000 additional British troops had arrived on the banks of the Mississippi, where they immediately bombarded the American earthworks. For three hours the two sides exchanged volleys. British cannon disabled three American guns and damaged Jackson's earthworks. Finally, the attack stopped when the British exhausted their ammunition. Unfortunately, Pakenham did not know that the weak east side of Jackson's line near the swamp had collapsed.

Pakenham's plan for the January 8, 1815, assault proved too complicated. He sent 780 soldiers across the river to attack American defenses on the west bank. Once the west bank attack had succeeded, the plans called for the British to turn their guns east and enfilade Jackson's entrenched position at Chalmette. However, because the west bank attack was delayed and then swept downriver by a fast current, by the time British troops captured the Americans' western position, the battle at Chalmette was over.

Too, Pakenham's plans needed tight coordination. As British forces attacked on the west bank, a column of British troops advanced along the river levee against Jackson's right. Another column attacked the American left near the cypress swamp. But nothing went right. The fascines (bundles of sticks bound together to fill in ditches) and ladders needed to get over Jackson's earthen walls went missing. Even so, Pakenham still felt confident, anticipating that the Americans would flee when they saw a disciplined British bayonet assault and that a cold morning fog would obscure British movements until his forces were on Jackson's line. But the element of surprise vanished when Pakenham ordered a single rocket be fired into the air to signal the beginning of the attack—which the Americans saw.

As the rising sun illuminated the battlefield, American defenders saw a sea of Redcoats and silver bayonets. Veteran British troops mounted a frontal assault, in a line-abreast formation, directly into Jackson's defensive entrenchments. American cannon shot seemed to be absorbed into the British ranks. As one soldier or group of soldiers fell, others immediately closed the gap. Dead and wounded British soldiers fell atop one another. At times the British advancing column stopped, reformed, and then lurched forward again.

On the American right British soldiers made their way to Jackson's line but could not breach it. Trying to inspire his troops, Pakenham personally encouraged them to advance toward the rampart, but his soldiers fled instead. At this moment the 93rd Scottish Highlanders, who had been kept in reserve, moved diagonally at a quick pace across the open battlefield from the American right toward the left. The sight of 900 tartan-clad Highlanders crossing the field bolstered British confidence. Then, without explanation, the Highlanders stopped 100 yards from the rampart, permitting American musket and cannon fire to sweep their ranks, killing 600 soldiers and wounding General John Keane. While trying to rally the Highlanders, Pakenham himself was mortally wounded.

The withering flurry of American artillery and rifle fire had produced devastating casualties among the British. Within thirty minutes 291 Redcoats, including Pakenham and General Samuel Gibbs, had been killed; 1,267 men, including Keene, had been wounded; and 484 had been captured or gone missing. The entirety of the British senior field command had fallen. Leaderless British survivors scurried for safety rather than face more murderous fire. In contrast, American casualties were negligible: thirteen dead, thirty-nine wounded, and nineteen missing. Jackson's makeshift defensive line and scraggly, heterogeneous army had easily withstood an arrogant British assault.

Over the following days, Admiral Cochrane tested the strength of the American Fort St. Philip downriver. On January 9, 1815, British ships began a ten-day bombardment of the fort, firing more than 1,000 rounds on the post but only killing two American soldiers. On January 18, 1815, British ships stopped attacking. During the bombardment, British troops had trickled out of their Mississippi River encampment. Seemingly within hours, the entire British army had disappeared, leaving behind wounded soldiers.

By the end of January, the British fleet had anchored off Mobile Bay, ready for the next phase of Cochrane's plan. On the morning of February 8, 1815, 1,400 British troops landed near Fort Bowyer off Mobile. During the next three days they slowly positioned their cannon to attack. American major William L. Lawrence's forces harassed the attackers, but they were overwhelmed by British firepower and could not resist. Before the final assault, Lawrence surrendered on February 11, 1815—two days before news of the Treaty of Ghent reached the Gulf Coast.

New Orleans had been saved by Jackson's dogged defense and British arrogance, while news of peace spared Mobile from attack. American success along the Gulf Coast thereafter would be used to paint the war as an American victory, since the conflict was officially over.

CONCLUSIONS

In 1807 Algiers had resumed its seizure of American ships in the Mediterranean. After the War of 1812, the United States sent a fleet to the region to deal with the trouble. Stephen

Decatur arrived first and turned Algerine tactics against the enemy by taking prisoners and demanding ransom and tribute for their return. By the end of summer 1815 Decatur had forced Algiers, Tunis, and Tripoli to accept peace and pay indemnities. Decatur then departed, leaving behind ships that would form the nucleus of a permanent Mediterranean naval squadron to protect American rights. But soon afterwards, Algiers repudiated the treaty and resumed warfare against commerce. A combined British-Dutch fleet ended the Algerine War in August 1816, breaking the power of the Barbary States once and for all.

During the period from 1781 to 1816 the United States confronted not only the Barbary problem but also tremendous turmoil in the Atlantic World. Intermittent fighting between Britain and France placed the United States and the Barbary States on the periphery, with each trying to maintain an independent course—one through free trade and the other through piracy. Ultimately, agricultural self-sufficiency, free trade, open markets, and the expansion of commerce provided economic freedom for the United States.

This era of seemingly continuous war ravaged every section of the United States and threatened American interests abroad through Barbary attacks in the Mediterranean; the French naval war in the Caribbean; Indian depredations in the Northwest; British raids in Maine, the Chesapeake, and the South Atlantic; and Spanish-encouraged Indian violence along the Gulf South. More than 450,000 militiamen served in the War of 1812, along with thousands of volunteers, some 50,000 regular soldiers, and 20,000 sailors. Of these men, only 2,260 men died and 4,500 were wounded in battle, although as many as 15,000 died from disease and other nonmilitary causes. War costs also totaled $158 million, increasing the national debt to at least $127 million by war's end and causing the country to teeter on the verge of financial collapse. But with peace, a new sense of nationalism quickly swept through the country. During the next century the United States would be consumed with internal developments and territorial expansion, both of which strengthened the nation and its armed forces.

Finally, news of the Battle of New Orleans boosted American morale. It was the country's greatest military accomplishment since George Washington's victory at Yorktown. It also represented the first great American victory, because Jackson's cosmopolitan, polyglot American army had fought together for the United States, preserving its independence. The victory also ushered in important domestic changes, as the South assumed a greater role in the nation's affairs, the power of New England and

TIMELINE

January 1787	Shays' Rebellion
May–September 1787	Constitutional Convention
October 1790–August 1795	Indian Wars in Old Northwest
1794	Whiskey Rebellion
1798–1800	Quasi-War with France
1801–1805	Tripolitan War
November 1811	Battle of Tippecanoe
1812–1815	War of 1812
December 1814–January 1815	New Orleans campaign
1815–1816	Algerine War

Federalism declined, and Andrew Jackson emerged as a national hero. Jacksonian America would embrace a new era of empire during which the nation's ebullient spirit would eventually lead it into its first expansionist war on foreign soil.

SUGGESTED READINGS

Crackel, Theodore. *Mr. Jefferson's Army: Political and Social Reform of the Military Establishment.* New York: New York University Press, 1987.

Cusick, James G. *The Other War of 1812: The Patriot War and the American Invasion of Spanish East Florida.* Gainesville: University Press of Florida, 2003.

DeConde, Alexander. *The Quasi-War: Politics and Diplomacy of the Undeclared War with France, 1797–1801.* New York: Charles Scribner's Sons, 1966.

Dowd, Gregory Evans. *A Spirited Resistance: The North American Indian Struggle for Unity, 1745–1815.* Baltimore: Johns Hopkins University Press, 1991.

Hickey, Donald R. *The War of 1812: A Forgotten Conflict.* Urbana: University of Illinois Press, 1989.

Kohn, Richard H. *Eagle and Sword: The Federalists and the Creation of the Military Establishment in America, 1783–1803.* New York: Free Press, 1975.

Lambert, Frank. *The Barbary Wars: American Independence in the Atlantic World.* New York: Hill and Wang, 2005.

McKee, Christopher. *A Gentlemanly and Honorable Profession: The Creation of the U.S. Naval Officer Corps, 1794–1815.* Annapolis, MD: Naval Institute Press, 1991.

Owsley, Frank L., Jr. *Struggle for the Gulf Borderlands: The Creek War and the Battle of New Orleans, 1812–1815.* Gainesville: University Press of Florida, 1982.

Quimby, Robert S. *The U.S. Army in the War of 1812: An Operational and Command Study.* East Lansing: Michigan State University Press, 1997.

Skeen, C. Edward. *Citizen Soldiers in the War of 1812.* Lexington: University of Kentucky Press, 1999.

Skelton, William B. *An American Profession of Arms: The Army Officer Corps, 1784–1861.* Lawrence: University Press of Kansas, 1992.

Smith, Gene A. *"For the Purposes of Defense": The Politics of the Jeffersonian Gunboat Program.* Newark: University of Delaware Press, 1995.

Symonds, Craig L. *Navalists and Antinavalists: The Naval Policy Debate in the United States, 1785–1827.* Newark: University of Delaware Press, 1980.

Szatmary, David P. *Shays' Rebellion.* Amherst: University of Massachusetts, 1980.

CHAPTER 6

EMPIRE OF EXPANSION

1810–1849

To Conquer Without War: The Gulf South • Reforming the Military • Following the Setting Sun • A Maritime Destiny • Trailing Tears: Indian Removal • Cherokees, Chickasaws, Choctaws, and Creeks • Black Hawk War • Second Seminole War • The Lone Star Republic • The War with Mexico

The ships of the tiny United States Pacific Squadron departed Callao, Peru, on September 7, 1842. Two days out, Commodore Thomas ap Catesby Jones invited the other commanders to his flagship, the frigate *United States*. Upon the arrival of his captain, James Armstrong, Commander Cornelius K. Stribling of the sloop *Cyane*, and Commander Thomas A. Dornin of the sloop *Dale*, Jones asked them: "Is the rumor of war between the United States and Mexico . . . and the cession of the Californias . . . to Great Britain, sufficiently probable to justify the withdrawal . . . of our naval force from the coast of Peru and Chile, to send to California?" Unanimously, they answered yes.

Jones's second question was more ambiguous. "Under what circumstances," he asked, "would it be proper for us to anticipate Great Britain in her contemplated military occupation of California?" After careful deliberation, the officers agreed that should the United States and Mexico enter into war, they should seize and defend every major port in California. They also concurred that should the "views of the late President Monroe, in his celebrated message to Congress, December 2, 1823," a reference to the Monroe Doctrine, still be considered the policy of the country, the United States should occupy California to prevent any other country from doing so.

The Pacific Squadron proceeded to the coast of California, and on October 20, 1842, sailors and marines went ashore in Monterey, seizing the port for the United States. The conquest occurred without a shot being fired, except for the thirty-six-gun salute that accompanied the raising of Old Glory. The following day, however, Jones learned that there were no hostilities between the United States and Mexico. He immediately returned the port to Mexican officials with the same pomp and ceremony that had been seen the previous day.

Although a mistake, Jones's seizure of Monterey set an important precedent for the United States. By basing their decision on the Monroe Doctrine, Jones and his officers indicated they were thinking of national policy rather than limited military tactics. National policy called for the extension of the area of freedom by expansion, a concept inextricably linked to the term "Manifest Destiny," coined by John L. O'Sullivan in the 1840s. Discussion of that process generally centered around not the act of extension itself, but rather the concept of "destiny." By the 1840s the U.S. public had widely accepted the ideas that Providence had destined the United States to continued growth and that expansion was a civilizing process based on moral progress rather than military might. But the "natural right" of expansion unquestionably lay in the power to conquer. What ultimately made expansion not only possible but manifest was not some transcendent destiny, but the absence of powerful neighbors to check such a process. By the 1850s American expansion had consumed Native American lands in the West, Mexican lands in the Southwest, and maroon communities that appeared threatening, creating conditions leading to sectional discord and civil war.

TO CONQUER WITHOUT WAR: THE GULF SOUTH

Presidents Thomas Jefferson, James Madison, and James Monroe all actively supported covert operations and filibustering attempts as means of promoting territorial expansion along the Gulf of Mexico. The beginnings of an independence movement in Mexico in 1810 provided the opportunity for the United States to strengthen its claim on Texas, an area Republicans believed to be part of the Louisiana Purchase. The September 1810 rebellion in Baton Rouge, which created the original "Lone Star" Republic of West Florida coincided with Madison's State Department providing "unofficial" financial and military assistance to Bernardo Gutiérrez de Lara, José Álvarez de Toledo y Dubois, and Augustus William Magee in their attempts to overthrow Spanish rule in Texas. In East Florida in 1812, American "patriots" began a revolution similar to the one in Baton Rouge, with filibusters seizing the settlement of Fernandina on St. Mary's Island. General George Mathews, a special agent under President Madison, subsequently formed the "Republic of Florida," organized a provisional government, and thereafter laid siege to the Spanish fort at St. Augustine. In fact, the Madison administration supported the patriots and provided them with military assistance until their actions threatened a war with Spain. Then the administration disavowed Mathews's activities and withdrew U.S. troops in the spring of 1813, leaving East Florida in Spanish hands. These filibuster attempts illustrated the government's position on local revolutions and the desire to bring like-minded movements into the American Union.

During the War of 1812 the United States strengthened its claim to southern lands by waging wars against Indians to promote expansion. General Andrew Jackson prosecuted a southern war against hostile Creeks and destroyed the Indian buffer zone between the United States and Spain's Florida colonies, opening lands for American settlers. Defeated Indians still hostile to the United States fled to Spanish Florida, where they were joined by runaway slaves. Together these groups threatened peace and stability in the region as they raided southern frontier farms, prompting the U.S. government to take action.

THE GULF COAST, 1816–1818

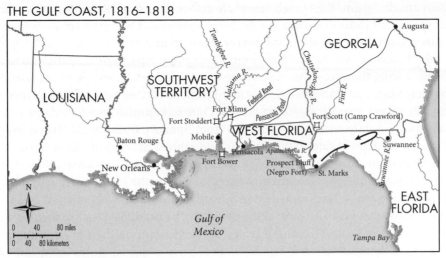

MAP 6.1 The Gulf Coast, 1816–1818

In late July 1816, American army and naval forces eliminated Negro Fort at Prospect Bluff on the Apalachicola River. Abandoned by the British, the heavily defended position had become a refuge for runaway slaves and served as a visible sign of opposition that threatened the southern plantation economy and future American expansion. American gunboats fired artillery on and destroyed the bastion, killing more than 300 African Americans. Although unauthorized by the Madison administration, the attack eliminated the fort and removed the threat.

In 1817 President Monroe provided unofficial support for Scotsman Gregor McGregor and his plan to seize Amelia Island, East Florida, in the mouth of the St. Mary's River as an operational base for Venezuelan revolutionaries. McGregor's revolt succeeded, and soon thereafter the island became a haven for pirates, smugglers, and slave traders. As long as Monroe's government believed the filibusters could take Florida from the Spanish without embroiling the United States in war, the administration waited. When privateer Louis Michel-Aury, acting on behalf of Mexican revolutionaries, seized the island in late September 1817, Monroe saw no advantage in continuing covert operations. Law and order deteriorated on Amelia Island, threatening the stability of the entire region. In late December 1817 Aury surrendered the island to U.S. army and naval forces without bloodshed and departed. The United States had acquired the territory at Spanish expense.

Andrew Jackson's invasion of Florida during the spring of 1818 provided the last impetus for Jeffersonian expansion. The aftermath of the War of 1812 had left Florida in an unsettled state and demonstrated Spain's lack of control over the territory. The Monroe administration authorized Jackson to pursue hostile Indians into Spanish Florida to bring peace to the region. Jackson, broadly interpreting his orders and contrary to instructions sent by one of his subordinates, seized both St. Mark's and Pensacola, Florida, claiming they served as bases for Indian attacks against the United States. He also executed two British subjects whom he claimed sponsored Indian violence. While the general would be criticized for exceeding his orders, his actions proved Spain could not control Florida.

Shortly thereafter, Secretary of State John Quincy Adams pressured Spain into negotiating a treaty. Facing the encroachment of Americans into Florida, revolts in Texas and other parts of New Spain, and uncertainties related to the ill-defined western boundaries of the Louisiana Purchase, Spanish diplomat Luis de Onís relinquished the Florida peninsula to create a firm boundary separating Louisiana from Spanish Texas. In the Transcontinental Treaty (also called the Adams–Onís Treaty), the United States paid $5 million in legal claims by American citizens against Spain and agreed to a precise stair-stepping boundary between American and Spanish lands that extended west to the Pacific coast. Florida became American territory while Texas remained in Spanish hands.

With the acquisition of Florida, the philosophy of Manifest Destiny seemed to have been realized in the South. All the lands east of the Mississippi River, in addition to those obtained through the Louisiana Purchase, had been acquired from European powers without war. Afterward, expansion focused westward, and within thirty years the nation controlled all of the lands between the Atlantic and the Pacific, as Jefferson had prophesied. The War of 1812, the military operation against Negro Fort, and Jackson's invasion of Florida destroyed the threats of southern Indians and free black settlements. With the destruction of America's weaker neighbors, the transcendent ideas represented by Manifest Destiny could flourish.

REFORMING THE MILITARY

In 1812 the United States had been drawn into a war for which it was unprepared, but by the end of that conflict most Americans thought it had been justified. The United States had not been defeated, the country had gained foreign respect, and the republic had survived. The country's administrative structure had faltered under the burden of war, but in the process of repairing it the federal government had become stronger, and the American people had pulled together despite factionalism and sectionalism. Americans had become aware of their differences from Europeans and had developed a separate identity with a selective memory, viewing their recent victories as great and their defeats as insignificant. Meanwhile, the country had adopted new heroes—Andrew Jackson, William Henry Harrison, Oliver Hazard Perry, and Thomas Macdonough—and a new set of nationalist ideals. Since most Americans believed that the country did not need a powerful permanent military force, they expressed themselves through economic policy and culture.

President Madison's December 1815 State of the Union Address suggested several steps the country should take to strengthen itself, and soon thereafter Congress passed legislation promoting (1) national economic self-sufficiency, (2) internal improvements, and (3) a strengthened national defense system. The new wave of economic nationalism sweeping the nation was manifested in the chartering of the Second Bank of the United States, along with the passage of a new protective tariff for manufacturing. Government support for internal improvements—the building of roads and development of water transportation—would facilitate not only the expansion of commerce but also the movement of soldiers across the country. But because of President Madison's constitutional scruples, most internal improvements over the next 100 years would be undertaken by state governments and private enterprise (the federal government didn't assume control over large-scale internal improvement projects until the Federal Highway Act of 1916).

National defense emerged again during the postwar period as a controversial issue, debated by professional military officers who had endured incompetent political appointments, the glacial pace of bureaucratic decision-making, and archaic administrative systems. Politicians highlighted the performance of Harrison's militia in Canada and Jackson's militia at New Orleans to argue that there was little need for a professional peacetime standing army. Leaders like General Winfield Scott used the postwar demobilization of the military to institute reforms and begin reorganizing the army. He based his reforms on Washington's 1783 idea to create a skeletal regimental structure that could be inflated or filled out over time with conscriptions, volunteers, or militiamen. President Madison, Secretary of War Monroe, and senior military leaders proposed a professional army of 20,000 troops, but ultimately Congress reduced the allotment to only 10,000 with the Army Reduction Act of 1815. This parsimonious decision reiterated the message that the militia would still play a major role in national defense. The reorganization permitted the new army to remove most of its generals, as the structure called for two major generals (Jacob Brown in the north and Andrew Jackson in the south) and four brigadier generals (Winfield Scott, Edmund P. Gaines, Alexander Macomb, and Eleazar Ripley). The nine infantry regiments, without cavalry, would be stationed across the frontier to provide protection in a way militia could not.

President Monroe and Secretary of War John C. Calhoun found their system tested almost immediately during the First Seminole War when General Jackson led troops into Spanish Florida, where they lacked food, equipment, and supplies. A breakdown in the supply system demanded another army reorganization. The creation of staff departments in Washington—including the offices of the Adjutant General, Paymaster General, Chief of Ordnance, Quartermaster General, Surgeon General, and Commissary General, with the already existing Corps of Engineers—between 1816 and 1818 addressed shortcomings in the army structure, although it created conflict within the service between line and staff officers. In 1820, when Congress demanded that Calhoun develop a plan to reduce the army to 6,000 men, the secretary of war suggested that the enlisted personnel of each company be cut to half strength, which would preserve the army's structure while allowing it to expand quickly to 19,000 men in case of emergency. This new "expansible army' concept protected the professional officer corps from being disbanded. With this reorganization, Calhoun acknowledged that the professional army and its officer corps, rather than militia, served as the nation's first line of defense.

Calhoun also worked with West Point superintendent Sylvanus Thayer to reform officer education and training. Major Thayer had traveled throughout Europe in 1815 to study European military education. When he returned he organized West Point cadets into tactical units, implemented a strict code of discipline that emphasized honor and integrity, created the Commandant of Cadets, reformed the curriculum, and introduced new models of educational instruction. During Thayer's tenure (1817–1833), these reforms transformed West Point into the premier engineering school in the country, securing for the superintendent the moniker of Father of the U.S. Military Academy. Calhoun's proposal for specialized training also resulted in schools for artillery at Fortress Monroe, Virginia, and for infantry at Jefferson Barracks, Missouri. The formalization of military education provided standardized doctrine and training for the professional army.

The navy's success during the War of 1812 and the Second Barbary War also spurred Congress to embrace legislation to fund construction of capital ships rather than gunboats, which had performed woefully during the War of 1812 and had not proven economical. The April 1816 Act for the Gradual Increase of the Navy authorized nine ships-of-the-line, twelve heavily armed frigates, and three steam batteries and represented the first and largest peacetime naval expansion program to that time. Much like the Humphrey super-frigates built during the 1790s, these new vessels would carry far more guns than their rating called for—the largest ship, the *Pennsylvania*, was rated to carry 80 to 100 guns but actually boasted more than 120. Once the vessels had been completed, most observers assumed that the United States Navy would become a first-rate naval power. Although these vessels never fired a shot during war, Congress by authorizing them had acknowledged the need for a seagoing naval force.

The U.S. Navy has traditionally implemented construction programs that reflect the last war the nation has fought rather than projecting its future needs. The capital ships authorized in 1816 soon became unsuitable for the navy's new mission. During the four decades after the War of 1812 the navy's ships needed to be nimble and quick, and to possess a shallow draft to defend American commerce and shipping from pirates and privateers in the Caribbean and Gulf, protect whalers in the Pacific, and fight the slave trade along the coast of Africa and Brazil. This changing mission made the large two-deck ships obsolete even before they were launched. Moreover, naval technology changed drastically as steam propulsion began replacing sails. In fact, American riverboat entrepreneurs and European navies experimented with both sidewheel and screw propulsion, while naval ordnance moved away from smoothbore cannons. After three centuries, exploding shells replaced solid shot. By the time of the war with Mexico in 1846, the War of 1812–era ships had already become technologically obsolete.

As specialized technology changed, the administration of the navy had to evolve as well. Because the secretary of the navy did not have the specialized training to make informed decisions about naval problems, in February 1815 administration of the navy was turned over to a three-officer Board of Navy Commissioners, who advised the department on all matters of technology, construction, and operation. The system functioned with mixed success until 1842, when it was replaced with the bureau system, which divided administrative responsibility between five organizational units (ordnance and hydrography; yards and docks; construction, equipment, and repair; provisions and clothing; and medicine and surgery). The establishment of the bureau system provided the navy with a professional, self-sustaining institutional structure for the future.

Finally, the war had taught the United States how inadequately it was defended. British naval units had entered most ports and easily raided the coastline. Since the country remained committed to a small navy, it needed a coastal and harbor fortification system to prevent an enemy from landing on American soil. In April 1816 President Madison appointed Napoleon's former top engineer, Simon Bernard, as the chief engineer of the army. Madison also established a board of engineers to study the nation's seaport defenses, which was ironic because Congress only appropriated $800,000 that year to repair decrepit and aging forts. The board's 1821 report recommended that defenses be put in place at fifty sites, stretching from Maine to Florida and across the Gulf Coast to the Mississippi River; eventually, sixty-nine fortifications were put in place or under construction by 1843. These sloping grassy earthworks backed by brick or stone walls and armed with heavy artillery (twenty-four- or thirty-two-pound cannon) embodied the "third fortification" system, which helped mollify Americans' fear of the next war. But much like navy ships, these forts had become obsolete by the time they were finished, and they were never used to protect the nation against a foreign invasion, although many were used well into the twentieth century.

FOLLOWING THE SETTING SUN

During the period after the War of 1812 army-trained engineers explored and surveyed the West, built roads and bridges, and constructed forts and stockades to protect settlers moving to the western frontier. West Point trained officers for both war and exploration, and by the late 1830s the Army Topographical Corps was staffed with Academy-trained officers who had studied a curriculum promoting engineering and expansion. Secretary Calhoun wanted to establish an army outpost on the Yellowstone River in 1818–1819, but distance and a lack of steamboat accessibility scuttled those plans. Instead, a scientific expedition under Colonel Henry Atkinson and the Army Topographical Corp's Major Stephen H. Long spent the winter of 1819–1820 at Council Bluffs before attempting to find the source of the Platte and Missouri rivers. While the expedition failed, Long's detailed report about the "Great Desert" (Great Plains) and its poor prospects for agriculture helped form American opinions about the land and culture of its inhabitants. His efforts also led to the creation of Fort Atkinson, the first U.S. Army post constructed west of the Missouri River. However, the lack of tangible expedition results, the difficulty of supplying far-removed military outposts, and the Panic of 1819 brought a temporary end to postwar military expansion.

Long later explored trade possibilities, examined the military situation, and cataloged scientific specimens during an expedition to the Upper Mississippi River Valley, the Minnesota River, the Red River of the North, and the Canadian borderlands in 1823. The army established Fort Leavenworth in 1827 as the first permanent post on the west side of the Missouri River, and it remains the oldest active army installation outside of Washington, D.C. The fort served as the forward base for surveyors, immigrants, and soldiers protecting and launching future expeditions along the Santa Fe and Oregon trails, including Captain Benjamin Bonneville's 1832–1835 exploration of the West. After temporarily resigning his army command, Bonneville, acting as a fur trader and private citizen, explored the Great Salt Lake and the Great Basin, crossed the Sierras into California, and moved north to the disputed

Oregon country. These rumblings of Manifest Destiny became louder during the early 1840s as thousands of settlers departed Independence, Missouri, on the Oregon Trail for the West along a path that army explorers had carved during the 1820s and 1830s.

A MARITIME DESTINY

The navy played a major role in American expansion during the period after the War of 1812. With its expanded size and new mission, the navy found itself in the vanguard of economic expansion, confronting challenges that larger fleets had traditionally encountered. With the beginning of revolution in Spain's western empire, privateers and pirates increased their activity in the Gulf of Mexico and the Caribbean. In 1818 the United States sent Oliver Hazard Perry to Venezuela, where he successfully urged revolutionaries to exercise more caution when issuing letters of marque. The following year Congress authorized navy ships to convoy commercial vessels and to attack pirates operating in the West Indies. This directive created the West Indies Squadron, which operated in the Caribbean and the Gulf from 1821 until it was combined with the Home Squadron in 1842. Learning that deep-water frigates and ships-of-the-line were not suitable for the shallow waters of the Gulf and Caribbean, the navy sent the schooners *Enterprise, Nonsuch,* and *Lynx* and two Jeffersonian gunboats (*No. 158* and *No. 168*) to the region; initially, each of them sailed individually until Captain James Biddle arrived as commander in late 1819. Operating from bases in Key West, Florida, and the Danish island of St. Thomas, Biddle faced a delicate diplomatic situation because of Spain's jealously guarded territoriality. Nonetheless, his squadron curtailed the activity of pirates and privateers in the Caribbean, captured slave traders and pirate ships off Louisiana and Spanish Texas, forced Louis Aury to abandon Amelia Island off the Georgia–Spanish Florida coast, and later drove Jean Lafitte's operations out of business on Galveston Island.

In February 1823 Captain David Porter replaced Biddle as commander of the squadron and immediately initiated changes. With great energy, he replaced all the deep-draught ships with smaller schooners and a Hudson River paddlewheel ferry renamed *Sea Gull*, the U.S. Navy's first steam warship to undertake missions. During Porter's first two years of command, this reengaged squadron captured seventy-nine vessels, greatly curtailing the activities of pirates and privateers. In late October 1824 a group of pirates sacked a warehouse on St. Thomas, reportedly taking $5,000 in loot to Fajardo on the island of Puerto Rico. Lieutenant Charles Platt learned of the theft and landed in Fajardo dressed as a civilian to investigate. Spanish officials captured him and accused him of being a spy, detaining him for hours. When Porter later discovered the affront, he led three ships to Fajardo, launched an armed landing party, threatened to destroy the town, and demanded an apology. Porter's aggressive action forced the Spanish to acknowledge their corruption, but it also led him to be tried by a naval court-martial, which found him guilty of exceeding his orders. Sentenced to a six-month suspension of duty, Porter instead resigned to become the commander-in-chief of the newly established Mexican navy.

In addition to the West Indies Squadron, the navy created five other distant stations, or squadrons, to protect American commercial interests abroad. While in these remote locations, naval officers often found themselves serving as the country's frontline diplomatic representatives. The Mediterranean Squadron, founded in 1815, was created in response to the reemergence of North African pirates, but the forceful suppression of the pirates in 1815–1816 limited the squadron's missions in the region to showing the flag. After Congress declared the international slave trade to be illegal and authorized the navy to interdict it, the navy created the African Squadron in 1821 to operate off the Guinea coast of equatorial West Africa. For two decades British and American naval vessels operated independent slave patrols because of the tensions involved in seizing ships flying the other's flag, which provided a boon to smugglers willing to switch flags at a moment's notice. The Webster-Ashburton Treaty of 1842 settled these outstanding difficulties, and the two countries carried out joint cruising operations to halt slave traders until the outbreak of the Civil War. By 1821 pleas from American merchants and whalers demanding protection also resulted in the Navy Department creating the Pacific Squadron, which cruised from the tip of South America to the coast of present-day California, including occasional voyages west to the Hawaiian Islands. With the Mexican War and the acquisition of California the squadron assumed a more active and important role, eventually dividing into the North and South Pacific Squadrons; the division revealed the growing importance of the Pacific and the emergence of a two-ocean navy. The final two squadrons, the Brazil Squadron, established in 1826, and the East India Squadron, established in 1835, both protected American trade in distant locations and showed the flag when necessary to protect American interests. These six stations spanned the globe, confirming by the mid-1830s that American seapower and naval philosophy embodied a broad maritime Manifest Destiny.

With stagnation within the naval officer corps, many aspiring young officers pursued scientific exploration as a way to gain promotion. Since the general public embraced the very popular concept of scientific inquiry as a tool to benefit society, Congress appropriated $300,000 for an expedition to explore the southern polar ice shelf and map the islands of the South Pacific. Despite the substantial sum of money, plans dragged, and officers declined the command. Finally junior Lieutenant Charles Wilkes accepted the command and for four years (August 1838–July 1842) the Great U.S. Exploring Expedition sailed more than 85,000 miles, charted 280 islands and 1,500 miles of the coast of Antarctica, and gathered a vast array of scientific specimens that ultimately became the core of the Smithsonian Collection. Subsequent naval expeditions explored the Dead Sea in 1848, conducted astronomical calculations in Chile (1849–1852), charted the Amazon Valley in 1851, and surveyed and explored the North Pacific and the rivers in southern South America in 1853 as well as the Panama area the following year. Perhaps the most important of these expeditions was Matthew Calbraith Perry's mission to Japan (1852–1854), which opened the island to American trade and made arrangements for stranded American sailors. This scientific-diplomatic-commercial mission embodied precisely the type of expedition the mid-nineteenth-century navy undertook, because it was "scientific" in nature but also aimed to survey the economic potential of the region, establish diplomatic relations, and note Japan's military disposition—an enterprise in the spirit of the United States' maritime Manifest Destiny.

THE UNITED STATES EXPLORING EXPEDITION, 1838–1842

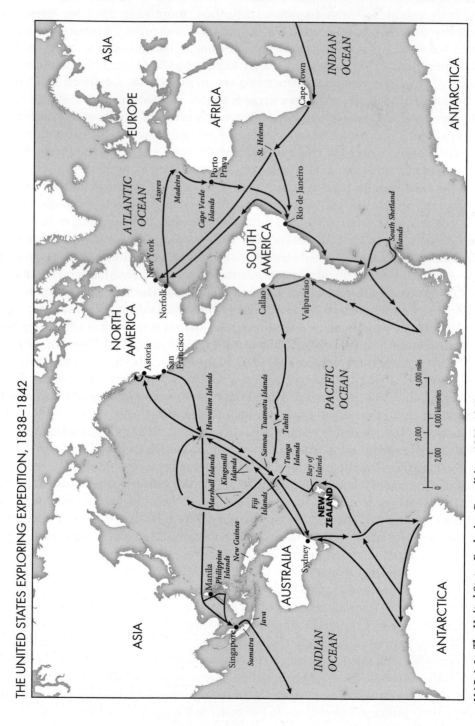

MAP 6.2 The United States Exploring Expedition, 1838–1842

TRAILING TEARS: INDIAN REMOVAL

Native Americans had presented a problem for the country since the colonial era, and continued westward expansion brought them into another contest that would end poorly for the tribes. Tense post War of 1812 relations forced the federal government to appoint Indian agents to maintain order along the frontier, resolve conflicts between settlers and Indians, and determine when violations of the law occurred. Agents also had responsibility for enforcing obligatory treaties, which proved difficult because of Indian discontent and white attempts to defraud the tribes. In remote areas, army officers often assumed the role of agent and used the military to carry out their responsibilities. Moreover, Indian agents often operated out of army posts, which made appointments appear to be part of the defense structure.

Army officers generally viewed Indians with contempt rather than as "noble savages." Shaped by their wartime experiences with Indians, they often described the natives in the most unflattering terms—as butchers or as indolent or uncivilized peoples. Some of these officers wanted to exterminate the Indians or at least remove them from the path of civilization. Many even believed that Indians were inferior because of their environment and stage of development. In this view, the most advanced, such as the Cherokees and other southeastern tribes, were an exception to the rule because they had adopted white culture and a settled agrarian way of life, and had tried to assimilate. Regardless, civilians wanted them removed as quickly as possible, and army officers had to protect Indians from aggressive settlers, greedy merchants, and others trying to take advantage of them. Unfortunately, the army never had enough frontier troops to do so.

Soldiers often found themselves on the wrong side when trying to protect Indians. Local laws and unscrupulous businessmen and traders tried to manipulate and drive Indians into debt so they would be forced to relinquish their lands. In 1824 Secretary of War Calhoun proposed a plan for Indian removal, and in January 1825 President Monroe created the Arkansas and Indian territories, in which eastern Indians could obtain land by agreeing to voluntarily swap their eastern territory. President John Quincy Adams was committed to nonforceful removal of the eastern Indians, but the state of Georgia wanted the Cherokees and Creeks removed immediately, and with force if necessary. The Cherokees insisted that their treaty with the United States recognized them as a separate and independent entity not subject to the laws or control of any state or nation; consequently, they declared that they planned to stay on their treaty lands.

CHEROKEES, CHICKASAWS, CHOCTAWS, AND CREEKS

President Andrew Jackson's inauguration in 1829 coincided with the discovery of gold in the mountains of northeast Georgia, and both events damaged the Cherokees' prospects. Jackson believed the Indians to be barbarians and thought that the only humane policy was to remove them to lands west of the Mississippi River. By 1830 Jackson had convinced Congress to pass the Indian Removal Act, which authorized the president to give Indians federal lands west of the Mississippi in exchange for voluntarily surrendered southern and eastern lands. At the same time, prospectors swept into north Georgia with the discovery of gold, staking claim to Cherokee lands. Playing the white man's litigious game, the Cherokees petitioned the Supreme Court to protect their lands, and in 1831 Chief Justice John Marshall ruled that the Cherokees embodied a "domestic dependent nation" with an unquestionable right to their lands. The state of Georgia, unhappy with the removal delay, passed an 1830 law requiring whites in Cherokee territory to obtain licenses to live in the area and to take an oath of allegiance to the state of Georgia. Two New England missionaries refused to do so and were convicted by Georgia and imprisoned; their appeal reached the Supreme Court, and in 1832 Chief Justice Marshall ruled once again that the Cherokees were a "distinct political community" over which Georgia law had no force. Jackson refused to uphold the Court's ruling, instead claiming he could not interfere in Georgia. Finally, some Cherokees felt they had no choice but to give up their land, which they did in 1835.

The army was the only governmental instrument big enough to carry out Indian removals. Believing careful organization would eliminate violence, protect the tribes, and move them efficiently, the army's commissary general of subsistence along with civilian superintendents supervised the wave of Indian removals, beginning with the Choctaws in 1830. The army established patrols along the removal route, repaired forts, and escorted the 13,000 Choctaws to the Arkansas Territory by 1838. The Creeks peacefully resisted removal, but by 1834 squatters and an aggressive Alabama state government had pressured them to move. Federal agents did little to protect the Creeks from fraudulent land speculators, who cheated them out of their land parcels. Then Georgia militiamen attacked Creek refugee camps, forcing warrior parties to raid white farms for sustenance. The violence produced the Creek War of 1836, in which General Thomas S. Jesup moved quickly against 400 recalcitrant Creek warriors and their leaders. General Winfield Scott directed troops to round up those Creeks who escaped Jesup's offensive. Within a few weeks most of the Creeks had been subdued, and the removal of 16,500 Creek men, women, and children began in July, with chiefs and warriors being transported in chains. The subsequent Chickasaw evacuation occurred without incident in 1837.

Cherokee removal proved problematic. The tribe had peacefully resisted, and the Supreme Court had ruled in its favor, but the executive branch nevertheless demanded the people's relocation. Tennessee, Georgia, and North Carolina militia, combined with the army, forced Cherokees from their homes and placed 17,000 in crude stockades that resembled concentration camps; 4,000 refugees died while there. Then army supply officers escorted the survivors along the 800-mile trail west—a path that became known as the "Trail of Tears." Along the way greedy civilians gouged Cherokees and army personnel alike, inflating prices for everything. The refugees suffered from exposure, disease, and starvation, as well as assault, robbery, and even rape. The 8,000 survivors who completed the forced march initially settled near Tahlequah, Oklahoma, and over time rebounded as a society. A very few Cherokees evaded federal forces, remaining in the eastern mountains and securing title to federal lands there. The episode unquestionably left a dark imprint on the U.S. government.

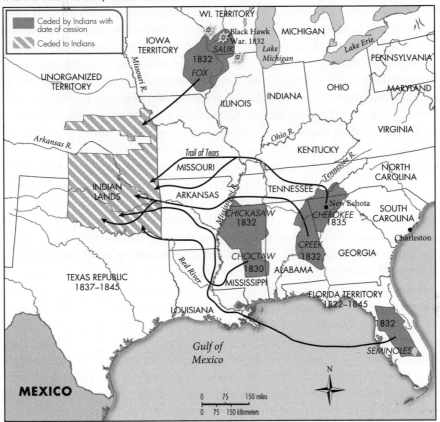

MAP 6.3 Indian Removal, 1820–1840

BLACK HAWK WAR

Indians were also forced to move out of the Old Northwest. In early April 1832 Sauk chief Black Hawk led a group of Sauks, Kickapoos, and Meskwakis—collectively known as the British Band—across the Mississippi River. Unhappy with a fraudulent 1804 treaty in which the Sauks had been cheated out of their Illinois lands, Black Hawk reportedly planned to reoccupy the territory that his tribe had lost. While he was accompanied by 500 armed warriors, he also brought an estimated 600 women and children with him, obviously signaling that his group was not a war party. The conflict that would subsequently emerge stemmed from intertribal violence that had been smoldering for decades, the disappearance of hunting lands, and a changing federal policy that emphasized moving Indians west of the Mississippi River, with force if necessary.

In April 1832 General Henry Atkinson departed St. Louis aboard a steamboat with 220 regulars just as Black Hawk's band crossed into Illinois. When Atkinson arrived at Fort Armstrong on Rock Island, he discovered Black Hawk's group was nearby and that most of the

Meskwakis he wanted to arrest were also present. Calling for volunteers, Atkinson assembled 2,100 troops, including twenty-three-year-old militia captain Abraham Lincoln.

War could have been avoided had the U.S. government not replaced experienced Indian agents who had good relationships with the tribes. Atkinson tried to negotiate with the British Band rather than take forceful decisive action, refusing to move until all risk had been eliminated. Black Hawk also hoped that other tribes, such as the Potawatomis and the Ho-Chunks, would support his cause, but he soon learned that they would not, and that he would not receive supplies from British Canada. Without support, Black Hawk acknowledged that he needed to negotiate to end the crisis. Yet an encounter with Illinois militia volunteers destroyed all hopes for peace.

On May 14, 1832, some 260 citizen-soldiers encountered part of Black Hawk's band near present-day Stillman Valley, Illinois. Although confusion remains as to how the battle began, a large militia force attacked forty warriors at dawn. The Battle of Stillman's Run apparently convinced Black Hawk of the need to avenge the reported attack on his warriors, who had been traveling under a flag of truce. President Jackson and Secretary of War Lewis Cass also refused to consider any diplomatic solution, wanting instead to make an example of Black Hawk to deter all other tribes considering similar action.

As Atkinson recruited additional volunteer militiamen and native allies, including Menominees, Dakotas, and some Ho-Chunks, Black Hawk began raiding settlements farther west in the hopes of drawing the Americans away from his encampments. In mid-June his band attacked near present-day South Wayne, Wisconsin, killing and scalping four whites. Militia colonel Henry Dodge pursued the attackers, cornering a small group in a bend of the Pecatonica River; in their first victory of the war, the Americans killed and scalped eleven Indians. During the remainder of June, Black Hawk attacked Apple River Fort and Kellogg's Grove twice, with the last attack on June 25 representing his final victory of the struggle.

Running low on food and supplies, Black Hawk decided to take his people west across the Mississippi River. President Jackson sent Winfield Scott to replace Atkinson, but he arrived too late to see combat in the last campaign. Illinois militia caught up with Black Hawk's greatly reduced band on July 21 near present-day Sauk City, Wisconsin. By attacking the militia in the Battle of Wisconsin Heights so that his women and children could cross the Wisconsin River, Black Hawk managed to hold off a much larger force but lost a substantial number of warriors. He believed that since he was crossing back into Indian Territory the fighting would stop. Instead, a steamboat armed with artillery arrived on August 2, and the vessel, along with the army, militia, and allied Indians, all fired on the defenseless British Band as it tried to cross the Mississippi River, butchering some 260 Indians in what came to be called the Battle of Bad Axe. On August 9 a band of Dakotas attacked the survivors of the British Band on the west side of the river, killing another sixty-eight. Ho-Chunks eventually hunted down the last survivors, taking between fifty and sixty scalps. Finally, on August 27, Black Hawk and nineteen other leaders surrendered; eventually they would be imprisoned at Fortress Monroe, Virginia.

Overall, some seventy-seven white settlers, militiamen, and soldiers were killed during the war, not including those who died from a cholera epidemic that Scott's soldiers had brought from the East. At least 600 of the British Band perished during the fighting.

IMAGE 6.1 Battle of Bad Axe River   This painting depicts the defeat of Black Hawk's Sac and Fox followers on August 2, 1832, at the Battle of Bad Axe River. By the end of August the war was over, ending armed Indian resistance in the Old Northwest Territory that had begun during the seventeenth century. The tribes were forced to sign treaties that dispossessed them of their lands and relocated them west.

The Black Hawk War concluded armed Indian resistance in the Old Northwest Territory, which had begun during the seventeenth century. Afterwards, government officials negotiated treaties to dispossess other tribes of their lands and relocate them west. Even tribes that had helped defeat Black Hawk eventually had to relocate. Drawing one final lesson from the struggle, the U.S. Army acknowledged that when fighting a mobile enemy such as Indians, cavalry were essential.

SECOND SEMINOLE WAR

The federal government's attempt to force the Seminoles to move west produced the Second Seminole War (1835–1842). Florida entered the Union as a territory in 1821, and almost instantly territorial officials acknowledged a problem with the estimated 22,000 Seminoles who lived there. This diverse group primarily occupied areas around the Apalachicola River, along the Suwannee River, and in the interior Alachua Prairie stretching south and westward to Tampa Bay. As white settlers moved into the area, relations between the United States and the tribe grew strained. In September 1823 Seminole and territorial officials signed the Treaty of Fort Moultrie, which created an interior reservation running from the Ocala area south to a line even with the southern end of Tampa Bay; some Seminole chiefs were also permitted to remain in the area of the Apalachicola River. The tribe's movement onto the reservation occurred slowly and with controversy, as Indians felt they were being cheated and forced onto substandard lands. The government insisted on the relocation and established Fort Brooke at Tampa Bay in 1824 and Fort King at Ocala in 1827.

Seminole chiefs vehemently opposed the claim that they had to relocate and later argued that they had been forced to sign the Treaty of Payne's Landing in 1833, which gave them three years to move west of the Mississippi. The federal government interpreted the treaty clock to have started in 1832, when Seminole chiefs first visited western lands to determine their suitability. The Seminoles interpreted the clock as having begun with the signing of the treaty in 1833. With its timeline calling for a move deadline of 1835, the federal government exerted pressure on the tribe, and Seminole agent Wiley Thompson demanded the Seminoles abide by the schedule. Eight Seminole chiefs finally agreed after being coerced by troops from Forts King and Brooke, but five prominent chiefs refused, with violence beginning in 1835.

Seminoles raided white plantations in autumn 1835, claiming that they needed food for the winter. In late December, the army sent Major Francis L. Dade with 110 soldiers from Fort Brooke to resupply and reinforce Fort King. Dade anticipated that Seminoles shadowing his movements would attack, but he thought the assault would occur at a river crossing or in thick forests. Once he passed these threatening areas, Dade recalled his scouts. Waiting for Chief Osceola to join them, 180 Seminoles attacked on December 28 when the soldiers were about twenty-five miles from Fort King, just south of present-day Bushnell, Florida. Crouching in the tall grasses, Seminoles watched as the soldiers pressed though an area thick with palmetto, palm, and oak trees. Then Chief Micanopy fired a shot that instantly killed Major Dade, knocking him from his horse. All of a sudden musket fire pelted the soldiers from the dense undergrowth, reportedly killing half their number. The survivors discarded

THE SEMINOLE WARS, 1817–1858

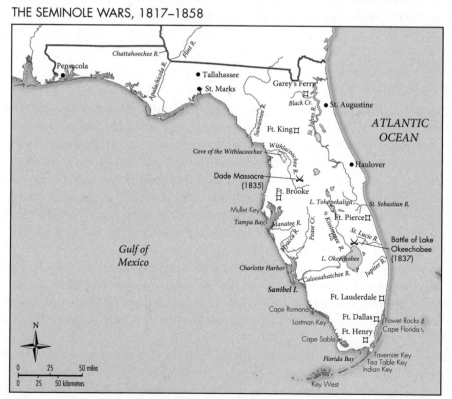

MAP 6.4   The Seminole Wars, 1817–1858

their heavy woolen coats and tried to scurry to cover. During the next four hours the Indians slowly picked off every survivor except for two soldiers and a black interpreter, who finally made their way back to Fort Brooke.

The massacre of Dade and his troops emboldened the Seminoles, who raided almost every Florida settlement, attacked army posts, and even burned the Cape Florida lighthouse. Osceola had not participated in Dade's massacre because on that same day—December 28— he had been occupied by an ambush of Seminole agent Wiley Thompson outside Fort King. Three days later Osceola ambushed 750 Florida militiamen, regulars, and volunteers as they crossed the rain-swollen Withlacoochee River in Citrus County. Without a boat or bridge, only a few troops could cross at a time. When a third of the force had crossed the river, the Indians attacked. The regulars who had already crossed prevented the Indians from driving them back into the river. By sunset the Indians had retreated back into the overgrowth.

Throughout the spring and summer of 1836, the Seminoles expanded their swath of destruction. Generals Duncan Clinch, Edmund Pendleton Gaines, and Winfield Scott initially led troops in pursuit of Seminole raiding parties. The War Department transferred Gaines to the Louisiana–Texas boundary, while Scott assembled troops and supplies at Fort Brooke. However, because of the remote location, Scott could not secure the materials he needed until April, and by this time the Seminoles had melted into the swamps. Hot, humid weather sapped the strength of the short-term enlistees, who returned home as soon as they could. Logistical problems also plagued Scott's efforts: although the army had adequately stocked depots, it was almost impossible to transport goods over the rough and watery terrain. Finally, the navy's West Indies Squadron, which had been instructed to assist in the removal of the Seminoles to the West, stepped in to offer assistance, assuming a combat and transportation role in the watery Everglades.

Operating near St. Augustine, Scott criticized Floridians' commitment to the struggle, calling them cowards. He also lamented the poor performance of local militiamen and volunteers. When the War Department sent him to suppress Indian violence in Alabama during the late spring of 1836, Floridians cheered. That fall General Thomas S. Jesup assumed command of Florida operations and changed the U.S. strategy. Instead of sending out large contingents of troops on mission, he tried drawing the Seminoles in. That failing, he assembled more than 9,000 regulars, volunteers, and militiamen, including a brigade of marines and navy and Revenue Service personnel who patrolled the coast and inland rivers and streams. Jesup successfully drove a wedge between the Seminoles and their escaped slave allies, promising freedom to the latter if they agreed to move west. He also lured Osceola into a conference in October 1837 under a flag of truce, only to take him captive—a move for which he received much criticism. Osceola died three months later in confinement.

Jesup sent multiple columns south from St. Augustine to apprehend and defeat the Seminoles. On Christmas Day, Colonel Zachary Taylor's 1,000-man force encountered 400 Seminole warriors on the north shore of Lake Okeechobee. The Seminoles had chosen an ideal position in a hammock (clump of trees) surrounded by five-foot-tall sawgrass and with a half mile of swamp between their position and that of the soldiers. Indian scouts perched in the trees relayed information about troop movements. Taylor decided to advance straight into the Seminole defenses, with his men wading through the swamp and sawgrass.

As they came into range, the Seminoles leveled a devastating barrage of fire. Taylor's volunteers initially retreated but were reformed and sent ahead once again, and after several hours, they forced the Seminoles to retreat. Taylor had had 26 men killed and 114 wounded, but he could claim victory in the Battle of Okeechobee—one of the largest and hardest-fought battles of the Second Seminole War.

Taylor succeeded Jesup as commander in Florida in May 1838. With a reduced army, Taylor's policy was to keep the Seminoles out of northern Florida. He constructed small posts at twenty-mile intervals across the peninsula connected by a grid of roads. This building program coincided with a lull in the war, prompting many in Washington to think the conflict was too costly and that the Seminoles should be permitted to remain in Florida. Finally the War Department sent General Alexander Macomb to negotiate a peace treaty, which was signed on May 19, 1839.

The peace agreement seemed stable until late July, when a Seminole faction attacked a trading post on the Caloosahatchee River, killing soldiers and civilians. Seminole chief Sam Jones, who had signed the treaty with Macomb, promised to relinquish those responsible for the attack but then did not, forcing the army to take action. While Taylor's system of forts kept the Seminoles out of northern Florida, he continually deployed small patrols and even purchased a pack of bloodhounds to track Indians. This harsh, unusual practice received unfavorable press coverage in Washington that forced the army to halt its usage before it paid dividends. Politicians instead demanded negotiations.

General Walker K. Armistead, who replaced Taylor in the summer of 1839, focused on negotiations, but they also failed. By the spring of 1841, Colonel William J. Worth had replaced Armistead, bringing with him an aggressive policy of warfare combined with continual appeals for the Seminoles to surrender. While most commanders suspended operations during the summer, when dysentery was prevalent, Worth actively campaigned during these months. He prevented Seminoles from planting, tending, and harvesting crops; destroyed food supplies and villages; and drove the Indians into swamps, where he used the navy's mosquito boats and dugout canoes to harass them further. The navy penetrated every river and creek and even entered the Everglades, keeping the Seminoles constantly on the run. By the end of the summer of 1841 many Seminoles had willingly surrendered and accepted removal rather than face starvation.

Worth's war of exhaustion succeeded. In early 1842 he secured permission to leave the remaining Seminoles on an informal reservation in southwestern Florida and to end the war, which he did on August 14, 1842. Those Seminoles outside the reservation were rounded up and sent west by the end of the year—only some 300 Seminoles remained on the reservation, and Worth claimed they did not pose a threat to white settlements. From December 1855 to May 1858, however, the remaining Seminoles again raided white settlements, and the army and state militia retaliated by burning and destroying their villages and crops. When the Third Seminole War ended in the spring of 1858, the army moved all but 100 Seminoles to the West; those who remained moved deeper into the Everglades to locations unwanted even by whites.

The Second Seminole War had lasted from 1835 to 1842, making it one of the longest Indian wars in American history. The guerrilla conflict (a form of irregular warfare in which small groups of combatants use tactics including ambushes, sabotage, and raids to fight a larger and less mobile traditional military) greatly strained the U.S. Army. Some 10,000 regulars and 30,000 volunteers fought in the struggle, which cost an estimated $40 million. Almost 1,600 soldiers died during the conflict, mostly from disease, but the army gained valuable experience in fighting an enemy and organizing for war. It also developed specialized equipment for the struggle and a corps of mechanics and laborers to keep it in operating condition. Moving away from unreliable private contractors, the army purchased steamboats and developed flat-bottomed bateaux for use in navigating shallow rivers, creeks, and swamps. The new equipment and lessons proved useful as the army mobilized for a struggle against Mexico.

THE LONE STAR REPUBLIC

Monroe's secretary of state, John Quincy Adams, negotiated the Adams–Onís Treaty on February 22, 1819, giving the United States the Florida peninsula and establishing a western boundary. Beginning in the summer of 1819 James Long made the last American effort to capture Texas, with the largest and best-equipped force to invade Texas since the Magee–Gutiérrez expedition of 1812. Long's expedition lasted in an irregular off-and-on fashion until the fall of 1821, when he finally surrendered and was taken to Mexico City, where a soldier supposedly accidently shot and killed him. Long's failure can be attributed to a changing U.S. policy under which government officials and the army prevented him from receiving supplies and reinforcements. This was the first time the U.S. Army had stopped an effort to seize Texas, and these actions demonstrated the army's growing constabulary duty in the borderlands, an indication of its changing mission in the region. Long's death also marked the end of early filibustering into Texas.

When Mexico secured its independence from Spain in 1821, Texas fell under Mexican control. With independence, Mexico attempted to attract foreign settlers to its vulnerable northern provinces. By 1821 some 200 Americans had settled on the Brazos River; by 1824 that number had grown to 2,000 Anglos in Texas, and by 1830 20,000 Americans had crossed into the territory. Within a decade the trickle-turned-flood threatened Mexican control, so beginning in 1830 the Mexican government issued proclamations to prevent American immigration. Nevertheless, by 1835 there were 30,000 Anglos in the province.

Friction in Texas began in 1832 when Americans demanded they be allowed to separate and form a state apart from the Mexican state of Coahuila. These settlers sent Stephen F. Austin to Mexico City to present their request to General Antonio López de Santa Anna, who had seized control of the Mexican government, abolished the federal system, and made himself dictator. Santa Anna had Austin imprisoned, and when Texans protested, he dispatched an army north to quell the unrest. In response Texans met in convention at Washington-on-the-Brazos and adopted the Declaration of Causes for taking up arms, pledging to uphold the Mexican Constitution of 1824. As Santa Anna's 4,000 soldiers advanced to Béxar (present-day San Antonio), Texans declared their independence on March 2, 1836.

Raiding bands of Comanche Indians and inclement weather—cold, snow, and heavy rains—delayed the progress of the Mexican army, which was unaccustomed to harsh winter

THE TEXAS REVOLUTION

MAP 6.5 The Texas Revolution

conditions. When Santa Anna reached Saltillo, he sent General José de Urrea with 550 soldiers to Goliad while he advanced on Béxar. Sam Houston, who had been appointed commander of the Texan army, had sent James Bowie to Béxar to remove cannon from the former mission known as the Alamo so they would not be captured by the Mexicans. Upon arriving, Bowie reported that Béxar had to be held because it was the only stronghold west of the Sabine River. In February William B. Travis arrived at the post with thirty cavalrymen, as did famed frontiersman and ex-congressman Davy Crockett and a small group of Tennessee volunteers, giving the Alamo approximately 187 defenders. In late February Mexican troops poured into Béxar, and during the next two weeks their numbers swelled to more than 4,000 soldiers. These troops fired artillery in an attempt to weaken the Texans' defenses and morale. Finally, on the morning of March 6, Santa Anna ordered an all-out assault on the former mission in order to send a strong message to other rebels in Texas. Storming the

Alamo, Mexican soldiers overwhelmed the defenders, and within an hour it had fallen. The attackers spared women and children but slaughtered almost every Texan combatant and captured a handful of survivors, whom they later executed. Though the Mexicans had won this insignificant tactical engagement, they suffered heavy casualties, including many officers. More importantly, Texans and Americans would "Remember the Alamo!"

Three weeks later, on Palm Sunday, March 27, Mexican general Urrea executed 342 captured Texans at Goliad and then moved to join with Santa Anna. Houston's ragtag volunteers at Gonzales, numbering fewer than 400 men, began retreating east toward Louisiana in a flight known as the Runaway Scrape. With Mexican forces in close pursuit, Houston's evacuation gathered an increasing number of women and children, who burned all that they could not eat or take, leaving Mexican troops without supplies. Meanwhile, Mexican colonel Juan Almonte pursued Texas president David Burnett and other officials south to the coast, where they escaped via boat to Galveston Island just before being captured. With the Texas Revolution teetering on the verge of collapse, Houston's troops captured a Mexican courier on April 18 carrying intelligence indicating that Santa Anna and a small contingent of soldiers planned to arrive soon at San Jacinto (near present-day Houston).

By mid-morning April 20, Houston had assembled 900 men at San Jacinto. Santa Anna's 700 Mexican soldiers arrived a few hours later, encamping on a plain bordered by woods on one side and a marsh and a lake on the other. During the late afternoon the two sides skirmished as the Texans tried to determine the true Mexican strength. Instead, the engagements convinced the Mexicans to strengthen their makeshift breastworks during the night using brush, saddles, and anything else they could find. At 9 o'clock the next morning, General Martín Perfecto de Cos arrived with 540 inexperienced reinforcements, who bolstered the Mexican army to about 1,200 men. During the early afternoon Santa Anna permitted his men to rest, eat, and bathe. Meanwhile Houston's men, having crawled through high grass and pulled their single cannon into fighting position, fired their first round at 4:30 in the afternoon, starting the Battle of San Jacinto.

After the first volley, the Texans broke ranks and charged the Mexican position, yelling, "Remember the Alamo! Remember Goliad!" They soon swept through the crude breastworks and engaged the Mexicans in fierce hand-to-hand combat. Mexican officers tried to rally their surprised troops and restore order, but chaos prevailed. Within eighteen minutes most Mexican soldiers had fled the field. For the next several hours the Texans pursued and killed stragglers—650 in total—and captured 300 Mexicans. During the battle only eleven Texans died, and thirty others suffered wounds. The following day Texan scouts captured a disguised Santa Anna and took him to meet the wounded Sam Houston. Santa Anna agreed to surrender and give the Republic of Texas its independence, setting the Rio Grande as its southern boundary, even though the Mexican Congress later repudiated the treaty. Through warfare the Lone Star Republic had been born.

The Republic of Texas and Mexico did not agree to an armistice until June 1843. Nonetheless Americans had rallied to the Texas cause. After the revolution, Texans anticipated a quick annexation into the United States and voted to accept entrance into the Union. But because of growing antislavery agitation in Congress President Andrew Jackson did not even recognize the Republic until his last day in office in March 1837. His successor, Martin Van

Buren, shied away from the question during his presidency, and Texas began pursuing an empire that would stretch to the Pacific and rival the United States, a policy possible because of trade relations with Britain and France and the availability of cheap Texas cotton. The Texas question remained controversial until the Republic joined the Union in December 1845, culminating a struggle to fulfill the United States' Manifest Destiny.

THE WAR WITH MEXICO

By the early 1840s the United States and Mexico were moving toward conflict. The American wave of immigration had pushed westward toward the Pacific Ocean, with settlers finding their way to the Oregon country, which was then also claimed by Great Britain. A scant few turned south to the paradise of Mexican California. Others crossed Louisiana's western border into the Republic of Texas, which many anticipated would soon join the Union. During the election of 1844 Democratic candidate James Knox Polk of Tennessee pledged himself to settling the Oregon boundary dispute and annexing Texas, and he privately acknowledged his desire to acquire California. Polk's presidential victory seemed to validate the American expansionist agenda.

President Polk had blustered during the campaign that the United States should take all of Oregon—"Fifty-four Forty or Fight," a slogan that referred to the territory's northernmost latitude. During his inaugural address he publicly announced that the American claim to Oregon was unquestionable. As president, Polk's saber rattling had diplomatic and military consequences. When he told Great Britain that the United States was abandoning previous offers to settle the Oregon boundary at the 49th parallel in favor of the more northern boundary, it appeared threatening and forced Britain to consider whether it was willing to fight for a distant and sparsely settled territory. By early 1846 the British government had agreed to accept the 49th parallel and in June signed the Buchanan-Pakenham Treaty. Polk's blustering and willingness to use military force convinced the British that cooperative diplomatic relations and trade were more important than fighting for an isolated colony.

During the last months of John Tyler's presidency he used Polk's presidential victory as a public mandate to annex Texas via a joint resolution of Congress, which required a simple majority vote in both houses of Congress rather than a two-thirds victory in the Senate. The measure passed on Tyler's last day as president, March 3, 1845, and Texas entered the Union on December 29, 1845, as the twenty-eighth state. Since 1836 Mexico had refused to recognize Texas's independence, and with annexation it broke diplomatic relations with the United States.

Polk nonetheless attempted to repair relations with Mexico. In November 1845 he sent John Slidell to Mexico on a secret mission with instructions to offer as much as $30 million to secure the Rio Grande as the Texas–Mexico border and to acquire California and New Mexico. Given political instability in Mexico, Slidell could not gain what Polk wanted, so he returned to Washington in March 1846. Meanwhile, diplomatic instructions had been sent to the U.S. consul in Monterey, California, Thomas Oliver Larkin, that he should make Californians aware that the United States would accept them as brothers; Larkin quietly lined up support. Finally, during the fall of 1845 Polk sent General Zachary Taylor and 3,500

ISSUES IN MILITARY HISTORY

RACE AND THE MEXICAN WAR

During the first half of the nineteenth century race became a hotly contested issue that divided the nation. While the country embraced territorial expansion, racial prejudice inevitably influenced American attitudes, and race became a major factor during the Mexican War. The predominantly light-skinned northern European-Americans saw themselves as an enlightened people who had achieved an advanced state of progress in agriculture, industry, commerce, and the fine arts. Democracy and Protestantism provided the dual foundation for this advanced race and society, which would capitalize on navigable rivers, roads, and railroads to transform Mexican territory into an American paradise.

In this view, Mexicans were seen as civilized but as falling far short of Euro-Americans. They were believed to have inherited a proclivity toward cruelty from the Spaniards, and their willingness to embrace monarchy, centralized government, and Catholicism only reinforced perceptions of their institutionalized barbarism. When Mexicans slaughtered combatants, such as the prisoners at Goliad and the defenders of the Alamo during the Texas Revolution, or killed wounded soldiers on the battlefield, such as at Puebla, their actions were used by Americans to demonstrate the weakness of their character. The Mexicans' failure to fully develop their lands, commerce, and industry also supposedly resulted from their mixed Spaniard, Indian, and African heritage and further highlighted their weakness. In fact, their lack of development convinced Americans that the Mexican allegiance to Rome had betrayed the republican ideals of the Enlightenment and of progress. As such, Mexicans deserved punishment.

Skin color served as an identifier for Americans once the war began. Since African Americans served as military servants in U.S. ranks, Euro-Americans encountered them frequently and concluded that the black race was superior to the biracial Mexicans, who could be anything from pure Spaniard to mulatto, quadroon, octoroon, or even pure Indian. After campaigning in Mexican territory, soldiers started believing that American slaveholders treated their chattel better than Mexicans treated their Indian laborers or peons. During campaigns U.S. troops also purchased abundant goods and services, which permitted those laborers and peons to buy their freedom and increase their standard of living. Ultimately, Americans believed that the invasion transformed soldiers from conquerors to liberators, freeing Mexico from tyranny and emancipating its wretched inhabitants.

Finally, it is generally accepted that American soldiers were racist, and certainly by modern standards they were. But their attitudes were also far more complicated, viewing race as more than skin color. In their view, the Protestant Christian God had blessed Americans with a bounty of opportunities, including the chance to take new lands from less civilized opponents and make those lands productive. Moreover, the Americans' acceptance of a divinely sanctioned racial caste system—based on skin color, religion, type of government, and other categories—reinforced their belief that they should be the masters of the North American continent. Their "one true" religion, which rested on religious free will, and their "one true" republican government, which embodied civic free will, connected government to religion and formed the foundations of Manifest Destiny. White Euro-American soldiers served as the agents of this movement and as the instruments of the Mexican War.

soldiers to the Nueces River in southern Texas. In early 1846 Polk ordered Taylor to move south to the Rio Grande, where he constructed a makeshift fort (Fort Texas) at the site of present-day Brownsville on the river across from the Mexican city of Matamoros. Mexico demanded the withdrawal of American troops north of the Nueces River, but Taylor ignored those demands.

On April 25, 1846, some 2,000 Mexican cavalry attacked Captain Seth Thornton's seventy-man patrol north of the Rio Grande in the disputed territory, killing eleven soldiers and taking the remainder as prisoners. A few days later, on May 3, Mexican artillery fired on Fort Texas. For almost seven days the barrage continued as Mexican troops surrounded the fort, wounding thirteen and killing two American troopers. On May 8, Taylor arrived with 2,400 soldiers to break the siege, only to be met by 3,700 Mexican troops under General Mariano Arista. During the resultant Battle of Palo Alto, Taylor's "flying artillery" (light mobile artillery mounted on horse carriages along with a gun crew mounted on horses) rapidly fired devastating volleys into Mexican infantry ranks. Mexican artillery failed to counter the barrage, and Arista's cavalry charges were repulsed by Taylor's guns. In the early afternoon a cannon wadding caught fire, igniting dry grass and taking several hours to burn out. With smoke obscuring the battlefield, both Arista and Taylor tried to turn the other's flank without success, and by sunset the fighting had stopped.

Suffering more than 300 killed and roughly 300 wounded, Arista retreated during the night and following morning to a dry riverbed five miles away called Resaca de la Palma. Taylor did not pursue the Mexican forces until the early afternoon of May 9, by which time the Mexicans had entrenched themselves in a narrow ravine with flanks protected by shallow ponds and thick and thorny underbrush. Taylor's flying artillery could not dislodge the Mexican defenses, so he sent troops into the undergrowth. As American dragoons and infantry overran Mexican guns, the demoralized Mexicans retreated across the Rio Grande. Taylor's soldiers, who had captured several artillery pieces, General Arista's writing desk and silver, and the colors of the famed Tampico Battalion, waited in Fort Texas until equipment and supplies could be brought forward for crossing the Rio Grande.

The Mexican government had announced in April that it would repel any invading army, and its April 25 attack on Thornton's patrol had tried to drive Americans from the disputed territory. With Slidell's failure to resolve the situation diplomatically, President Polk became convinced that the two countries were moving toward war. On May 9, the same day as the Battle of Resaca de la Palma, Polk received notification of the Mexican attack on April 25. He immediately sent a message to Congress claiming that Mexican forces had killed American soldiers on U.S. soil. Congress voted overwhelmingly to declare war, even though New Englanders voiced strong opposition. During December 1847 an obscure Illinois Whig congressman named Abraham Lincoln also introduced a series of proposals collectively known as the "spot resolution" that sought to identify exactly the spot where American blood had been shed. In reality, that spot was not on American soil, but in disputed territory desired by an expansionist nation.

President Polk's war objectives called for seizing lands north of the Rio Grande and the Gila River and occupying western lands to the Pacific, including California. Working with General Winfield Scott and Secretary of War William Marcy, he developed plans for invading Mexico. General Zachary Taylor, affectionately known to his troops as "Old Rough and Ready," would cross the Rio Grande, occupy Matamoros, and then march west toward Monterrey. General John Wool would lead a second expedition from San Antonio to attack the Mexican city of Saltillo. Finally, Colonel Stephen Kearny would depart Fort Leavenworth to capture Santa Fe (New Mexico) and then proceed to California while volunteer Colonel

THE MEXICAN WAR

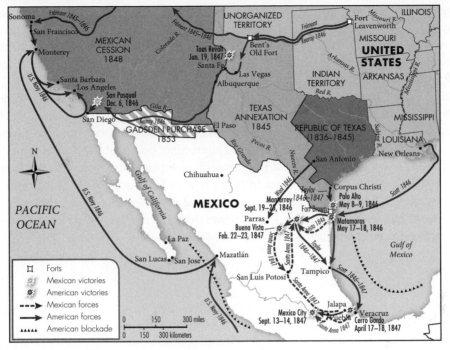

MAP 6.6 The Mexican War

Alexander Doniphan advanced through El Paso toward Chihuahua. If necessary, further plans called for an American amphibious landing on the Gulf Coast near Vera Cruz and the subsequent invasion of the central valley of Mexico. While General Scott seemed a natural choice to command armies in Mexico, Polk feared such an appointment would make him a potential presidential candidate. Instead, Taylor's victories at Palo Alto and Resaca de la Palma convinced Polk to promote him to the brevet rank of major general and give him command of the invasion of Mexico.

THE BEAR FLAG REVOLT

Brevet Captain John C. Frémont, the son-in-law of expansionist Missouri senator Thomas Hart Benton, had crossed the Sierra Nevada range in December 1845 with sixty-two men on a topographical expedition to survey and map the region. While traveling south to Monterey, the capital of Mexican Alta California, the armed party threatened Californian officials, especially Commandante General José Castro. Frémont reportedly traveled to Monterey because he had secret instructions for U.S. consul Thomas Oliver Larkin regarding an impending war. Castro did not like an armed group encamping outside the pueblo, so he demanded that Frémont leave California immediately or Mexican forces would drive him out.

Unwilling to provoke a war, Frémont departed for the Oregon Territory, but while in northern California, he learned that American settlers had captured horses bound for the Mexican military. On June 14, 1846, these settlers seized the pueblo of Sonoma along with Mariano Guadalupe Vallejo, the military commander of Alta California. Fearing that Castro was massing an army, the group mimicked the Texas revolutionaries, proclaiming the Bear Flag Republic. Frémont and his men joined the cause.

Commodore John D. Sloat, commander of the navy's Pacific Squadron, had been in Monterey Harbor since July 1, waiting for war news. Given what had happened in 1842 to Thomas ap Catesby Jones, he had refused to take presumptive action, but after learning of Frémont's actions and speaking with Consul Larkin, Sloat occupied the port of Monterey on July 7, 1846. Two days later, the Bear Flag Republic abruptly ended when the American flag was raised in Sonoma, in Yerba Buena (present-day San Francisco), and at John Sutter's fort in Sacramento. When Robert Stockton replaced Sloat, the aggressive commander joined his forces with Frémont's to seize San Diego, Santa Barbara, and Los Angeles. California was incorporated into the American Union in short order.

THE SANTA FE EXPEDITION

General Stephen Kearny departed Fort Leavenworth on June 2, 1846. Crossing plains, mountains, and deserts, Kearny's 1,700 soldiers arrived at Santa Fe in mid-August, capturing the pueblo without firing a shot. Having received intelligence from California that the province had already fallen to U.S. forces, Kearny established a civilian territorial government in Santa Fe and departed with 100 men for California. After marching through mountains and deserts, Kearny's exhausted men arrived in California in early December, where they learned that Californians were still revolting.

As the Americans neared San Diego on December 6, 1846, they encountered heavy rains and an encampment of Andres Pico's 100 Californians at nearby San Pasqual. Despite wet weapons and damp powder, Kearny believed the Californians to be cowards, so he pushed ahead too quickly. Spoiling for an engagement, his order to advance at a trot was misconstrued. Instead his mounted men charged ahead, outpacing his infantry and stretching his lines too far. Mounted Californians with long lancers and lassos descended on the disorganized American attack and during fifteen minutes of bloody combat successfully engaged the Americans, inflicted serious casualties (twenty-one dead and seventeen wounded of fifty engaged), and simply rode away. Kearny had seriously underestimated his enemy and its ability, and he had attacked in bad weather without information regarding the terrain. Pico almost surrounded Kearny a few days later near Rancho San Bernardo, but Stockton's marines and sailors arrived to escort the American force to San Diego. On January 8, 1847, Kearny, commanding sailors, marines, and dragoons, finally defeated the Californians at the Battle of the San Gabriel River, bringing an end to the revolt in California.

Colonel Doniphan had waited for the arrival of General Sterling Price before he departed with 500 men for Chihuahua, where he planned to unite with General Wool's column coming from San Antonio. On Christmas Day, Doniphan stopped at about 1 p.m.

at Brazito on the Rio Grande, nine miles south of present-day Las Cruces, New Mexico. Noticing an approaching cloud of dust, Doniphan immediately formed his men for battle. Mexican major Antonio Ponce de Leon's 1,200 men—infantry and lancers, armed with a single howitzer—offered Doniphan the chance to surrender. Instead, Doniphan used the time to finalize his preparations for battle, forming his lines and instructing his men to hold their fire until the Mexicans were within fifty yards. Advancing Mexican infantry fired three unanswered volleys, as the Americans held as instructed. Then suddenly Doniphan's guns erupted, immediately breaking the attack. Meanwhile, American teamsters repelled the lancers' attack. Adding insult to injury, Apache Indians harassed the Mexicans as they retreated.

On December 27 Doniphan arrived at El Paso, where he gathered additional men, supplies, and transportation. Hearing that Wool had abandoned his advance, Doniphan nonetheless departed El Paso, arriving near Chihuahua on the last day of February. Mexican general Jose A. Heredia had assembled more than 4,000 men and artillery to defend the city, positioning them fifteen miles north of its boundaries where a road crossed the Sacramento River. Seeing the Mexican position, Doniphan chose to use his cavalry to screen his infantry movements. He also positioned American artillery to silence Mexican guns and to drive off Mexican lancers. Then, advancing against the southernmost earthworks, out of range of most Mexican guns, Doniphan's infantrymen slugged their way through the lines. Mexican attempts to counterattack were beaten back by American artillery, and by late afternoon Heredia's troops had retreated. Doniphan marched into Chihuahua on March 1, 1847, occupying the city until late April, when he joined Taylor at Saltillo.

TAYLOR'S CAMPAIGN

By the time Taylor launched his campaign in Mexico, the war had spread to New Mexico and California. Taylor had waited because he did not have the necessary equipment—boats and wagons—for the invasion. After finally crossing the Rio Grande, Taylor found the Mexicans had abandoned Matamoros. He secured 1,500 pack mules and moved his army west to Camargo, where he awaited additional reinforcements, supplies, and transportation. Men poured into the unhealthy and muddy town, swelling his ranks to 15,000. But many of the recruits had short-term enlistments, and others became sick in the hot and humid climate. Leaving in late August with some 6,250 regulars and volunteers, Taylor's army lumbered west, reaching Monterrey on September 19, 1846.

Monterrey was strongly fortified. It had a citadel on the north end of town and a river on the south, and it was ringed with forts with abundant artillery. Taylor decided to cut off the western road to Saltillo, so he sent regulars and 400 Texas Rangers to do so. These men suffered through a miserable rainy night but finally secured the road on September 21, with substantial losses. Using artillery to subdue the citadel, Taylor's infantry then fought its way into the town. By the third day, the Americans were forced to struggle building to building, and even to engage in "mouse holing" (breaking holes through walls between buildings), to avoid remaining exposed in open streets; Americans would use these tactics a century later while fighting in Italian and German towns. Texas Rangers, also known as Devil Texans (Tejanos), knocked down doors, threw in incendiary devices, and then advanced house to house rather than through the streets. As Taylor used howitzers and a ten-inch mortar to force the Mexican commander to negotiate, Mexican troops retreated into the city center.

On September 24, Taylor accepted Monterrey's surrender, an unimpeded withdrawal of Mexican troops, and an eight-week armistice. Upon learning of Taylor's generous terms, President Polk ordered the armistice terminated. In mid-November Taylor sent 1,000 men to occupy the important crossroads of Saltillo to extend the Americans' strong defensive line across northern Mexico that stretched from Monterrey to Victoria.

The U.S. Navy found itself in the unusual situation of being the dominant naval force of the war. Instead of trying to break a blockade, as in the War of 1812, the navy enforced one and attacked the Mexican coast. Commodore David Conner, commander of the Gulf Squadron, tried to use his larger ships to capture the port of Alvarado during the summer and fall of 1846, but because his ships could not cross the sandbar, they could not protect the Americans' smaller vessels, which Mexican batteries repeatedly drove off. In October Commodore Matthew C. Perry used smaller craft to seize the port of Frontera and then moved up the Grijalva River to bombard Tabasco. Using the same tactics, in mid-November Conner took sailors and marines to Tampico, only to find that the Mexicans had abandoned it. The navy then extended Taylor's defensive line south and east to the coast.

President Polk did not fully understand the barren terrain of northern Mexico, believing that Taylor could march south and live off the land. In reality the semi-arid environment stopped Taylor in his tracks, because without water, food, and transport, his army would wither away. Polk also mistakenly believed a promise by General Santa Anna, living in exile in Cuba, to make a deal with the United States: in return for Polk allowing Santa Anna to return to Mexico, the general pledged to end the war and sell disputed territories to the United States at a reasonable price. Santa Anna had also pledged to Mexican president Valentín Gómez Farías that he had no presidential aspirations, and that he would use his military skill to drive the gringos from Mexico. Both Polk and Farías believed Santa Anna, but he deceived them. Polk arranged for Santa Anna to land at Veracruz, but once there, he proclaimed himself president and organized an army to march against Taylor. Polk had also concluded that Taylor could not be trusted, so he ordered a second front be opened in Mexico under General Winfield Scott.

Santa Anna recruited 25,000 men and advanced northward to meet Taylor. By November he had reached San Luis Potosí, but he wanted more information about the Americans. Santa Anna soon learned of a split among the Americans resulting from General Scott's decision to take 4,000 men from the north for his invasion of Veracruz, a move that left an angry Taylor with only 6,000 troops, mostly volunteers. Sending General Jose de Urrea and cavalry to retake Ciudad Victoria and isolate Monterrey, Santa Anna departed San Luis Potosí in late January with 21,500 ill-trained troops. By the time the Mexican army had marched the 280 miles to Saltillo Santa Anna's force had shrunk to 15,000 exhausted men. Taylor had only 4,650 volunteers, leaving the Americans outnumbered three to one.

On February 22, 1847, Taylor's cavalry located Santa Anna's army, prompting an American retreat to a position near the Hacienda San Juan de la Buena Vista—a location dominated by a narrow road running through a valley and lined by ravines and arroyos. Taylor mounted his artillery on the road, positioned his infantry and cavalry on a wide eastern plateau, and waited. Santa Anna disliked Taylor's position because it did not permit the use of his cavalry. While he offered Taylor the chance to surrender, he positioned his artillery on the road and on high ground east of the road. Taylor declined.

Mexican artillery opened fire about three o'clock. Throughout the late afternoon, Santa Anna tried to take the American left, and repeatedly Kentucky, Arkansas, and Indiana volunteers fell back but held. Shortly before sunset, Mexican forces appeared to be positioning to sweep the American right, and Taylor reinforced his line with Major Braxton Bragg's two field guns. Fighting stopped at sunset, but during the night Santa Anna moved five eight-pound cannon to high ground above the American left with the intention of flanking the position the following morning.

Fighting resumed at sunrise on February 23, when Santa Anna tried to rout the American right. Once it became clear that the American artillery would not collapse, Santa Anna focused on the American left. Indiana volunteers, supported by three cannon, held for thirty minutes before beginning to retreat, a withdrawal that quickly turned chaotic as nearby units broke and ran for more than a mile to the walls of a hacienda. Santa Anna sent his cavalry to pursue the fleeing Americans, but the horsemen were blunted by Colonel Jefferson Davis's Mississippi Rifles and Bragg's artillery. As the battle raged, an afternoon thunderstorm and hailstorm showed no mercy to either side.

Just when it appeared the Americans would drive the Mexicans back, Santa Anna committed two reserve divisions to strike against Taylor's middle. This immediate Mexican advantage of fresh troops forced the American center to retreat. Then suddenly Davis's Mississippians and the Indianans overran the Mexican right and rear, driving them into the ravines off the road. Attacked on three sides, Mexicans scurried to any protection they could find. As the sun set, Santa Anna retreated toward San Luis Potosí, having suffered 600 killed, more than 1,000 wounded, and 1,900 missing. Taylor's losses included 267 killed, 387 wounded, and 6 missing. Taylor retreated, but in victory.

While Taylor had not planned for the battle or made effective use of intelligence, he had shown great courage in combat. Positioned conspicuously in the middle of the American line, he led by example, disregarding danger. His constant movement of artillery and willingness to attack at every opportunity turned the battle several times during the day. He won admiration and respect from his troops, although the War Department reprimanded him for disobeying orders. Taylor, knowing that victory in this battle had brought him recognition and opportunity, returned home to a hero's welcome. Zachary Taylor had political ambitions.

SCOTT'S INVASION

Polk selected Winfield Scott, derisively known to his troops as "Old Fuss and Feathers," to command the second Mexican front because he did not think the general was a political threat. Immediately Scott and Commodore David Conner began planning for the invasion of Veracruz—the strongest fortification in North America—which would be the first large-scale amphibious operation by the U.S. military.

During early March, Scott personally reconnoitered the harbor to select a landing site, choosing Collado Beach three miles south of Veracruz and safely beyond the range of the fort's guns. On March 9, 1847, Conner assembled his fleet of capital ships, small armed vessels, and 141 specially designed stackable flatboats for an amphibious landing, and at 5:30 the invasion began. For six hours small armed vessels covered the navy's landing of 10,000 soldiers. In fact, the entire invasion force landed without firing or receiving a shot.

The landing troops quickly moved inland across the sand dunes without much Mexican opposition. During the following days, additional troops, artillery, supplies, and horses landed, and only stormy weather delayed Americans operations for four days. Once ashore, Scott's troops constructed siege lines stretching from north of the city south to Collado Beach. By March 22, American artillery had readied for a landward attack on Veracruz's harbor fort. For five days land and naval artillery pounded Fort San Juan de Ulúa. As Scott planned to assault the city, Mexican leaders requested a cease-fire to evacuate women and children. When Scott refused, the Mexicans surrendered the city on March 29, 1847. Army and navy cooperation had delivered a near-bloodless victory.

Leaving some troops in Veracruz, on April 8 Scott departed the coastal fever region for the mountain city of Jalapa along the same path Hernán Cortéz had taken 300 years before. After his defeat by Taylor at Buena Vista, Santa Anna had reformed his army, recruiting 12,000 soldiers, and prepared fortifications at the mountain pass of Cerro Gordo. He then occupied the peak of El Telegrafo, where he intended to trap Scott's invasion. Learning of the trap, Scott's army advanced slowly and deliberately, prompting Mexican artillery to fire before the Americans came into range. Lieutenant P.G.T. Beauregard of the engineers quickly surveyed defenses and suggested that Atalaya Hill on the Mexican left could be scaled, giving American artillery an advantage. Captain Robert E. Lee determined the approach to take and during the night engineers cut paths though the brush and forest, pulled artillery through and up ravines, and by April 17 had secured the top of Atalaya Hill.

Santa Anna knew of American intentions but believed that the artillery protecting his flank could silence American guns. He proved mistaken. On the morning of April 18, American field artillery fired while infantry attacked the Mexican rear and front along the Jalapa road. The Mexican forces, surrounded in only three hours, quickly surrendered or hastily retreated. Americans overran Santa Anna's camp so quickly that he mounted a horse without his artificial leg (he had lost the leg leading troops during a brief war with France in 1838, the so-called Pastry War), which was captured by Illinois troops and remains on display in the Illinois State Military Museum.

Scott moved to Jalapa but had to wait for further action. The enlistments of seven of his ten volunteer regiments were expiring, and only a few soldiers reenlisted. With fever season about to hit Vera Cruz, the others returned home immediately. When these troops left, along with the wounded and sick, Scott's army shrank to fewer than 6,000 men. With this reduced force, Scott moved ahead cautiously, reaching Puebla by mid-May.

Scott spent much of the summer waiting for reinforcements and supplies and protecting his supply and communication lines from guerrilla attacks. As the leader of an occupying army in enemy territory, Scott made sure that his soldiers treated civilians fairly and with respect to prevent popular uprisings. He also learned that U.S. State Department official Nicholas

Trist had arrived with instructions to negotiate an end to the war. Trist had made contact with Santa Anna and even arranged a down payment of $10,000 to purchase peace. But Santa Anna, who had just been elected president of Mexico for a second time, reneged again, forcing Scott's hand. In August the general abandoned his lines and moved inland toward Mexico City. Learning of this decision, the aging Duke of Wellington, who had defeated Napoleon in 1815, commented from Europe, "Scott is lost!" because he had severed his supply lines while in the middle of enemy territory. Within three days Scott's army had arrived in Ayolta, on the plateau overlooking the central valley of Mexico. Mexico City lay fourteen miles ahead.

Scott observed that the eastern approach to the city had been strongly fortified. Consequently, he decided to attack Mexico City from the west, meaning he would have to make a flanking movement to the south and west, navigating between lakes, mountains, and the fifteen-mile Pedregal lava bed. Robert E. Lee found a mule path across the Pedregal's southwestern tip that entered the village of Contreras. After improving the path into an army-worthy road, Scott's advance forces approached Contreras on August 19, finding Mexican reinforcements and heavy artillery, including a sixty-eight-pound howitzer. Scott's engineers then found an approach that led to the rear of the Mexican line, and during the night American reinforcements streamed through the gully during a torrential downpour to reach the Mexican rear by dawn. Early on the morning of August 20, forces simultaneously struck the Mexican front and rear. Within seventeen minutes, 700 Mexicans had died, 800 had been captured (including four generals), and Contreras had been captured.

Santa Anna's survivors retreated to the nearby village of Churubusco, where the general seized a stone church and convent, converting them into strong fortifications. Scott's army followed in quick pursuit but surprisingly ran into musket fire from well-entrenched Mexican forces. For almost three hours, the Americans gained no ground, as their attacks were repeatedly driven back. Finally they broke through when the Mexicans ran low on ammunition and several of their cannons melted from repeated fire. As the Americans entered the church and convent they encountered soldiers of the Mexican San Patricio (Saint Patrick) Battalion, a group of several hundred foreigners, mainly Irishmen who had deserted the U.S. Army because of the U.S. treatment of Catholics; while most had been killed, almost 100 were captured, and many were later executed for desertion. By the end of the day, Mexican losses numbered 4,000 killed and wounded, while the Americans had had 155 men killed and 876 wounded, totaling some 12 percent of the American army.

After the Mexican defeat at Churubusco, Santa Anna requested a cease-fire to reopen diplomatic negotiations. For two weeks, Nicholas Trist and Mexican officials discussed peace terms, but they could not agree on provisions. The armistice provided time for each side to replenish their fighting forces and for Mexicans to strengthen their defenses. Finally, on September 6, Scott terminated discussions and made plans for the final assault on Mexico City.

Nearby sat the Castle of Chapultepec, positioned on a high bluff and guarding the western entrance into the city. On September 13, Scott launched an assault over the causeways at the foot of Chapultepec, and soldiers scaled the rugged sides of the bluff. American soldiers and marines took a hail of musket fire, but they slowly fought their way up to the castle, which was defended by teenage cadets of the Mexican military academy. These boy soldiers defended the castle for two hours before being ordered to retreat. Six of the *Héroes Niños*

Nebel, *Storming of Chapultepec—Quitman's Attack.*

IMAGE 6.2 **Battle of Chalpultec** Carl Nebel's depiction of the American storming Chalpultec Castle on September 13, 1847 conveys the difficulty in taking this Mexican position. Because of the fierce fighting and loss of life, American Marines have commemorated this engagement in the opening line of the Marine's Hymn, "From the Halls of Montezuma."

(Boy Heroes), refusing to retreat, continued fighting; legend contends that the last survivor, Juan Escutia, wrapped himself in the Mexican flag and jumped from the roof of the castle to keep it from falling into American hands. The Marine Hymn, "From the Halls of Montezuma," honors the marines who participated in this battle, and the red stripe (blood stripe) worn on the trousers of officers and noncommissioned officers supposedly commemorates the high number of casualties Americans suffered while storming the castle. In reality, very few marines participated in the assault.

Scott advanced toward the city center, and by nightfall the Americans controlled two gates into the city. The following day, September 14, Scott's invasion fought house to house, driving deeper into the city before the Mexicans finally surrendered. Santa Anna had fled with the remainder of his army as he tried to sever Scott's supply and communication lines to the coast, and he surrendered after his defeat near Puebla on October 9. Scott meanwhile occupied Mexico City and declared martial law, waiting for diplomats to end the war.

Mexican guerrilla raids continued until early February 1848, when Trist and Mexican officials signed the Treaty of Guadalupe Hidalgo, which gave the United States unquestioned control over Texas, established the Rio Grande as the U.S.–Mexican border, and relinquished to the United States the southwestern territory that incorporates the present-day states of California,

Nevada, Utah, New Mexico, Arizona, and parts of Colorado and Wyoming. In return, the United States paid Mexico $15 million and agreed to assume $3.25 million in debts that the Mexican government owed to U.S. citizens. Polk had angrily recalled Trist to the United States in October 1847, but the diplomat had stayed, believing it better to continue negotiations rather than risk a continued war. Unhappy with the negotiated treaty because he believed payments implied guilt, Polk nonetheless submitted it to the Senate, which ratified it on March 10, 1848.

LEGACY OF WAR AND EXPANSION

Undoubtedly, the Mexican-American conflict was part of a war for territorial expansion in the spirit of Manifest Destiny. The conflict gave West Point graduates like Robert E. Lee, Ulysses S. Grant, George McClellan, George Meade, Thomas Jackson, William Sherman, Joseph Johnston, and Braxton Bragg their first opportunities to gain firsthand experience of battle. The country's first successful foreign war was characterized by better-trained officers making sound battlefield decisions, more and better equipment, and more sound tactics and strategy. President Polk had enlarged Thomas Jefferson's "Empire of Liberty," but no luster from that shining victory reflected on him. Instead, Zachary Taylor and Winfield Scott gained fame and military glory, and the war was soon overshadowed by the growing sectional conflict.

The war was overwhelmingly costly in real terms. The government spent $97.7 million on the conflict, plus treaty costs. More important, the human costs were staggering—1,721 died from combat, while another 11,155 died from disease. Of the more than 115,000 troops who served, 4,102 suffered immediately from debilitating wounds and disease. For years after the war former soldiers suffered from diseases they had contracted during the conflict. Some estimates suggest that total casualties may have reached as high as 40 percent if those who died later from injury- or disease-related maladies are counted. Additionally, many of those who returned home did so as broken men—a precursor to what civilians would witness in far greater numbers two decades later.

Militarily, the Mexican War was the country's first successful international offensive war. Two invasions of Mexico—one of which was the first large-scale amphibious operation—resulted in the first capture of a foreign capital. Soldiers and marines also implemented martial law on foreign soil for the first time. And, for the first time, correspondents traveled with the troops to report on the war. The military victories and publicity describing those successes that these reporters sent home initially unleashed a wave of patriotic national pride. But as military commanders bickered with one another during the postwar years about perceived affronts and charges of incompetency, Americans turned their attention to the growing sectional disputes. Territorial acquisitions from the war also reopened the debate about slavery, pushing the country toward civil war.

CONCLUSIONS

By the 1850s a sense of professionalism and an *esprit d'corps* had developed within the American military, manifested in the appearance of a military subculture and idea of professional ethics. West Point graduates filled the officer ranks of the army. Since the U.S. Naval Academy did not start accepting midshipmen until October 1845, the navy still relied on an apprentice system to train its officers. Annapolis-trained officers would play a role in the wars that followed.

TIMELINE

1810–1818	American expansion along Gulf of Mexico
1818–1825	Mosquito War in the Caribbean
1830–1850	Removal of Indians from southeastern lands to the West
1832	Black Hawk War
1835–1842	Second Seminole War
1836	Texas Revolution
1838–1842	Great U.S. Exploring Expedition in the South Pacific
1846–1848	Mexican War
September 1847	U.S. conquest of Mexico City
February 1848	Treaty of Guadalupe Hidalgo

Technology, however, changed the navy far quicker than it did the army. Advancements in steam propulsion produced a need for specialized technicians and different tactics and strategy. Army artillery changed as well, but the method of firing a cannon did not differ much between 1815 and 1850. Infantry tactics continued to follow the Napoleonic principles of the early nineteenth century, even though armies became more efficient at killing soldiers.

The army did develop manuals on military thought and strategy, such as Henry W. Halleck's *Elements of Military Art and Science*, which applied the Napoleonic principles of Frenchman Antoine Henri Jomini to the American strategic situation. But frontier constabulary duty and Indian warfare did not lend themselves to theoretical solutions. Denis Hart Mahan, who studied at West Point under Sylvanus Thayer, taught warfare and engineering from a Jomini perspective at the U.S. Military Academy from 1832 to 1871, ultimately shaping the thought and influencing the tactics and strategy of army officers who fought in both the Mexican War and the American Civil War. His son, Alfred Thayer Mahan, would become the most important American naval strategist of the late nineteenth century (see chapter 10), promulgating ideas that shaped the naval strategies of the United States, Great Britain, Germany, and Japan and led to the naval arms race of the 1890s. Much like American society, the military developed standards of professionalization, and army officers came to view themselves as part of a group that had a purpose and a mission. The navy did not foster this sense of standardized professionalism for another generation—after the American Civil War had divided the nation.

SUGGESTED READINGS

Eisenhower, John S. D. *So Far from God: The U.S. War with Mexico*. New York: Random House, 1989.

Goetzman, William H. *Army Exploration in the American West, 1803–1863*. New York: Macmillan, 1969.

Heidler, David S., and Jeanne T. Heidler. *Old Hickory's War: Andrew Jackson and the Quest for Empire*. Baton Rouge: Louisiana State University Press, 2003.

Johnson, Robert Erwin. *Thence Round Cape Horn: The Story of United States Naval Forces on Pacific Station, 1818–1923*. Annapolis, MD: Naval Institute Press, 1963.

Jung, Patrick J. *The Black Hawk War of 1832*. Norman: University of Oklahoma Press, 2007.

Long, David F. *Gold Braids and Foreign Relations: Diplomatic Activities of U.S. Naval Officers, 1798–1883*. Annapolis, MD: Naval Institute Press, 1988.

Mahon, John K. *History of the Second Seminole War, 1839–1843*. Gainesville: University Press of Florida, 1985.

May, Robert E. *Manifest Destiny's Underworld: Filibustering in Antebellum America*. Chapel Hill: University of North Carolina Press, 2002.

McCaffrey, James M. *Army of Manifest Destiny: The American Solider in the Mexican War, 1846–1848*. New York: New York University Press, 1992.

Prucha, Francis Paul. *The Sword of the Republic: The United States Army on the Frontier, 1782–1846*. New York: Macmillan, 1968.

Schroeder, John H. *Shaping a Maritime Empire: The Commercial and Diplomatic Role of the American Navy, 1829–1861*. Westport, CT: Greenwood Press, 1985.

Skelton, William B. *An American Profession of Arms: The Army Officer Corps, 1784–1861*. Lawrence: University Press of Kansas, 1992.

Smith, Mark A. *Engineering Security: The Corps of Engineers and Third System Defense Policy, 1815–1861*. Tuscaloosa: University of Alabama Press, 2009.

Watson, Samuel J. *Peacekeepers and Conquerors: The Army Officer Corps on the American Frontier, 1821–1846*. Lawrence: University Press of Kansas, 2013.

Winders, Richard Bruce. *Mr. Polk's Army: The American Military Experience in the Mexican War*. College Station: Texas A&M University Press, 1997.

CHAPTER 7

DISUNION

1849–1861

The Military at Midcentury • The Indian Frontier • An Imperial Navy • The Sectional Crisis • War • First Fights • Troubled Waters • Turning Points

In his insightful and informative handbook for westward pioneers, *The Prairie Traveler*, published by the War Department in 1859, Captain Randolph Marcy shared his many years of experience exploring the West and described in pleasant, matter-of-fact prose how best to navigate the great trails of the vast frontier. He also touched on the expansive role of the army and the myriad challenges it faced in the wake of the war with Mexico, writing:

> A regiment is stationed to-day on the borders of tropical Mexico; to-morrow, the war-whoop, borne on a gale from the northwest, compels its presence in the frozen latitudes of Puget's [*sic*] Sound. The very limited numerical strength of our army, scattered as it is over a vast area of territory, necessitates constant changes of stations, long and toilsome marches, a promptitude of action, and a tireless energy and self-reliance that can only be acquired through an intimate acquaintance with the sphere in which we act and move.

Marcy and other army officers were largely responsible for establishing that acquaintance for the host of settlers, prospectors, and dreamers who soon spread across the continent. It was just one of the roles soldiers played in the newly expanded nation.

For Marcy and most of the other officers of this small professional service, West Point training did little to prepare them for the realities of army life. "The education of our officers at the Military Academy is doubtless well adapted to the art of civilized war," Marcy wrote, "but can not [*sic*] familiarize them with the diversified details of border service." Soldiers had to "improvise new expedients to meet novel emergencies." It is not surprising, then, that the years between the war with Mexico and the Civil War produced a good deal of improvisation and innovation.

While Marcy astutely conveyed many of the new realities facing America's military establishment, he also stood as a vivid example of the systemic quandaries that plagued the officer corps and induced a number of gifted young men to resign their commissions for lucrative careers in the private sector. When he published *The Prairie Traveler* in 1859, Marcy was forty-seven years old but still just a captain, having last been promoted in 1846. Superannuated officers clogged the rolls, leading to a glacial pace of advancement and causing younger men to chase brevet promotions or simply leave the service. This situation became a compelling factor in 1861 when the fledging Confederacy offered loftier grades to ambitious officers. Prior to that development, poor pay and distant assignments made army life less than appealing. Somehow, though, the army managed to retain a cadre of fine line officers and, as Marcy would soon prove, capable staff men. After years on the frontier, and following the publication of *The Prairie Traveler*, Randolph Marcy, who became perhaps better known as George McClellan's father-in-law, spent the rest of his career in lackluster staff assignments, mostly in the Inspector General's Office, which he headed with the rank of brigadier general at the time of his retirement in 1881, just shy of fifty years on active duty.

THE MILITARY AT MIDCENTURY

The Civil War (1861–1865) remains the greatest challenge the United States has ever faced. The secession of eleven southern states and the two sides' inability to negotiate an end to the resultant crisis brought to North America a military conflict of unimagined proportions, one that would leave the South devastated for years to come and cost well more than 600,000 lives. It became the ultimate watershed moment in the nation's history, at once settling the inflammatory question of slavery and confirming forever the idea of perpetual union, a principle from which President Abraham Lincoln never wavered. The period provides arguably the most studied and most storied aspect of U.S. history and remains controversial, spawning differing interpretations of and continued arguments over the war's causes and effects—indeed, over its very meaning. Although the war continues to loom large in the national memory, it was a war which, at the outset, the United States and the upstart Confederacy proved completely unprepared to fight, with disastrous consequences. And although some might argue that the decade preceding the war offered numerous hints of premeditated preparation for an inevitable regional confrontation, the military events of 1849 to 1860 demonstrate a concerted effort to forge a much different future. By 1860 the army had established itself as an effective frontier constabulary, tried and tested in dozens of contests against the formidable tribes of the American West, and the navy had emerged as a prolific agent of empire.

The breathtaking success of the United States' conquest of Mexico and the consequent Treaty of Guadalupe Hidalgo added a massive amount of land to the nation. When combined with the prior annexation of Texas, the settlement of the Oregon boundary issue with Great Britain, and the 1853 Gadsden Purchase, the Mexican Cession essentially completed the quest known as "Manifest Destiny," the desire of American expansionists to control the continent from coast to coast. The new territorial acquisitions also provided the final pieces of the contiguous United States of the present. At the same time, the U.S. Navy extended its reach—as well as American influence—to new regions of the world, especially in the Pacific, opening markets and adding vital coaling stations to support its growing steam-powered fleet and its mission. Yet with vast new lands and enhanced global reach came equally vast new responsibilities for America's soldiers and sailors.

Even before the territorial additions, the army faced the increasingly daunting task of pacifying, protecting, and patrolling the ever-advancing western frontier against an increasingly resistant Indian population. The new lands—which covered more than a million square miles—only increased these demands, especially after the 1848 discovery of gold in California. The onslaught of thousands of westward-bound settlers severely complicated matters. The addition of California fostered plans for new transcontinental railroads, while the growing numbers of overland emigrants demanded better routes west, all of which placed a premium on the army's topographical engineers. The army's widening duties came to include numerous exploration, mapping, and surveying expeditions, as well as thankless security details along the emigrant trails to Oregon, California, and other emerging mining regions. Mundane but necessary jobs such as fort building and supply transport over lengthening lines of communication also added to the burden. And, of course, fighting intensified as the frontier pushed onto the Great Plains and into the Southwest after Texas joined the Union in 1845. To complicate things further, the American West presented a land of great diversity and breadth that challenged human ability. Deserts, mountains, endless plains, little water, intense heat, subzero cold, and unpredictable storms of every variety made living and working in these new lands all the more demanding.

Despite the dramatic expansion of their mission and jurisdiction, soldiers found little support from Washington, where a traditionally tightfisted Congress continued to limit military appropriations. What had for decades been an aversion to a large standing military as a threat to liberty by the 1850s had become a philosophy of fiscal restraint that expressed itself in an unwillingness to invest in an undermanned military establishment that continued nevertheless to prove its worth. Southern fear of northern domination also discouraged military growth. By the time the army completed its conversion to peacetime standing in 1849, it numbered fewer than 10,000 officers and men, and yet it had much more land to cover, including the border with an aggrieved Mexico and a new Indian frontier in the Southwest that brought into play the fearsome and formidable Comanches, Kiowas, Apaches, and Navajos. The potential for conflict was especially high since one of the most desirable possible routes for a transcontinental railroad skirted that border and ran through the lands of some of the fiercest warriors the army had ever encountered.

The regular army's postwar configuration—eight regiments of infantry, the 1st and 2nd Dragoons, the Regiment of Mounted Rifles, and four regiments of artillery—could in no way meet preexisting demands let alone their new responsibilities. Pressure from inside the army and from sympathetic politicians brought some, albeit totally inadequate, relief. An expansion of the size of the company, the army's principal operational unit, increased the authorized strength of the force to almost 13,000 by 1851. But with such distances to cover and a highly mobile foe in the offing, the old array of units proved simply unreasonable. While infantry, long the mainstay of the army and far more cost-effective than mounted troops, could perform garrison duties and support military exploration, it stood no chance in the hot pursuit of well-mounted Cheyenne or Lakota raiders. Artillery was practically useless on the frontier, as Indians rarely fought in large concentrated formations. Under intense pressure from hardworking Secretary of War Jefferson Davis of Mississippi, Congress in 1855 finally consented to substantive additions in the form of four new regiments, the 9th and 10th Infantry and the 1st and 2nd Cavalry (the first time U.S. mounted units carried such a designation), which raised the army's authorized strength to more than 16,000, although it never approached this number in practice. The new mounted regiments were an important official recognition of the need for a more mobile force.

The new cavalry regiments became legendary and from the start boasted rosters packed with future Civil War generals. The elite 2nd Cavalry, also known, perhaps derisively, as "Jeff Davis's Own" for its high percentage of southern officers, produced sixteen Civil War generals, including Albert Sidney Johnston, Robert E. Lee, George H. Thomas, and John Bell Hood. The 1st Cavalry offered an equally impressive profile, including Joseph E. Johnston, George McClellan, and J.E.B. Stuart. These handpicked units drew the toughest assignments of the 1850s: the 1st Cavalry deployed to Kansas, while Texas became home to the 2nd.

New regiments also addressed a persistent problem in the regular army—a dearth of opportunities for talented young officers. Robert E. Lee had more than twenty-five years in the service, mostly employed on engineering projects and a thirty-month stint as superintendent at West Point, and although a colonel by brevet (by virtue of his stellar performance in Mexico), his substantive rank remained captain until he earned the appointment to lieutenant colonel of the 2nd Cavalry. Slow promotion, low pay, and a lack of opportunity, combined with a seniority system that clogged the commissioned ranks with older, often ineffective men, drove a number of promising young officers such as McClellan and Thomas J. Jackson from the service.

Force augmentation, while welcomed, did not address all of the concerns weighing on America's leaders. Although easy to overlook as a period between two wars, the 1850s proved to be an important decade in terms of the evolution of the U.S. military establishment. During this time America's soldiers and civilian officials began to shake off years of intellectual stagnation and to embrace new technology and new, more efficient operations. Not all of these experiments worked.

The daunting logistical challenges involved in supplying America's far-flung posts gobbled up both time and treasure. The transformative Secretary Davis looked outside the continent for a more effective and less expensive way to move supplies through the hostile Southwest, especially along the all-important route from San Antonio, Texas, to California. Davis's search led to one of the most unique experiments in American military history—the use of camels. Intrigued by the possibilities these animals offered (they could carry more than horses or mules over longer distances) and their durability, tolerance for high heat, and ability to exist on little water, Davis sought and received congressional funding for what he hoped would become a "Camel Corps." He then sent an agent to the Middle East, where he procured some seventy camels and hired several handlers. After a long trip by sea to Texas, the beasts journeyed overland to their new home at Camp Verde, outside of San Antonio. Although the camels proved useful in limited trials, enthusiasm for the project waned, and the coming of the Civil War dealt a final blow to the enterprise. The camels were either sold off to zoos or circuses or left to roam the desert.

Certainly more important to the military evolution was Davis's commitment to embracing new technology in the area of weaponry, which coincided with a number of important

IMAGE 7.1A AND 7.1B (a) Unidentified Union Soldier (b) African American Soldier Guarding a 12-Pounder "Napoleon" Gun Top: This unidentified Union soldier is well armed with modern weapons of war, including a new .58 caliber rifle musket, revolver, and bayonet. Bottom: An unidentified African American soldier stands guard near a 12-ponder "Napoleon" gun, probably near Petersburg, Virginia.

developments in the field, especially those pertaining to the musket. Davis moved boldly to replace his troops' outmoded and often ineffective smoothbore muskets with new rifles; to adopt the much more reliable and easy-to-use percussion cap, which replaced the flintlock as the ignition system in firearms; and to use the so-called Minié ball, a conical lead projectile with a hollowed base that expanded to provide a tighter fit in rifling, which in turn produced higher muzzle velocity and better accuracy, essentially tripling the musket's effective range to up to 600 yards. In 1855 the government armories at Springfield, Massachusetts, and Harpers Ferry, Virginia, began to produce rifles exclusively. The .58-caliber Springfield muzzle-loading rifle musket became the standard and most widely used model during the Civil War. Cavalry units carried an assortment of carbines. As metallic cartridge ammunition became available in the late 1850s, it spawned the concurrent development of breech-loading rifles and carbines, of which the Sharps and later the Spencer became the preferred models. Metallic cartridges were expensive, however, so breech-loading technology wasn't applied widely in the infantry until after the Civil War.

Colt revolvers earned quite a reputation in Mexico, and by the 1850s, cap-and-ball revolvers had found favor in the regular army's mounted units. Colt and its competitors, namely Remington, produced a number of models for military application. Although metallic cartridge revolvers became available prior to the Civil War, they saw only limited use in the war and would not be adopted by the army until the 1870s.

Military ordnance also saw major development during this period, with the first rifled guns put into service on land

and at sea. The work of naval officer John A. Dahlgren and army artillerist Thomas J. Rodman led to the production of better large guns. Although still muzzle-loading, these new pieces would remain the standard in the navy and in the army's seacoast fortifications for almost four decades. Robert P. Parrott's work on rifled guns led to their wide employment during the Civil War. Indeed, the excellent U.S. three-inch Ordnance Rifle made up a large percentage of the Federal inventory by 1863. But the most prolific field-piece of the war, introduced in 1857, became the twelve-pounder, smoothbore gun-howitzer, better known as the Napoleon, after the man credited with its design, Emperor Napoleon III of France. Artillerists prized the rugged bronze Napoleon for its ease of deployment and its ability to fire solid shot and shell as well as canister (a collection of two dozen or more steel balls, that created a giant shotgun effect when packed into the tube). Canister-spewing Napoleons thus became one of the most devastating antipersonnel weapons of the Civil War.

While the 1850s produced a significant evolution in weapons technology, military leaders and theorists continued to embrace the lessons of the past and did not substantially alter their tactics to confront the new realities ushered forth by the rifle and Minié ball. Dennis Hart Mahan, the legendary West Point instructor, emphasized the tactics of Napoleon Bonaparte as rendered by French theorist Antoine Henri Jomini. Mahan's influence endured in the writings of his students, including Henry W. Halleck and William J. Hardee. Recent scholarship indeed suggests that because the military continued to rely on the same tactics, the extensive use of rifles, contrary to popular belief, did little to change the dynamics of battle or produce increased casualties during the Civil War. And while these same leaders remained enamored of European-style conventional warfare, even sending a delegation to observe the Crimean War, America's soldiers faced an all too different reality of limited, unconventional, guerrilla fighting over vast and forbidding lands and became increasingly, perhaps surprisingly, proficient at small war.

The Mexican War had provided a brief and in many ways exhilarating diversion from the ongoing conflict with the American Indians, but that conflict now intensified. The 1850s featured a number of distinct "wars" that produced more than 200 armed clashes between U.S. soldiers, both regular and irregular, and various tribes. Not all of the fighting took place in the West. A third and final confrontation with the Seminoles in Florida (1855–1858) ended with most of the remaining members of the tribe agreeing to relocate to Indian Territory. The Florida campaign drew considerable military attention at a time when the army found itself hard-pressed on numerous fronts. Artillery companies still manned a number of coastal fortifications, but the West drew by far the majority of the nation's military resources.

THE INDIAN FRONTIER

For decades American leaders had imagined a permanent Indian reserve in the West, but despite the establishment of the Indian Territory (later Oklahoma) it never became reality, as the tide of white migration never subsided. Even natural boundaries such as the Mississippi could not restrict the push, and no human-imposed boundary could achieve what nature could not. Even as the war in Mexico unfolded, American emigrants and soldiers moved westward in ever-growing numbers along the legendary Santa Fe and Oregon trails. With the end of the war came time to consolidate the bounty of new territory and to cultivate new opportunities. Much of this work fell to the army.

The small regular army addressed its manifold responsibilities remarkably well. Whether conducting multiple surveying expeditions, mostly to identify future railroad routes, or escorting settlers, the soldiers had their hands full. The fact that these activities brought soldiers and civilians alike into contact with native tribesmen, disrupted hunting patterns and bison herds, and generally threatened the existence of tens of thousands of western Indians ensured that conflict remained ceaseless.

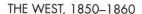

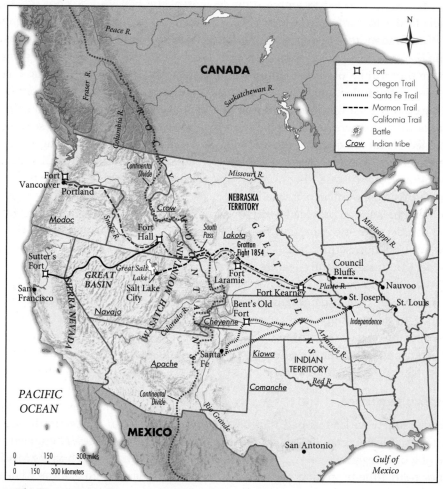

MAP 7.1   The West, 1850–1860

As the army moved deeper into new lands, it put down roots, so to speak, establishing forts, camps, and outposts that served a variety of roles. Forts allowed the army to project its influence into areas in which the United States previously had no official presence. Forts, camps, and cantonments became bases of operation, supply centers, and often the genesis for new settlements, offering security for settlers and peaceful Indians alike. Consequently, soldiers frequently found themselves protecting local Indians from encroaching civilization. It was a delicate act, to be sure. It comes as no surprise, then, that much of the military effort in the West involved fort construction, with fifty-two being built between 1848 and 1854 alone. Many quickly became obsolete as the settlement line passed them by. Still, by 1860, the army operated some sixty-five major posts and dozens of smaller ones in the trans-Mississippi West, mostly along emigrant trails and the Mexican border and in places where the Indian populations proved especially threatening. Texas alone required two distinctive lines of forts, one running along the Rio Grande that also protected the vital San Antonio to California road and another west of the settlement line along the Indian frontier. These bases came in all styles and sizes and were usually constructed of materials available at or near the site. Consequently, some were built of timber, some of stone, and some merely of earth. Most were simply a collection of buildings: barracks, officers' quarters, storage warehouses, corrals, mess halls, and hospitals. Few resembled the symmetrical stockades of film and television. Because there were so many forts spread over so much land, troop complements at most posts were small, usually one or two undersized companies. Rarely did an entire regiment occupy a western fort.

The thankless tasks associated with exploration, fort construction, and garrison life claimed most of the hours in a soldier's life and accounted for high rates of desertion—especially near mining areas—and drunkenness. But life on the frontier also brought danger and uncertainty. Although most of the fighting that occurred between 1849 and 1861 involved small engagements, the period also produced a number of major campaigns, with fighting in all corners of the West. As soldiers occupied recently acquired lands or moved into less settled areas such as Minnesota, they encountered stubborn resistance from the tribes they met, in many cases for the first time. Even surveying operations often attracted a violent reaction. In the Southwest, the army found considerable opposition from the Navajos and various Apache bands. Near Fort Laramie on the Platte River in 1854 Lakota warriors overwhelmed an army detachment under recent West Point graduate Lieutenant John Grattan, killing or mortally wounding all thirty men; the assault prompted a punitive response that resulted in the killing of eighty-six Lakotas.

In Kansas, through which three major emigrant trails passed, white encroachment posed a major threat to the Southern Cheyennes, who pushed back with predictable fury. In response, the 1st Cavalry, supported by infantry and artillery, conducted a major campaign under the venerable Colonel Edwin V. Sumner that culminated in a costly defeat for the Cheyennes on the Solomon River in 1857 and featured one of the few saber charges recorded during the Indian Wars. Significant fighting also occurred in the Northwest, where Yakima, Chinook, and Nez Perce warriors forcefully resisted the onslaught of civilization. Mining and ranching operations in northern California also brought considerable hardship, including degrading exploitation, to Indians of the region, who pushed back, often violently, only to face military retribution. A sad case in point occurred in May 1850, when a detachment of dragoons supported by local militia attacked a party of Pomo Indians at Clear Lake in Lake County, killing at least 150, and probably many more, mostly old men, women, and children in what became known as the Bloody Island Massacre; a subsequent slaughter on the nearby Russian River yielded similar results.

Nowhere did the army face a more challenging foe than it did in Texas and the surrounding areas, where arguably the most talented and terrifying Indians of the West—the Comanches—long tormented settlers on both sides of the Rio Grande. In the army's first major operation against the Comanches, Major Earl Van Dorn of the 2nd Cavalry led troops into Indian Territory and the Texas Panhandle to discourage the marauders, with some notable but temporary success. The last important Indian action before the Civil War was a punitive expedition against the Navajos in 1860. Although the Indians inflicted some damage and obstructed certain movements, U.S. soldiers generally proved more effective in battle.

Not all of the army's attention was directed toward the Indians of the West. The largest operation of the period unfolded in Utah Territory. After being driven from one community after another east of the Mississippi and following the murder of founder Joseph Smith, members of the Church of Jesus Christ of Latter-Day Saints selected lands in the distant West to create a Mormon state that would lie outside the jurisdiction of the United States and began the long migration to Utah in 1847, when the region was still technically part of Mexico. But the hope of an unattached domain ended when the Treaty of Guadalupe Hidalgo ceded the land to the United States. The Compromise of 1850 that conferred statehood on California also created Utah Territory, with Mormon leader Brigham Young appointed territorial governor. Mormon defiance of federal authority and their controversial practice of polygamy, combined with reports of poor treatment of westbound emigrants, compelled President James Buchanan to order a large expedition to Utah in 1857 with the purpose of establishing federal authority, constructing military bases, and installing a new governor.

The expedition, under the overall command of Colonel Albert Sidney Johnston, left Fort Leavenworth in July and reached Utah that fall. Mormons, alarmed by the approach of troops and suspicious of their intent, conducted a campaign of scorched earth resistance that included the burning of several army supply wagons, which caused a food crisis in Johnston's command that winter. What became known as the Utah War or Mormon War involved a number of unfortunate incidents, such as the infamous Mountain Meadows Massacre, in which Mormon militiamen murdered more than 100 members of a wagon train en route to California. But Johnston and his regulars displayed great restraint and largely avoided confrontation, ultimately relying on diplomacy and a strong show of force to prevail. In June 1858 Johnston and 2,500 troops occupied Salt Lake City largely without trouble. A force that represented almost a sixth of the army's total strength remained in Utah until the outbreak of the Civil War.

AN IMPERIAL NAVY

For years before and after the war with Mexico, the U.S. Navy's bold pursuit of overseas markets and its protection of American lives and property vividly anticipated the nation's imperialist pursuits of the late nineteenth and early twentieth centuries. During the 1830s and 1840s the navy aggressively projected American interests abroad, especially in the Pacific, where it opened trade agreements with China and the East Indies. As it continued its conversion to steam propulsion, however, the navy needed new partners to facilitate trade and provide access for coaling stations. Japan, which had been almost completely closed off to the rest of the world for two centuries, became the chief object of American desire. The navy had attempted to engage the Japanese on previous occasions, but it took a grand display of Western industrial power and the diplomatic grandeur of Commodore Matthew Calbraith Perry to convince the Japanese to open their islands to U.S. trade and diplomatic relations. In July 1853 Perry's flotilla of four ships—the sidewheel steamers *Mississippi* and *Susquehanna* and sloops of war *Plymouth* and *Saratoga*—entered the waters off Tokyo with guns loaded and rolled out. Most of the isolated Japanese had never seen steam warships. After much posturing Perry presented the U.S. requests and vowed to return for Japan's answer within months. Returning with a considerably larger squadron in February 1854, the commodore secured land for a coaling station and signed the Treaty of Kanagawa, which opened two Japanese ports to U.S. trade, provided for the establishment of a consulate, and promised safe harbor for shipwrecked American sailors. The "opening" of Japan proved to be a major turning point in global dynamics.

THE AMERICAN EXPEDITION, UNDER COMMODORE PERRY, LANDING IN JAPAN.

IMAGE 7.2 Perry's "Opening" of Japan This artist's rendering of U.S. Navy officer Matthew C. Perry's momentous 1853 landing in Japan reflects the importance of the event. Perry's "opening" of Japan proved immensely consequential for both nations.

Certainly, the navy, like the army, filled numerous roles and took on a fascinating array of challenges, including exploration, scientific experimentation, and diplomacy, during this period. Its expeditions sailed the world's seas from the Arctic to the Amazon and from China to West Africa. It conducted surveys of South America's Rio de la Plata and numerous other waterways, charted ocean currents and winds, and explored the Darien Isthmus (Panama) for a possible canal route. Perhaps most telling of eventual American designs were the numerous punitive affairs in which the navy participated. U.S. sailors and marines landed at Okinawa, Buenos Aires, Hong Kong, Shanghai, Montevideo, Portuguese West Africa (Angola), and Fiji to protect American lives and property. In 1854, after an attack on a U.S. consulate, the sloop-of-war *Cyane* virtually destroyed the Nicaraguan port of San Juan del Norte (present-day Greytown). Two years later, American warships arrived at Canton during the Taiping Rebellion and launched an attack on the four barrier forts, destroying them and 176 guns and inflicting more than 400 casualties while suffering only 42. And in 1858 the U.S. Brazil Squadron of nineteen ships attacked Paraguay for firing on the exploration ship *Water Witch* three years before, securing an indemnity and a new trade treaty. American warships, often working in concert with the Royal Navy, also participated in pirate suppression activities and seized a number of slave ships off West Africa.

Like the army, the navy pursued technological advances that would pay major dividends during the Civil War. In addition to steam propulsion, the screw propeller provided an improvement over the sidewheel operation, while the significant upgrades in naval gunnery mentioned previously led to enhanced effectiveness and efficiency. The Crimean War foreshadowed the rise of iron-hulled and ironclad warships, and the United States found itself uniquely situated to develop both. And, like the army, the navy embraced professionalism, emphasizing education and abolishing corporal punishment in hopes of attracting better sailors. The Naval School at Annapolis, Maryland, established in 1845 to train officers, was formally designated the United States Naval Academy (USNA) in 1850; the following year the academy adopted a four-year curriculum with training cruises in the summers. Although widely dispersed, the navy by 1861 had better positioned itself intellectually and operationally for the coming conflict.

THE SECTIONAL CRISIS

The political machinations of the 1850s and the unrest occasioned by the intensifying slavery crisis finally led to the involvement of the army. The Kansas-Nebraska Territorial Act opened the floodgates of violence when the doctrine of popular sovereignty invited a war for the future of Kansas between proslavery and antislavery forces known to history as "Bleeding Kansas." In May 1856 proslavery forces sacked the free-state town of Lawrence, which triggered murderous retribution at Pottawatomie by abolitionist John Brown and ignited a guerrilla war that claimed some 200 lives and caused more than $2 million in property damage before army troops arrived to restore order. Soldiers subsequently stayed on to ensure valid elections in the coming years.

It seems as if every event of the period, from the war in Mexico to the election of 1860, influenced or was influenced by the debate over slavery. The conflict stymied development, such as railroad construction, and generally cast a gloom over the nation. Up until the mid-1850s, the military remained outside the political fray, but the events in Kansas proved impossible to ignore. Once involved, the army did a remarkable job of remaining professionally detached, even as politicians allowed the country to unravel. In the South, fear of a major slave revolt left people on edge. A heavy-handed military approach in Kansas would only exacerbate concerns of a northern conspiracy to abolish slavery. On the other hand, northerners found the attempt to extend slavery to the territories increasingly intolerable. Into this cauldron of fear and distrust sprang the fugitive abolitionist zealot John Brown, who had been in hiding since leading the 1856 raid on Pottawatomie and was now planning to deliver a great blow for the antislavery cause.

Along with twenty-two followers, in October 1859 Brown crossed the Potomac River from Maryland and seized the government arsenal at Harpers Ferry, Virginia, taking hostages. His goal had been to inspire and then support a slave revolt, but in reality he had no plan for achieving such an aim. Soon Brown and his men, including five African Americans, found themselves trapped, surrounded by local militiamen and angry citizens. The next day a detachment of marines arrived from Washington, D.C., led by Lieutenant Colonel Robert E. Lee, who happened to be on leave visiting his home in nearby Arlington when the alarm sounded. Assisted by another furloughed soldier, Lieutenant J.E.B. Stuart, Lee directed an assault that captured Brown and brought the incident to a close, with ten of the raiders, including two of Brown's sons, killed and seven taken prisoner. One marine died in the operation, along with four citizens. Brown and six others were convicted of treason and hanged by year's end. To many southerners, Brown's act confirmed their worst fears; to many northerners he became a martyr of the antislavery cause. This relatively minor event, which had had little chance of producing anything more than Brown's martyrdom, nonetheless became the final blow to hopes for sectional reconciliation.

As the presidential election of 1860 neared, southern leaders, hardened by the increasingly fervent abolitionist rhetoric of the rising Republican Party, began to discuss secession in earnest. Ignoring nominee Abraham Lincoln's more moderate stance, they vowed to leave the Union should the Republican win the election. On Election Day, the Democrats, Stephen Douglas and John C. Breckinridge, split the vote north and south, respectively, and another candidate, John Bell, took the all-important border states of Tennessee, Kentucky, and Virginia, allowing Lincoln, with only 40 percent of the popular vote, to score a resounding victory—without a single electoral vote from a slave state. What southerners had feared most had occurred: the slaveholding South no longer controlled its own destiny. True to their word, South Carolina secessionists met in December and voted to dissolve all ties to the United States; the six Deep South states of Georgia, Florida, Alabama, Mississippi, Louisiana, and Texas followed suit. A nation long divided over the issue of slavery had now divided in fact. The seven states sent delegates to Montgomery, Alabama, in February 1861 to form a provisional government for the Confederate States of America, with former senator and secretary of war Jefferson Davis as president.

Secession posed serious concerns for the United States. It threatened northern access to the Mississippi, it invited European intervention, and it held the very real prospect of war. Compromise could avert a permanent split, but it would require cooler heads, and those were in short supply. Secession became especially problematic for the War Department. The army operated coastal fortifications in several southern states, including South Carolina and Florida. In Texas, a significant military department, a large percentage of the army, occupied more than a dozen posts and staffed a headquarters in San Antonio. In each case the seceded states demanded the surrender of federal property and the evacuation of loyal soldiers. Acting without orders, the commander of the Department of Texas, Brevet Major General David Twiggs, a southerner, surrendered all federal property and stores but failed to alert the various garrisons around the state to his decision. Some, such as the men at Fort Chadbourne in West Texas, were incredulous when Texas troops showed up to take possession but stood down when Twiggs's actions had been confirmed. Somehow, the situation in Texas failed to produce the conflagration that appeared likely. This, regrettably, was not the case in South Carolina.

The United States was by no stretch of the imagination prepared for this stunning turn of events. With lame duck president James Buchanan in the White House until March 1861, the response to secession and the challenge it posed to federal authority was tempered by that reality. In December 1860 the army on paper numbered roughly 16,000 men, with fewer than 10 percent, mostly in artillery companies, stationed east of the Mississippi; the navy was stretched around the world. In Charleston, Major Robert Anderson moved his small garrison from the vulnerable Fort Moultrie to a not yet completed Fort Sumter, located on an island in the harbor and thus isolated from the South Carolina mainland. Still, South Carolina demanded the removal of federal troops. President Buchanan refused to comply and even attempted to send reinforcements. On January 9 the transport ship *Star of the West*, carrying 200 federal troops, approached Fort Sumter. Carolina batteries opened fire on the vessel. Major Anderson wisely refused to reply. Once constituted, the Confederate government ordered General P.G.T. Beauregard, one of the many officers to resign his U.S. commission, to assume command of the troops gathered at Charleston.

When Abraham Lincoln took office in March, he vowed not to interfere with slavery where it existed but also pledged to hold property still in federal possession. In Charleston Harbor, though, Anderson ran low on supplies. Sumter had to be evacuated or resupplied. Yet surrender conferred a legitimacy on the Confederacy that Lincoln refused to recognize, while resupply invited a violent response. Lincoln shifted the burden to the Confederacy by advising South Carolina that he intended to send humanitarian aid in unarmed ships. Confederate leaders refused to allow the mission and demanded the immediate surrender of Fort Sumter. When Anderson rejected Beauregard's ultimatum at 4:30 a.m. on April 12, 1861, the big guns around Charleston Harbor opened fire on the fort, and the outgunned Sumter answered. After a bombardment of more than thirty hours during which the two sides exchanged more than 4,000 rounds, Anderson surrendered. Remarkably, not a single soldier on either side perished in the barrage, although two men died when a cannon exploded during a final salute to the U.S. flag.

IMAGE 7.3 Fort Sumter A *Harper's Weekly* depiction of the Confederate bombardment of Fort Sumter in Charleston Harbor that initiated the American Civil War. After more than a day of steady pounding the fort surrendered on April 13, 1861.

WAR

The attack on Fort Sumter caused an outpouring of anger in the North and a great deal of excitement in the South. With the United States' regular army too small and too dispersed, President Lincoln immediately called upon the loyal states to raise 75,000 ninety-day volunteers to quell the rebellion. Days later he proclaimed a blockade of southern ports from South Carolina to Texas. The free states enthusiastically complied with Lincoln's call for troops, easily exceeding their quotas, while the eight slave states remaining in the Union largely rejected the call, considering Lincoln's response rather than the attack on Sumter the first act of war. Four Upper South states—Arkansas, North Carolina, and the immensely important Virginia and Tennessee—now joined the seven other southern states in the Confederacy. With Virginia's secession, the Confederate government opted to move its capital to Richmond, located little more than 100 miles from Washington. Maryland, given its proximity to Washington and Virginia's defection to the Confederate camp, had to be retained by force, lest the U.S. capital become an island between two hostile states. Kentucky and Missouri, both bitterly divided on the issue of secession, ultimately remained loyal, although thousands of their numbers joined the Confederacy. Delaware never wavered in its devotion to the Union. Pro-Union sentiment also ran high in the mountainous areas of East Tennessee and western Virginia.

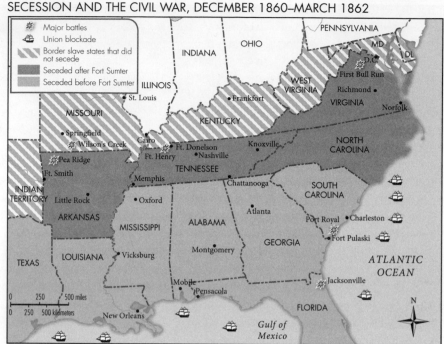

SECESSION AND THE CIVIL WAR, DECEMBER 1860–MARCH 1862

MAP 7.2 Secession and the Civil War, December 1860–March 1862

As the two sides came into focus, it became clear that the Union possessed a wealth of advantages. Its population of roughly 22.5 million included more than 4.5 million men of military age (eighteen to thirty-five), and that number would grow with a steady flow of immigrants in the coming years. Additionally, loyal slave states counted around 300,000 slaves. The Confederacy had a total population of 9 million, of which close to 3.7 million were slaves, leaving a white population of 5.3 million and only 1.1 million men of military age. This four to one advantage in military-age men only increased during the course of the war. The Union states also accounted for some 90 percent of the United States' industrial capacity, 80 percent of its prewar wealth, and at least two-thirds of its railroad mileage. The twenty-two loyal states enjoyed diverse economies and robust agriculture. Importantly, they produced food. The southern economy, ever reliant on slave labor and cash crop exports, could not meet the demands of a protracted war, especially after the Union blockade tightened its grip, and lacked manufacturing facilities to be fully self-sufficient. Finally, although diminished by the loss of eleven states, the United States' government remained intact, with an established treasury and state department. It had a standing army, albeit one that was small and scattered, and a navy of forty-two active ships with the capacity to produce many more.

The Confederacy did boast a few advantages, among them the South's sheer size. But this became as much of a burden as it was a blessing, in that it eventually meant more land to protect with fewer men to protect it. The South, it was traditionally argued, also possessed a stronger martial tradition than did the North, although this assertion has long been disputed by historians. Still, more than a quarter of the U.S. Army's regular officers resigned their commissions to join the Confederacy, 125 of whom became general officers. Other Confederate officers had attended West Point or one of the South's many military schools, such as the Citadel or the Virginia Military Institute, or had served in the regular army in Mexico or the Indian campaigns. The southern horse culture also contributed to the early superiority of Confederate cavalry. The Confederates' greatest advantage lay in the fact that they only had to defend their turf—or, better yet, do nothing at all and hope to be left alone. The United States, on the other hand, in order to restore the Union would have to conquer the South.

These comparisons only mattered in the case of a large, protracted war, which few Americans anticipated. Men on both sides predicted early battlefield success and a quick resolution. But neither side devoted the attention or resources required to produce such decisive results. Steeped as they were in Napoleonic lore, leaders thought in terms of grand armies and large set piece battles yet relied on masses of largely untrained men led by inexperienced officers. The kind of war these men wanted to fight took practice and patience, but both of these qualities were in short supply. Not a single man in either army had the experience the war would demand. No one, except the ancient heroes of Mexico—Winfield Scott (who was seventy-four when the Civil War began) and John Wool (who was seventy-seven)—had commanded anything larger than a regiment in battle, and few had even done that. Scott, the Union's commanding general and a Virginian by birth, was one of the few to advocate a less direct confrontation. Still sharp but too infirm to take the field, Scott suggested that a combination of a tight blockade and Union control of the big rivers of the South—especially the Mississippi—would eventually squeeze the Confederacy out of existence. But in the country's superheated political environment, Scott's strategic vision, called by critics the "Anaconda Plan," fell on deaf ears. Leaders, both military and political, instead favored a strategy that emphasized capturing or holding capital cities and other important centers. Richmond became the target for Union leaders, who also grew obsessed with protecting Washington. Confederate leaders in the short term concentrated on defense, but to an ultimately fatal extent devoted most of their attention and resources to the Eastern Theater.

Initially, both sides relied on temporary volunteer armies to fight the war. Lincoln's call for 75,000 militiamen provided the Union only short-term manpower, as by law these men were limited to ninety-day enlistments. With the U.S. Congress out of session until July, Lincoln acted unilaterally (and extralegally) to shore up the nation's defenses, ordering the addition of 22,714 men to the regular army and 18,000 to the navy and calling for forty regiments of volunteers (42,000 men) to serve three-year enlistments. In July Congress confirmed Lincoln's actions and authorized another 500,000 three-year volunteers. President Davis had called for 60,000 men prior to the attack on Fort Sumter, and, like Lincoln, he would later call for more.

For the Union, the regular army remained intact as a separate entity and would serve in various capacities during the war, but the bulk of the fighting would fall to the U.S. Volunteers. Although the Confederacy created a regular army, it never truly materialized, and the South relied almost exclusively on a provisional force. In both cases, the central governments charged the states with raising a given number of regiments, with quotas based on population. Across the various states volunteers joined companies, usually formed of individuals from the same town, county, region, or, in large cities, neighborhood, and, particularly in the North, of the same ethnic background. Ten companies then formed a regiment. Once activated regiments received a numerical designation: 1st Texas Infantry, 6th Pennsylvania Cavalry, 2nd Connecticut Heavy Artillery. Artillery regiments were usually divided into batteries and deployed as such. Democratic traditions in both the North and the South meant that the soldiers commonly elected their company officers (lieutenants and captains) and sometimes even their field grade offices (majors and colonels); however, governors normally appointed the latter, which provided state executives with plenty of opportunities for dispensing patronage. As the war progressed it became useful for junior officers from the Union's regular army to take leaves of absence to accept volunteer commissions at a higher grade.

Regiments became the building blocks of the field armies of the Civil War. Two or more regiments—usually four, and quite often from the same state—formed a brigade, which would be commanded by a colonel or brigadier general; two or more brigades—again, usually four—formed a division. As the war grew and even larger formations became necessary, two or more divisions were combined to form a corps. In the Union divisions were headed by a brigadier general or a major general; the latter usually commanded corps. In the Confederacy divisions usually warranted a major general, while corps command dictated a lieutenant general. (The Union did not authorize the lieutenant general grade until 1864, when Ulysses S. Grant became commanding general.) Finally, field armies contained either multiple divisions or two or more corps. In the Union system a major general commanded an army; in the Confederate service after 1861 armies were led by full generals (the equivalent of a modern four-star general). Confederate brigades, divisions, and corps, while assigned numerical designations, frequently were identified by the commander's name: Hood's Texas Brigade, Cleburne's Division, Longstreet's Corps. Confederate armies also drew their names from the region in which they primarily operated: the Army of Tennessee, the Army of Northern Virginia. Union brigades, divisions, and corps, by contrast, went by numerical designations within a given army, which was itself identified with the most prominent waterway within its proposed area of operation: First Brigade, Second Division, Sixth Corps, Army of the Potomac.

Both armies relied on general officers appointed by the respective presidents. These appointments involved a delicate mix of politics and patronage and produced an often-unhealthy blend of professional and nonprofessional soldiers. Both presidents appointed politicians whose support they needed or coveted, men who represented vital interests or unique constituencies, such as the German, Irish, or Polish communities of the North. Lincoln, a man of very limited military experience and with little knowledge of his army, found himself reliant on officers who had their own agendas and was somewhat hamstrung by the regular army's seniority system until he decided to bypass it altogether. Davis had far more flexibility in appointing general officers, and as a graduate of West Point, a veteran of Mexico, and a former secretary of war, he had considerably more familiarity with the officer cadre of the old army as well as the numerous citizen-soldiers with whom he had served in Mexico.

Davis also benefited from the talent of those who defected from the old army, especially after Virginia joined the Confederacy. Secession forced a difficult, often heartbreaking choice on men in uniform. While an overwhelming majority of southerners in the old army resigned their commissions and offered their services to their home states and ultimately the Confederacy, some chose to remain loyal. Robert E. Lee, General Scott's favored choice to lead the Federal army, instead went with Virginia, turning away from the country that had provided his education and employed him for more than thirty years. Lee's 2nd Cavalry colleague and fellow Virginian George H. Thomas, on the other hand, stayed loyal to the Union, a decision for which his family never forgave him. John Gibbon, raised in North Carolina, also stuck with the Union, but his brothers fought for the Confederacy. Conversely, more than a few northern men, such as John C. Pemberton, who had developed ties to the South, offered their services to the Confederacy. In this way, the war shattered families and friendships.

In addition to the pull of home and family, men had selfish reasons for joining the Rebel cause. For many officers the Confederacy offered opportunity for advancement and glory after years of stagnation in the old army. Captains and lieutenants now became colonels and generals. The same inducements applied to Union officers who left the regular army for volunteer commissions. The dramatic military expansion that followed the firing on Fort Sumter also offered a second chance to hundreds of men who had left the service but whose training made them suddenly attractive. Grant's promising career, for example, had come to an end when loneliness-induced drinking forced his resignation from the U.S. Army. After a series of failures in private life, the war beckoned, and he made the most of his second chance. William T. Sherman, too, had previously left the army, only to suffer embarrassment in the civilian world. Together, Grant and Sherman, both seen by many prior to the war as failures, became the war's winning combination. On the Confederate side, West Point–trained Leonidas Polk had left the army only months after graduation to pursue an Episcopal priesthood. He subsequently rose to become bishop of Louisiana and one of the founders of the University of the South. Yet almost thirty-five years after resigning his commission, he offered his sword to his old friend Jefferson Davis. And for no group did the opportunity resonate more than it did among politicians. Dozens of political and civic leaders pursued Civil War commands. Far too many proved unequal to the task, with some proving outright disastrous, but others, such as congressmen John A. Logan of Illinois, Francis P. Blair, Jr., of Missouri, and Iowa railroad man Grenville Dodge, proved perfectly capable.

Perhaps the most interesting members of the officer corps on both sides were the pure amateurs, men who often had some social standing and resources but little or no military experience. Wade Hampton of South Carolina, one of the South's wealthiest planters, proved to be a natural soldier. Tennessee's Nathan Bedford Forrest, who had made a fortune selling slaves, among other endeavors, became a legend of the saddle. Twenty-two-year-old Nelson A. Miles, a Massachusetts store clerk, went on to become one of America's great soldiers.

For both Lincoln and Davis the selection of leaders involved a great deal of speculation. Certainly, each president could choose from rosters of accomplished officers whose résumés were filled with West Point training and trials under fire in Mexico or on the frontier, but none of these experiences prepared them for the coming war. Previous military experience might very well help, but neither it nor a West Point pedigree nor service in Mexico was a guarantee of success. As the war would reveal, youthful enthusiasm, raw physical courage, and even personal magnetism became just as valuable. The challenge for Lincoln and Davis, as it developed, was not to rely on experience or education but to cultivate leadership talent within the crucible of war. This, of course, took time and a good bit of trial and error, which proved costly but sadly unavoidable as Americans raced to war.

FIRST FIGHTS

It is not surprising that the initial armed clashes of the war took place in the disputed border regions. The first casualties from fire occurred just days after Sumter, when a prosecession mob in Baltimore attacked a regiment of Massachusetts troops en route to Washington. Four soldiers and twelve townspeople died in the melee. Aggressive actions by pro-Union forces in Missouri led by Captain Nathaniel Lyon prevented secessionists from controlling the state, but not without bloodshed; one riot in St. Louis claimed more than thirty lives and left Missouri perhaps the most bitterly divided state, a fracture that would endure for the duration of the conflict and years beyond. In the northwestern portion of Virginia, where opposition to secession ran high, Federal troops led by General George McClellan, a former soldier turned railroad executive turned soldier again, drove Confederate forces from the region, allowing its secession from Virginia and the eventual formation of the state of West Virginia. Kentucky managed briefly to retain a tenuous neutral status, with both the Union and Confederacy respecting its boundaries, but not for long.

After its secession, Virginia moved quickly to seize federal assets within the state. While Virginian forces failed to take the formidable Fort Monroe at the tip of the peninsula between the York and James rivers, they did secure Norfolk Naval Yard across the waters from Hampton Roads, taking more than 100 guns, some old vessels, and the remains of the steam frigate USS *Merrimack*, which had been left in flames by evacuating Federal sailors. Burned down to its waterline, the *Merrimack* in Confederate hands would be refitted as an armored ram and christened *Virginia*.

With the Confederate capital now at Richmond, that city became the obsession of northern leaders, and "On to Richmond" became the theme as voices both inside and outside the government at Washington agitated for a decisive battle to settle the conflict. The first of many failed attempts to take Richmond came in June, when a force of 3,500 men under Massachusetts politician-turned-general Benjamin Butler advanced up the Virginia Peninsula from Fort Monroe, only to be turned back by well-entrenched Rebels at Big Bethel Church well short of the Confederate capital. Although a minor affair, the clash at Big Bethel pointed to a major problem faced by both sides: the inability to distinguish friend from foe. The rapid mobilizations had not allowed for anything like standardized uniforms. On both sides of the line shades of blue and gray mixed with the festive reds and greens of the

Zouave units, who sported French-inspired outfits that featured baggy trousers, short vests, and fezzes or turbans. Similar uniforms and flags would cause great confusion in the early battles of the war.

As pressure for a Union advance on Richmond mounted quickly, it fell solidly on the shoulders of the man who commanded Federal troops in Northern Virginia, General Irvin McDowell. McDowell, a career staff officer who had never led troops in battle, understood his volunteer army needed more training and begged for time, only to be ordered to move. After a sluggish march on July 21, McDowell's 35,000 Federal troops approached the Confederate position some twenty-five miles southwest of Washington. There, along a small stream called Bull Run, General Beauregard's 20,000 men, reinforced by rail with General Joseph Johnston's smaller command from the Shenandoah Valley (which managed to elude the Union force assigned to prevent such an occurrence), defended the railroad junction at Manassas. McDowell's attack made some headway, but battlefield confusion and a stubborn Confederate stand anchored by the Virginia brigade of General Thomas J. Jackson, who earned one of history's great nicknames—"Stonewall"—for the effort, stemmed the Federal advance. A counterattack featuring the devilish "Rebel Yell" turned the tide. The battle soon became a rout as Yankee soldiers broke and ran, scattering the many spectators who had come out from Washington to witness the events. As McDowell's unprepared force retreated to the safety of Washington, the Confederates celebrated victory.

By the terms of future Civil War battles, the Battle of Bull Run (or Manassas to the Confederates) was a minor affair. Union casualties (killed, wounded, and missing or captured) numbered almost 3,000 to some 2,000 for the Confederates. As the first major engagement of the war, however, Bull Run produced many revelations: the armies needed better organization and training, too many variations in flags and uniforms made it difficult to distinguish friend from foe, and railroads and telegraphic communication would play significant roles in the conflict. And although the battle proved a clear victory for the upstart Confederacy, it was in no way decisive. The Union army would fight again. This fact became the single greatest lesson of the war's first big battle: Civil War battles were rarely decisive, because the combatants, even in victory, suffered so much damage that pursuit and annihilation of a defeated foe proved almost impossible. For the South particularly, the inability to produce a decisive victory spelled doom. But for the moment, Confederate victory seemed to confirm the South's sense of martial superiority. It had won the first major confrontation of the war.

For the Union, the turn of events produced a new resolve. President Lincoln and Congress now prepared for a long war and began to marshal the nation's resources to that end. Lincoln demoted the hapless McDowell and passed over dozens of senior officers to name George McClellan, fresh off his success in western Virginia, to command Union forces in Virginia. McClellan, who only months before had been a railroad executive, was now a major general in the regular army. He undertook the recruitment, training, and organization of what soon became one of the largest, most well-equipped, and most well-trained armies in the world—the Army of the Potomac. By November, McClellan had replaced Winfield Scott as general-in-chief. Handsome, brilliant, a gifted organizer, and immensely popular among his men, McClellan appeared to be the savior Lincoln sought. Unfortunately for Lincoln, appearances are often deceiving.

Meanwhile, as both governments and much of the press remained fixated on Virginia and the Confederate success there, the war took a decided turn in favor of the Union in the Trans-Mississippi West and along the southern coastline. In August, pro-Confederate Missourians reinforced by troops from Arkansas defeated a small Federal army at the Battle of Wilson's Creek in the southwestern corner of Missouri, killing early Union hero Nathaniel Lyon. The Confederates advanced into Missouri before being driven out of the state by Union reinforcements. The following spring Union forces under General Samuel Curtis delivered a sound beating to the Confederates at Pea Ridge in northwestern Arkansas. Thereafter, Union control of Missouri was never seriously challenged. Farther to the west, a Confederate force from Texas invaded New Mexico Territory, pushing up the Rio Grande in the fall of 1861 in hopes of securing that region and perhaps parts of California for the southern cause. After a string of small victories during which the Rebels occupied Albuquerque and Santa Fe, Federal troops supported by Colorado volunteers destroyed the Confederates' supply train during an otherwise inconclusive fight at Glorieta Pass northeast of Santa Fe in March 1862. The Confederate bid for empire ended in a desperate retreat back to Texas.

TROUBLED WATERS

The Federal blockade of the southern coastline, proclaimed just days after the firing on Fort Sumter, initially presented little threat to Confederate commerce, but as the navy added ships to the effort its effectiveness grew. Within months hundreds of ships patrolled the south Atlantic and Gulf seacoasts. Although far more ships got through the blockade than were apprehended, Confederate policy actually contributed to the appearance of its effectiveness. As part of what has been called "King Cotton diplomacy," the Confederacy opted to hold its 1861 cotton shipments, believing that withholding the goods from Britain's cotton-hungry textile industry would create higher demand and hasten British recognition of the Confederacy, but bumper crops in previous years and emerging new sources of cotton allowed the British to call the southern bluff. Consequently, the cotton embargo instead gave the impression that the blockade was working and was thus legitimate in the eyes of foreign powers. As the blockade tightened the South became increasingly reliant on fast, steam-powered blockade runners to ship out cotton and other goods in order to acquire and bring in badly needed supplies from Europe.

Although Britain recognized the blockade and clung to its neutral status, an event at sea almost brought the British into the war. In November 1861, Federal Captain Charles Wilkes, commanding the steam frigate *San Jacinto*, on his own authority stopped the British mail packet *Trent* in Caribbean waters. A boarding party removed from the *Trent* Confederate diplomats James Mason and John Slidell, both of whom were bound for their respective diplomatic posts in England and France. The British responded angrily, demanding an apology and the release of the two diplomats. Some in the government and the press called for war, but cooler heads prevailed and the crisis passed when the United States released Mason and Slidell and, short of apologizing, admitted that Wilkes had acted without orders.

Even as the *Trent* affair played out, the U.S. Navy had its first success in the East when a flotilla led by Flag Officer Samuel DuPont sailed into South Carolina's Port Royal Sound and subdued the Confederate garrison there. Transports then disgorged 13,000 troops, who took control of a large area that now became a Federal base that could provide badly needed support for the ships blockading Charleston and Savannah, Georgia. The Port Royal beachhead also served as a staging area for future ground operations in South Carolina. In February 1862 another Federal flotilla of shallow-draft gunboats under Flag Officer Louis Goldsborough steamed into the North Carolina Sounds escorting transports that carried 10,000 soldiers under the command of General Ambrose Burnside, who subsequently occupied Roanoke Island. This operation led to Federal control of the Sounds, which rendered the upper Carolina coastline and its many inlets and bays almost useless to the Confederates. The blockade got even stronger after Union operations along the Georgia coast produced the surrender of Fort Pulaski, which closed off Savannah.

While the Confederates could not hope to compete with the U.S. Navy or the industrial output of the United States, they were not without naval success. Confederate naval victories came primarily from two very different sources: innovation and interruption. During the course of the war, southerners experimented with and mastered the use of floating mines, called torpedoes, which inflicted serious damage upon Union warships. The Confederates also produced the first operational submarine, *H. L. Hunley*, which sank a Union blockading ship on its first and only mission by using a long spur to drive an explosive device into the hull. *Hunley* never made it back to its base. But the Confederates' most important contribution to naval warfare grew from the wreckage of the captured U.S. steam frigate *Merrimack*, which would become the first ironclad warship to engage another warship in battle.

An ironclad warship was not a new idea. The French and British had produced working models that had yet to be proven in battle, and, in fact, the Union already had a number of armored ships in operation, with several—namely, the formidable *Cairo-* or City-class ironclads—playing a major role in the successful February 1862 Fort Henry–Fort Donelson Campaign. But an engagement between ironclad ships had never before occurred. Confederate engineers took what was left of *Merrimack* and its unreliable steam engine, constructed a deck along the waterline, and covered it with a casement of thick wood and four inches of iron plate, slanted inward to promote glancing blows. Rechristened *Virginia*, the ship mounted ten heavy guns, but it was large, slow, and hard to maneuver. Still, against it, the wooden-hulled ships of the blockading squadron stood no chance. On March 8, 1862, under the command of Captain Franklin Buchanan, *Virginia* steamed down the James River into Hampton Roads, where the James drains into the Chesapeake Bay, to attack the Union blockade. It opened fire on the sloop-of-war *Cumberland*, killing dozens before ramming the helpless ship, which went down with 121 men. *Virginia* then turned its attention to the frigate *Congress*, which ran aground and was pounded by the Confederate ship's heavy guns.

Heated projectiles known as hot shot left *Congress* in flames, which eventually caused the explosion of its powder magazine, taking the ship down with all hands. Late in the day and in need of repairs, *Virginia* suspended the attack.

The U.S. Navy possessed a revolutionary weapon of its own, and it was steaming for Hampton Roads even as *Virginia* savaged the blockade. USS *Monitor*, the creation of engineer John Ericsson, was something altogether different from *Virginia*. Its steam engine and screw propulsion system were entirely underwater, encased in an iron hull. Its deck floated just above the waterline. On deck only a small pilothouse and a large rotating turret could be seen. Within the innovative turret, protected by eight inches of iron plate, two eleven-inch Dahlgren guns provided all of *Monitor's* firepower. *Monitor* arrived in Hampton Roads during the night, guided to the ghastly scene by the flames from *Congress*, and took station near the big frigate *Minnesota*, which had run aground trying to evade the Confederate monster.

When the next day *Virginia* emerged to finish off the wooden ships of the blockade, it instead found *Monitor*. Their encounter—the first duel between ironclad warships in history—marked a watershed moment in naval history and rendered wooden warships obsolete. The two ships pounded away at each other for hours, doing considerable damage but failing to inflict a terminal wound. The lighter and more maneuverable *Monitor* and the more heavily

IMAGE 7.4 *Monitor v. Virginia* This highly stylized lithograph captures the first clash between ironclad warships, the Battle of Hampton Roads in Chesapeake Bay on March 9, 1862. The duel between the U.S.S. *Monitor* and the C.S.S. *Virginia* ended in a draw but ushered in a new era of naval warfare.

ISSUES IN MILITARY HISTORY

WAS THE CIVIL WAR THE FIRST MODERN WAR?

"Modern war" is, of course, a relative term. What makes a war modern? The Civil War has been called the first modern war because it unfolded during a time of great technological innovation and industrial expansion, which greatly increased the availability of rifled weapons, steam propulsion, armored warships, telegraphic communication, and even military aviation in the form of observation balloons. During this war both sides relied on large national armies and resorted to large-scale conscription. But a similar argument can be made for the Crimean War (1853–1856) as well. Conversely, the Civil War can be viewed as a continuation of an earlier military era, as the men who led its regiments, brigades, and divisions, as well as its mighty field armies, studied and applied lessons from the Napoleonic era to deal with the conflict they faced. The Civil War, then, might best be considered a transition from one era to another, as the stalemate around Richmond and Petersburg in the final year of the war certainly anticipated the trench warfare of World War I.

While Civil War officers and the men they led enjoyed access to an array of technology, they often did not know how to employ it effectively. For example, it became widely accepted that the rifle musket and the Minié bullet revolutionized warfare and rendered Napoleonic tactics obsolete, and that because leaders failed to adapt to this new technology, casualties soared. But more recent scholarship by historians such as Earl J. Hess downplays the effect of the rifle on tactics. The rifle did dramatically improve range and accuracy, but Civil War soldiers rarely called upon these capabilities, preferring instead short-range engagement. Nor did rifles necessarily account for greater casualty rates than did the old smoothbore musket. The rifle did not, as it was traditionally assumed, ultimately discourage the employment of cavalry as a main battle component, as evidenced by General Philip Sheridan's successful use of the mounted arm late in the war, or materially degrade the effectiveness of artillery. And while railroads and telegraphic communication played considerable roles in the Civil War, they did not significantly influence many of its great campaigns.

Without doubt, the advent of ironclad warships revolutionized naval warfare and led to an evolutionary process in shipbuilding that lasted well into the twentieth century. And clearly the Civil War's massive mobilization of manpower—roughly 10 percent of the total population—provided a preview of the giant national armies that would fight the world wars. The Civil War should therefore not properly be considered the first modern war or the last Napoleonic conflict, but rather a significant transitionary event, one from which future leaders regrettably learned far too little.

armed *Virginia* fought to a draw. *Virginia* then steamed back into the James to loom as a continued threat to the blockade until its own demise two months later, when it was destroyed to keep it from falling into Federal hands. *Monitor*, never particularly suited for the high seas, went down in a storm off the North Carolina coast later that year. Both ships served as models for future ironclad construction.

TURNING POINTS

As the conflict developed, so too did distinctive theaters of war. The Eastern Theater encompassed the seaboard states from the mid-Atlantic to Florida, but most of its fighting took place in Virginia. The Western Theater stretched from the Appalachian range to the

Mississippi, and included Tennessee, Kentucky, Georgia, Alabama, Mississippi, and eastern Louisiana. The Trans-Mississippi Theater embraced western Louisiana, Arkansas, Missouri, Texas, and the Southwest. While the Eastern Theater, containing as it did both capitals and most major cities, attracted by far the most attention, and the Trans-Mississippi witnessed few events of consequence, it was in the Western Theater where Union forces produced their first important victories and in so doing changed the course of the war. Although the war would last for four years, it may fairly be argued that for the Confederates it was lost early on and in the West.

The Western Theater presented numerous challenges for the Confederacy: its rivers offered potential routes of invasion, and Tennessee's border with Kentucky, which was more than 300 miles long and stretched from the Cumberland Gap to the Mississippi, could not be adequately defended. As long as both sides recognized Kentucky's claim of neutrality and upheld their vows to not enter the commonwealth, the South enjoyed a tremendous buffer. But in September 1861 the Confederates squandered that advantage when Leonidas Polk, the Episcopal bishop turned general, on his own initiative moved his forces into Kentucky to occupy the bluffs along the Mississippi at Columbus, violating the state's tenuous neutrality. Polk's move dashed any hope among southerners that the Bluegrass State might finally join the Confederacy. Instead, it acted quickly to affirm its affiliation with the Union and invited Federal troops to secure the state.

The Federal commander at Cairo, Illinois, which sat upriver from Columbus at the confluence of the Mississippi and the Ohio, readily seized the opportunity. General Ulysses S. Grant, a West Point graduate and Mexican War veteran who had been forced in 1854 to resign his commission or face court-martial over charges of drunkenness, had benefited from the political influence of Congressman Elihu Washburne in securing his volunteer appointment and his promotion to regional command. Grant sent forces to occupy Paducah and Smithland, Kentucky, where the Tennessee and Cumberland rivers respectively entered the Ohio. In November he put 3,000 troops on transports and moved down the Mississippi to engage Confederate forces at Belmont, Missouri, opposite Columbus. After a back-and-forth fight in which his forces were almost overwhelmed, Grant managed a skillful withdrawal and returned to Cairo.

Undaunted, Grant devised another way to compromise the Confederate position at Columbus. The Union enjoyed a clear advantage on water, and the navy had proved adept at working with the army to achieve important objectives, as evidenced by the Port Royal operation. Grant turned to Flag Officer Andrew Foote, who commanded a squadron of river gunboats, including four new City-class ironclads, to mount a combined expedition against the forts guarding the Tennessee and Cumberland rivers. In February 1862, Foote's gunboats, trailed by army transports, steamed up the Tennessee River to engage the Confederates at the ill-conceived Fort Henry, just below the Kentucky line. Having dropped the soldiers off several miles north of the fort, Foote attacked on the morning of February 6. The Confederate commander at Fort Henry, General Lloyd Tilghman, had already recognized the hopelessness of the situation and had sent most of his men overland to Fort Donelson on the Cumberland, retaining only a small crew of volunteers to man Fort Henry's few guns. After a brief exchange Tilghman raised the white flag. The battle was over before Grant's soldiers even arrived. For such a small engagement, the Battle of Fort Henry became a major victory for the Union and a true turning point in the war. It opened the Confederate heartland to invasion, it isolated West Tennessee, it rendered Polk's position at Columbus untenable, and most importantly, it gave the Union a badly needed victory.

While Foote's flotilla steamed back down the Tennessee to the Ohio and over to ascend the Cumberland, Grant's army of 17,000 men moved overland to invest Fort Donelson. This fort, which was much better positioned and better armed than Fort Henry, included strong river batteries as well as extensive earthworks that formed a large perimeter around the post. General Albert Sidney Johnston, a particular favorite of Jefferson Davis, had inherited an impossible situation when he took command of all Confederate troops in the Western Theater, with his forces scattered and unprepared for the riverborne threats that now confronted them, Still, from his headquarters in Bowling Green, Kentucky, he made the curious decision to reinforce Donelson in hopes of buying time to withdraw from Kentucky. Reinforced, Fort Donelson held fewer than 20,000 men.

The weather turned bitterly cold as Grant's soldiers invested Fort Donelson. On February 14, Foote's gunboats attacked as planned, but the well-placed Confederate guns pounded the ironclads, driving them away with serious damage and wounding Foote. Grant called up reinforcements of his own, bringing his numbers to around 27,000 men. The next day the Confederates attempted a breakout, but oddly, after opening a gap in the Union line, they pulled back into the fort. Grant ordered a counterattack that afternoon that compromised a portion of the Rebel fortifications before nightfall suspended the operation. That night, in a comedy of incompetence, the Confederate commanders opted to surrender, but senior Brigadier John Floyd of Virginia, a former U.S. secretary of war, passed command to his second, Gideon Pillow, fearing he would be hanged for treason. Pillow, a Tennessee politician, then for similar reasons passed the command to Kentuckian Simon Bolivar Buckner, the only professional soldier of the three. Floyd and Pillow escaped with some of their men, as did several hundred of Colonel Nathan Bedford Forrest's cavalry command. Left with little alternative, Buckner, an old army friend of Grant's, asked for terms of surrender. Grant's reply became one of the most famous lines of the war: "No terms except an immediate and unconditional surrender can be accepted. I propose to move immediately upon your works." Buckner had no choice but to accept, and with the surrender of Fort Donelson and the almost 13,000 Confederate soldiers within it, the North had a second stunning victory in as many weeks, and the Union discovered a new and much-needed hero in "Unconditional Surrender" Grant.

Like the victory at Fort Henry, the fall of Fort Donelson produced major repercussions. The Cumberland River now lay open all the way to Nashville, which became the first Confederate capital to fall on February 25. Confederate troops had by this time been forced from Kentucky and most of Tennessee, and now they fell all the way back to Corinth, Mississippi, where Johnston gathered his scattered forces. Grant's campaign, coupled with the amphibious operations along the Carolina coast, also confirmed the wisdom of Winfield Scott's "Anaconda Plan." As spring approached, Union forces took aim at the Mississippi River.

Although it had been a rough winter for the Confederates, events in Virginia, or a lack thereof, gave them reason for optimism. Back East, McClellan had failed to deliver a victory or even hint at offensive action. The undeniably gifted "Young Napoleon" had built a magnificent army of upwards of 150,000 men and yet remained convinced he needed more, always believing himself outnumbered. To an increasingly frustrated President Lincoln, the arrogant and condescending "Little Mac," having so carefully created the Army of the Potomac, appeared unwilling or unable to expose it in combat. McClellan's apprehensions notwithstanding, citizens and soldiers on both sides would soon witness the unimaginable carnage of modern warfare in North America.

CONCLUSIONS

The decade that followed the war with Mexico and preceded the Civil War proved to be anything but the calm between two storms. It was, in fact, quite a formative and important period in the evolution of America's military establishment. The army continued to refine its position within the greater society even as it faced major challenges such as massive territorial expansion, Indian unrest, and intensifying sectional strife. As a small professional organization, it relied on the government's frugal civilian leadership to finance its expansive mission and made some modest progress in force augmentation and technological development, including the establishment of the army's first designated cavalry regiments, the adoption of rifled weaponry, and the widespread employment of the army in support of civilian endeavors. Geography and industrial development continued in many ways to define the army's numerous roles, which ranged from escorting westward pioneers to surveying land for future railroads. America's soldiers spread across vast new lands, establishing forts and opening new areas for settlement. Rapid westward expansion brought inevitable confrontation with the fierce tribes of the Great Plains and the Far West, with soldiers growing increasingly adept at asymmetrical warfare. As Captain Marcy noted, little in the army officer's West Point education prepared him for life on the frontier. Instead, soldiers learned on the job and did so remarkably well.

The navy, too, experienced daunting new demands and responded with impressive achievements. The acquisition of California and its fine deepwater ports made further exploitation of the Pacific a foregone conclusion. With increasing bellicosity, the navy engaged in profitable as well as punitive campaigns, forging important relationships but also forcefully protecting U.S. interests. Like the army, the navy experienced rapid technological advancement, in steam and screw propulsion, armor, and rifled guns. Just as army engineers mapped the West, navy men charted the seas and explored new, distant regions.

Still, despite notable progress in professionalism and proficiency, weaponry, and leadership, the military establishment was shaken like the rest of the country when South Carolina began the secession movement that triggered the Civil War. The demands of that war soon proved far too great for the small professional force and the navy to meet and once again required the government to call forth a citizen army, one far larger and mightier than most Americans could have fathomed. Once at war, the two Americas fielded great bodies of amateur soldiers who were controlled by civilian authorities who had little grasp of how to prosecute such a conflict and generals who, like the young lieutenant on the prewar frontier, were forced to learn on the job. As a result, the leaders on both sides of this regrettable war struggled to articulate strategy or to execute it once it had been defined.

The Civil War unfolded at a time when industrial progress yielded great technological advancements that should have materially altered the way wars were fought or discouraged them altogether. This did not occur. Generals continued to rely on tactics derived from the Napoleonic era, and soldiers failed to adjust to the possibilities presented by their improved muskets and ammunition. Thus, the Civil War was fought much like previous wars had been fought, with large, linear formations engaging at short distances with predictably heavy casualties. The first year of the war, though, offered only a small sample of the horrors to come.

TIMELINE

1850	U.S. Naval Academy established
1853–1854	Matthew C. Perry's "opening" of Japan
1855–1858	Third Seminole War
1855	1st and 2nd Cavalry Regiments established
1855	U.S. armories begin exclusive production of rifle muskets
1856–1858	"Bleeding" Kansas
1857	Twelve-Pounder "Napoleon" gun introduced into U.S. arsenal
1857–1858	Utah expedition (Mormon War)
October 1859	John Brown's raid on Harpers Ferry
November 1860	Abraham Lincoln elected president
December 1860	South Carolina secedes from Union
February 1861	Seven southern states form Confederate States of America
April 1861	Confederate forces fire on Fort Sumter; Lincoln calls for volunteers
July 1861	First Battle of Bull Run
November 1861	George McClellan appointed general in chief of Union forces
February 1862	Confederate Forts Henry and Donelson fall to U.S. forces
March 1862	USS *Monitor* and CSS *Virginia* fight first engagement between ironclad warships

SUGGESTED READINGS

Beatie, Russel H. *Army of the Potomac*, vol. 2: *McClellan Takes Command, September 1861–February 1862*. Cambridge, MA: Da Capo Press, 2004.

Bigler, David L., and Will Bagley. *The Mormon Rebellion: America's First Civil War, 1857–1858*. Norman: University of Oklahoma Press, 2011.

Chalfant, William Y. *Cheyennes and Horse Soldiers: The 1857 Expedition and the Battle of Solomon's Fork*. Norman: University of Oklahoma Press, 1989.

Feifer, George. *Breaking Open Japan: Commodore Perry, Lord Abe, and American Imperialism in 1853*. Washington, D.C.: Smithsonian, 2006.

Goetzmann, William H. *Exploration and Empire: The Explorer and the Scientist in the Winning of the American West*. New York: W. W. Norton, 1978.

Hess, Earl J. *The Rifle Musket in Civil War Combat: Reality and Myth.* Lawrence: University Press of Kansas, 2008.

Horwitz, Tony. *Midnight Rising: John Brown and the Raid that Sparked the Civil War.* New York: Henry Holt and Company, 2011.

Longacre, Edward G. *The Early Morning of War: Bull Run, 1861.* Norman: University of Oklahoma Press, 2014.

Madley, Benjamin. *An American Genocide: The United States and the California Indian Catastrophe.* New Haven, CT: Yale University Press, 2016.

Smith, Gene A. *Iron and Heavy Guns: The Duel Between the* Monitor *and the* Merrimac. Abilene, TX: McWhiney Foundation Press, 1998.

Smith, Timothy B. *Grant Invades Tennessee: The 1862 Battles of Forts Henry and Donelson.* Lawrence: University Press of Kansas, 2016.

Utley, Robert M. *Frontiersmen in Blue: The United States Army and the Indian, 1848–1865.* New York: Macmillan, 1967.

CHAPTER 8

HARD WAR
1862–1865

The Western Theater: 1862 • *The Eastern Theater: 1862* • *The Rise of Robert E. Lee*
• *The Eastern Theater: 1863* • *Conscription* • *The Western Theater: 1863* • *Black Troops*
• *Prisoners of War* • *Decisions* • *The Eastern Theater: 1864* • *The Western Theater: 1864*
• *"Damn the Torpedoes": Naval Actions of 1864* • *The Final Acts: 1865*

The Civil War offered a career-defining proving ground for two generations of professional soldiers. Men like Grant and Lee, Jackson and Sherman became the stars of this monumental conflict, but professionals constituted only a fraction of those engaged. More than 3 million men served in the war, the vast majority of whom were volunteers or draftees from civilian life with little or no military experience. An astonishing number of these men became very good soldiers and contributed mightily to the war effort despite the hostility they often encountered from their professional comrades. Talented amateurs Nathan Bedford Forrest, Wade Hampton, and Richard Taylor amassed impressive records as lieutenant generals in the Confederate army. On the Union side much negative attention has accrued to "political generals" such as Nathaniel Banks, Benjamin Butler, and Daniel Sickles, all of whom struggled in high command, but the North also derived a wealth of excellence from its citizen-soldiers. Men like Nelson A. Miles, Francis C. Barlow, and John A. Logan became prolific warriors. The wartime experience of nonprofessionals contributed greatly to the postwar proliferation of veterans' organizations and patriotic societies and helped drive significant changes in the postwar regular army as a number of these men received commissions and transitioned into the professional ranks.

Although something of a cliché now, thanks to his own self-aggrandizing prose and the admiring treatment of historians, novelists, documentarians, and filmmakers, Joshua Lawrence Chamberlain of Maine represents the Civil War's ideal citizen-soldier. A Bowdoin College professor when he took leave to accept a volunteer commission with the 20th Maine Infantry, Chamberlain took command of his regiment just two weeks before the Battle of Gettysburg, where he and his men famously helped defend Little Round Top, a feat for which he was awarded the Medal of Honor in 1893. After being wounded several times, dangerously so at Petersburg, and earning promotion to brigadier general, he went on to command a brigade in the Army of the Potomac in the final stages of the war.

A capable self-promoter like Chamberlain, John Brown Gordon also wrote stirringly of his war experience. Born into a prosperous Georgia family, he attended the University of Georgia but never finished. He then studied law but instead became engaged in the lucrative family coal business. An outspoken advocate of secession, he raised a company of volunteers that became part of the 6th Alabama Infantry, with Gordon as its captain. While fighting in the Eastern Theater, this dynamic natural leader rose steadily through the ranks, becoming colonel in April 1862. After being severely wounded at Antietam, he was promoted to brigadier general and thereafter took on an increasingly prominent role in General Lee's Army of Northern Virginia, rising to major general and corps command. By war's end he was arguably Lee's most capable subordinate, and during the final Appomattox Campaign he directed more than half of the army. Rather inexplicably, he never received the appropriate promotion to lieutenant general that he so richly earned.

It was fitting, then, that these two self-made warriors should create a final bit of drama on a narrow lane in Appomattox County, Virginia. On April 12, 1865, three days after the fateful meeting between Lee and Grant, the official surrender took place, with the proud remnants of Lee's army filing past elements of the victorious Army of the Potomac's V Corps, stacking their arms, and yielding their battle-torn banners. Lee, Grant, and almost every other top general had already departed, but there remained some unfinished business to settle. According to his eloquent and evocative account *The Passing of the Armies: An Account of the Final Campaign of the Army of the Potomac, Based upon Personal Reminiscences of the Fifth Army Corps* (1915), Chamberlain had been designated by Grant to preside over the final surrender. If this was indeed the case, it was a curious choice, as Chamberlain was not the senior officer on hand. No such curiosity would have accompanied the appointment of the man who led the Confederate column in this final sad parade: John Gordon, whose perfect posture remained intact as he rode at the head of his corps though lines of Union veterans. As Gordon passed, Chamberlain ordered a salute from his assembled men. Gordon, recognizing the gesture, directed his soldiers to return the salute—"honor answering honor," as Chamberlain put it. "On our part," he recalled, there was "not a sound of trumpet more, nor roll of drum; not a cheer, nor word nor whisper of vain-glorying . . . but an awed stillness rather and a breath-holding, as if it were the passing of the dead." In the spirit of Grant's generous surrender terms, Chamberlain's actions further promoted national reconciliation.

Both Chamberlain and Gordon parleyed their military experience into successful postwar careers. Chamberlain served four one-year terms as governor of Maine before returning to Bowdoin College as president. He spent the final years of his life as the government-appointed surveyor of the port at Portland, Maine, and died in 1914 of complications from his Petersburg wound, which had never fully healed and for fifty years caused him great discomfort. General Gordon became one of many former Confederates to rise to prominence as a "Redeemer" in the Democratic Party. He served in the U.S. Senate and as governor of Georgia. Immensely popular among veterans, he enjoyed a successful speaking career and published a highly romanticized if somewhat factually dubious memoir. He died in 1904.

PRINCIPAL CAMPAIGNS OF THE CIVIL WAR, 1862–1865

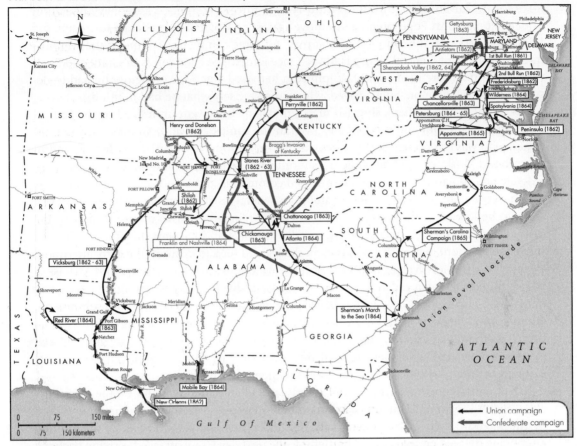

MAP 8.1 Principal Campaigns of the Civil War, 1862–1865

THE WESTERN THEATER: 1862

With the arrival of April the war approached its first anniversary. Fighting had spread from the Carolina coast to New Mexico, but Americans had yet to witness the big, decisive battle that many expected, one that would settle the question of southern independence one way or the other. Apart from Grant, whose aggressive riverine campaign continued to make inroads in the South, few commanders appeared interested in a fight. Outside of Washington, General McClellan continued to balk when prodded by President Lincoln. His giant army stood dormant for months. Confederate forces in Virginia appeared no more eager to engage, content to await McClellan's move. But out West Grant maintained the initiative, moving his growing army unmolested along the Tennessee River toward his next objective, the critical railroad hub of Corinth, Mississippi, where his adversary Sidney Johnston had cobbled together a force of more than 40,000.

Early in the month Grant's army of 35,000 soldiers, supported by two river gunboats, encamped along the Tennessee at Pittsburg Landing, just north of the Mississippi line, awaiting the army of General Don Carlos Buell, which after taking Nashville planned to join Grant's force for the advance on Corinth. A third Federal force, a combined army-navy operation under General John Pope, prepared to move against an isolated Confederate fortress in the Mississippi to begin the conquest of that river. All three commands fell under the administrative umbrella of General Henry Halleck. Once joined, the commands of Grant and Buell would number more than 60,000. If Johnston harbored any hope of victory he had to destroy Grant's wing before Buell arrived, which was precisely what he had in mind.

On April 6, 1862, after a sluggish march that somehow went unnoticed by the Federal army, Johnston's four corps struck and overran the camps of five of Grant's six divisions. Grant, who was not present at the attack, rushed to the scene to organize a defensive perimeter around Pittsburg Landing while his subordinates bought valuable time. A flawed Confederate attack plan led to badly intermingled commands and a poor distribution of force, which were complicated by pockets of stubborn Federal resistance, notably the position that came to be known as the Hornets' Nest, where the remnants of two divisions held up the Confederate advance for hours. Trying to rally his force and reorient the attack, Johnston moved to the front, where he was struck in the leg and bled to death in the early afternoon. Command then devolved upon P.G.T. Beauregard, the hero of Fort Sumter and Manassas, who had recently been exiled to the West because of his inability to get along with President Davis. Finally, the Confederates blasted the men in the Hornets' Nest into submission, taking some 2,000 prisoners. But by that time, Grant had developed a strong defensive position at the landing, where the remnants of five divisions and more than sixty guns, as well as two "timber-clad" gunboats, awaited the final Confederate onslaught that never came. Content with the day's victory, Beauregard suspended the attack.

That night, ignoring the advice of subordinates to cross the river and escape, Grant decided instead to attack. Reinforced by the quickly deploying divisions of Buell's army and by the wayward division of General Lew Wallace, which had missed most of the fighting after being delayed en route to the battlefield, the next day Grant attacked, driving back the Confederates and recovering his overrun camps. Beauregard had no choice but to retreat back to Corinth. The Battle of Shiloh or Pittsburg Landing became the first of many epic bloodbaths of the war and the largest battle to that point in American history. At the time it seemed unimaginable that American men could unleash such horror on each other. Out of roughly 100,000 men engaged, more than a quarter had been killed, wounded, or taken prisoner, including some 1,700 killed on each side, among them General Johnston, who became and remained the highest-ranking officer to perish in the Civil War. Moreover, Shiloh became the tragic prototype for Civil War battles: massed armies, mass confusion, high casualties, and an utter lack of decisiveness. Going forward, the model would be repeated often, with the carnage only compounded. These battles featured such ferocity that their victors rarely realized a meaningful opportunity to exploit the triumph and almost never managed to do so. So, while Shiloh gave America its first taste of slaughter on a grand scale, it was only the beginning.

For his part, Grant escaped catastrophe, but not by much. His army had been surprised and could well have been destroyed. He suffered much criticism and many calls for his head and even considered resigning, only to be convinced otherwise by his friend and subordinate

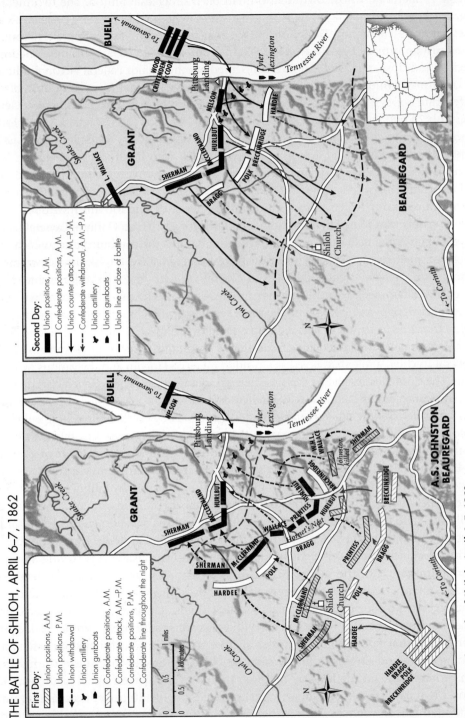

THE BATTLE OF SHILOH, APRIL 6–7, 1862

First Day:

- Union positions, A.M.
- Union positions, P.M.
- Union withdrawal
- Union artillery
- Union gunboats
- Confederate positions, A.M.
- Confederate attack, A.M.–P.M.
- Confederate positions, P.M.
- Confederate line throughout the night

Second Day:

- Union positions, A.M.
- Confederate positions, A.M.
- Union counter attack, A.M.–P.M.
- Confederate withdrawal, A.M.–P.M.
- Union artillery
- Union gunboats
- Union line at close of battle

MAP 8.2 The Battle of Shiloh, April 6–7, 1862

William T. Sherman, whose own division had been savaged at Shiloh. The two men now formed a bond—a martial partnership—that ultimately would win the war. Grant's early success at Forts Henry and Donelson likely saved his job, but something else about him helped sustain him; as Lincoln replied to Grant's critics: "I can't spare this man. He fights." Criticism and close calls aside, Shiloh represented another major Federal victory in the West and confirmed Union control of Tennessee. It was also the first hit of a double blow to Confederate hopes in the West. The day after Beauregard retreated from Tennessee, General Pope, with 23,000 men and Flag Officer Foote's gunboats, took the Confederate river fortress known as Island # 10 that was supposed to prevent Federal access to the lower Mississippi. Island # 10, its garrison, and dozens of heavy guns fell with hardly a fight. Whereas in the East no coherent strategy had emerged on either side, in the West Union forces had developed a formula for success that involved the conquest of the South's navigable rivers and key communications centers, forcing the Confederates to defend too much with too little.

Pope's army now joined those of Grant and Buell for a strike on Corinth. General Halleck, a respected military intellectual, arrived to take command of the combined force, which he led in an incomprehensibly slow and unreasonably cautious advance. It took almost two months for troops to cover the twenty-odd miles to Corinth, only to find it abandoned on May 30. Halleck now attempted to consolidate his gains, leaving Grant's Army of the Tennessee to hold northern Mississippi and West Tennessee while sending Buell's command, now designated the Army of the Ohio, eastward to take the railroad and river hub of Chattanooga. In July, Lincoln called Halleck to Washington, where his talents as an administrator could be put to better use as general-in-chief, a role that served as a conduit between Lincoln and the various field commands. The Confederates had by this time fallen back to Tupelo, where General Braxton Bragg replaced Beauregard after the latter was relieved for taking an unauthorized break from the army. Bragg wasted little time in seizing the initiative. Making excellent use of the railroad, he moved most of his force to Chattanooga via Montgomery, Alabama, beating Buell to the prize.

Bragg then moved northward from Chattanooga, while a separate Confederate command under General Edmund Kirby Smith advanced into eastern Kentucky from Knoxville, forcing the cautious Buell to protect his lines of communication by falling back all the way to Louisville. After briefly occupying Kentucky's capital at Frankfort but failing substantially to rally the state to the Confederate cause, Bragg found his position suddenly precarious. After being strongly reinforced, Buell finally moved against the invaders. Despite neither side showing any particular interest in fighting, they nonetheless clashed at Perryville, southwest of Lexington, on October 8 in a confused, disjointed affair in which neither general could bring his full force to bear on the enemy. Bragg fell back into Tennessee via the Cumberland Gap unmolested by Buell, who marched toward Nashville. Lincoln had by now seen enough of Buell and replaced him with General William Rosecrans, himself coming off lackluster performances that fall in Union victories at Iuka and Corinth in Mississippi. After much prodding Bragg and Rosecrans finally came to blows on Stones River near Murfreesboro, south of Nashville, on the last day of 1862. In one of the fiercest fights of the war, each side over two days (they took January 1 off) suffered roughly 30 percent casualties (almost 25,000 men killed, wounded, or missing of the 82,000 engaged). Yet the battle yielded no advantage to either side, and both armies went into winter quarters.

Meanwhile the navy tightened its grip on the Deep South. One force under Captain Charles Davis, who had replaced the wounded Foote, steamed southward down the Mississippi, neutralizing Fort Pillow above Memphis and taking the city itself by early June before moving to the mouth of the Yazoo, just miles upriver from Vicksburg. Another force concurrently moved up the Mississippi from the Gulf of Mexico. Commodore David G. Farragut, with a squadron of eight steam sloops, mortar rafts, and gunboats, along with transports carrying 10,000 soldiers under General Benjamin Butler, first engaged the two forts protecting the approaches to New Orleans on April 24, destroying nine Rebel gunboats and taking New Orleans without a fight the next day. Butler's men then arrived to begin the unhappy occupation of the South's largest city and the repository of much of its tangible wealth. Soon Baton Rouge, a second capital, and Natchez also fell to the unstoppable combined arms of the United States. By May, Vicksburg stood as the last important Confederate bastion on the Mississippi. The Confederacy's inability to defend important cities like New Orleans and Memphis pointed to the problems of geography but also to the superiority of the Federal navy, to which the Rebels had no real answer.

Vicksburg now became General Grant's singular objective. Having concentrated his Army of the Tennessee east of Memphis, in November he advanced into Mississippi but found his operation hampered by Confederate cavalry raids on his lines of communication. The sacking of the Federals' newly established forward supply base at Holly Springs by General Earl Van Dorn's raiders eventually compelled Grant to pull his army back by year's end. Still, he hoped for better news from a secondary expedition, an amphibious operation led by Sherman and his naval counterpart Commander David Dixon Porter that landed near the mouth of the Yazoo on Christmas Day. The Confederate defenders on the bluffs above Chickasaw Bayou, however, easily repulsed Sherman's attack on December 29. It had been an impressive year for Grant and Federal forces in the West, but it ended in frustration, with the general no closer to taking the "Gibraltar of the Mississippi" than he had been months before.

THE EASTERN THEATER: 1862

Since taking command of the Army of the Potomac George McClellan had built what appeared to be a magnificent force, with orderly camps, well-trained soldiers, and notably high morale, but had done little to inspire Lincoln's confidence. His army sat idle through the fall and winter, as Little Mac continued to believe his force dramatically outnumbered, although it never would be. Felled by a bout of typhoid fever during the winter, he showed no sign of newfound aggressiveness as spring approached. By March 1862, President Lincoln had had enough and ordered an advance. McClellan responded with an ambitious proposal to move his army of more than 150,000 by water via the Chesapeake Bay to Urbanna on the Rappahannock River, less than fifty miles east of Richmond, hoping to catch the Confederates in Northern Virginia off guard. But Joseph Johnston, the top Confederate commander in Virginia, learned of the plan and quickly pulled his army back to cover the capital. Still committed to a waterborne operation, McClellan shifted his landing target to the Union-held Fort Monroe at the tip of the peninsula formed by the York and James rivers more than seventy miles southeast of Richmond. In March, promising Lincoln that Washington had adequate protection, McClellan began the massive movement of troops toward the peninsula. But a minor engagement in the distant Shenandoah Valley changed the whole complexion of the campaign and likely altered the course of the war.

On March 23 a small Rebel command under Stonewall Jackson attacked a much larger Federal force at Kernstown in the lower valley near Winchester. Although his forces were repulsed, Jackson made a strong impression, convincing Federal authorities that he possessed a much larger force than he had and that he posed a significant threat to Washington. Lincoln, who had relieved McClellan of his overall command, now assumed a more active role in directing operations and ordered the rerouting of Federal assets to the Shenandoah. Among those assets were the 30,000 men of Irvin McDowell's corps, who had been earmarked to support McClellan's effort at Richmond.

Jackson's Shenandoah Valley Campaign featured a remarkable combination of rapid marching, hard fighting, and sheer intimidation. With reinforcements swelling the Rebel ranks to 18,000 men, between April 30 and June 9 Jackson fought and won four battles and numerous skirmishes, marched almost 700 miles, and tied up three separate Union commands while inflicting 8,000 casualties to 2,500 of his own. Most importantly, he prevented at least 30,000 men from joining McClellan at Richmond.

On the Virginia Peninsula, McClellan's 90,000 men began a slow advance on Richmond but quickly found their path blocked at Yorktown, the site of the British surrender in 1781, by a Confederate barricade manned by no more than 15,000. The Confederate commander, John B. Magruder, employed a number of ruses, including felled trees painted to resemble cannon, to deceive the already cautious McClellan, who easily could have punched through the Rebel works. Instead, he wasted a month waiting for siege artillery. Fortunately for the Federals, Confederate general Joseph Johnston, who arrived to assume overall command and was, if possible, just as timid as McClellan, ordered his forces to fall back toward Richmond. The Army of the Potomac followed, with McClellan convinced as ever that he was outnumbered. Despite the glacially slow advance, Federal forces reached the outskirts of Richmond on May 25. With the army deployed roughly equally on both sides of the Chickahominy River, Johnston seized the opportunity to attack McClellan's divided command on May 31. In the Battle of Seven Pines or Fair Oaks, the Federals beat back piecemeal Confederate assaults over two days of fighting th   casualties numbered 5,000, while the Confe   nificantly, Johnston, who was badly wounde

THE RISE OF ROBERT E. LEE

With a large yet docile Federal army practically at Richmond's gates and his top commander incapacitated, President Davis, seeing no logical alternative on the field, appointed his military advisor General Robert E. Lee to command the forces around Richmond. Thus far, the war had not favored Lee. Western Virginia had fallen to Union forces on his watch, a development for which he was widely criticized, even ridiculed. After an unceremonious tour of Confederate fortifications, Lee had been ordered to Richmond. Once perhaps the most highly regarded soldier in the old army, he now had his shot at redemption.

Lee designated his new command the Army of Northern Virginia; called in reinforcements, bringing Jackson's troops from the valley; and sent out his cavalry under dashing young General J.E.B. "Jeb" Stuart on a ride around McClellan's army during which Stuart's men destroyed tons of supplies and gathered much valuable information about McClellan's dispositions. For most of three weeks McClellan failed to make a major move, giving Lee plenty of time to plan and prepare. When the fighting finally began, the odds were roughly equal, with Lee commanding some 97,000 men in and around Richmond and McClellan overseeing about 104,000. On June 25, McClellan ordered an ineffectual probe of Lee's main line, but Lee countered by stripping that line in order to concentrate the bulk of his forces on the single Federal corps north of the Chickahominy. These actions began a series of furious fights known as the Seven Days Battles.

On June 26, Lee launched a massive but badly uncoordinated attack on General Fitz John Porter's V Corps at Mechanicsville. Porter held and inflicted heavy casualties on the Confederates but soon withdrew to a stronger position at Gaines's Mill. Again Lee unleashed a ferocious frontal assault, and again Porter held until late afternoon, when General John Bell Hood's Texas Brigade pierced the Federal line; however, the Rebels could not exploit the breach. Porter's corps withdrew during the night, uniting with the rest of the army, which McClellan now ordered to retreat. Completely unnerved by the intensity of Lee's offensive, he opted to save his army rather than continue the conquest of Richmond. The Federals beat back savage assaults on June 29 and 30, falling back to an excellent position at Malvern Hill, where Lee again attacked on July 1 and again suffered frightful losses. Despite a clear victory in this last of the Seven Days Battles, during which he inflicted casualties on a two-to-one basis, McClellan continued the retreat to a prepared position on the James River at Harrison's Landing. The Confederates had suffered almost 20,000 killed and wounded to fewer than 10,000 among the Federals, but the Army of Northern Virginia had saved Richmond and taken 6,000 Yankee prisoners in the process. Robert E. Lee emerged as a hero who inspired awe in the South and fear among his adversaries. Nevertheless, the Seven Days boldly demonstrated a troubling truth: Lee's brand of fighting was unsustainable unless he could deliver the elusive decisive victory.

Lincoln, bitterly disappointed by McClellan's failure, created a second major field force in Virginia, the Army of Virginia, and summoned John Pope from the West to command it. With Pope's army in Northern Virginia and McClellan's still on the peninsula, Lee left troops to cover Richmond and moved northward with his reorganized army to confront Pope. After much maneuvering Lee found Pope where he wanted him, near the old Bull Run battlefield. Here Lee employed a vintage Napoleonic move, enticing his opponent to attack an inviting portion of his army while hitting his enemy's exposed flank with the other portion. On August 29 Pope obliged, attacking Jackson's corps and allowing General James Longstreet's corps to strike his flank unprepared. The tactic drove the Federals from the field and ultimately to the safety of Washington's defenses. Even in a complete victory, Lee lost 10,000 men killed, wounded, and missing to Pope's 16,000, so he could not mount a meaningful pursuit. Pope was reassigned to distant Minnesota, and his short-lived army would be absorbed into the Army of the Potomac when it returned from the peninsula.

ANTIETAM, SEPTEMBER 17, 1862

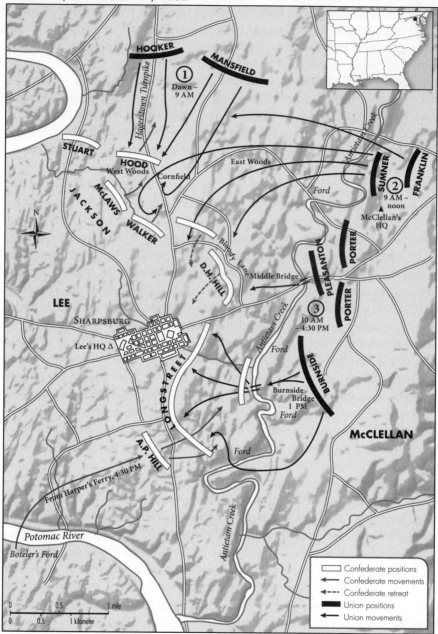

MAP 8.3   Antietam, September 17, 1862

Already something of a military legend, Lee had within three months saved Richmond and routed a second Federal army, but he had also amassed monumental casualties, his army was suffering from a serious lack of coordination and good staff work, and his men badly needed rest and resupply. Nevertheless, Lee instead chose to assume the offensive, deciding to take the war into the North, where he hoped to gain recruits and secure a decisive victory on northern soil that would attract foreign recognition if not direct intervention. On September 4, the 55,000-strong Army of Northern Virginia crossed the Potomac River and moved into Maryland, concentrating at Frederick three days later. There Lee divided the army, sending Jackson to take nearby Harpers Ferry. Back in Washington, McClellan, recently restored to command, led his 95,000 men in pursuit. On September 12, McClellan's forces recovered a lost copy of Lee's marching orders. He now had Lee's army badly divided but once again failed to act decisively.

Lee desperately attempted to concentrate at Sharpsburg while portions of his command fought holding actions in the hills between that town and Frederick. After taking Harpers Ferry and more than 10,000 Federal prisoners, Jackson left the division of General A. P. Hill to finish up while marching with the rest of his command to Sharpsburg. For two days, McClellan failed to move against Lee, allowing the Confederates to prepare a strong position along Antietam Creek. The Battle of Antietam or Sharpsburg presented McClellan, who had almost double the men Lee did, with an ideal opportunity to destroy Lee's army. Yet in typical McClellan fashion he failed to seize the moment. When he finally attacked on September 17, he sent his corps into battle piecemeal, never adding available weight to the attack. This move allowed Lee to shift men to threatened spots along his line. A prime example of the economy of force principle, Lee's army fought stubbornly against long odds, often holding back entire corps with a single brigade. At almost any moment collapse appeared inevitable, but McClellan never committed his reserves. Finally, in the early afternoon, General Ambrose Burnside's IX Corps forced a crossing of Antietam Creek and appeared poised to crush Lee's right flank, but Burnside delayed, allowing A. P. Hill's division to arrive after a forced march from Harpers Ferry and stymie the assault. At the end of the day, Lee's small army had fought McClellan's massive host to a standstill. McClellan had failed to insert 20,000 men, who stood idle throughout the deadly contest. The casualties for the single day well exceeded 20,000, including 4,000 killed. It remains the deadliest one-day battle in American history.

After standing inactive the next day, McClellan permitted Lee to retreat back into Virginia without pursuit, missing still another opportunity. The Battle of Antietam, while disappointing to Lincoln by almost any measure, was nonetheless an important strategic victory for the Union. Lee had achieved nothing and had suffered heavy losses. Maryland had not rallied to the Confederate cause, nor had Marylanders joined Lee's shrinking ranks. A victory in any form was welcome, and Lincoln used the occasion to issue a preliminary Emancipation Proclamation, the final version of which would become law in January 1863. Although the proclamation in reality freed only a fraction of the nation's slaves, limited as it was to those living in the states still in rebellion, it did make the abolition of slavery a stated objective for the Union, and, importantly, it included a provision that allowed the United States to induct African American men into military service. By war's end more than 200,000 black men would serve in the army and navy, representing about one-tenth of the total number of men who served for the Union.

The missed opportunity at Antietam ushered in a winter of considerable discontent for President Lincoln and the Union. McClellan's continued inaction compelled the president in November to remove the still-popular general and replace him with another professional,

IMAGE 8.1 Antietam Dead   The September 17, 1862 Battle of Antietam remains the single deadliest day in American military history. The battlefield became one of the first to be extensively photographed in the wake of the fighting. This Alexander Gardner print vividly captured the carnage.

Ambrose Burnside, who had enjoyed some success early in the war but openly doubted his own fitness for high command. Burnside understood all too well what Lincoln expected of him. He assembled the massive Army of the Potomac, comprising more than 120,000 men divided into three "Grand Divisions" of two corps each—the only time such a configuration was used during the war—and moved toward Richmond via Fredericksburg. Reaching that lightly defended town on the Rappahannock River in mid-November, Burnside wasted a week awaiting the arrival of pontoons and another two weeks getting the bridges in place. This delay allowed Lee to unite his army, which had been restored to almost 80,000 men and more than 200 guns, on the high ground behind Fredericksburg. The Federal crossing began on December 11, impeded by Confederate snipers. Two days later the fighting began, promisingly enough, south of Fredericksburg, where two Union divisions managed to temporarily breach Jackson's line, only to be halted and driven back. Burnside's other, and much more memorable, attack was made against Longstreet's corps at Marye's Heights, where the Confederates held a powerful defensive position in a sunken road protected by a strong stone wall, behind which riflemen lined up three or four deep. Above them artillery covered the entire approach. Relegated to an impossibly narrow advance, the Union attack on the heights became a series of brigade-sized assaults—fourteen of them—that ended in senseless slaughter. By the end of the day Federal casualties exceeded 12,400, while Lee's army had suffered less than half that number. Fredericksburg became one of the most one-sided victories of the war, but again there was no meaningful follow-up by Lee. A second Union attempt to get around Lee's army in early January proved impossible thanks to knee-deep mud, a rather appropriate end to the winter campaign.

THE EASTERN THEATER: 1863

By now, a definite trend had emerged in the Eastern Theater: a large Federal army would march on Richmond, get defeated by a smaller, more aggressive Confederate force, and retreat. Lincoln had tried four generals with the same results. In January 1863, he turned to a fifth, General Joseph Hooker. "Fighting Joe" Hooker, a capable corps commander with a reputation for drinking and womanizing, worked quickly to reorganize and reinvigorate the Army of the Potomac in preparation for the spring campaign season. His army of almost 115,000 men had wintered near Fredericksburg in close proximity to Lee's force of roughly 60,000. Lee, coping as usual with meager resources, had sent most of Longstreet's corps to winter in the less war-torn southern part of the state, leaving the rest of the army particularly vulnerable to a forceful Federal advance.

Hooker devised a strong campaign strategy that involved holding Lee's army at Fredericksburg with a small portion of his command while a large cavalry raid toward Richmond further distracted the Confederate general, allowing Hooker to march with the bulk of his force around Lee's left flank to attack the exposed Confederate rear. The campaign opened with initial success in late April as three corps executed an excellent march, crossing the Rappahannock and Rapidan rivers and securing vital fords for the trailing corps. Hooker then concentrated in the densely wooded area west of Fredericksburg known as the Wilderness. The cavalry raid, though, accomplished nothing and left Hooker blind to his opponent's movements, which were daring, to say the least. After consolidating his army, Hooker began his advance, expecting Lee to retreat. When he was confronted instead by a small Confederate force on May 1, Hooker appears to have lost confidence, spurring him to fall back into the Wilderness to establish a defensive position around a crossroads community known as Chancellorsville.

Facing monumental odds, Lee had already divided his army, keeping an augmented division in Fredericksburg to discourage a Federal advance in that sector and moving with 40,000 men to the Wilderness to face Hooker. Lee's cavalry kept the general well abreast of Hooker's movements, altering him that the Federal right flank in the Wilderness appeared vulnerable. On May 2 Lee ordered the unthinkable, sending Jackson with 27,000 men on a wide flanking movement while keeping only 15,000 to face Hooker's 75,000-strong main body. At any moment Hooker could have attacked and likely destroyed the Confederates in the Wilderness and at Fredericksburg, but he remained idle, giving Jackson the time he needed to locate the Union flank. At 5:30 that afternoon, Jackson's men surprised the Federal XI Corps, rolling up the flank and threatening a total rout, but time and daylight ran out. After 9 p.m., attempting to press the attack, Jackson and several other officers were fired upon by confused troops of their own command, wounding Jackson. As the attack died out, Jackson's wing remained separated from Lee's. That night doctors amputated the general's shattered left arm, and cavalry commander Jeb Stuart assumed temporary command of Jackson's wing. In desperate fighting on May 3 Lee united with Stuart, but Federal troops under General John Sedgwick drove the Confederate forces from the heights at Fredericksburg and then moved to support Hooker at Chancellorsville. In response, Lee split his force again, driving back Sedgwick on May 4 at Salem Church. The next day Hooker began his withdrawal from the Wilderness. Union casualties approached 17,000 killed, wounded, and captured or missing, while the Confederates lost almost 13,000. Another Union advance had failed, and so too had another Union general. The Battle of Chancellorsville, often referred to as "Lee's Masterpiece," indeed featured an audacious Confederate performance but yielded the South no real advantage—only another bloodbath. Clearly, neither side possessed a winning strategy or the capability to deliver a truly decisive victory.

As he had done the previous year, Lee chose to seize the initiative and once again take the war into the North. Unlike the previous year, however, he would be marching northward without his most trusted subordinate, Stonewall Jackson. Jackson, who had been expected to recover from his Chancellorsville wound, instead contracted pneumonia and died on May 10, leaving Lee with a command crisis and no heir apparent to the lost general. Lee nonetheless decided to reorganize his army into three corps and selected fellow Virginians Richard Ewell and A. P. Hill to command the 2nd and 3rd Corps, respectively, with Longstreet retaining the steady 1st Corps. Ewell and Hill presented curious choices. Ewell had been out of action for more than a year recovering from a lost leg, and Hill, while a grand fighter, was plagued by serious health issues and was unreliable at best. Lee therefore headed into hostile territory with two-thirds of his army under new commanders, but this was only one of his problems.

On June 3, 1863, the Army of Northern Virginia moved northward through the Shenandoah Valley, with Stuart's cavalry screening the advance. But on June 9 Federal cavalry under General Alfred Pleasanton surprised Stuart's forces at Brandy Station. The resultant battle proved significant in three ways: one, for the first time Federal cavalry in the East equaled Rebel horsemen in battle; two, the position of Stuart's men betrayed Lee's intentions; and, three, an embarrassed Stuart, seeking to restore his reputation after the drawn fight, subsequently led his men on a long, quixotic raid that took him out of contact with Lee at a most inopportune time. Alerted to Lee's movement, Hooker put the Army of the Potomac in pursuit. By late June Lee's three corps were in Pennsylvania, but separated, with Federal forces closing in and no word from Stuart. At the same time long-running differences between Hooker and the Lincoln administration came to a head. Overplaying his hand, Hooker offered his resignation. Remarkably, on the eve of what promised to be a major battle, Lincoln accepted and appointed General George G. Meade commander. Finally alerted by a spy to the location of the Federal army, Lee ordered his forces to concentrate, precipitating the greatest battle ever fought in North America.

On July 1, 1863, a division from A. P. Hill's corps approached the crossroads village of Gettysburg in southeastern Pennsylvania, where two Federal cavalry brigades under General John Buford stood in its path. The Yankee troopers put up a stiff fight, buying time for the

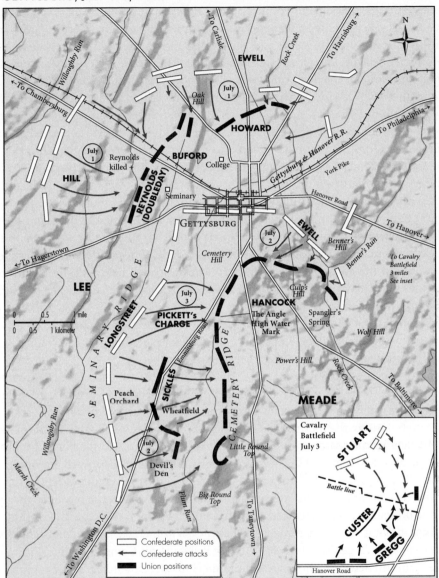

MAP 8.4 Gettysburg, July 1–3, 1863

infantry to arrive. What started as a skirmish (Lee had hoped to avoid a general engagement until he had more information about his enemy's movements) quickly became a fierce battle as the rest of Hill's corps arrived from the west and Ewell's corps struck from the north, driving two outnumbered Federal corps through the town but, importantly, onto high ground, where the Federals formed an excellent position around Cemetery Hill and Culp's Hill and then extended their line southward during the night along Cemetery Ridge. As the Federal corps settled in, their disposition came to resemble an inverted fishhook. Overall, the first day at Gettysburg featured plenty of determined fighting, with results that favored the Confederates but also represented a lost opportunity for which Lee's men would pay dearly.

On July 2, Lee hoped to strike and roll up the Federal left, which was anchored on a largely undefended hill known as Little Round Top. The attack took hours to organize, because responsibility for it fell to Longstreet, whose corps was still arriving on the field. In the meantime, the Union III Corps, which held the Federal left and was commanded by a publicity seeking political general named Daniel Sickles, advanced without orders, abandoning superior ground and exposing the entire Federal line to rout. When Longstreet did attack, he exploited Sickles's unauthorized redeployment with promising results. Hood's division crashed the flank and charged through the incongruous boulder-laden ground known as Devil's Den and up Little Round Top, but the quick response of the nearby Federal II Corps and fine work by the Yankee artillery saved the main line while Chief Engineer Gouverneur Warren on Little Round Top could rush reinforcements to the embattled hill in time to halt the Rebel advance. A supporting attack by Ewell's corps on the north end of the line made some headway but failed to dislodge the well dug-in Federal troops. Fighting continued into the night, but at the end of the day, the Union position had held, and thousands of men lay dead and wounded, including perhaps Lee's best fighting general, Hood, who suffered a horrible arm wound.

Having tried both flanks and believing Meade to have reinforced them at the expense of his center, Lee planned to hit the middle of the Union line with a massive artillery barrage followed by a three-division assault directed by Longstreet while Ewell again attacked the north end of the line and Stuart's cavalry, which had finally arrived on July 2, attempted to strike the Federal rear. But as events unfolded on July 3, nothing went according to plan. Longstreet delayed his attack, Ewell's morning attack amounted to nothing, and Stuart's effort was rebuffed by the increasingly confident Federal cavalry. Finally in early afternoon some 140 Rebel guns roared to life, blasting away at Cemetery Ridge but doing little real damage. At about 3 p.m., 12,000 Confederate soldiers moved forward in what became known as "Pickett's Charge" (after General George Pickett, commander of one of the attacking divisions). Crossing three-quarters of a mile of open ground in the July heat, the advance soon came under fire from Federal artillery that ripped through the Rebel lines, which nonetheless kept moving, now under intense rifle fire, even as men fell by the hundreds. Still they came even as double canister spewed from Yankee guns on Cemetery Ridge. Entire formations were annihilated. Somehow a few hundred Confederate soldiers made it to the Union line, only to fall or surrender. The attack claimed almost half of the men who went forward, including a number of generals and a frighteningly high percentage of company and field grade officers. The remnants of three divisions struggled rearward. The Battle of Gettysburg was over. In three days of intense fighting the Army of the Potomac had suffered 23,000 casualties, including more than 3,000 killed. The Army of Northern Virginia had lost as many as 28,000 men, including almost 4,000 killed.

Once again, two giant armies had waged a large and unthinkably bloody but ultimately indecisive battle in the Eastern Theater. Meade failed to mount a vigorous pursuit, for which he was criticized—rather unfairly—and Lee managed to get the remnants of his proud force back to Virginia. So devastating was Gettysburg that neither army managed another serious effort for ten months. Gettysburg was not a turning point as such, but it did expose Lee's limitations. He had made mistakes. But for once, the Army of the Potomac had won a clear victory and was now living up to its promise.

CONSCRIPTION

During the Civil War both governments passed and implemented conscription laws after initial enthusiasm for volunteering waned. The Confederate Congress passed the first conscription act in April 1862, and two subsequent laws expanded the scope of the legislation, requiring all white males ages eighteen to thirty-five to serve for a period of three years or the duration of the war and extending the enlistments of men already serving under volunteer enlistments to three years or the duration of the war. The Confederate government also continued to encourage volunteer enlistment by allowing enlistees certain privileges and paying them bounties. National conscription proved quite controversial in the South, as it ran counter to cherished beliefs about states' rights. Even more controversial were provisions that allowed for exemptions for certain men, the ability to hire substitutes, and the onerous "Twenty Negro Law," which exempted any planter who owned twenty or more slaves from the requirement to serve. Such exemptions rightly invited the indictment of the conflict as a "rich man's war, poor man's fight." Opposition to conscription was widespread but particularly acute in areas of strong Unionist sentiment. In March 1863 the U.S. Congress passed the first of several Enrollment Acts that established a military draft. As in the South, these outlined a number of exemptions and allowed individuals to escape service by paying a $300 fee or hiring a substitute. In the wake of the Emancipation Proclamation, with the abolition of slavery now a stated war aim, the prospect of being drafted to fight to free slaves who would then become economic competition did not sit well with working-class whites. A number of draft-related riots erupted in the North, the most infamous of which occurred in New York City in July 1863. During this clash, which was in reality a race riot, a mob consisting mostly of disgruntled Irish laborers attacked government buildings and the Republican Party headquarters before going after African American citizens, their homes, and their businesses, killing dozens and wounding hundreds before troops arrived from Gettysburg to restore order.

THE WESTERN THEATER: 1863

In the West, General Grant continued his focus on Vicksburg but abandoned any overland operation from Tennessee. He instead turned his attention to the Mississippi River and how best to position his army to get at the bastion. He reasoned that the only way to do so was to approach from the interior, but the Confederates and various natural obstructions made that almost impossible from the North or from the river itself. Landing his army south of Vicksburg would involve running the city's mighty batteries. Although discouraged by geography and nature, Grant remained determined, trying a number of approaches, including digging a canal that would allow the navy and his transport ships to bypass Vicksburg's heavy guns. By April Grant had concentrated his forces on the Louisiana side of the river at Milliken's Bend and begun moving his men southward to a position opposite Grand

Gulf, roughly forty miles below Vicksburg. Admiral Porter in a series of bold actions ran his gunboats and transports past Vicksburg's defenses to unite with Grant's army and provide a means of crossing the river. Grant now staged several distractions to draw Confederate attention from his intended crossing. The most famous and successful of these was a brigade-sized cavalry raid led by Colonel Benjamin Grierson that departed from La Grange, Tennessee, on April 17. Thus far, Federal cavalry had done little in the way of raiding and certainly paled in comparison to the Confederate raiders of Jeb Stuart and Nathan Bedford Forrest, but "Grierson's Raid" reversed that trend. In sixteen days, Grierson's command rode 600 miles through the heart of Mississippi, destroying miles of railroad and telegraph lines as well as rolling stock and valuable stores. The raid netted some 600 Confederate casualties to Grierson's own 27. Most important, it occupied and otherwise distracted thousands of Confederate troops while Grant crossed his army to the east bank of the Mississippi. Grierson's troopers entered Federal lines at Baton Rouge, Louisiana, on May 2.

On April 30, Grant's infantry completed the crossing, landing at Bruinsburg. The next day Federal forces defeated the Confederate garrison at Port Gibson. Turning inland, abandoning its communications, and living off the land, the Army of the Tennessee advanced on Jackson, defeating a Rebel force at Raymond on May 12. Two days later it drove the Confederates from Jackson and occupied the city, doing considerable damage to the railroad. Then, turning westward toward Vicksburg, Grant engaged and routed the main Confederate army of General John C. Pemberton on May 16 at Champion Hill. The next day, Federal troops compelled the Confederates to abandon their Big Black River position and fall back into Vicksburg's formidable defenses. In less than three weeks, Grant's army had marched almost 200 miles, won five large engagements and several smaller ones, and inflicted more than 8,000 casualties—almost twice as many as it suffered. Now, it had 30,000 Confederate troops trapped in their river fortress with nowhere to go and no way to sustain themselves.

After two costly and unsuccessful assaults, Grant settled for a siege, investing Vicksburg and mercilessly bombarding the Confederate position. Soldiers and civilians alike endured grimly in caves and tunnels, subsisting on meager food stocks and eventually anything that could be found, praying for relief. Those prayers went unanswered. General Joseph Johnston, sent by President Davis to command all Confederate forces in the Western Theater, had assembled a small army of about 30,000 men near Jackson but made no attempt to engage Grant or to at least ease the pressure on Vicksburg. With supplies exhausted and no hope of relief, on July 4, the very day Lee's defeated army marched away from Gettysburg, Pemberton surrendered his starving garrison of almost 30,000 men. His conquest of Vicksburg complete, Grant closed the book on one of the greatest campaigns in American military history. Through sheer determination and great skill, Grant had dealt the Confederacy its most damaging wound to date. Complete Federal control of the Mississippi opened the river to commerce and severed the Trans-Mississippi from the rest of the Confederacy, leaving Texas and its vast and badly needed resources isolated and largely unreachable.

As Grant tightened his grip on Vicksburg, one of the most interesting and overlooked events of the war unfolded in Tennessee, where General Rosecrans's Union Army of the Cumberland after months of inactivity finally moved against Bragg's Confederate Army of Tennessee. During the almost bloodless Tullahoma Campaign, which lasted from June 23 to

July 2, Rosecrans managed to maneuver Bragg's forces out of Middle Tennessee and back into Chattanooga. In August Rosecrans moved against Bragg's vital rail connection to Atlanta, forcing the Confederates to abandon Chattanooga and move into northwestern Georgia. At the same time, the Federal Army of the Ohio under Ambrose Burnside advanced from Kentucky toward Knoxville preparatory to a link-up with Rosecrans that, due to bad weather and poor roads, never occurred. Confederate authorities, sensing an opportunity to destroy Rosecrans's force, detached James Longstreet's corps from the largely idle Army of Northern Virginia and sent it by rail to reinforce Bragg in Georgia, which brought Bragg's troop total to more than 70,000 to Rosecrans's 60,000. It would be one of the few times the Confederates enjoyed a numerical advantage in battle. The opposing armies clashed in a densely wooded area along Chickamauga Creek a few miles south of Chattanooga on September 19. Fierce fighting yielded no advantage for either side, but the following day bungled orders resulted in a shift in the center of the Federal line just as Longstreet launched a particularly forceful attack, which allowed the Confederates to plunge through the gap, shattering the Federal line. General George Thomas, commanding the XIV Corps on the Union left, rallied enough of the army to make a stand, repelling repeated Confederate attacks and allowing the Army of the Cumberland, which reported more than 16,000 casualties, including almost 5,000 missing or captured, to withdraw in good order to Chattanooga. Bragg, who sustained almost 18,500 casualties, offered no pursuit. The Battle of Chickamauga stood out as one of the hardest-fought and bloodiest battles of the war but, like the other great slaughters, yielded no decisive results.

A badly unnerved Rosecrans held Chattanooga but soon found the town and his army surrounded by Bragg's forces and cut off from supplies and support. Burnside at Knoxville was unable to advance, and although two corps from the Army of the Potomac under General Hooker were rushed by rail to Chattanooga, they could not get through. The situation soon grew desperate as supplies dwindled and winter approached. At the same time dissension in the Confederate high command created major problems for Bragg and caused morale, already low, to plummet. The result was a strange paralysis on both sides that only ended with the appointment on October 17 of Grant as the Union's overall commander in the West. Grant slipped into Chattanooga a week later, having already relieved Rosecrans, whom he replaced with Thomas, and quickly ordered an operation that opened a gap in the Confederate siege line, through which Hooker's two corps passed into the city, bringing badly needed supplies. Soon, Sherman arrived from Mississippi with the Army of the Tennessee. With elements of three field armies, Grant now outnumbered Bragg by a considerable margin, especially after Bragg sent Longstreet's detachment of roughly 17,000 men on a fruitless mission to oust Burnside from Knoxville.

With the situation radically changed, on November 24 Grant ordered the first attacks on Bragg's strong positions on Lookout Mountain and Missionary Ridge. Hooker's men fought their way up Lookout Mountain, rising some 1,500 feet above the valley below, and rather easily displaced the Confederates there. East of Chattanooga, Sherman hit the Confederate right on Missionary Ridge but made no progress. The next day Hooker renewed his attack on the Confederate left as Sherman again attacked the right, with neither gaining ground against Bragg's now-consolidated line on Missionary Ridge. That afternoon, Thomas sent the Army of the Cumberland forward to threaten the Rebel center by taking the first line of works at the base of the ridge. The Cumberlanders, many of whom had experienced the embarrassment of Chickamauga, quickly achieved their objective but under heavy fire from the second and third lines on the ridge kept advancing without orders. Now, the steepness of the ridge worked against the defenders, as they were unable to adjust their artillery and rifle fire to compensate for the rise, and Federal troops pressed to the top, piercing the Confederate line, which soon crumbled. Nightfall and a stubborn rearguard stand by General Patrick Cleburne's excellent division saved Bragg's force, which escaped into Georgia.

By Civil War standards, the Battle of Chattanooga featured comparatively light casualties, with 5,800 for Grant and 6,700 for Bragg, the majority of which were listed as missing or captured. But the victory confirmed forever the Union hold on Tennessee. Control of the important railroad hub provided an excellent jumping-off point for the coming conquest of the Deep South. Finally, the victory, coming on the heels of Vicksburg, marked Grant as the undisputed champion of the Union effort. Indeed, most of what had been won to this point in the conflict came on Grant's watch. But as the war entered its fourth year, final victory appeared no closer, and for Lincoln, entering the last year of his term with reelection very much in doubt, time was running out.

BLACK TROOPS

Union commanders in in occupied areas of the South had begun to organize "contraband" units out of runaway slaves early in the war, but the Emancipation Proclamation allowed the official enlistment of black soldiers and sailors. Among the first black regiments raised in the North, the 54th Massachusetts Infantry was also among the first to see action, suffering staggering casualties in a fruitless attack on Fort Wagner near Charleston in the summer of 1863. Most African American units were organized into regiments of the United States Colored Troops (USCT) and officered by white volunteers. The arming of black troops—both freemen and former slaves—brought vitriolic denouncements from the Confederacy, which vowed to execute any captured black man or white officer of black troops. While this drastic measure was never officially taken, untold numbers of black men and freemen seized by Confederates during operations were subsequently enslaved. Black troops were also subject to atrocities such as the murder of surrendering black soldiers at Fort Pillow in Tennessee and the unchecked slaughter of black soldiers during battle. While most black troops performed labor and other services or served in rear areas guarding railroads and warehouses, by the end of the war the Union army had mustered entire divisions of black troops that went on to play a substantive role in the final campaigns. More than 180,000 black men served in the Union armies, and at least 18,000 served in the navy, accounting for almost 10 percent of the total Federal force. Only late in the war did the Confederacy embrace the idea of arming slaves to fight in exchange for their freedom, but hostilities ended before any black regiments were organized.

PRISONERS OF WAR

The treatment of black prisoners was a contributing factor in one of the most controversial and unsavory chapters of the war. During the first two years of the war, both armies had cooperated on the exchange of prisoners or issued paroles under which surrendered soldiers were allowed to return home if they agreed not to take up arms for a specified period. These systems had worked well until the Confederacy's declaration that it would execute any black prisoners. That move, combined with widespread abuse of parole agreements, especially after the large-scale surrender at Vicksburg, caused the Lincoln administration to suspend exchanges in 1863. Neither government was prepared for the surge of prisoners that overwhelmed prison facilities both North and South in 1864, creating myriad horrors. With its economy in shambles and unable to feed and clothe its own soldiers and civilians, the Confederate government was particularly hard-pressed to care for Yankee prisoners. The most infamous example of this ugly reality was the Andersonville stockade in Georgia, where some 13,000 Union soldiers died of disease, exposure, or starvation. Even in the bountiful Union, prisons were scenes of unspeakable neglect, wretched sanitation, and scarce food.

DECISIONS

The winter of 1863–1864 found the war no closer to resolution than it had been the previous year. Despite Union victories, an economic collapse, and food shortages occasioned by an ever-tightening blockade, the Confederacy remained defiant. In Washington, President Lincoln, faced with rising dissent from antiwar Democrats and a general public weariness with the war, entered an election year facing the real prospect of defeat. Three years into the war neither army had produced anything like the knockout blow that so many had expected back in 1861. But while a decisive victory remained elusive, Lincoln showed himself still capable of decisive military action. In March he appointed U.S. Grant general-in-chief of the Armies of the United States, giving him command of all Union forces and direction of the war along with the newly authorized grade of lieutenant general. In Grant, Lincoln had at last found a partner who could deliver victory.

No desk general, Grant intended to lead from the field, and in Virginia at that, a move that set the stage for a showdown between the war's two most successful commanders. Although Meade remained in charge of the Army of the Potomac, Grant would direct its operations as well as those of all other Federal forces. He retained General Halleck as de facto chief of staff in Washington, a role in which he coordinated the actions of the various field armies and at which Halleck excelled. In the Western Theater Grant's long-time subordinate and trusted friend William T. Sherman replaced him as the head of the large army group outside of Chattanooga.

Grant's plan, which was remarkably simple, called for all Union armies to attack and keep attacking until the Confederate forces capitulated. The destruction of Confederate field armies now became the singular objective of Union forces. Once the beginning of spring allowed operations to resume, the Army of the Potomac would move against Lee's Army of Northern Virginia, while Sherman, with George Thomas's Army of the Cumberland, General James B. McPherson's Army of the Tennessee, and General John M. Schofield's Army of the Ohio, would advance against the Confederate Army of Tennessee, now under Joseph Johnston, who had replaced the hapless and much-despised Bragg, in northern Georgia. In distant Louisiana, a plan to invade Texas known as the Red River Campaign came to nothing, while an effort by Federal forces in the Shenandoah Valley to neutralize that region's usefulness to the Confederacy also met with disappointment.

IMAGE 8.2A AND 8.2B   (a) Lee, (b) Grant   Confederate General Robert E. Lee (left) became arguably the most revered commander of the war, while General U.S. Grant rose from obscurity to lead the United States to victory. Their epic struggles in final year of the war ended with Lee's surrender to Grant at Appomattox Court House.

For the Confederates, the losses of 1863 dashed any hopes of foreign intervention and severely limited the options open to President Davis and his commanders. Gone too were hopes for a major victory that might compel a peace settlement. Indeed, the only real hope that remained was to extend the hostilities until the North grew tired and sued for peace. But that approach required resources that the Confederates simply did not possess. Already running out of men, food, horses, and even support in some sectors, the Confederates faced grim prospects.

THE EASTERN THEATER: 1864

On May 4, in a movement quite similar to Hooker's a year before, the 100,000-man Army of the Potomac crossed the Rapidan and moved into the Wilderness. The next day Lee reacted quickly with his 60,000 men to block Grant's advance and trap him where the dense woods somewhat checked the Federal advantages in men and artillery, attempting to replicate his previous success. A hellish two days of fighting in the woods left 30,000 men (18,000 Federals and 12,000 Confederates) killed and wounded, some of whom were burned alive by fires ignited by exploding shells, and no clear victor. But Grant was not Hooker. Rather than retreat, he ordered an advance around Lee's right flank, forcing Lee to counter. The Battle of the Wilderness thus established the character of what became known as the Overland Campaign—large, brutal battles followed by a Federal advance and a Confederate response that constituted a bloody dance of death through the heart of Virginia.

Lee's troops outraced Grant's vanguard to the crossroads village of Spotsylvania Court House a few miles southeast of the Wilderness, where they fortified a strong position that featured a large salient in the middle of the line that came to be known as the "Mule Shoe." Arriving on May 8, Grant launched repeated attacks on the Confederate force, including a rapid concentrated strike against the Mule Shoe directed by young Colonel Emory Upton that pierced the Rebel line but lacked the weight to exploit the success. Although the Confederates doggedly restored their line, Upton's attack inspired Grant. He ordered a repeat performance, but this time with the entire II Corps. The assault on the Mule Shoe on May 12 again temporarily pierced Lee's line before a savage Confederate counterattack sealed the breakthrough. After a week of stalemate, Grant moved again around the Confederate right, forcing yet another Lee countermeasure. Ten days of fighting at Spotsylvania produced another staggering casualty total, with close to 18,000 Federal and 12,000 Confederates killed, wounded, captured, or missing. The first two weeks of the campaign had produced no fewer than 60,000 casualties. Such was the new reality in this war.

Taking advantage of the standoff at Spotsylvania, Grant unleashed his powerful 10,000-strong Cavalry Corps, recently reorganized under the fiery General Philip Sheridan, on a raid toward Richmond. Stuart's Rebel horsemen, with fewer than half of Sheridan's number, rode in pursuit and made contact with Sheridan's force at Yellow Tavern just north of Richmond on May 11. The battle yielded a clear Union victory but little else, as Sheridan opted not to press the initiative. Among the 1,000 Confederate casualties, though, was the young cavalier Jeb Stuart, who fell mortally wounded, another major blow for General Lee.

In late May Lee blocked Grant's advance at the North Anna River, and once more, Grant moved around Lee's right, pressing ever closer to the Confederate capital. Lee in the meantime rushed to Cold Harbor, just east of Richmond, where he established a strong position. An impatient Grant flung his army at the improved Confederate lines at Cold Harbor in a series of costly and futile assaults that left 7,000 Federal troops killed and wounded in less than an hour—an attack the general would lament for the rest of his life.

Having been thwarted by Lee, Grant decided to bypass Richmond in a bold move across the James River to strike the important railroad hub of Petersburg, an operation that, if it succeeded, would cut Lee's communication lines and isolate his army. The massive movement required stealth and deception, both to hold Lee in place north of the James and to keep him distracted with diversions. To these ends, Grant carefully disguised his withdrawal from Cold Harbor and sent Sheridan on a long raid toward Charlottesville. Sheridan succeeded in drawing off most of Lee's cavalry, now under General Wade Hampton, but achieved little else. The resulting Battle of Trevilian Station became the largest all-cavalry engagement of the war. At its close Sheridan withdrew and eventually rejoined Grant's forces, which by then had invested Petersburg.

The Army of the Potomac began its ambitious movement south on June 12, with several corps traveling overland to the James and another corps by water, landing at the Federal beachhead at Bermuda Hundred. The II Corps crossed the James on boats on June 14, while engineers completed a massive pontoon bridge over which the rest of the army crossed during the next two days. The army's rapid and well-concealed relocation caught Lee off guard, but the final Federal advance on Petersburg lacked alacrity, allowing General

Beauregard and a small force to buy valuable time for Lee to adjust and send reinforcements. Grant was bitterly disappointed by the lost opportunity.

Lee, facing a number of urgent challenges, had already dispatched most of his Second Corps under General Jubal Early to deal with an emerging Federal threat in the Shenandoah Valley. In May, a ragtag Rebel force had defeated a small Union army in the Battle of New Market, which featured the notable participation of cadets from the Virginia Military Institute (VMI), but a renewed Federal effort under General David Hunter had produced a couple of minor victories, including the sacking of Lexington, where the Yankees burned VMI before marching on Lynchburg. Early's veterans arrived in time to help turn back Hunter. Incorporating troops from the valley into his command, Early then seized the initiative, moving northward through the valley in late June and becoming a serious concern for Union leaders. After crossing the Potomac into Maryland, he cleared Frederick on July 9, with little standing between his army of 12,000 and Washington. Federal General Lew Wallace managed to scrape together a force of about 6,000 and blocked Early's advance at the Monocacy River, buying precious time for reinforcements to reach Washington. By the time Early approached Washington's defenses on July 11, the mighty VI Corps from the Army of the Potomac had arrived. The Confederates retreated into the Shenandoah but remained a threat.

IMAGE 8.3 Confederate Fortifications at Petersburg   Bitter siege conditions that existed late in the war left Richmond and Petersburg in Virginia ringed with miles of trenches and defensive works. Petersburg became the scene of particularly intense fighting, including the July 1864 Battle of the Crater.

To counter that threat, Grant created the new Military Department of the Shenandoah, uniting four separate commands under thirty-three-year-old Philip Sheridan. After some initial posturing, Sheridan's cavalry-heavy Army of the Shenandoah defeated Early's army in an intense battle at Winchester on September 19 and again at Fisher's Hill three days later. Sheridan, on Grant's instructions, then presided over the destruction of the valley itself, during which his troops destroyed barns, mills, crops, and livestock in a controversial effort to erode public support for the Confederate cause and render the fertile valley useless to the Confederate war effort. Having largely completed his work, Sheridan left his army for a conference in Washington. On October 19 Early launched a surprise attack on the Federal camps at Cedar Creek, quickly overrunning most of the army before elements of the VI Corps established a new line. Sheridan, arriving on the field after a dramatic ride, launched a devastating counterattack that drove the remnants of Early's forces from the field. The success of Sheridan's Shenandoah Valley Campaign provided the first really good news in the East since the campaign season began and combined with big victories by Sherman in Georgia all but guaranteed President Lincoln's reelection.

On the Richmond–Petersburg front, Grant quickly enveloped Lee's positions, forcing him to extend his lines to cover his tenuous rail connections. For his part, Lee turned the area into a vast complex of trenches, breastworks, and other fortifications, manned by his dwindling and hungry army. Attempting to break through, Grant combined siege operations with numerous probes and thrusts that failed to yield results, the most spectacular of which involved the explosion of a mine dug under the Confederate line at Petersburg and packed with gunpowder. During the resultant Battle of the Crater on July 30, poorly led Federal troops failed to exploit the breach the explosion produced. The battle became infamous for its desperate fighting, much of which took place in the massive hole blasted in the earth, and the large-scale deployment of black troops, who became convenient targets for vengeful men in that pit of death. The Army of the Potomac continued through the hot summer and fall to extend Lee's lines, but somehow Lee managed to keep his rail connections open. The battle for Petersburg and Richmond came to feature the extensive construction on both sides of elaborate trench systems from which the armies sniped at each other continuously. The nightmare of this trench warfare in some ways anticipated the horror of the Great War. Still, as winter came on there remained no end in sight.

THE WESTERN THEATER: 1864

Like Grant in Virginia, in early May Sherman kicked off his campaign against the Confederates, advancing on Joseph Johnston's reinforced army in northern Georgia. Unlike Grant, Sherman would rely chiefly on maneuver rather than meat-grinder battles to achieve his ends, and he had a willing accomplice in Johnston, who had long displayed a preference for retreat. Using his large force to advantage, Sherman turned Johnston out of one strong position after another, forcing the Confederates southward, ever closer to the railroad and supply center at Atlanta. By late June, Johnston had assumed a formidable position at Kennesaw Mountain. For once Sherman lost patience and launched a costly attack that he quickly regretted; nevertheless, he forced Johnston to fall back to the outskirts of Atlanta by early July. Frustrated by Johnston's refusal to take the offensive and his apparent willingness to yield Atlanta, something Davis could not accept, on July 17 the Confederate president controversially removed the popular general and replaced him with John Bell Hood, a bold fighter who had learned his craft under Lee in Virginia.

At thirty-three, Hood had lost the use of his left arm at Gettysburg and had his right leg amputated after suffering a dangerous wound at Chickamauga. No one in this war, with the exception of Lee defending Richmond in 1862, had inherited a more desperate situation than did Hood, with his army's back against Atlanta and three Federal armies converging. Hood understood that Davis expected him to fight. And fight he did, launching three major attacks in eight days. With Sherman's armies advancing on different fronts and widely separated, Hood attempted to isolate one army at a time, attacking the Army of the Cumberland as it crossed Peachtree Creek north of Atlanta on July 20. After achieving initial success, the attack faltered and the Confederates fell back to their prepared defensive works in Atlanta. Two days later, Hood ordered a bold flanking move on the Army of the Tennessee east of the city, surprising the Federal troops. During the attack General McPherson was killed when he accidentally rode into Confederate troops, making him the only Federal army commander killed in action. After a confused and ferocious back-and-forth fight, in which politician-turned-general John A. Logan rallied the shaken Army of the Tennessee, Sherman's men repulsed the attack with heavy losses. A poorly coordinated attack on the same Army of the Tennessee west of Atlanta at Ezra Church ended Hood's offensive series, but his aggressiveness had slowed Sherman, who now cautiously worked to extend the Confederate line to its breaking point. Atlanta thus came to resemble Petersburg. The Federal goal had been to destroy Confederate armies but once again became focused on conquering important population centers. After Confederate cavalry emphatically rejected a series of Union raids, Sherman finally exploited his superior numbers. Leaving one corps to occupy his trenches, Sherman marched with the bulk of his force on a wide wheel west of Atlanta, a movement that Hood's forces could do nothing to stop. After a final rather meaningless engagement at Jonesboro, the Yankees cut the last rail line into Atlanta, forcing Hood to evacuate, destroying tons of valuable stores and ammunition, and leaving Atlanta in flames. Sherman's men occupied the city the following day. The fall of Atlanta gave Lincoln and the Union their first major victory of 1864 and changed the momentum of the presidential election.

After vacating Atlanta, Hood marched northward and then westward into Alabama, hoping to draw Sherman out of Georgia. But Sherman had enough resources to dispatch a sizable component of his army under Thomas to deal with Hood, while he abandoned his supply line and marched with more than 65,000 hardened veterans through Georgia, bringing total war to the southern heartland. During his brutally effective "March to the Sea," Sherman ordered his army to cut a swath fifty miles wide though one of the South's most productive regions, destroying crops, barns, and livestock, before reaching Savannah in December. Accepting the city's surrender without a fight, Sherman presented the lovely prize to the recently reelected President Lincoln as a Christmas gift. As Sheridan had done in the Shenandoah, Sherman brought unprecedented devastation to Georgia's civilian population in hopes of discouraging support for the war, but his march instead left bitterness and an enduring hatred in his wake. Sherman's actions also did much to demoralize thousands of Deep South troops in Lee's army, who now feared for their homes and families. Confederate desertion thus became a major byproduct of what Sherman termed "hard war."

Hood, having failed to lure Sherman out of Georgia, marched into Tennessee with scarcely 50,000 men, hoping to reclaim Nashville and take the war into Kentucky. At Nashville Thomas gathered Union troops from across the South and awaited Hood's arrival. In November, a Federal field force under John Schofield attempted to slow Hood's progress but barely escaped a Confederate trap at Spring Hill before assuming a strong defensive position at Franklin, just south of Nashville. Hood, angered by the missed opportunity, pushed on to Franklin, where, without waiting for his full force or most of his artillery, he flung his two available corps at the Federal line in what became one of the most desperate and devastating battles of the war. Fighting lasted into the night as casualties mounted. Eventually Schofield managed to withdraw under cover of darkness to join Thomas at Nashville, having lost 2,300 men. Hood held the field, but his army was gutted. His 7,000 total casualties included many of his best troops. Six generals, including Irishman Patrick Cleburne, the army's outstanding division commander, had been killed or mortally wounded, and five more badly injured. Undaunted, Hood pushed on to Nashville, occupying the hills south of the city as winter set in. While Grant pressured Thomas to attack, that meticulous commander took time to prepare his army and await favorable weather. When he finally attacked on December 15, Hood had nothing left with which to resist. Falling back, he attempted to hold his new position with fewer than 30,000 men, but a second Federal attack on December 16 shattered the Confederate line. Hood lost more than 5,000 men, most of whom were captured. His army disintegrated and, hotly pursued, retreated all the way back into Mississippi, where Hood resigned. For all intents and purposes, the war in the Western Theater was over.

"DAMN THE TORPEDOES": NAVAL ACTIONS OF 1864

The U.S. Navy and cooperating army units had devoted considerable attention to tightening the blockade and shutting off southern ports, with mixed results. While Charleston had been largely isolated by 1864, inventive southerners nonetheless made history in its harbor when in February the manually propelled Confederate submarine *Hunley* drove a torpedo into the hull of the steam frigate *Housatonic*, sinking the warship but going down itself in the wake with all hands. The Confederacy could not hope to compete with the U.S. Navy and its rapid wartime expansion, but it did manage to construct a number of formidable ironclad rams, such as the *Albemarle*, which menaced Federal ships along North Carolina's coast until it was torpedoed and sunk in October. Far more successful were the fast ships acquired by the Confederacy in England early in the conflict. These commerce raiders, notably the *Florida* and *Alabama*, preyed on Union merchant and whaling fleets for much of the war. *Alabama*, captained by the dashing Raphael Semmes, took more than sixty merchant vessels and sank one warship before it was battered and sunk by the USS *Kearsarge* off Cherbourg, France, in June 1864. Blockade running, long the lifeblood of the Confederacy, had become much more difficult by 1864, with only a few ports still operational. One of those, at Mobile, became the target of Admiral Farragut's squadron in August 1864, when his flotilla of four ironclad monitors and fourteen wooden warships steamed into heavily defended Mobile Bay. When one of his monitors struck a torpedo (mine), Farragut, shouting, "Damn the torpedoes, full speed ahead," led his wooden flagship *Hartford* and the others

FALLACIES OF THE "LOST CAUSE"

One of the most pervasive tenets of what came to be known as the Lost Cause narrative arose from General Robert E. Lee's official farewell to his soldiers. Of his surrender to General Ulysses S. Grant, Lee wrote, "The Army of Northern Virginia has been compelled to yield to overwhelming numbers and resources." This simple statement planted the idea that Lee and his army had not been defeated militarily but simply overcome by the manpower and material might of the Union. Within weeks of Lee's surrender, purveyors of the Lost Cause, including former generals such as Jubal Early, crafted an appealing alternative history to explain how a superior culture, a superior form of manhood, could have lost such a noble fight. The Lost Cause narrative by definition held that the Confederacy never had a chance of succeeding. It also deemphasized the role of slavery in bringing about secession and offered up an idealized memory of the antebellum South. These ideas, like Lee's assertion, stuck, as did the belief that southern soldiers, especially Lee and the martyred "Stonewall" Jackson, were clearly superior to their Yankee counterparts.

Lee represents a special case. Revered in both the North and South, and often endowed with superhuman qualities, he is viewed by many as the perfect southern gentleman warrior. He is arguably the most admired soldier in American history, but he was also a flawed man and a flawed general who has only in recent years received the critical examination he deserves. His deification came largely at the expense of Grant and other Union leaders, whose reputations suffered. In the larger debate about Civil War leadership, the long-held belief that the Confederacy possessed better generals is simply preposterous. Each side had competent, even excellent general officers, and each side had many others who did not measure up.

Furthermore, like the idea of the Lost Cause itself, the assertion that the United States won the war simply because of its overwhelming manpower and material resources is not supported by fact. This argument has been upended numerous times throughout history (Vietnam and Afghanistan provide more recent examples). If success had been based solely on numbers and resources, General McClellan would have won the war in 1862. He did not, nor did a dozen other army commanders blessed with superior manpower and resources. The Union won because of incredible military and political determination, inspired leadership, and steady execution. Certainly, Grant and his subordinates enjoyed abundant manpower and resources, but it took leadership and will to employ those resources in order to defeat a tenacious foe.

In truth, nothing about the Lost Cause narrative holds up. Yet for a number of reasons, not the least of which was reconciliation, the Lost Cause appeal gained traction and became a generally accepted interpretation of the war, despite the objections of Union veterans and African American leaders such as Frederick Douglass. By the 1920s its message and the imagery it inspired held sway in popular culture, in films like *Birth of a Nation* and *Gone with the Wind* and in twentieth-century historical treatments of the Civil War such as the writings of Douglas Southall Freeman and Bruce Catton, among others. The influential Catton believed that "the legend of the Lost Cause has served the entire country well." But it did not serve the entire country well; on the contrary, it dishonored the men—including 200,000 African Americans—who served the Union, it allowed the country to look away as white southerners systematically disenfranchised the black population while reasserting white supremacy, and it proved detrimental to a comprehensive understanding of a war that was much more complex and complicated than the legend would allow.

through the remaining mines and past the heavy guns of Fort Morgan. Once in the bay, Farragut engaged the Confederate ironclad ram *Tennessee*, which fought valiantly until subdued. The Federals now choked off Mobile. In December, Union forces moved against the Confederacy's last open port on the Atlantic at Wilmington, North Carolina. With Admiral David Porter's squadron providing support, Union troops under the disappointing political general Benjamin Butler failed to neutralize Fort Fisher, which covered the approaches to Wilmington. A second effort in January 1865 directed by the capable General Alfred Terry took Fort Fisher and closed off Wilmington.

THE FINAL ACTS: 1865

As 1865 arrived Federal resources, both human and material, proved simply overwhelming. While the Union had enjoyed great advantages in manpower and material from the beginning, victory required the willful application of those advantages, which is what occurred once Grant took overall command. Throughout 1864 Federal army and naval forces applied relentless pressure on almost every point of the Confederacy, birthing new divisions and corps seemingly at will and adding warships by the dozen. Conversely, the Confederacy was running out of time and just about everything else.

Belatedly, and with no real chance of it making a difference, President Davis appointed Lee general-in-chief, giving him control of the entire Confederate war effort. Lee in turn recalled Joseph Johnston and tasked him with organizing what remained of Confederate forces in the Carolinas and other parts of the South in an effort to prevent Sherman's hard-marching army from uniting with Grant's already massive command in Virginia. A small army still held Mobile, and Nathan Bedford Forrest's cavalry remained on the loose. But the situation proved hopeless.

By February, Sherman's forces had reached Columbia, South Carolina, which had been largely destroyed by fires, likely set by retreating Confederates. Sherman's men completed the destruction of the cradle of secession and moved into North Carolina, while a second Union force took Wilmington and marched inland. On March 19, Johnston attacked a portion of Sherman's superior force at Bentonville but was compelled to withdraw the next day when confronted with Sherman's full army. This would be the last major engagement between Sherman and Johnston. In late March, Sherman's army united with General John Schofield's troops advancing from Wilmington. Sherman ordered a halt for rest and to allow the roads to improve before moving on to Petersburg.

Also that March, General George Thomas, still at Nashville, sent General James H. Wilson's giant cavalry force—more than 13,000 men—on a raid to destroy remaining war-making infrastructure in Alabama and Georgia. Wilson's troopers defeated a small force led by Forrest at Selma, an important industrial and supply center, which they systematically destroyed before moving on to Montgomery and into Georgia, doing much damage along the way.

In Virginia, the Richmond–Petersburg front presented an awesome spectacle—the vision of modern war. Miles of interconnected trenches faced each other, cut into land stripped of vegetation. The Union lines, linked by telegraph wires and supplied by a specially built military railroad, contained vast amounts of cannon and ammunition and abundant stocks of almost everything imaginable. Grant's improvised headquarters at City Point—once a small village at the confluence of the James and Appomattox rivers—had become a military-industrial city of staggering proportions, one of the busiest ports in the world. Inside the Confederate lines soldiers and civilians battled hunger and disease, desertion and declining morale. With Wilmington lost and Carolina occupied, Lee lost his last two sources of supply. Beginning in February, Grant resumed his probes and punches, extending Lee's lines as he attempted to cut the Confederates' last rail links. Amazingly, Lee's army, now less than 60,000 strong, still showed plenty of fight, as evidenced by its attack on Fort Stedman on March 25, a bold attempt to break Grant's hold on Petersburg directed by General John B. Gordon. A civilian volunteer when the war began, Gordon now commanded half of Lee's army, but his attack—the last offensive move ordered by Lee—ended in failure.

The next day Sheridan arrived from the Shenandoah Valley, adding his large and victorious Cavalry Corps to Grant's already awesome arsenal. The extra weight and mobility afforded by Sheridan's arrival allowed Grant to close the trap. On April 1, Sheridan, supported by the V Corps, destroyed the Confederate right flank in the decisive Battle of Five Forks. With his position compromised, Lee advised President Davis and his cabinet to evacuate, which they did on one of the last trains to get out of Richmond. The next day, an all-out attack on Petersburg pierced the Confederate lines in numerous places. General A. P. Hill was killed trying to rally his men. A desperate stand allowed the Rebels to hold until nightfall, when Lee ordered Richmond and Petersburg abandoned. Fires set by departing soldiers destroyed much of both cities.

Moving his scattered army westward by numerous routes, Lee hoped to reach food supplies in the countryside and eventually link with Johnston's forces in North Carolina. In a frenetic campaign during which neither side found much food or rest, Lee's dwindling army fought off the rapidly closing Federals at a number of points, but on April 6 at Sayler's Creek, Sheridan's cavalry cut off a large portion of the force, compelling more than 6,000 to surrender. Hoping to feed his starving army, Lee had ordered rations sent by rail to Appomattox Station, but Sheridan's troopers arrived first, blocking Lee's continued movement. As Lee's men arrived, so too did fast-marching Federal infantry. A last bloodbath was avoided when Lee wrote to Grant asking for a meeting to discuss terms of surrender. In one of the great moments in American history, on April 9 Grant and Lee met at Appomattox Court House. To Lee's surprise Grant offered generous terms, which the Confederate general accepted. Lee, his officers, and his men could go home. Their war was over. Grant also had rations issued to Lee's hungry soldiers, fewer than 30,000 of whom remained.

After touring war-ravaged Richmond, President Lincoln returned to Washington. On April 14 he and his wife attended a play at Ford's Theater. There, a popular actor and Confederate sympathizer named John Wilkes Booth shot Lincoln in the head. The president died the following morning. Booth, the leader of a conspiracy that also involved the attempted murder of Secretary of State William H. Seward, escaped into the countryside, where he was located and killed by a Federal soldier on April 26. By that time Johnston had surrendered to Sherman in North Carolina. In Alabama, General Richard Taylor, son of President Zachary Taylor, surrendered the remaining Confederate troops east of the Mississippi on May 4. On May 10, General Wilson's cavalry apprehended Jefferson Davis in Georgia. And on May 26, at New Orleans, General Simon Bolivar Buckner, the man who had surrendered to Grant at Fort Donelson back in 1862, surrendered the Confederate Trans-Mississippi Department. The war was over.

THE APPOMATTOX CAMPAIGN

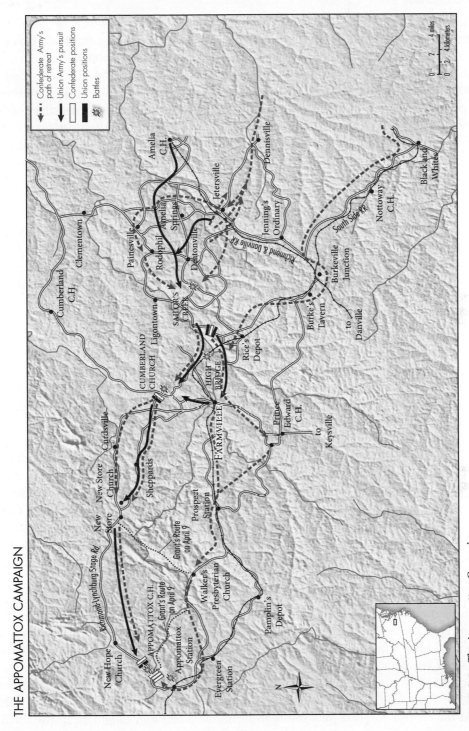

MAP 8.5 The Appomattox Campaign

CONCLUSIONS

The American Civil War was a hugely destructive event. Because Confederate records are incomplete, the total number of casualties is not known with certainty, but historians estimate that the war accounted for at least 625,000 deaths, more than 400,000 of which did not occur in battle. Recent studies suggest that the actual number of deaths was closer to 750,000. More than 500,000 men were wounded, many desperately so. Tens of thousands lost arms, legs, or eyes. By any measure, it was the deadliest and most destructive conflict in American history. For the South, the war proved particularly devastating. It laid waste to southern infrastructure, destroyed agriculture and railroads, and killed almost a quarter of southern white men of military age. And with the end of the fighting came the humiliation of military occupation, emancipation, and white disenfranchisement that accompanied Reconstruction.

During the Civil War, American leaders on both sides relied once again on temporary volunteer armies drawn from the civilian population. This reliance on amateur soldiers no doubt contributed to high casualties and helped to prolong the war, but perhaps not as much as has been assumed in the past. Both sides learned the intricacies of combat and became generally proficient in warfare as the conflict continued. New technologies also played a significant role in this war. The extensive use or railroads and telegraphic communication, the widespread adoption and employment of ironclad warships, and the embrace of improved artillery and small arms added new capabilities. But despite technological advancements, commanders did not significantly alter the way they fought battles. Nor was the Civil War proportionally bloodier than other American conflicts, although in terms of scale it certainly was. Both sides struggled to develop coherent strategy. The Federal success on the southern waterways and the increasingly effective blockade confirmed the wisdom of Winfield Scott's early strategic vision, but this approach did not materially affect the situation in the East until much later in the war. Therefore, in a very real sense, for the Union the war was won in the West, where the Confederacy simply could not protect its heartland and rivers. For his part, Lincoln proved be a gifted commander-in-chief. He displayed an ability to learn from his mistakes and to mature in his leadership role. He could be too patient and also not patient enough. Ultimately, his partnership with Grant sealed the Union victory. Once the Union leaders opted to focus on the destruction of Confederate field armies, apply unrelenting pressure across the South, and fight a war of attrition in which they finally marshaled their considerable advantages, the Confederacy was doomed.

Jefferson Davis, despite his military experience, never adopted a solid strategic approach to the war and often proved incapable of controlling his generals. Confederate insistence on protecting Richmond and other population centers, combined with an inability to control southern rivers, left too much area open to exploitation. A fixation on the Eastern Theater clearly plagued both sides but proved fatal to the Confederates. Their demise therefore can legitimately be traced to the fall of Fort Henry and Fort Donelson. Ultimately, the Confederates established an unsustainable form of government that limited the central government's ability to prosecute a war and fought an unsustainable brand of warfare that required resources the South could not provide. Lee's victories were often almost as costly as his defeats. He ran out of men and the means to support those he had. As mentioned earlier, the Union did not win the war simply because of superior manpower and resources, but once the war stretched into a fourth year these advantages became overwhelming. The Confederates perhaps could have won the war had they achieved an early decisive victory or had the Federals experienced a catastrophic failure, but neither occurred, and in the end they could not hope to win a war of attrition. Union victory undoubtedly required vast resources but also demanded great execution and unprecedented sacrifice.

Union success reaffirmed the vitality of republican government and the commitment to civilian control of the military. For the United States, the war effort and its many manifestations brought profound changes to American society, American culture, and America's military establishment.

TIMELINE

March 1862	"Stonewall" Jackson's Shenandoah Valley campaign
March–July 1862	Peninsula campaign and Seven Days Battles
April 1862	Battle of Shiloh; death of A. S. Johnston; New Orleans falls to Federal forces
June 1862	Robert E. Lee assumes command of Army of Northern Virginia
August 1862	Second Battle of Bull Run
September 1862	Lee's Maryland campaign; Battle of Antietam
December 1862	Battle of Fredericksburg
December 1862–Janary 1863	Battle of Stones River
January 1863	Lincoln's Emancipation Proclamation takes effect
May 1863	Battle of Chancellorsville; death of Stonewall Jackson
July 1863	Battle of Gettysburg; Confederates surrender Vicksburg
September 1863	Battle of Chickamauga
November 1863	Battle of Chattanooga
March 1864	U. S. Grant appointed commander of all U.S. forces
May–June 1864	Overland campaign in Virginia; Battles of the Wilderness and Spotsylvania Court House
May–September 1864	Atlanta campaign
July 1864	Confederate raid on Washington
September 1864–March 1865	Shenandoah Valley campaign
November–December 1864	Confederate invasion of Tennessee; Battles of Franklin and Nashville
April 1865	Battle of Five Forks; fall of Richmond and Petersburg; Appomattox campaign; Lee's surrender to Grant; Lincoln assassinated at Ford's Theater
May 1865	Final surrenders of major Confederate field forces

SUGGESTED READINGS

Ballard, Michael B. *Vicksburg: The Campaign that Opened the Mississippi.* Chapel Hill: University of North Carolina Press, 2010.

Brands, H. W. *The Man Who Saved the Union: Ulysses Grant in War and Peace.* New York: Doubleday, 2012.

Castel, Albert. *Decision in the West: The Atlanta Campaign of 1864.* Lawrence: University Press of Kansas, 1992.

Coffey, David. *Sheridan's Lieutenants: Phil Sheridan, His Generals, and the Final Year of the Civil War.* Lanham, MD: Rowman and Littlefield, 2005.

Hess, Earl J. *Civil War Infantry Tactics: Training, Combat, and Small-Unit Effectiveness.* Baton Rouge: Louisiana State University Press, 2015.

McPherson, James M. *Battle Cry of Freedom: The Civil War Era.* New York: Oxford University Press, 1988.

Sears, Stephen W. *Gettysburg.* Boston: Houghton, Mifflin, 2003.

Sears, Stephen W. *Landscape Turned Red: The Battle of Antietam.* Boston: Houghton, Mifflin, 1983.

Smith, Timothy B. *Shiloh: Conquer or Perish.* Lawrence: University Press of Kansas, 2014.

Stoker, Donald. *The Grand Design: Strategy and the U.S. Civil War.* New York: Oxford University Press, 2010.

Thomas, Emory M. *Robert E. Lee: A Biography.* New York: W. W. Norton, 1995.

Trudeau, Noah Andre. *Bloody Roads South: The Wilderness to Cold Harbor, May–June 1864.* Boston: Little, Brown, 1989.

Trudeau, Noah Andre. *The Last Citadel: Petersburg, Virginia, June 1864–April 1865.* Boston: Little, Brown, 1991.

Trudeau, Noah Andre. *Like Men of War: Black Troops in the Civil War: 1862–1865.* Boston: Little, Brown, 1998.

Trudeau, Noah Andre. *Southern Storm: Sherman's March to the Sea.* New York: Harper-Collins, 2008.

Tucker, Spencer C. *A Short History of the Civil War at Sea.* Lanham, MD: Scholarly Resources, 2002.

Woodworth, Steven E. *Jefferson Davis and His Generals: The Failure of Confederate Command in the West.* Lawrence: University Press of Kansas, 1990.

Woodworth, Steven E. *This Great Struggle: America's Civil War.* Lanham, MD: Rowman and Littlefield, 2011.

CHAPTER 9

RECONSTRUCTION AND CONQUEST
1865–1890

*Unfinished Business • Demobilization and the New Regular Army • Reconstruction
• Expanded Role • Technology • The Last Indian Wars • Professionalism*

Lieutenant Charles Gatewood's short career as a professional soldier on the frontier offers a case study in the vicissitudes of army life during the closing decades of the nineteenth century. Among the first generation of southern men to be admitted to the United States Military Academy in the postwar period, the Virginia-born son of a Confederate soldier graduated in 1877 and, as a freshly minted second lieutenant in the 6th Cavalry, traveled to the Southwest, where he would spend the next ten years in some of the most demanding work in the service. During his first major campaign, Gatewood led Indian scouts in the arduous Victorio War (1878–1880). Early on he showed great interest in Native American culture and language, and as commander of a detachment of Apache scouts he devoted considerable effort to learning the ways of his men and in the process earned their trust and even admiration. When General George Crook took charge of the Department of Arizona in 1882, he selected gifted young officers such as Gatewood to administer the various reservations. Gatewood, now a first lieutenant, took charge of the difficult White Mountain Agency at Fort Apache. The young officer and the innovative Crook shared a sympathy for their Indian charges but soon fell out when Crook failed to provide the levels of support Gatewood deemed necessary.

In 1886, after massive campaigns directed by Crook and his successor, Nelson Miles, failed to capture the recalcitrant Geronimo and his meager but much-feared band of followers, Miles sent Gatewood and two of his trusted Apache scouts into Mexico to obtain Geronimo's surrender. After a grueling trek that took a toll on his already precarious health, Gatewood succeeded when most likely no other soldier could have. But instead of praise and promotion, both of which he richly deserved, Gatewood found himself isolated—the ambitious Miles apparently fearful that Gatewood, not he, would get the lion's share of the credit for Geronimo's surrender. Subsequently transferred with his regiment to the Dakota Territory during the Ghost Dance scare of 1890, Gatewood was badly wounded and disabled in an 1892 explosion at Fort McKinney, Wyoming, during the Johnson County Range War.

Unfit for field duty, he went on medical leave but developed severe abdominal pain and was assigned to the medical facility at Fort Monroe in his native Virginia. He died there of stomach cancer in May 1896. He was only forty-three years old and still a lieutenant after almost twenty years in the army.

UNFINISHED BUSINESS

On May 23 the victorious Army of the Potomac paraded down Washington's Pennsylvania Avenue in a Grand Review before an excited public and invited dignitaries that lasted for hours; the next day Sherman's hard-marching men repeated the spectacle. But the war was not quite over, and the process of putting the nation back together had hardly begun. Soon the Union's great volunteer army would be dismantled, and almost a million men would return to civilian life. The mighty U.S. Navy, which had grown to 700 ships and some 60,000 officers and men, would experience not only a major downsizing but also a retreat from the technological advances it had embraced during the war. A voracious budget-cutting mindset quickly replaced the philosophy of wartime excess in the halls of Congress. Fiscal restraint and concerns over the continued existence of a large standing army led to deep cuts in the military establishment at a time when its mission, while certainly changing, remained complex, demanding, and expansive. Reconstruction policy placed heavy burdens on the army, while westward expansion mandated its speedy return to the frontier. America's overseas interests also still required naval support. Despite myriad challenges and the dearth of government investment, the postwar years proved to be tremendously formative for the nation's military. The army experienced a marked rise in professionalism, thanks to an experienced officer corps and exceptional continuity in the command ranks. Although the U.S. military lagged behind those of the European powers in terms of technological advancement and organization, it managed to make laudable progress during the decades following the Civil War.

Conspicuously absent from the grand review was General Philip Sheridan. On May 17, 1865, Grant ordered Sheridan to take charge of the situation west of the Mississippi, where the Confederates had yet to yield. Sheridan's mission served two purposes: to compel the surrender of the last major Rebel command and to apply pressure on the unwelcome French-sponsored regime in Mexico. Under the guise of debt collection and taking advantage of a United States distracted by civil war, Emperor Napoleon III had moved to reestablish a French presence in North America. French troops invaded Mexico in 1862 and, despite a setback in the Battle of Puebla on May 5 (Cinco de Mayo), had occupied much of the country by 1863, ousting the legitimate government of Benito Juárez and establishing a puppet monarchy under the young Austrian archduke Maximilian, a clear violation of the Monroe Doctrine. The Confederates in the Trans-Mississippi capitulated to the Union before Sheridan even arrived in the region, but he pursued the second part of his charge with considerable vigor.

Supplied with three infantry corps and two divisions of cavalry, with the latter under the command of his wartime favorites George Armstrong Custer and Wesley Merritt, Sheridan garrisoned key positions in Texas and placed a large force along the Rio Grande. By deploying Sheridan and 50,000 Union soldiers to Texas, Grant sent a compelling message to Maximilian and France. Although U.S. troops did not engage Maximilian's forces directly, Sheridan nonetheless schemed with mercenaries and loyal Mexican operatives to destabilize the regime while overtly threatening U.S. intervention. On Sheridan's watch tons of surplus U.S. war materiel fell into the grateful hands of Juárez's republican armies. Sheridan's intimidation tactics and Secretary of State William H. Seward's measured diplomacy often conflicted, but the combination worked. In 1866 Napoleon ordered his French troops out of Mexico, leaving the hapless Maximilian essentially undefended. In May 1867, General Mariano Escobedo's Juarista troops, many carrying U.S. Springfield muskets and wearing Yankee blue jackets, cornered Maximilian's small imperial force at Querétaro. A month later, Maximilian went before a Mexican firing squad. By that time, Sheridan's role and that of the army had taken on new dimensions.

DEMOBILIZATION AND THE NEW REGULAR ARMY

In May 1865, at the close of the Civil War, the Armies of the United States—comprising regulars, volunteers, and the U.S. Colored Troops—numbered more than 1 million men, but demobilization occurred at a rapid pace as volunteer units mustered out of service. All volunteers would be gone within the next two years, leaving once again only a small regular army to resume its old duties and to confront the new challenges of the postwar era. Grant and others perceived that if the army returned to its old organization as essentially a frontier constabulary, it could no longer meet the manifold responsibilities presented by Reconstruction and western expansion. The "Old Army" had to expand, and with this expansion America could find suitable positions for the heroes of the Civil War.

Unfortunately for Grant's plan, things did not quite work out that way. Congress, dealing with the staggering debt generated during the war, was in no mood to fund a large standing army. After something of a compromise, in July 1866 Congress passed a bill to establish the size and configuration of the postwar army. Reflecting the various constituencies involved in war making in a democracy, Congress tried to accommodate everyone but succeeded in pleasing very few. First, the government tripled the authorized strength of the army to 54,000, adding twenty-six infantry regiments and four cavalry regiments (the more professional artillery remained at five regiments). To reward the nonprofessional citizen-soldiers who, contrary to popular belief, had performed exceptionally well as a whole, and in deference to the many political generals now sitting in the capitol who harbored great disdain for West Point–trained officers, half of the new officer commissions went to accomplished amateurs, men like Nelson A. Miles and Benjamin Grierson; the other half went to worthy professionals, among them the "Boy Generals" such as Custer and R. S. Mackenzie. The inclusion of former volunteer officers in the reorganized regular army had far-reaching implications, most of which were positive. An excellent example of the move's intent and how it played out was Samuel B. M. Young of Pennsylvania, who had volunteered as a private in 1861 and by 1865 had risen to command of a regiment of cavalry and then briefly a brigade during the Appomattox Campaign. Offered a commission, he joined the regular army as a second lieutenant in 1866 and rose through the ranks to command a division in Cuba during the war with Spain before becoming the army's first chief of the general staff in 1903.

Of the new regiments, six—four infantry (38th–41st) and two cavalry (9th and 10th)—were to be composed of black soldiers, in recognition of their considerable contribution to the Union victory. Four regiments (the 42nd–45th), known as the Veteran Reserve Corps, were to be composed of wounded and disabled officers and men. In 1869 Congress slashed the number of infantry regiments from forty-five to twenty-five, with the black units consolidated into the 24th and 25th Infantry regiments and the Veteran Reserve Corps dissolved altogether. By 1876 the total authorized strength of the army had dwindled to 27,442, a level at which it would remain, more or less, for the next twenty years

The demobilization of the U.S. Volunteers meant that officers who had held lofty grades in that organization during the war returned to their regular ranks and regiments or to civilian life. For younger men without seniority in the regular army, the impact was demoralizing. Men such as Wesley Merritt and George Crook, who had been full-rank major generals in the Volunteers, reverted to the regular rank of captain. Those who had entered the war from civilian life and had risen to general officer rank in the volunteer establishment had no regular rank to fall back on. The seriously flawed brevet system complicated matters further. Brevets had been issued liberally throughout the war as a reward for outstanding performance, but also for simply being part of an operation or a unit. They had been issued for excellent staff work, for wounds received, and, at the end, for war service and had been used to elevate better-performing junior officers over men senior in service. The government had dispensed brevets in both the regular and volunteer organizations, and some officers had accrued brevets in both organizations. At the end of the war, the aforementioned Ranald Mackenzie, for example, held the full rank of brigadier general in the U.S. Volunteers and was a major general of volunteers and brigadier general in the regular army by brevet—but his substantive rank remained captain of engineers. The folding of the volunteer establishment in 1866 kicked off a race for position and promotion that lasted into the twentieth century. Men who had been generals, who had commanded corps, divisions, or brigades through the greatest war in American history, now faced life as lieutenants, captains, and majors at some far-flung western post or as the head of a detachment of occupation troops in the Deep South, charged with upholding the newly granted civil rights of freed slaves. Most of these men understandably wanted to be generals again, a desire that ignited the remarkable competition among officers that characterized the postwar era.

What to do with so many generals? At the end of the Civil War, the Union army contained hundreds of general officers and hundreds more who could claim to be a general by brevet. Clearly there would not be room for all of them in the new, albeit larger, regular army. In 1866 Congress, in the name of a grateful nation, awarded Grant a fourth star, making him the first full general in the United States Army. Predictably, Sherman moved up to lieutenant general. The law also provided for four major generals and eleven brigadiers of the line. Generals also headed eight staff departments as surgeon general, paymaster general, chief of ordnance, commissary general of subsistence, judge advocate general, chief of engineers, quartermaster general, and adjutant general. Both the inspector general and the chief signal officer held the rank of colonel. When Grant became president in 1869, he vacated the position of commanding general, which went to Sherman, who held the job for fifteen years. President Grant then made one of his many controversial moves as chief executive, promoting Sheridan to lieutenant general over senior major generals Henry Halleck, George Meade, George Thomas, and Winfield Scott Hancock. Sheridan succeeded Sherman as commanding general in 1883. Together, Sherman and Sheridan directed the army through an extremely formative period, including the successful conclusion of the Indian Wars, and shaped its future well into the twentieth century, although neither had much stomach for the immediate demands of Reconstruction.

RECONSTRUCTION

By war's end, the army had been involved in reconstruction activities for some time, having essentially governed occupied areas for much of the war. In March 1865 Congress created the Bureau of Refugees, Freedmen, and Abandoned Lands, commonly known as the Freedmen's Bureau, under the direction of the army. Under the leadership of General O. O. Howard, the bureau was charged with protecting, assisting, and uplifting former slaves. This organization provided food, medicine, education, and in many cases physical protection to the hundreds of thousands of freed people throughout the South but increasingly attracted the hatred of southern whites and became targets of violence from for terrorist organizations such as the Ku Klux Klan. Failing to accrue the resources and manpower it required for its numerous responsibilities, the bureau was disbanded in 1871.

With the war's end in sight, Lincoln had begun to formulate policy for readmitting the seceded states to the Union, but his assassination left implementation of that policy to Andrew Johnson, a Union-loyal former Tennessee senator who, in the eyes of many in the North, especially those who had served, took Lincoln's plans for a lenient reconstruction too far. Under Johnson's plan former Confederate states seamlessly reentered the Union, but in a decidedly defiant and unrepentant fashion. The southern states promptly packed congressional delegations and statehouses with former Confederate officials and army officers, passed discriminatory laws called Black Codes that all but returned the former slaves to a state of servitude, and severely restricted African Americans' civil rights.

Finding that Johnson's policies threatened to undo what Union soldiers had accomplished on the battlefield, Grant and Secretary of War Edwin Stanton allied with Radical Republicans in Congress to reject the reconstruction plans and congressional delegations approved by Johnson and impose its own much more severe plan. Congressional Reconstruction equaled military Reconstruction. After garnering even more seats in the 1866 midterm elections, Radical Republicans in Congress ushered in military Reconstruction in ten of the former Confederate states (Tennessee had already been accepted back into the Union), which were divided into five military districts, each commanded by an army general. Virginia became the First Military District; the Carolinas the Second; Florida, Georgia, and Alabama the Third; Mississippi and Arkansas the Fourth; and Texas and Louisiana the Fifth. Congress also, over Johnson's veto, laid the groundwork for the Fourteenth Amendment and passed two important acts that directly affected the military: the Command of the Army Act, which formalized the chain of command and made Senate approval mandatory for the removal of the general-in-chief (Grant), and the Tenure of Office Act, which mandated Senate approval to remove a cabinet official. The Tenure of Office Act triggered a showdown when Johnson fired Stanton without Senate approval in 1868. The House of Representatives responded with impeachment. Johnson fell one vote short of conviction and removal from office after a contentious trial in the Senate.

Reconstruction duties weighed heavily on the army and occupied about one-third of its available manpower after 1866, when Congress capped it at 54,000 officers and men. Called upon to serve as police and nation-builders, the soldiers faced intense hatred, abuse, and even death. Black soldiers in the South had it worse than their white counterparts. But as states gradually qualified for readmission, and as Congress chipped away at the army's authorized strength, reducing its size to only 27,000 by 1876, the army's commitment in the South waned. The nation's commitment to Reconstruction waned as well. Resistance in the South coupled with indifference elsewhere led to the political arrangement that ended Reconstruction. As the result of contested presidential election results in 1876, Republican candidate and former Union general Rutherford B. Hayes agreed to end Reconstruction and remove the last federal troops from civic and law enforcement duties in the South in exchange for the Democrats' support of his election.

MILITARY RECONSTRUCTION

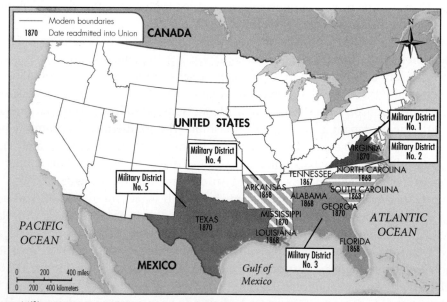

MAP 9.1 **Military Reconstruction**

EXPANDED ROLE

Hayes's ascendancy ushered in the Gilded Age, a period of unrestrained capitalism that witnessed the liberal employment of the regular army in an extramilitary capacity. During Reconstruction, the army intervened repeatedly in support of local and federal law enforcement agencies, but the deployment of federal troops to quell domestic disturbances associated with labor unrest and abuses of power marked a dangerous expansion of the professional military's authority. In 1877 President Hayes ordered the army into action to protect federal property during widespread railroad strikes. The disciplined, well-led regulars helped restore order—significantly, without suffering or inflicting any casualties. In 1892 troopers from the 6th Cavalry intervened in a violent confrontation between gunmen hired by the wealthy members of the Wyoming Stock Growers Association and small growers in Johnson County, Wyoming, to protect the former's "regulators" from a local mob. President Benjamin Harrison later dispatched six companies of the 9th Cavalry to protect the association's interests. The army, and occasionally marines and sailors, was called upon numerous times during the period, with the most controversial deployment coming during the 1894 Pullman Strike, when President Grover Cleveland ordered federal troops into action in Illinois and other states against the wishes of state authorities, setting a troubling precedent. Under the guise of ensuring the delivery of mail, soldiers served as strikebreakers and, unlike the 1877 troubles, this time inflicted casualties. These unwelcomed domestic interventions were duties better assigned to state militias, which in many cases had deteriorated after the Civil War.

Indeed, domestic unrest provided the impetus for the creation of what became the National Guard. The desire to create well-armed, well-trained militias led to the founding of the National Guard Association in 1879. At a time when the regular army struggled to attract and retain soldiers, Americans found the part-time commitment required by a militia unit attractive. Militias and eventually the National Guard offered men the opportunity for patriotic expression, physical exertion, and fraternal interaction. By 1890 the National Guard movement had produced impressive results, gaining additional appropriations as well as acceptance.

The military establishment during this period extended well beyond police actions and the nation-building duties of Reconstruction. The Corps of Engineers continued its work on improving the nation's rivers and harbors, supervised construction of numerous structures in Washington, including the Library of Congress and the Washington Monument, and continued to explore and map the continent. With the 1867 acquisition of Alaska, the army took on administrative responsibilities for the new territory. The engineers and officers of the Signal Corps mounted or supported several explorations of the Yukon country and the Arctic. Engineer and signal officers also conducted valuable geological surveys and established a weather service. Although these services eventually moved to civilian control, the army's scientific endeavors proved invaluable, while the army's Medical Department assumed an important role in advancing that profession by significantly enhancing its library and museum collections, establishing both as important research facilities.

With the establishment in 1872 of Yellowstone National Park, the army began a long and critical role as protector of this treasure and many others in what became the National Parks system. As commander of the vast Military Division of the Missouri, General Philip Sheridan took a keen interest in Yellowstone and used his already burdened resources to battle the park's exploitation. In 1883, he led a massive expedition into the park that included President Chester Arthur and other dignitaries to witness the wonders of the land but also the effects of environmental degradation and other human abuses. Sheridan's forceful advocacy no doubt contributed to the army assuming official responsibility for the park's administration in 1886. Park administration remained an army duty until the 1916 creation of the National Park Service. By that time the army had grown adept at a number of civil functions, from fighting fires and floods to confronting major natural disasters such as the hurricane that devastated Galveston, Texas, in 1900 and the 1906 San Francisco earthquake.

TECHNOLOGY

During the post–Civil War years, both the army and the navy retreated from technological advancement or simply failed to keep pace with available improvements. Frugality and a surplus of equipment dictated an avoidance of costly new systems. During the immediate postwar years, the army's infantrymen continued to carry the prolific Springfield .58-caliber rifle musket as U.S. armories converted thousands of these weapons into breech-loaders. The cavalry units wielded a variety of carbines, including the popular Spencer repeater, which saw extensive use during the war, as well as a range of cap and ball revolvers. But much to the displeasure of the troopers, an army board in 1872 tested dozens of rifles, both single shot and repeaters, before adopting the Springfield entry, a single-shot breech-loading rifle and carbine that fired .45-caliber black powder metallic cartridge ammunition. The army also sought a standard sidearm to replace the cap and ball pistols, most of which had been converted to take cartridge ammunition. The 1872 Colt six-shot .45-caliber revolver became the clear preference. The Springfield rifle and carbine would remain the standard in the regular army until the 1890s, as would the Colt revolver.

During the postwar years the army found limited use for artillery, and consequently artillery development lagged. The popular twelve-pounder mountain howitzer remained in service but was eclipsed in the mid-1870s by the lightweight and durable Hotchkiss gun, a 1.65-inch steel breech-loading rifle that had a range of 4,000 yards and could be carried on pack mules or easily pulled by a single horse. The Hotchkiss gun was widely used in the West. Although the army experimented with a number of systems for weaponry, including hydraulics and pneumatics, it did not adopt smokeless powder until the 1890s, long after European powers had made it standard. First introduced during the Civil War but not widely accepted or employed, the Gatling gun was a crank-operated mechanical gun mounted on an artillery carriage that could fire more than 300 rounds per minute with its rotating barrels. Designed by Christopher Gatling, the gun underwent a number of improvements before the army acquired 100 units of six- and ten-barrel models. In the frontier army, the Gatling gun was categorized as artillery and performed well in several engagements, although some

IMAGE 9.1 Hotchkiss Gun In the years following the Civil War, the army adopted breech loading small arms and artillery as well as cartridge ammunition. In this photograph from 1890 artillerists and Lakota scouts stand with one of the lightweight Hotchkiss guns that rained death in the Battle of Wounded Knee.

officers shunned it in the field as too unwieldy. Custer notoriously refused to include a Gatling detachment during his ill-fated march to the Little Bighorn in 1876. Gatling guns remained in the army arsenal until they were replaced by the modern machine gun during the First World War.

THE LAST INDIAN WARS

During the twenty-five years that followed the American Civil War, a steadily shrinking regular army performed onerous Reconstruction duty, conducted numerous surveys, and quelled civil unrest, but its main function during this period was the final subjugation of the American Indians of the West. The prewar conditions that sparked a series of Indian uprisings in the 1850s—westward migration, mining, and misunderstanding—only intensified in the postwar years. Westward migration onto the Great Plains and across them to Oregon and California reached overwhelming proportions for the tribes into whose hunting grounds these pioneers intruded. Fifteen years of pent-up energy and delayed dreams gave way to feverish railroad construction. Soon steel rails cut across the prairies and valleys of the frontier, bringing with them civilization—farmers, ranchers, merchants, ministers, and miners—and seriously disrupting the lives of the Indians and the great bison herds that sustained them. Professional hunters lured by the lucrative trade in buffalo robes, which were all the rage back East and in Europe, descended on the plains, encouraged by the government and the railroads, and slaughtered the great beasts in alarming numbers, leaving the earth littered with stripped carcasses and mounds of bones. Herds that once numbered in the millions all but disappeared by 1880, as the buffalo was hunted almost to extinction. Faced with such monumental threats to their ways of life and their very existence, the nomadic tribes of the West responded with understandable urgency and determination.

The spreading railroad network would eventually improve the logistical nightmare the army confronted in returning to the West, and the reduction of the buffalo herds undoubtedly played a large supporting role in subduing the tribes of the plains, but the army faced an incredibly difficult and often ill-defined task in taming the vast region west of the Mississippi. The years 1865 to 1890 saw more than 1,000 military actions of all sizes. Most of these involved the regular army, augmented on occasion by hired auxiliaries and almost always by Indian scouts. Throughout this time, the army dealt with a manpower shortage that was never adequately addressed. In 1874 Congress cut the enlistment ceiling to 25,000, but in fact the frontier army never approached that number in active, on-duty troops. During the Reconstruction years, occupation duties claimed roughly one-third of the available force, while the responsibility of garrisoning coastal fortifications also drained valuable resources, as did the many other duties the officers and men performed. During the busy and productive 1870s the army was scarcely able to muster 9,000 men for frontier duty. Illness (always a problem), desertion, and detached duty cut deeply into that number. Gone were the days of divisions and brigades. Regiments again became the largest operational formations, but they almost never served as a whole. In the West, the company—or cavalry troop—became the main tactical unit. With 430 companies to man more than 200 posts, the frontier army spread itself thin. Mounted regiments became essential and provided the main striking force in every campaign of the Indian Wars period. The mounted arm had been reorganized at the onset of the Civil War, when the old Dragoon and Mounted Rifle regiments were redesignated as "cavalry"; thus, the 1st and 2nd Dragoons became the 1st and 2nd Cavalry, the Mounted Rifles became the 3rd Cavalry, the 1st and 2nd Cavalry became the 4th and 5th Cavalry, and the new 6th Cavalry was added as well. Postwar expansion created the 7th and 8th and the African American 9th and 10th Cavalry. Each of these regiments saw extensive service on the frontier.

Manpower was but one of the soldiers' concerns. Poor, irregular pay, inconsistent rations, shoddy equipment, and harsh climates plagued the army. Inadequate, inconsistent training and high rates of turnover due to expired enlistments and desertion cut into operational effectiveness. While the army had an abundance of fine officers and managed to achieve high levels of retention and continuity in the field and company grades, attracting and retaining enlisted soldiers remained a serious problem throughout the Indian Wars period. During such a dynamic time, soldiering simply did not offer attractive prospects for most men. For many, though, especially immigrants and African Americans, the army represented a solid professional opportunity. Between 1866 and 1874 half of all enlisted men were foreign-born, mostly Irish and German, and most of these were veterans of one war or another. Immigrants also supplied a high percentage of quality noncommissioned officers, the corporals and sergeants who formed the backbone of the army.

BUFFALO SOLDIERS

In an army plagued by low morale and high desertion rates, African American regiments became exceptions to the rule. Not only did these units perform well in the field, but they also boasted lower desertion and higher reenlistment rates than their white counterparts. Soldiers in the 9th and 10th Cavalry and, after consolidation, the 24th and 25th Infantry regiments also experienced long periods of service, notably high esprit de corps, and great continuity of leadership. Benjamin Grierson commanded the 10th Cavalry from 1866 until his retirement in 1890. Although Henry O. Flipper (who became the first African American to graduate from the U.S. Military Academy at West Point in 1877) served as a lieutenant in the 10th Cavalry before his career was ended by a court-martial over questionable charges in 1882, most officers of the black regiments were white. While Indians of the West made little distinction between black and white soldiers—soldiers were soldiers—they did come to refer to the troopers of the 10th Cavalry as "Buffalo Soldiers," a label that carried the utmost respect. The term stuck with the 10th and was later extended to the other African American

IMAGE 9.2 Buffalo Soldiers In recognition of the service of African American soldiers during the Civil War, Congress authorized the formation of permanent black regiments in the regular army. Their Indian adversaries in the West dubbed them "Buffalo Soldiers." Here, men of the 25th Infantry pose at Fort Keogh, Montana, circa 1890.

regiments. Despite the fact that black soldiers endured discrimination and racial hatred, often garrisoned the most forbidding posts, and usually received the worst equipment and horseflesh, they performed well beyond the expectations of their many critics and in so doing played an important role in the closing of the West and the nation's military history.

FRONTIER CONSTABULARY

This army was a strange mix of immigrants and African Americans, of experienced sergeants and gifted, ambitious officers, led at the top by men who had secured Union victory in the Civil War through an irresistible combination of military execution and willful application of total war. Under William T. Sherman and Philip H. Sheridan, the army would apply the lessons of the late war to the realities of the frontier. Talented young officers such as Ranald Mackenzie and Nelson Miles, both of whom were barely twenty-five and serving as general officers when the Civil War ended, became the lords of the plains, fighting in pursuit of renewed glory, while thoughtful George Crook honestly attempted to learn from and work with his Indian adversaries. While proven warriors, these men in particular were also benevolent conquerors who tried to honor the terms of the subjugation they enforced, only to see the government continue to betray its promises. All too often, the regular army was the only thing that stood between Manifest Destiny and the extinction of the American Indians.

THE INDIANS

It is estimated that after the Civil War about 250,000 Indians inhabited the Trans-Mississippi West, roughly 100,000 of whom the U.S. government considered hostile because they had not accepted life on a barren reservation where they would be dependent on government handouts. Nomadic and reliant on the horse and buffalo, the tribes of the Great Plains and the mountain West resisted white encroachment in various ways, but as pressure on them mounted, fighting became the preferred alternative to life on a reservation. Victims of an inevitable clash of incompatible cultures, the Indians clung to their land and their ways. What white leaders failed to grasp was that they expected the Indians to relinquish things no white man would willingly consider surrendering: life, liberty, land. Yet as white civilization spread, the only space left available for the Indians was that which held no value for whites. Treaties and professions of peace had proven worthless. Although certainly not all Indians and not all whites embraced the warring culture that defined both peoples, enough members of both human tribes found the temptation to use force irresistible.

The United States' small regular army relied on discipline and firepower in battle, while Indians preferred hit-and-run tactics; not tied as the soldiers were to supply trains and bases of operation, the latter used their great mobility, space, and distance to their advantage. Indian warriors mastered individual combat but often performed poorly in coordinated action and usually avoided a stand-up fight. The persistent cliché that the Plains Indians were the "finest light cavalry in the world" is a misnomer. Excellent horsemen who could fight effectively on horseback they were, but a truly fine cavalry presents a level of organization, discipline, and tactical application that Indians rarely achieved in battle. Indian fighters excelled at guerrilla warfare and raiding but on occasion did manage large coordinated action as well as impressive fire discipline and tactical application. Indian society, though, was riven by intertribal rivalries and historical animosities that whites easily exploited. There is no denying the fact that the army's job would have been immeasurably more difficult without the assistance of Indian allies, auxiliaries, and scouts. Furthermore, unlike the soldiers, Indian forces had to protect their families and villages, which usually remained near the fighting. Indian villages were particularly vulnerable to winter attack, as it was customary for their inhabitants to stock up on supplies and wait out the cold months. Thus, Indian villages became ready targets once the army applied its total war practices to the frontier.

Ultimately white civilization proved unable to understand and appreciate the distinctive nature of Indian life. Reformers hoped to turn nomadic hunters whose very understanding of manhood rested on their prowess in battle into Christian farmers. Yet the government repeatedly settled Indians on land that was not suitable for farming or much else. Government contractors consistently failed to provide agreed-upon support. Corruption reigned. White leaders made treaties without offering Indians a firm understanding of what they entailed and then responded punitively when Indians continued to hunt on the ceded land. It was an old story, as old as Anglo-Indian relations. Differing concepts of leadership also caused problems. White culture vested power in recognized leaders, and a deal signed between leaders bound the leaders' subjects to the agreement. Most Indian groups had no such understanding. A treaty entered into by a tribal elder or chief and recognized by white authorities did not necessarily bind the young men of the band to the agreement, an outlook that led to repeated "violations." For the Indians and the army alike, treaties usually produced more problems than solutions. Ultimately the Indians' cherished ways of life proved unsustainable against the onslaught of insatiable humanity.

IMAGE 9.3A AND 9.3B (a) Sitting Bull, (b) Chief Joseph Indian Leaders: Lakota Holy Man Sitting Bull whose forces inflicted a major defeat on the army in the Battle of Little Bighorn; Gifted Nez Perce leader Joseph led his people on an epic quest for freedom.

IMAGE 9.3C AND 9.3D (c) Geronimo, (d) Red Cloud   Indian Leaders: the Apache warrior Geronimo confounded two of the army's best commanders before ultimately surrendering; Lakota Chief Red Cloud, who successfully contested the Bozeman Trail.

PRECURSORS

The conflict between western settlers and the various Indian tribes did not end when the Civil War erupted. Although most of the regular army was withdrawn from western posts, volunteer militia took up the duties of frontier defense. In Confederate Texas, the settlement line retracted in places for lack of manpower, but in Minnesota, Indians attempted to throw back the tide of settlement and failed, while in the Southwest local authorities took advantage of the absence of regular troops to wage punitive campaigns against native groups.

In Minnesota the disruption of life caused by white settlement resulted in starvation conditions. The Dakota people (Santee Sioux), who had been relegated to a small reservation, sought relief but received only ridicule and scorn. In August 1862, the Dakotas lashed out, killing hundreds of settlers over the course of several weeks before being overwhelmed by Minnesota militia in the Battle of Wood Lake on September 23. After a speedy trial during which the Indians had no representation, 303 men were convicted of numerous crimes and sentenced to death. President Lincoln commuted the death sentence for all but thirty-nine men, who were hanged at Mankato on December 26 in the largest public execution in U.S. history. In the Southwest, longstanding unrest caused by white settlement and mining activities compelled the authorities in the newly established Arizona Territory to remove the Navajos from their traditional homelands to a reservation in eastern New Mexico known as Bosque Redondo. Beginning in June 1863 territorial militia under famed frontiersman Colonel Christopher "Kit" Carson conducted a scorched earth campaign that left the Navajos in a dire condition. After a climactic engagement in Cañon de Chelly, the Navajos submitted and were marched more than 300 miles overland to the barren reservation. Some 1,000 Navajos died on this "Long Walk." After years of suffering, members of the tribe were allowed to reclaim a portion of their ancestral lands as part of a new reservation in Arizona.

Although not the deadliest episode involving Indians during the Civil War, perhaps the most controversial event took place in eastern Colorado Territory on November 29, 1864, when Colorado militia under the ambitious Colonel John Chivington attacked the village of Cheyenne chief Black Kettle on Sand Creek. Like the Dakotas in Minnesota, the Cheyenne bands of the southern plains had seen their lives disrupted by the encroachment of white settlement, which interfered with buffalo and other game essential to their lives and as a result made food scarce. Young warriors began to raid in search of food, causing alarm in settlements that were all too familiar with what had occurred in Minnesota. Hoping to avoid further conflict, Black Kettle moved his village to the site on Sand Creek near Fort Lyon, where he believed it came under government protection. The villagers were unprepared for Chivington's attack, which disproportionately struck old people, women, and children, many of whom were raped and mutilated. At least 150 Cheyennes and Arapahos were killed, and probably many more. Black Kettle, who during the attack waved an American flag and a flag of truce to try to halt the slaughter, managed to escape, but the Sand Creek Massacre left an indelible memory in the minds of the southern plains Indians.

With the close of the Civil War the regular army gradually returned to its role as the guardian of the frontier, but not without considerable adjustment. Old posts had to be reoccupied and refreshed; new posts had to be built. Many of the officers would be serving on the frontier for the first time, a completely new experience for the heroes of the Civil War. Generals Grant and Sherman had little experience with Indians, nor did General Winfield Scott Hancock, who directed one of the early campaigns on the southern plains that vividly revealed the army's lack of preparation. Of the bright young stars who now led regiments Wesley Merritt, Nelson Miles, and Ranald Mackenzie had entered the Civil War from West Point or, in the case of Miles, civilian life and thus had had no exposure to Indian fighting, yet all would emerge as proficient and prolific warriors. Quickly, the pressures of western expansion pressed hard upon the returning regulars.

BOZEMAN TRAIL SETBACK

Previous gold strikes in Montana had brought demands for a more direct route from the Oregon Trail to Virginia City. The so-called Bozeman Trail offered that direct route, but it cut through Lakota (Sioux) and Northern Cheyenne lands. Government efforts to craft a treaty with the local tribes produced only mixed results, with some bands agreeing to allow the construction of forts and the passage of prospectors, some remaining aloof, and others, such as the highly respected Lakota leader Red Cloud, proving completely defiant. In June 1866 Colonel Henry B. Carrington marched from Fort Laramie to begin establishing the planned string of forts, igniting the first sizable confrontation of the postwar period. After replacing the volunteer garrison at Fort Reno, Carrington established Fort Phil Kearny and Fort C. F. Smith in the Bighorn Mountain country of northern Wyoming and southern Montana. In December 1866 a large body of Lakota and Cheyenne warriors led by the talented Crazy Horse attacked a wood-cutting party outside of Fort Phil Kearny. When the impetuous Captain William Fetterman led a relief column into a cleverly disguised ambush, he and all eighty of his men were killed in the so-called Fetterman Massacre. On August 1, 1867, twenty-five soldiers and civilians of a hay detail held off a much larger Indian force near Fort C. F. Smith, sustaining only six casualties in the Hayfield Fight. The next day near Fort Phil Kearny Captain James Powell and a detachment of twenty-seven soldiers guarding a wood-cutting party endured a four-hour onslaught by hundreds of Lakota warriors. Fighting from wagon boxes removed from their wheel assemblies, they lost only six men killed and two wounded while inflicting several dozen casualties. Although the Hayfield and Wagon Box fights discouraged the Indians, continued pressure compelled the army to abandon its three Bozeman Trail forts in 1868.

SOUTHERN PLAINS

General Sheridan's Department of the Missouri included the busy Kansas prairie, where rail-road construction and disruptions of the buffalo herds struck the Indians most acutely. Activity in the region escalated rapidly after General Hancock's abortive but nonetheless invasive campaign of 1867 and the largely unsuccessful Medicine Lodge treaty negotiations. The area, long the domain of the Southern Cheyenne and Arapaho tribes as well as roaming Kiowa and Comanche bands, presented numerous challenges that the far-flung posts and dispersed

MAP 9.2 The West, 1860–1890

companies could not address to the aggressive Sheridan's satisfaction. The general ordered his longtime aide Major George "Sandy" Forsyth to hire fifty frontiersmen as a mobile strike force against marauding Indians in Kansas. In September 1868, Forsyth's scouts came under attack by a force of some 600 Cheyenne and Arapaho warriors and took up a position on an island in a dry riverbed on a fork of the Republican River, where they held out during repeated attacks over three days, suffering six killed and fifteen wounded, including Forsyth himself, while inflicting considerably more casualties on the attacking Indians. The Battle of Beecher's Island, named for Lieutenant Frederick Beecher, who was killed in the fighting, ended when a relief column of Buffalo Soldiers from the 10th Cavalry arrived.

Although it had become government policy to concentrate western Indians on reservations, the practice created additional problems. Many of the bands raiding Kansas settlements in 1867 and 1868 did so from reservations in western Indian Territory (present-day Oklahoma). Many groups would gladly accept rations and even winter on reservations only to return to traditional hunting grounds in the spring. The government's persistent inability to honor its treaty commitments or to do so in a satisfactory fashion caused many an exodus from the reservations. In an attempt to stop the attacks on Kansas settlements and railroad crews, Sheridan devised a campaign strategy that would be employed often and usually with positive results: a brutal combination of converging columns and total war. This approach proved especially effective in the winter months, when Indian villages entered into a state of near hibernation, with large stocks of food accumulated and pony herds close at hand.

The targets of Sheridan's winter campaign of 1868 were the Cheyenne and Arapaho villages along the Washita and Canadian rivers in western Indian Territory, just east of the vast Comanche stronghold in the Texas Panhandle. Sheridan began his campaign by moving in columns from forts in New Mexico, Colorado, and Kansas. At dawn on November 27 the Kansas column, Lieutenant Colonel George A. Custer's 7th Cavalry, surrounded the village of the unlucky Black Kettle on the Washita River. While Black Kettle had continued to profess his peaceful intentions, others in his village continued their warring ways, making the winter encampment a legitimate military target in the government's mind. In deep snow and subfreezing temperatures, as Custer's regimental band tried to play his signature "Garryowen" on frozen instruments, the soldiers attacked, killing dozens in fierce fighting, including Black Kettle and his wife. Custer's men then burned the lodges and shot hundreds of ponies but were soon threatened by warriors from neighboring villages, which forced Custer's command to withdraw during the night with more than fifty women and children captives. Unknown to Custer at the time, Major Joel Elliott and a detachment of fifteen men in pursuit of fleeing fighters were ambushed and killed. Custer's total losses amounted to two officers and nineteen men killed, with another fourteen officers and men wounded. Legitimate though his attack may have been in military terms—especially under Sheridan's total war approach—Custer could not escape comparisons to Chivington at Sand Creek. But Custer had his supporters too, and many openly approved of his Washita attack.

Sheridan's winter campaign did not produce the desired effect. The following spring the southern plains experienced a rash of violence, which continued until 1875 and required a major concentration of troops to quell the unrest. Kiowa and Comanche warriors operating out of reservations in Indian Territory and from canyon strongholds in the Texas Panhandle plagued settlements in Texas, Kansas, and New Mexico. Texas became a particular concern, as it presented three long and hostile fronts that invited attacks from not only the Kiowas and Comanches from across the Red River, but also Kickapoo and Lipan bands operating out of Mexico and roaming Apaches in the trans-Pecos area of West Texas. The army had constructed a string of forts along the western frontier and another string along the Rio Grande, as well as others protecting the San Antonio to El Paso road. Texas, then, became the scene of the army's next major effort.

Compounding the issue as far as the army was concerned were the well-intentioned but disastrously flawed peace initiatives that accompanied Grant's move to the White House in 1869. Eastern reformers and grandstanding politicians demonized the army, with some justification, for its wanton acts of violence and harsh treatment of the Indians. Conflict between the Bureau of Indian Affairs within the Department of the Interior and the army within the Department of War hampered cooperation and led each agency to blame the other for various transgressions. President Grant embraced a reform agenda with a peace policy that involved placing reservations under the guidance of benevolent religious groups. The enduring but elusive idea of turning America's Indians into Christian farmers proved disastrous, as many bands continued to live and receive rations on the reservations while raiding at will, only to return to their refuge to avoid persecution. The most graphic case in point occurred in Texas in May 1871.

TEXAS

General Sherman had been bombarded by complaints about Indian depredations from Texas citizens and their political representatives. Although incredulous, he decided to go to Texas to observe the situation firsthand. He toured the frontier, visiting several posts with no fanfare and only a small escort, but found no sign of the much-advertised hostile activity. Confirmed in his belief that the complaints were no more than hyperbole, he was nearing the end of his journey when he stopped at Fort Richardson, about sixty miles northwest of the town of Fort Worth. Unknown to Sherman, he and his escort had traversed a small valley under the watchful eyes of a large Kiowa raiding party. Later that day, the party, led by Kiowa chieftain Satanta, struck a supply train, killing and mutilating teamsters and making off with mules and much bounty before returning to the reservation near Fort Sill in Indian Territory. A badly wounded survivor managed to reach Fort Richardson to alert the post of the attack. The next day a visibly disturbed Sherman examined the site of the so-called Warren Wagon Train Massacre and understood that the stories he had heard were indeed true. Sherman sent Colonel Mackenzie with several companies of his 4th Cavalry in pursuit of the culprits, but, believing that the raiders had made for secret hideouts on the Llano Estacado (the Staked Plains of the Texas Panhandle), the troopers apprehended no one; they did, however, accumulate a wealth of knowledge about the previously mysterious region. In a strange twist of fate, Sherman moved on to Fort Sill, where he found himself confronting Satanta and the other leaders of the raid, who had openly boasted of their successful attack. Backed by 10th Cavalry Buffalo Soldiers, Sherman had Satanta and two others arrested and sent to Texas for trial. Thereafter, Texas became the scene of constant campaigning that brought the state and most of the southern plains under control by 1875.

Mackenzie, whom Grant considered the "most promising young officer" of the Civil War, had hardly passed thirty years of age when he became the army's primary troubleshooter in Texas. Having suffered six wounds in the war, including the loss of two fingers on his right hand—for which the Indians called him "Bad Hand"—Mackenzie was known for his toughness and had turned the 4th Cavalry into an elite unit. Throughout 1872 and 1873, Mackenzie's troopers campaigned relentlessly in Texas and beyond. In May 1873, in response to a number of raids by Kickapoo and Lipan bands operating out of Mexico, but with only a verbal order from General Sheridan, Mackenzie led six companies of the 4th Cavalry and a detachment of Indian scouts across the Rio Grande without the blessing of the Mexican government. Mackenzie's men drove seventy miles into Mexico, destroyed two Indian villages, and returned to Texas with dozens of women and children prisoners, covering an amazing 160 miles in only thirty-two hours. Raids from Mexico all but ceased.

The 4th Cavalry also played a leading role in the climactic conflict on the southern plains. In 1874 Sheridan, who now commanded the vast Military Division of the Missouri, coordinated a five-pronged campaign directed against the Kiowa and Comanche strongholds in the Texas Panhandle, in which columns converged from Kansas to the north, New Mexico from the west, and Indian Territory from the east while two pushed northward from forts in Texas. In one of the largest efforts the army had mounted in the West, Sheridan committed some 3,000 troops to the fall campaign, which also featured conspicuous contributions from Colonel Nelson A. Miles, who, like Mackenzie, was emerging as one of the army's premier Indian fighters. In September, Mackenzie, moving from Fort Concho in West Texas, located a sizable Comanche winter encampment in the large, deep,

IMAGE 9.4A AND 9.4B (a) Mackenzie, (b) Miles Lords of the Plains: Oft wounded Ranald S. Mackenzie became the army's frontier troubleshooter; ambitious and prolific Nelson A. Miles had a role in most of the important events of the post-Civil War period.

IMAGE 9.4C AND 9.4D (c) Sheridan, (d) Crook   Lords of the Plains: Much of the fighting during the Indian Wars period came under the direction of former Civil War hero Philip Sheridan; Unconventional George Crook produced some notable successes but experienced serious setbacks as well.

and rugged Palo Duro Canyon, just south of present-day Amarillo, Texas. After a harrowing descent into the canyon on a narrow trail, the 4th Cavalry swept through the village, quickly gaining control of many lodges and the large pony herd. With very few casualties on either side, Mackenzie achieved a stunning victory. After destroying the village and its invaluable accumulated supplies and allowing his scouts to take a few of the ponies, Mackenzie ordered the rest of the herd—some 1,500 horses—destroyed to prevent recapture. The Battle of Palo Duro Canyon proved to be the death blow for the Comanches and Kiowas. Relentless winter campaigning by Mackenzie, Miles, and others finally broke the fiercest tribes the southern plains had known. The following spring, the great Comanche leader Quanah Parker, himself the son of a white captive, surrendered to Mackenzie and accepted what turned out to be a prosperous existence on the reservation in Indian Territory. With Quanah's submission the Texas frontier, along with Indian Territory and much of the southern plains, was for all intents and purposes pacified.

NORTHERN PLAINS

Even as the southern plains quieted, the north remained troubled. An 1874 army-led expedition into the Black Hills of the Dakota Territory had confirmed the presence of gold, which led to an onslaught of prospectors and others seeking opportunity and wealth on lands belonging by treaty to the Lakota people. The government's failure to honor treaty obligations and to protect Lakota land caused a great deal of unrest as thousands of Lakotas, Cheyennes, and Arapahos left their reservations to join those Indians still roaming free in the mountains and valleys of the Yellowstone country of Montana and Wyoming. Bureau of Indian Affairs agents grew alarmed at the mass exodus and issued orders for all reservation-registered groups to return to their agencies. Few complied, however, and the bureau reluctantly turned to the army for assistance. In the spring of 1876 General Sheridan took up the matter, devising a multipronged campaign like the one that proved so successful in Texas.

A March campaign to the Powder River Valley identified the location of Indian camps but accomplished little else. A more robust effort, which involved three columns converging on the Yellowstone River and its tributaries, the Rosebud and the Little Bighorn, came to fruition in June. That campaign began in April when a mixed column of cavalry and infantry commanded by Colonel John Gibbon moved eastward from Fort Ellis in Montana. Then, in May, a large force of fifteen cavalry, five infantry companies, and around 300 Crow and Shoshone auxiliaries under General George Crook advanced from Fort Fetterman on the North Platte, while General Alfred Terry's column, spearheaded by eleven companies of Custer's 7th Cavalry, pushed westward from Fort Abraham Lincoln near Bismarck. Unknown to the army, an unprecedented number of highly motivated warriors and their families had camped in the valley of the Little Bighorn under the inspirational Lakota leader Sitting Bull. Upward of 12,000 Lakota, Cheyenne, and Arapaho people, among whom were as many as 3,000 fighting men under battle-tested veterans such as Crazy Horse, Gall, and Crow King, awaited the soldiers.

On June 17 a Lakota-Cheyenne force of more than 1,200 under Crazy Horse attacked Crook's 1,300-strong column on the Rosebud, just across the Montana line. Fierce fighting lasted for more than six hours, as the Indians engaged in an uncharacteristic stand-up battle, displaying a level of tenacity and discipline that took the soldiers by surprise. The Battle of the Rosebud was one of the largest engagements of the Indian Wars and featured high casualties on both sides. Although the Indians withdrew, the damage to Crook's force and, more important, his confidence compelled him to fall back on his supply base and await reinforcements, thus removing his large contingent from the campaign. Meanwhile, Gibbon's and Terry's columns advanced unaware of Crook's setback. Terry met with Gibbon and Custer on June 21, settling on a plan to trap the rebellious Indians—whose strength the commanders still had not determined—between the two wings and force them to submit. No action was to be taken until all elements of the operation were in place. Before moving out, Custer declined the assistance of four companies of cavalry from Gibbon's command and a section of Gatling guns that he feared would only slow him down.

On June 25 Custer approached the Little Bighorn valley. His scouts identified an Indian village but could not make out its size or exact location. Clear signs of Indian movement convinced Custer that his presence was known and that the Indians threatened to escape his grasp. Without waiting for Gibbon, who was still a day out, Custer moved on the suspected Indian village. He knew almost nothing about the object of his attack. He could not see the hundreds of lodges that stretched for miles along the Little Bighorn, and he could not know that at least 2,000 warriors, many fresh off the successful battle with Crook, awaited his regiment. Still, Custer determined to attack. Compounding that error in judgment, he divided his regiment, sending Captain Frederick Benteen with three companies on a circuitous route to block his adversaries' suspected flight while Major Marcus Reno struck the head of the village with three companies and a group of Indian scouts. Custer would attack the other end

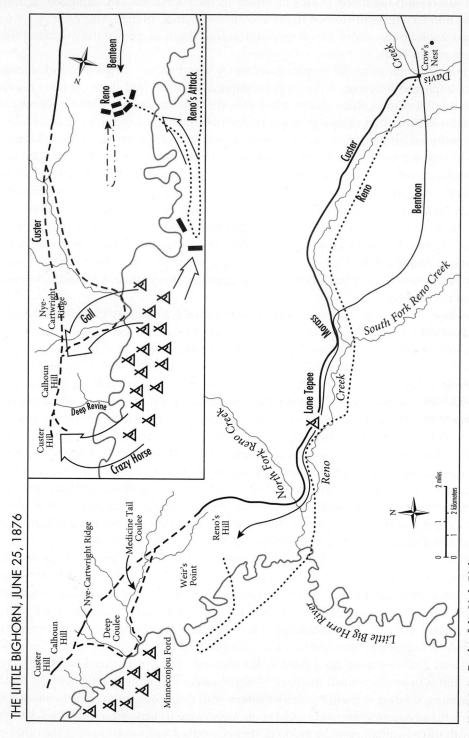

THE LITTLE BIGHORN, JUNE 25, 1876

Custer Hill
Calhoun Hill
Nye-Cartwright Ridge
Deep Coulee
Minneconjou Ford
Medicine Tail Coulee
Weir's Point
Reno's Hill
North Fork Reno Creek
Lone Tepee
Reno
Morass
South Fork Reno Creek
Creek
Benteen
Reno
Custer
Crow's Nest
Davis
Creek
Little Big Horn River

N

0   1   2 miles
0   1   2 kilometers

Custer
Nye-Cartwright Ridge
Gall
Calhoun Hill
Deep Revine
Custer Hill
Crazy Horse
Reno
Benteen
Reno's Attack
N

MAP 9.3   Battle of the Little Bighorn

of the village with the remaining five companies. While en route, he sent orders recalling Benteen and the regiment's pack train.

Reno's afternoon attack met a bloody demise. His troopers charged the village only to find a horde of vengeful warriors wielding great firepower, including fine repeating Winchesters. Rather than scattering as expected, once again the Indians stood and fought, inflicting heavy losses and driving off Reno's devastated battalion. Reno withdrew his command to the bluffs across the river and assumed a strong defensive position. Later joined by Benteen and the pack train, this remnant of the regiment would hold out, unable to support Custer as he continued his advance, ignorant of Reno's repulse.

As Custer and his 225 men mounted a ridge above the village, they were confronted by perhaps 1,500 well-armed Lakota and Cheyenne warriors. In a fight that is believed to have lasted about an hour, Custer and his entire battalion were killed, with many of the bodies subsequently plundered and mutilated. Back at Reno's position, the attack resumed, but the survivors held on during the night and the following day until relieved by Gibbon's men on June 27. More than half the men of the 7th Cavalry had been killed or wounded. Indian losses remain unknown.

News of the bloody defeat on the Montana prairie sent shock waves through a nation preparing to celebrate its centennial. The Battle of the Little Bighorn became famous as "Custer's Last Stand," and the martyred Custer was transformed once more into a national hero, destined for a starring role in the American narrative. The unexpected Indian victory, the greatest of the post–Civil War period, only invited massive retaliation. The government's response was rapid and decisive. Sheridan summoned Mackenzie's crack 4th Cavalry from Texas and Nelson Miles's 5th Infantry from Kansas to launch a winter campaign under the overall command of General Crook. In an awesome application of total war, the army campaigned relentlessly during the bitter winter of 1876–1877. In late November 1876, Mackenzie's ten companies of cavalry launched a dawn attack in subzero temperatures on Dull Knife's Cheyenne village on a tributary of the Powder River in Wyoming Territory. In desperate fighting both sides suffered heavy casualties—unusual for Mackenzie—but the soldiers secured the village, finding souvenirs of Little Bighorn before destroying all of the food and shelter the fleeing Cheyennes could not carry off and herding away most of their ponies. The destitute survivors suffered miserably before ultimately being forcibly relocated to the Indian Territory. In September 1878 Dull Knife led a forlorn attempt to return to the northern plains. After eluding several army units sent in pursuit, he surrendered near Camp Robinson, Nebraska, only to be subjected to a cruel captivity. Dozens of men, women, and children died in an attempted breakout. Finally, Dull Knife and a few survivors were allowed to settle at the Pine Ridge Agency in Dakota Territory.

In January 1877, after a grueling campaign, Miles, with 500 infantrymen mounted in wagons and two pieces of artillery, fought forces led by Crazy Horse at Wolf Mountain near the Wyoming–Montana line. Miles continued to apply pressure, and by spring most of the holdout Lakota and Cheyenne bands had surrendered or returned to their various reservations. Sitting Bull led a number of his followers to Canada. By summer the so-called Great Sioux War was over, but lingering unrest continued until 1881, when Sitting Bull returned and took up residence under the watchful eye of the army.

THE FAR WEST

California had experienced a good deal of hostile Indian activity for years as white settlement became overwhelming for the native populations, and it was in northern California that one of the most bizarre incidents of the post–Civil War period occurred. Again, reservation issues fueled the conflict. The Modocs of the Tule Lake area in far northern California had a long and tumultuous relationship with settlers in the region but by treaty had agreed to settle on a reservation in southern Oregon shared with the adversarial Klamaths. In late 1872 a militant faction of Modocs led by Kintpuash, known to local white miners as Captain Jack, returned to the traditional Modoc lands in the Lost River Basin, upsetting the settlers there, who demanded their removal. A botched military-civilian response led to an armed uprising in which more than a dozen civilians were killed, beginning a war that featured embarrassingly futile efforts by the army and Modoc treachery. With only some sixty warriors, the Modocs holed up in a natural stronghold in the forbidding lava beds south of Tule Lake. A much-reinforced army found little success in confronting them, forcing the government to attempt negotiations. General E.R.S Canby, commander of the Military Department of the Columbia, assumed control of the talks but in April 1873 during a face-to-face meeting Captain Jack shot and killed Canby and a civilian negotiator. Canby thus became the only regular army general officer to be killed in the line of duty during the Indian Wars. Colonel Jefferson C. Davis then assumed command of a renewed military effort. Betrayed by a fellow Modoc leader, Captain Jack was captured in June. He and three others were hanged, while most of his followers were sent to Indian Territory. The Modoc episode dealt a severe blow to President Grant's peace initiative.

Beginning in far northeastern Oregon and ending 1,500 miles away in the mountains of northern Montana, the Nez Perce War ranks as one of the most remarkable military campaigns in American history. For years a band of Nez Perces had occupied land in the Wallowa Valley in northeastern Oregon, near the Washington border, in largely friendly defiance of an 1863 treaty that had relocated most Nez Perce bands to a reservation in Idaho. But by the mid-1870s mounting pressure from white settlers in the region finally prompted the government to compel the Wallowa Valley Nez Perces to move to the reservation. In May 1877 General Oliver O. Howard, commanding the Department of the Columbia, delivered the unhappy ultimatum that the Nez Perces would have to move or be moved. After much deliberation, Nez Perce leaders, including brothers Joseph and Ollokot, agreed to the relocation, but after wayward young Nez Perce men killed several settlers, events quickly spiraled out of control. The army unit sent to bring in the culprits instead fired on a Nez Perce peace delegation, precipitating an engagement during which the Indians demonstrated great determination in driving away the soldiers. Joseph now led his people into the mountains, hoping to evade the army. General Howard, who had lost an arm during the Civil War, in turn called out more troops and personally led the pursuit. One of Howard's detachments attacked the Nez Perce village of Looking Glass, whose residents had not been involved in the previous events but now joined Joseph's flight, bringing the Nez Perce numbers to roughly 700, among whom were some 200 fighting men.

Howard's large command, consisting of 500 soldiers in detachments of cavalry, infantry, and artillery, attacked the Nez Perce position on the Clearwater River in Idaho on July 11. During the two-day battle, Nez Perce warriors demonstrated a discipline, tenacity, and tactical ability that would mark the entire campaign. Indian battles rarely involved sustained and controlled fighting, but the Nez Perce warriors maintained pressure on Howard's soldiers and inflicted heavy casualties with well-aimed volley fire. Howard was compelled to deploy his artillery to avoid being overwhelmed. In all, he suffered seventeen men killed and twenty-seven wounded. Nez Perce sources put Indian casualties at four killed and six wounded, but Howard believed them to be much higher. With army reinforcements arriving, the Nez Perces escaped eastward into the Bitterroot Mountains, hoping to reach the buffalo range beyond. Managing to put some distance between themselves and Howard's sluggish column, they entered the Bitterroot Valley and, at the insistence of Looking Glass, stopped for rest on the Big Hole River. There, on August 9, a separate army column out of Montana led by Colonel John Gibbon surprised and overran the Nez Perce camp. Gibbon's command, comprising 160 officers and men as well as 45 civilian volunteers and a number of scouts, quickly occupied the camp as the Indians scrambled for the nearby woods, where they reorganized and opened a withering fire on Gibbon's men before launching a furious counterattack that regained the village. Fighting continued the next day, but after buying enough time for noncombatants to escape, the warriors disengaged and followed. Gibbon's command suffered mightily, with twenty-eight killed and thirty-nine, including Colonel Gibbon, wounded. As many as ninety Nez Perce men, women, and children died, most during the initial attack.

By this time, negative press coverage had savaged Howard and other officers while elevating Joseph to great-captain status. After fighting another engagement on August 20 just west of Yellowstone, the weary Nez Perces passed through the national park, alarming tourists. Determined to reach refuge in Canada, they then turned northward, still trailed by Howard and his badly used-up command. Hoping to head off Joseph's people before they could reach sanctuary, Howard ordered Colonel Nelson Miles at Fort Keogh in western Montana to intercept them. On September 30, Miles, with around 400 men, mostly from the 2nd and 7th Cavalry regiments, attacked the Indians as they rested in the Bear Paw Mountains, less than forty miles from the Canadian border. After an initial melee in which both sides suffered heavy casualties, including Ollokot, who was killed, Miles settled in for a siege. Perhaps 300 Nez Perces managed to slip away and make it to Canada, while Joseph and the others dug in and endured sniper fire, which ultimately killed Looking Glass. On October 5, with most of his fighting men dead and with Howard's long-suffering column having finally reached the field, Joseph surrendered to Miles, famously exclaiming: "From where the sun now stands I will fight no more forever." Despite Miles's assurances, Joseph and his people were sent to Indian Territory, where they endured great hardship before finally being allowed to settle on reservations in Idaho and Washington.

Indian conflict in the Northwest did not conclude with the Nez Perce drama. In 1878 and 1879 the army mounted sizable operations to quell unrest in Idaho, where the Bannocks and Sheepeaters had responded to the pressures of white settlement by engaging in separate but relatively minor uprisings. Southward in Utah and Colorado, the formidable Utes threatened war only to be dissuaded by an impressive show of military force staged by Colonel Mackenzie that ended the conflict without bloodshed.

For the army, the most frustrating theater of the Indian Wars was the desert Southwest, where the various Apache groups had confounded the very best officers the army had to offer. Complicating matters was the international border, which the Indians used quite effectively to evade both U.S. and Mexican troops. Here, as elsewhere in the West, the army faced the loathsome burden of separating peaceful bands from hostile ones and the thankless task of protecting the former against often-murderous white civilians. In 1871, for example, a group of Apaches living under the supposed protection of the army at Camp Grant was attacked by a civilian force out of Tucson. More than 100 Apaches, mostly women and children, were murdered in the so-called Camp Grant Massacre, and several dozen children taken during the attack were sold into slavery in Mexico.

In 1872 General Howard, the deeply religious former head of the Freedmen's Bureau, took charge of affairs in the Southwest. Howard's sympathy for the Indians' plight led to productive talks with vaunted Apache chieftain Cochise that ended the much-feared warrior's fighting career. But recalcitrant bands continued to raid on both sides of the border, which occasioned a major campaign by the inventive General George Crook. Crook's unconventional tactics included the liberal use of Apache scouts and pack mules instead of wagon trains, and he also dealt earnestly and honestly with Indian leaders. The combination of Howard's diplomacy and Crook's relentless campaigning brought relative order to the region, but Cochise's death in 1874 opened the way for a new generation of Apache leaders, including men known on both sides of the border as Geronimo and Victorio.

The government's failed reservation policy contributed to renewed unrest in 1876, when several hundred Apaches left the agency to raid settlements in Arizona and New Mexico as well as the Mexican states of Sonora and Chihuahua. By 1879 Victorio's bloody exploits had drawn considerable military attention from the United States and Mexico. Apaches proved to be particularly difficult to defeat because they combined highly effective hit-and-run guerrilla warfare with an incredible physical endurance that had been well cultivated in the harsh desert climate. They were not as dependent on the horse as were the plains tribes and fought well on foot in the rocky environment of the border country, which provided numerous natural fortresses. Victorio's rampage came to an end in 1880 when, hounded by the Buffalo Soldiers of the 9th and 10th Cavalry regiments, the Apaches fell prey to Mexican irregulars. By that time, the United States and Mexico had established a productive relationship. Under President Porfirio Díaz, Mexico adopted a much more friendly posture toward its neighbor to the north that eventually facilitated cross-border pursuit by U.S. troops. This repaired relationship paid major dividends in the waning days of the Apache wars.

Despite their fierce resistance, by 1880 most Indians in the American West had submitted to U.S. authority. Only the Apaches remained defiant, with Geronimo and others continuing to confound the army's top Indian fighters. A toxic combination of deplorable conditions and a heavy-handed army response to a provocative religious message of rebellion contributed to a deadly confrontation at Cibecue Creek on the San Carlos Reservation when Apache scouts turned on soldiers of Colonel Eugene Carr's 6th Cavalry. Geronimo and fewer than 100 others subsequently left the reservation for Mexico, from which they raided settlements in Arizona and New Mexico. General Crook returned in 1882 and mounted a sizable expedition into northern Mexico the following year that finally compelled Geronimo and his followers to return to the reservation in 1884. Crook's success was short-lived, however, as Geronimo bolted the reservation in May 1885 and once again began raiding extensively throughout the region. After Crook sent two large expeditions into Mexico and manned strategic points along the border, Geronimo agreed to surrender and famously met with Crook in March 1886, only to back out of the agreement. Disheartened, Crook asked to be relieved and was replaced by the prolific Nelson Miles, who mounted a massive effort against the Apache leader, sending a heavy column into Mexico, but to no avail. Geronimo's tiny contingent tied up several thousand regular army troops throughout the summer of 1886. Finally, Miles reluctantly sent Lieutenant Charles Gatewood and a complement of Apache scouts after the troublesome Geronimo. In the meantime, Miles also sent the families of the warring Chiricahua and Warm Springs peoples by rail to prisons in Florida. Gatewood's scouts soon located Geronimo, and the lieutenant convinced him to come in. The last great Apache leader surrendered to Miles at Skeleton Canyon, Arizona, in September. Geronimo, his followers, and the loyal Apache scouts were all sent to prisons in Florida. Geronimo gained minor celebrity status during his later years and eventually took up a peaceful residence at Fort Sill in Oklahoma.

The final act in the long and tragic war between the United States and the American Indians came as the result of a religious uprising that unfolded on the reservations of the West. The hopeful vision of Indian revival and regeneration first promulgated by the Paiute holy man Wovoka spread to the Lakota reservations in the Dakotas by 1890. There, what had become known as the Ghost Dance movement took on a more militant expression, with many dancers donning "Ghost Shirts" that they believed could not be penetrated by soldiers' bullets. As reservation agents grew concerned, they called for military assistance to discourage an uprising. General Miles, now commanding the Military Division of the Missouri, ordered several important Lakota leaders to be detained. On December 15, Lakota tribal police attempted to arrest the revered Sitting Bull, who was killed in the melee. Fear spread through the Lakota communities. When influential leader Big Foot attempted to relocate his band from the Cheyenne River Reservation to the Pine Ridge Reservation, his movement was arrested by Colonel James Forsyth's 7th Cavalry, which confronted the Lakotas at Wounded Knee Creek in southern South Dakota on December 29. Five hundred troopers backed by a section of breech-loading Hotchkiss guns moved in to disarm the ailing Big Foot's warriors, many of whom carried fine Winchester repeaters. During the disarming process, tensions escalated and many men refused to surrender their weapons. When soldiers attempted to take the rifle of an agitated warrior the gun discharged and chaos erupted. Lakota warriors opened fire on two companies of dismounted soldiers, inflicting heavy losses. The soldiers responded, firing into the massed Indians. The situation soon devolved into a gruesome hand-to-hand struggle as noncombatants sought to escape the carnage. Then the Hotchkiss guns opened. When the killing finally stopped at least 146 Lakotas, and likely many more, including Big Foot and sixty women and children, lay dead on the frozen ground. Another 50 had been wounded, and perhaps 150 escaped. Twenty-five troopers of the ill-fated 7th Cavalry had been killed in the action, and another thirty-nine wounded. Although often referred to as a massacre, the slaughter at Wounded Knee was certainly not intended. It was nonetheless the last military engagement of the Indian Wars.

IMAGE 9.5 Wounded Knee   The aftermath of the tragedy at Wounded Knee in 1890: soldiers and civilian contractors bury Lakota dead, including women and children, in mass graves. Wounded Knee marked the end of the Indian Wars.

PROFESSIONALISM

Military professionalism grew steadily under Commanding General William T. Sherman (1869–1883) and his successors Philip H. Sheridan (1883–1888) and John M. Schofield (1888–1895). During Sherman's long tenure, he promoted postgraduate education for the officer corps. The Artillery School at Fort Monroe was reopened in 1868; a school for signal officers opened that year as well. In 1881 Sherman founded the School of Application for Infantry and Cavalry at Fort Leavenworth. The Engineer School of Application opened in 1885, and the Army Medical School followed in 1893. Military intellectualism also flourished during this period, led chiefly by Colonel Emory Upton. Upton, a dynamic young officer who had been badly wounded during the Civil War, worked extensively on tactical development and organization. He served as commandant of cadets at West Point and as an instructor at the Artillery School, and conducted a lengthy tour of Europe and Asia to study the top military establishments there, growing particularly impressed with the German model. Upton wrote extensively, and his theories became quite popular among

ISSUES IN MILITARY HISTORY

WAS THE TRAGEDY AT WOUNDED KNEE A MASSACRE?

Despite the many ways in which it is employed, the noun "massacre" lacks a comprehensive definition. According to the Cambridge English Dictionary, a massacre is "the killing of a large number of people, especially people who are not involved in any fighting or have no way of defending themselves." Merriam-Webster's definitions include "a wholesale slaughter." Certainly, the events at Wounded Knee included examples of both definitions. Also implied in the term are elements of willfulness and premeditation. The Sand Creek Massacre, for example, had all of these characteristics and is therefore easier to categorize. The same argument could be applied to Vietnam's infamous My Lai Massacre.

One problem with defining Wounded Knee as a massacre is that the soldiers involved neither had orders to attack nor were predisposed to do so. They outnumbered the warriors almost five to one, which should have discouraged Indian resistance. But army leaders badly misjudged the volatility of the moment. Another problem was that the Lakotas were well armed, many wielding fifteen-shot Winchester repeaters, and refused to yield their prized weapons when ordered to surrender all firearms. Finally, and most damaging to the massacre argument, the Indians delivered the first lethal volleys of the event, firing into the soldiers' ranks and felling dozens. By that time it was too late to prevent the inevitable slaughter. For many involved, any semblance of restraint vanished.

Wounded Knee was a monumental tragedy and a sad final episode in the long and lamentable war between European-Americans and the American Indians that dated to the earliest years of colonization. Clearly, army leaders' decision to employ a heavy-handed approach to an already explosive situation set the stage for disaster. Sending in the long-aggrieved 7th Cavalry to disarm potential veterans of the Battle of Little Bighorn only exacerbated tensions, and the fact that many of the troopers were raw recruits who had never been exposed to combat conditions no doubt also played a role, as it did at My Lai seventy-eight years later.

What happened at Wounded Knee was nothing more than what had happened dozens of times throughout the brutal history of the Indian Wars. It was the result of perpetual misunderstanding, mistrust, and mistakes, of one culture exercising overwhelming advantage over another, of failure of leadership. Once a preventable exchange became a full-blown firefight, not enough was done to stop it or to protect innocents. In this regard neither side was blameless. Was Wounded Knee a massacre? Like so much about the Indian Wars, there is simply not an easy answer. The situation was far too complicated to boil down to a single word.

progressive officers in the army. Published long after his 1881 suicide, his *Military Policy of the United States* offered a forceful argument for a strong professional army and an equally strong indictment of the militia system and the traditional volunteer army approach. He advanced the idea of an expansible regular army that could be augmented by volunteers and militia but remain under professional officers. Upton also advocated merit-based promotion to replace the flawed seniority system and the creation of a general staff based on the German model to address the corrosive relationship between line and staff. Finally, he advocated an American military establishment free of political oversight, a controversial idea that stood no chance of becoming reality. But by the time of its publication in

1904, much of what Upton advanced in *Military Policy of the United States* had been embraced, including the formation of a general staff and greater federal control of militias. Upton's efforts coincided with a general trend toward intellectual expression, as a number of professional organizations, including the U.S. Naval Institute, the U.S. Cavalry Association, and the Association of Military Surgeons, began to publish journals. The army's postgraduate schools at Fort Monroe and Fort Leavenworth also produced publications of their own.

In 1882 Congress passed legislation requiring compulsory retirement for all officers at sixty-four years of age. This law forced out General Sherman and several still-competent officers but also created opportunities for advancement for others. So while many heroes of the Civil War slipped into retirement, many more who rose to prominence as young men during that conflict brought the influence of the Civil War generation into the next century as America's agents of expansion and empire.

CONCLUSIONS

The year 1890 not only marked the end of the Indian Wars but also signaled the closing of the frontier. The national census that year declared as much. Although the army continued to man dozens of posts across the West, its role as a frontier constabulary was ending as well. During the twenty-five-year period that followed the Civil War the army experienced a great deal of continuity in leadership under Sherman and Sheridan and completed its transition into an effective fighting force under gifted regimental and company commanders. Men who had gained notoriety on the battlefields of Virginia and Tennessee transformed themselves into competent, even outstanding, frontier officers; some—most notably Mackenzie and Miles—produced stunning results. A number of regiments, such as Mackenzie's 4th Cavalry, approached elite status. Likewise, Crook's innovative campaigns and humanitarian administration set an example of professionalism for the next generation of officers, an example that would not always be followed in the vexing pursuit of empire.

With the final major confrontation at Wounded Knee, a military conflict that had lasted almost 300 years came to a close. The defeat and subjugation of the indigenous peoples of North America ended a long, tragic, and hugely traumatic chapter in American history, one that has been largely neglected or often misrepresented. As a continuous military event, the post–Civil War campaign against the many western tribes proved both fruitful and frustrating for the regular army, which experienced a good deal of failure alongside its notable successes. Much of the army's work in the late nineteenth century went unnoticed or was easily forgotten, eclipsed by a romanticized narrative of "Custer's Last Stand" and caricatures of Indians of the "Wild West." This narrative of good versus bad ignored the complexities of the struggle. In the end, a small professional military force prevailed over a more numerous and often better-armed adversary who had been forced to contend with a number of complicating factors: the wave of white settlement, the destruction of the buffalo, the constant need to protect family, and the devastating impact of the army's use of Indian allies.

Despite relatively little tactical and technological development, the soldiers of the West adeptly applied the lessons of the Civil War to a new theater, staging large campaigns that featured converging columns and relentless pressure and made it increasingly impossible for the Indians to resist. One by one, the fiercest tribes on the continent succumbed. The army's experiment with racial integration continued as well and produced largely positive results, as the Buffalo Soldiers acquitted themselves quite favorably, often in the most hostile climates—both physical and cultural. As unsavory as Indian fighting was for many soldiers, the deployment of regular army units in domestic disputes involving labor and agrarian unrest raised troubling questions of propriety. Certainly, the mustering of federal military might on behalf of capitalist interests posed serious concerns. Such concerns only grew during the nation's evolution into empire.

TIMELINE

August–December 1862	Dakota (Sioux) uprising in Minnesota
November 1864	Sand Creek Massacre in Colorado
1866	Authorization for African American regiments in the regular army
1866–1868	Lakota Bozeman Trail campaign
1866–1877	Military Reconstruction
May 1867	End of Maximilian's rule in Mexico
November 1868	Battle of the Washita
May 1871	Warren Wagon Train Massacre
April 1873	Modoc War; General E.R.S Canby killed
1874	Black Hills expedition
1874–1875	Red River War; Battle of Palo Duro Canyon
1876–1877	Great Sioux War (Centennial Campaign)
June 1876	Battle of Little Bighorn
June–October 1877	Nez Perce War
1879–1886	Apache War
September 1886	Geronimo's final surrender
1890	Ghost Dance movement on northern plains reservations
December 1890	Battle of Wounded Knee

SUGGESTED READINGS

Cozzens, Peter. *The Earth Is Weeping: The Epic Story of the Indian Wars for the American West.* New York: Alfred A. Knopf, 2016.

DeMontravel, Peter R. *A Hero to His Fighting Men: Nelson A. Miles, 1839–1925.* Kent, OH: Kent State University Press, 1998.

Downs, Gregory P. *After Appomattox: Military Occupation and the Ends of War.* Cambridge, MA: Harvard University Press, 2015.

Fitzpatrick, David J. *Emory Upton: Misunderstood Reformer.* Norman: University of Oklahoma Press, 2017.

Foner, Eric. *Reconstruction: America's Unfinished Revolution.* Updated ed. New York: Harper Perennial, 2014.

Haley, James L. *The Buffalo War: The History of the Red River Indian Uprising of 1874.* Garden City, NY: Doubleday, 1976.

Hutton, Paul Andrew. *Phil Sheridan and His Army.* Lincoln: University of Nebraska Press, 1985.

Lavender, David. *Let Me Be Free: The Nez Perce Tragedy.* New York: HarperCollins, 1993.

Leckie, William H., and Shirley A. Leckie. *The Buffalo Soldiers: A Narrative of the Negro Cavalry in the West.* Rev. ed. Norman: Oklahoma University Press, 2003.

Leckie, William H., and Shirley A. Leckie. *Unlikely Warriors: General Benjamin Grierson and His Family.* Norman: University of Oklahoma Press, 1984.

Pierce, Michael D. *The Most Promising Young Officer: A Life of Ranald Slidell Mackenzie.* Norman: University of Oklahoma Press, 1993.

Tate, Michael L. *The Frontier Army in the Settlement of the West.* Norman: University of Oklahoma Press, 1999.

Utley, Robert M. *Cavalier in Buckskin: George Armstrong Custer and the Western Military Frontier.* Rev. ed. Norman: University of Oklahoma Press, 2001.

Utley, Robert M. *Frontier Regulars: The United States Army and the Indian, 1866–1891.* New York: Macmillan, 1973.

CHAPTER 10

EMPIRE AND INTERVENTION

1890–1917

An Imperial Navy Again • A Splendid Little War • The Ugly War • The Boxer Rebellion • The Big Stick • Punitive Expedition • Technology • Organization • Separate but Not Equal

" I Was a Racketeer," wrote retired general Smedley Butler in the progressive magazine *Common Sense* in 1935. "I spent 33 years and 4 months in active service as a member of our country's most agile military force—the Marine Corps. . . . And during that period I spent most of my time being a high-class muscle man for Big Business, for Wall Street and for the bankers. In short, I was a racketeer for capitalism." Perhaps no career better exemplified the new imperial mission of the United States military than Butler's. Born into a prominent Philadelphia Quaker family, Butler enlisted in the marines in 1898 and as a teenage lieutenant served in the Philippines. He fought conspicuously in the Boxer uprising in China, in the 1914 occupation of Veracruz, Mexico, and in the Caco insurgency in Haiti. The oft-wounded recipient of two Medals of Honor, he went on to serve in Europe during the First World War, rising to the rank of major general. During the Prohibition era, he took leave from the corps to direct law enforcement efforts in Philadelphia.

However, after leaving the service, Butler became a pacifist and an outspoken critic of American imperialism. As he wrote of his extraordinary experiences:

I helped make Mexico and especially Tampico safe for American oil interests in 1914. I helped make Haiti and Cuba a decent place for the National City Bank boys to collect revenues in. I helped in the raping of half a dozen Central American republics for the benefit of Wall Street. The record of racketeering is long. I helped purify Nicaragua for the international banking house of Brown Brothers [in] 1909–12. I brought light to the Dominican Republic for American sugar interests in 1916. I helped make Honduras "right" for American fruit companies in 1903. In China in 1927 I helped see to it that Standard Oil went its way unmolested.

He even likened his activities to those of the most notorious criminal of the day: "Looking back on it, I feel I might have given Al Capone a few hints. The best he could do was to operate his racket in three city districts. We Marines operated on three continents."

Certainly, Butler's transformation from Third World warrior to antiwar, anticapitalist crusader was unusual, but it also illuminates the struggle the nation's service personnel faced as the military's mission shifted from conquering the continent to projecting American political and economic influence into vast and distant new regions. In fact, though, the mission had not really changed; it had only grown larger and more complex. As General Butler noted, "Let us remember that the military deal of our country has never been defensive warfare. Since the Revolution, only the United Kingdom has beaten our record for square miles of territory acquired by military conquest. Our exploits against the American Indian, against the Filipinos, the Mexicans, and against Spain are on a par with the campaigns of Genghis Khan, the Japanese in Manchuria and the African attack of Mussolini."

AN IMPERIAL NAVY AGAIN

As the army's frontier mission came to a close and it drifted toward an uncertain future, the navy emerged from a long period of decline and neglect to join the ranks of the world's finest fleets. Thus the closing of one frontier coincided, not coincidentally, with the opening of another, as the United States spread its influence in the Pacific and cast covetous eyes on the Caribbean. Even as European powers and Japan hotly engaged in imperial expansion, the United States had remained relatively isolated, and the feverish pace of imperial development in Africa and Asia threatened to leave the nation shut out and alone if its leaders failed to join the race. However, the 1867 acquisitions of Alaska and Midway gave the United States a presence in the Pacific, and by the 1890s Samoa and Hawaii simply awaited formal annexation before entering a growing American empire. A new Manifest Destiny emerged as American expansionists called for more overseas engagement and a mighty navy to support it and rekindled dreams of a trans-isthmian water route through Central America. The large leap from isolated continental power to overseas empire required a significant contribution from America's military establishment, an establishment that proved more than willing, if not always prepared, for the task. By the turn of the century, the United States had acquired valuable new lands by conquest, and within the first quarter of the new century it would intervene militarily and economically in nations throughout the Caribbean and Central America, fully realizing the expansionists' imperial dreams.

After years of neglect and regression during which the navy sold off or mothballed most of its wartime fleet, including its more advanced vessels, and stubbornly avoided steam in favor of sail, seapower advocates began to chip away at the reactionary attitudes in Congress and within the navy. Beginning in the 1880s, Congress authorized incremental upgrades in the nation's naval inventory. The new reality meant steam-powered ships with steel, compartmentalized hulls, screw propulsion, breech-loading rifled guns, and no sail riggings. Bigger and faster ships to protect and project U.S. interests became a major focus of expansionist rhetoric. But for seapower advocates, the importance of upgrades extended well beyond the business of protection and projection to the capability of fighting the frontline fleets of the world. A powerful nation demanded a modern, powerful navy, as well as a great merchant fleet, abundant coaling stations, and strategically located bases. Expansionists pursued all of these aims with impressive gusto.

Like the army during the same period, the navy experienced a notable rise in professionalism, highlighted by the 1885 establishment of the Naval War College under the direction of Rear Admiral Stephen B. Luce. Luce had been at the forefront of naval reform since the establishment of the U.S. Naval Institute in 1873. The institute's publication, *Proceedings*, became an important venue for progressive naval thought. For the new Naval War College, Luce envisioned a curriculum heavy on naval history and doctrine and hired intellectual Commander Alfred Thayer Mahan to deliver these subjects. Mahan, the son of legendary West Point instructor and mentor to generations of officers Dennis Hart Mahan, was a natural fit for the role. His lectures proved progressive and impactful. Following Luce's departure for sea duty in 1886, Mahan became president of the college. After being promoted to captain, he published his hugely influential *The Influence of Sea Power upon History, 1660–1783* in 1890. Like the census also published that year, it produced far-reaching effects. His argument that great empires relied on control of the seas could be boiled down to a simple formula: a great empire required an equally great navy. The success of the British offered the most recent example. Much more than a simple history lesson, the book became a treatise on American imperial and naval expansion, contending that the rising emphasis on foreign trade and overseas markets demanded a large merchant fleet, coaling stations, and overseas bases, and all of these required a large, modern navy for protection. Mahan's views resonated in Europe, especially in Britain and Germany, and Japan, but for American imperialists they were tantamount to a new Manifest Destiny, one that would allow the United States to spread its influence across the Pacific and throughout the Caribbean. Mahan's emphasis on capital ships—big battleships and cruisers—capable of deepwater operations marked a turn away from the past emphasis on fixed coastal fortifications, coastal defense ships, and commerce raiders. The nation had in fact already begun the conversion, but Mahan's book as well as several international dustups gave big-navy advocates and expansionists the impetus to go all in on their mission.

Prodded by pronavy writings in *Proceedings* and other publications and by the recommendations of the Naval Advisory Board, Congress took the first steps toward building a modern navy. For many, the state of the navy had reached embarrassing levels. In 1880 the U.S. Navy rated outside the top-ten world fleets and trailed the Chilean force in the Western Hemisphere; its forty-eight nearly obsolete vessels proved completely inadequate to meet the demands of a growing nation. In 1883 Congress appropriated funds for four new steel-hulled warships: the protected cruisers *Atlanta*, *Boston*, and *Chicago*, which were lightly armored and smaller than their European counterparts; and the dispatch ship *Dolphin*. Together, these vessels became known as the ABCD ships. None of them were state-of-the-art, but they marked a move in the right direction. Although they possessed steel, compartmentalized hulls and were electrified, they still carried sail riggings and lacked the advanced armor and armament of British designs. In 1885 the navy secured two more bigger and faster protected cruisers, the *Charleston* and *Newark*, the last large American warships with full sail rigs.

One impediment to naval construction was the inability of the American steel industry to produce armor on a large enough scale, but by 1886 this issue had been surmounted. Built from British designs, the *Texas* and *Maine* carried the designation of second-class battleships but were actually armored cruisers. In 1889 and 1890 Secretary of the Navy Benjamin Tracy, who fully embraced Mahan's teachings and his preference for capital ships, pushed a major naval expansion agenda, maintaining that even while the navy's role remained defensive it must possess the capability of winning a naval war. To that end he proposed an ambitious shipbuilding program, but Congress approved only three new vessels, America's first true battleships, the *Indiana, Massachusetts,* and *Oregon.* At more than 10,000 tons and mounting an array of ordnance, including thirteen-inch guns, these "*Indiana*-class" ships signaled the U.S. Navy's successful transition to a modern deepwater fleet.

Two incidents in Latin America furthered enthusiasm for naval expansion. In 1891 an altercation in the Chilean port of Valparaiso left two sailors dead and eighteen wounded. The threat of war triggered the uncomfortable realization that Chile boasted a superior navy and was capable of striking vulnerable cities on the California coast. Similarly, a boundary dispute between Great Britain and Venezuela in 1896 brought the United States into a potential conflict with the British. Although cooler heads prevailed, the threat of conflict led to funding for more ships. Between 1892 and 1896, with a slight disruption caused by the Panic of 1893, the navy added the battleships *Iowa, Kentucky, Kearsarge, Alabama, Illinois,* and *Wisconsin* to its fleet. The navy's enhanced profile and a new commitment to recruiting also produced a notable improvement in the profile and quality of sailors. By the close of the century, the United States Navy, so recently a subject of derision, had become a point of national pride and a force more than capable of projecting American power around the globe.

A SPLENDID LITTLE WAR

The U.S. war with Spain, often known as the Spanish-American War, resulted from a confluence of events and influences. Rising expansionist nationalism, ideas of social Darwinism and racial superiority, hyperbolic journalism, and a romantic notion of war all contributed to the outbreak of this unfortunate but, from a U.S. perspective, fabulously successful war. Ostensibly fought to secure Cuba's independence from Spain, the war became a boon to America's imperial aspirations.

Cuba had long held special appeal for American expansionists. Its proximity to the United States and its slave-based plantation economy had inspired filibustering attempts in the years before the Civil War. Later, the United States made serious bids to acquire the island. At various times, particularly after 1895, Americans grew interested in the Cuban struggle for independence, a conflict that attracted the attention of expansionists and humanitarians alike. As the rebellion intensified, calls for U.S. intervention became louder, but President Grover Cleveland and his successor, William McKinley, resisted, instead applying diplomatic pressure to foster Cuban autonomy. Direct U.S. intervention would represent a violation of the nation's cherished Monroe Doctrine, in which President James Monroe had pledged not to interfere with European colonies remaining in the Western Hemisphere. McKinley, a Civil War veteran, worked particularly hard to avoid a conflict, but it became increasingly difficult.

In an effort to quell the insurrection, Spain sent the well-regarded General Valeriano Weyler to take charge in Cuba. Weyler's *Reconcentrado* policy, an ill-fated attempt to isolate the rebels by settling noncombatants in fortified hamlets that were essentially concentration camps, resulted in much suffering and death. Any Cubans remaining outside of the camps were considered rebels and subject to destruction. The misery in Cuba provided ready fodder for the "yellow journalism" of the rival newspaper empires of William Randolph Hearst and Joseph Pulitzer, which demonized Weyler and called for U.S. intervention to compel Spain to relinquish its colony.

The insurrection and intensified concerns over the safety of U.S. citizens and business interests in Cuba pushed the reluctant McKinley closer to action. In February 1898 he ordered the USS *Maine* to take station in the waters off Havana. Only days after its arrival a massive explosion sank the vessel, killing 266 sailors and marines. Immediately newspapers and war hawks in and out of government blamed the Spanish for the disaster. A preliminary investigation by the navy suggested that the tragedy had been caused by an external explosion, which only served to confirm suspicions of Spanish treachery, although no cause could be identified. Much later, an advanced study of the wreck revealed that an internal explosion, probably in the highly combustible coal hold, had brought down the *Maine*. Even if the true cause of the explosion had been discovered at the time, it likely would have stood little chance of quieting the bellicose hawks. For men like Assistant Secretary of the Navy Theodore Roosevelt, the nation needed a war. Soon enough it had one.

Still, McKinley tried to avoid military conflict, pursuing a more deliberate diplomatic line, but when Spain failed to accept U.S. mediation or discuss Cuban independence, he asked Congress for the authority to use force in the pursuit of Cuban independence. Congress on April 19 passed a joint resolution that declared Cuba independent and granted McKinley the power to use force toward achieving that end. McKinley quickly ordered a blockade of Cuban ports. Spain had no choice but to declare war on April 23. Congress passed its war declaration on April 25, but, not to be outdone, made it retroactive to April 21 to predate the Spanish declaration.

With war declared, the nation found itself remarkably unprepared to fight. Suddenly overwhelmed by the realities of the situation, the McKinley administration began a chaotic and confounding mobilization, fraught with political interference that recalled the early days of the Civil War. Spain, too, was woefully unprepared for war, with a population in 1898 of fewer than 19 million, compared to a U.S. population of 76 million. Spain's army numbered almost 500,000, but more than 70 percent of it was tied up in overseas deployments in Cuba, the Philippines, and Puerto Rico. Cuba alone attracted almost 57 percent of the army, some 278,000 men. This army, top heavy with officers and badly politicized, lacked adequate training and supply but was armed with the excellent Spanish Mauser rifle, which was superior to its American counterparts. Like the U.S. Navy, the Spanish fleet had experienced a period of neglect and decline but had in recent years seen some, albeit inadequate, augmentation and modernization. On paper, the Spanish inventory appeared formidable, but its ships lagged behind other European and American vessels in armor and armament, and many were simply outdated. By 1898 the Spanish simply could not match the vastly improved American navy.

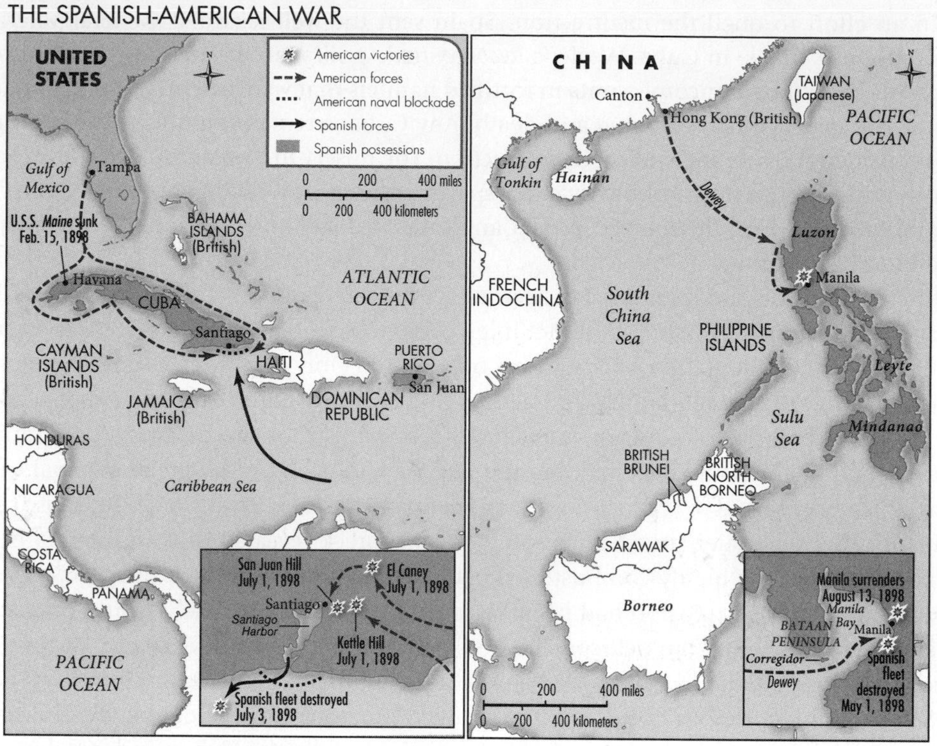

THE SPANISH-AMERICAN WAR

MAP 10.1 The Spanish-American War

But while the U.S. naval expansion and modernization of the previous decade had well prepared that service for the coming conflict, with assets positioned to strike mighty blows quickly, the regular army could muster only roughly 27,000 men scattered across the country in undermanned companies and battalions. The army had no plans for a large-scale mobilization or any opportunity to train a large force. The senior leadership was dominated by aging Civil War veterans, such as Commanding General Nelson Miles, Wesley Merritt, and William R. Shafter. The far-larger National Guard had not yet been integrated into a cohesive military network, and there were questions about the legality of sending guardsmen overseas. Like the Civil War and the Mexican War before it, the war with Spain would be fought by the regular army as well as by a separate temporary volunteer force. Congress initially authorized 125,000 volunteers for the conflict but soon raised that number to 200,000 and also provided for an expansion of the regular army to 65,000. In all, some 275,000 men were mobilized—a force that the War Department completely lacked the ability to train, equip, and support. And, as had occurred during the two previous wars, politics heavily influenced the process of selecting officers for the volunteer units. McKinley even seized an opportunity for national reconciliation by appointing former Confederates, including Fitzhugh Lee (Robert E. Lee's nephew) and Joseph Wheeler, a prominent cavalry officer, who would play an important role in the coming fight.

McKinley also authorized special federal volunteer regiments such as the colorful and charismatic 1st U.S. Volunteer Cavalry, better known to history as the "Rough Riders."

Recruited and organized by Theodore Roosevelt, who resigned his position as assistant secretary of the navy to become the unit's second-in-command, the regiment trained at San Antonio, Texas, in anticipation of the tropical heat expected in Cuba. The Rough Riders came from an astonishing array of backgrounds. By design the regiment included cowboys and Indians, lawmen and outlaws, western adventurers to be sure, but also a complement of Ivy League athletes and the scions of some of America's most prominent families. Unlike most other volunteer outfits, the Rough Riders received the best equipment and were directed by capable leaders, including their commander, Colonel Leonard Wood, a surgeon by training and veteran of the Indian Wars. In many ways, though, the Riders were Teddy Roosevelt's regiment, and they captured the public's imagination thanks to the attention they received from the many journalists who covered this quintessentially American story.

From the start, regular army officers clashed with politicians over everything from urgency to strategy. General Miles favored a systematic preparation followed by, if necessary, a campaign that relied heavily on the regulars. Most American leaders hoped that the blockade and U.S. support for the Cuban rebels would compel Spain to exit the island; few foresaw a major ground war in Cuba. This measured approach required patience, but politics and public pressure demanded a speedy mobilization and a rush to war, which proved devastating. Enthusiastic volunteers quickly filled the ranks, but the country simply could not provide for such a rapid mobilization. Clothing and food shortages, a lack of modern weapons, and ill-prepared facilities created nightmares of supply and sanitation even after the fighting ended. Illness and exposure became far greater threats than the prospect of death in battle. War fever aside, it would take weeks to get ground troops into battle. Fortunately for the United States, its navy stood uniquely prepared to act.

An effusive advocate of the war, Theodore Roosevelt had before leaving the Navy Department positioned his maritime assets advantageously. Most importantly, he had ordered Commodore George Dewey's Asiatic Squadron to Hong Kong in preparation for a strike against the Spanish fleet in the Philippines. Once war was declared, Dewey, a well-regarded Civil War veteran with extensive experience at sea, steamed for Manila Bay. Arriving in Philippine waters on April 30, Dewey's flotilla slipped into the bay, avoiding potentially devastating mines. On May 1, his six modern warships in a meticulous operation that even allowed a break for breakfast inflicted a stunning defeat on the outmatched Spanish in a matter of hours, destroying seven ships, silencing shore batteries, and killing or wounding 370 men while losing no ships and suffering a single fatality, that to heat exhaustion. Although the navy had occupied Manila Bay, it did not possess the resources to engage the Spanish troops on land, so Manila remained in Spanish control while Dewey opened communication with Filipino rebels and awaited ground forces from the United States. Dewey's complete but somewhat surprising victory—surprising in that it occurred across the globe from Cuba—made him the first hero of this new war and earned him speedy promotion to admiral. America's investment in its navy had returned lucrative dividends.

In the Caribbean, Admiral William Sampson's North Atlantic Squadron established a firm blockade of Havana, but without the force necessary to mount an invasion of the well-defended capital, attention shifted to the southern side of the island and the port of Santiago de Cuba. In an ill-advised move, Spanish authorities ordered the naval squadron of Admiral

Pascual Cervera y Topete to Santiago, where it soon was bottled up by a U.S. blockading force. The army and navy differed widely over how to attack Santiago, which seriously compromised cooperation, but the army's preference for a move inland to invest Santiago from the interior prevailed. The task fell to General Shafter's V Corps, which included a heavy complement of regular forces as well as the Rough Riders, who rushed by train from San Antonio to Tampa to be part of the invasion. At Tampa, the jumping-off point for the Cuba campaign, logistical failings and a lack of transport capacity seriously limited the size and shape of the invasion force. Almost all of the cavalry horses had to be left behind, so the Rough Riders and other cavalry units would be fighting dismounted.

Although the navy had made laudable advances in ship construction leading up to the war, the army's technological development lagged. Smokeless powder had been invented in the 1880s but had not been enthusiastically pursued by the army, which did not adopt the Krag-Jørgensen rifle until 1892. The Danish-designed bolt-action rifle and carbine, which fired a .30-caliber smokeless powder cartridge and held five rounds, offered an upgrade over the Springfield, which remained in service into the 1890s, but limited inventory and insufficient ammunition supplies meant that only the regular units and a few special volunteer regiments such as the Rough Riders received "Krags." Most volunteers carried the old Springfields, which still fired black powder ammunition, a significant disadvantage in battle. In artillery there had been no significant upgrades. The Hotchkiss and Gatling guns of the Indian Wars era, as well as a 3.2 inch breech-loader that required a powder bag and separate projectile rather than a single cartridge, all fired black powder ammunition. The Spanish, whose modern systems fired smokeless powder ammunition, thus enjoyed an advantage in small arms and artillery.

On June 22, 1898, Shafter's roughly 17,000-strong command landed at Daiquirí and Siboney, just east of Santiago. General Joseph Wheeler's cavalry division engaged Spanish troops in a sharp clash at Las Guásimas on June 24, after which the Spanish fell back on Santiago with American troops in pursuit. As U.S. troops closed in on Santiago, badly outnumbered but well-positioned and well-armed Spanish soldiers blocked the eastern approaches to the port city. On July 1, despite a more than ten-to-one advantage, General Henry Lawton's division took all day to take control of the town of El Caney, defended by fewer than 600 men. The tough fight at El Caney kept Lawton's soldiers from supporting a separate attack on the San Juan Heights, where another 500 Spaniards held fortified positions on Kettle Hill and San Juan Hill. There, some 8,000 soldiers in the infantry division of General Jacob F. Kent and Wheeler's dismounted cavalry division, temporarily commanded by General Samuel Sumner, advanced after an ineffective artillery preparation. The outnumbered Spaniards put up a stout fight, but a dramatic advance up Kettle Hill, which featured Roosevelt and the Rough Riders and excellent fire support from Lieutenant John Parker's four Gatling guns, carried the position. The Spaniards abandoned San Juan Hill shortly thereafter. In accounts of this episode the Rough Riders attracted most of the attention, and in truth the regiment performed well, but the focus on Colonel Teddy's boys overshadowed the fine work of the other units involved in the attacks, including the Buffalo Soldiers of the 9th and 10th Cavalry regiments. During the fighting on July 1 the Americans suffered 205 killed and almost 1,200 wounded while inflicting roughly 600 casualties on the Spanish defenders. U.S. forces now closed in on Santiago.

IMAGE 10.1   Rough Riders   Members of the 1st United States Volunteer Cavalry, better known as the Rough Riders, with their leader, future president Theodore Roosevelt (center), after their successful campaign in Cuba during the 1898 U.S. War with Spain.

The Spanish leaders at Santiago, surrounded on land and blockaded at sea, desperately ordered Admiral Cervera with his six ships to try to cut his way through the blockade. Hopelessly outgunned and with little chance of success, Cervera followed orders with predictable results. In the Battle of Santiago de Cuba on July 3, the American fleet completely overwhelmed the Spanish flotilla, sinking or disabling all six of its vessels, killing more than 300 sailors and marines, and wounding another 150. The Americans also took 1,700 prisoners, including Admiral Cervera, all at a cost of one man killed and one wounded. On land, U.S. reinforcements under General Miles bolstered the siege. Ultimately, the weight of U.S. numbers and the threat of a bombardment of Santiago compelled the Spanish to surrender on July 16, for all intents and purposes ending the conflict in Cuba, but not the war.

In late July General Miles departed Cuba with a small invasion force bound for the Spanish colony of Puerto Rico, where plans called for him to be joined by additional troops from the United States. Miles's forces landed at several points on the southern side of the island, avoiding the main Spanish concentration around San Juan. With more time to prepare, Miles's command was much better equipped than Shafter's invasion force, enjoyed a full complement of artillery, and had thus far largely avoided the tropical afflictions that had devastated the troops in Cuba. With 17,000 men in four columns, the Americans pressed inland with the goal of capturing San Juan. Miles made excellent progress, suffering few casualties in a handful of heated engagements but finding little resistance. Before he could take San Juan, on August 12 Miles learned that the United States and Spain had reached an agreement to end hostilities. The conquest of Puerto Rico cost the United States four soldiers killed and forty wounded. Total Spanish casualties numbered roughly 400.

In the Philippines, Admiral Dewey and his ships controlled Manila Bay while Spanish troops still held the capital, surrounded by 10,000 Filipino rebels under Emilio Aguinaldo y Famy. Back in the United States, the Philippines Expeditionary Force, designated the VIII Corps, assembled in San Francisco, but a lack of transport capacity delayed its departure. By comparison with the Cuba campaign, preparation for the Philippines campaign was orderly and thorough, with soldiers well cared for. General Wesley Merritt, a gifted cavalry commander and veteran of the Civil War and Indian Wars, commanded the expedition, which, divided into three separate lifts, steamed for the Philippines, with the first contingent landing on June 30. By late July the entire force, a mix of regulars and volunteers some 12,000 strong, had arrived. Meanwhile, Dewey had opened negotiations with the Spanish officers at Manila, hoping to secure their surrender. The situation was delicate, however, as Merritt's orders specifically forbade him from including Filipino nationalists in any negotiations or allowing them to take part in the capture of the city, restrictions that soon made the Filipinos apprehensive of American intentions. Furthermore, with telegraphic communications temporarily cut, neither the Americans nor the Spaniards had ready contact with authorities in Washington or Madrid. On August 9 Merritt and Dewey issued an ultimatum to Spanish authorities in Manila. With food supplies nearly exhausted and the city cut off from any support, the Spanish commander agreed to surrender, but only to the Americans and only after fighting a final staged limited engagement that would preserve Spanish honor. For the Americans, the tricky part became keeping the Filipinos out of the battle. The engagement took place on August 13 and turned out to be a good bit more than a face-saving show, especially when Filipino troops entered the fray, but by the end of the day, U.S. troops had occupied Manila, taking 13,000 Spanish prisoners and large stocks of weapons and ammunition. The Americans suffered 17 men killed and more than 100 wounded. Unknown to those involved in the Philippines, the previous day the United States and Spain had agreed to a peace protocol ending the brief conflict. Spain's claim in subsequent negotiations that the Manila surrender, coming as it did after the armistice, should not stand failed to reverse the situation.

American troops continued an uneasy occupation at Manila while Filipino resentment rose to dangerous levels. But to American leaders, the Philippines were simply too valuable to relinquish. A war that the United States had entered ostensibly to liberate Cuba had instead delivered an American empire. In the Treaty of Paris signed that fall, Spain ceded to the United States the islands of Puerto Rico and Guam as well as the Philippines, for which the United States paid $20 million. The human costs of the conflict were more than acceptable for such an outcome. Fewer than 400 Americans had been killed in action, with some 1,500 wounded. Much less acceptable were the 5,000 deaths attributed to disease, poor hygiene, and poor sanitation in Cuba and at camps in the United States. The inadequate medical service as well as the poor provisioning of the army led to a major investigation headed by former Civil War general and railroad magnate Grenville Dodge. The so-called Dodge Commission ultimately rendered a number of recommendations for improving the medical service and military hygiene.

Although the United States honored its pledge not to annex Cuba, it maintained an occupation force there until 1902, when American officials handed over control of the island to the Cubans. While many Cubans disapproved of the continued occupation, it was not without benefits. Under military governors Generals John R. Brooke and Leonard Wood, the army completed numerous internal improvements; built schools, hospitals, and railroads; modernized sanitation systems; and fought disease. Indeed, army surgeon Walter Reed led a team of physicians that finally associated the mosquito with the deadly plague of yellow fever. Reed's work and that of Colonel William C. Gorgas significantly reduced the threat of tropical diseases such as yellow fever and malaria. Less palatable to the Cubans was the so-called Platt Amendment, a set of provisions attached to Cuba's 1901 constitution at the insistence of the United States that placed heavy restrictions on the Cuban government and gave the United States the right to intervene in Cuba and to establish military bases or coaling stations on the island, which resulted in the construction of the naval base at Guantanamo Bay. Over the next three decades the U.S. military intervened repeatedly in Cuba, while investment and business expansion ensured America's continued domination of the new nation.

THE UGLY WAR

If indeed the brief struggle with Spain was, in the words of Secretary of State John Hay, a "splendid little war," the unwelcome fight for control of the Philippines became anything but. Filipino hopes for independence vanished with the Treaty of Paris, and the resultant anger prompted thousands to resume their rebellion, only now against the occupying Americans. Having already declared independence from Spain, General Aguinaldo in January 1899 formally established the Philippine Republic, with a new constitution, a new capital at Malolos, and himself as president. What followed was a nasty undeclared war that proved far longer and costlier than the war that had spawned it, one that Americans would largely wipe from the national memory, with disastrous consequences for the future.

The Philippines archipelago consists of several large islands and hundreds of small ones occupied by diverse peoples speaking a dozen different languages, which presented a major problem for the United States. On one hand, the task of pacifying the Philippines recalled the Americans' experience in the Indian Wars; on the other, it represented something altogether new—nation building in a distant land. As in Cuba, the army busied itself with infrastructure and public works projects with a special emphasis on education and health care, pursuing what President McKinley called benevolent assimilation. But as American leaders would discover decades later in Southeast Asia, winning the hearts and minds of a beleaguered population is a difficult proposition during an active military campaign. Once known as the Philippine Insurrection, the Philippine-American War began in February 1899 with an altercation between U.S. troops and Filipino nationalists at an American outpost near Manila, where some 40,000 rebels significantly outnumbered the 12,000 Americans now commanded by General Elwell Otis. The resultant Second Battle of Manila produced 250 American and some 2,000

Filipino casualties. Attempting to fight an essentially conventional war, Aguinaldo's poorly armed and indifferently trained force was at a severe disadvantage to the well-armed and more disciplined American army. By the end of March the Americans had secured Manila and driven the rebels northward. Otis next sent two columns under generals Arthur MacArthur

THE PHILIPPINE-AMERICAN WAR

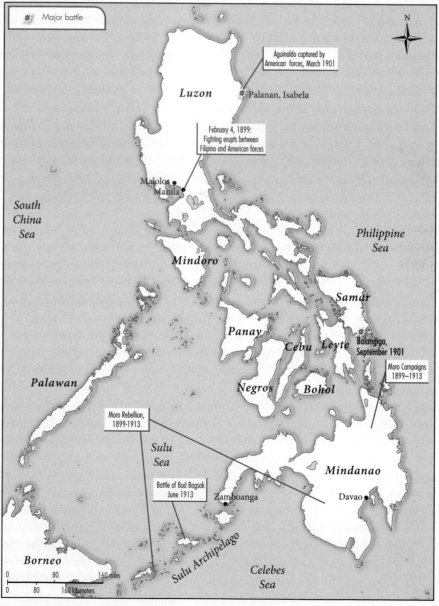

MAP 10.2 The Philippine-American War

and Henry Lawton into the northern portion of the main island of Luzon. MacArthur's troops quickly took the capital of Malolos; other victories followed. A fall campaign brought most population centers and lines of communication under U.S. control. Recognizing the futility of fighting a conventional war, Aguinaldo in November 1899 disbanded the Filipino army in favor of smaller guerrilla units that could be used to advantage.

The guerrilla war proved much more successful for the Filipinos, who inflicted serious casualties on U.S. troops during the first months of 1900. Surprise attacks and ambushes as well as sabotage and booby traps became major concerns for U.S. forces. Guerrillas also targeted Filipino civilians who cooperated with the Americans. General Otis interpreted the change of tactics as a sign of American success, but the new guerrilla war brought a renewed intensity to the fighting. In this atmosphere both sides committed atrocities. MacArthur, a teenaged Civil War hero and Medal of Honor recipient, replaced Otis in May 1900 and aggressively confronted the new reality. He ordered intensified action on all fronts, ramping up the military commitment as well as public works and development efforts. He also liberalized the use of Filipino scouts, which paid dividends in March 1901, when General Frederick Funston, a colorful figure in his own right, infiltrated Aguinaldo's camp by posing as a captive with the help of native scouts and captured the elusive leader. Far less successful was the policy of concentration, an ill-fated attempt to isolate the guerrillas by relocating civilians into fortified camps. Importantly, the conflict in the Philippines, like those in the Caribbean, unfolded during a time of overt racism, driven by ideas of social Darwinism and white superiority. As the fighting intensified and atrocities mounted, racism on the part of American soldiers became more pronounced and contributed to the horror that so marked the Filipino campaign.

Aguinaldo's capture and subsequent acceptance of U.S. sovereignty dampened but did not destroy the guerrilla movement. As persistent pressure brought more areas under American control and as more and more guerrillas gave up the fight, President McKinley in the summer of 1901 transferred power to civil authority, appointing respected jurist William Howard Taft governor of the Philippines. General Adna Chaffee replaced MacArthur and oversaw the final brutal campaigns of the war in the Batangas region of southern Luzon and on the island of Samar. Drawing a clear distinction between legitimate conventional warfare and illegitimate guerrilla warfare, American troops exercised broad discretion in crushing resistance, with civilians often caught in the middle. A relentless effort directed by General Franklin Bell finally ended the guerrilla action in Batangas, but rebels in Samar proved particularly difficult to subdue. In September 1901 Filipinos wielding machetes, axes, and other farm implements attacked an unprepared garrison of American troops at Balangiga, hacking to death more than fifty soldiers in what became known as the Balangiga Massacre. In retaliation, General Jacob Smith conducted a scorched earth campaign that made little distinction between civilian noncombatants and guerrillas. Even in this war of wanton brutality, the intensity of Smith's actions stood out. Smith ultimately faced court-martial and was forced from the army.

President Theodore Roosevelt declared the war in the Philippines over on July 4, 1902. By that time more than 125,000 American soldiers, sailors, and marines had served in the islands. Almost 4,500 had died and another 2,800 had been wounded in action. The Filipinos had suffered an estimated 16,000 military deaths. A civilian death total is unknown, but estimates range from 200,000 to 1 million, devastating by any measure. But the conflict was not over. Pockets of resistance remained, especially on the southern island of Mindanao, where the fierce Moros—Muslim Filipinos known for their stubborn resistance to Spanish rule—mounted furious challenges to American authority until 1913, when U.S. troops under General John J. Pershing inflicted a final defeat on them in the Battle of Bud Bagsak. The Philippine experience proved largely a success for the United States, with the military developing sound counterinsurgency practices and positive nation-building programs. Unfortunately, the hard-won lessons of the conflict would be lost on future generations.

ISSUES IN MILITARY HISTORY

UNLEARNED LESSONS OF SMALL WARS

As discussed in this and previous chapters, the United States military over the years grew proficient at what came to be known as "small war." The term "small war" applies more to the nature of the opponents and the style of engagement than to the scale of the conflict. The U.S.-Philippine War certainly was not "small" in terms of troops deployed or resources committed, but it involved the broad application of guerrilla tactics and, consequently, extensive counterinsurgency measures on the part of U.S. forces. In the Boxer uprising, the U.S. contingent battled a decidedly irregular foe. And certainly the army's long war with the Indians of the American West involved few large battles but a good deal of what is often, although not altogether accurately, called "asymmetrical warfare." Similarly, the United States' many interventions in the Caribbean and Central America provided the the Marine Corps with abundant opportunities to hone its small war doctrine during the first third of the twentieth century.

Throughout these various commitments, professional soldiers with no formal training in counterinsurgency or guerrilla warfare learned on the job and, despite some notable exceptions, became quite good at small war. Big-war veterans like George Crook, Ranald Mackenzie, and Nelson Miles became masters of irregular warfare, but the army made no real effort to embrace this mode of fighting in its official training or doctrinal development, content to focus on the next big conventional war. The Marine Corps, though, absorbed the lessons of such engagements and eventually produced its insightful *Small Wars Manual*, a how-to book for conducting successful campaigns against stealthy insurgents amid large noncombatant populations in challenging environments. Indeed, the American military experience up to World War II provided many valuable lessons for fighting small wars, some of them gained at great expense and not without devastating failures.

Despite their frequency, small wars have traditionally held little appeal to the soldiers involved or to the American public and have more often than not been conducted out of sight, which made the world wars, like the Civil War before them, all the more alluring to late-twentieth-century professional soldiers, who largely ignored the lessons learned by their predecessors. This reality came into focus in Vietnam, where American leaders like General William Westmoreland directed a big-war approach to an essentially small-war situation, with predictable results. How could a conflict like Vietnam, one of the longest in American history, one to which at its peak the United States committed more than half a million military personnel, be considered a small war? Commentator and author Max Boot makes a convincing case for this designation in his eye-opening book *The Savage Wars of Piece: Small Wars and the Rise of American Power*. Vietnam presented the challenges of a small war, he argues, yet American leaders applied a decidedly big-war approach to it, relying on massive firepower and attrition and overlooking the capabilities of the Vietnamese or the conditions of Southeast Asia. By choosing to fight a big war in a small-war situation, American leaders failed to embrace the lessons of the nation's own military past.

THE BOXER REBELLION

Involvement in the Philippines made the United States a player in Asia and the Pacific Rim and soon sparked a keen interest in China. China, rocked by internal disruptions and a stunning military defeat by Japan, increasingly found itself vulnerable to foreign domination as Japan, Russia, and several European powers attempted to carve out spheres of influence within the once-great empire. For many Chinese, especially young nationalists, the influx of foreign economic and religious influence became intolerable. A secret antiforeigner society emerged, the Righteous and Harmonious Movement or Band, known to Westerners as the "Boxers" (a reference to their martial arts prowess). The Boxers, encouraged by the aged Manchu empress and often supported by imperial Chinese troops, began striking foreign nationals, particularly Christian missionaries and their Chinese converts, near the end of the century. In the summer of 1900 the Boxers, supported by imperial troops, besieged the diplomatic compound in Peking (Beijing), where most of the foreign nationals had banded together in the walled British Legation and would ultimately hold out for fifty-five days, during which time seven U.S. Marine guards were killed and fourteen wounded.

In his "Open Door" notes, U.S. Secretary of State John Hay had gone on record opposing the foreign appropriation of China and encouraging the various nations involved to respect China's political and territorial integrity. But with American lives and interests at stake, U.S. leaders agreed to support a multinational relief effort—one of the few times since the American Revolution that the United States had participated in a multinational military operation. The first attempt to reach Peking with a force of 2,000 men, including 112 U.S. sailors and marines, was turned back by heavy Chinese resistance. A much larger international force, designated the China Relief Expedition, consisted of Japanese, Russian, French, British, German, Austrian, and Italian troops as well as 2,500 Americans sent from the Philippines under General Adna Chaffee, with more coming from California. Once assembled the American contingent included the 9th and 14th Infantry regiments, the 6th Cavalry, an artillery battery, and a marine battalion. Advancing northward from the Taku Forts on the East China Sea, the expedition captured the port city of Tientsin (Tianjin) on July 14, but it took another month of marching and fighting in difficult conditions before it reached the besieged legation in Peking. On August 14 Japanese, Russian, and American troops attacked Peking's outer walls, with American participation especially conspicuous, while the British contingent waded through a water gate to relieve the legation. The next day, U.S. artillery blasted open the gates to the Imperial City (Inner City) before action was suspended. American forces suffered some 200 casualties in the affair.

Participation in a multinational coalition completed a major shift in American policy, one that began with the acquisition of foreign lands and grew more defined as the fighting raged in the Philippines. By now, the United States clearly possessed an overseas empire and vested interests throughout the world, most directly in Asia, the Caribbean, and Central America. Such imperial reach required a much grander military commitment. The suppression of the Boxer uprising revealed the challenges of multinational cooperation. The whole campaign could well have ended differently had the Chinese been better armed and more disciplined. Superior allied firepower often compensated for numerical disadvantages and disorganization, but it was no guarantee of success. American leaders and their soldiers, sailors, and marines continued to adapt as their mission continued to evolve.

For the United States, adaptation to the new role of imperial power occurred remarkably quickly. New lands and ongoing strife in the Philippines and the Caribbean meant no shortage of military obligations. Military commitment also received a boost after the assassination of William McKinley in 1901 brought forty-two-year-old Theodore Roosevelt to the presidency. Roosevelt possessed an abiding devotion to Alfred Thayer Mahan's expansive vision for a great navy, overseas bases, and a canal through Central America, as well as a commitment to protecting American interests and projecting American power in the Western Hemisphere and beyond. He aggressively pursued the objective of establishing a Central American canal, considering an option in Nicaragua before settling on Colombia's Isthmus of Darien, or Panama. When Colombia refused to ratify the treaty that would establish an American-controlled canal zone Roosevelt supported Panamanian rebels' 1903 breakaway by sending the navy to discourage a Colombian response and quickly recognizing Panama's independence. Secretary Hay subsequently concluded the canal deal with the new republic, and soon work was underway on one of the great engineering projects of history, in which the army played a significant role. Appointed to oversee the project in 1907, Colonel George Goethals of the Corps of Engineers completed the herculean job in 1914. As they had done in Cuba, army doctors under the direction of Colonel William Gorgas tackled tropical diseases, largely eliminating malaria and yellow fever, which had killed thousands and threatened to derail the project.

Both during construction and after its completion, the canal required a significant military commitment, including a sizable garrison and considerable fortifications. Once opened, however, it represented maximized potential for the navy, cutting the time required to move ships from the Atlantic to the Pacific by weeks and eliminating the need to maintain separate large fleets. Ensuring the canal's security added yet another dimension to America's imperial profile. Such a monumental investment and invaluable asset had to be protected. Regional defense thus became a paramount concern for Roosevelt and the driving rationale behind his self-described approach to hemispheric security: "Speak softly but carry a big stick."

THE BIG STICK

Fear of foreign encroachment and the ongoing need to protect national interests led Roosevelt in 1904 to issue his own take on the 1823 Monroe Doctrine. In what came to be known as the Roosevelt Corollary, which was essentially an extension of the Platt Amendment, the president claimed "international police power" and an unequivocal right to intervene in the historically unstable nations of the Caribbean and Central America for the purpose of maintaining order. Perpetual debt issues in places such as Haiti and the Dominican Republic offered a pretext for European intervention, so ensuring fiscal as well as political stability in the developing nations of the region became a new mission for the navy. This "gunboat diplomacy" combined military occupation with customs receivership and, often, public works programs. Between 1902 and 1934 the United States intervened repeatedly in Latin America and the Caribbean.

THE UNITED STATES IN CENTRAL AMERICA AND THE CARIBBEAN, 1898–1933

MAP 10.3 The United States in Central America and the Caribbean, 1898–1933

In 1906 a rebellion against the nascent U.S.-influenced government in Cuba brought the first of four interventions over a sixteen year period. Nicaragua, where political unrest erupted into civil war, experienced the heavy hand of the marines during two long and acrimonious occupations (1912-1925 and 1926-1933). The first U.S. intervention, which lasted from 1912 to 1925, involved the extended deployment of a large legation guard. The second, from 1926 to 1933, featured a bitter five-year fight against a guerrilla army led by the charismatic Augusto Cesar Sandino, whose opposition to America's influence and military presence made him a hero to future leftist guerrilla leaders and inspired the Sandinista revolution in the 1970s. Civil wars in Haiti (1915) and the Dominican Republic (1916) also resulted in military intervention and extended occupations. Pacification operations usually fell to the marines, who became masters of such colonialist duties. In the process they carved out a distinctive profile within the American military establishment and contributed some of the most colorful warriors in the nation's history.

A number of marines cemented their reputations while fighting insurgent forces and bandits on the island of Hispañola and in the jungles of Central America. Some, such as Smedley Butler, mentioned at the beginning of this chapter, became legendary icons of the U.S. Marine Corps in their own right, while others played substantial roles in shaping the corps and defining its place within the military establishment. John Lejeune, the son of a Confederate veteran and graduate of the Naval Academy, joined the marines in 1890 and

IMAGE 10.2 Marine Legends   Marine Legends John A. Lejeune (front, second from left) Littleton W. T. Waller (front, center) and Smedley D. Butler (front, second from right) during the U.S. occupation of Veracruz, Mexico, in 1914.

became the prototypical imperial warrior. He served around the world and during the Great War commanded the 2nd Division in France, the first marine to head an army division, before capping his almost forty years in the corps as its commandant. Marine Camp Lejeune in North Carolina is named in his honor. Although considerably older (he joined the corps in 1880), Littleton W. T. "Tony" Waller shared many adventures with Butler and Lejeune and developed a close personal friendship with Butler, even serving as his best man. Although a decorated and well-regarded marine, Waller faced court-martial for an excessively brutal campaign he led in Samar during the Philippine-American War. When it became clear that Waller had followed the orders of his superior, an army general, he was acquitted and resumed his illustrious career. As a collective force, Butler, Lejeune, and Waller contributed mightily to the creation of the modern Marine Corps. Gunnery Sergeant Daniel Daly, a diminutive 5'6" and 130 pounds, became a living legend after defending the Tartar Wall during the Boxer uprising and served with distinction under Butler in Haiti. Like Butler, he earned two Medals of Honor among a host of other decorations. Finally, as an acting lieutenant in the Haitian Gendarmerie and later as a marine officer in Nicaragua, future World War

II and Korean War hero Lewis "Chesty" Puller honed the leadership skills that would make him one of the most decorated warriors in American history. For Puller and others of his generation, service in Latin America and particularly in Haiti provided excellent preparation for the major wars to come.

One feature of U.S. interventions in the region that proved even more onerous than the presence of marines for the peoples of Central America and the Caribbean was the development of native constabularies, usually called national guards, in each of the countries that experienced lengthy occupations. Trained and armed by the United States and initially officered by marines, these forces were based on the idea that a small professional military posed less of a threat to the democratic process than traditional large standing armies. In most cases, though, the guards became repressive tools of their officers, who used them to seize power in Nicaragua, Panama, Haiti, the Dominican Republic, and Cuba, resulting in longstanding, brutal dictatorships that became a sad legacy of the era of intervention.

PUNITIVE EXPEDITION

Mexico experienced unwanted and unwelcomed U.S. intervention twice. Both occurred in the context of the Mexican Revolution: the first, the occupation of the main port of Veracruz, had a direct impact on the nation's political and military order, while the second came in response to an attack on U.S. soil by disgruntled revolutionary leader Francisco "Pancho" Villa. Between 1876 and 1911 the United States and Mexico enjoyed a period of relatively positive relations, thanks in part to the long U.S.-friendly rule of President Porfirio Díaz, a former general who had helped topple the Maximilian regime. Díaz allowed cross-border military operations against the Apaches and encouraged U.S. business development in Mexico, particularly in the railroad, mining, and petroleum sectors. He also fostered a focus on internal improvements and law and order, bringing a previously unknown level of stability to Mexico. But behind this façade of order and progress, most Mexicans still suffered from poverty and a lack of opportunity. After indicating a willingness to step aside in the election of 1910, the aged Díaz reneged on his promise, which ignited the first phase of the revolution. Rebel forces rose in opposition, and fighting erupted in 1911 in Ciudad Juárez, across the Rio Grande from El Paso, Texas. Compelled to yield, Don Porfirio left the country.

After Díaz's departure, reform-minded Francisco Madero assumed the presidency, but he proved too ineffectual for many in Mexico, particularly American and British businessmen who feared that he could not or would not protect foreign interests. In February 1913 U.S. ambassador Henry Lane Wilson, himself deeply concerned about Madero, conspired with Mexican general Victoriano Huerta to overthrow the president, whom Huerta then had murdered. The general, who pledged to protect foreign investments, assumed the presidency but, rather surprisingly, failed to garner U.S. recognition. Lame duck president William Howard Taft refused to act, and his successor, Woodrow Wilson, citing the illegitimate nature of Huerta's ascent to the presidency, denied him recognition outright. Meanwhile, a war between Huerta's army and revolutionary forces ripped Mexico apart. Wilson resisted intervention but pressured Huerta to resign and imposed an embargo on the sale of arms and equipment to the regime. While he waited for a legitimate leader to emerge, he also ordered a large buildup of troops along the Mexican border and grudgingly allowed the sale of arms to the rebels. Wilson initially favored Pancho Villa, a colorful, Robin Hood-like figure from the northern state of Chihuahua, for Huerta's replacement, and Villa courted the U.S. president's support by refusing to condemn the violent U.S. occupation of Veracruz.

In April 1914 sailors from a U.S. Navy warship were detained in Tampico, Mexico's oil port on the Gulf of Mexico. Although the sailors were released with an apology from the local authorities, Admiral Henry Mayo demanded a formal public apology and a salute to the American flag, which Huerta found excessive. Wilson sustained Mayo and saw an opportunity to intervene. Before anything else came of the Tampico affair, Wilson learned that a German cargo ship carrying arms for the Huerta regime was headed for Veracruz and, naïvely believing the Mexicans at Veracruz would welcome U.S. intervention, ordered the immediate seizure of the port there to prevent their unloading. On April 21 the first U.S. contingent arrived at Veracruz and quickly seized the customs house and docks. The port city where Winfield Scott had begun his campaign in 1847 was defended by a force mostly made up of local militia and townspeople, who were unsure of what was happening and, in the absence of any real leadership, fought back. What began as an occupation of port facilities soon became the conquest of the entire city. In hazardous house-to-house street fighting, the Americans completed the occupation of Veracruz in two days while suffering nineteen killed and seventy-one wounded. At least 200 Mexicans died in the fighting, and an estimated 300 were wounded, mostly noncombatants. Huerta condemned the attack, as did rebel leaders Venustiano Carranza, Álvaro Obregón, and Emiliano Zapata. With no civil authority willing to cooperate with the Americans, Admiral Frank F. Fletcher declared martial law. Soon 8,000 American soldiers and marines held the city, with officers handling all governmental functions. General Frederick Funston soon arrived to assume command. Under pressure, Huerta resigned in July and Carranza claimed the presidency, but the occupation continued until November 1914, when all American forces departed, leaving behind a large stock of military supplies that fell into the hands of Carranza's army.

Once Carranza assumed the presidency Villa rose in opposition, and Mexico's catastrophic civil war continued. Wilson maintained his "watchful waiting" approach until 1915, when Carranza's well-armed and well-led forces inflicted a series of bloody defeats on Villa's troops. That October Wilson reluctantly recognized Carranza as Mexico's president, a "betrayal" that infuriated Villa. One reason behind the recognition was Wilson's belief that Carranza would do a better job of protecting foreign interests, lives, and property than would Villa or another revolutionary leader, but Villa intended to prove otherwise. Although no longer a national power, he still controlled an army of several hundred dedicated followers. In January 1916 Villa and his men stopped a train in northern Mexico and removed and murdered eighteen employees of an American mining firm. On March 9, with roughly 500 men, he crossed the international boundary west of El Paso and attacked the small railroad town of Columbus, New Mexico, killing seventeen people and burning much of the town, but a nearby detachment of troopers from the 13th Cavalry responded quickly and inflicted heavy casualties on the Villistas, who slipped back into Mexico with the cavalry in hot pursuit. During the chase, which penetrated fifteen miles into Mexico, Major Frank Thompson's troopers killed another 70 to 100 of Villa's men, losing no one.

In response to this attack on American soil, President Wilson ordered a military incursion into Mexico to capture Villa and break up his army. Command of the Punitive Expedition went to one of the army's rising stars, General John J. "Black Jack" Pershing, who was the commander at nearby Fort Bliss. As a junior officer Pershing had fought Indians on the frontier, taught at West Point, led 10th Cavalry Buffalo Soldiers at San Juan Heights in Cuba, and participated in the suppression of the Moros in the Philippines. He had also won praise for his benevolent administration while commanding in Mindanao and had served as an observer of the Russo-Japanese War. Pershing so impressed Theodore Roosevelt that the president had him promoted directly from captain to brigadier general, a controversial move that saw Pershing leapfrog hundreds of senior officers. His colorful nickname dated to his time at West Point, when cadets unhappy with his demanding style and dark demeanor labeled him Black Jack in a pejorative reference to his days leading black troopers of the 10th Cavalry. Having recently lost his wife and three daughters to a house fire at the Presidio in San Francisco, Pershing threw himself into his new assignment.

Pershing's force—initially fewer than 5,000 soldiers—assembled at Columbus, and on March 15 the first elements moved out, crossing into Mexico. Spearheaded by four cavalry regiments, the expedition advanced rapidly. On March 27 the 7th Cavalry, Custer's old regiment, struck a Villista camp at Guerrero, Chihuahua, more than 200 miles from Columbus, killing fifty-six and suffering just five wounded. Villa escaped into the mountains. Soon the expedition included 10,000 troops, with infantry and artillery added to the mix. Logistical problems caused by Mexico's refusal to allow Pershing access to the railroads meant that the army had to rely on motorized transportation for the first time, and dozens of trucks were acquired and sent to Mexico. Another first was the deployment of military aviation in an active operation. The 1st Aero Squadron of the Signal Corps provided useful reconnaissance and communications support before all eight of its inferior planes broke down. Chihuahua itself also presented major challenges, with a vast desert, large mountains, and an often-inhospitable climate. To make matters worse, the expedition had to deal with a hostile population. It soon became clear, too, that Pershing and his men faced a much greater threat from Carranza's troops than they did from Villa's scattered bands. Indeed, two of the largest engagements of the campaign involved Carranza's forces.

Deep inside Chihuahua at Parral in April, angry citizens attacked a 100-man detachment of the 13th Cavalry that was attempting to buy supplies in town. As the troopers fought their way out of Parral, they encountered more than 500 government troops. Surrounded and badly outnumbered, the troopers held on until relieved by a squadron of Buffalo Soldiers from the 10th Cavalry. During this engagement the Americans suffered two men killed in action and six wounded, while the Mexicans sustained at least forty casualties. The fighting at Parral brought the two nations to the brink of war. President Wilson federalized the National Guard, and soon more than 100,000 guardsmen patrolled the border. A second clash between U.S. and Mexican forces occurred at Carrizal in June. This time two troops of the 10th Cavalry containing only seventy-nine men, three officers, and two civilian guides impudently and against orders attacked some 400 Mexican soldiers—and got mauled. Twelve men, including all three officers, died in the battle, ten more were wounded, and twenty-four became prisoners of the Mexican government. Fortunately, neither Wilson nor Carranza wanted a war. Rather than escalate hostilities, Wilson demanded the release of the prisoners, and Mexico quickly complied. Both sides agreed to form a joint commission to discuss various grievances. Carrizal was the last major engagement of the Punitive Expedition. U.S. troops stayed in Mexico for seven more months but remained mostly inert, the soldiers busying themselves with drill, sports, and other recreational pursuits. Wilson, with an eye on Europe and particularly the U.S. relationship with Germany, which was nearing a breaking point, would not permit any action that might trigger a war in Mexico. Pershing, while bitterly disappointed, followed orders. U.S troops began to leave Mexican soil in January 1917, and by February 5 the last soldiers had crossed the border. The expedition failed to capture Villa, but it did do considerable if temporary damage to his forces. Perhaps the main benefit of the expedition was the experience Pershing, his officers, and his men received.

TECHNOLOGY

Another clear benefit of the Punitive Expedition was the exposure it offered the army to the latest in military technology, from airplanes to automobiles, limited radio communication, and an array of new firepower. Following its experiences in Cuba and the Philippines, the army sought more effective small arms, adopting the excellent M1903 Springfield, an extremely accurate .30-06-caliber bolt-action rifle with a five-shot magazine, to replace the Krag-Jørgensen. The Mauser-inspired 1903 Springfield remained in service through World War II and beyond. In 1917 the prolific gun designer John Browning introduced the Browning Automatic Rifle (BAR), a .30-06-caliber magazine-fed light machine gun that could be carried by individual soldiers. The BAR was issued during the Great War and saw extensive use in World War II. With regard to handguns, Colt introduced a .38-caliber service revolver in 1898, but that model proved inadequate, particularly in actions against the Moros in the Philippines. The army tested a number of semiautomatic handguns before adopting the outstanding M1911 Colt, a powerful and reliable .45-caliber weapon designed by John Browning that remained the standard sidearm in the United States and elsewhere until the 1990s. American-born Hiram Maxim developed the first truly automatic machine gun in the 1880s, but the United States was slow to embrace the new technology, continuing to rely on the Gatling gun. Crew-served and usually belt-fed machine guns, both air-cooled and water-cooled and capable of firing 400 to 600 rounds per minute, significantly altered the battlefield equation and had unfathomable implications for the future. The Maxim gun saw extensive use in the British army's colonial conflicts. A Browning design produced by Colt was adopted by the U.S. Navy and employed by marine units in the Philippines, during the Boxer uprising, and in the various Central American and Caribbean interventions. The army eventually adopted a French model that proved inadequate. During the Great War, American troops employed several different models before settling on new Browning .30- and .50-caliber designs that would become the standards during World War II. The long-neglected artillery finally received an upgrade with the 1902 adoption of a new three-inch gun with a recoil mechanism and improved sights that compared favorably with the popular French 75-millimeter gun. These developments completed the U.S. army's transition to a smokeless powder arsenal by the early 1900s.

In the area of military aviation, the United States lagged behind European powers. Military balloons had been used for decades, and dirigibles offered advantages over airplanes in terms of range and time aloft, but reluctance to fund new technology as well as a simple aversion to the concept of air warfare slowed development. Congress appropriated funds for an aviation section of the Signal Corps in 1908, but funding hardly kept pace with advancements in the field or with the lavish investments of several European powers. The poor performance of the eight Curtiss aircraft during the Punitive Expedition did not increase enthusiasm. On the eve of its entry into the Great War, the United States trailed the other combatants in every aspect of military aviation.

ORGANIZATION

As its mission expanded, the regular army grew steadily during the first fifteen years of the twentieth century to more than 100,000 by 1915. It also underwent major organizational changes that had been long pursued by reformers. The lessons of the Spanish-American War provided the impetus for

IMAGE 10.3 Browning Machine Gun Prolific gun designer John M. Browning's M1917 .30 caliber machine gun being demonstrated by the designer's son Lieutenant Valmore Browning in France during the First World War. Browning designed automatic weapons included the M1911 Colt .45 semiautomatic pistol and the Browning Automatic Rifle (BAR) which remained in service for decades.

these shifts, while transformational Secretary of War Elihu Root (1899–1905) provided the leadership. It was Root who published the unfinished manuscript of the late Emory Upton—*The Military Policy of the United States*—which provided a forceful argument for a strong, professional army that was capable of fighting and winning modern wars. Organizationally and administratively, the army had been plagued by an unhealthy relationship between the commanding general and the War Department, in which the commanding general controlled field operations and supervised line officers while the secretary of war dealt with the staff officers who headed the various military bureaus. Root proposed doing away with the position of commanding general in favor of a general staff headed by a chief of staff, who would serve as the top advisor to the civilian authorities. This organization, based heavily on the German model, would in theory achieve better coordination between the bureaus and a more integrated command structure while eliminating the conflict between line and staff. Over much opposition Congress approved the change in 1903, and in August of that year General S.B.M. Young, a Civil War veteran, became the first chief of staff. The position was solidified in 1910 with the appointment of General Leonard Wood. The army also reorganized its service schools and added the General Staff and Service College at Fort Leavenworth and the Army War College. Schools were added or reorganized over the next few years as leaders continued to emphasize education and preparedness. Staff departments were also consolidated in the interest of efficiency.

During this period the National Guard received much-needed attention and a good deal of political support. Pressure by Secretary Root resulted in the passage of the so-called Dick Act, named after Congressman Charles Dick, a National Guard officer himself. The Dick Act represented the first serious revision of the 1792 Militia Act and established two separate militia organizations: the Organized Militia, known as the National Guard, and the Reserve Militia. It also more closely tied the National Guard to the regular army and provided robust funding for equipment and enhanced training. Provisions allowed for regular officers to be detailed to Guard units and mandated joint exercises. Subsequent bills removed restrictions on the ways the Guard could be deployed and where it could be sent, even allowing Guardsmen to be sent overseas as federalized units.

IMAGE 10.4 Great White Fleet U.S.S. *Connecticut*, flagship of the "Great White Fleet." From December 1907 to February 1909 sixteen U.S. Navy battleships sailed around the world in a display of military power ordered by President Theodore Roosevelt.

The navy's role in national military strategy continued to grow with the acquisition of overseas territories. Its rapid development and stellar performance during the Spanish-American War only enhanced its profile and congressional support. With the encouragement of President Roosevelt and other "big navy" advocates, the navy continued to grow and modernize, with an emphasis on battleships; its capital ships got bigger and faster, became capable of carrying ample fuel for long cruses, and mounted larger guns. The quality of steel armor and ammunition also improved greatly. The advent of the internal combustion engine and improved electrical systems facilitated the rise of submarines, which the navy viewed primarily as a coastal defense weapon. The ranks of sailors grew steadily as well, from 16,000 in 1900 to 60,000 by 1915. The marines more than tripled during the same period to a total of 10,000. But nothing so dramatically signaled the navy's ascent as the around-the-world cruise of the "Great White Fleet" from 1907 to 1909. During this expedition sixteen battleships painted a brilliant white traveled 45,000 miles and made pointed stops in Japan and China. By the time the United States entered the Great War, its navy ranked behind only those of Great Britain and Germany. But it lacked adequate bases and balance within the battleship-heavy fleet. And, like the army, it trailed its European counterparts in naval aviation.

SEPARATE BUT NOT EQUAL

The inclusion of African American soldiers and sailors in the post–Civil War regular establishments carried the appearance of progressive advancement, as the military offered a solid profession and improved stature for many black men. As noted, the army's four permanent African American regiments participated conspicuously in the Indian Wars, in Cuba and the Philippines, and in the Punitive Expedition, and black men would participate in large numbers in the coming Great War. But despite the appearance of progress, black units remained largely officered by white men, often endured the most unpleasant assignments, and routinely faced racial discrimination and overt hatred both within the service and in the communities in which they were stationed. Discrimination and racial tension grew more acute with the rise of Jim Crow and conservative rule in the former Confederate states, particularly after the Supreme Court's 1896 decision in *Plessy v. Ferguson* that recognized the constitutionality of racial segregation under the guise of "separate but equal."

By that time the navy had adopted a rigid system of segregation that essentially limited black men to mess attendant and steward billets. The army had long maintained segregation in garrisons, but during active operations black and white men frequently fought side by side. Racism was rampant in the segregated army, while equality proved illusory at best. Two incidents in the former Confederate state of Texas highlight the precarious nature of military service for African Americans. In the summer of 1906 three companies of the 25th Infantry Regiment took station at Fort Brown at Brownsville on the Rio Grande. The presence of these black soldiers near the volatile border town inflamed racial tensions. During the night of August 13 unidentified perpetrators fired dozens of shots into homes and businesses in Brownsville, killing one man and badly wounding another. Residents implicated soldiers from Fort Brown. Subsequent investigations failed to identify the culprits, and the soldiers—almost 170 of them—refused to offer up any of their own, which angered army investigators, who recommended that the soldiers be dismissed for what was termed a "conspiracy of silence." Rather surprisingly President Theodore Roosevelt in November ordered the summary discharge "without honor" of 167 enlisted men of the 25th Infantry—the largest such discharge in the army's history. Many of the discharged were career soldiers who now lost everything. In 1972 Congress, following the release of a comprehensive study and its own investigation, overturned Roosevelt's order, but it was far too late for the soldiers whose lives were destroyed.

The Houston Riot of 1917 resulted in much more bloodshed and a much stiffer penalty for those involved. That July, following the U.S. entry into the First World War, a battalion of the 24th Infantry Regiment arrived at the newly established Camp Logan near Houston. The presence of black soldiers in the racially segregated former Confederate state quickly triggered unrest. Soldiers accustomed to encountering discrimination and open hostility found the situation increasingly intolerable. Less than a month into this troubled deployment, an incident of police brutality involving a local black woman and two soldiers exploded into violence as more than 100 soldiers, angry and fearing for their safely, mutinied and marched into a Houston neighborhood, firing wildly as they went. The rioters soon lost cohesion and disbanded, but not before sixteen people, including four policemen and an Illinois National Guard officer, had been killed or mortally wounded, with many more hurt in the rampage. The next day the soldiers were loaded on trains and rushed away, but 118 men were later implicated and faced court-martial. Because the nation was at war, the convicted men received severe sentences. Despite a lack of strong evidence, nineteen soldiers were hanged and sixty-three received life sentences. Soon the trauma was absorbed by war fever and largely forgotten, but the sad reality of racial injustice lingered.

CONCLUSIONS

With rather remarkable agility, after 1890 the United States military establishment transformed itself into an international fighting force capable of projecting power on a global scale. The rapid ascent of the navy and its breathtaking success in the war with Spain established it as a frontline fleet. Not altogether seamlessly but nonetheless rather impressively, the army evolved from a frontier constabulary to an imperial fighting force, winning land wars in the Caribbean and the Philippines in short order. In the Asia-Pacific realm, though, the army mission often resembled the force's prior experience on the U.S. frontier, as men who had subdued Lakotas and Apaches brought that experience to bear against Filipino guerrillas and Chinese nationalists. Just as Civil War veterans carried the military establishment into the twentieth century, the Indian fighters led the charge in Cuba and the Philippines. Under a group of dynamic officers and with a new imperial mission at hand the Marine Corps gained definition and purpose and stood poised to become an even more formidable and more autonomous fighting force. For the first time, Americans fought in large numbers and prevailed far from their homeland, administering new provinces filled with unfamiliar peoples, engaging in large-scale nation-building efforts, and doing a good amount of work in the interest of big business. For the first time since the Revolution, the United States participated in a multinational military coalition. A nation born out of opposition to empire now presided over one of its own.

After years of stagnation and failure to embrace technological advances, the army and navy made considerable gains. The navy's adoption of modern warships allowed it to compete with the world's great fleets. While the army trailed its European counterparts in the development of armor and military aviation, it made significant gains in small arms and machine guns. But as involvement in a great global conflict loomed, the United States found itself dependent upon European allies for warplanes, tanks, and often even artillery and machine guns.

Reform and expansion of the army, navy, marines, and National Guard, coupled with meaningful experiences in the field and at sea, prepared the American military establishment for its next great challenge—war in Europe. Lessons learned from the flawed mobilization of the Spanish-American War would prove valuable as the nation prepared to enter its largest conflict to date. The era of empire and intervention produced breath-

TIMELINE

1890	A. T. Mahan's *The Influence of Sea Power upon History* published
April–August 1898	U.S. war with Spain
May 1898	U.S. Navy captures Manila Bay in the Philippines
June–July 1898	Cuba and Puerto Rico campaigns
1898–1933	U.S. military interventions in Central America and Caribbean
1899–1902	U.S.-Philippine War
November 1899–September 1901	Boxer uprising and suppression
1903	General staff model adopted; S.B.M. Young made first chief of staff
December 1907–February 1909	Cruise of the Great White Fleet
1911–1917	Mexican Revolution
1913	Last fights in the Philippines; Battle of Bud Bagsak
April–November 1914	U.S. occupation of Veracruz
August 1914	Panama Canal opened
March 1916	Francisco "Pancho" Villa's attack on Columbus, New Mexico
April 1916–February 1917	Punitive Expedition in Mexico

taking expansion, adaptation, and innovation within the U.S. military, an achievement that complemented the nation's incredible economic and industrial expansion during the time. The United States emerged from this period a world power with as yet unrealized potential.

SUGGESTED READINGS

Boot, Max. *The Savage Wars of Peace: Small Wars and the Rise of American Power.* New York: Basic Books, 2002.

Clendenen, Clarence C. *Blood on the Border: The United States Army and the Mexican Irregulars.* New York: Macmillan, 1969.

Cosmas, Graham A. *An Army for Empire: The United States Army in the Spanish-American War.* College Station: Texas A&M University Press, 1998.

Eisenhower, John S. D. *Intervention: The United States and the Mexican Revolution.* New York: W. W. Norton, 1993.

Linn, Brian McAllister. *The Philippine War, 1899–1902.* Lawrence: University Press of Kansas, 2000.

Longley, Kyle. *In the Eagle's Shadow: The United States and Latin America.* Wheeling, IL: Harlan Davidson, 2002.

O'Toole, G.J.A. *The Spanish War: An American Epic—1898.* New York: W. W. Norton, 1984.

Schmidt, Hans. *Maverick Marine: General Smedley D. Butler and the Contradictions of American Military History.* Lexington: University Press of Kentucky, 1987.

Trask, David F. *The War with Spain in 1898.* Lincoln: University of Nebraska Press, 1981.

Vandiver, Frank E. *Black Jack: The Life and Times of John J. Pershing,* 2 vols. College Station: Texas A&M University Press, 1977.

Wimmel, Kenneth. *Theodore Roosevelt and the Great White Fleet: American Sea Power Comes of Age.* Washington, D.C.: Brassey's, 2000.

CHAPTER 11

THE GREAT WAR AND BEYOND

1917–1940

The Great War • The African American Experience • Airpower • Final Allied Offensives
• The Interwar Years • The National Defense Act of 1920 • Retreat from Intervention
• Billy Mitchell and the Pursuit of Airpower • Descent into War

The American military experience has over the years affected social and cultural change in the United States and beyond. The robust participation of African Americans in the Civil War and the subsequent establishment of black regiments in the regular army fostered hopes for greater black attainment, even equality—hopes that the establishment dashed repeatedly. The Great War offered yet another opportunity for black Americans to establish their worth and take an unequivocal stance against racial discrimination and injustice. And many men jumped at the opportunity. But while military service by black men had become generally accepted and even celebrated on occasion by 1917, there had been little progress in creating officers' billets for African Americans. Between 1870 and 1887 only three black men graduated from the military academy at West Point; after 1887, with Jim Crow limitations firmly in place, appointments of African Americans to the academy ceased altogether. The army remained segregated, although most officers of the black regiments were still white. When the excellent performance of the army's only serving black officer, Charles Young, raised the possibility of an African American man commanding white men, the War Department went to rather extraordinary lengths to keep that from happening, forcing Lieutenant Colonel Young's temporary retirement on the basis of unfounded medical concerns.

Understandably, the promotion of a black officer corps became a signature cause of several civil rights organizations. Given that tens of thousands of African Americans were likely to serve in the coming war, advocates such as W.E.B. Du Bois agitated to have qualified black officers leading black troops. With the declaration of war in April 1917 the idea assumed a greater urgency and found greater acceptance. Soon thereafter Secretary of War Newton Baker announced the establishment of Fort Des Moines Training Camp for Colored Officers, the first substantial officer-training program for African Americans in the nation's history.

In May 1917 1,250 men, made up of 1,000 college graduates and professionals and 250 noncommissioned officers from the four black regiments of the regular army, assembled at the former cavalry post in Iowa. After a difficult and demanding training course, 639 men graduated from the program and accepted commissions in the army. Many of these men soon shipped out to France as members of the segregated 92nd Infantry Division. The men of the 92nd Division found the wartime experience in France both enlightening and immensely disappointing. They enjoyed greater social mobility and acceptance in France than they had in the United States and often marveled at the lack of racism there, yet they also confronted bitter resentment and degrading racial hostility from white Americans in Europe. In a war billed as a fight for democracy over autocracy, liberty over oppression, African American soldiers could not fail to recognize the hypocrisy, and many vowed to fight it when they returned to the States.

Charles Hamilton Houston was one of many black officers who returned to America to pursue careers in law, education, or advocacy. An Amherst College graduate and former English instructor at Howard University, Houston had already launched a promising career before joining the fight against Germany. After returning from France, he entered Harvard Law School, beginning a stellar legal career. He quickly emerged as a leading litigator and strategist in the civil rights struggle, mentoring a generation of young black attorneys such as Thurgood Marshall and playing a significant role in challenging the prevailing "separate but equal" standard that had been codified in the 1896 *Plessy v. Ferguson* ruling. Indeed, it was Houston's strategic approach that led to the landmark *Brown v. Board of Education of Topeka, Kansas* decision in 1954, four years after his premature death in 1950.

The Great War thus served as a catalyst for dozens of young black men to become leaders in the modern civil rights movement. Charles Hamilton Houston and his fellow soldiers recognized the obvious contradictions in their own nation's patriotic rhetoric and responded with a commitment to attack those contradictions in court and in the classroom. In this way the Fort Des Moines experiment more than fulfilled its promise.

THE GREAT WAR

By the time the last of General Pershing's Punitive Expedition crossed the Mexican border and returned to U.S. soil, the Great War had been raging for almost three years. While the United States had established an overseas empire and had participated in coalition warfare, it had not thus far entered into an entangling alliance with other world powers, and although it had seen some military expansion, it had not experienced the hypermilitarism of Germany and Japan. It was these issues—imperial rivalry, binding alliances, and rampant militarism—that, when combined with the emergence of a modern industrial society, produced the largest and most ghastly conflict to date in human history. The advent of new weaponry and an inexplicable failure to adjust to the destructive potential of such instruments of death contributed to slaughter on an unfathomable scale. Prior to 1917, Americans had largely avoided the horrors of this war by clinging to a tenuous neutrality, but a series of events ultimately pushed the United States to the brink. Soon it would join allied Britain and France in a monumental struggle against the Germany-led Central Powers. In so doing the United States became the decisive force in bringing the conflict to a close.

It was unimaginable for a great many people that a conflict of such staggering magnitude could erupt during an era of extraordinary human progress. But it did, and with a relative suddenness that reflected the pace of progress in the industrial world. On June 28, 1914, Hapsburg archduke Franz Ferdinand, heir to the throne of the dual monarchy of Austria-Hungary, was assassinated by a Serbian youth during a visit to Sarajevo in Bosnia. Austria-Hungary threatened retaliation against nearby Serbia, where the ultranationalist terrorist group the Black Hand had planned the assassination. Austria-Hungary's subsequent mobilization prompted Russia to mobilize in support of Serbia, which was its ally. Germany then threw its support behind Austria-Hungary and used the threatened conflict with Russia to justify striking Russia's ally and longtime German adversary France, which it attacked through neutral Belgium, prompting Great Britain to declare war on Germany. Soon the Allied Powers—Britain, France, Russia, and Italy (as well as others)—were at war with the Central Powers of Germany, Austria-Hungary, Bulgaria, and the Ottoman Empire, with each side mobilizing giant national armies. The German attack on France lost steam, however, and soon a massive front in eastern France stretched from Switzerland to the North Sea. Other fronts developed along Russia's western frontier and in northern Italy along the border of Austria. From Europe war spread to distant lands and to the seas of the world.

The war quickly devolved into a stalemate, with elaborate trench works on each side of a deadly killing ground. European military leaders had not paid sufficient attention to the lessons of America's Civil War or, for that matter, the Franco-Prussian War of the 1870s or the Russo-Japanese War of 1904. If they had, they chose to ignore those lessons, flinging their giant conscripted armies against modern defenses that included machine guns, long-range artillery, and barbed wire. Added to these horrors were such new and hellish weapons as flamethrowers and poison gas. Airplanes and dirigibles brought death from above. Motorized tanks, little more than tractors with armor and a gun, demonstrated the evolving potential of the internal combustion engine. At sea, the great battleship navies witnessed a major paradigm shift with the advent of viable submersibles—U-boats.

Epic battles produced obscene casualties. The Battle of Verdun, which lasted from February to December 1916, accounted for almost a million French and German casualties; the 1916 Battle of the Somme was even worse, lasting almost half a year and producing almost 1.3 million casualties. On a single day in July the British suffered 60,000 casualties, of which almost 20,000 were deaths. In the ill-conceived 1917 Passchendaele Offensive (also known as the Third Battle of Ypres), the British suffered another 300,000 losses, including significant casualties among New Zealand and Canadian troops, over the course of three months of fighting. In all, more than 60 million men fought in the war. Almost half became casualties. At least 9 million died. The horrors of war extended to the oceans of the world, where the Royal Navy dominated the surface but stealthy German U-boats lurked beneath, making the Atlantic a deadly place for combatant ships as well as passenger liners and merchant vessels.

Americans displayed a variety of responses to the war. Many still had close ties to Europe, including a sizable minority of German and Irish Americans, who initially favored the Central Powers. Most Americans embraced the nation's historic connections with Britain and France. The vast majority of U.S. citizens preferred neutrality, but a good many saw the potential of great profits in trading with both sides. Soon, however, a British blockade of

German ports made it impossible to maintain trade with the Central Powers, while German U-boats operating in the Atlantic made shipping a precarious business. Both actions angered American leaders, but President Wilson stuck to diplomacy. Rather quickly, American sentiment turned against Germany. Germany, after all, posed the greatest threat to U.S. interests in the Caribbean and Latin America, and British propaganda was particularly effective at depicting German atrocities. However, it was the threat of U-boat attacks that had the greatest effect in pulling the United States away from its neutral stance.

Having warned the Allies of the danger their U-boats posed to shipping, the Germans felt justified in attacking any ship bound for Britain or France, including those of neutral nations. Unrestricted submarine warfare became a deadly menace to America's merchant fleet and Americans traveling on Allied vessels. The destructive potential of submarine warfare found graphic expression in May 1915 when a U-boat sank the British luxury liner *Lusitania* off the coast of Ireland, killing 1,200 people, including 128 Americans. *Lusitania*, as it turned out, had been carrying weapons and war materiel in its cargo hold, making it a legitimate target. Nevertheless, outraged Americans called for action. Wilson demanded an end to unrestricted submarine warfare and threatened to sever diplomatic ties with Germany. Since Wilson chose, more or less, to accept the British blockade while condemning German U-boat attacks, by 1916 the United States was providing essential funding and vast amounts of raw materials and other goods to the Allies while sending almost nothing to the Central Powers. Although most Americans still wished to remain out of the war, the nation began a slow mobilization, which prompted Secretary of State William Jennings Bryan to resign in protest.

To a certain extent, the United States had been mobilizing for some time, but the sinking of *Lusitania* and U.S. merchant vessels pushed the nation closer to a true war footing. Certainly, the Punitive Expedition in Mexico and the deployment of the National Guard to the border represented such a shift. Wilson, while maintaining his stance on neutrality, also recognized the need to improve military preparedness. He advocated a major naval buildup, an expanded army and National Guard, and increased officer training. Congress responded with the National Defense Act of 1916, which provided for a significant increase in the regular army, an expansion of the National Guard to 400,000, and the establishment of well-defined standards for organization, training, and deployment. It also brought the Guard more seamlessly under federal authority, mandated the establishment of a reserve force, established provisions for a wartime volunteer army, and created the Reserve Officer Training Corps (ROTC) to encourage officer training on college campuses. Finally, the act granted the executive branch the power to create a wartime economy. The accompanying Naval Act of 1916 provided for a substantial expansion of the navy's surface fleet with a continued emphasis on capital ships in an effort to challenge the great Royal Navy, but America would continue to lag behind the European powers in submarine development and doctrine. Subsequent actions by Congress included the creation of the civilian Council of National Defense and the Shipping Board.

These acts, while in theory improving the American military establishment's capabilities and preparedness, in no way prepared it for meaningful participation in Europe, where the scope of conflict and carnage continued to mount. In addition to the brutal stalemates at

Verdun and the Somme, heavy fighting broke out on the Eastern Front and in Italy. The British suffered a bitter setback at the hands of the Turks at Gallipoli. At sea, the Royal Navy and the German High Seas Fleet slugged it out in the Battle of Jutland. In February 1917 U-boats resumed unrestricted submarine warfare, sinking almost 800,000 tons of Allied and neutral shipping in a single month. Staggering casualties forced the Germans to assume a largely defensive posture on land while relying on submarine warfare to strangle and starve Britain and France, a strategy that almost succeeded.

The resumption of unrestricted submarine warfare finally pushed Wilson to break diplomatic ties with Germany, a first step toward direct U.S. involvement in the war. The next step came as a result of a British-intercepted German telegram from diplomat Arthur Zimmermann that proposed an alliance between Germany and Mexico and suggested that should the United States enter the war, Mexico should attack its northern neighbor. In return, once Germany finished off the Allies, it would help Mexico regain its lost provinces in the American Southwest. Once released to the public, the so-called Zimmermann Telegram stirred outrage but failed to induce a war declaration. That final step occurred in April 1917 when U-boats sank five U.S. merchant ships, killing fifteen Americans.

The United States may have declared war, but it was nowhere close to being ready to fight one. Yet time appeared to be running out for the Allies. A dire situation developed in 1917 when a revolution in Russia toppled czarist rule and led to a civil war in which the communist Bolsheviks seized precarious control. The new regime cut a separate deal with Germany and eventually exited the war, allowing Germany to focus its attention and manpower on the Western Front. Then, on the Western Front mutiny swept through the French army, which placed an additional burden on the British and contributed to the disastrous Ypres campaign that fall. Also that fall, Italian forces crumbled in the Battle of Caporetto, surrendering almost 300,000 troops to the Austrians. All the while, German U-boats maintained pressure on Britain and France, threatening to starve the Allies into submission. Although the United States had little to offer when it entered the war, its few contributions quickly made a difference.

THE NAVY

The mobilization of American ground forces would take months and was never fully realized, but the navy offered some immediate assistance. Admiral William Sims helped to implement what turned out to be an effective counter to the submarine threat—the convoy system, which used warships to escort merchant vessels from North America to Britain and France. By May 1917 the U.S. Navy had become an active participant in this system, significantly reducing losses at sea and allowing badly needed supplies to reach Europe. At the outset of U.S. involvement, the navy appeared formidable, with more than 300 vessels of all types in service, including thirty dreadnaughts and smaller battleships, but many of the ships were outdated or in need of repair. Consequently, the navy embarked upon an aggressive shipbuilding program that would double the size of the fleet by the end of the war. Particular attention went to destroyers and subchasers, which were used for the antisubmarine campaign. By the end of 1917 the U.S. Navy had fifty-two destroyers and a handful of battleships operating in

European waters. The navy also deployed submarines and eventually the planes of the Naval Air Service to Europe, both mostly in support of the antisubmarine effort. Finally, it engaged in extensive mine-laying work in the North Sea between Scotland and Norway, creating the so-called Northern Barrage. The antisubmarine campaign in both Europe and the Western Hemisphere paid huge dividends, which along with the convoy system allowed the United States to ship millions of men and millions of tons of supplies to Europe. Indeed, thanks to the effectiveness of the convoy system, not a single U.S. troop ship was lost en route to France. By the end of the war, naval personnel strength had expanded more than fivefold to almost 500,000 and for the first time included women, albeit in predominantly administrative roles. The U.S. Navy fought no large battle like Jutland or the giant carrier battles of World War II, but it contributed mightily to the Allied victory.

AMERICAN EXPEDITIONARY FORCES

Many Americans hoped to limit the nation's involvement in the war to naval and material support, but it soon became clear that American ground forces would also be required.

IMAGE 11.1 Pershing General John J. "Black Jack" Pershing. During a remarkable career he commanded 10th Cavalry Buffalo Soldiers on the frontier and alongside the Rough Riders in Cuba; he later served in the Philippines and led the Punitive Expedition in Mexico before assuming command of American Expeditionary Forces in World War I.

At the time of the U.S. entry into the war, the army numbered only 200,000, counting National Guard troops under federal control, with another 100,000 Guardsmen still in state service, posted mostly along the Mexican border. After some substantial increases, the Marine Corps numbered some 30,000 in 1917. While the government ramped up its war-making capacity, the War Department began the buildup of manpower, but it would take months before anything like the numbers required could be raised, equipped, trained, and sent to Europe. As it had been in previous wars, America's mobilization was often haphazard. Again, the War Department would rely on a largely temporary volunteer fighting force to support the regular army, the marines, and the Guard. Training camps were established across the country, and in the spring and summer of 1917 Congress passed and then expanded the Selective Service Act to require all men aged eighteen to forty-five to register and serve if drafted. Conscription came under civilian control, handled by local draft boards. Some 24 million men registered, with more than half of the army's wartime strength of 5 million drawn from conscription. Conscription spurred volunteer enlistments as well. The act also raised the regular army to its authorized wartime strength of 286,000 and the National Guard to its authorized strength of almost 450,000, based on the National Defense Act of 1916, and provided for the establishment of a volunteer army, to which most conscripts would be assigned. Finally, the act addressed conscientious objectors, allowing them to perform noncombat duties, and provided for deferments and exemptions for certain vocations and family situations. Significantly, it did not include the mechanisms for hiring substitutes or paid exemptions that had proved so controversial during the Civil War.

It would be months before American ground troops could contribute meaningfully to the Allied effort, but it was important for President Wilson to provide a morale-lifting U.S. military presence in Europe. To that end the War Department established the American Expeditionary Forces (AEF). Wilson selected the experienced General Pershing over several senior officers to lead the new organization. Soon promoted to four-star rank, Pershing became one of the most powerful officers in American history. A token force was pulled together from the regular units serving along the Mexican border and brought to strength with new recruits. The first units sailed for France in June 1917 and arrived in time for the 16th Infantry Regiment to parade down the Champs Élysées on the Fourth of July, a symbolic gesture that allowed the Americans to pay tribute to the French contribution to the Revolutionary War with a ceremony at the tomb of the Marquis de Lafayette. The Yanks had come to repay their debt. But the Americans went immediately into training and not the trenches, much to the chagrin of the Allies.

British and French officials hoped to muster American troops as fillers for their depleted ranks and had offered to train and equip American soldiers for that role, but American leaders refused to allow it on principle (although American troops did serve essentially as fillers during emergencies). Insisting that the Americans would need months of training and would then fight as distinctively American formations, not as subordinate elements of the Allied army, Pershing disappointed his French and British counterparts. President Wilson also opposed amalgamation, as he considered a clearly identifiable American contribution essential to postwar U.S. bargaining power. Assuming success, such an American effort would bolster public support for the war effort and elicit national pride. Pershing, recognizing the dire nature of affairs and the political need to placate British and French leaders, quickly called for 1 million fighting men to be sent to France, admitting that this would likely be only the beginning of a much larger U.S. contribution. In June of 1918 he requested that 3 million men be in France by the following spring.

One factor that hampered mobilization was the size of the American divisions, which at 28,000 were twice as large as those of the European armies. Each division included two infantry brigades of two regiments each, an artillery brigade, combat engineers, three machine gun battalions, and various support troops. The American military establishment also lacked most of the instruments of modern war—tanks, machine guns, chemical weapons, heavy artillery, and warplanes—and would have to rely on the French and British to supply them. Only in small arms were the Americans initially well supplied. Although it took time, U.S. industry rose to the challenge and by mid-1918 was producing the necessary equipment. American-made aircraft appeared in Europe late in the conflict, as did excellent Browning machine guns and automatic rifles. For tanks and most artillery, the AEF remained dependent upon the Allies.

Training, too, presented a major challenge. Past experience more than testified to the importance of preparation, and the army recognized that the training of officers, noncommissioned officers, and enlisted men would provide many positive returns. Former chief of staff General Leonard Wood had previously promoted the idea of summer training camps, offering military instruction to college students as a way of preparing for a future mobilization. He had also supported a similar project for civilian professionals at Plattsburg Barracks in New York known as the "Plattsburg Idea." Now, the success of this approach infused the army's numerous officer training camps, where civilians and reservists received three months of training before being commissioned in the volunteer army. The regular army also recruited officers from the enlisted ranks and ROTC programs. These so-called "ninety-day wonders" made significant contributions to the American war effort. Training for enlisted men lasted for months in the United States, with those sent overseas receiving additional training in France before being assigned to a quiet sector of the front for additional seasoning. Initially, this training encompassed more than just military matters: the War Department and the general staff also placed a heavy emphasis on character development, hygiene, and even sex education. Months of such preparation taxed the patience of British and French leaders, who badly needed the men in action. That time arrived in the spring of 1918. Getting millions of American troops to Europe stretched shipping capacities beyond limits, but a herculean effort assisted by the British finally brought 2 million Americans safely to France by the end of the conflict.

Although the mobilization presented numerous challenges and was not without major obstacles, it was an impressive accomplishment. Much of the credit for its execution belonged to General Peyton C. March, who was appointed chief of staff in May 1918. March, handpicked by Secretary of War Newton Baker, had been Pershing's chief of artillery before being recalled to overhaul the general staff. A gifted administrator, he oversaw the training, supply, and deployment of the AEF. After being promoted to four-star rank, he also reorganized the general staff and clearly asserted the primacy of the chief of staff position within the army high command, bringing the long-troublesome bureau chiefs in line and making them fully subordinate to his office. Although he clashed with Pershing on many issues, the two forged a winning partnership. March established a model for modern wartime management and served as a mentor to future chiefs.

Without a heavy American presence in the field, British and French leaders had to cling to the defensive and await the availability of a trained American army. Fortunately for the Allies, renewed tensions between Germany and Russia kept dozens of experienced German divisions tied up on the Eastern Front and thus unable to add weight to the spring offensives in the west. Like the British and the French—indeed, all of the European combatants—the Germans were on the verge of exhaustion. The prospect of a large and fresh American army entering the fray meant that the Germans needed a decisive victory to end the war before the Americans could turn the tide. To that end General Erich Ludendorff assembled a massive force on the Western Front, pulling divisions from Italy and some from the east. His plan was to drive a wedge between the British and French sectors of the front and then turn on and destroy the British forces. The attack would rely on shock and the application of infiltration tactics, which had first been employed successfully in the east by General Oscar von Hutier. The so-called Hutier tactics involved extensive cooperation between artillery and infantry, stealth, and speed. After a brief initial artillery preparation designed to disrupt opposing troop positions, well-concealed light infantry would strike weakly defended portions of the line, bypassing and isolating strong points and maintaining the initiative; a second wave of infantry supported by artillery and machine guns would then reduce the strong points. Success depended on the weight of numbers and surprise as well as the ability to sustain the attack. The initial employment of these tactics in France stunningly confirmed their potential, but the Allies adjusted with laudable alacrity.

The attacks began in March and quickly produced desirable results, driving a deep wedge into the British lines, but stiff British resistance and the late but pivotal arrival of French support managed to prevent disaster, and the offensive ground to a halt, having produced almost 250,000 casualties on each side. This offensive also witnessed the Germans' use of an incredible new weapon, the "Paris Gun," a giant artillery piece with a 117-foot-long barrel that gave it an effective range of more than seventy miles and allowed the Germans to bombard Paris from positions sixty-five miles distant. Early German success led to an important development in Allied leadership, when French general Ferdinand Foch was named supreme commander of Allied forces in France, uniting the Allied command structure for the first time in the war—an equally important development for the AEF. A second German offensive in April, also in the British sector, failed as well, with another 200,000 combined casualties. The third German offensive in May finally spurred the large-scale commitment of American troops.

The German attack in May collapsed the Allied line on the Aisne River and pushed to the Marne, creating a deep salient and posing a serious threat to Paris, less than fifty miles from the tip of the salient at Château-Thierry. General Pershing responded to the crisis by offering Foch the use of U.S. troops. The 3rd Division was rushed in trucks and by rail to Château-Thierry on the Marne, while the 2nd Division moved into positions to the west on the main road to Paris. But it was the 1st Division, posted well north of the Marne in the Amiens salient, which saw the first heavy fighting by American troops in the war when it attacked the German forward position at Cantigny—an effort planned by operations officer and rising star George C. Marshall. After taking the village on May 28, the Americans, supported by French tanks and artillery, fought off furious counterattacks into the following day, suffering more than 1,500 casualties. It was an auspicious beginning for the Americans, but the events around Château-Thierry would soon eclipse those at Cantigny and establish the AEF as a formidable fighting force.

On May 31 the 3rd Division's machine gun battalions began to arrive by truck at Château-Thierry to bolster French units there. The remainder of the division arrived shortly thereafter to relieve the French, who fell back to refit. Over the first three days of June, the 3rd Division doggedly held out against determined assaults, preventing the Germans from securing a crossing on the Marne. The Americans then counterattacked with French support, driving the Germans from Château-Thierry and ending the threat in that sector. This stand earned the division the sobriquet it continues to hold—"Rock of the Marne." To the

THE WESTERN FRONT, MAY–NOVEMBER 1918

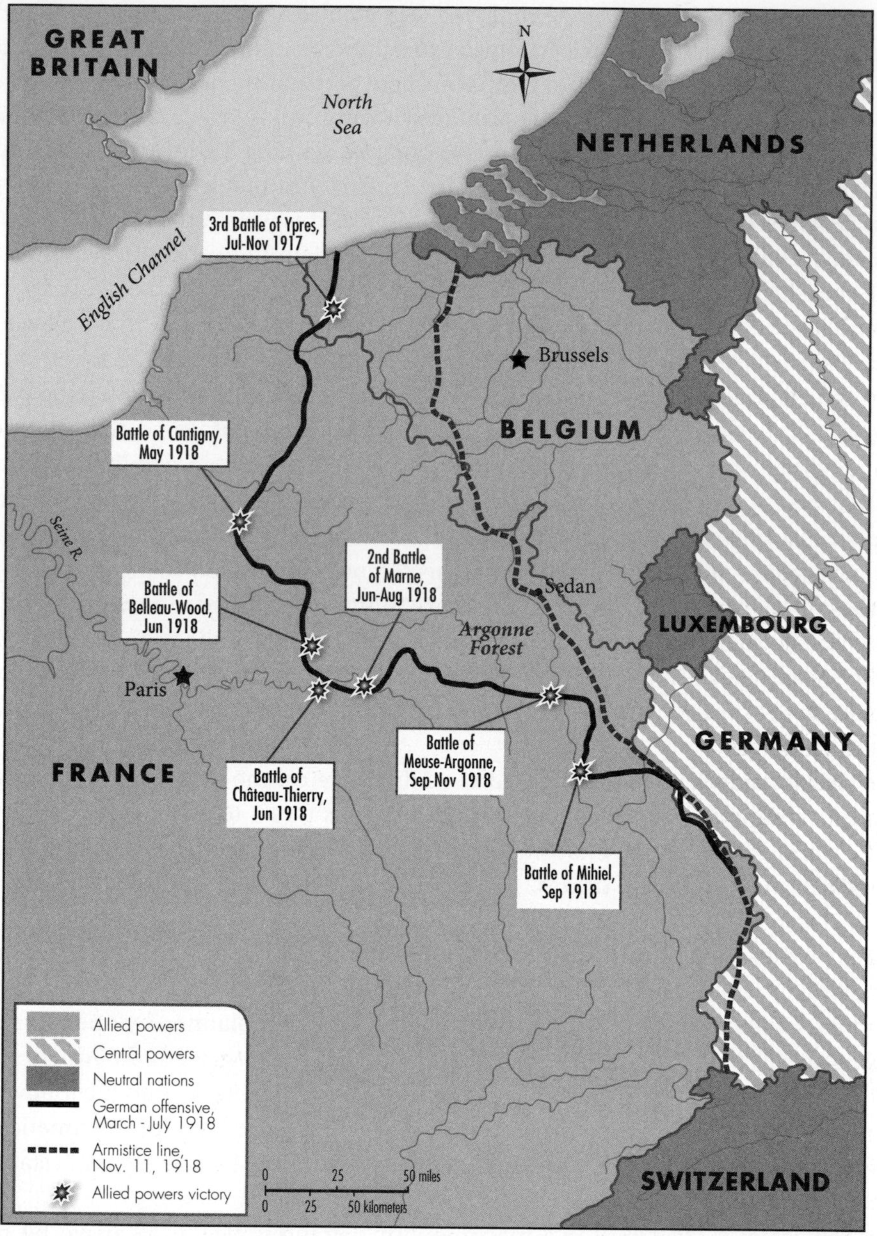

MAP 11.1 The Western Front, 1918

west, the 2nd Division moved in to relieve French troops on the line between Monneaux and Belleau, opposite Belleau Wood. On June 6, still under French direction, the division was sent forward to take Belleau Wood, which French leaders mistakenly believed to be lightly defended. The 4th Marine Brigade spearheaded the attack, initiating three weeks of bitter fighting for which the marines earned high praise for their tenacity and toughness. By June 26 the woods had been secured at the cost of some 5,000 casualties, which were particularly heavy in the two marine regiments. Although likely apocryphal, according to legend the Germans bestowed upon the marines the cherished title of "Devil Dogs." Regardless of the story's truth, the marines' introduction to the ground war in Europe continued their evolution as an increasingly important component of the U.S. military establishment.

The victories at Cantigny, Château-Thierry, and Belleau Wood contributed mightily to the defeat of the "Ludendorff Offensives" of spring 1918. In July the 3rd Division mounted another stout defense of the Marne that allowed the Allies to seize the initiative. At that point, the Allies went on the attack. During the Aisne-Marne Offensive, which lasted from July 18 to August 5, the American 1st and 2nd Divisions fought in the French Tenth Army and spearheaded the initial advance. Seven other American divisions also participated, recovering much valuable land and ending the threat to Paris for good by compelling the Germans to abandon the Marne salient. German hopes of dealing the Allies a fatal blow before the Americans entered the war in significant numbers evaporated. In fact, American contributions to ending the crisis on the Marne and then throwing back the German line did much to revive the Allies' spirits and clearly improved morale.

The AEF had by now been organized into three corps. General Hunter Liggett's I Corps and General Robert Bullard's III Corps saw action in the Aisne-Marne campaign, while the two divisions of General George Read's II Corps served under British command in another sector. With the success of the Allied offensive, Pershing pushed for a separate American field army with its own area of operations. With more than a million troops in France, the Americans could assume a much larger role. To that end, Pershing in August activated the U.S. First Army, consisting of I and III Corps. Although Pershing had refused to allow American troops to be used as fillers in the Allied armies, he did allow his soldiers and marines to fight in French and British organizations. During the crisis on the Marne he willingly placed American divisions under French control. The II Corps remained under British direction throughout the conflict. In these cases, Pershing insisted that the American divisions remain intact and distinctively American and thus that they not be amalgamated into Allied armies. He made an exception with the African American 93rd Division.

THE AFRICAN AMERICAN EXPERIENCE

Roughly 400,000 African Americans served in the armed forces during the Great War, approximately half of whom went to Europe as part of the AEF. In a military establishment rife with racism and committed to segregation, it is not surprising that American leaders had little desire to employ African Americans in a combat role. In fact, a high percentage of black servicemen performed labor in the AEF's vast logistics system with no hope of seeing action on the frontlines, but under pressure from African American leaders and civil rights advocates, the army created two combat divisions made up of African American soldiers and a number of officers, although most officers continued to be white. The 92nd Division served in the

American First Army but because of inadequate training and troubled leadership did not perform particularly well, although it did have some notable successes. The 93rd Division, on the other hand, performed splendidly—in the French army. As Pershing's one exception to amalgamation, the four regiments of the 93rd (the 369th, 370th, 371st, and 372nd) were permitted to serve essentially as French troops, within French divisions, and were largely equipped by the French army. While all of the regiments served with distinction and drew the praise of French commanders, the 369th Infantry gained legendary status as the "Harlem Hellfighters." This regiment amassed an outstanding record in France, serving in the front-lines longer than any other American unit, for which the men received high honors from the French government. Service in France proved a particularly eye-opening experience for many African Americans, who found far more acceptance and much less discrimination in Europe than in the United States. Furthermore, the French and British armies' inclusion of large numbers of troops from colonial possessions in Africa, India, and elsewhere allowed for the seamless incorporation of black troops.

IMAGE 11.2 Harlem Hellfighters "Harlem Hellfighters," members of the 369th Infantry Regiment in France during World War I. The African American regiment fought in the French army and was among the most heavily engaged and most decorated American units in the war. These soldiers wear the prestigious French Croix de Guerre, awarded for valor.

AIRPOWER

Airpower was very much an evolving doctrine when war broke out in 1914. With the outbreak of hostilities, the European powers massively expanded their air capabilities. The Americans lagged behind. The sad flying experience during the Punitive Expedition did nothing to promote enthusiasm. However, the war in Europe attracted a number of American aviators, who volunteered for service with the British or the French, most famously in the LaFayette Escadrille in the French air service, which attracted much notoriety. These pilots provided the nucleus of American experience when the United States finally entered the conflict.

As the United States prepared for war, the Aviation Section of the Signal Corps was reorganized as the Army Air Service for deployment to Europe, but it lacked equipment and tactical development. Once in France, the pilots received training and participated in operations in quiet sectors prior to assuming an enhanced role. Flying mostly French and later British planes Americans soon engaged in a variety of missions, ranging from observation and reconnaissance to artillery spotting and bombardment. Aerial combat offered the war's greatest risk and renown, and flyers eagerly sought "ace" status. America's top ace, Eddie Rickenbacker, became one of the nation's most recognized war heroes, registering twenty-six kills. When the AEF entered combat in earnest in 1918, the Air Service performed well in support of ground operations. During the Saint-Mihiel Offensive, in the largest concentration of airpower to that point, General William "Billy" Mitchell directed 1,500 aircraft in more than 3,000 bombing and strafing sorties, achieving clear air superiority. Some 600 American pilots also supported the final Meuse-Argonne Offensive. By war's end the Air Service counted more than 700 planes, a number of balloons, and almost 800 pilots, as well as ground personnel, gunners, and observers. During the conflict it lost some 300 aircraft, 50 balloons, and more than 200 flying men.

FINAL ALLIED OFFENSIVES

In August 1918 a British-French effort, with the assistance of the American II Corps, reduced the German Amiens and Lys salients, which severely degraded and demoralized the German army. In the meantime, Pershing planned the first offensive for the new American First Army: the reduction of the Saint-Mihiel salient, which would become the largest American military operation to date. Supported by a large multinational air force commanded by American Billy Mitchell and several hundred tanks, many manned by Americans of Lieutenant Colonel George Patton's 304th Tank Brigade, 600,000 Allied troops made up of the First Army assisted by the French II Colonial Corps converged upon the salient on September 12. After a massive bombardment by almost 3,000 guns, the infantry made great progress, as the Germans were already in the process of withdrawing. On September 16 the battle concluded with the Allies claiming 16,000 German prisoners and more than 400 guns at a cost of 7,000 casualties. Pershing hoped to press on and capture Metz, but Marshal Foch wanted instead to shift the Americans northward for what became the final campaign of the war.

The Meuse-Argonne Offensive developed as part of a larger Allied campaign all along the Western Front. The American First Army, supported again by French troops, had as its objective clearing the Germans from the Meuse River–Argonne Forest region between Verdun and Reims. To be able to launch his assault on September 26, Pershing had to oversee a massive redeployment of troops and overcome daunting logistical obstacles. Divisions used at Saint-Mihiel had to be exchanged for fresh yet unproven divisions, and thousands of tons of supplies had to be moved over poor roads in deteriorating weather. In something of a miracle, Pershing's operations officer, Colonel George Marshall, managed to get everything in place north of Verdun on time. Again, the effort would be supported by tanks, artillery, and planes supplied by the British and French. The Allied army for this campaign numbered more than a million men in the American First Army and the French Fourth Army, which gave Pershing a considerable manpower advantage, but the hilly, thickly forested region, which would be difficult to navigate on its own, was made even more imposing by extensive German defensive works, including bunkers and multiple trench lines. The initial attacks made some headway but soon bogged down due to a combination of inexperience, terrain, stubborn German resistance, and weather. Having made laudable progress but now facing the difficulty of fighting in the dense Argonne, Pershing halted to reorganize. Elsewhere on the Western Front, Americans in the 27th and 30th Divisions of the II Corps participated in the successful British-led advance on the Somme.

At the start of October, Pershing, having replaced some of his inexperienced divisions with more seasoned troops, launched the second phase of the campaign. Fighting in the Argonne continued to be a hellish experience. In one notable episode, a machine gun battalion of the 77th Division found itself cut off and surrounded by German troops. It took five harrowing days for rescuers to reach the survivors of the "Lost Battalion." Only 194 of the 504 men in the unit emerged unscathed; 111 were killed, and another 199 wounded, missing, or captured. In a related event, another unit attempting to rescue the Lost Battalion came under German attack and suffered heavy losses, but Corporal Alvin C. York of Tennessee, who had attempted to avoid military service for religious reasons, led a squad of fifteen men against the German position. An excellent shot, York quickly neutralized a machine gun emplacement and dispatched a group of attacking Germans at close range. The German officer commanding the unit then surrendered with 131 officers and men to York and his seven unwounded comrades. Twenty-five Germans had been killed in the clash. Promoted to sergeant, York was featured in an article in the *Saturday Evening Post* and became the most celebrated enlisted man of the war.

In addition to the struggles in the Argonne Forrest, German fire from the east bank of the Meuse caused serious problems. To address this concern, Pershing created the Second Army under General Bullard; General Liggett took over the First Army, as Pershing assumed overall command of the new American army group. On October 10 the First Army cleared the Argonne, but it took the rest of the month to overcome the final line of German defenses. By that time, the Central Powers had dissolved, with Bulgaria, Turkey, and Austria-Hungary quitting the fight. With the beginning of November, a general Allied advance pressed the Germans at every point, and they quickly gave ground. The First Army moved forward swiftly, soon reaching the Meuse near Sedan, close to its objective, the vital German railroad and logistics center at Mézières. From the heights above Sedan, the Americans brought the Mézières railroad under artillery fire. But the First Army was not allowed to take Sedan, the site of an embarrassing French loss to the Prussians in 1870, as Marshal Foch understandably gave that honor to French troops. Then, after so much death and destruction, the fighting abruptly ended with an armistice that took effect at 11 a.m. on November 11. More than 1.2 million Americans had fought in the Meuse-Argonne Offensive, by far the largest operation to that point in American history. The casualties in the two American armies totaled 120,000, with some 26,000 killed in action.

The Great War would later be eclipsed by the Second World War in almost every way, but in November 1918 few could imagine

IMAGE 11.3 Alvin York Tennessean Alvin C. York opposed military service on religious grounds yet won the Medal of Honor for his exploits in battle during World War I. Among America's most decorated soldiers, Sergeant York also became one of the nation's most famous enlisted men.

anything more catastrophic than the conflict that had just ended. The scale of destruction, unequalled in human history, left Europe and other parts of the world in ruin. More than 60 million people fought in World War I, and more than half became casualties. At least 9 million men died. A flu pandemic that swept the world in 1918 and 1919 killed at least 25 million more, including thousands of servicemen. The Americans did not win the war for the Allies, but it is highly unlikely that there would have been an Allied victory without the robust contributions of the United States in the final year of the conflict. The United States ultimately mobilized approximately 5 million military personnel for the war, with 2 million making it to Europe and 1.5 million seeing action. U.S. forces suffered in excess of 300,000 casualties, including 114,000 deaths. Certainly, by comparison to the massive bloodshed experienced in the European armies, the American losses were small, but considering the limited duration of the U.S. combat role, they were significant and reflect the intensity of the American contribution. Although the Germans and even the Allies themselves downplayed that contribution, the late-arriving Americans provided the decisive force in the Allied victory.

DID AMERICA PROVIDE THE DECISIVE FORCE IN WORLD WAR I?

German General Erich Ludendorff believed that the Americans changed the course of World War I. Citing the sheer numbers of Americans arriving in France in 1918 and the large size of AEF divisions, which was double that of their European counterparts, Ludendorff proclaimed the United States "the decisive power in the war." But Ludendorff and others downplayed the military prowess of the Americans in maintaining that their main contribution was psychological. By late 1918 Germany for all intents and purposes stood alone against the resilient and now robustly reinforced Allies, and having exhausted their resources and failed in the massive spring offensives to deliver a knockout blow, war-weary German soldiers found the arrival of tens of thousands of fresh, enthusiastic Americans too much to overcome. Americans certainly felt they had played a large, even decisive, role in securing the Allied victory and looked with great pride on the accomplishment. Not so the Europeans and many other observers.

With victory secured, Europeans generally demonstrated a lack of appreciation for the U.S. contribution to victory, citing the fact that America had entered the war late, borne only a fraction of its costs, and suffered far fewer casualties than the European armies. Nor had the American homeland suffered the ravages of war. How could the Americans have been the decisive force considering these qualifiers? This is a legitimate question. But could the Allies have won without the American contribution? Probably not.

Certainly, the arrival of large numbers of fresh American troops in Europe both bolstered the Allies and discouraged the Germans, who at that point simply had nothing with which to counter the American deployment. Furthermore, when the fighting abruptly stopped in November 1918, the AEF had twenty-nine large divisions in Europe, with more in the pipeline, a discouraging reality for the Germans. But even ignoring those factors or the pivotal role the U.S. Navy played in securing the Atlantic or the timely insertion of AEF troops during the German offensives of 1918 or, finally, the tremendous U.S. effort in the Meuse-Argonne Offensive, the largest military operation in American history to that point, General Ludendorff's assessment that the U.S. contribution was indeed decisive remains compelling. War is never simply a matter of numbers. As with the Union armies in the Civil War, numbers are meaningless without determined leadership and battlefield execution. By fighting in Europe, American forces proved themselves capable of competing with the world's great military establishments.

THE INTERWAR YEARS

The years between the world wars saw an interesting variety of operations for the American military establishment. Most immediately, American troops participated in occupation duties in Germany. The Treaty of Versailles, concluded in June 1919, proved disappointing to many Americans, including President Wilson, who experienced the embarrassing rejection of his hopeful Fourteen Points. His emphasis on self-determination, territorial integrity, and peace fell prey to the vengeful desire of European leaders to hold Germany accountable for the war. The punitive nature of the treaty virtually ensured a second world war. President Wilson fared no better at home, where Congress rejected both the treaty and Wilson's pet project, the League of Nations. The United States eventually concluded a separate peace with Germany, and the last American occupation troops departed Germany in 1923.

The sudden conclusion of the war sent shock waves across the globe, prompting numerous regional conflicts and civil wars. In the United States, much social unrest, including race riots and labor clashes, ensued, some of which required military intervention. Overproduction had damaged the economy, and rapid demobilization caused widespread unemployment. Despite the great victory in Europe, a general sense of malaise settled over the country. Many Americans preferred disengagement to continued involvement on the world stage. Congress rejected War Department requests for a much larger regular army, and the American public showed little interest in funding a large standing military that might be dragged into another faraway conflict. The speedy demobilization and appropriations cutbacks brought the army to just 225,000 officers and men by the end of 1919. Once again it became an all-volunteer force. The navy received slightly better treatment, as the government viewed it as the nation's first line of defense and, along with the marines, as the primary players in the dirty work of intervention.

Disengagement, though, proved hard to achieve in an increasingly complex world. Events in Russia drew American forces into a delicate and largely unfruitful episode. After the demise of czarist rule, a bitter civil war erupted, pitting the Bolshevik "Reds" against a variety of opposition groups under the "White" banner. Even before the fighting ended in France, American troops were dispatched to two points in Russia on two differing missions. A small British-French-American force under British command deployed to northern Russia in June 1918, ostensibly to retrieve supplies and weapons provided to the czarist regime by the Allies in order to prevent them from falling into German hands. The expedition soon became embroiled in the civil war on the side of the Whites. The American regiment involved saw a good deal of action and suffered about 400 casualties during its unhappy year in Russia before it was evacuated in August 1919. American forces also launched an expedition to Siberia with the twofold objective of rescuing the Czech Legion, a large and formidable force made up of ethnic Czechs in Russia and prisoners-of-war from the Austro-Hungarian army, which was operating against the Bolsheviks, and discouraging Japanese aggression in the region. Two regiments landed at Vladivostok in August 1918. With strict orders not to interfere with Russian affairs, the Americans guarded the Trans-Siberian Railroad's approaches to Vladivostok, clashing occasionally with White and Red contingents and barely avoiding a showdown with the Japanese, who occupied the port. Once the Czechs were evacuated by sea, the American mission ended, and the troops departed in April 1920, having avoided serious conflict and suffering fewer than 100 casualties.

THE NATIONAL DEFENSE ACT OF 1920

Despite the fact that Congress rejected War Department requests for a much larger regular army, it did pass significant military legislation in the form of the National Defense Act of 1920. This act established the "Army of the United States," which was to include a regular army, the National Guard, and a reserve force made up of the Enlisted Reserve Corps and the Officers' Reserve Corps. In the regular army the act provided for a total authorized enlisted strength of 280,000 men and almost 18,000 officers and added new branches that reflected new realities—air, chemical, and financial. Interestingly, the Tank Corps, which had been established during the war, was not assigned its own branch but was absorbed into the infantry, where it languished before the cavalry eventually took an interest in it. The Guard's strength was capped at more than 400,000, although all strength limits were to be established by annual appropriations bills; force totals in both the regulars and the Guard would see deep cuts in the 1920s and early 1930s. A major emphasis on preparedness now tied the regular army to the training of the Guard. Furthermore, ROTC programs that were expanded under the act and the four-week Citizens' Military Training Camps assured a ready supply of trained officers. Training was extended to a number of branch-specific and advanced schools, such as the Command and General Staff School at Fort Leavenworth, the Army War College, and Army Industrial College in Washington. The act also assigned to the War Department the responsibility for planning and mobilization in the event of another war. During the interwar years extensive effort went into war planning, including great emphasis on the industrial needs of modern warfare. Army and navy staffers developed a range of "color plans" to anticipate various scenarios, such as, most significantly, War Plan ORANGE for a potential war in the Pacific with Japan.

General Pershing replaced Peyton March as chief of staff in 1921 and reorganized the general staff based on his wartime headquarters structure into five divisions: G-1, personnel; G-2, intelligence; G-3, training and operations; G-4, supply; and War Plans. The army in the United States was spread among nine corps, each with assigned divisions (one regular, two Guard, and three reserve). The army continued to patrol the Mexican border, garrisoned bases throughout the country, and maintained forces in the Philippines, Hawaii, and Panama, as well as, until 1938, a rather large garrison at Tientsin, China. During the 1930s the army completed the transition from horses to mechanized transport and limited the size of its divisions to roughly half that of Great War divisions, more in line with other armies of the world. Among the myriad roles performed by the army on American soil, one proved onerous to many Americans, while another demonstrated the utility of the service.

The Great Depression occasioned unprecedented suffering in the United States and undoubtedly affected military development. Among the struggling citizenry were thousands of veterans of the Great War, who marched on Washington in hopes of receiving early payment of a bonus promised to them by the government for their service in the war. Denied the early payment by Congress, the "Bonus Army" remained near the Capitol in an improvised village that became something of an embarrassment to President Herbert Hoover's administration. In July 1932, after a violent clash between the veterans and local law enforcement personnel, President Hoover ordered the regulars to evict the "Bonus Army." With Chief of Staff General Douglas MacArthur personally leading the detachment, 600 officers and men, including future World War II heroes Major Dwight D. Eisenhower and Major George S. Patton, supported by tanks, swept through the encampment and drove the veterans from the capital without firing a shot, although a number of bonus marchers were roughed up. From a public perspective, however, the use of regular army troops against civilians—veterans, no less—represented a dangerous abuse of executive power that damaged the army's reputation and that of President Hoover.

IMAGE 11.4   CCC   Between the two World Wars, army personnel were called upon to support the Civilian Conservation Corps, an ambitious New Deal program that employed thousands of young men on an array of projects, including conservation work and infrastructure improvements in the nation's state and national parks.

A much more positive and productive employment of the army involved the organization and operation of the Civilian Conservation Corps (CCC), the first of the major make-work programs of President Franklin D. Roosevelt's New Deal. Beginning in 1933 the army established more than 1,300 camps to house some 310,000 previously unemployed young men, who for a small wage completed a variety of public works projects around the country, building roads, improving state and national parks, and taking part in many other worthwhile endeavors. The regular army detailed 3,000 officers and noncommissioned officers to run the camps and supervise the various projects. Although it was a considerable drain on the operational effectiveness of the army, CCC duty offered participants valuable organizational and administrative experience. Even without military instruction, the military-like conditions helped prepare tens of thousands of men for future service.

RETREAT FROM INTERVENTION

Although U.S. intervention in the Caribbean, Central America, and Asia did not cease during the war, American leaders steadily lost enthusiasm for such activities. Marine occupation troops departed the Dominican Republic in 1924 and left Nicaragua the following year, only to be drawn back in during widespread unrest in 1926 (see chapter 10). In 1930 President Hoover made public a State Department memorandum drafted by Undersecretary J. Reuben

Clark that disavowed the U.S. right to intervene in the region under the Monroe Doctrine. President Franklin Roosevelt further distanced the nation from interventionism when he adopted the so-called Good Neighbor Policy to promote hemispheric harmony and solidarity. In 1934 Roosevelt concluded a treaty that abrogated the Platt Amendment and the U.S. right to intervene in Cuba. By then the last of the marines had left Nicaragua and Haiti. With the exception of China, where marines remained until 1941, these withdrawals marked the end of an era. The retreat from such distasteful colonial duties allowed the Marine Corps to refocus its attention on its next mission.

Despite its expanded role during the Great War, its mastery of small wars, and its documentation of that success in its own manual, the corps was in danger of becoming typecast as an expeditionary constabulary. The threat of war in the Pacific with Japan prompted military leaders to develop a theoretical response to such a conflict, which became War Plan Orange. The plan evolved over the years, but a key component involved the acquisition of advance bases for the navy. To this end, marine strategists such as Commandant John Lejeune began to develop doctrine for amphibious assault. While the lack of men—the corps numbered fewer than 20,000 men during most of the interwar period—and required equipment such as landing craft prevented plans from being put into actual practice, strategists were able to study recent examples of amphibious attacks, such as the British disaster at Gallipoli, to advance ideas that ultimately produced the successful amphibious warfare of World War II. Also, in 1933 the Navy Department created the Fleet Marine Force and later published the *Tentative Manual for Landing Operations*, commitments that paid dividends in the years ahead.

The retreat from engagement applied to all branches of service and in many ways produced positive results. One major initiative of the interwar years was the placement of limits on the size of fleets and regulation of the production and employment of capital ships, including aircraft carriers, to avoid the kind of escalation that had preceded the Great War. Achieving reductions in the navy required a delicate balancing act, as leaders still viewed the navy as "the first line of defense." The United States hosted a multinational conference in Washington in 1921–1922 that produced several agreements regarding the size and composition of fleets. One limited the tonnage of capital ships, which required the United States to scrap a number of battleships in service and in production. Another limited those ships' number and gun size. Limiting fleets, it was hoped, would prevent a war in the Pacific. To further ease Japanese concerns the United States also agreed to not establish new bases in the Pacific. Another conference in London imposed additional limits on submarines, cruisers, and destroyers but included an opt-out mechanism if a signatory nation felt threatened. The U.S. Navy, owing to economic restraints, did not reach its authorized limits until long after Japan had disavowed the agreements.

When he assumed office in 1933, navy enthusiast Franklin Roosevelt reversed this course and embraced naval expansion by making shipbuilding a New Deal priority. The buildup accelerated dramatically in the late 1930s. Improvements to the internal combustion engine and electronics were especially important in the development of fleet submarines, which became capable of taking part in long missions in support of fleet operations in the Pacific. Both those vessels and the rapidly advancing aircraft carriers dramatically enhanced the navy's capabilities. By the time the world again plunged into war, the navy was modern, well led, and well positioned to act.

The retrenchment experienced during the interwar years could be attributed to fiscal conservatism and a return to isolationist tendencies, but after 1929 the Great Depression also slowed progress in terms of technological development and the introduction of new weapons systems. Despite clear evidence that tanks held the potential to alter ground warfare substantially, American leaders both in the military and in Washington displayed little enthusiasm for these vehicles. Rather than recognizing the ever-improving tank's revolutionary ability to deliver shock, penetration, and exploitation, American leaders continued to view armor as essentially infantry support. Even with the horse almost completely phased out of military service, the obvious cavalry-like applications of armor and other forms of mechanized warfare went mostly unexplored. As a result, armor development, in terms of doctrine and application, languished during the interwar years. The United States did not produce a battle-worthy tank until the eve of World War II and thus entered the war at a serious disadvantage in armor. Successful large-scale military exercises conducted in Louisiana and North Carolina in 1941 opened some eyes to the potential of this equipment and featured fine performances by a cadre of senior field grade officers, which in turn heavily influenced future doctrine and deployment related to tanks, antitank weapons, and other motorized equipment during the coming war. But this all took time. The only significant weapons upgrades during the 1930s were the adoption of the outstanding M1 Garand, a .30-caliber semiautomatic rifle with an eight-round magazine, improved mortars, and the excellent 105-millimeter howitzer, all of which became mainstays of the American forces in World War II. In the field of aviation, though, the United States managed to make impressive progress.

BILLY MITCHELL AND THE PURSUIT OF AIRPOWER

The generally positive performance of the Air Service during the Great War did little to solidify its role in the postwar military establishment. Considerable disagreement arose over the place of military aviation, its uses, and its capabilities. The army, navy, and marines all possessed aviation sections, and each had enthusiastic supporters. A community of vocal airpower advocates who argued for the primacy of military aviation in the post–Great War world slowly emerged. In the United States the most forceful advocate of airpower, General Billy Mitchell, who had directed major air campaigns during the war, assumed an almost evangelical zeal during the interwar years. To Mitchell, the United States' approach to airpower amounted to negligence. The British had established an independent Royal Air Force, and Mitchell and others believed the United States should as well, but conservatives in the War Department and Congress resisted. Like the influential Italian Giulio Douhet, Mitchell believed that airpower would become the preeminent military force of the future, rendering traditional land and naval warfare obsolete. He also held, as did Douhet, that wars might be won with strategic bombing alone by expanding missions beyond military-industrial targets to strike population centers. In 1921 Mitchell staged a bombing demonstration for the navy in which Air Service planes attacked a stationary, unmanned former German battleship in the waters off Virginia. Although the pilots successfully sank the ship with aerial bombardment, the navy observers remained unmoved, pointing to the controlled nature of the experiment. When the army and navy refused to accede to Mitchell's vision, he publicly criticized both branches. For his insubordination he was demoted to colonel and transferred to Texas. In 1925 Mitchell's continued criticism resulted in a court-martial during which he assailed the military establishment's failure to embrace airpower as utter incompetence and negligence bordering on treason. Mitchell then resigned, but his influence continued. In 1926 the War Department established the Army Air Corps and later the Air Corps Tactical School. As the 1930s progressed the quality of Air Corps warplanes and personnel improved rapidly, and the conversion to single-wing, fully enclosed, metal fuselage aircraft, with vastly more powerful engines and greater payload capacity, ensured that the Air Corps and later the Army Air Forces were well equipped for the next war. An excellent example of the triumph of Billy Mitchell's influence and the rise of strategic bombing doctrine was the introduction of America's first heavy bomber, the B-17, a four-engine, long-range warplane designed to deliver large payloads and absorb much punishment. A "self-defending" ship, it mounted .50-caliber machine guns in turrets atop and beneath the fuselage as well as in mounts in the nose, tail, and sides. The B-17 had to be sold to Congress as a coastal defense measure. In addition to bombers, the War Department and the Navy Department introduced planes for observation, pursuit, and air combat. Both the navy and the U.S. Marine Corps dramatically expanded their aviation capabilities, developing tactical doctrine for carrier-based operations and close air support of ground operations. The idea of decisive, strategic bombing took hold among many of America's aviators and strategists, and it would play an important and controversial, although hardly decisive, role in the coming war. By the outbreak of World War II, the United States had fully emerged as an air power, although Mitchell's dream of an independent Air Force remained elusive.

DESCENT INTO WAR

The hopes of avoiding war fostered by the naval disarmament treaties of Washington and London faded quickly amid the rise of hypernationalist, militaristic regimes in Italy, Germany, and Japan. In Italy, the Fascist Benito Mussolini took power in 1922. In Germany the Nazi Party gained control of the government in the early 1930s. There Adolf Hitler seized upon poverty and despair as well as anger and resentment over the Treaty of Versailles to exercise dictatorial power by 1934. Persecution of Jews and other minorities ensued. Hitler pulled Germany out of the League of Nations and began to rearm its military in defiance of the Versailles treaty. In 1935 Italy invaded Ethiopia with impunity, while Germany reclaimed the vital Saar Basin. The following year German troops occupied the Rhineland, again in open defiance of the country's treaty obligations. At the same time, Spain erupted in a brutal civil war, which provided Hitler the opportunity to support the Fascist cause. Spain soon became a proving ground for Germany's new weapons and tactics. By 1938 Germany was gobbling up Europe, forcing a union with Austria and occupying the Sudetenland in Czechoslovakia. British and French leaders made little effort to control the Nazi aggression, adopting instead a policy of appeasement in hopes that the acquisition of lands with historic ties to Germany would satisfy Hitler. But in 1939 the Germans took the rest of Czechoslovakia and moved into Lithuania; during the same year the Spanish republic collapsed and Italy invaded Albania. The Germans also concluded a nonaggression pact with the Soviet Union, which facilitated the invasion of Poland on September 1. France and Britain now rose to defend their ally, but by this time it was far too late.

The world now witnessed blitzkrieg—lightning war on a grand scale. Unlike the United States, Germany had invested in armor and armor doctrine. Mechanized war, free of the horrid trenches of the Western Front, came to Denmark in the form of well-coordinated strikes and impressive cooperation between Germany's air, land, and sea assets. In another new application of airpower, airborne troops played a significant role in securing Norway and access to Scandinavia's vital resources. Finally, German troops swept through the Low Countries of Belgium and the Netherlands, driving British, French, and other Allied troops to the coast at Dunkirk. A massive sealift involving almost every available craft in England managed to rescue more than 300,000 men, but now nothing stood before the German army and its mighty panzer divisions. Paris, which the Germans had failed to take during the four years of the Great War, fell in June. German warplanes then began a relentless attack on England known as the Battle of Britain. The British grimly hung on, buoyed by the daring work of their fighter pilots, but Britain now stood alone.

By the time the Germans invaded Poland, what came to be known as World War II had already begun halfway across the world. Under a government dominated by hardline militarists, Japan had been increasingly aggressive in East Asia. Having long since annexed Korea, it occupied Manchuria in 1931. In the otherwise distracted outside world, China's call for assistance fell on deaf ears. When a Japanese attack on Shanghai in 1933 brought some condemnation in the League of Nations, the Japanese quit the league. The next year Japan renounced the naval disarmament treaties and continued to build a war fleet that posed a serious threat to U.S. interests. Indeed, by 1939 Japan possessed a larger fleet than the United States, surpassing America in every category except battleships. Japan continued its aggressive actions on the mainland, taking advantage of a civil war between Chinese nationalists and the rising communists. Then, in July 1937, Japanese and Chinese forces clashed near Beijing, igniting the Second World War. The continued conquest of China and events such as the wanton "rape" of Nanking did nothing to ease fears about Japanese intentions.

The United States took a cautious approach to the escalation of hostilities. Most Americans rejected the idea of another war, more concerned with the ravages of the Great Depression. As with the Great War, in the United States "neutrality" was little more than a word. The nation moved decisively to provide military aid to China. The Neutrality Act of 1939, though, hampered the nation's ability to offer unfettered aid to Britain and France, mandating the establishment of a cash-and-carry arrangement. After the fall of France, though, President Roosevelt moved boldly to support Britain and to prepare his nation for war. He released dozens of aged destroyers to the Royal Navy in exchange for base concessions. In September 1940 he introduced the first peacetime draft in American history. After winning an unprecedented third term Roosevelt announced that the United States would become the "Arsenal of Democracy" and bolstered aid to Great Britain, but Britain was running out of time and money. Congress responded with a program that came to be known as Lend-Lease, which allowed the United States to extend robust support to any nation at war with Germany or Japan and removed cash-and-carry restrictions. Meanwhile, the war continued to expand. German forces moved into Greece and eastern Europe. Field Marshal Erwin Rommel's armored divisions ran roughshod across North Africa, driving the British into Egypt. It seemed that nothing could stop the insatiable German war machine, but in June 1941 Hitler committed one of the greatest blunders in human history when he ordered a massive invasion of the Soviet Union, bringing a mighty and mightily aggrieved population into the war. The United States now extended aid to the Soviets, while the U.S. Navy intensified its presence in the Atlantic, protecting shipments to Britain and inviting confrontation with German U-boats. At the same time Congress removed most restrictions on shipping and authorized the arming of merchant vessels.

In the Pacific events moved steadily toward a confrontation with Japan. Even while threatening American interests, Japan remained reliant on the United States for raw materials, steel, and fuel, but after Japanese forces invaded French Indochina (Vietnam), the Roosevelt administration moved to restrict strategic imports to Japan. After Japan proclaimed a protectorate over Indochina, Roosevelt froze Japanese assets in the United States and cut oil exports to the Pacific nation. In the Philippines, General Douglas MacArthur began to organize defenses in preparation for an attack. The United States now demanded that Japan withdraw from China and Indochina. In Japan the prowar hardliners who dominated the government planned a strike against the U.S. Navy in Hawaii and the army in the Philippines and also forced out the moderate premier, who had sought a compromise with the United States. American leaders feared an imminent attack on U.S. forces in the Pacific yet considered Hawaii an unlikely target. But a new weapon of war, the aircraft carrier, which had only been in its infancy during the Great War, made almost any target a possibility.

CONCLUSIONS

Aside from the considerable human cost of the conflict, the United States emerged from the Great War largely unscathed, with its infrastructure fully intact. Although it would experience a brief economic downturn and social unrest, the United States escaped the massive disruptions that continued to plague Europe. Now the world's preeminent economic power, it assumed the status of martial titan, although many observers still questioned its military prowess. Lessons learned in the mobilization process, in dealings with allies, and in the sheer effort that went into fighting a foreign war were instrumental in preparing for the next global conflict, which quickly appeared inevitable. But the distractions of the interwar years, including a profound turn toward isolationism and the Great Depression, hampered the United States' application of many important lessons. Thus, the nation was not as prepared as it could have been when it was finally dragged into the next, even larger, fight.

During the interwar years the navy made huge strides in developing aircraft carriers and long-distance fleet submarines and cultivated a crop of outstanding command personnel. The marines continued to evolve their mission and expand their role by developing, albeit largely theoretically, amphibious warfare doctrine and stood poised to become its chief practitioners. These developments allowed the United States to assume a competitive edge in the Pacific once the fighting began. Like the navy, the army boasted a core of experienced and innovative officers who would rise swiftly to the next challenge, but it lagged well behind the forces of other large nations, most notably Germany, in armor and armored warfare doctrine. The army, navy, and marines also all became enamored of airpower's potential and made investments in the types of planes that could support amphibious warfare, duel with carrier-launched fight-

TIMELINE

June 1914	World War I begins
May 1915	*Lusitania* sunk by German U-boats
April 1917	U-boats sink five U.S. merchant ships
April 1917	U.S declaration of war
July 1917	First elements of American Expeditionary Forces arrive in France
March–June 1918	German offensives on the Western Front
May 1918	Battle of Cantigny
June 1918	Battles of Chateau Thierry and Belleau Wood
June 1918–April 1920	Russia expeditions
July–August 1918	Allied Aisne-Marne Offensive
September 1918	Allied Saint-Mihiel Offensive
September–November 1918	Allied Meuse-Argonne Offensive
March 1930	Clark Memorandum made public
July 1932	Bonus Army expelled from Washington, D.C.
1933	U.S. military interventions in Central America and Caribbean end
April 1933	Civilian Conservation Corps established
July 1937	Japanese and Chinese forces clash near Beijing, initiating World War II in Asia
September 1939	German invasion of Poland begins World War II in Europe

ers, and sustain strategic bombing campaigns. Once again, American industry and scientific innovation allowed the nation to enjoy an unsurpassed technological advantage once it was called upon.

SUGGESTED READINGS

Boot, Max. *The Savage Wars of Peace: Small Wars and the Rise of American Power*. New York: Basic Books, 2002.

Carroll, Andrew. *My Fellow Soldiers: General John Pershing and the Americans Who Helped Win the Great War*. New York: Penguin Press, 2017.

Coffman, Edward M. *The War to End All Wars: The American Military Experience in World War I*. Lexington: University Press of Kentucky, 1998.

Dickson, Paul, and Thomas B. Allen. *The Bonus Army: An American Epic.* New York: Walker, 2004.

Hurley, Alfred F. *Billy Mitchell: Crusader for Air Power.* Rev. ed. Bloomington: Indiana University Press, 1975.

Lee, David D. *Sergeant York: An American Hero.* Lexington: University Press of Kentucky, 1985.

Lengel, Edward G. *To Conquer Hell: The Meuse-Argonne, 1918.* New York: Henry Holt, 2008.

Maher, Neil M. *Nature's New Deal: The Civilian Conservation Corps and the Roots of the American Environmental Movement.* New York: Oxford University Press, 2009.

Murray, Williamson, and Alan R. Millett, eds. *Military Innovation in the Inter-War Period.* New York: Cambridge University Press, 1996.

Roberts, Frank E. *The American Foreign Legion: Black Soldiers of the 93d in World War I.* Annapolis, MD: Naval Institute Press, 2004.

Strachan, Hew. *The First World War.* New York: Simon & Schuster, 2003.

Tucker, Spencer C. The *Great War, 1914–1918.* Bloomington: Indiana University Press, 1998.

Vandiver, Frank E. *Black Jack: The Life and Times of John J. Pershing,* 2 vols. College Station: Texas A&M University Press, 1977.

Willett, Robert L. *Russian Sideshow: America's Undeclared War, 1918–1920.* London: Brassey's, 2003.

Wilson, Adam P. *African American Army Officers of World War I: A Vanguard of Equality in War and Beyond.* Jefferson, NC: McFarland, 2015.

CHAPTER 12

SAVING THE WORLD FROM EVIL
1939–1945

The Road to War and American Unpreparedness, 1939–1941 • *No Certain Victory: War in Europe, 1942* • *Turning Point: May 1943–May 1944* • *Flexing Newly Found Muscles* • *We Are Americans!* • *American Women at War* • *The Final Push* • *Final Victory*

On June 6, 1944, thousands of young men waited on the deck of the troopship *Empire Javelin*. The weather was cold and dreary as the members of Company A of the 116th Regiment of the army's 29th Division checked their gear after finishing a breakfast of pancakes, eggs, and coffee. Many stared off in the distance toward the Normandy shore. Among them were thirty-four men from the small town of Bedford, Virginia. Most had joined the National Guard during the Depression to supplement the meager incomes of impoverished southeastern Virginia. They had never anticipated being federalized in 1941 and shipping off to training camps. Some were brothers and cousins; several were husbands and fathers. All had endured endless training in preparation for D-Day. Different people handled the situation in distinctive ways, including twin brothers Roy and Ray Stevens. They had been assigned to different landing craft, so on deck Ray stuck out his hand to Roy, but his brother refused to take it, saying, "I'll shake your hand in Vierville-sur-Mer," where they intended to rendezvous. Ray tried again, telling his brother, "I'm not going to make it." Roy rejected the extended hand once more, but his brother's fear had clearly gripped him.

While many remained lost in thought or sought friendly assurances that they would make it, the loudspeaker suddenly blared: "This is it, men. Pick it up and put it on. You've got a one-way ticket, and this is the end of the line." Down the ropes they went, weighted down by equipment, and the Bedford boys boarded boats heading for different points on Omaha Beach. Everyone remained comparatively silent as they approached the landing zones, many praying for protection. Roy Stevens watched a series of rocket flashes and yelled, "Take a good look! This is something you will tell your grandchildren." A friend, John Barnes, thought to himself, "Sure, if we live." Not long after, a wave swamped their boat, and they treaded water until they could be rescued.

As the landing craft neared the beach and the German pillboxes and imposing obstacles came into focus, trepidation heightened. Then enemy fire began falling nearby. In one boat, a shell tore off the arm of Frank Draper, who bled to death on the deck of the landing craft amid vomit and seawater. Finally, the landing craft hit the beach, and troops poured out, searching for cover but finding none. The battle-hardened German 352nd Division waited and then, on command, unleashed a deadly volley of machine gun and rifle fire. In the first wave, Captain Taylor Fellers, a former road construction manager, led his fellow Virginians forward. But the Germans slaughtered many of them immediately, including Dickie Abbott, Clifton Lee, Gordon Henry White, Nick Gillaspie, and Wallace Carter.

All over Omaha Beach, the Bedford boys fell. Bedford and Raymond Hoback died at the water's edge. Somewhere along the way, Earl Parker perished, leaving behind a child he never met. Roy Stevens was wounded, and as he lay on the ground, he thought that the invasion had failed. But the tenacity and the bravery of the Americans eventually won the day, and they slowly advanced inland. By the end of the day, nineteen Bedford boys lay dead. Another four would die over the next few weeks of the Normandy campaign.

It took a month, but finally news of the devastating losses at Normandy began to filter back to Bedford through letters and word of mouth. On July 17, the young operator of the Western Union Teletype machine at Green's Pharmacy, Elizabeth Teass, turned it on. Within a short time, the chattering of the machine became incessant. Her heart dropped as she read the first line, "The Secretary of War desires to express his deep regret." The messages just kept coming as Teass recruited people to run them to the families of the fallen before word leaked out. Throughout the day, people fanned out through the community, carrying the bad news.

Eventually some of the survivors fought their way across Europe and returned home, many carrying physical and psychological wounds. They joined the families of Bedford County's fallen in honoring the dead, first with the dedication of a memorial on the courthouse lawn in 1954 and then with the opening of the national D-Day Memorial on June 6, 2001. All over the country, many others hosted homecoming parades, erected memorials, and remembered those who had died in Europe.

THE ROAD TO WAR AND AMERICAN UNPREPAREDNESS, 1939–1941

Storm clouds brewed in Europe and Asia throughout the 1930s, culminating in Germany's invasion of Poland in September 1939, an act that sparked war in Europe. For two years afterward, the United States watched the Germans steamroll over Europe. Woefully unprepared for such a conflict, Washington began military preparations while sending assistance to the British and, after 1941, the Russians. In 1939, the United States could field only a small force outside of a good-sized navy. However, by the end of 1941, a large, albeit untried, army existed. It proved to be a sleeping giant that awoke on December 7, 1941.

THE STATE OF MILITARY UNPREPAREDNESS

The unsatisfactory outcome of World War I and the onset of the Great Depression had ensured an American turn toward isolationism. The military shrank significantly in the interwar period, particularly during the Depression, when government expenditures plummeted in response to domestic considerations. In 1939, the U.S. Army had 200,000 soldiers supplemented by 200,000 Guardsmen. For armor, the army counted 329 light tanks and just over 1,800 aircraft, most inferior to those wielded by potential enemies. That year, the U.S. Army ranked seventeenth in size globally, just barely ahead of the Albanian army.

The navy fared better, as President Franklin Roosevelt strongly supported the force (often referring to the navy as "we" and the army as "them"), believing in its ability to protect American shores and far-flung outposts in Asia. The expansion of the navy began even before the outbreak of hostilities in Europe. In 1938, Congress approved a ten-year $1.1 billion program to construct three modern battleships and two carriers, as well as 3,000 aircraft. When the Germans attacked Poland in September 1939, the U.S. Navy had two fleets (one in the Pacific and one in the Atlantic) with 15 battleships, 5 aircraft carriers, 36 cruisers, 104 destroyers, and 56 submarines. However, many of the capital ships were of World War I vintage. Also, many manpower shortages remained in 1939, and naval planners pointed out that potential enemies, especially Japan, had larger forces.

SHOCKED INTO ACTION

The rapid defeat of Poland in September 1939 surprised few observers. However, debates over preparedness arose when the Germans rolled through France in the spring of 1940 and left Great Britain isolated. By the summer of 1940, the United States had begun increasing defense spending. In July, a congressional appropriation doubled the size of the U.S. fleet to include nine battleships, eleven carriers, and forty-four cruisers. In addition, Roosevelt chose World War I veteran General George Marshall to lead the efforts to build up the army. Marshall increased procurement efficiency, federalized the National Guard, and pushed Congress to adopt a peacetime draft to induct civilians into the military forces. By 1941, the United States had 1.4 million men in arms.

Equally as important, the American industrial base began producing war materials at a brisk pace. Massive government spending caused companies like Ford and Chrysler, Boeing and Northrup, and Kaiser Shipyards to ramp up their efforts. From New York to Los Angeles and many places in between, the war industry sent millions to work, giving the impression that a mighty sleeping giant had awoken. Some began characterizing the country as the "Arsenal of Democracy."

Disagreements soon arose, however, over what to do with the materials. Some groups, such as America First, called for stockpiling arms in preparation for a Nazi attack on American shores. Others, including Roosevelt and prominent journalist William Allen White, argued that the best way to help America was to support the British.

In late 1940, the president sent fifty World War I–vintage destroyers to help the British combat Nazi U-boats. In return, London granted the United States leases on strategic bases in the Caribbean. When London ran out of funds to meet the cash-and-carry requirement of the 1939 Neutrality Act, Roosevelt announced a Lend-Lease program in the spring of 1941 that allowed the president to "sell, transfer, exchange, lease, lend or otherwise dispose of . . . war material" to allied powers. While denounced by some for draining U.S. reserves, the program proved popular with many Americans, who increasingly supported the British.

THE UNDECLARED WAR

The U.S. military began playing an active role in the European conflict in 1941. Early on, Hitler sought to avoid provoking the United States, particularly with submarines. However, when Roosevelt expanded U.S. support to Britain, he moved the United States closer to war. By late 1941, an undeclared war began in the North Atlantic.

America's first step toward war occurred in April 1941, when Roosevelt shifted twenty ships from the Pacific Fleet to the Atlantic, extended the U.S. defensive perimeter to 26 degrees west, and ordered U.S. vessels to patrol the area. Unknown to most Americans, U.S. ships began shadowing German U-boats to give their locations to the British. Roosevelt also replaced Danish forces on Greenland with U.S. troops and soon expanded the American presence to Iceland.

He justified such actions by warning that new technologies had changed America's natural defensive perimeters. "If you hold your fire until you see the whites of their eyes, you will never know what hit you," he counseled. By June, he further extended the defensive perimeter and secretly initiated talks with British military strategists about priorities when the United States entered the conflict. Each month, Washington inched closer to war.

However, many Americans wanted to avoid war, at least until the mobilization of U.S. industrial might and manpower reached much higher levels. Captive to public opinion, Roosevelt ignored several German provocations. In early September, a German submarine fired on the USS *Greer* after it reported the U-boat's location to British planes, which subsequently dropped depth charges on the German vessel. The Germans missed, but Roosevelt disingenuously characterized the episode as an unprovoked attack. Other incidents followed, including the torpedoing of the USS *Kearny*, which caused the deaths of eleven sailors. Not long after, a submarine sank the USS *Reuben James* as it provided convoy protection, with the loss of 115 Americans.

Still, Congress and the president hesitated to declare war, trying to buy more time as the German war machine ground down in wintry Russia. No German invasion of England appeared imminent. In North Africa, battles raged as U.S. supplies assisted the Allied forces. Thus, the United States waited, providing assistance when possible but avoiding a direct confrontation.

Despite these calculations, the war began on a totally different front on December 7, 1941, when the Japanese attacked U.S. forces at Pearl Harbor, Hawaii. However, it was not until four days later that Hitler declared war on the United States, a delay that honored Germany's alliance with Japan. The United States reciprocated, igniting a full-scale conflict.

NO CERTAIN VICTORY: WAR IN EUROPE, 1942

When the United States entered the war in 1941, the Allies still faced an uphill battle in Europe. For a year, they hung on while the Americans mobilized. Soon U.S. forces began arriving in Europe and North Africa, engaging the enemy on land, at sea, and in the sky. However, U.S. forces struggled against the more experienced and often better-equipped Axis forces, and the conflict's outcome remained very much in doubt, even through the end of 1942.

THE ARSENAL OF DEMOCRACY

The U.S. industrial might was a major contribution to the Allied effort in World War II. While industries had begun transitioning to a state of war before December 1941, more substantial changes occurred in 1942. Government agencies tried to ensure maximum output to support the nation's massive manpower buildup. The United States hoped its technology and the sheer volume of production would overwhelm its enemies.

After December 1941, Roosevelt and his advisors pushed for centralized controls to manage the distribution of raw materials to strategic industries. In early 1942, the White House created the War Production Board (WPB, later the Office of War Management), which allocated resources to vital war industries and rationed important goods such as gasoline, paper, sugar, tobacco, and coffee. The WPB even created new industries, including a synthetic rubber industry to replace natural supplies lost in Southeast Asia. By the end of the war, the country produced 800,000 tons of rubber annually. The board also worked with other government agencies including the Office of Economic Stabilization to control prices and wages to prevent inflation and to raise income taxes to fund the war effort. The government needed the revenues, as its size increased from 950,000 personnel in 1939 to 3.8 million six years later. Its expenditures swelled from $9 billion to $98 billion in the same time.

The results of all these efforts were significant. From July 1940 to August 1945, U.S. factories produced more than 86,000 tanks, 1,200 warships, 96,000 bombers, 88,000 fighters, 14 million shoulder weapons, and 120,000 artillery pieces. The "Arsenal of Democracy" had become the "Factory for Victory" in one of the greatest mobilizations in history.

A BLOODY WAR IN THE ATLANTIC

In the first years of the war, the nation's major challenge was the transportation of materials to Britain and its allies. To do so, it relied heavily on the U.S. Merchant Marine. With only 55,000 men in late 1941, the Merchant Marine's numbers peaked at 215,000 several years later. Its mission was dangerous. German U-boats as well as bombers operating from bases in Norway harassed the slow-moving transports, some submarines operating as far south as the Caribbean, sinking an average of thirty-three ships a week in 1942.

In the North Atlantic and Artic Circle, ice caked the ships, and navigation and other sensitive equipment froze. If the vessels sank, crewmen could survive only a few minutes, as frostbite and hypothermia struck quickly. It was not a duty anyone chose willingly, but tens of thousands endured it. One of the worst duties was supplying the Soviets. Convoys often began in Iceland and headed north of Norway and Sweden for the Soviet ports of Murmansk and Archangel. There, the Soviets unloaded the ships and sent the materials to the Soviet armies operating far to the south, sustaining the forces through the dark times of 1942.

The best example of the dangers faced by the Merchant Marine occurred in July 1942. A convoy designated PQ 17 left Iceland with thirty-five ships bound for Archangel under heavy guard by the Royal Navy. However, on July 4, the convoy commander suddenly ordered the ships to scatter and proceed on their own after receiving reports that the German battleship *Tirpitz* had departed its base to attack PQ 17.

The slow-moving merchantmen proceeded with limited defensive capabilities. When German reconnaissance planes located the ships, a slaughter followed, exacerbated by the arrival of German submarines and bombers. The ships steamed forward, but few avoided the massacre. The billowing smoke of dying ships littered the skies. The attacks became so bad that one crew refused rescue and chose to stay in lifeboats rather than board another doomed freighter. Eventually the Germans sank twenty-four of the thirty-five ships, sending to the sea's bottom more than 210 bombers, 430 tanks, 3,350 vehicles, and 100,000 tons of munitions. The Germans only lost six aircraft. Among Allied losses were 153 sailors killed, with many more suffering frostbite and losing limbs as surgeons amputated the dead extremities.

Shipping losses continued throughout 1942 and into early 1943. One U.S. Coast Guardsman characterized the North Atlantic during that time as "the bloodstained sea." By early 1943, some planners in Washington and London worried that the staggering losses would close down the shipping lanes. The German U-boats made life on the seas miserable, and the Allies searched desperately for a means to deal with them.

IMAGE 12.1 The Sinking of U.S. Ships by German U-Boats In the early years of World War II, many allied transportation ships faced risk of German U-Boat attacks. For the unidentified U.S. tanker above, tragedy was narrowly avoided thanks to swift efforts by the crew to tame the growing fire, and aid from a US navy ship, which towed the tanker to land.

INTO THE DESERT

As the battle in the North Atlantic raged, American soldiers headed to Europe and North Africa. While many Americans wanted a cross-Channel attack, the British pushed fighting in the Mediterranean because they feared attacking mainland Europe before they were ready, especially after a disastrous raid at Dieppe in August 1942. Ultimately London won the day, with some support from General Dwight D. Eisenhower.

The first major American effort in North Africa, Operation TORCH, began in November 1942. When the Americans and British hit the beaches near Oran, Casablanca, and Algiers, they encountered ferocious fighting from French Vichy soldiers. However, the U.S. soldiers, as well as naval and air forces, fought well, and within a short time, the Americans occupied the cities and initiated a two-front war against the Axis forces in North Africa.

While the press praised the operation, some commanders worried about their troops' capabilities. American general Lucian Truscott warned that the landing "would have spelled disaster against a well-armed enemy intent on resistance." The British shared such an attitude. One observer at Fort Jackson, South Carolina, in the summer of 1942 fretted that "murder" would follow if the Americans faced the Germans. General Harold Alexander complained that the Americans were "soft, green, and quite untrained. . . . They have no hatred of Germans and show no eagerness to get in and kill them." Some Brits even complained that the Americans were becoming the Allies' "Italians."

Such opinions received validation when German forces crashed headlong into a small group of untested American engineers and tankers at Kasserine Pass in mid-February 1943.

Inexperienced and poorly led, the Americans never deployed their mines and barbed wire and quickly surrendered the high ground. U.S. soldiers also failed to dig foxholes deep enough to prevent German tanks from crushing them. With superior firepower from their 88-millimeter artillery pieces and tanks, including the new Panther, the Germans easily routed the Americans. The engagement was a bloodbath, with hundreds of tanks destroyed, thousands wounded and killed, and more than 4,000 captured.

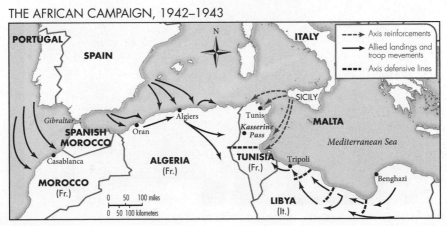

THE AFRICAN CAMPAIGN, 1942–1943

MAP 12.1 The African Campaign, 1942–1943

The small town of Red Oak, Iowa, alone lost forty-five young men at Kasserine. More than 100 separate telegrams were sent to residents reporting people missing in action, although many ended up in German prisoner of war (POW) camps. Others surrounding communities including Clarinda, Council Bluffs, Glenwood, and Shenandoah also suffered heavy losses. This first major defeat shook the country.

The U.S. performance also undermined Allied confidence, even though German field marshal Erwin Rommel never fully exploited his advantage. In the aftermath of Kasserine, Eisenhower and his staff reevaluated U.S. forces and concluded that poor leadership, lack of combat experience, and an absence of coordination of artillery and aerial support had ensured defeat. Others critiqued the poor quality of the infantry, and especially its officer corps. Among recruits, the air force and navy generally received first choice, ensuring that many junior army officers and the mass of infantry were often drawn from the lowest rungs of American society.

To its credit, the U.S. Army rebounded quickly, following the British example after a string of defeats in North Africa and Europe prior to U.S. arrival. More experienced British advisors began training officers, and the U.S. Army built off its strengths in artillery and sheer numbers. Troops also increasingly learned on the job against Rommel's Afrika Corps.

Most important, Eisenhower seized the chance to reorganize his command. No officer rose more in this reorganization than General George Patton, who took over the units decimated at Kasserine. A West Point graduate, Patton had a reputation for foul language and

IMAGE 12.2 George Patton in Sicily   Nicknamed "Old Blood and Guts," General George Patton was notorious for his bold and aggressive military leadership. Here, he is seen instructing troops in Sicily.

bravado. His close associate General Omar Bradley described him as "the most fiercely ambitious man and the strangest duck I have ever known." A British colleague characterized him as "a dashing, courageous, wild and unbalanced leader, good for operations requiring thrust and push but at a loss in any operation requiring skill and judgment." Patton soon implemented strict discipline and drove his men forward, dramatically improving many units.

After Kasserine, the U.S. forces performed better, pushing back the Germans and Italians at numerous places. In the air, the Americans and the British sustained numerical superiority, sometimes outnumbering the Germans twenty to one. American artillery remained a bright spot for its accuracy and ability to deliver devastating cover. Certain units like the 1st Infantry Division, known as the "Big Red One," established their fighting credentials, but more work remained as the Allies prepared bigger operations.

By early May 1943, the two-pronged attack from east and west bottled up the Axis armies around Tunis. Soon, the Germans began evacuating even as thousands surrendered, raising anything white, including underwear. "Germans were everywhere. It made me a little light-headed," war correspondent Ernie Pyle reported. In the end, more than 200,000 Axis soldiers headed to POW camps, many located in the United States. It was a spectacular German defeat. Some American soldiers serenaded the defeated German troops in a broken Yiddish-English song:

Are ve not der Supermen?
Ya, ve is der Supermen, super-dooper Supermen . . .

Combined with the German defeat at Stalingrad, the perceived invincibility of the German army suddenly crashed to the ground.

WAY UP THERE IN THE WILD BLUE YONDER

The learning curve for the U.S. Army Air Corps paralleled that of the other branches early in the war. While many U.S. leaders remained infatuated with airpower, reflecting the continuing American fascination with technology, growing pains occurred in tactics and leadership. Like the other branches, the Army Air Corps had a difficult 1942.

The first chances for the Americans to test their pilots and equipment occurred in North Africa. When the United States arrived in the region, the *Luftwaffe* commanded North Africa's skies. Its veteran pilots operated from bases in the desert as well as in Sicily. With their advanced ME-109 and FW-190 fighters, as well as Stuka dive-bombers capable of providing accurate ground support, the Germans made life miserable for U.S. ground troops.

In contrast, American pilots lacked experience and worked off dusty airfields often far from the frontlines that turned into mud during the rainy season. Early on, U.S. pilots lost twice as many planes to accidents as to combat. Nevertheless, learning on the job in their heavily armed B-17 bombers, P-40 and P-38 fighters (the latter called the "twin forked devil" by the Germans), and borrowed Spitfires, the Americans and their allies eventually overwhelmed the Germans with their numbers.

Yet the problems of coordinating air operations and ground forces remained. In one engagement near Medjez-el-Bab, a group of American tank destroyers attacked across open ground when they saw P-38s sweeping in low, only to be repeatedly strafed by their own planes. The pilots worked efficiently, destroying almost every vehicle, killing five, and wounding another sixteen. In response, a company commander ordered his men to shoot at anything larger than a goose.

Confrontations frequently occurred between ground and air commanders, often over a failure to protect soldiers. One of the most famous unfolded after General Patton lost one of his top aides to enemy planes. He fired off a report to the high command, complaining bitterly, "Forward troops have been continuously bombed all morning. . . . Total lack of air cover for our units has allowed German air force to operate almost at will."

The Allied air commander, Air Vice Marshal Arthur Coningham of New Zealand, responded quickly, calling Patton's claims "inaccurate and exaggerated . . . false cry of wolf." He added that the American's message "was first assumed to be a seasonal 1st April joke . . . . It can be assumed that 2nd Corps personnel concerned are not battleworthy in terms of present operations." The message sent Patton into a rage, prompting Eisenhower to order a retraction from Coningham and send Air Marshall Arthur Tedder and General Carl Spaatz to Gafsa to meet Patton.

IMAGE 12.3   Air War in Europe   The United States Air Force conducts a bombing raid over an unknown German city, circa May 1944.

At their meeting, as the general launched into a profanity-laden speech, three German fighters suddenly appeared, riddling the command post with bullets and bomb fragments. An infuriated Patton headed outside, where he took his ivory-handled revolvers and fired at the attackers. When the assault ended, Tedder asked Patton if he had staged the attack. The American simply growled, "I'll be damned if I know, but if I could find the sonsabitches who flew those planes, I'd mail each of them a medal."

Despite such trials, by the time the Germans and Italians surrendered in North Africa in May 1943, the Allies controlled the skies. From the air, they sank fleeing Axis ships and prevented reinforcements and supplies from reaching southern Europe. Heavy bombing of Sicily and the Italian mainland also began in preparation for the next military operations against southern Europe. While much work remained to coordinate the next campaigns, greater experience and the sheer number of Allied planes sweeping through the skies changed attitudes among many GIs toward the fighter and bomber pilots.

ISSUES IN MILITARY HISTORY

THE EFFECTIVENESS OF THE STRATEGIC BOMBING CAMPAIGN OVER EUROPE

During World War II and its aftermath, the air war over Europe sparked the U.S. public's imagination. Documentaries such as *Memphis Belle* (1944) and movies such as *12 O'Clock High* (1949) praised the sacrifices and valor of the bomber crews. With this renewed focus on airpower, the U.S. military's reliance on the new technology became more concentrated.

Over time, however, debates over the uses and ethics of bombing arose. One of the first was related to the effect of Allied bombing on Germany's ability to wage war. A series of studies known as the Strategic Bombing Survey, led by statisticians and analysts, including future Secretary of Defense Robert McNamara, found that in Europe, only a small percentage of bombs actually hit their target. Furthermore, they found that the bombing did little to limit German war production. Instead, they argued that the Germans' lack of fuel and the contributions of ground troops, particularly Russians, were more important factors in defeating the Germans.

Other debates focused on the morality of bombing. In particular, controversies flourished around the use of firebombs and the targeting of civilians as part of terror campaigns. These debates raged throughout the postwar era, peaking with the publication of Kurt Vonnegut's classic novel *Slaughterhouse-Five* (1969) and the U.S. involvement in Vietnam. During the latter conflict, more people questioned the ability of airpower to significantly alter the enemy's ability to wage war. With the United States dropping nearly 2.5 times more tonnage in Southeast Asia than it had in all of World War II, critics (including many within the military) raised doubts about how effective bombing could be in breaking the will of the enemy and radically affecting its ability to conduct military operations.

All of these debates led the military to develop more precision bombing techniques, including the use of "smart" bombs and missiles. However, arguments continue today over the effectiveness of bombing as a primary weapon to achieve military success and its morality, especially with the introduction of new weapons such as drones as tools of modern warfare.

EUROPE FROM ABOVE

Many American pilots cut their teeth in North Africa, but most people in Washington focused on the bombing of France and Germany. No group inspired the nation's imagination as much as the pilots and crews of the 8th Air Force, who suffered heavy losses and learned hard lessons. Overall, it took time for the U.S. air war to evolve and have an effect, although the actual results remain a hotly contested issue.

For nearly twenty years preceding American entry into the war in Europe, U.S. strategists prepared to fight in the skies over the continent. Early airpower proponents, strongly influenced by Billy Mitchell, sought to destroy the enemy's will to fight. In 1926, U.S. doctrine characterized such attacks as "a method of imposing will by terrorizing the whole population . . . while conserving life and property to the greatest extent." They later replaced "terrorizing" with "attacks to intimidate civil populations." Few debates considered such actions' morality.

In the 1930s, Army Air Forces (AAF) leaders focused on bombers, believing that they could serve as a defensive weapon against invading forces and as an offensive weapon against enemy industries. Many supported building aircraft such as the heavily armed four-engine B-17 "Flying Fortress," which became a mainstay of the U.S. forces in Europe, as well as the B-24 "Liberator."

After entering the war, the United States planned to focus on precision daylight bombing using its advanced Norden bombsights. While both the British and the Germans had abandoned this approach after heavy losses, U.S. leaders argued that their more heavily armed bombers could provide overlapping protection to limit German fighter effectiveness. While the British preferred to rely on area bombings at night, the American "can do" attitude won the day.

Thus, when the U.S. forces arrived in large numbers in England in mid-1942, the commander of the 8th Air Force, General Spaatz, implemented daylight attacks. On August 17, 1942, the force launched its first operation when a dozen B-17s accompanied by British fighters struck a railyard in Rouen, France. Problems arose as more than 80 percent of the bombs missed their target, causing nearly 400 civilian casualties. But there were no American losses, and U.S. leaders declared the raid a resounding success.

Subsequently, however, the force's mission became much more difficult. A lack of experience led to accidents, most of which occurred on takeoff or landing, problems exacerbated by often-miserable weather conditions. The range of P-47 "Thunderbolt," P-38 "Lightning," and P-51 "Mustang" fighters limited the Americans' operations over enemy territory, allowing veteran German pilots to mercilessly attack the U.S. bombers.

These challenges intensified on June 10, 1943, when the 8th Air Force attacked German petroleum manufacturers, ball-bearing plants, and airfields. Without fighter protection, the bombers faced a tough task. The Luftwaffe had a complex early warning system and solid anti-aircraft gun defenses at strategic locations that claimed many victims and disrupted bombing runs. And, of course, the German fighter pilots had developed strategies for tearing through the layers of American bombers, including firing rockets into the formations while staying out of firing range.

Several missions highlighted the German resolve to protect their homeland. On August 17, two different divisions of U.S. bombers headed to Regensburg and Schweinfurt in a multiwave attack. The first group, commanded by General Curtis LeMay, focused on the Me-109 plant at Regensburg. Heavy German resistance led to the loss of twenty-four bombers, with many more damaged. The second wave encountered even more challenges, as weather forced its planes to a lower altitude of 17,000 feet, where enemy anti-aircraft and fighters were more effective. The waiting Germans pounced, downing thirty-six bombers as the Americans fought their way back to England during the nine-hour attack. The devastating losses caused one American navigator, Elmer Bendiner, to write, "All across Germany, Holland and Belgium the terrible landscape of burning planes unrolled beneath us. It seemed that we were littering Europe with our dead."

He was correct. By the mission's conclusion, the Americans had lost sixty bombers and six fighter planes, and eleven bombers were so damaged that they had to be scrapped. Additionally, 102 crewmembers died and 381 became prisoners, with some facing internment in Switzerland. Nearly 20 percent of the force had been lost, an unsustainable outcome. The Germans lost forty-seven planes and only sixteen pilots while the U.S. crews claimed 288 Germans. The Americans tried again a few months later with similar losses, failing to achieve their goals as production facilities quickly recovered from the attacks.

These stunning costs caused U.S. generals to question their commitment to daylight precision bombing. Such operations continued, although in smaller numbers, until early 1944. But, sometimes it produced miraculous stories, such as that of the B-17 *The Pub*, piloted by American Charlie Brown who led his first mission on December 20, joined by 475 other bombers. The target was the FW-190 production facility at Bremen.

From the beginning, problems arose, as three of the seven planes in Brown's unit had mechanical failures, severely weakening the unit's ability to provide protective overlapping firepower. As the planes neared Bremen, heavy flak flew upward, hitting first the nose of the *Pub* and then a wing, knocking out an engine, and causing another to run wildly. Still, the plane moved forward, ultimately dropping its twelve 500-pound bombs. Brown then turned toward the North Sea with his fellow bombers. However, his plane fell behind as its engines sputtered. Then the dreaded call of "Bandits" came over the intercom. Enemy guns chewed up the plane, further damaging its controls and killing the rear gunner. Other crewmembers suffered wounds as they desperately fired their fifty calibers until knocked out of commission or their guns froze.

Desperately trying to flee, Brown started spinning the plane in a circle toward the ground. Ultimately, he leveled off, a maneuver that shaking shook off most of the enemy fighters, who stayed at higher altitudes to pound the Americans. Once done, he headed out to sea, knowing that enemy anti-aircraft awaited on the shoreline. He had few options, although the crew debated bailing out.

Not far away, a German ME 109 carrying Franz Stigler, a veteran with twenty-two kills, headed toward the *Pub*. As Stigler neared the plane, he froze as no one fired at him. Then he saw the craft, its left stabilizer gone and bullet and cannon holes riddling the fuselage. It was not a fair fight, and he knew it. At that moment, he made a fateful decision: he pulled alongside the plane and began to escort it toward the shoreline. Once, he motioned toward Sweden, indicating that the crew should accept internment rather than dying in the North Atlantic. However, Brown never pondered the choice but continued through the anti-aircraft kill zone, accompanied all the way by the ME 109, which kept the Germans from firing on the American plane. At sea, the two separated, with Brown desperately fighting to reach his base. He ultimately returned, much to the amazement of everyone who saw the remnants of the *Pub*.

Stigler, of course, told no one, fearing execution. Brown and his crew reported the bizarre event but received strict orders not to tell anyone, because commanders feared that others would gamble on receiving such mercy rather than firing on the enemy. Years later, Brown and Stigler reunited and shared their miraculous story.

TURNING POINT: MAY 1943–MAY 1944

In early 1943, an Allied victory appeared far from secure. The Germans still held most of Europe, and the fate of the Battle of Stalingrad remained in the balance, although Axis casualties mounted. In the North Atlantic, German U-boats continued their onslaught, severely weakening the Allied war effort. Finally, in the air war over Europe, the Germans continued to inflict heavy losses on U.S. bomber groups. Yet changes were on the horizon.

VICTORY IN THE NORTH ATLANTIC

As late as March 1943, German U-boats exacted huge losses on Allied shipping. That month, German wolf packs devastated two convoys, which lost twenty-two ships and tons of supplies for the war effort. One analyst noted, "Everybody . . . says we cannot sustain losses like this. The system is broken down."

But suddenly, in less than two months, the tide turned. A number of conditions favored the Allies, including the introduction of a new radar system. Later, German Admiral Karl Dönitz acknowledged, "The lack of means of counteracting this radar location undoubtedly left the boats in an inferior and, indeed, hopeless position." Furthermore, the Allies began to employ more long-range bombers and small escort aircraft carriers. As the planes covered the slower merchant ships, patrolling the surrounding waters with the new radar, the aircraft kept the Germans submerged for fear of being bombed or depth charged from above.

Soon, the Germans staggered under heavy losses. In May, they lost more than twenty subs. Dönitz acknowledged that events "had shown beyond dispute that the anti-submarine organization of the two great sea powers was more than a match for our U-boats." Feeling helpless, he met his senior commanders to discuss whether the submarines should withdraw completely. They refused to quit, although they diminished their operations and shifted them to peripheral areas. The German U-boats never again posed the threat seen in 1942, and the Allies could now transport massive amounts of supplies and men across the Atlantic for operations in Italy and France.

TAKING CONTROL OF THE SKIES

While Allied losses and bad weather in the winter of 1943 forced American bombers to restrict their operations, a new command structure arrived, bringing a new attitude. The famous General Jimmy Doolittle came in under General Henry "Hap" Arnold, who issued a Christmas message telling the AAF to "destroy the enemy air force wherever you find them, in the air, on the ground, and in the factories."

Throughout 1943–1944, the U.S. force's numbers of B-17s and B-24s swelled, as did its numbers of P-47s and P-38s carrying drop tanks that increased their range, which by August 1943 had extended to 375 miles. A crucial change occurred with the introduction of large numbers of P-51 "Mustangs" in early 1944. The Mustang's replacement of an Allison engine with a British Rolls-Royce Merlin engine enhanced its speed, turning it into the fastest plane in the sky. Working in tandem with the resilient P-47, the U.S. fighters began inflicting heavy losses.

Equally as important, Assistant Secretary of War Robert Lovett pushed the AAF to provide sufficient fighter coverage for its bombers. He worked with General Barney Giles and North American Aviation (the P-51 manufacturer) to remove a heavy radio and replace it with a 100-gallon tank. When combined with drop tanks, the Mustang operated farther than ever before into Germany by March 1944. It was the best fighter in the air until the Germans introduced the Me-262 jet late in the war.

With fighter protection and reserves to throw at Germany, the Allies took the offensive on February 20, 1944, with the "Big Week." On the first day, more than 1,000 bombers departed on missions, escorted by 885 fighters. They met little opposition, but those that followed encountered stiff resistance from a desperate Luftwaffe. On February 24, the AAF lost 66 bombers and 10 fighters, but the next day only 17 out of 800 were lost.

During this time, U.S. airpower inflicted heavy casualties on the German fighters. In February, when the Mustangs and Thunderbolts accompanied the bombers, the Luftwaffe lost one-third of its single-engine fighters. While production stayed high despite the attacks, the German force also lost 17.9 percent of its pilots. Increasingly, raw pilots straight out of training headed into the Allied line of fire.

By March 4, the onslaught had reached Berlin. The appearance of the Americans overhead during daylight hours shook German leaders, who saw losses mount to 22 percent of pilots in March, including two commanders, one with 102 kills and another with 161. Within a few months, the German resistance had virtually collapsed under the weight of relentless daytime and nighttime bombing. As the Allies landed in Europe in June and established more air bases on the continent, German losses and destruction of the homeland only increased.

FLEXING NEWLY FOUND MUSCLES

After the campaign in North Africa and a successful coordinated operation in Sicily, the Allies prepared to invade Italy before invading France and beginning the long march to Berlin. They planned to squeeze the Germans between this eastward push and the Soviets, whose victories at Stalingrad and Kursk had the Axis Powers on their heels.

Millions of young Americans joined the veterans of North Africa and Sicily as they prepared to assault Europe, both in the Mediterranean and across the English Channel. The numbers swelled especially in England, where the British complained about the "Yanks" being "overpaid, oversexed, and over here." In 1943, George Orwell complained, "It is difficult to go anywhere in London without having the feeling that Britain is now Occupied Territory." Of course, that perception ignored the hard slogging of American GIs in North Africa and Sicily.

THE ITALIAN CAMPAIGN, 1943–1945

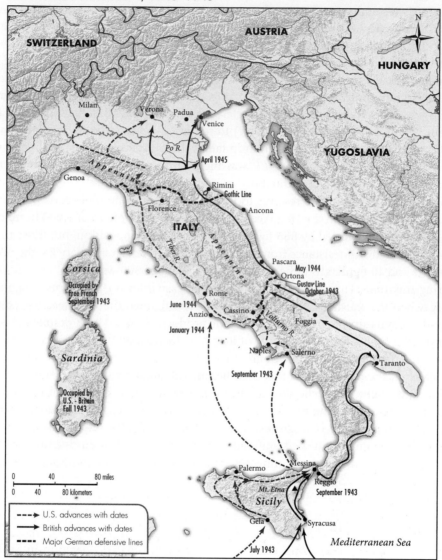

MAP 12.2 The Italian Campaign, 1943–1945

In the fall of 1943, a new front opened in Italy. On September 3, the British met little resistance during Operation BAYTOWN, during which they crossed the Straits of Messina and occupied Calabria. General Albrecht Kesserling, commander of German forces in Italy, correctly saw the operation as a precursor to a larger one, so he braced himself for the main thrust.

On September 10, a large armada of ships appeared off the coast of the small seaport of Salerno, not far from Naples, to launch Operation AVALANCHE. General Mark Clark, called by his admirers the "American Eagle," led the operation of 70,000 men divided between two locations ten miles apart and separated by a river. The Germans waited in good defensive positions in the hills with artillery already pinpointed on locations exiting the beachhead. Some, including Bradley, warned beforehand that the "situation seemed ripe for disaster."

From the start, the Germans inflicted heavy casualties. As U.S. troops advanced, a German loudspeaker called out, "Come on in and give up. We have you covered." German planes strafed the Americans, mines destroyed landing craft, and artillery pounded the pines and olive tree groves near the landing zones. The green 36th Division, a unit primarily composed of nationalized Texas National Guardsmen, bogged down under the withering fire and by the end of the first day, the Allies were holding on precariously.

Fortunately, the Germans faltered in launching a counterattack, limited as they were by fuel shortages and deceived by the belief that the Allies planned a bigger operation nearer Naples. However, on September 13, the Germans crashed through the American lines. One battalion surrendered and two others disintegrated. One observer noted seeing a "rabble of shocked and demoralized soldiery." Desperate, Clark ordered the 82nd Airborne dropped within his lines and planned an evacuation as the enemy neared his command post.

But the Germans misread the terrain and found themselves bottlenecked between the river and U.S. positions. U.S. artillery, both land and naval, sent thousands of rounds into the stalled German forces, breaking the attack. The Germans retreated, allowing thousands of paratroopers to reinforce the beachhead and helping turn the tide. By October 1, Allied forces marched into Naples.

With a foothold and the British 8th Army driving up the coast, the Allies focused on Rome. From the start, some strategists warned about the obstacles of such an operation, including the Gustav Line, where Kesserling planned to bleed the Allies dry. With infantry moving to England to prepare for the invasion of France, Allied commanders faced an arduous test. No battle better demonstrated the challenges of driving the Germans out of Italy than the battles fought around the abbey atop the 5,000-foot-high Monte Cassino. From February to May, the Allies mounted four large assaults on this sanctuary with limited success.

The first attack occurred on January 20, when GIs of the hard-luck 36th Division rowed across the Rapido River in twelve-man plywood boats and twenty-four-man rubber dinghies. Before they arrived, the Germans spotted them from their high perches on Monte Cassino and called in murderous fire. When U.S. engineers tried to build a bridge, the trucks carrying the materials bogged down in the mud. They could only construct small footbridges, which soon became slick with American blood.

Ultimately, a few hundred Americans reached the north side of the river, but they ran into minefields that stopped their advance. German defenders poured out heavy rifle fire and artillery. One of the young soldiers wrote: "I remember this kid being hit by machine gun fire; the bullets hitting him pushed his body forward like a tin can."

By January 25, the Americans lost the foothold. They negotiated a temporary truce to gather their dead, with one observer recalling that "limbless, headless torsos were stacked like firewood . . . to await collection." The 36th incurred 1,681 casualties and another shock to its fragile condition, both materially and psychologically.

The urgency on the Gustav Line increased when desperate Allied commanders under pressure to capture Rome launched an amphibious assault on the small port city of Anzio near the capital city. Code-named Operation SHINGLE, the effort involved a large force of Americans surprising the Germans. However, the undermanned U.S. forces moved cautiously, afraid of overextending their lines. Once the Germans regrouped, they bottled up the Allied forces in the beachhead and constantly bombarded the rear echelon areas to such an extent that many GIs found it safer in the frontlines. Churchill complained, "I thought we were landing a Tiger cat; instead all we have is stranded whale."

For months, the Allies tried to break through the Gustav Line and out of Anzio, but neither side could break the stalemate. Frustrated, the Allies even bombed the abbey at Monte Cassino, completely obliterating it with 1,200 tons of bombs and 195,000 artillery shells. Instead of helping, it actually made the site more impregnable. Finally, in late May, the British pieced together a maneuver that broke through the line while the Americans pushed forward. Clark's desire to capture Rome allowed a large part of the German Army to escape, but on June 5, 1944, Allied tanks and troops rolled into the Italian capital. It had been a terrible slog, but that day, the Allies celebrated. Few knew that another great struggle would begin the following day.

Once the Allies took Rome, the fighting in Italy continued, as natural defensive positions provided the Germans a way to exact heavy casualties on their enemy. Furthermore, as priorities shifted to Western Europe with the invasion of Normandy, the Italian campaign became an afterthought for the Allies. Nonetheless, thousands of Americans and their allies continued to die as the soft underbelly of Europe proved anything but an easy point of penetration.

EVERYONE TO THE FRONT

To support the offensives in Italy and France, the United States required massive numbers of men. While volunteers flooded into the military after Pearl Harbor, they were insufficient. After September 1940, the Selective Service sent out millions of draft notices requiring men to submit to tests for classification unless local draft boards deemed them to the war effort on the home front. Some failed these tests because of mental or physical defects, but millions of citizen soldiers entered the U.S. military. The war required the greatest mobilization in American history and affected men of many different ethnic backgrounds, as well as women.

THE DOUBLE V

Given the United States' significant population of African Americans, the U.S. military relied on black men to fill its ranks. However, the relationship between the military and African Americans was complex, dating back to the American Civil War, when African Americans served in large numbers, but almost always under white officers. Some units had distinguished themselves over time, particularly the Buffalo Soldiers in the American West and the Harlem Hellfighters in World War I. Nonetheless, as the United States entered World War II, social norms kept African Americans segregated and often limited to service duties.

After Pearl Harbor, African Americans volunteered in large numbers and submitted to the draft, with many hoping to thereby earn equal citizenship. Early on, problems arose as

African Americans sought to defeat both fascism and Jim Crow in a "Double V" campaign. Many white officers avoided duty with African American units, and frontline commanders often refused to utilize them. Thus, by spring 1943, of the more than half a million African Americans in the army, only 79,000 were serving overseas, with the 92nd Infantry seeing the most action in Italy.

But, many African Americans ultimately did serve, particularly during such difficult engagements as the Battle of the Bulge. Some individuals distinguished themselves, including Lieutenant John Fox, who acted heroically in the Sericho Valley in Italy in December 1944. The day after Christmas, Fox and his troops held a house as he called in artillery against enemy forces. Greatly outnumbered, everyone retreated but Fox, who requested more fire. The artillery inched closer to his position, and finally he asked for it to be directed toward the house. When an artillery commander told him that would be suicide, Fox yelled, "Fire it!" He died in the rain of steel, surrounded by nearly 100 German dead. A commander put in his name for a Distinguished Service Cross (DSC), but the army lost the paperwork, and his family only received a Bronze Star and Purple Heart. In 1982, he finally received the DSC. In 1996, it was upgraded along with six others to a Medal of Honor, with an acknowledgement that racism had prevented him from receiving the nation's highest honor. Fox's wife, Arlene, attended a special ceremony at the White House to receive her husband's medal.

IMAGE 12.4 Anzio Supplies make their way to Allied troops stationed onshore Anzio, Italy. The Battle of Anzio would stretch from the initial landings on January 22nd to June 5th 1994. Critics largely point to U.S. Major General John P Lucas's lack of confidence in the Allies' strategic plan, and hesitancy to invest in his offensive forces, as a major cause of this prolonged period.

Other African Americans bravely served in the air, with the most famous group being the 99th Pursuit Squadron and the 332nd Fighter group, also known as the Tuskegee Airmen. These soldiers received training in Alabama, despite arguments that African Americans lacked the skills to fly. Ultimately, they deployed to the Mediterranean, where they flew P-40s and eventually P-47s and P-51s with noses and rudders painted red to distinguish them. On April 24, 1943, Lieutenant Charles B. Hall became the first African American to record a victory during combat over Sicily, shooting down an FW-190. His victory became one of hundreds as the Tuskegee Airmen flew over Europe, participating in the invasion at Anzio, where their pilots knocked down twelve planes in two days while protecting the landing zone. The group also produced several future leaders of the U.S. Air Force, among them Benjamin O. Davis, who became the first African American general in the service. The West Point graduate distinguished himself as a pilot and commander during the war, winning a Silver Star and Distinguished Flying Cross.

The actions of the Tuskegee Airmen and other African American units, including the 761st Tank Battalion (also called Patton's Panthers), ensured some progress. Many African American veterans returned home to lobby for equal rights, arguing that their willingness to risk their lives for their country required better treatment. Changes occurred over time, with the most important military-related development being President Harry Truman's Executive Order 9981, which ended segregation in the military on July 26, 1948.

WE ARE AMERICANS!

Not only African Americans, but also Latinos, including a significant number of Puerto Ricans drafted from the commonwealth, and Native Americans fought in large numbers in the U.S. military during World War II. Many distinguished themselves, including seventeen Medal of Honor winners, a number of whom were born in Mexico. They faced prejudice in integrated units but fought courageously nonetheless. However, the group with the most to prove was Japanese Americans. When World War II erupted, the Roosevelt administration placed many of these individuals in concentration camps under Executive Order 9066. Families lost homes and farms, receiving only a short time to report to deportation centers, carrying their only belongings in suitcases. The Japanese internment constituted one of the greatest violations of civil liberties in American history.

Ironically, when many of the young men confined in the camps received their Selective Service notice, they volunteered or reported to draft boards. Tens of thousands left their families behind the barbed wire fences of the camps and headed into the U.S. military, striving to prove their loyalty. Most fought in segregated units led initially by white officers. The most famous, the 442nd Regimental Combat Team, fought in Europe and became the most decorated U.S. army unit of the war. By war's end, its members had received more than 9,000 Purple Hearts and another 5,000 medals for bravery. The force also won eight Presidential Unit Citations. Its list of accomplishments included rescuing the 300 men of the "Lost Battalion" near Biffontaine, France, after the Germans encircled them in October 1944. The Japanese Americans attacked in rough terrain, at one point launching a charge during which some of the young men screamed, "Banzai." The casualties were heavy, with one platoon losing all its men except two. Yet they relieved the beleaguered force. Many of the men were surprised to see Japanese Americans coming to their rescue.

Japanese Americans' individual of acts of bravery astounded the American public. Sadao Munemori provided one such example. Raised in Glendale, California, the son of Japanese immigrants, he joined the army in November 1941. When the war broke out, the army removed him from combat training and assigned him to menial jobs, and his parents were sent to the concentration camp of Manzanar. However, in 1943, Munemori joined the 442nd in Europe and helped rescue the Lost Battalion. Then he headed to Italy, where the Americans were fighting along the Gothic Line. Only a month before the war ended, his unit attacked. The enemy pinned down his squad. Undeterred, Munemori rose and single-handedly attacked, knocking out two enemy machine guns. As he moved toward a crater occupied by two colleagues, an enemy grenade hit his helmet and fell into the hole. He jumped on it and absorbed the blast, dying on the spot. For his bravery, he received the Medal of Honor, the only one awarded to a member of the 442nd during the war, although the awards of nineteen others were upgraded in 2000.

At the end of the war, President Truman personally recognized the men of the 442nd for their bravery. The 1951 movie *Go For Broke* also honored the unit and its exploits. A number of its members went on to prominence, including Daniel Inouye, a DSC recipient whose shattered arm prevented him from fulfilling his dream of becoming a surgeon. Instead, he became a politician, winning his first election to the U.S. Senate in 1962. In 2000 his DSC was upgraded to a Medal of Honor. He died in 2012 after fifty years of distinguished service in the Senate.

AMERICAN WOMEN AT WAR

Race mattered a great deal in the U.S. war effort, but gender also counted. While the Soviets actively incorporated women into combat roles as snipers and fighter pilots, the United States resisted employing women in such ways. However, women did serve in various capacities, including traditional roles as nurses and support staff, and to a greater degree than at any point in American history.

When war broke out, a number of vocal Americans called for utilizing women in the military. A War Department study found that 50 percent of jobs in the military were gender-neutral. Eleanor Roosevelt and Representative Edith Nourse Rogers, a Republican from Massachusetts, pushed for more female involvement in the war, even though Secretary of War Henry Stimson complained that by nature women were pacifists. Eventually, the military allowed women without children and over the age of sixteen to join the Women's Army Auxiliary Corps (WAAC, later shortened to WAC) and the navy version, the WAVEs. Ultimately, more than 100,000 women found their way into the military, with approximately 16 percent serving overseas.

These women encountered resistance in many quarters. Opponents tried to portray the volunteers as promiscuous in both heterosexual and homosexual ways. despite the fact that rates of sexually transmitted diseases were significantly lower among women than among men. Sexual harassment was also common. Still, women performed tasks such as munitions disposal, codebreaking, and the transportation of planes to war zones with great skill. Yet only 2 percent of the military were women, and the country never realized their potential to fill manpower needs, even as shortages cropped up after D-Day.

THE FINAL PUSH

By the spring of 1944, the Allies were planning to open a second front in Western Europe to put more pressure on the Germans. The Soviets, fighting on a long front, were progressively wearing down the Germans, pushing them closer to their homeland. The Americans and British finally believed that they had the forces and materials to launch a cross-Channel attack. With air superiority and supplies flowing uninterrupted across the Atlantic, it was time to make the much-anticipated assault. Once this task was completed, it was not long before the Allies took Paris and ultimately marched into Germany.

OPERATION OVERLORD

For years, Soviet leader Josef Stalin had pressured Churchill and Roosevelt to launch a cross-Channel attack to relieve pressure on the Russians. He could not grasp its difficulty, never fully appreciating the huge logistical issues involved in launching an amphibious assault against heavily defended beaches. As the British and Canadians had demonstrated during the disastrous raid at Dieppe in 1942, such an invasion was a significant undertaking.

Under the command of Dwight Eisenhower, the Allied forces prepared to attack the beaches in France at Normandy in Operation Overlord. With thirty-five divisions at his disposal (less than the Germans had in France), Eisenhower relied heavily on airpower to limit German movements and deception to convince the Germans that Calais, not Normandy, was the target landing area. General Patton, who had been relieved of his field command, was assigned to head a fictitious army complete with fake landing craft and rubber tanks arrayed on the fields of England.

MAP 12.3 The Western Europe Campaign, June 1944–May 1945

IMAGE 12.5　D-Day　On June 6th, 1944 over 150,000 Allied troops landed on the shores of Normandy, France with the mission to gain ground on the European mainland. The operation was successful and marked the beginning of the end of the war, though this came as a result of great bloodshed. It is estimated that over 425,000 Allied and German troops were killed or wounded.

After several false starts, on June 5, the invasion force sailed with more than 150,000 American, British, and Canadian troops. On the night of June 6, paratroopers in lumbering transport planes and gliders dropped near the beaches at Normandy. Many landed outside of their drop zones but regrouped and disrupted German efforts to move reinforcements. In the morning, a massive air and sea bombardment of the German positions began. Afterward, landing craft headed to the beaches carrying the infantrymen; some were swamped by the high seas en route, sending soldiers overboard to drown. Nonetheless, thousands waded ashore on the five beaches, often facing murderous fire. The Americans were assigned to storm the well-defended Omaha and Utah beaches. Casualties were high, especially at Omaha Beach. However, the Allies established strong positions at Gold, Juno, Sword, and Utah beaches, moving inland and allowing more men and vast quantities of supplies to unload. Tenaciously, the Allies inched slowly out into the French countryside. The Germans fought stubbornly and sometimes viciously; SS units in particular executed hundreds of

Allied POWs. As reinforcements arrived, Allied planes continued to pound the Germans, with the fighter-bombers proving especially deadly.

By July, a breakout had occurred, led by Patton's newly activated Third Army, which nearly encircled the Germans. With superior intelligence derived from codebreaking efforts, the Allies anticipated German movements and counterattacks, allowing them to advance. By mid-August, Allied troops had landed in southern France in Operation Dragoon, capturing the vital port of Marseille. Not long after, the Allies liberated Paris as the Germans retreated to defensive lines nearer Germany.

TWO TALES

For eleven months, the Allies marched across Europe as American GIs bore the brunt of the fighting and dying. The Germans often possessed better tanks, artillery, and machine guns than the Allies and inflicted heavy casualties. While grousing about the challenges they faced, the Americans fought bravely and effectively. Only a small percentage of the 25 million Americans in the military during the war fought their way to Germany, and those who survived returned home with remarkable stories that inspired generations. But these stories were also marked by significant contrasts, perhaps none more so than those of Audie Murphy and Eddie Slovik. One became a famous movie star, and the other was charged with desertion and died in front of a firing squad in late January 1945. Both came from humble beginnings, but their paths parted once they entered combat.

Murphy rose from extremely modest roots in rural Texas, staying in school only through the fifth grade before starting to work to support his family. A crack shot, he often hunted to provide meals. When World War II broke out, he tried to join the marines and navy, but they rejected him because of his diminutive size and age. Ultimately, army recruiters accepted him after he falsified his birth records. Thus, in June 1942 he entered the war at age seventeen.

After basic training, he shipped out to North Africa and ultimately Sicily. He rose through the ranks to sergeant, winning a Bronze Star for his heroics at Anzio, where he knocked out a German tank with rifle grenades. During Operation Dragoon in August 1944, two Germans feigned surrender and then killed one of Murphy's friends; in response, the enraged Texan wounded several Germans, killed six, and captured nearly a dozen. He received a Distinguished Service Cross for his actions. For other heroic acts during the campaign, Murphy won a Purple Heart, a Silver Star, and other commendations. He also received a battlefield officer commission and rose to first lieutenant, all the while battling several wounds in both legs and gangrene that caused the removal of part of his hip. But he kept fighting, returning to his unit in a command position at age nineteen. On January 26, 1945, near Holtzwihr, France, a large enemy force attacked. The Germans hit a tank destroyer, setting it on fire. Holding his ground to cover his soldiers' retreat to a defensive line, Murphy called in fire. At one point, the artillery commander asked about the position of the Germans. Murphy screamed back, "Just hold the phone and I'll let you talk to one of the bastards!" Then, to stem the enemy advance, he jumped onto the burning tank destroyer, whose .50-caliber guns remained operational. Atop the turret, Murphy peppered the Germans with machine gun fire, partly aided by the smoke that shielded his position. From the treeline, his troops wondered why the tank did not explode. Murphy later admitted thinking, "How come I'm not dead?" He continued firing until he ran out of ammunition and then, having been wounded severely in the leg by shrapnel, returned to his men and organized a counterattack that pushed the Germans back. One of the soldiers noted that it was "the greatest display of guts and courage I have ever seen."

For his actions, Murphy received the Medal of Honor, and his face appeared on the cover of *Life* magazine. He wrote a best-selling book, *To Hell and Back*, and had a movie career that spanned two decades and forty films. In the movie about his exploits, one of the highest-grossing movies of 1955, he played himself. Privately, he dealt with nightmares and flashbacks, ultimately acknowledging his post-traumatic stress disorder (PTSD) in the 1960s, but his life changed dramatically as a result of his military service.

At the other end of the spectrum was Slovik. Raised in a modest Polish American home in Detroit, he got into trouble at an early age. Arrested at twelve for theft, he went in and out of jail for much of his teens and early twenties. Originally declared unfit for service, Slovik entered the military in 1944 at a time when the demand for soldiers was high. He arrived in Europe in August 1944 as a replacement in the 109th Infantry Regiment. Once there, he avoided the frontlines and requested rear echelon duty, citing his fear of dying. The captain refused, so on the way to his unit Slovik deserted, preferring prison to combat. He left behind a note admitting to his crime and promised to flee again if sent forward.

IMAGE 12.6   A Damaged German Tank After the Battle of the Bulge   Months after the conclusion of Battle of the Bulge, what is believed to be a German Panzer V "Panther" German tank lies overturned in Houffalize, Belgium. This photograph, taken in June 1945, displays the level of ruin left in the wake of Germany's last major assault.

Soon captured, Slovik was brought before a military tribunal in November. With his own admission as evidence, it took the jury only a short time to find him guilty and sentence him to death. Other deserters had also received this verdict, but none had been executed. However, Slovik's timing was horrible. In mid-December, the Germans launched a massive counteroffensive at the Battle of the Bulge. With the military facing more than 20,000 desertions by that time, manpower shortages became more acute. Commanders who could have suspended the sentence felt they needed to make an example to warn others.

On January 31, 1945, near the French village of Sainte-Marie-aux-Mines, servicemen escorted Slovik to a courtyard where twelve soldiers awaited. They tied Slovik to a stake, placed a black hood over his head, and stepped away. He remained defiant to the end, chastising the army for executing him because he had a criminal record. The soldiers then fired their M-1 rifles, killing him instantly. They buried him in a cemetery in an unmarked grave alongside others killed for murder or rape. Slovik became the only American executed for desertion during the war.

While Murphy became a hero, Slovik became a symbol of cowardice. Both arose from humble roots, as did many of the GIs crossing Europe at the time. The vast majority of these soldiers fought for survival and their buddies, drawn together as a true band of brothers and ultimately given the title of the Greatest Generation.

LIGHT AT THE END OF THE TUNNEL

The Allied rush across Europe caught the Germans in a vise that tightened every day. Overhead, the Luftwaffe had virtually disappeared by the end of 1944. While aircraft production remained high, Germany ran out of experienced aviators. Fuel increasingly became scarce, a major weakness in the German military machine. Targets also became increasingly difficult to find as the Allies focused on killing pilots, both on the ground and in the air. Still, many people died in the last six months of the war as the Germans fought tenaciously and prepared a major counterattack in late 1944. Despite warnings of German troop concentrations in the Ardennes, which they had stormed through in 1940, few Allied senior commanders were prepared for the ferocious offensive that struck on December 16, 1944. Aided by snowy weather and overcast skies that cancelled out Allied air superiority, veteran German soldiers with large numbers of tanks crashed through the U.S. lines, killing and capturing thousands and initiating the Battle of the Bulge.

Desperately, the Americans fought back as their engineers destroyed bridges and oil depots to slow the German advance. A huge salient grew as the Germans marched toward Antwerp. Hitler hoped to divide the Allied forces, compelling them to sue for peace so that he could concentrate on the advancing Soviets. He was delusional. Eisenhower and General Omar Bradley threw in their few available reserves, the battle-hardened 101st and 82nd Airborne Divisions, while Patton's army redirected its attack, moving toward U.S. forces surrounded at Bastogne, where the 101st held its position tenaciously, and then across the Ardennes. Enraged by German massacres of POWs at Malmedy, the Americans stubbornly resisted. Slowly, the German offensive ground to a halt, largely because of the tenacity of the American GIs and fuel shortages. Then the skies cleared and Allied fighters and bombers pounded the German units. Patton declared that it was "a clear cold Christmas, lovely for killing Germans."

By the second week of January, the Allies had regained most of the ground lost. In doing so, they lost more than 19,000 men killed, 47,000 wounded, and 15,000 captured. However, the Germans suffered 100,000 casualties, destroying their last reserves. Now the door was open for the drive into Germany, as the Russians began their final winter offensive in Poland. It was only a matter of time before the Germans collapsed.

THE SLAUGHTERHOUSE

Some in the British and American bomber command sought to accelerate Germany's collapse. Deploying large numbers of bombers and fighters, they intensified attacks on fuel, logistical, and communication centers, although such targets became increasingly limited as the range of destruction spread. Such assaults affected the Nazis' ability to fight. However, more Allied leaders increasingly focused on civilian populations, hoping to break the German people's will. In this effort the British took the lead, stoking controversy in the process. No one bombing mission stirred more feelings than the attack on Dresden on February 13–14, 1945. On the first night, the British dropped 650,000 incendiary bombs. Fires started throughout the city, which until that point had avoided massive destruction. People fled to bomb shelters, where they died from asphyxiation as the firestorms sucked out the air. Some headed to the Elbe River to escape the intense heat under a curtain of black rain. However, the heat simply melted their flesh. As the day unfolded, American bombers dropped tons of bombs on the railways. Blinded by the rising smoke, rescue workers and survivors were killed as the American ordnance landed on the stricken city. Ultimately, more than 25,000 civilians perished; many others suffered wounds and trauma. Some 75,000 homes were destroyed and another 18,000 badly damaged, creating more than 18 million cubic meters of rubble. Half the population fled, leaving behind a shell of the town once described as "Florence on the Elbe."

Immediately, controversy arose as the Germans reported the destruction of civilian targets at Dresden as well as Berlin and Munich. An Allied spokesman reported that the bombers had employed a "deliberate terror-bombing of German population centres as a ruthless expedient of hastening Hitler's doom." Fearing a public backlash, one officer called for the Allies to avoid "indiscriminate homicide and destruction." He argued that according to such a strategy, it logically followed that the Allied ground forces "similarly, should be directed to kill all civilians and demolish all buildings in the Reich."

Afterward, senior U.S. commanders reemphasized their commitment to precision bombing. However, no real controversy developed in the United States. Most Americans only wanted to kill the enemy to end the war as soon as possible so their sons, husbands, and fathers could return home. Many never differentiated between killing soldiers and killing civilians. Only after the war, when people appraised the success of the bombing campaign, would the moral issues become more sharply focused.

FINAL VICTORY

By the spring, the Americans and British were closing in from the west while the Soviet army approached from the east, squeezing the increasingly desperate Germans in the middle.

As the Germans retreated, they threw everyone into battle, including young men in their early teens. In the skies, their poorly trained pilots were often killed during their first missions. By early May, the Russians had surrounded Berlin, and Hitler committed suicide. Soon after, Germany surrendered.

With V-E Day—May 8, 1945—the war officially ended in Europe. Millions of American servicemen in Europe now planned to transfer to the Pacific for the invasion of Japan. For the majority, however, the war was over. Still, for many it never truly ended, as those returning home carried physical and psychological scars. New leaders emerged, including Eisenhower who rode his position into the presidency. Those who fought and died earned the designation of the Greatest Generation, something they never surrendered in the postwar era.

CONCLUSIONS

The citizen-soldier won the day during World War II as millions of young men and women flooded into the U.S. military. Driven by patriotism and the draft, many fought in campaigns in North Africa, Italy, and western Europe, helping ensure the defeat of the Axis Powers. Led by generals who adapted to the various fronts with new strategies that relied increasingly on mobility and air-ground operations, the U.S. Army and its Air Forces became an effective fighting force.

Americans at war benefited from the massive scale of production on the home front, where factories produced large quantities of rifles, tanks, artillery, ships, and planes. Allied research groups produced new technologies such as improved radar, long-range fighters able to swoop into the skies over Germany, and mobile aircraft carriers able to protect convoys. The sheer volume of production, together with the powerful Red Army, overwhelmed the Axis Powers.

But World War II in Europe also ushered in significant changes. German submarines and the introduction of long-range rockets further signaled to U.S. strategic thinkers the importance of an integrated world where national security required the extension of defensive perimeters. The conflict in Europe, in tandem with the one unfolding in the Pacific, forever transformed the U.S. military and created a new way of thinking about its role in everyday American life.

TIMELINE

September 1939–May 1945	Battle of the Atlantic
1941	Lend-Lease implemented
December 1941	Japanese attack on Pearl Harbor
November 1942	Operation TORCH in North Africa begins
February 1943	Battle of Kasserine Pass; Soviet victory at Stalingrad
July 1943	Allied invasion of Sicily
September 1943	Allied Italy campaign begins
June 1944	Operation OVERLORD launches invasion of Normandy; Allies liberate Rome
August 1944	Allies liberate Paris
December 1944	Battle of the Bulge
May 1945	Berlin falls to Red Army
May 1945	V-E Day

SUGGESTED READINGS

Atkinson, Rick. *An Army at Dawn: The War in North Africa, 1942–1943*. New York: Henry Holt, 2002.

Crane, Conrad C. *Bombs, Cities, and Civilians: American Airpower Strategy in World War II*. Lawrence: University Press of Kansas, 1993.

Holman, Lynn M., and Thomas Reilly. *Black Knights: The Story of the Tuskegee Airmen*. Gretna, LA: Pelican, 2001.

Kennett, Lee B. *G. I.: The American Soldier in World War II*. New York: Scribner's, 1987.

Meyer, Leisa D. *Creating GI Jane: Sexuality and Power in the Women's Army Corps During World War II*. New York: Columbia University Press, 1997.

Morrison, Samuel Elliot. *The Battle of the Atlantic: September 1939–May 1945*. Reprint ed. Edison, NJ: Castle Books, 2001.

Murray, Williamson, and Allan R. Millett. *A War to Be Won: Fighting in the Second World War*. Cambridge, MA: Belknap Press of Harvard University Press, 2000.

Porch, Douglas. *The Path to Victory: The Mediterranean Theater in World War II*. New York: Farrar, Straus, & Giroux, 2004.

Sparrow, Bartholomew. *From the Outside In: World War II and the American State*. Princeton, NJ: Princeton University Press, 1996.

Yenne, Bill. *Rising Sons: The Japanese American GIs Who Fought for the United States in World War II*. New York: Thomas Dunne Books, 2007.

CHAPTER 13

WAR WITHOUT MERCY: FIGHTING IN THE PACIFIC

1942–1945

The State of Unpreparedness • From Defeat to Victory: June 1942–October 1944 • The Sleeping Giant Awakened • Island Hopping • The War over Japan • The End of the Ground War • The Final Steps

On January 3, 1942, the five Sullivan brothers of Waterloo, Iowa, marched down to a naval recruiting station in Des Moines. After passing the required tests with flying colors, Albert, Francis, George, Joseph, and Madison boarded a train for the Great Lake Naval Training Station in North Chicago. When a reporter asked them why they had joined, George responded, "You see, a buddy of ours was killed in the Pearl Harbor attack, Bill Ball of Fredericksburg, Iowa." Francis added, "That's where we want to go now, to Pearl Harbor." George and Frank had previously served several years in the navy but had left in May 1941. Still, they repeated training and asked to stay with their brothers, in line with the family motto, "We Stick Together." While typically opposed to such requests, the navy relented. All five ultimately joined the crew of the cruiser *Juneau* operating near Guadalcanal in late 1942. On November 13, a Japanese submarine torpedoed the ship. As the *Juneau* retreated for repairs, it was struck by another Japanese submarine. This time, the ship sank quickly with most of the crew.

Captain Gilbert Hoover, commander of the flotilla, feared stopping because of the lurking Japanese submarine. He ordered a plane to report the sinking so commanders could dispatch rescue ships. However, the information failed to reach the right authorities for several days as the 100 survivors floated in the Pacific Ocean, enduring dehydration and shark attacks. Only a few survived until they were rescued eight days later. These survivors reported that Frank, Joe, and Matt had died instantly when the cruiser's ammunition magazine exploded. They remembered Al drowning the next day and George surviving four days, until he succumbed to delirium and simply disappeared from the raft.

Nearly two months later, the navy finally released the information of the Sullivan boys' deaths to the family. The parents had suspected something was wrong when letters stopped arriving and a neighbor received a message from a relative who wrote, "Isn't it too bad about the Sullivan boys? I heard that their ship was sunk." On January 21, three naval officers arrived at the family home at 98 Adams Street. The boys' father, Thomas Sullivan, met them as they exited their black sedan and asked them whom they had come to discuss. "I'm sorry, all five," Lieutenant Commander Truman Jones replied.

Soon other family members, including Al's wife, had gathered in the living room, where Commander Jones read, "The Navy Department regrets to inform you that your sons, Albert, Francis, George, Joseph and Madison Sullivan are missing in action in the South Pacific." While some held out hope because of the word "missing," deep down they instinctively knew the worst. Thomas Sullivan, who worked on the freight trains that transported military goods, tried to stay strong, asking his wife, Alleta, whether he should go into work. "It's all right, Tom," she told him. "It's the right thing to do. The boys would want you to. . . . There isn't anything you can do at home."

The Sullivans soon gained notoriety for their sacrifice. In September 1943, the navy commissioned the USS *Sullivans*, which was christened by the boys' grandmother. Alleta Sullivan regularly attended war bond events, and in 1944 Hollywood released a movie called *The Fighting Sullivans*. In response to this and several similar tragedies, the military created its sole survivor policy, which allowed families to request removal of their children from military service after significant losses.

The Sullivan brothers and many other soldiers and sailors fought and died in the Pacific, where the war differed in many ways from that waged in Europe. Many of the battles of the Pacific theater occurred at sea, accompanied by ferocious amphibious assaults and brutal jungle fighting. The Japanese fought to the death, inflicting heavy casualties. As both sides stereotyped the other, a war without mercy developed. U.S. bombers laid waste to the Japanese homeland, whose buildings were primarily constructed of wood and paper. By the end of the conflict, cities including Nagasaki, Tokyo, and Hiroshima lay in ruins. Millions had died, and the landscape of Asia had been changed dramatically.

THE STATE OF UNPREPAREDNESS

In 1941, in the vast Pacific region, the United States lacked both men and equipment to match the Japanese, reflecting a longer-term strategic commitment to Europe and a belief that the Germans and their allies posed a greater threat than the Asian nation, a conclusion aided by the physical expansiveness of the Pacific. Tokyo had advantages over Washington in all areas, including its massive battleships, the *Yamato* and *Masashi*, which displaced 72,800 tons and bore huge 18.1-inch guns. The Japanese also had numerous heavy cruisers, destroyers, and submarines, as well as a dozen light and heavy carriers. In contrast, the United States had only a few aircraft carriers, a host of old battleships, and fewer ships of all types. The shifting of some vessels to the North Atlantic in 1941 further weakened U.S. capabilities in the Pacific. Chief of Naval Operations Harold Stark warned that the U.S. fleet was "inferior to the Japanese fleet and cannot undertake an unlimited strategic offensive in the Western Pacific."

On land, the United States had bases in Hawaii, some troops in Guam, and other scattered outposts at places such as Wake and the Midway Islands. In the Philippines, the key U.S. asset in the region, General Douglas MacArthur had one regular U.S. army division complemented by several National Guard units and a large untrained force of Filipino militiamen. The naval force there was also fairly small, with three cruisers and thirteen destroyers. MacArthur had some aircraft, including new B-17 bombers, but the Japanese clearly outnumbered the Americans and had experienced pilots flying superior Zero fighters.

The road to war unfolded over a decade. For years, the Japanese had provoked widespread condemnation for their actions in China, where the United States supported Chiang Kai-shek and his regime. In 1940, Tokyo took control of Indochina after the French surrendered to Hitler. The Vichy government retained nominal control over the colony in return for allowing the Japanese to operate military bases there, an agreement that sparked a confrontation with Washington, which responded with an embargo on oil. The Japanese faced a dilemma: capitulate or run out of petroleum and other war materials within eighteen months. Instead,

IMAGE 13.1 Pearl Harbor Within a span of ninety minutes on the morning of December 7, 1941 Japanese military forces struck and destroyed the *U.S.S Arizona*, shown here, and went on to sink or damage twenty additional ships. The attack resulted in the loss of 2,390 American lives, and facilitated U.S. entry into the Second World War.

they chose a third option, planning an operation like one they had employed against the Russian fleet in Port Arthur in 1904, in which they had attacked three hours before declaring war. By November 1941, a similar plan to confront the United States was ready, and America's military and civilian leaders were totally unprepared for the onslaught.

THE PERFECT DISASTER

On the beautiful Sunday morning of December 7, 1941, American soldiers at Pearl Harbor, Hawaii, awoke early to enjoy paradise. The two major American commanders at the base, Admiral Husband Kimmel and General Walter Short, prepared to play golf. On the ships in the harbor, crews stirred while sentries marched leisurely around air bases. While American intelligence had predicted an impending Japanese strike, most U.S. leaders thought it would unfold in the Philippines.

At 7:55 a.m., U.S. Navy Commander Logan Ramsay saw an airplane barreling across the harbor. He planned to report the dangerous pilot until he noticed a rising sun on the plane. Running to the radio room, he sent a simple message: "Air raid, Pearl Harbor. This is not a drill." Throughout the fleet, alarms went off. On board the battleship *Arizona*, the speaker blared, "General Quarters, this is no drill!" Sailors jumped out of their bunks, grabbed their gear, and headed to their battle stations. As they emerged on deck, they saw the fearsome sight of 100 Japanese dive- and torpedo-bombers accompanied by Zero fighters. Within moments, bombs rained down on the *Arizona*. One hit its mark, penetrating the armored deck and passing into the ship's magazine. One sailor remembered a "blinding flash. It was gigantic." A Japanese pilot recalled looking down on a "hateful, mean-looking red flame" reaching into the sky. The explosion ripped apart the ship, killing most of the 1,000 sailors aboard.

For two hours, the Japanese laid waste to the U.S. ships and installations. Nonetheless, individual Americans performed heroically, including Doris Miller, an African American mess attendant on the *West Virginia*. When the attack began, Miller helped his fellow wounded crewmen and the captain to safety. Then he manned an anti-aircraft gun and began firing. For Miller's heroism, Admiral Chester Nimitz awarded him the Navy Cross, noting: "This marks the first time in this conflict that such high tribute has been made in the Pacific Fleet to a member of his race and I'm sure that the future will see others similarly honored for brave acts."

Despite such efforts, the Japanese achieved total victory, leading President Roosevelt to call it a "date which will live in infamy." They sank or severely damaged twenty-one ships, including the battleships *Arizona*, *California*, *Maryland*, *Nevada*, *Oklahoma*, *Pennsylvania*, *West Virginia*, and *Tennessee* (six ultimately returned to combat). Their pilots destroyed or severely damaged more than 320 aircraft, and 2,390 Americans died, with another 1,178 wounded. In contrast, the Japanese lost only twenty-nine planes, five midget submarines, and a total of sixty-four men. They achieved complete surprise, partly through good luck but also because of poor American intelligence and leadership. Their only regret was that three American carriers had escaped the onslaught. Admiral Isoroku Yamamoto, Japan's premier military leader, also worried that the Japanese had awoken a sleeping giant and feared that failing to achieve peace quickly would ensure Japan's demise.

THE ALLIES ON THEIR HEELS

From the beginning of the war in the Pacific, the Allies retreated as the Japanese quickly defeated the British and Dutch in Malaysia and Indonesia. The Japanese captured Guam on December 8 and set their sights on Wake Island. After bombing nearly wiped out the island's fighter protection on December 8, its American defenders prepared for Japanese invasion. On December 11, a large force of Japanese ships, including three cruisers, arrived off Wake. The Americans watched the Japanese move closer to their shore batteries, holding their fire. Then they unleashed a furious barrage, assisted by the remaining Wildcat fighters, that sank several destroyers. The Japanese beat a hasty retreat, providing the U.S. public with a little good news at a dark time.

Nearly two weeks later, on December 23, the Japanese returned to Wake with an aircraft carrier and a bigger landing force. For a day, the Americans fought valiantly, inflicting more than 1,100 casualties, sinking two destroyers and two transports, and heavily damaging a cruiser. One pilot, Captain Henry T. Elrod, won the Medal of Honor for destroying an enemy destroyer and several planes. However, the garrison was soon overwhelmed and running out of supplies, and surrendered. More than 1,500 headed into captivity, many of whom would die from starvation and disease. The Japanese held the island until 1945, when the small garrison there capitulated to the Allies.

The most serious U.S. defeat occurred in the Philippines. The conflict started badly. Despite having nine hours' advance knowledge, U.S. commanders left many B-17s and P-40 fighters on the ground at Clark Field. The enemy destroyed half of the force and killed pilots and support crew. Afterward, the Japanese controlled the skies and inflicted heavy casualties on U.S. forces and Filipino civilians. General MacArthur then exacerbated problems when he ignored prewar plans that called for a retreat to the Bataan Peninsula to fight until reinforcements arrived. Instead, he spread out his forces and failed to stockpile supplies on Bataan. The decision proved disastrous when the Japanese forced the Americans and Filipinos to the peninsula. During the engagement MacArthur stayed in the bowels of Corregidor in Manila Harbor, leaving most operations to General Jonathan Wainwright. While the press worshiped him, his own solders referred to him as "Dugout Doug" and criticized the stockpiling of food and materials at Corregidor while they suffered. The one time that MacArthur visited Bataan, he refused to meet with soldiers and avoided the frontlines.

On the peninsula, the Americans and Filipinos held various defensive lines for weeks, all the while staggering to field a force on half rations that shrank to 1,000 calories a day. Finally, on April 9, a gaunt Wainwright surrendered. The Japanese then forced the 12,000 Americans and 60,000 Filipinos on a long death march that saw thousands die from beatings, beheadings, and exhaustion.

Meanwhile, MacArthur left Corregidor on Roosevelt's orders in mid-March aboard a patrol torpedo–boat, promising, "I shall return." The defenders of Corregidor held out until May 6, when a massive Japanese assault overwhelmed them. Nonetheless, Filipino guerrillas waged a war from the mountains and jungles until 1944, when MacArthur finally returned. The United States and its allies had lost more than 25,000 killed and 100,000 captured during the campaign, a staggering defeat.

FROM DEFEAT TO VICTORY: JUNE 1942–OCTOBER 1944

In the first six months of the war, bad news plagued the United States and its allies in the Pacific. Everywhere, the Japanese marched forward, driving close to Australia and threatening Hawaii and Alaska. But the tide turned in early June 1942 at the Battle of Midway. From that point forward, the Americans never ceded the offensive, although many hard-fought battles occurred in the South Pacific in little-known places such as Guadalcanal.

THE BATTLE OF MIDWAY

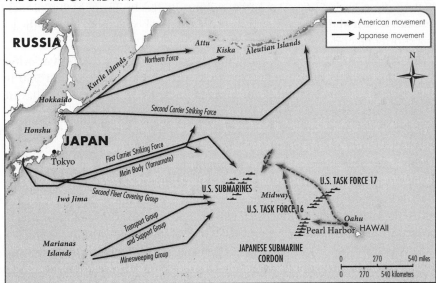

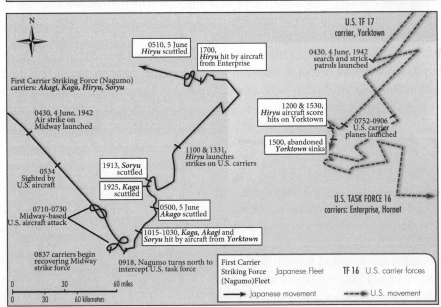

MAP 13.1   The Battle of Midway

WITH LOVE FROM SHANGRI-LA

With little good news from the Far East, Roosevelt sought a way to retaliate and raise morale among the civilian population. In late December 1941, he ordered a review of a potential bombing attack on Japan that would send a message to the Japanese people that their leaders could not protect them. However, without stable bases in China the logistics of such an effort were daunting, and no one wanted to risk an aircraft carrier by launching an attack close to the Japanese mainland. Ultimately, the navy presented a plan to launch long-range B-25 bombers off the deck of an aircraft carrier to bomb Japan and then head for unsure landings at Chinese bases. Army Air Forces volunteers led by Lieutenant Colonel Jimmy Doolittle, a famed test and racing pilot, stripped down the bombers to lighten the load and allow for a shorter takeoff.

After intensive training in South Carolina, the crews boarded the *Hornet*, which sped across the Pacific with its escorts, planning to launch the bombers within 550 miles of Japan. However, the Japanese spotted the armada on April 18, about 200 miles from the desired launch point. After conferring, Doolittle decided to launch immediately for fear of endangering the task force. Despite never having taken off on an aircraft carrier, all sixteen planes successfully got up in the air and headed toward their targets, primarily Tokyo, but also Kobe and Yokohama. The attack caught the Japanese flat-footed. All the B-25s dropped their payloads, and most hit their targets. Only one plane suffered damage from anti-aircraft fire, while American gunners shot down a Japanese fighter. After dropping their bombs, the planes headed to China, where allies promised to man homing beacons on temporary air bases where the Americans could refuel before heading to the Nationalists' capital. Miscommunication stymied the last stage of the operation, and most of the pilots ran low on fuel and simply parachuted out of their planes or crash-landed them. One headed to the Soviet Union, where he was interned. Ultimately, the Chinese rescued most of the crewmen, although the Japanese captured eight, eventually executing three for war crimes.

When Doolittle learned about the losses, he feared a court-martial. Instead, he and his crewmen became national heroes. Roosevelt taunted the Japanese with reports that the attacks had originated in the mythical city of Shangri-La. Incensed, the Japanese launched operations in China to find the air bases, diverting resources from other theaters. The attack shook the Japanese high command and accelerated its plans to attack Midway and ultimately Hawaii.

THE INVINCIBLE LAID LOW

Less than a month later, Allied forces won a strategic victory that stalled the Japanese advance toward Australia. When a Japanese invasion force left Rabaul and headed toward Port Moresby, American admiral Frank Fletcher moved in his forces to intercept. His armada included two carriers, the *Lexington* (the oldest carrier in the fleet) and the *Yorktown*. The latter's planes pounded the invasion force, bringing a large Japanese fleet to the Coral Sea. For two days, May 7 and 8, 1942, the Japanese and Americans fought, although surface ships never directly engaged each other. The Americans sank a light carrier, damaged a heavy one, and depleted the pilots of a third while losing the *Lexington*. The Japanese damaged the *Yorktown*, which limped back to Pearl Harbor for repairs. Both sides, but especially the Japanese, lost large numbers of pilots and airplanes. Finally, late on May 8, both sides disengaged and Yamamoto ordered the invasion fleet to return to base because of the lack of air cover.

In terms of losses, the Japanese had won the battle. However, it constituted a strategic and moral victory for the Americans, who had successfully repelled an invasion fleet. Equally as important, the damage the Americans inflicted on *Shokaku* and the depletion of the aircrews of the *Zuikaku* denied Admiral Yamamoto two carriers for his offensive against Midway. Thus, the Battle of the Coral Sea served as the undercard for the main battle in the mid-Pacific, as the Japanese prepared to invade Midway Island, northwest of Hawaii. Yamamoto hoped to draw the United States into a major sea battle and destroy much of its remaining fleet, especially its aircraft carriers. This would leave the Americans vulnerable in the Pacific, possibly provoking a crisis in confidence and an opening for negotiations in which the Japanese would have the upper hand.

Strategically, the Japanese wanted to catch the Americans in a trap. However, U.S. intelligence uncovered the Japanese plan to attack the Aleutian Islands as a diversion while executing the main thrust at Midway. The information was so good that a staff member skillfully predicted: "They'll come in from the northwest on a bearing 325 degree and they will be sighted at about 175 miles from Midway, and the time will be about Midway time." He missed the exact approach by only fifteen miles. On the basis of these reports, the Americans prepared further defenses at Midway, which already possessed formidable coastal defenses and more than 100 fighters and bombers. So many forces arrived on the small atoll that some defenders joked that it might sink if more landed. Nimitz supplemented those forces with two aircraft carrier task forces. One included the *Yorktown*, which after three days of massive repairs had headed back to sea, joining the *Hornet* and *Enterprise* to give Nimitz a potent force. Admiral Raymond Spruance replaced Admiral William "Bull" Halsey, who lay in a Honolulu hospital with acute dermatitis, as commander of Midway's naval forces. Spruance inherited an experienced carrier command structure and proved extremely capable.

On the Japanese side, Yamamoto personally led his forces, with Admiral Chuichi Naguno heading the carrier task force. By June 1, more than 145 Japanese ships were steaming toward Midway and the Aleutians, including the massive *Yamato* and four heavy carriers. Thousands of troops packed into transport ships, so confident of their success that they arranged to have their mail forwarded to them at the "Island of the Rising Sun," the name given to Midway.

On June 3, the American and Japanese fleets converged, although Yamamoto and Naguno lacked any knowledge about the American fleet. The first attacks began on Dutch Harbor in the Aleutians, while most of the Americans waited anxiously on the ships at Midway. One lieutenant on the *Yorktown* told his comrades: "The fate of the United States now rests in the hands of 240 pilots." The real battle began on June 4, when Naguno launched a heavy strike against Midway. The Japanese destroyed the marine command post and damaged fuel storage facilities but inflicted only a few casualties, and the airfield remained operational. They also lost thirty-eight planes, with thirty others damaged. As the strike commander left the scene, he radioed: "There is need for a second attack." By this time, torpedo bombers from Midway had attacked the main Japanese task force, although none struck their targets, and most of the bombs fell into the ocean. Additional sorties appeared likely, but Naguno lacked any intelligence about the U.S. ships. At that point, he made the decision to rearm his remaining planes for another assault on Midway. It would prove fateful.

No efforts represented the futility of the early American attacks at Midway better than those of Torpedo Squadron 8. At 3:30 a.m. on June 4, the crews had gathered in the briefing room, waiting for directions. Finally, around daybreak, their commander dismissed them for breakfast. Not long after, the loudspeaker sounded, "All pilots to ready room." There, a message waited: "Enemy units sighted. Looks like this is it." Within a short time, the crews had taken off the deck of the *Hornet* in their antiquated "Devastators." For two hours, they barreled toward the enemy fleet. A Japanese plane spotted them 100 miles out, ensuring a welcome from Zeroes. Without fighter escorts, the American pilots knew their slow-moving planes provided easy targets, but they kept going, hoping that a simultaneous assault by dive-bombers might draw away enemy fire.

Then, over the horizon, the vast Japanese armada appeared, with enemy planes being refueled and rearmed on the decks. The American squadron's leader, John C. Waldron, targeted the carrier *Soryu*. In a charge reminiscent of that of the Light Brigade during the Crimean War, Squadron 8 skimmed right above the water into Japanese fire. Large charges fired right ahead of the planes sent up walls of water to knock down the Americans. One by one, the enemy fighters and anti-aircraft brought the American planes down. Finally, only one remained: that of George "Tex" Gay, who fulfilled Waldron's final wish that "if there is only one plane left to make a final run in, I want that man to go in and get a hit." With Gay's gunner already dead, he closed to within 800 yards of the *Soryu* and released his torpedoes, barely clearing the carrier's bridge. The Zeroes then sent him tumbling into the sea, less than a half mile away. He climbed out and put a seat cushion over himself to hide from strafing pilots. He was the only survivor of Torpedo 8—and he had reserved himself a seat to fifteen minutes of the greatest show in U.S. naval history.

To that point, the Japanese had fought off eight consecutive attacks without suffering a single hit. On their decks, planes readied to take off for Midway. The battle was clearly in their favor, but that changed in an instant. The eight attacks had succeeded in myriad ways. First, evasive maneuvers had broken up the fleet's overlapping defenses, limiting anti-aircraft effectiveness. More important, the attacks had brought the covering fighters down to sea level to beat off the torpedo planes. Then, at 10:24 a.m., with the decks of the Japanese aircraft carriers littered with contact explosive bombs from the rearming and fuel lines from the refueling, two groups of American "Dauntless" dive-bombers from the *Yorktown* and *Enterprise* arrived to wreak havoc. Once above their target, they began steep dives from 10,000 feet, relatively unmolested by the Zeroes. One Japanese pilot sitting on the deck of the *Akagi* remembered, "The terrifying scream of the dive bombers reached me first, followed by the crashing of a direct hit." Soon, he recalled, "I was horrified at the destruction that had been wrought in a matter of seconds." Four bombs hit the *Kaga*, engulfing it in flames. The *Soryu* took three direct hits, sending the ship's elevator onto the deck. Planes on deck and in the hangar burned, and bombs and fuel lines exploded, contributing to the massive destruction. At the cost of forty-seven planes, the U.S. aviators sent three of Japan's most advanced carriers to the bottom of the ocean.

Nevertheless, the battle continued as the remaining carrier *Hiryu* launched its planes against the *Yorktown*. Two successive Japanese bomber attacks found their marks, forcing the *Yorktown*'s captain to abandon ship. However, the Americans evened the scored when the dive-bombers of the *Enterprise* found the *Hiryu* and set it ablaze. Just past midnight, the crew abandoned ship after removing the emperor's picture and receiving a speech from Admiral Tamon Yamaguchi, who led them in singing the "Kimigayo," the Japanese national anthem. Then Yamaguchi retired to his quarters to commit *seppuku*.

Recalling his carriers from the Aleutians and believing that the Americans only had one carrier left, Yamamoto ordered his ships to close on the enemy, but Spruance refused to take the bait. On the morning of June 5, Yamamoto ordered a retreat. When observation planes confirmed the withdrawal, Admiral Nimitz proudly sent a message, "You who have participated in the Battle of Midway today have written a glorious page in our history."

With the exception of the occupation of the Aleutians, the Japanese failed at Midway because of their arrogance and poor planning. Superior U.S. intelligence, the bravery of American pilots, and good luck ensured an American victory. The Japanese lost four carriers, a heavy cruiser, and hundreds of highly skilled pilots. Admiral Ernest King, chief of naval operations in Washington, concluded: "The Battle of Midway was the first decisive defeat suffered by the Japanese in 350 years. Furthermore, it put an end to the long period of Japanese offensive action, and restored the balance of naval power in the Pacific."

THE SLEEPING GIANT AWAKENED

Admiral Yamamoto clearly understood from his own travels in the United States that America's industrial base and ability to adapt to new technology would allow the Americans to eclipse the Japanese war effort if Tokyo failed to achieve a quick victory or negotiated

IMAGE 13.2 Battle of Midway U.S. Navy Fighter planes strike Japanese ships during the Battle of Midway. Occurring six months after the attack on Pearl Harbor, the Battle of Midway was a major success in the history of American naval warfare, and represented a turning point in the Pacific theatre of the war.

settlement. After Midway, he believed that the Japanese navy still had superiority in ships, including carriers and battleships, but he understood that chances of a quick naval victory were slim.

Yamamoto correctly appraised the situation. The gap in arms between the two sides narrowed quickly. In 1941, the Japanese built 5,088 aircraft, while U.S. factories poured out 26,277. By 1944, the discrepancy had increased to 96,318 American aircraft to 28,180 Japanese. The disparity extended to other areas as well. In 1941, the United States produced 544 military ships to 49 for the Japanese. By 1944 that number had jumped to 2,654 American ships versus 248 Japanese. That same year, the Japanese produced only 401 tanks, while U.S. factories built 17,565. After Midway, the Japanese faced a substantial uphill battle to keep pace with the Americans, particularly once it had to fight on a second front in China.

Such differences ensured that the Japanese had little chance of achieving a quick victory. With superior production, vast numbers of civilian volunteers and draftees entering the military, and a desire for vengeance, the United States never surrendered the initiative, and its forces painstakingly clawed their way across the vast expanse of the Pacific toward Japan.

THE FIRST STEP TOWARD TOKYO

Only a few months after Midway, the U.S. military took the offensive in the Solomon Islands, focusing on creating bases to move its forces across the middle of the Pacific. On August 6, a U.S. invasion force landed on Guadalcanal and Tulagi. With only nominal resistance, the

IMAGE 13.3 Guadalcanal Japanese soldiers lie dead on the shore after the Battle of the Tenaru. By the end of the Guadalcanal offensive, Japan had lost an estimated two-thirds of the 31,400 troops originally stationed on the island.

marines easily captured an unfinished air base at Guadalcanal. They then moved inland and established a defensive perimeter. On Tulagi, the 2nd Raider Battalion encountered fierce resistance from 2,000 defenders, who fought fanatically until only 23 remained. It was the Americans' first taste of a unique pattern of Japanese resistance.

The operation surprised the Japanese, but they soon recovered and sent a naval force with army reinforcements to the area. When U.S. forces were alerted to the approach of a large Japanese force, Admiral Robert Ghormley retreated without unloading most of the units' heavy equipment, including artillery, as well as munitions and foodstuffs. Unfortunately, his forces encountered those of Admiral Gunichi Mikawa near Savo Island in the darkness on August 8. The Japanese pounded the unprepared Americans and Australians. Within short order, they sank three cruisers and left another a smoking wreck. Only a small force stood between the Japanese and the transports, but Mikawa withdrew, worried about U.S. bombers catching him in the open at daybreak. He missed an opportunity to completely disrupt the operation.

With 16,000 marines in place, U.S. commander General Alexander Vandergrift set about his task of securing Guadalcanal. The marines used captured Japanese equipment to finish construction of their airfield, dubbed Henderson Field after a fallen torpedo-bomber pilot. General Millard Harmon, commander of army forces in the South Pacific, wired General Marshall in Washington that his men had "seized a strategic position" but added, "Can the marines hold it? There is considerable room for doubt!"

Soon after, the enemy tested the proposition. 1,000 battle-hardened Japanese soldiers landed with only one week's provisions and began to march across the island. Underestimating the Americans' strength, the Japanese commander planned to overwhelm the marines and capture the airfield. Alerted to their approach by a brave Solomon Island scout, Vandergrift correctly anticipated the enemy route across the Tenaru River. On the night of August 19, the Japanese repeatedly attacked marine positions, yelling "Banzai." The attack, which one officer described as a "housefly attacking a tortoise," soon became a massacre. After several hours, U.S. light tanks had obliterated the survivors. Near the end of the engagement, the Japanese commander knelt down on a beach and committed *hara-kiri*. The Americans lost 35 men, while 800 Japanese troops died, many crushed under tank treads.

For two months, Guadalcanal became the focal point of fighting in the Pacific. Both sides poured tens of thousands of troops into the area as the marines held on precariously to their beachhead and the airfield. Time after time, the Japanese launched wave attacks against marine positions such as "Bloody Ridge," but with little success. The island proved a horrible place to live, with the pestilential swamps claiming many or more lives than did bullets. Meanwhile, at sea, the two navies pounded each other to prevent resupply and draw the other into combat. Almost nightly, Japanese ships sped down the "Slot" to drop off supplies and troops and shell the Americans, avoiding the daylight, when Allied planes patrolled the region. As ships and planes piled up on the ocean floor, among them the U.S. carriers *Hornet* and *Wasp*, the area around Guadalcanal became known as Iron-Bottom Sound.

The engagement became a war of attrition, a strategy of bleeding the enemy to the point of exhaustion. Such a policy favored the Americans, whose factories completed new ships and planes faster than the Japanese. The deaths of thousands of the cream of the Imperial

Japanese Army, chewed up by U.S. machine guns, artillery, and rifles, further diminished Japan's prospects. Overhead, the Cactus Air Force at Henderson Field slowly but surely came to control the skies. When Admiral Halsey took command at Guadalcanal, he reinvigorated the U.S. forces, telling the men to "kill Japs, kill Japs and keep killing Japs."

In mid-November, the Japanese made a final desperate attempt to land a large number of troops on the island. However, they lost two battleships, a heavy cruiser, and eleven transports in the process. Soon after, the Japanese navy withdrew its support for the army on Guadalcanal. Fighting continued, but the troops slowly starved and lost combat effectiveness, leading the Japanese soldiers to characterize it as the "Island of Death." By January, the battle had ended. The Japanese had lost at least 23,000, many from disease and malnutrition. Admiral Raizo Tanaka observed, "There is no question that Japan's doom was sealed with the closing struggle for Guadalcanal. Just as it betokened the military character and strength of her opponent, so it presaged Japan's weakness and lack of planning that would spell her military defeat."

THE ISLAND HOPPING CAMPAIGN

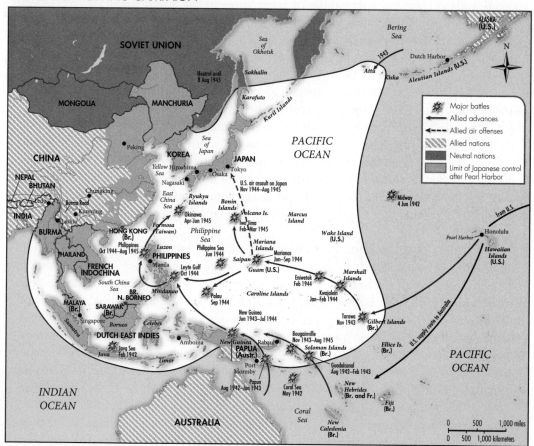

MAP 13.2   The Island Hopping Campaign

ISLAND HOPPING

With Guadalcanal conquered and Allied forces advancing in New Guinea, the U.S. command settled on a strategy of occupying islands that would bypass strongholds at Rabual and Truk to prevent a large loss of life. Forward air and submarine bases would also attack Japanese shipping and ultimately the mainland, with reclaiming the Philippines remaining an important goal. However, the Japanese ferociously defended the islands of Tarawa, Saipan, Peleliu, Einwetok, and Kwajelein, fighting to the last man behind heavy fortifications. U.S. troops suffered heavy casualties, both from enemy fire and from local maladies. Pictures of dead American bodies floating in lagoons and laying on sandy beaches reached home alongside letters and reports describing the horrible conditions and the fanaticism of the Japanese soldiers.

It was a war without mercy. At Tarawa, nearly 1,700 Americans died and 2,000 were wounded, including 600 sailors on board the sunken *Lipscombe Bay*. The Japanese lost 4,690 dead, with only 17 remaining to surrender. At Saipan, more than 3,400 Americans died and nearly 10,000 suffered wounds, while the Japanese lost nearly 29,000 soldiers, many of whom chose to commit suicide by jumping from cliffs rather than submit. Some 22,000 civilians died as well. The fighting extracted a heavy toll on survivors as well. After Tarawa,

IMAGE 13.4 Saipan American marines throw grenades towards Japanese soldiers during the 1944 Battle of Saipan. After a month of fighting, U.S. forces were able to take the island.

Marine General Holland Smith commented, "I passed boys who had lived yesterday a thousand times and looked older than their fathers. Dirty, unshaven, with gaunt, almost sightless eyes, they had survived the ordeal, but it had chilled their souls."

The land battles also largely ended the influence of the Japanese navy. During the invasion of Saipan, the Japanese made a last-ditch effort to destroy the U.S. fleet and disrupt American landings. Attempting to engage the Americans in a decisive sea battle, the aggressive Admiral Jisaburo Ozawa headed to the Philippine Sea with a force of nine carriers, including Japan's newest and most advanced vessel, the *Taiho*, six battleships, and forty-one support ships, carrying nearly 500 planes and more than 1,000 land-based aircraft. He would face U.S. Navy Task Force 58 under Admiral Spruance, which had 106 ships, including 15 carriers, 7 battleships, and numerous destroyers and cruisers. On the carriers, nearly 900 planes waited, including the new F6F Hellcats, designed specifically to outfly and outgun the Zeros. Spruance also had numerical and intelligence superiority over the approaching Japanese.

From the beginning on June 19, the Americans dominated. Ozawa, relying on faulty intelligence and poorly coordinated land-based aircraft, sent forces toward one segment of the U.S. fleet. However, U.S. radar alerted the ships well in advance, and squadrons of Hellcats ambushed the attackers, sending most plummeting into the sea. Those who survived faced a wall of anti-aircraft fire that sent many crashing into the water. In the first wave, only twenty-eight of the seventy Japanese planes survived. At the same time, the *Albacore* launched torpedoes that struck the mighty *Taiho*. As gas fumes built up in the damaged ship, it continued forward, having launched its planes. Like before, the Hellcats pounced and the anti-aircraft gunners threw up a steel curtain around the U.S. ships, sending 99 of the 130 Japanese planes into the ocean. Two more waves followed with similar results, leading the U.S. airmen to characterize the battle as "The Great Marianas Turkey Shoot." The Japanese situation went from bad to worse when the *Cavella* fired a spread of torpedoes that crippled the carrier *Shokaku*. Soon after, the fumes in the *Taiho* ignited, sending the ship below the waves with more than 1,600 crewmen. Not long after, the dive- and torpedo-bombers of Task Force 58 sent a light carrier and three tankers to the bottom and badly damaged two heavy cruisers. While Spruance failed to pursue the remainder of the Japanese fleet and completely destroy it, the damage he inflicted was significant. The remnants of Japan's once-powerful naval aviation branch were

IMAGE 13.5 U.S. Submarines A USS S-44 Submarine targets Japanese ships. Despite a slow start in the early section of the Pacific War, submarines would play a momentous role in the naval weakening and ultimate defeat of Japanese forces.

barely functional. Two more carriers had disappeared, ones not easily replaced, and the Japanese returned to Okinawa crippled. Saipan fell soon after.

DEATH FROM BELOW

The Battle of the Philippines Sea highlighted the significant contribution of the submarine force to the U.S. war effort. Throughout the war in the Pacific, submarines not only played a combat role, but also devastated Japan's merchant marine, rescued downed pilots, and dropped off coast watchers and commandos. The submarines proved extremely important in the defeat of Japan. However, during the early stages of the war, the submarine command performed poorly. Despite having all-volunteer professional crews that enjoyed elite status and relaxed discipline, many commanders wilted when confronting the enemy. As a result, the navy removed nearly 30 percent of the captains in 1942 and replaced them with younger, more aggressive officers. Furthermore, major technical problems plagued the Mark-14 torpedo, although the overall abilities of the *Tambor* class (and its successors) proved more than sufficient. Designed to explode near a ship's hull in response to changes in the earth's magnetic field, these torpedoes often failed to detonate properly because of a poor understanding of different fields in the South Pacific. The torpedoes also had faulty depth apparatuses and firing mechanisms.

In 1942 the Japanese built enough ships to replace those destroyed by submarines. But by the end of 1943, the American submarines were exacting a much heavier toll on Japanese vessels, thanks to new tactics, including wolf packs, and improved intelligence. Finally, alterations to the M-14 and the introduction of the Mark-17 torpedo gave submarine captains more lethal weapons. Increasingly, merchantmen and tankers became primary targets, which left Japan starved for resources such as petroleum, rubber, and iron. By 1944 submarines had effectively isolated Japan. That year, they sank 600 ships for a total of nearly 2.7 million tons. This removed half of Japan's merchant ships and nearly two-thirds of its oil tankers. Even as targets disappeared in 1945, the submarines continued disrupting Japanese efforts to supply their troops in far-flung places and move supplies to their homeland.

Despite the extreme hardships of living on submarines and the high death rate among crews (22 percent of those on patrol failed to return, with a loss of more than forty vessels), the submarine service made an invaluable contribution to the American war effort. As one observer noted, "The U.S. submarine offensive against Japan was one of the most decisive elements in ensuring the empire's defeat." Submarines accounted for 55 percent of Japan's naval losses (including a battleship and eight aircraft carriers), despite only constituting 2 percent of the navy's personnel. They helped weaken war production and prevented reinforcement and resupply of the outposts that the United States ultimately conquered or bypassed and let slowly starve. Never had so few made such a great contribution.

THE WAR OVER JAPAN

In the latter stages of the war, the Army Air Forces rushed to play a role in defeating Japan. Their leaders worried that the hard work of the marines and the navy would eclipse their own contributions and affect the nation's postwar military planning. Ultimately, the AAF did manage to make a significant impact in the last nine months of the war.

As early as the 1920s, proponents of airpower had speculated on what would occur in a fight between Japan and the United States. Billy Mitchell wrote in one of his last public speeches that the Japanese considered the United States "a decadent military . . . as easy to attack as a large jellyfish." Yet he also presciently underscored Japan's vulnerabilities. "These towns are built largely of wood and paper to resist the devastations of earthquakes and form the greatest aerial targets the world has ever seen," he noted. "Incendiary projectiles would burn the cities to the ground in short order."

By the mid-1930s, the command and general staffs had developed plans for a potential conflict in Japan that focused on the use of technology to reduce casualties for Americans and ensure victory. In a study called "The Psychology of the Japanese Soldier," planners argued that "meeting Japan's bayonets with bayonets is playing into her hand" and pushed airpower, especially strategic bombing. Mechanical superiority would save lives as well as unleash "the tremendous striking power of an air force directed at the paper cities of congested Japan." The report emphasized that against U.S. bombers, "samurai swords will be found rusty and their rice mustardized."

However, when the war began, land-based planes played a very small role. They provided air support against the Japanese in New Guinea and Guadalcanal, but naval aviators inflicted the lion's share of damage. During the island-hopping campaigns, long-range bombers and fighters had some successes, but most people focused on the ground troops and the navy pilots in the skies. However, as U.S. forces neared the Japanese mainland, new technology in the form of the massive B-29 Superfortress changed the potential of the Army Air Forces. A marvel of engineering, the plane had pressurized cabins, heavy armaments, and an ability to fly at very high altitudes for long distances. Yet it also offered many challenges. In a rush to get the B-29 in the air, engineers often failed to overcome known problems. In the engines, fires started without warning, and electrical systems often shorted out, leading one commander to stress that the B-29 "had as many bugs as the entomological department of the Smithsonian." The rash of accidents that occurred during testing made pilots skeptical. It got so bad that project director Lieutenant Colonel Paul Tibbets trained two of the prettiest WASPs (Women Airforce Service Pilots) to fly the Superfortress to shame "all those college athletes" who refused to fly it. Furthermore, until the capture of Saipan and Guam, few bases existed that could accommodate the new plane. The army experimented with bases in China, but they were hard to supply, and the Chinese often could not provide adequate security. Ultimately, AAF leaders focused on the island bases.

Until mid-1944, the B-29 had limited value, as the AAF relied more on B-17s and B-24s to support ground offensives. It was not until November 24, 1944, that B-29s finally attacked Tokyo. On that day, 110 Superfortresses took off, led by the *Dauntless Dotty*, piloted by General Rosie O'Donnell and his co-pilot, Major Robert Morgan of *Memphis Belle* fame. The attackers endured heavy flak, but most reached their target, the Musashino aircraft factory. However, very few hit it, and mechanical problems caused seventeen planes to turn home before arriving at their destination.

The Japanese desperately fought these massive bombers, but they lacked effective weapons or experienced pilots and so resorted to removing armor plating and weapons from existing planes and trying to ram the B-29s. In one case, the Japanese struck at the B-29 base on Saipan. One pilot strafed the airfield, landed his plane, pulled out his revolver, and waged a gun battle with the ground crew until he was shot dead. Bomber commander General Haywood Hansell survived the insanity by hiding under a jeep during the surprise raid.

For months, the bomber command faltered, until the arrival of General Curtis LeMay, the pugnacious, hard-driving veteran of the war in Europe christened by some pilots "Iron Ass." Before arriving, LeMay received a note from General "Hap" Arnold: "The B-29 project is important to me, because I am convinced that it is vital to the future of the Army Air Forces." The bombing in Europe had raised the AAF's stature, but in the Pacific, the force had proved less significant than the navy, marines, and army ground forces. The fledgling service needed to prove its worth.

LeMay pushed his pilots while changing tactics. With high-altitude runs and the dispersion of Japanese factories producing negligible results, he settled on attacking civilian centers. The weapon of choice became the M-69 incendiary bomb, a small napalm weapon that was dropped in clusters of thousands at a time. The primarily wooden Japanese cities provided rich targets for this approach, described by LeMay as "bomb and burn 'em till they quit." Ironically, Admiral Yamamoto had predicted years before Pearl Harbor that in a conflict between Japan and the United States, "Tokyo will probably be burnt to the ground."

IMAGE 13.6 **Fire-bombing of Japan** Osaka, Japan, after a string of fire-bombing attacks by the Allied forces. Massive loss of civilian life as a result of the Allies' extensive air raid campaign and use of nuclear weapons would prompt later debates of the ethical impacts of such weapons.

The first grand experiment of the new tactics began on a large scale on March 9, 1945. In Operation Meetinghouse, LeMay sent 235 B-29s, each carrying between 10,000 and 14,000 pounds of incendiaries, against Tokyo. As his pilots prepared to leave, he told them: "You're going to deliver the biggest firecracker the Japanese have ever seen." A perfect storm of factors soon ensured U.S. success. As Pathfinders laid down the first bombs from low altitudes to increase accuracy, a powerful wind blew, spreading flames with alarming speed. Just after midnight, the main contingent of bombers arrived. Some of the late-arriving planes had their bellies caked in the soot of the massive wall of flame reaching skyward. The fires raged for hours, killing nearly 90,000 people, most from asphyxiation as temperatures reached 1,800 degrees Fahrenheit. The fires destroyed six square miles of the city, leaving a barren landscape in their wake. In the end, the Americans lost only twelve planes, with another forty damaged by flak. Afterwards, Arnold wrote LeMay: "I want you and your people to understand fully my admiration for your fine work. . . . Your recent incendiary missions were brilliantly planned and executed."

With this new strategy, the B-29s went on to attack the largest Japanese cities, including Osaka, Kobe, and Nagoya. Besides continuing firebombing operations until war's end, the B-29s also attacked airfields in preparation for the invasion of Okinawa and sowed mines in inland waters. While LeMay and some colleagues worried about an outcry over such methods, none developed until after the war. In this conflict of extreme brutality, few Americans cared what happened as long as it ended the war sooner.

THE END OF THE GROUND WAR

By late 1944, the Japanese had retreated everywhere except in China, where Nationalist leader Chiang Kai-shek appeared more concerned with fighting the Chinese Communists than combating the Japanese. He clashed often with U.S. general Joe Stillwell, who declared, "The crazy little bastard would sabotage the whole damn project—men, money, material, time and sweat we have put into it for two and half years." Stillwell and others devoted prodigious amounts of time and energy to supplying and training the Nationalists, with Allied pilots flying their cargo planes over "the Hump" of the Himalayas because the Japanese had severed all ground transportation.

Despite the poor combat performance of the Nationalists (as opposed to the Communists, who elicited support among some Americans for their aggressiveness and bravery), the Japanese devoted significant resources to China. They also stationed large numbers of troops near the Manchurian border in 1945, fearful of a Soviet attack. This concentration prevented them from reinforcing their garrisons in the Pacific.

The ground war in Burma also involved Americans, although the British primarily shouldered the burden of reconquering their former colony and protecting their prize possession of India. Those Americans who did fight received recognition for their efforts, particularly the members of "Merrill's Marauders" (the 5307th Composite Unit, a provisional unit commanded by General Frank Merrill), who often worked behind enemy lines to interdict supplies and disrupt enemy operations. Usually armed with only automatic weapons and sixty-millimeter mortars, the unit won fame for fighting against overwhelming odds and winning victories.

While fighting on the periphery consumed a good deal of attention, the main focus of U.S. forces in 1944 was recapturing the Philippines, where nearly 250,000 Japanese troops waited. By late October, U.S. forces had massed off Leyte. After a massive bombardment, the Americans waded ashore unopposed. Immediately, MacArthur and President Sergio Osmeña, accompanied by a gaggle of reporters and dignitaries, followed. Once on the beach, MacArthur approached a microphone already set up by the Signal Corps and proudly announced: "People of the Philippines, I have returned! . . . Rally to me! Let the indomitable spirit of Bataan and Corregidor lead on. . . . The guidance of divine God points the way. Follow in His Name to the Holy Grail of righteous victory."

Little did MacArthur know that a near catastrophe lay on the horizon. In a last-ditch effort to destroy the invaders, the Japanese navy had planned a diversion of several lightly manned carriers to draw away the main American forces and allow heavy battleships, including the *Yamato*, to sail into Leyte Gulf and destroy the Americans. This maneuver would initiate a four-day battle, the largest in modern naval history.

The Japanese plan got off to a rocky start when U.S. pilots inflicted heavy damage on Japan's forces in the Sibuyan Sea. Perhaps most significantly, they hit the 72,800-ton *Musashi* with seventeen bombs and nineteen torpedoes, eventually sending the huge ship to the bottom. Not long after, in night action in Surigao Strait, U.S. battleships and patrol-torpedo boats caused further harm to the Japanese fleet. However, when the Japanese embarked on their diversion, Admiral Halsey took the bait and chased the nearly empty carriers, leaving the landing force protected primarily by a small group of destroyers and escort carriers designated "Taffy 3." The latter were lightly armed and carried only twenty planes each, designed more for antisubmarine actions than combating huge capital ships. Yet Taffy 3 fought heroically, causing the Japanese to think that they had encountered heavy carriers. Destroyers created smoke screens and raced forth to fire torpedoes. The 200 aircraft attacked without ceasing, running out of bombs but returning on dry runs to force the fleet to dodge them. The large guns of the *Yamato* hit and sank the escort carrier *Gambier Bay*, but U.S. planes significantly damaged the attacking battleships and forced their retreat.

The Battle of Leyte Gulf was also notable for the Japanese introduction of a frightening new weapon: the kamikazes, volunteers who sacrificed their lives to crash their bomb-laden planes into U.S. ships. Attacking in large groups, the kamikazes often overwhelmed defenses. Launching from bases on Luzon, they sortied against the U.S. fleet on October 24. Early on, a Zero crashed into the light carrier *Princeton*. It scored a direct hit on the flight deck, setting off fires that ultimately hit the ammunition magazine and sank the ship—the first of many lost to the kamikazes. But despite this new weapon and near victory, the Battle of Leyte Gulf broke the back of the Japanese navy. It lost four carriers, three battleships, six cruisers, twelve destroyers, and hundreds of planes. In turn, the U.S. Navy lost a light aircraft carrier, an escort carrier, three destroyers, and 200 aircraft. No longer would the Japanese navy pose a real threat to U.S. forces.

The invasion of Leyte ended in December after U.S. troops destroyed the Japanese ground forces of nearly 70,000 at a loss of 3,500 killed and nearly 12,000 wounded. Then, in January, the Americans stormed ashore at Luzon. There, they faced a large enemy force led by the infamous General Tomoyuki Yamashita, who had defeated U.S. forces in 1942. In preparation for the American attack, he had placed his troops throughout the island to guard prominent airfields and defensive fortifications, including Corregidor. The fighting proved to be fierce, with the worst occurring around Manila. By early February, American forces and Filipino guerrillas were on the outskirts of the capital. Yamashita ordered his troops to make Manila an open city, but Admiral Sanji Iwabachi instead gathered nearly 20,000 men and ordered them to fight to the death. A slaughter followed as the Japanese fanatically resisted the invaders, helping to destroy the city once characterized as the "Pearl of the Orient." To try to prevent casualties, MacArthur provided little air support for the often house-to-house fighting. Even so, more than 100,000 Filipinos died in the crossfire, and it took weeks to clear the Japanese from the city.

In the Philippines, many units distinguished themselves, including the 158th Infantry Regiment, known as the "Bushmasters." Originally an Arizona National Guard unit, its members included many tough, hard-nosed young Mexican Americans and Native Americans from the mining communities and small towns that dotted the state. They had trained in Panama before deploying to the Pacific. During operations in New Guinea, they had established their reputation as tireless fighters, skilled in jungle warfare. Their insignia was a pit viper wrapped around a machete, one of their favorite weapons. As one journalist covering the unit emphasized, "The Bushmaster bows to no man in the art of hand-to-hand fighting and any unwary Jap who crosses his path would probably never know what hit him." In the campaign in the Philippines, they proved themselves again. Although they suffered heavy casualties in assaults on Japanese forces during the invasion of Luzon, they won acclaim for capturing a fourteen-inch coastal gun that had been firing on American ships and ground troops, receiving a Presidential Unit Citation. Such actions led General MacArthur to conclude: "No greater fighting combat team has ever deployed for battle."

THE FINAL STEPS

The final push toward Japan began when the marines stormed ashore at Iwo Jima in February 1945. After a month of heavy fighting, nearly 7,000 marines perished and 18,000 were wounded on the black sand beaches and in the heavily fortified hills of the small island. Almost the entire Japanese force on the island, more than 20,000, died. The iconic images of U.S. Marines raising the American flag over Mount Siribachi became a fundamental part of American military lore. Once in the hands of the United States, the two airfields on the island provided new bases for fighters to escort B-29s and emergency landing strips for the Superfortresses. Indeed, even before the island was fully secured, B-29s returning from Japan had made emergency landings on Iwo Jima.

Not long after, on April 1, 1945, Easter Sunday, a massive armada of 1,200 American ships anchored off the shores of the large island of Okinawa, only 350 miles southwest of Japan. On the island, 80,000 Japanese soldiers waited for the attack by the more than 180,000 Americans of General Simon Bolivar Buckner, Jr.'s Tenth Army. It had been somewhat controversial to give command of this operation to an army general when marines had done so much of the heavy lifting in the Pacific. Regardless, Buckner and his troops faced a daunting task. Lieutenant General Mitsura Ushijima had created a series of defensive lines across the sixty-mile-long island, many of which traversed caves and other natural obstacles. After a massive initial bombardment, the Americans landed unopposed and moved inland. At one point, an excited commander radioed Pearl Harbor: "I may be crazy but it looks like the Japanese have quit the war, at least in this sector." Immediately, someone on Admiral Nimitz's staff responded, "Delete all after 'crazy.'"

Pearl Harbor was correct. Within a few days, the U.S. troops hit Ushijima's first defensive line, and the offensive ground to a halt in the heavy mud and difficult terrain. The Japanese fought ferociously, contesting every yard and grinding up U.S. forces. Intermittently, they launched counteroffensives aided by superior artillery and air and naval support. The slow war of attrition wore down the attacking Americans. Fighting offshore proved just as fierce, as waves of Japanese kamikazes and supporting bombers and fighters launched attacks from Formosa and southern Japan. The destroyers bore the brunt of the attacks, as they acted as warning pickets for the main forces. In mid-April, the *Laffey* endured more than twenty individual attacks, with six suicide planes hitting the ship. The crew fought the resultant fires by flooding compartments, never leaving the battle until forced to retreat for repairs. *Laffey* survived, although twelve other destroyers went to the bottom during the battle. The kamikazes also severely damaged a number of ships, including Admiral Spruance's flagship, the *New Mexico*. Furthermore, the fatigue of waiting for attacks exacted a heavy toll on soldiers. One journalist observed, "The strain of waiting, the anticipated terror, made vivid by past experience, sent some men into hysteria, insanity, breakdown." Such feelings sometimes led to comic relief: after one hard-fought battle, sailors on one destroyer on the picket line "set up a huge arrow-shaped sign pointing rearward and reading, 'Carriers this way.'"

It took U.S. forces nearly three months to finally secure Okinawa. The price of the victory was high. Nearly 7,000 died on land, and a staggering 32,000 were wounded. The dead included the commander General Buckner, who was lost to enemy artillery during the final days of fighting. Buckner, like MacArthur the son of a Civil War veteran, became the highest-ranking American officer lost to enemy fire during the war. But to many, the greatest loss was the famed war correspondent Ernie Pyle. Known as the "infantry's journalist" for his folksy tales of those serving on the frontlines, Pyle had endeared himself to GIs throughout the world. Upon his death, President Truman wrote: "No man in this war has so well told the story of the American fighting man as American fighting men wanted it told. He deserves the gratitude of all his countrymen."

The horrifying losses also included 70,000 Japanese and at least 80,000 Okinawans caught in the crossfire. Such costs convinced American planners that the United States and its Allies would incur huge casualties during the anticipated invasion of Japan, perhaps a million men. By the end of June, the plans for the invasion of the main island were gearing up as troops from Europe began being funneled to the Pacific. Meanwhile, the massive air assault and blockade continued.

ISSUES IN MILITARY HISTORY

THE DROPPING OF THE ATOMIC BOMB

Few issues in military history have been more contentious than the decision by President Harry Truman to drop two atomic bombs on Hiroshima and Nagasaki at the end of World War II. At the time, few questioned the decision to lay waste to the Japanese, believing that it was these attacks that had forced them to surrender, thus saving American lives. However, a small minority raised warning flags, arguing that the bombings had ushered in a new chapter of savagery in war and had not been necessary, as Japan had been ready to surrender.

For the most part, from the early Cold War through the early 1960s, the majority of people writing about the use of atomic weapons followed the standard narrative given by President Truman that he had bombed Hiroshima and Nagasaki to shorten the war and prevent further casualties. Some pointed to the ferocious resistance on Okinawa and the refusal of the Japanese government to surrender for a week after the dropping of the second bomb to justify the decision. But by the early 1960s, a small but influential group of antinuclear and New Left activists and scholars had begun to question the basic assumptions of Truman's justification. The publication of the controversial *Atomic Diplomacy* (1963) by Gar Alperovitz opened new debates. Using declassified documents and memoirs of the participants, Alperovitz questioned those who said that Truman's decision had been rooted in his desire to end the war. Instead, he argued that Truman had wanted to intimidate the Soviet Union in the opening salvo of the Cold War, hoping to stymie Soviet expansionism throughout Europe and Asia.

Since the 1960s, the issue has remained a contentious one. Antiwar groups, including those in Japan, have focused on the U.S. dropping of the bombs, and the creation of memorials to those killed in the attacks have given rise to regular debates over the decision. One of the most contentious occurred around the exhibition of the *Enola Gay* at the Smithsonian on the fiftieth anniversary of the bombings in 1995. The exhibit focused on the plane and the bomb but failed to contextualize the events at Hiroshima and Nagasaki, including their long-term effects on the world. Today, the struggle to define these actions through the lens of war, especially one often characterized in the United States as the "Good War," shows the importance of the struggle to write and preserve the history of events related to the use of military force, especially such revolutionary and ferocious ones.

"I AM BECOME DEATH"

While the Allies prepared for an invasion of Japan, a new devastating weapon entered the U.S. arsenal. For years, the government had funded top-secret experiments at various sites across the country to build an atomic bomb. Headed by General Leslie Groves, the "Manhattan Project" cost nearly $2 billion. By the summer of 1945, successful testing in the New Mexico desert had showed the weapon's awesome power. Afterward, leading scientist Robert Oppenheimer quoted Hindi scripture, "I am become death, the destroyer of worlds."

With the Japanese showing no indication of surrendering, even as the Soviets planned an attack, the Truman administration made the decision to deploy atomic bombs. The prediction that a million Americans would be killed or wounded if forced to invade Japan clearly played a significant role in the decision. Few protested the enormous implications of the act; some U.S. policymakers even argued that the bombing would serve as a warning

IMAGE 13.7   Atomic Bomb   Atomic bomb mushroom cloud over Nagasaki, Japan. The closing of World War Two saw nuclear bombs used for the first time in history. First, with the dropping of the bomb named "Little Boy" over Hiroshima, then "Fat Boy" over Nagasaki.

to future enemies, including wartime allies the Soviets. Thus, the War Department ferried the weapon to Saipan and dispatched specially trained crews led by Colonel Paul Tibbets to make practice runs over Japanese cities during which they dropped simulated atomic weapons.

On August 6, the *Enola Gay*, piloted by Tibbets, headed toward Hiroshima. On board was the weapon nicknamed "Little Boy," which one crewman described as "an elongated trash can with fins." After several hours of flying, the *Enola Gay* arrived over the target. People below barely noticed the small group of B-29s. At 8:15 a.m., bombardier Major Thomas Ferebee released the bomb while Tibbets immediately banked hard to escape the blast. "Little Boy" fell from 31,000 feet to 1,900 feet, where it exploded just above Shima Hospital. A huge mushroom cloud rose as the weapon generated the force of 12,500 tons of dynamite, sending ground-zero temperatures soaring to 5,400 degrees Fahrenheit. Some people were simply vaporized, while others had their skin completely removed or scorched black. Tibbets reported that the scene looked like a pot of water, "black and boiling underneath with a steam haze on top of it." Radiation, which would have ruinous effects over time, quickly spread. An estimated 80,000 people died; less than 7 percent of the city's buildings remained standing.

Upon learning of the results, President Truman proudly exclaimed, "This is the greatest thing in history." Others expressed similar feelings as scientists at Los Alamos called Santa Fe restaurants to schedule celebration dinners. Soldiers throughout the Pacific and those being transferred from Europe wholeheartedly supported the president's decision, which they believed would end the war and allow them to return home. But not everyone saw the bombing as a positive. Journalist Hanson Baldwin emphasized: "Yesterday, we clinched victory in the Pacific, but we sowed the whirlwind." A letter writer to the *New York Times* characterized Hiroshima as "a stain on our national life. When the exhilaration of this wonderful discovery has passed, we will think with shame on the first use."

But Japan still refused to capitulate, so on August 9, another B-29 named *Bock's Car*, piloted by Major Charles Sweeney, headed toward Kokura, but weather and the ash from an earlier firebombing obscured the target, so it diverted to Nagasaki. *Bock's Car* carried the "Fat Boy" bomb, which it released on the unsuspecting city just after 11 a.m. The bomb incinerated the city, killing as many as 50,000 people, including eight American POWs. While not as deadly as the Hiroshima bomb, partly because hills shielded sections of the city, it exacted a heavy toll. The two blasts, when combined with the Soviet invasion of Manchuria, finally compelled Emperor Hirohito to surrender.

The formal ceremony ending the war occurred on September 2, 1945, when Japanese representatives signed a declaration of surrender on the decks of the USS *Missouri* in Tokyo Harbor. By that point, more than 2 million Japanese had died, with many more wounded. The United States had lost more than 100,000 men in the Pacific, and three times as many had been wounded. China had suffered the most, losing as many as 5 million (the exact number is unknown). The war had devastated all the opponents and significantly changed the region.

CONCLUSIONS

Savagery characterized the war in the Pacific, and while U.S. casualties in the region were less than those in Europe, the conflict against Japan fundamentally shaped the consciousness of many Americans regarding the conflict. Japan's defeat also altered geopolitics in the region and set the stage for future wars, including those in Korea and Vietnam.

The war also demonstrated the importance of technology and the ability to adapt to different geographies. The U.S. Navy in particular changed quickly as new and plentiful weapons shifted the tide against the Japanese, who in 1941 had had the most powerful navy in the Pacific. Former civilians jumped into cockpits, went deep into the bellies of ships, and waded ashore to fight in the vicious campaigns of the South Pacific, ultimately wearing down the Japanese. In the skies massive bombers and advanced fighter planes worked together with submarines and surface ships to starve Japan and its troops. Ultimately, the most terrifying technology to arise was the atomic bomb, which was dropped on Hiroshima and Nagasaki, sparking a new era in warfare that created an even more dangerous world than had existed before 1941.

While civilian leaders during World War II made a strategic choice to focus on Europe first, American anger toward Japan never dissipated, as the public sought revenge for the treachery at Pearl Harbor. This hatred contributed to military decisions such as the dropping of the atomic bombs and demands for unconditional surrender. In the end, the United States established a preeminence that had previously belonged to the Japanese and the British. The conflict laid the groundwork for a new U.S. role in the region after 1945.

TIMELINE

December 1941	Japanese attack on Pearl Harbor
March 1942	MacArthur ordered to leave Philippines
April 1942	Doolittle's raid on Japan
May 1942	U.S. and Filipino troops surrender to Japanese forces; Battle of Coral Sea
June 1942	Battle of Midway
August 1942	Battle of Guadalcanal
November 1943	Battle of Tarawa
October 1944	MacArthur's return to Philippines; Battle of Leyte Gulf
February–March 1945	Battle of Iwo Jima
April–June 1945	Battle of Okinawa
August 1945	Nuclear bomb attacks on Hiroshima and Nagasaki; Japanese surrender
September 1945	Formal Japanese surrender aboard USS *Missouri*

SUGGESTED READINGS

Costello, John. *The Pacific War, 1941–1945.* New York: Harper Perennial, 2009.

Dower, John. *War Without Mercy: Race and Power in the Pacific War.* New York: Pantheon Books, 1987.

Hastings, Max. *Retribution: The Battle for Japan, 1944–45.* New York: Alfred A. Knopf, 2009.

Hopkins, William B. *The Pacific War: The Strategy, Politics, and Players that Won the War.* Minneapolis: Zenith Press, 2010.

Norman, Michael, and Elizabeth Norman. *Tears in the Darkness: The Story of the Bataan Death March and Its Aftermath.* New York: Farrar, Straus, Giroux, 2009.

O'Neill, Robert. *The Pacific War: From Pearl Harbor to Okinawa.* Oxford, UK: Osprey, 2015.

Spector, Ronald H. *Eagle Against the Sun: The American War with Japan.* New York: Free Press, 1985.

Tillman, Barrett. *Whirlwind: The Air War Against Japan, 1942–1945.* New York: Simon and Schuster, 2010.

Toll, Ian W. *The Conquering Tide: War in the Pacific Islands, 1942–1944.* New York: W. W. Norton, 2015.

Urwin, Gregory J. W. *Facing Fearful Odds: The Siege of Wake Island.* Lincoln: University of Nebraska Press, 2002.

CHAPTER 14

DIFFERENT KIND OF WAR: THE EARLY COLD WAR AND THE FORGOTTEN WAR

1945–1951

From World War to Cold War • *Toward a National Security State* • *A Brave New World*
• *The Forgotten War: The Bloody War in Korea* • *Snatching Defeat from the Jaws of
Victory: November 1950–March 1951* • *The Air War*

The thought of war crossed the minds of few American soldiers stationed around the world in the late 1940s. Most performed relatively cushy garrison duties with limited training, easy access to creature comforts, and travel to exotic locations. These included postwar Japan, where the compliant Japanese had accepted the rule of General Douglas MacArthur, who proved a benevolent dictator as he rebuilt the nation as a bulwark against communism. However, in late June 1950, soldiers enjoying these comfortable positions received a rude awakening when North Korean dictator Kim Il-Sung invaded his southern neighbor. Suddenly, the United States found itself rushing to assist Syngman Rhee's South Korean government, whose forces had collapsed. Soon, Americans were fighting under the flag of the United Nations.

Immediately, a mobilization began in Japan, the closest source of U.S. forces. Members of the 21st Regiment of the 24th Infantry Division boarded transport planes and flew to Pusan, South Korea. Amid cheers and unfurled banners, they boarded trains for a trip north, during which they were ravaged by mosquitoes, heat, and the foul stench of rice paddies fertilized by human and animal feces. Some expected the mere appearance of U.S. troops to dissuade the enemy, but this proved a false hope.

By June 5, the 400 dazed men, codenamed "Task Force Smith," after their commander, Lieutenant Colonel Brad Smith, had arrived at the front. Someone described them as "Leonidas and the Spartans in olive drab." There, they dug foxholes on the hills overlooking a main road near

Osan and waited. One commander noted that these raw recruits, most under twenty and few with combat experience, "looked like a bunch of Boy Scouts." They lacked mines, barbed wire, and other defensive weapons, as well as any real intelligence on the enemy. At dawn on this rainy day, the cold and tired young men peered out onto the valley. Around 7 a.m., someone spotted Russian-supplied T-34 tanks advancing. An officer called in artillery, but the gunners lacked armor-piercing rounds. "Jesus Christ, they're still coming!" one soldier exclaimed. Lieutenant Ollie Connor moved forward with a hand-held bazooka and fired twenty-two rounds, often from less than fifteen yards away. The antiquated ordnance mostly bounced off the armor of the North Korean tanks, thirty of which passed through the American lines.

A few hours later, three more tanks appeared, accompanied by infantry in mustard-colored uniforms. Mortar fire temporarily stopped the advance, but the tanks pressed forward, and the infantry swarmed the American lines. Cut phone lines and inoperable radios prevented Smith from calling in artillery, and soon the enemy started gunning down his command. Facing encirclement, the colonel ordered a retreat. Soon the U.S. troops were racing down the slopes and into rice paddies and along narrow farm paths, hoping to escape. They left the dead and the severely wounded behind, leaving only an unnamed medic to care for them, and desperately discarded weapons, clothing, and anything else that might lighten their load. Some units fared better than others, relying on ingenuity and good luck. Others simply surrendered, never to be seen again.

Within five days, the survivors had found each other and the battalion regrouped, although only 185 of the original 403 remained. Others eventually rejoined the unit, but nearly 200 never returned. It was a horrible disaster. The unprepared and woefully equipped Task Force Smith had performed poorly against a peasant army, albeit one that was relatively well supplied and experienced. This episode became characteristic of the fighting performance of the U.S. Army in the early stages of the war.

FROM WORLD WAR TO COLD WAR

From the end of World War II until the beginning of the Korean War, the United States demobilized. However, unlike its course after World War I or other conflicts, it maintained war footing in preparation for a perceived inevitable conflict with the Soviet Union and its communist allies. Almost immediately, the United States assumed responsibility for military defenses on a global level as the Cold War began and heated up through 1950. For the first time in its history, the United States maintained a large standing military and expanded its national security state in a time of peace, a dramatic departure from precedent ushered in by new technologies and a shrinking world.

THE NEW WAR

As the war ended in Europe, U.S. suspicions of the Soviet Union reemerged as Stalin imposed communist regimes on the nations of Eastern Europe and the Balkans. Some Americans immediately called for demonstrations of strength against the Soviets to stop the aggression. Just after Germany surrendered, General George Patton, who often referred to the Soviets as

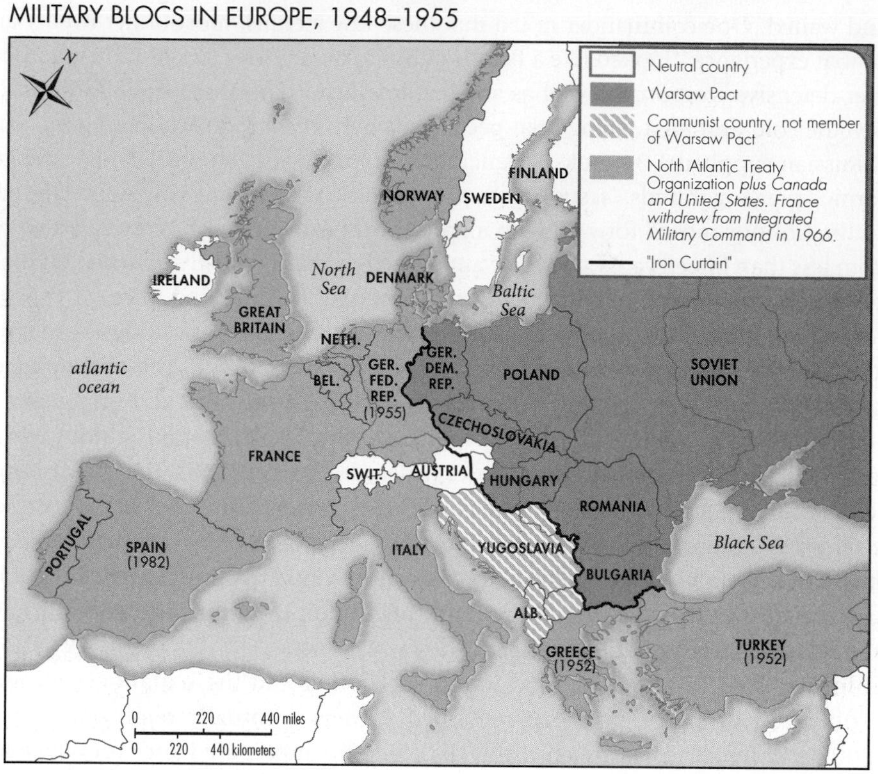

MILITARY BLOCS IN EUROPE, 1948–1955

MAP 14.1 **Military Blocs in Europe, 1948–1955**

"Mongols," boldly told a War Department official, "Let's keep our boots polished, bayonets sharpened, and present a picture of force and strength to the Red Army. This is the only language they understand and respect." Many others shared his viewpoint, including new president Harry Truman, whose black-and-white view of the world clashed significantly with Roosevelt's more nuanced vision. Hardliners came to dominate the military and the State Department as General George Marshall stressed, "We are now concerned with the peace of the entire world."

These concepts corresponded with the rise of those pushing a new American age among civilian leaders in the government and media. In 1941, prominent publisher Henry Luce stated: "It is in this spirit that all of us are called, each to his own measure of capacity, and each in the widest horizon of his vision, to create the first great American Century." Such ideals blended well with those of Archibald MacLeish, who emphasized in 1945, "We have . . . the abundant means to bring our boldest dreams to pass—to create for ourselves whatever world we have the courage to desire." Thus, in 1945 and 1946, military debates centered less on quick demobilization and a return to isolation, and more on global issues and America's role in them. The postwar competition with the Soviet Union clearly set the United States on a different path than it had taken after previous wars, especially World War I.

PREPARING FOR THE PEACE

While some Americans focused on future conflicts with the Soviet Union, many preferred to concentrate on a return to normalcy after years of economic depression and war. With millions in the armed services, many others employed in the defense industries, hundreds of thousands dead, and millions wounded, the country faced significant obstacles in preventing a recurrence of the major dislocations that had caused economic problems after World War I.

One of the first challenges was how to handle the mass demobilization of the more than 20 million military personnel who were serving in the armed forces at the end of the war. In early 1944, the Roosevelt administration worked in tandem with Harry W. Colmery, the former head of the American Legion, and congressional leaders, including Democratic senator Ernest McFarland of Arizona and Republican representative Edith Nourse Rogers of Massachusetts, to push through the G.I. Bill (formally called the Servicemen's Readjustment Act). While the government had paid pensions and bonuses for military service as well as for medical care after World War I, the G.I. Bill went much further. It provided unemployment insurance to returning veterans, gave them low-interest loans to buy homes and start businesses, and paid stipends for tuition and living costs for servicemen attending college. In this way leaders sought to distribute veterans throughout the economy and prevent the same high unemployment experienced after World War I. They proved largely successful, although minorities rarely received equal benefits, especially in the South and Southwest. The G.I. Bill fostered 14 Nobel Prize winners, dozens of senators and Pulitzer Prize winners, 450,000 engineers, 67,000 doctors, and hundreds of thousands of teachers, scientists, accountants, businessmen, and nurses. It also helped create a significant middle class in postwar America that affected the growth of the economy and influenced culture well into the 1980s.

Beyond the G.I. Bill, American taxpayers paid a significant price for helping those who had been wounded and disabled in the war. The Veterans Administration (VA) faced a huge burden in dealing with the hundreds of thousands of men who had been horribly wounded, both physically and mentally. Hospitals for veterans sprang up across the country to provide treatment, although they often suffered from staff shortages and lacked the established quality controls and equipment of private hospitals. The VA also provided rehabilitation for disabled veterans, many of whom had been blinded or burned or had lost limbs, and provided job training and counseling from psychiatrists, social workers, and rehab specialists. More than 600,000 veterans went through the VA. The wounded received sympathetic portrayals in films including *The Best Years of Our Lives* and *Pride of the Marines*, although the road to recovery and reintegration was a long, difficult one. Many never completed it, battling the demons of war with alcohol and drugs and succumbing to them early in life.

TOWARD A NATIONAL SECURITY STATE

Although Americans were eager to put the war behind them and focus on a brighter future, the specter of the Soviet Union haunted efforts to demobilize. Instead, rumblings arose about the threat from Moscow to the American way of life. Nothing symbolized these warnings more than the "Long Telegram" sent by State Department official George Kennan in February 1946 from the embassy in Moscow. A long-time analyst of the Soviet Union,

Kennan argued forcefully that the Soviets possessed a "neurotic" view of the world and were "committed fanatically to the belief that with [the] U.S. there can be no permanent modus vivendi." Predicting long-term tensions with the Soviet Union, he encouraged the Truman administration to build up major industrial and military centers in Western Europe, Japan, and the United States as a containment strategy.

As attitudes toward Moscow hardened throughout the U.S. government, the Truman administration made a momentous decision in early 1947. Ongoing civil wars in Greece and Turkey, reportedly supported by Moscow, concerned the British, who in turn alerted the Americans. Thus, Truman went to Congress in March to declare: "I believe that it must be the policy of the United States to support free peoples who are resisting attempted subjugation by armed minorities or by outside pressures." He also requested $400 million for the task, which Congress easily approved, even though critics warned it was a dangerous first step toward universal commitments to authoritarian regimes such as the royalist one in Greece. Nevertheless, this orientation, known as the Truman Doctrine, became the cornerstone of the U.S. containment policy, one that would be replicated throughout the Third World during the early Cold War. Soon, it also became accepted military policy to funnel billions of dollars to pro-American governments across the globe.

As tensions rose, more people, including the president, clamored for military preparedness. As early as October 1945, Truman called for a single military department coordinated by a civilian secretary. By late 1946, competing bills to reorganize the national security structure were making their way through Congress, leading to the passage of the National Security Act of 1947, described by one person as the "Magna Carta of the national security state." This legislation created several new entities, including the National Security Council (NSC) and the Central Intelligence Agency (CIA), both with strong ties to the executive branch. While not the centralized system envisioned by Truman, the act also brought together the services, which now included an independent air force (separate from the army), and created the Joint Chiefs of Staff (JCS) to work with the redesignated secretary of defense and Congress to outline priorities in planning and development. Secretary of War Robert Patterson refused the initial posting as secretary of defense, so it fell to Admiral James Forrestal, a long-time hardline anticommunist and navy supporter. Unfortunately, the new legislation failed to end interservice rivalry, as envisioned by Truman, and instead often intensified competition for funds and bases subject to congressional appropriations. The navy in particular fared well, as it avoided the loss of its aviation component to the new air force and was permitted to sustain a large naval fleet by peacetime standards.

One of the most resounding victories during the bureaucratic battles of 1947 was won by the marines. A group of prominent officers known as the Chowder Society launched a political guerrilla war against the president, who wanted the marines' role in the armed services diminished. Members of the group employed numerous methods to block this effort, going so far as to steal secret documents and distribute them to supporters in the press and Congress. The Chowder Society benefited from a strong public relations campaign that included movies and the political work of several former marines, including senators Paul Douglas, Mike Mansfield, and Joseph McCarthy. In the end, the Marine Corps survived, maintaining a mission to support naval operations and its own air wing. Marines flourished in the postwar period as they established a reputation for toughness and elitism.

Many more battles arose as the president and his advisors fought to consolidate more power into the hands of the White House and Pentagon. However, the primary missions of the different branches of the U.S. military remained the same for many years afterward, although interservice rivalry and competition with new agencies such as the NSC and CIA deepened over time.

OFF WE GO INTO THE WILD BLUE YONDER

The newly formed United States Air Force fared well after winning its independence from the army in 1947. It soon got a chance to exercise its power with missions such as the Strategic Air Command (SAC), which controlled continental air defenses. Bases sprang up throughout the country to house bombers and fighters as the country prepared for the ultimate conflict with the Soviet Union. More important, the SAC became the primary source of delivering nuclear weapons, including over 400 atomic bombs, stockpiled in the U.S. arsenal by 1951. While it took years to build up the organization, led by General Curtis LeMay beginning in 1948, the air force established a prominent position in strategic planning that it rarely relinquished.

During the postwar era, the air force captured the country's imagination with its technology and the role it had played in defeating the Axis Powers in World War II. This fascination persisted despite various strategic assessments that questioned the effectiveness of the bombing in breaking the Axis Powers. Studies showed that the air force had failed to interrupt the enemy's production capabilities or undermine its will to fight, in contrast to the success attributed to it by its proponents.

CANDY BOMBERS

The air force did enjoy some major successes after the war. An important one that stirred people's imaginations unfolded in 1948. When the Allies in West Germany consolidated their sectors and organized a constitutional government, Stalin decided to test their will by cutting off the narrow road and rail routes to the isolated outpost of Berlin, sitting 100 miles inside the Soviet sector. Unwilling to ignite a war with the Soviets over Berlin, Truman turned to the U.S. Air Force. In 1945, the Soviets had agreed to a twenty-three-mile-wide air corridor into Berlin. Now, the United States and its British allies resolved to airlift all necessary goods into the city of more than 2 million people. Soon cargo planes began arriving from all over the world in an operation that became known as the Berlin Airlift.

For more than a year, cargo planes ferried goods to Berlin, sometimes as often as every three minutes. Pilots became known as Candy Bombers for dropping sweets to children from the planes. Ultimately more than 275,000 flights delivered 2.3 million tons of supplies to Berlin in an effort that became a symbol of U.S. innovation and commitment. While accidents occurred that cost the lives of sixty pilots and their crews, the effort was a resounding success, and Stalin eventually ended the blockade. This success endeared the air force to the American people, which came to be seen as even more important a few months later, when air force reconnaissance planes detected radiation over Siberia, where the Soviets

Berlin "Airlift" of 1948-49 broke through Soviet blockade of city by non-stop supply shipments to beleaguered garrisons and 2½ million civilian population of West Berlin.

IMAGE 14.1   Berlin Airlift   A Douglas C-54 Skymaster lands at Tempelhof Airport, while a crowd looks on from below. This iconic photograph shows the beginning of the "Berlin Airlift," an initiative in which the Allies supplied West Berlin with food and other essential items.

had exploded their first atomic bomb. When the United States' nuclear monopoly ended in August 1949, the real stakes of war with the Soviet Union rose. Now, the mission of the SAC and the U.S. Air Force became even more valuable, as the Soviets could only deliver the weapon via bomber at this time. The air force now became the first line of defense in an increasingly dangerous world.

A BRAVE NEW WORLD

The Soviet explosion of the atomic bomb scared Americans, and the triumph of the Communists under Mao Zedong in China that same year further confirmed American fears of a grand communist conspiracy for worldwide domination. Both events ensured more defense spending, which renewed bureaucratic battles over resources. This struggle sparked a major confrontation between civilian and military authorities as President Truman sought to consolidate power under the secretary of defense and the chairman of the JCS and to undermine the individual secretaries of the army, air force, and navy. This conflict came to a head in 1949, when Admiral Forrestal resigned after suffering a nervous breakdown. His successor, Louis A. Johnson, a former infantry officer and assistant secretary of war, immediately angered the navy by approving an air force request for thirty-six B-36 bombers. Then he further infuriated the admirals by cancelling the construction of the *United States*, a 65,000-ton supercarrier with strategic bombing capabilities. In response, naval officers went on the offensive in the "Revolt of the Admirals." Navy Secretary John L. Sullivan resigned, and officers accused Johnson and Secretary of the Air Force Stuart Symington of falsifying documents to promote the B-36 and leaking them to the House Armed Services Committee. When that failed, Admiral Arthur Radford convinced Democratic senator Carl Vinson of Georgia, chairman of the Senate Armed Services Committee, to hold hearings that would allow senior navy officers, including admirals William Halsey and Ernest King, to make a case against Johnson and the air force.

The hearings were a spectacular failure for the navy. Symington effectively parried Radford and his colleagues' charges. New chairman of the JCS General Omar Bradley dressed down the navy, going so far as to accuse its leaders of undermining civilian control of the military. In retaliation, all of the active officers involved in the revolt besides Captain Arleigh Burke received punishments. But while the navy had suffered a substantial defeat, it remained popular in Congress and among the public.

While the service rivalries continued, a consensus developed on the U.S. role in the postwar world. A communist coup in Czechoslovakia and the Berlin Airlift had pushed Western Europeans and Americans closer together. British foreign secretary Ernest Bevin emphasized that "political and indeed spiritual forces must be mobilized in our defence." In July 1948, talks began in Washington on forming an alliance. The United States joined the North Atlantic Treaty Organization (NATO) in 1949, committing to a military alliance in which every member nation agreed to take "such actions as it deems necessary, including the use of armed force," if another signatory were attacked. NATO's charter members included England, Norway, France, Denmark, Canada, and Portugal, as well as the United States—the first time the Americans had joined a formal military alliance since 1800. The organization's first secretary general, Lord Hasting Ismay, emphasized that it existed to "keep the Americans in, the Russians out, and Germans down."

During the early Cold War, no document more than NSC-68 highlighted the changes in attitudes that had occurred among Americans and the nation's new strategic vision. Prepared by the NSC, the "United States Objectives and Programs for National Security" reached President Truman's desk on April 14, 1950, and sparked a vocal internal debate unlike any that had been seen since Kennan's Long Telegram. NSC-68 predicted that the Soviets would become more aggressive once they achieved superiority in weapons and stressed Moscow's "combination of ideological zeal and fighting power." It called for the United States to "strike out on a bold and massive program of rebuilding the West's defensive potential to surpass the Soviet world, and of meeting each fresh challenge promptly and unequivocally." It concluded: "The integrity of our system will not be jeopardized by any measures, covert or overt, violent or nonviolent, which serve the purposes of frustrating the Kremlin design." It was a call to action that events unfolding in the Far East accelerated.

THE KOREAN WAR THROUGH OCTOBER 1950

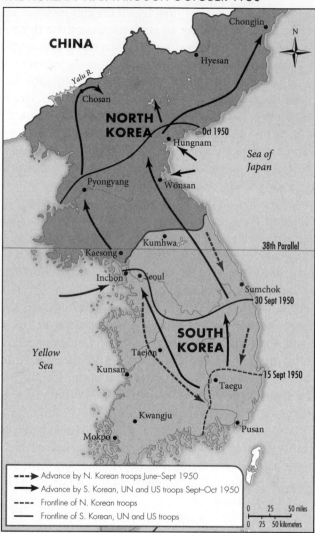

MAP 14.2 The Korean War through October 1950

THE FORGOTTEN WAR: THE BLOODY WAR IN KOREA

Few wars that cost so much in blood and gold as the Korean War have been relegated to the deepest recesses of the national memory. In this conflict the United States fought on the little-known peninsula from 1950 until an armistice in 1953. Operating in very difficult terrain and extreme weather against determined foes, Americans participated in the first real shooting match of the early Cold War. Strategic blunders and the resulting stalemate soon caused many Americans to reevaluate the nation's global commitments. But instead, most simply pushed the experience into the background, much to the consternation of those who had fought.

THE ROAD TO WAR

Most Americans, including many policymakers, could not have located Korea on a map in June 1950. Yet after 1945, the United States played a significant role in the country's realignment after six decades of Japanese dominance. Ultimately, U.S. leaders made numerous mistakes in this involvement, leading to problems that plagued the United States for many years afterward.

As World War II ended in August 1945, the United States pushed the Soviets to accept the 38th Parallel as a demarcation line between different spheres on the Korean Peninsula. While Soviet forces had drawn near the region after the invasion of Manchuria, they acceded to the demand on August 15. However, they began supporting Kim Il-Sung, a fanatical communist who had fought with Mao's forces against the Japanese. With Soviet support, the Korean leader built up a formidable military and a repressive political system.

Meanwhile, soldiers of the XXIV Corps landed in South Korea under General John R. Hodge to administer the former Japanese colony. They found a very alien nation with little in the way of government or facilities. Throughout the fall of 1945, Hodge struggled to stabilize matters. He openly fraternized with Japanese officers, who one observer noted "were viewed as cooperative, orderly and docile while the Koreans were seen as headstrong, unruly, and obstreperous." With little understanding of the local culture and determined to limit communist influence, the United States threw its support behind the Princeton-educated reactionary Syngmun Rhee. The aging Rhee soon seized power by relying heavily on former Japanese collaborators, especially in the military and civil service. Over time, he became more dictatorial and repressive but received little pushback from Hodge, who liked the firm hand he kept on the South Koreans.

As the 1948 elections approached and the withdrawal of troops grew closer, Hodge and his staff doubled down on their support for Rhee. On July 24, 1948, U.S. troops lowered their flag from the capitol building in Seoul. While attending the ceremony, General MacArthur told the Koreans, "An artificial barrier has divided your land. This barrier must and shall be torn down." Two months later, Kim Il-Sung proclaimed the Democratic People's Republic of Korea in Pyongyang under the guidance of the Soviets.

For nearly two years, both Rhee and Kim Il-Sung consolidated power and built up armies. While some Americans questioned U.S. support for Rhee, military and economic assistance continued to flow into the South. Meanwhile, the Soviets helped build an imposing force in North Korea. Border skirmishes occurred, but the United States was more focused on Europe and the Middle East than northeast Asia. By June 1950, relations between the North and the South had deteriorated. Commander of the Korean Military Assistance Group General W. L. Roberts reported: "If South Korea is called upon to defend herself against aggression, its ground army is capable of doing an excellent job." He predicted that the force would have even more success if U.S. officers accompanied the Koreans, declaring: "The advisers will almost command except in name." He was wrong on both accounts.

SURPRISE AND RETREAT

On June 25, the North Koreans, with Soviet support, dashed across the 38th Parallel in a well-coordinated mass attack. Their T-34 tanks led the way, followed by thousands of infantry supported by artillery. It was a rout, forcing the poorly led and -equipped South Koreans to retreat across the country.

Alarm bells went off in Washington. U.S. leaders immediately blamed the Soviets. Secretary of State Dean Acheson wrote: "It was an open, undisguised challenge to our internationally accepted position as the protector of South Korea. . . . To back away from this challenge . . . would be highly destructive of the power and prestige of the United States." The Truman administration immediately submitted the issue to the United Nations (UN), asking for a condemnation of the North Koreans and the promise of an international force to combat the aggression. With the Soviets boycotting the UN because of its refusal to recognize communist China as a legitimate member, the United States easily pushed through the resolution, and the United Nations joined Washington in challenging North Korean aggression.

Despite some optimism that Western troops might stem the tide, the introduction to the peninsula of the first U.S. troops, including Task Force Smith, failed. Not long after the debacle at Osan, the 24th Division arrived from Japan and sent the 34th Regiment to the front with nearly 2,000 men, anticipating success. But due to a lack of effective bazookas and heavy tanks, limited high-explosive anti-tank (HEAT) shells, and inexperienced officers and men, the 24th Division collapsed in its first actions on July 6. For a while the only thing that slowed the North Koreans in their advance was the terrain, overextension of supply lines, and the flood of refugees clogging the roads. A pattern of conflict soon developed in which the North Koreans would confront entrenched U.S. forces by moving forward with tanks while infantry flanked the U.S. infantry by climbing adjacent hills. The North Koreans often attacked in waves at night, trying to avoid U.S. airpower, which was itself limited by poor ground control and pilot inexperience. The spooked Americans often withdrew in short order. However, some did display bravery and leadership under duress. General William Dean personally led a bazooka team that stalked tanks in the streets of Taejon. His men scored successes, but eventually the North Koreans forced the general to run. He evaded them for nearly a month, desperately marching back to UN lines, but the enemy eventually managed to capture and incarcerate him for three years.

All of the U.S. units underperformed, but none received more scrutiny than the 24th Infantry Regiment of the 25th Division. This all-black unit remained a symbol of the recalcitrant army leadership that refused to honor President Truman's 1948 executive order desegregating the military. At one point, so many of its soldiers were fleeing that officers set up roadblocks behind their position to turn them back. The men's poor performance finally led the army to discard all-black units.

Throughout the retreat back toward Pusan, the southeastern port city where the 8th Army resided, the U.S. forces continued to perform poorly. One reporter wrote, "I saw young Americans turn and bolt in battle or throw down their arms, cursing the government for what they thought was embroilment in a hopeless cause." Panic also spread as the North Koreans slaughtered POWs, some of whom were found shot with their hands tied with barbed wire and dumped along the roadside. The conflict had rapidly become one of the worst routs in U.S. history.

STANDING THEIR GROUND

Slowly the U.S. Army and South Korean troops, with the assistance of international forces, including the British, established a perimeter around Pusan. General Walton H. Walker, a World War I and World War II veteran, took command of the 8th Army in South Korea. A no-nonsense, hard-driving Texan, Walker hated retreating and had little tolerance for those who did so. Soon, he had issued a "stand or die" order, pushing his men to hold the line. When meeting a senior field officer, he told him: "If I see you back here again, it better be in a coffin."

The North Koreans intensified their offensive against Pusan in August, wanting to score a decisive victory before more UN forces arrived, but the Allies held steady and built up their force, amassing nearly 170,000 troops by the end of August. By then, they possessed a five to one superiority in tanks and significant advantages in artillery, including offshore U.S. naval ships. Still, the outcome of the offensive remained in doubt. From the beginning, the UN forces controlled the skies, although weather and poor coordination limited their effectiveness. However, as more planes arrived (many flying off aircraft carriers), providing ground support and attacking enemy supply lines, the tide turned. B-29s flying from Japan dropped hundreds of thousands of tons of ordnance on railway lines, destroyed important bridges and transportation centers, and pounded enemy concentrations near Pusan. Airpower ultimately proved the decisive factor in stymying the overextended North Koreans.

At the end of August, the North Koreans launched a last offensive that quickly petered out. With overextended supply lines and troops dispersed in operations aimed at terrorizing the southern populace, the Communists faced a rapidly expanding force ready to take the offensive against them. The forceful nature of General Walker clearly made a difference, as the Allies' defeatism dissipated and resolve stiffened.

THE IMMACULATE ASSAULT

With the Pusan perimeter stabilizing, General MacArthur, as supreme commander for the Allied powers, formulated one of the most audacious maneuvers in U.S. military history. Wanting to relieve the pressure on Pusan and flank the enemy, MacArthur proposed an amphibious assault on the port city of Inchon near Seoul. From the beginning, his plan faced opposition, with many wanting to use the marines to break out of Pusan. Critics feared Inchon's tricky waterways and limited tides, and no one knew much about the North Korean defenses. Yet MacArthur persevered. At one meeting with navy planners, he prodded them: "I never thought the day would come, that the Navy would be unable to support the Army in its operation." Then, in dramatic fashion, he told them: "I can almost hear the ticking of the second hand of destiny. We must act now or we will die. . . . We shall land at Inchon, and I shall crush them." At the end of the meeting, the chief of naval operations responded: "General, the Navy will get you to Inchon."

IMAGE 14.2   Landing at Inchon   On September 15th, 1950, Major General Oliver P. Smith led the 1st Marine Division in a surprise assault, at Inchon, South Korea. The successful operation at Inchon made way to a key recapture of Seoul.

Military commanders scheduled Operation Chromite to launch on September 15. The marines, who needed to reestablish their position as an invaluable force in the postwar era, would serve as the point of the spear. Planners anticipated high losses; one order went out to continue the operation even if casualties reached as high as 82.3 percent. As one marine noted, "God, what kind of idiot would write an order putting in a decimal point like that?"

On September 12, the invasion fleet left Japan. During the trip, a typhoon struck with pounding winds and high waves, making many of the nearly 77,000 Americans seasick. But they persevered and arrived in the waters off Inchon late on September 14, ready to attack through the treacherous waterways and narrow inlets. On September 15 at 3 a.m., lights flashed in the troop compartments as sergeants paraded up and down, yelling: "On your feet, you guys! Time to saddle up for a beach party!" The marines ate a meal of powdered scrambled eggs and dry toast, although many just stared at their food, too nervous to eat. Each knew the horror stories of World War II in the Pacific, where thousands had died hitting the beaches under withering Japanese fire. Before the marines boarded their landing craft, the navy and its British allies put on a brilliant pyrotechnic show of heavy bombardment. U.S. forces then quickly captured the strategic island of Wolmi-do as the attackers waited for the rising tides of the late afternoon. Fortunately, the Communists had few troops in Inchon and had never mined the harbor.

At 5:30 p.m., the marines began moving forward in slow-moving landing craft, but confusion spread amid a drizzle and heavy smoke from the bombardment. At one point, an officer, studying his map, asked the driver, "Do you have a compass?" The driver looked at the display panel and responded: "Beats me, sir, I don't know much about this tub. Six weeks ago, I was driving a bus in San Francisco." Despite these challenges, U.S. forces hit the beaches and began using scaling ladders to top the seawall. The North Koreans occasionally offered spirited resistance, although the hard-charging marines, aided by close air support and naval fire, soon dispersed them. As the evening went on, the landing craft unloaded thousands of Americans and dropped off tanks and artillery as well as supplies.

By the end of the day, U.S. forces had advanced far inland. Only twenty-five miles from Seoul, the North Koreans reacted slowly, completely surprised. MacArthur waded ashore, his triumph acknowledged by everyone, including himself. Simultaneously, UN forces around Pusan launched a major offensive that sent the North Koreans reeling. Across South Korea, enemy forces surrendered by the thousands or simply retreated to the mountains to wage a guerrilla war. As the troops advanced, heavy fighting broke out around Seoul. Some strategists urged an enveloping move to spare the destruction of a direct assault, but MacArthur refused, wanting to enter the city quickly and triumphantly. Thousands died as the North Koreans fought ferociously while the U.S. Air Force and artillery pounded away at them, leading to high civilian casualties.

On September 27, MacArthur entered the devastated city. Standing alongside Rhee, he announced: "By the grace of merciful Providence, our forces fighting under the standard of that greatest hope and inspiration of mankind, the United Nations, have liberated this capital city of Korea." Turning to Rhee he said, "Mr. President, my officers and I will now resume our military duties and leave you and your government to the discharge of the civil responsibility." As they shook hands, the emotional Rhee responded: "We admire you. We love you as the savior of our race."

SNATCHING DEFEAT FROM THE JAWS OF VICTORY: NOVEMBER 1950–MARCH 1951

In the next stage of the war the United States and its allies moved to chase the panic-stricken North Koreans above the 38th Parallel. MacArthur hoped to conquer the entire peninsula for Rhee, and despite repeated warnings of possible Chinese intervention, U.S. officials pushed further, overextending their lines and separating their forces. By the onset of winter, U.S. fortunes had changed dramatically and the pursuers became the pursued when hundreds of thousands of Chinese troops joined the North Koreans in their fight, turning an anticipated victory parade by Christmas into a rout and a stalemate.

TO THE YALU AND THE LONG RETREAT

In late June 1950, Truman issued a directive that stated that MacArthur had "all the authority he needs . . . to keep the North Koreans from killing the people we are trying to save." There was one caveat: "He is not to go north of the 38th parallel." However, as U.S. forces advanced in September, the president and his advisors changed their minds. By October 9, the 8th Army had crossed the 38th Parallel and plunged headlong northward while the marines marched up the eastern half of the peninsula.

On October 15, President Truman traveled to Wake Island to meet with MacArthur. The general dismissed warnings of a Chinese buildup on the Yalu River, the border between China and North Korea. "Formal resistance," MacArthur emphasized, would end by Thanksgiving, and there was "very little" chance of Chinese intervention. If Mao sent troops, it would be small numbers easily matched by UN forces. Truman left the meeting confident in the plan to liberate North Korea. But MacArthur proved disastrously wrong. On October 2, the Chinese Politburo in a raucous meeting decided to commit Chinese troops to Korea. Classifying them as "volunteers," the Chinese moved hundreds of thousands of soldiers into Manchuria near the Yalu River. By October 19, six divisions had crossed into Korea, with six more arriving a week later. More followed over the next few weeks, totaling more than 350,000, as opposed to the expected 70,000 maximum predicted by MacArthur.

Instead of solidifying their lines in anticipation of the Chinese offensive, MacArthur and General Edward Almond steamrolled north, believing U.S. troops could return home by Christmas. Soon the Chinese were exploiting the gaps in the American lines, their troops crashing through them and isolating units. Panic spread among those who feared Chinese encirclement. One soldier reported that it was "every man for himself! Then there was really chaos. Everybody just bugged out." Another complained bitterly: "We had believed that it was all over. Yet now we knew the war would be over no time soon." He commented about the Chinese, "There's no end to them—the more you kill, the more they come." A headlong retreat followed as the 8th Army simply melted away in a mad dash back toward the 38th Parallel.

ISSUES IN MILITARY HISTORY

PRESIDENT TRUMAN AND THE FIRING OF DOUGLAS MACARTHUR

The controversy surrounding President Harry Truman's firing of General Douglas MacArthur over Korean strategy sparked debates in April 1951 that continue today. On one side, Truman's defenders justified the firing on the basis of the general's insubordination and the need to reinforce civilian control of an apolitical military. They agreed with the president's statement: "I fired him because he wouldn't respect the authority of the President. . . . I didn't fire him because he was a dumb son of a bitch, although he was." They also praised the president for preventing an expansion of the conflict that might have triggered World War III. On the other side, MacArthur's defenders accused Truman of having a defeatist attitude that emboldened the Soviet and Chinese communists as well as leftist movements worldwide. The failure to allow MacArthur to take the war to the enemy prevented the United States from fully waging a war to not only contain communism but roll it back in Asia after the staggering loss in China in 1949.

After the initial furor died down, the issue temporarily receded in the American consciousness. But biographers of both Truman and MacArthur, including William Manchester and David McCullough, revived the debates, which became louder with the release of additional declassified documents and new memoirs by principal participants. The battle lines broke to a large degree as they had in earlier years, with praise for Truman focusing on the concept of civilian control and criticism of him calling his action impulsive and poorly managed. The disagreement paralleled more contemporary debates over Vietnam and its leadership.

Over time, new issues assumed more centrality. The most important concerned the expansion of the war that MacArthur had sought and its potential to have started a massive conflagration that would have claimed millions of lives and possibly provoked a nuclear confrontation. People who supported this stance agreed with chairman of the Joint Chiefs of Staff General Omar Bradley, who said that MacArthur's strategy would "involve us in the wrong war, in the wrong place, at the wrong time and with the wrong enemy."

The debates over MacArthur's firing will likely continue, although it appears that most people in hindsight side with Truman's decision to fire MacArthur as an act reinforcing the proper role of military leaders in American society. Still, while MacArthur told Congress in April 1951 that "old soldiers never die, they just fade away," that seems unlikely to occur in his case.

THE BLOODY ROAD

On the eastern half of North Korea, the marines soon encountered similar conditions. They landed at Wonsan on October 25 and quickly advanced northward toward the large Chosin Reservoir. However, on November 2, they encountered the first units of the Chinese army, who waited until nightfall to launch heavy attacks that sought tactical breakthroughs to disrupt command and logistical support. The Chinese also wanted to avoid UN planes dropping napalm, which created sheets of flame that incinerated victims, its jellied residues burning them even after the initial blast.

Unlike Almond's army troops in the western half of the country, the marines slowed their advance as they encountered the Chinese. The weather turned against the Americans, with

IMAGE 14.3 **Chosin Reservoir** During the Battle of Chosin Reservoir, located in the mountains of North Korea, U.S. marines, soldiers, and allied troops found themselves vastly outnumbered by Chinese units, fighting in freezing conditions. Although the two week ordeal ended with the evacuation of American and U.N. forces from the territory, the battle is widely regarded as pride-point for the U.S. Marine Corps, and seen as an exemplification of the tenacity Marines demonstrate against extreme odds.

temperatures falling on November 11 to –8 degrees. With the 8th Army disintegrating on his left flank, General Oliver P. Smith requested and received permission to start withdrawing, telling his commanders that it was "an attack in another direction." For weeks, the marines fought ferociously, leapfrogging each other as they moved southward while inflicting heavy casualties on the Chinese. Stories of the astronomical odds they overcame entered marine lore. In one, legendary marine general Lewis "Chesty" Puller told his troops after being surrounded: "All right, they're on our left, they're on our right, they're in front of us, they're behind us. . . . They can't get away this time."

There were some bright spots in the retreat. The G Company of the Third Battalion, 1st Marines, performed particularly heroically. Reconstituted at Camp Pendleton in August 1950 with reservists and men from garrison duties, the unit headed to Korea in September, arriving in time to fight at Inchon and Seoul before joining the marines landing at Wonsan. In November, they participated in the "attack in another direction." At one point, William B. Baugh won the Medal of Honor for diving onto a grenade and absorbing the blast to protect his comrades in a truck. Frostbite became a major concern, and many died or suffered wounds in the retreat. By the time it arrived at Hagura to regroup, the company had lost a significant number of men as well as much equipment. With no time to rest or outfit, the men entered the frontlines, surviving on Tootsie Rolls and heated cans of fruit cocktail. Led by Captain Carl Sitter, they received orders to take the East Hill, a 1,500-foot promontory overlooking the surrounded marines and their hastily constructed airfield. On November 29, they trudged up the hill under heavy enemy fire, ultimately securing it and setting up defensive positions for the inevitable counterattack. Facing an enemy unit of more than 2,000 soldiers, the Company endured sniper fire and mortar attacks. Unable to break the frozen ground, they piled up dead North Koreans for cover. As they readied for the night on November 30, Captain Sitter barked out, "What are we going to do? You're going to fight, damn it! You must fight or you aren't getting out of here. It's that simple."

Later that night, the Chinese filled the air with flares and the sounds of bugles and whistles as officers pushed their men forward, urging them to "Shā! Shā! Shā!" ("Kill! Kill! Kill!"). Outnumbered ten to one, the marines fought ferociously, even as their machine guns froze, some of the men urinating on the weapons to warm them. Soon, the enemy's dead stacked up in front of the .30-calibers. Throughout the night, the Communists attacked in full force, raking the marines with .50-caliber machine gun fire and killing many Americans. One died after he suffered a compound fracture, went into shock, and simply froze to death. In another case, a soldier went blind when the blood from a head wound froze over his eyes. Desperately the marines threw cooks, bakers, and office personnel into the fight, as well as the British Royal Commandos, the last reserves. The wounded Captain Sitter and his officers rallied the troops. At one point, a marine asked him, "Captain, what happens if we are surrounded?" He simply replied, "We're going to fight like hell!"

By dawn, the survivors had held the hill and the Chinese moved to withdraw. Around 9 a.m., marine Corsairs arrived and dropped napalm on the retreating Chinese. The soldiers of G Company had survived the night, turning back a large attack and inflicting heavy casualties. A few days later, they joined the other marines in reaching the safety of Hungnam. For his bravery, Sitter received the Medal of Honor.

By the time the marines finally loaded onto ships, they had suffered nearly 7,000 casualties, many to frostbite. Nearly 200 ships carried the troops, much of their heavy equipment, and many civilians from Hungnam, with the last U.S. forces destroying the port facilities. The U.S. forces had lived to fight another day in one of the greatest evacuations in U.S. military history.

SHOWDOWN BETWEEN TITANS

The "Great Bug Out" of the north by the 8th Army and the marines gave the Chinese and the newly reconstituted North Korean army the initiative. On New Year's Eve, they launched a major offensive that pushed the UN forces more than sixty miles south of the 38th Parallel and allowed the Communists to again capture Seoul. However, the UN lines stabilized by the middle of January, largely aided by the constant pounding of their warplanes, which worked day and night to destroy supply lines and kill the enemy with strafing and napalm.

The introduction of General Matthew Ridgway as commander of the 8th Army and the fully incorporated marines helped change UN fortunes. A well-respected paratrooper and World War II veteran, Ridgway instilled a new confidence in UN forces, telling his troops

IMAGE 14.4   Combat in Korea   American soldiers utilize nearby rocks to protect themselves from flying mortar shells in Central Korea.

early on that "the issue now joined here in Korea is whether Communism or individual freedom shall prevail." Then, he pledged: "You will have my utmost. I shall expect yours." Under his command, the UN forces changed tactics, jettisoning the principles of MacArthur and Almond to focus not on gaining ground, but on destroying the enemy. He sought to drive the Communists into the open and inflict heavy casualties through enveloping maneuvers, probing attacks, and reliance on "meat grinder" tactics. By March, Ridgway's forces had driven the Chinese and North Koreans back across the 38th Parallel, liberating Seoul once more on March 15. Soon, UN forces had established defensive lines just inside North Korea in preparation for an anticipated enemy spring offensive.

Brewing below the surface, however, was a major battle between MacArthur and President Truman. In late December, Truman had sent a directive to the general changing the armed forces' mission from restoring "international peace and security" to "defend[ing] in successive positions" and "inflicting such damage to hostile forces in Korea as is possible, subject to the primary consideration of the safety of your troops." MacArthur chafed at the instructions, possibly hoping to incorporate Chiang Kai-Shek's Chinese forces on Taiwan into the equation in a strategy that some called "unleash the Nationalists." But by early

1951, Truman had settled on negotiating a way out of Korea rather than taking the fight to the Chinese and engaging in bombing in Manchuria. MacArthur opposed negotiations and denounced "further military restrictions."

Frustrated, MacArthur issued statements that had not been cleared by the White House on March 24 mocking the Chinese Communist army as overrated and unable to maintain "even moderate air and naval power [or] . . . an industrial base," hinting at the potential use of atomic weapons, and predicting that if the UN forces took the fight into China, the government there would collapse and Nationalists would retake the continent. He also wrote a letter to Congressman Joseph W. Martin, Jr., the Republican House minority leader, agreeing with his position on unleashing the Nationalists. After complaining that the United States was focusing on Europe at the expense of Asia, MacArthur stressed: "We must win. There is no substitute for victory." Martin read the letter on the House floor on April 5, infuriating Truman. In response, Truman declared that "the time ha[s] come to draw the line. MacArthur's letter to Congressman Martin showed the general was not only in disagreement with the policy of the government but was challenging this policy in open insubordination to his Commander in Chief." For a couple of weeks, Truman mulled over his options for responding to one of the greatest challenges to civilian control of the military in U.S. history. Finally, after conferring with the JCS and Secretary of Defense George Marshall, he decided to fire MacArthur. On April 12, Secretary of the Army Frank Pace planned to deliver the news to the commander personally, but miscommunication and an internal leak allowed MacArthur to learn of his firing via Japanese radio. Soon he left for home while Ridgway assumed his position and General James Van Fleet took control of the 8th Army.

Truman faced heavy criticism for his move, although many praised him for countering the threat to civilian control of the military. Once home, parades were organized in MacArthur's honor in Washington and New York City. Partisans rushed to his defense, allowing him to speak before Congress to promote his ideas and conclude: "Old soldiers never die; they just fade away." One Republican congressman characterized MacArthur as "the voice of God," while Truman said privately that the general's statements were "a bunch of bullshit." Hearings followed, producing 2 million words of testimony, but after the initial praise for the general, most people lost interest or recognized MacArthur's arrogance and the threats he posed to the established order. Then he simply faded away.

THE AIR WAR

While the conflict stalemated in mid-1951 and a two-year period of negotiations began, the war continued in the air. From the beginning, the air force and navy, along with the marine air wing, played an important, albeit debated, role in the fighting. They clearly assisted the war effort by providing close air support, although the enemy rarely fought during the day, which limited UN efforts. They also succeeded in attacking Communist supply lines, but the Chinese adapted to these measures by traveling at night and using low-tech methods of transportation, including hundreds of thousands of porters. Large-scale bombing by B-29s of North Korea's small industrial bases and cities produced some additional success. Finally, as in previous wars, the efforts of fighter pilots sparked the American public's imagination. Their dogfights, especially in the so-called MiG Alley, became the source of legend.

The Communists typically maintained numerical superiority in the air throughout the war and sometimes inflicted heavy casualties on the slower-moving Allied bombers with northern targets. However, UN forces swept the Communist planes from the skies over the frontlines and rarely allowed penetration of rear areas. The fighting was often fierce, as Chinese and Russian pilots

IMAGE 14.5　US Air Force in Korea　One aircraft model used extensively in the Korean War was the F-84, shown above. The Thunderjet, as it is also referred to, was commonly used for targeted ground attacks, as opposed to air-to-air combat.

working from bases in Manchuria often outnumbered UN pilots and flew advanced Russian aircraft, but the UN pilots, most of whom were American, usually prevailed. After receiving alerts from radar stations in the Yellow Sea, they would meet the enemy in traditional dogfights, sometimes diving at speeds exceeding the sound barrier. Well trained and often veterans of World War II, the Americans usually forced the enemy to retreat back into the safe zones of China. By the war's end, the fighters had accounted for 792 enemy fighter kills at the loss of only seventy-eight of their own. Captain Joseph McConnell led the pack with sixteen confirmed kills.

Airpower also saw the introduction of a new player in Korea: the helicopter. With their ability to range long distances over land and sea, helicopters became an important way to rescue downed pilots, reducing the airman attrition rate compared to World War II. They also performed significant duties in transporting the wounded to hospitals in rear areas, dramatically reducing the number of deaths among UN soldiers who would have died in previous wars.

Many stories of the air war over Korea were told, but one reflected ongoing changes in the U.S. military regarding race. In 1950, African American Frank E. Petersen, Jr., joined the navy and took the required exams. He called the tests "relatively unremarkable," but a few days later a petty officer called and asked: "Would you mind retaking the examination?" He complied, knowing that the petty officer suspected him of cheating. But he aced it again, and the officer exclaimed: "Petersen, my boy, the navy has opportunities for you. . . . My, God, man, what a great steward you'd make." Undeterred, Petersen served as a seaman's apprentice and electronics technician, but he dreamed of becoming an aviator, inspired by Jesse L. Brown, the navy's first African American aviator, who died in combat in 1950. In 1951, the navy accepted him into its aviation cadet program. He experienced prejudice throughout the process. During training, bus drivers ordered him to the back of the bus, and he could not join other cadets in restaurants and theaters. However, when instructors tried to minimize his performance, fellow students came to his defense. Finally, he received a commission as a second lieutenant in the Marine Corps, becoming the first African American aviator in corps history. He immediately shipped out to Korea, where he flew sixty-four combat missions in 1953, earning six air medals and the Distinguished Flying Cross for heroism. Later, in Vietnam he flew more than 300 missions, earning a Purple Heart for his service in North

THE KOREAN PENINSULA IN 1953

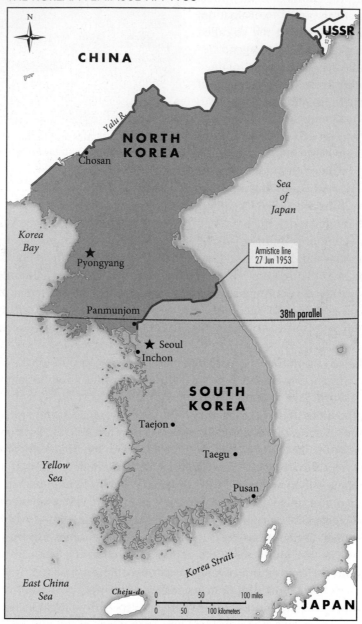

MAP 14.3 The Korean Peninsula in 1953

Vietnam. In 1979, he became the first African American general in the Marine Corps and then the first African American commander at Quantico Marine Base. He retired a lieutenant general in 1988 after winning twenty medals for heroism. The path opened by Truman's Executive Order 9981 had definitely changed his own course.

FIGHTING WHILE NEGOTIATING

By the end of July 1951, Allied forces had stabilized their lines north of the 38th Parallel and established air superiority. Simultaneously, U.S. officials had reached out through Soviet officials to jumpstart the peace process, since the United States maintained no formal relations with North Korea or China. After some talking, both sides agreed to discuss major issues, including borders, future bases, and POWs. Negotiators began meeting in Panmunjom just north of the 38th Parallel. Unfortunately, the posturing of both sides, especially the Communists, ensured little progress, as did the refusal of many Chinese and North Korean POWs to return home. Within a short time, both sides walked away. It would take excruciating months for talks to restart and years for a final settlement to be reached.

From this point forward, neither side sought an outright victory, as most people recognized that it would not happen. Thus, most of the fighting came to center on seeking strategic advantages to force the other side to make concessions and thereby ensure an end to the hostilities. Meanwhile, the dying continued, particularly in the moun-

IMAGE 14.6 **US POWs** This cartoon taps into the country's frustration surrounding the release of POWs during the Korean War, and general public discontent of "The Forgotten War." Trucks labeled "The Few to Return" move through the valley of the shadow of death, while an ominous figure of a dead soldier looms above. While prisoners of war were finally being released, many would never return, and the ones who did return brought trauma from the war with them.

tainous areas of the Kansas Line just north of the 38th Parallel. Promontories such as Heartbreak Ridge and Old Baldy became well known to the U.S. public, while others, such as Hill 981, became noted simply for their height. Battles around them became meat grinder affairs, with neither side winning a major advantage.

Few conflicts during the Korean War took on a more symbolic value in American military history and popular culture than the battles fought at Pork Chop Hill during the spring and summer of 1953. Pork Chop Hill, also called Hill 255, was located in an area often described as a "moonscape" because of its lack of vegetation and the pockmarks in the earth created by heavy artillery. It had ceased to be a strategic site after the Chinese took Old Baldy, which overlooked it. Nevertheless, the Americans and their allies refused to abandon it. Distinguished historian S.L.A. Marshall stressed: "That concession would have been in the interest of line-straightening without sacrifice of a dependable anchor. But national pride, bruised by the loss of Old Baldy, asserted itself, and Pork Chop was held."

The Chinese attacked the hill on the night of April 16. A U.S. patrol encountered two enemy companies sweeping toward the undermanned Americans, who were holding their position with fewer than 100 men. The Communists had cut communication lines, so Lieutenant Thomas Harrold called in heavy artillery using flares, slowing the Chinese momentarily. After hours of savage fighting, often hand-to-hand, the Chinese took most of the hill outside of the high ground and a few isolated pockets. Several attempts by the Americans to reinforce their men failed. The next day, both the Americans and the Chinese began pouring troops into the battle, with the U.S. commanders determined to deny the Chinese a propaganda victory. Artillery and mortars pounded the hillside, with the Americans firing more than 110,000 rounds in two days. At one point, Lieutenant Earle Denton, holding the command post, found himself surrounded, leading him to fire directly up through the roof and call for artillery strikes directly on the position. Just as the engagement appeared over, a risky move by one American platoon directly up the face of the hill led to relief. The fighting continued until the early morning of April 18, when U.S. reinforcements repelled a Chinese assault. Driven back, the Chinese conceded tactical defeat, and the zone cooled dramatically for several months. Losses were heavy, with more than 100 Americans dead; one group of the 31st Infantry had only seven survivors. In 1959 the semifictionalized movie *Pork Chop Hill*, starring Gregory Peck, would immortalize the Americans who fought on the site.

The hill remained an important propaganda tool through the end of negotiation leading to the armistice, which was prolonged by the machinations of President Rhee, who released

IMAGE 14.7 Helicopters in Korea   Soldiers ready a wounded comrade for medical evacuation by helicopter. Helicopters proved pivotal in the Korean War as a means to transport wounded soldiers, and rescue pilots shot down by the enemy.

enemy POWs who had refused repatriation. On July 6, the Communists launched another massive attack on the hill, now held by a larger U.S. force. For four days, the two sides battled, fighting hand-to-hand in the trenches and the bunkers. A series of attacks and counterattacks wore down the U.S. 7th Division, which lost four of its thirteen company commanders. On July 11, U.S. commanders decided to stop the bloodbath, which had already claimed more than 240 UN soldiers and another 1,000 wounded. U.S. forces withdrew to better defensive positions, and on July 27, the warring sides signed an armistice, ending three years of brutal fighting.

CONCLUSIONS

The Korean War frustrated Americans like no other, quickly becoming known as the "Forgotten War." It resulted in many dead and wounded, and even more bearing the psychological and physical wounds imposed by war. It caused Americans to question why many of their POWs collaborated with the enemy, to ask why technology could not carry the country to victory, and to confront weaknesses demonstrated while fighting an Asian enemy. It also committed the United States to a long-term relationship with South Korea, where its troops remain today. The war, neither a triumphal victory like World War II nor a defeat, faded quickly in the American consciousness, which had a hard time processing it.

But the Korean conflict reflected the rapidly changing nature of the U.S. military in everyday American life. With the onset of the Cold War, the United States chose to maintain a large standing military. The rapid expansion of alliances such as NATO and the commitment of U.S. troops to defend far-flung outposts such as Korea sustained the need for more than the skeleton force that had typically characterized the U.S. military after a major conflict. Furthermore, the new technologies of the early Cold War, such as long-range bombers, dramatically reduced the natural barriers, such as the vast oceans, on which the United States had relied to avoid conflict over the years. The war forced upon Washington the need for new strategies that would take into account global conditions in many new areas of the world such as the Middle East, where U.S. planners now concentrated on containing the perceived Soviet threat. It also forced an evolution of the military, which was now called upon to prepare for a potential global thermonuclear conflict, leading to tensions between military and civilian leaders. The world in which the United States now found itself was indeed a brave new world, but one that was increasingly small and dangerous.

TIMELINE

January 1944	Passage of G.I. Bill
February 1946	Kennan's Long Telegram
March 1947	Announcement of Truman Doctrine
September 1947	Passage of National Security Act
June 1948–May 1949	Berlin Airlift
April 1949	NATO founded
April 1950	NSC-68 report issued
June 1950	Korean War starts
September 1950	Inchon landing
October 1950	Truman fires MacArthur
July 1953	Armistice in Korea

SUGGESTED READINGS

Cherny, Andrei. *The Candy Bombers: The Untold Story of the Berlin Airlift and America's Finest Hour.* New York: Putnam, 2008.

Edwards, Paul M. *United Nations Participants in the Korean War: The Contributions of 45 Member Countries.* Jefferson, NC: McFarland, 2013.

Fehrenback, T. R. *This Kind of War: The Classic Korean War History.* Updated ed. Washington, D.C.: Brassey's, 2000.

Haruki, Wada. *The Korean War: An International History.* Lanham, MD: Rowman & Littlefield, 2014.

McWilliams, Bill. *On Hallowed Ground: The Last Battle for Pork Chop Hill.* New York: Berkeley Caliber Books, 2004.

Mettler, Suzanne. *Soldiers to Citizens: The G.I. Bill and the Making of the Greatest Generation.* New York: Oxford University Press, 2005.

O'Donnell, Patrick K. *Give Me Tomorrow: The Korean War's Greatest Untold Story—The Epic Stand of the Marines of George Company.* Cambridge, MA: Da Capo Press, 2010.

Pearlman, Michael D. *Truman and MacArthur: Policy, Politics, and the Hunger for Honor and Renown.* Bloomington: Indiana University Press, 2008.

Stokesbury, James L. *A Short History of the Korean War.* New York: William Morrow, 1988.

Stueck, William. *The Korean War: An International History.* Princeton, NJ: Princeton University Press, 1997.

CHAPTER 15

FROM THE TOP OF THE WORLD
TO A QUAGMIRE

1953–1975

*Dwight Eisenhower and the New Look, 1953–1961 • Dipping in Their Toe in Indochina
• Other Flashpoints • The Military-Industrial Complex • Pay Any Price, Bear Any Burden
• Limited Partnership in South Vietnam • The Big Juicy Worm on the Hook: Major U.S.
Involvement, 1963–1968 • The Year of the Continuous Nightmare: 1968 • We've Gotta Get
Out of This Place: Vietnamization and Withdrawal, 1969–1975 • Looking into the Mirror*

A bright sun rose over the red mountains in the small copper mining camp of Morenci, Arizona (population 5,000), on July 4, 1966. While others prepared for a day of festivities, a group of nine young men waited at the local bus stop with their friends and families. There were significant contrasts between them: the red-haired, fair-skinned Stan King, who stood 6'5" and weighed 230 pounds, could not have looked more different from Leroy Cisneros, who was 5'4" and 140 pounds with dark hair and a dark complexion. Despite those differences, they shared many things in common: their fathers all toiled in the Phelps Dodge Company mine or smelter, their families all lived in segregated company housing, and they all followed a schedule driven by shifts of twenty-six days on, two days off. All of them had also volunteered for military service in March when a Marine Corps recruiter had arrived and spun tales of heroism while also offering a chance to escape the drudgery of work in the massive open-pit mine.

The young men, who became known as the Morenci Nine, said their last goodbyes and boarded the bus for San Diego. There, marine drill instructors immediately pounced on them, yelling obscenities, questioning their sexuality, and ordering them onto yellow footsteps painted on the ground, heels together and toes pointed out, with barely any room in front of or behind them. Tens of thousands of young men had preceded them, and many more followed.

The nine spent the next eight weeks in boot camp in Platoon 1055. Friends provided encouragement to the heavier-set Bobby Draper, who sometimes fell behind on long runs under the baking summer sun. They also saved Van Whitmer, who had cut through a different platoon lined up for dinner, from a vicious beating after a melee broke out. Finally, in early September, they all graduated and headed to advance training.

Over the next three years, all of these citizen-soldiers eventually fought in Vietnam. Their stories were miraculous at times. Cisneros survived more than forty missions as a reconnaissance point man and several times barely missed being blown apart by enemy grenades or gunfire. Joe Sorrelman received relatively cushy duty guarding an airfield but requested a transfer to the fighting. The marines granted the request, sending him to Con Thien in the summer of 1967. Only a small miracle kept him from death. After leaving Vietnam to return home for a family medical emergency, he learned that the enemy had nearly wiped out his squad the day after his departure.

Not everyone proved so lucky. Bobby Dale Draper, a former All-State linebacker, on August 2, 1967, walked into a Viet Cong ambush that killed him and everyone in his squad. Two months later, King fell during Operation Essex, having only arrived two weeks earlier. Five months later, an enemy sniper shot Whitmer near Hue, and Larry West fell during an operation on Goi Noi Island, just a few months after starting his second tour. The following month, the handsome Robert Moncayo died near Khe Sanh after arriving eighteen days earlier. Morenci, already reeling from a company lockout, found itself mourning the loss of five young men within nine months.

For a short while, the deaths stopped. Mike Cranford miraculously survived his tour and mustered out along with Cisneros and Sorrelman. That left only Clive Garcia in the marines. While he had originally been assigned to serve in Guam and San Diego, he repeatedly asked to transfer to Vietnam to avenge his friends' deaths. Ultimately, the marines honored his request, and in late November 1969, he died defusing an enemy booby trap.

On December 9, the media, including ABC News and *Time* magazine, descended on the little Arizona town for Garcia's burial. Dark clouds hung over Morenci as the community packed the Catholic church to honor him, ultimately laying his body next to Moncayo's. One person noted, "It's just like this town been the butt of a twisted joke. The bodies just keep coming in—one at a time." Garcia's mother, Julia, simply told a reporter, "He died for . . . this cause of freedom." The community would never forget the sacrifice.

Many more young Americans landed in Vietnam before and after the Morenci Nine. By its end, the war had killed more than 58,000 Americans and 2 million Vietnamese. By 1968, after years of fighting an unpopular war, the United States sought an exit that left behind its Army of the Republic of Vietnam (ARVN) comrades to fight the Viet Cong and North Vietnamese. Ultimately, in 1975, two years after the United States officially withdrew, enemy tanks battered down the gates of the presidential palace in Saigon, ending a sad chapter in American military history, one that had begun many years earlier during the Truman and Eisenhower administrations.

DWIGHT EISENHOWER AND THE NEW LOOK, 1953–1961

While problems in Indochina festered, President Eisenhower vowed during the 1952 election to travel to Korea and terminate the interminable war there. In late November, he visited the peninsula, and eight months later, the war ended. The former general then turned his focus to domestic politics, which included restructuring the military to make it less costly. However, by the time Eisenhower left the White House in 1961, the military had grown exponentially and had become more embedded in the nation's social fabric, leading him in his Farewell Address to lament the creation of a "military-industrial complex."

From the beginning, Eisenhower had focused on reducing federal spending to balance the budget. Once the U.S. military had disengaged from Korea, he and his advisors concentrated on cutting military costs to commit the United States to a more fiscally conservative course after years of expansion of the federal government. What evolved was a "New Look" that stressed nuclear deterrence over costly conventional weapons and large formations, a reorientation that accelerated the development of technology during the postwar era. In December 1953, Eisenhower instructed Secretary of Defense Charles Wilson "to establish personnel ceilings in each service that will place everything on an austerity basis." Anticipating complaints, he stressed: "We are no longer fighting in Korea, and the Defense establishment should show its appreciation of this fact without wailing about the mission they have to accomplish." Shortly thereafter, Secretary of State John Foster Dulles made a speech, one personally vetted by the president, that emphasized the administration's commitment to less costly measures "by placing more reliance on deterrent power, and less dependence on local defensive power." He also emphasized that the United States wanted to avoid fighting localized wars.

Results occurred quickly. Within a couple of years, the army had shrunk from 1.5 million personnel to 1 million, while the navy and marines went from 1 million to 870,000. Only the air force grew, from 950,000 to 970,000. Investments in nuclear weapons, including intercontinental ballistic missiles (ICBMs), soaked up the lion's share of new expenditures as terms like "brinksmanship" and "massive retaliation" entered the American lexicon. Overall, U.S. nuclear arsenals grew from 1,161 warheads in 1953 to 12,305 by 1959, reflecting a strategic realignment that played to U.S. strengths in industrial output to counteract the Soviet advantages in manpower. Eisenhower also relied on covert operations rather than military concentrations in countries like Iran and Guatemala to achieve regime change.

There were many critics of the new policy, including army chief of staff Matthew Ridgway, who publicly criticized the move to cut conventional forces. Eisenhower responded by refusing to renew his term in the summer of 1955. His replacement, General Maxwell Taylor, critiqued the administration in his book *The Uncertain Trumpet*. He left soon after, ultimately returning to serve the Kennedy administration. But despite the critiques, U.S. military forces remained by far the largest they had ever been during peacetime in U.S. history.

DIPPING IN THEIR TOE IN INDOCHINA

Despite focusing on nuclear weapons, the White House did consider using conventional forces in several hotspots. In Indochina, the United States backed French efforts to reestablish control after their defeat in 1940. In this task the French faced a potent enemy in the communist Viet Minh, led by Ho Chi Minh, who had received U.S. aid during World War II. Despite its earlier support, Washington threw its weight behind Paris in a Cold War move meant to counteract a perceived communist threat. After 1946, the Viet Minh settled in for a long struggle, retreating to the countryside to wage a guerrilla war. Ho warned: "It will be a war of tiger and an elephant. If ever the tiger stops, the elephant will pierce him with his tusks. Only the tiger doesn't stop. . . . He will leap onto the elephant and rip his back to shreds before disappearing . . . and the elephant will die from exhaustion and loss of blood."

For years, the United States had supported France, buying its loyalty by building up European defenses. In 1949, Mao's Communist victory in China increased the pressure on U.S. leaders to support the French in Indochina with more military aid. By the end of 1950, the United States had committed more than $133 million in arms. Accompanying American aid was the U.S. Military Assistance Advisory Group (MAAG), which evaluated French requests for hardware and provided training for the French and their Vietnamese allies. Victories by the Viet Minh in 1950 and the Korean War led to increased support, with totals reaching $385 million in 1953 as President Dwight Eisenhower took office. The amounts only increased in 1954 as the French launched an offensive to defeat the Viet Minh. By this point, the Americans were paying for more than three-fourths of the costs of the war.

In 1954, General Henri Navarre arrived in Indochina with nine new French battalions to build up a Vietnamese army that would initiate an offensive. Secretary of State Dulles proudly proclaimed that Navarre's plan would "break the organized body of Communist aggression by the end of the 1955 fighting season." He was wrong. Navarre, with the support of American planners, sent 12,000 French and Vietnamese troops far inland to draw out the Viet Minh at Dien Bien Phu. Viet Minh general Vo Nguyen Giap obliged and surrounded the French position in March 1954. For fifty days, the Viet Minh slowly strangled the garrison. Desperate, Paris begged for U.S. support. In late March JCS chairman Admiral Arthur Radford proposed Operation Vulture, in which sixty U.S. B-29s would bomb the Viet Minh. To cover up U.S. involvement, planners called for French flight crews and French markings on American planes. Some even discussed using tactical nuclear weapons to break the siege.

Critics within the military immediately arose. General Ridgway warned that bombing alone could not save the French and expressed fears about committing U.S. troops in such difficult conditions. One military analyst worried about mission creep, noting: "One cannot go over Niagara Falls in a barrel only slightly."

President Eisenhower briefly toyed with the idea of aiding the garrison but resisted the impulse. On May 7, the French surrendered and soon agreed to the Geneva Accords, something opposed by the U.S. administration. Washington threw its support behind sustaining a noncommunist South Vietnam, one patterned after South Korea. Dulles told the press that "the important thing [was] not to mourn the past but seize the future opportunity to prevent the loss in Northern Vietnam from leading to the extension of communism throughout Southeast Asia and the Southwest Pacific."

A GOOD STOUT EFFORT

The Eisenhower administration faced huge obstacles in South Vietnam, especially those related to nation building. Dulles told congressmen that the United States must "put up a good stout effort even though it is by no means certain that we will succeed." Privately, he acknowledged that the United States had only a one in ten chance of success. Dissenting voices soon surfaced. Secretary of Defense Wilson called for the United States to extricate itself from the region as "completely and as soon as possible," declaring that he could foresee "nothing but grief in store for us if we remain . . . in the area."

Despite these warnings, the Eisenhower administration backed Ngo Dinh Diem, a fervent nationalist and Catholic with powerful benefactors in the United States, including Senator John F. Kennedy. General Walter Bedell Smith expressed hope that Diem would become a "modern political Joan of Arc" who could "rally the country behind him." Others opposed the choice, however, with one diplomat complaining that Diem was a "messiah without a message" whose only "formulated policy is to ask immediate American assistance in every form." General Lawton Collins sent a cable in the spring of 1955 that noted: "It would be a major error in judgment to continue to support a man who has demonstrated such a marked inability to understand the political, economic and military problems associated with Vietnam."

By mid-1955, the last chance to jettison Diem had passed, and the administration concentrated on building up the Army of the Republic of Vietnam. MAAG now transitioned into a new role led by General Samuel Williams that focused on preparing the ARVN to fight internal enemies using counterinsurgency tactics derived from past experiences in the Philippines and the Caribbean, as well as British and French models that reflected a recognition of the importance of small wars in the Third World during the Cold War. Simultaneously, the advisory group prepared the ARVN for an inevitable fight with the North Vietnamese.

In these tasks the Americans faced many challenges, some not of their own making. When the French withdrew, they took the best equipment and Vietnamese soldiers with them. Furthermore, Diem perpetually interfered by putting his political cronies, who lacked fighting skills and were often only interested in enriching themselves, in important leadership roles. One person noted that "generals and colonels, it was said jokingly in Saigon, were the only first-class travelers in Vietnam." Simultaneously, the Americans battled their own prejudices, calling the Vietnamese "natives" and treating them with a mix of condescension and contempt. An official U.S. Army report underscored these biases, characterizing "the long-standing nature of the Vietnamese people" as "passive, submissive, fatalistic, accustomed to being led . . . pastoral and non-mechanical."

Despite the challenges, General Williams set about his task. Borrowing heavily from their experiences in South Korea, the Americans built up a 150,000-person army, constructed bases, and even paid the soldiers' salaries. But the interest in security went beyond building the military. The U.S. government also recruited an advisory group from Michigan State University to train local police in methods of interrogation and riot control. However, Diem and MAAG pushed the university team to focus on training a 60,000-person Civil Guard, despite protests that this task would exceed its members' capabilities and undermine the primary effectiveness of the mission. From the beginning, the Americans struggled to transform the Guard into an effective force, but Diem undermined their efforts by using it as a dumping ground for ARVN officer castoffs. Furthermore, while armed with some bazookas and armored cars, the Guard typically received inferior weapons. Its performance underwhelmed evaluators. Colonel Edward Lansdale complained that Guard officers were "pathetically unready for the realities of the Vietnamese countryside. A squad of Civil Guard policemen, armed with whistles, night sticks and .38 caliber revolvers, could hardly be expected to arrest a band of guerrillas armed with submachine guns, rifles, grenades and mortars."

Despite signs to the contrary, by 1960, the MAAG was crowing that the United States had accomplished a "minor miracle" by turning "little more than a marginal collection of armed men" into a modern army capable of resisting communist aggression in South Vietnam. But the reality was often different. One prominent historian notes, "Through luck as much as anything else, the Eisenhower administration helped keep the Diem regime afloat for six years." Its successes created a dependent society, and, as a Vietnam veteran underscored, the impression of success "trapped Eisenhower and subsequent U.S. presidents in a frustrating and futile effort to define and defend U.S. interests in Vietnam."

OTHER FLASHPOINTS

During this period there were other Asian hot spots beyond Indochina, including Taiwan. Confrontations occurred on the two small Nationalist islands of Quemoy and Matsu, which lay just off the Chinese coast, in the fall of 1954 and more seriously in 1958, when Chiang moved 100,000 troops there. Beijing responded by shelling the islands. In Washington, Deputy Secretary of Defense Donald Quarles worried out loud: "The Orientals can be very devious. If we give Chiang our full support he would then call the tune."

Despite personal misgivings, Eisenhower sent U.S. vessels to resupply the Nationalists as part of a continuing evolution of U.S. strategy toward the provision of more support to regional alliances in Asia and the Middle East. For several months, tensions remained high, although the Chinese deliberately avoided provoking the Americans. In mid-September, the JCS informed the president that the islands were not key to the defense of Taiwan. Eisenhower announced in a television address, "There is not going to be any appeasement," but also declared, "I believe there is not going to be any war." Chiang ultimately reduced the number of troops on the islands while the Communists bombarded them every other day to allow for resupply. Eisenhower wrote, "I wondered if we were in a Gilbert and Sullivan war."

Simultaneously, Eisenhower's administration deployed ground troops overseas for the only time during his eight-year tenure. For years, the White House had worried about rising Arab nationalism under Gamal Abdel Nasser in Egypt. In response, in the spring of 1957, the president received congressional approval to announce the "Eisenhower Doctrine," which granted him the power to use force in the Middle East if governments there requested protection against "overt armed aggression from any nation controlled by International Communism." In the summer of 1957, a military coup in Iraq brought to power a "republican" regime that after taking power moved closer to the Soviet Union. Many analysts feared that Lebanon would follow. Soon, the Lebanese president had requested protection from the United States. Air Force general Nathan Farragut Twining bragged to Dulles that the "Russians aren't going to jump us," and "if they do come in, they couldn't pick a better time because we've got them by the whing whang and they know it." In July 1958, Eisenhower ordered 14,000 marines ashore in Lebanon.

For three months, the marines patrolled without incident before finally withdrawing in late 1958. When combined with strong U.S. support for Israel, this action revealed Washington as a major player in the Middle East, one who sought to protect valuable oil reserves and prevent Soviet aggression. In the process, however, the United States alienated nationalists

IMAGE 15.1 **Marines in Lebanon** A U.S. Marine aims a machine gun towards Beirut, Lebanon. Marines arrived in the region in 1958, after Lebanese president Camille Chamoun requested aid from the United States.

in Egypt and Syria, who moved more firmly into the Soviet sphere, and drained significant time and energy in the often-tumultuous region.

THE MILITARY-INDUSTRIAL COMPLEX

Throughout the Eisenhower years, relations with the Soviet Union and China remained tense. Although Eisenhower won some victories in limiting nuclear testing, other problems arose late in his term over the 1960 Soviet downing of a U-2 spy plane piloted by Francis Gary Powers. Still, the administration generally avoided being dragged into major confrontations like the one in Korea. Nonetheless, the American appetite for defense appropriations only grew as American society became ever more dependent on military spending. Across the country, military bases from Charleston, South Carolina, to Abilene, Texas, came to rely on government spending as service personnel at the large bases poured valuable dollars into local economies. Defense industries also prospered in cities such as Wichita, Kansas, and Bath, Maine. Small businesses providing services to these larger companies sprang up nationwide, ensuring more congressional support for defense spending. Companies such as Boeing began employing lobbyists to guarantee contracts to provide arms to U.S. allies.

Military spending reached into other areas that were less obvious. One of the most important initiatives during the Eisenhower administration was the creation of the Interstate Highway System. General Lucius Clay, chairman of the President's Advisory Committee on a National Highway System, argued that "a safe and efficient highway network is essential to America's military and civil defense." In June 1956, Congress passed a $25 billion twelve-year appropriation to start construction. Builders even made sure to add long stretches of straight road without overhead hazards to provide emergency airstrips during war.

More domestic spending poured into military activities in October 1957 after the Soviets launched an unmanned satellite, *Sputnik*, which orbited the earth. The perceived science gap led to the National Defense Education Act of 1958, which sent money into schools for the study of math and sciences as well as foreign languages. Large research universities benefited as billions of dollars flowed to them. By the early 1960s, 20 percent of their monies came from federal grants, much of it for military research.

The military's reach extended even further as large numbers of U.S. troops spread into regions where before 1941 the United States had shown little interest. The increased burden of maintaining these troops was exacerbated by the increasing costs of new technologies, including nuclear weapons, jet fighters and bombers, and research and development for future systems. For the first time in its history, the United States became reliant on defense spending during peacetime.

Even as he oversaw this rise in defense spending, Eisenhower worried about its effects on the country. As he left office, he gave a Farewell Address that focused primarily on the development of the "military-industrial complex." In it, he warned that while before World War II the United States had no defense industry, the Cold War had created "a permanent armaments industry of vast proportions" that included more than 3.5 million people spread across the world. At the same time, annual spending on military security had risen above the net income of all U.S. corporations. He warned: "In the councils of government, we must guard against the acquisition of unwarranted influence, whether sought or unsought, by the military industrial complex. The potential for the disastrous rise of misplaced power exists and will persist." Eisenhower concluded by stressing that the country "must avoid becoming a community of dreadful fear and hate, and be, instead, a proud confederation of mutual trust and respect."

It was a prescient warning for an industry that continued evolving relatively unabated, although the next chapter in Vietnam definitely caused some reflection. The former general clearly recognized the inherent dangers of such a course. As his director of defense research and engineering Herbert York explained, Eisenhower understood both "the necessity of having a military-industrial complex and . . . the problems and dangers it brought with it."

PAY ANY PRICE, BEAR ANY BURDEN

By early 1961, John F. Kennedy had brought to the White House a new charisma and energy. To many the young war hero represented a time of change and hope. This optimism extended to foreign affairs: in his Inaugural Address, Kennedy announced: "Let every nation know, whether it wishes us well or ill, that we shall pay any price, bear any burden, meet any hardship, support any friend, oppose any foe, in order to assure the survival and success of liberty." He concluded with the immortal words: "Ask not what your country can do for you—ask what you can do for your country." To some, the new president stood in great contrast to his predecessor.

THE CUBAN MISSILE CRISIS, 1962

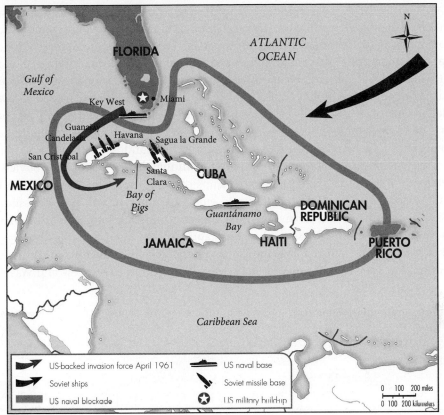

MAP 15.1 The Cuban Missile Crisis

To fulfill Kennedy's promise of a "flexible response" in foreign policy and military affairs, the Pentagon, under the leadership of Secretary of Defense Robert McNamara, continued building up nuclear forces for deterrence but increasingly focused on counterinsurgency and nation building to combat Third World enemies. Efforts included the promotion of the "Green Berets," soldiers who received special training in language, small arms, and civil affairs. Although the Green Berets had been created in the Eisenhower period, they became a symbol of the new efforts of the Kennedy administration.

Early on, conflicts in Laos, Berlin, and especially Cuba received the lion's share of Kennedy's attention. In April 1961 he approved the disastrous Bay of Pigs operation that sent Cuban exiles to a devastating defeat by the forces of Fidel Castro. The embarrassed administration responded with CIA Operation Mongoose, which sought to overthrow Castro through sabotage and assassination. Matters came to a head in October 1962 when a U-2 reconnaissance plane on a routine mission photographed missile sites in Cuba. By that time, the Soviets had placed forty-two nuclear weapons in the country. Kennedy immediately declared, "He can't do that to me," seeing the act as a test of wills with Soviet premier Nikita Khrushchev.

The president then set up an executive committee of his most trusted advisors to formulate a response. During the debates, former secretary of state Dean Acheson recommended surgical air strikes on the missiles, while the JCS pushed for a full-scale invasion to remove both the weapons and Castro. Others, including Attorney General Robert Kennedy, pressed for a naval blockade, a "quarantine" that would prevent additional missiles from arriving.

After much debate, the president settled on the "quarantine," even though he knew that such a provocation on the high seas could bring war. As U.S. forces massed in southern Florida, on October 22, Kennedy called on the Soviets to end their "deliberately provocative" actions and remove their weapons from Cuba. He also promised massive retaliation against the Soviet Union if any missiles were launched from the island.

In what one person characterized as "an international war of nerves," the Soviets chose the prudent course. On October 26, Soviet ships carrying more weapons to Cuba turned around. Moscow also used intermediaries to guarantee the removal of the missiles if the United States promised not to invade Cuba and removed U.S. Jupiter missiles in Turkey. After some anxious moments, Kennedy agreed, and tensions dissipated quickly.

Most observers recognized that the Cuban Missile Crisis had taken the world to the brink of nuclear war. To try to prevent future misunderstandings, Moscow and Washington

IMAGE 15.2 Cuban Missile Crisis The world faced near nuclear war in October of 1962 after Washington discovered the presence of Soviet nuclear missile sites in Cuba. For thirteen days, John F. Kennedy and advisors carefully analyzed potential strategies and outcomes and engaged in a tense standoff with the Soviet Union. Resolution came when Soviet leader Nikita Khrushchev agreed to dismantle the missiles in return for the promise that the United States would not invade Cuba.

established a hotline to allow for direct communication between the president and the premier. However, the crisis sparked changes in the Soviet Union, including shifts in leadership. Khrushchev's successors were determined to not have to back down in a clash with the United States, which led to a renewed nuclear arms race that created massive stockpiles of weapons and raised tensions over time.

LIMITED PARTNERSHIP IN SOUTH VIETNAM

After the Cuban Missile Crisis passed, Kennedy quickly turned his attention to Vietnam in early 1963. The Viet Cong had successes, largely related to Diem's authoritarian actions, particularly the persecution of Buddhists. He was also increasingly alienating more South Vietnamese, particularly those in the countryside and among the intelligentsia. To stem the tide, Kennedy increased U.S. involvement in Vietnam. By the spring of 1961, he had sent 100 additional advisors and 400 counterinsurgency specialists to the region. The administration also prodded the ARVN to begin clandestine operations against North Vietnamese strategic targets.

Not long after, Kennedy sent two close advisors, General Maxwell Taylor and NSC advisor Walt Rostow, to Vietnam. When they arrived in late 1961, they found a dispirited ARVN led by cautious political appointees. Taylor concluded that "no one felt that the situation was helpless" but warned that the problems posed by the North Vietnamese were serious and required action. Kennedy ultimately responded with more advisors but resisted calls for combat troops, telling his confidant Arthur M. Schlesinger, Jr.: "The troops will march in: the bands will play; the crowds will cheer . . . and in four days everyone will have forgotten. Then we will be told we have to send in more troops. It's like taking a drink. The effect wears off, and you have to have another."

Under the newly organized Military Assistance Command, Vietnam (MACV), General Paul Harkins and his lieutenants dove into their jobs. The number of Americans in Vietnam jumped from 3,205 in late December 1961 to more than 9,000 a year later. American advisors, many of whom were veterans of World War II and Korea, often flew helicopters and planes on missions and fought alongside the South Vietnamese. While the administration downplayed these individuals' direct involvement, journalists increasingly reported the active role they were taking.

U.S. strategists in many agencies, including the military, also worked with Diem to undermine Viet Cong support in the countryside with the Strategic Hamlet Program. Strongly influenced by British activities in Malaya in the 1950s, this program resettled peasants into fortified hamlets ringed by moats and barbed wire. Funding for housing and food flowed from the United States but often ended up in the hands of corrupt government officials. By September 1962, the government had relocated more than 4.3 million people, one-third of the southern population. While Diem and some Americans, including McNamara, praised the policy, others sounded a warning note. One RAND researcher cautioned against being distracted by "statistical razzle-dazzle" that ignored those affected by the resettlements. One American soldier complained that those implementing the program "only want to please the regime. They haven't the faintest idea of what makes peasants tick—and how can they? They're city boys who earned promotions by kissing the asses of their bosses." Ultimately, the program failed miserably, largely because its leader, Colonel Pham Ngoc Thao, was a Viet Cong agent who knew that it alienated the peasants.

Despite reported successes, Harkins continued requesting more materials and advisors. The number of American advisors in Vietnam peaked at 16,000 in 1963, when McNamara visited Saigon in April and announced: "Every quantitative assessment we have shows we are winning this war." Although Kennedy called for reductions before his death, the move was more in response to perceptions of improvements than a commitment to a full U.S. withdrawal.

LOVERS, NOT FIGHTERS

One of the most visible Americans to land in Vietnam in the early 1960s was the outspoken Lieutenant Colonel John Paul Vann. The Korean War veteran had close relationships with some of the most prominent American journalists covering the war, including David Halberstam of the *New York Times* and Neil Sheehan of United Press International. A dynamic maverick, Vann initially championed the ARVN when he arrived in 1962. He told a reporter that the South Vietnamese "may be the world's greatest lovers, but they're not the world's greatest fighters. But they're good people, and they can win a war if someone shows them how." At the same time, he declared that the Viet Cong could be defeated "if they would only stand and fight."

Despite this optimism, Vann soon became extremely critical of the ARVN, particularly after the Battle of Ap Bac on January 2, 1963. That day, 1,200 South Vietnamese soldiers, supported by helicopters and heavy artillery, moved against 400 Viet Cong in trenches armed only with machine guns and mortars. From the outset, ARVN leaders advanced cautiously. Infuriated, Vann pushed for more aggressive action as overhead American helicopters flew into a hail of Viet Cong bullets that brought down five. All day long, the American advisors drove the ARVN forward, but with little success. Finally, at sundown, the Viet Cong simply melted away into the jungle, having inflicted heavy casualties, including more than eighty killed and hundreds wounded. In addition, three Americans died and eight suffered wounds. The enemy only lost eighteen men, with nearly forty wounded, despite being pounded by helicopter gunships, heavy artillery, and bombers. An enraged Vann quipped to one journalist that the ARVN had given "a miserable fucking performance, just like it always [does]." In contrast, he described the Viet Cong as "brave men" who "gave a good account of themselves today." While MACV claimed victory, Vann complained bitterly to his superiors and journalists, arguing for new officers and better training. Nevertheless, he greatly feared an American buildup. "We'd end up shooting at everything—men, women, kids, and the buffalos," he warned. Ultimately, his admonitions fell on deaf ears.

JETTISONING DIEM

As conditions worsened, Kennedy explored options. McNamara and Harkins continued to voice confidence in Diem, but the arrival of new U.S. ambassador Henry Cabot Lodge signaled a change. Rumors circulated around Saigon of an impending coup in October 1963. Lodge communicated with army officers that while the United States would not "stimulate" an overthrow, it would not "thwart a change of government or deny economic and military assistance to a new regime if it appeared capable of increasing [the] effectiveness of the military effort, ensuring popular support to win [the] war."

On November 1, the generals leapt into action, seizing major military installations and government offices. Within a short time, they had apprehended Diem and murdered him and his brother. The assassins then deposited the bodies in unmarked graves in a cemetery next to the U.S. ambassador's residence.

VIETNAM, 1965–1967

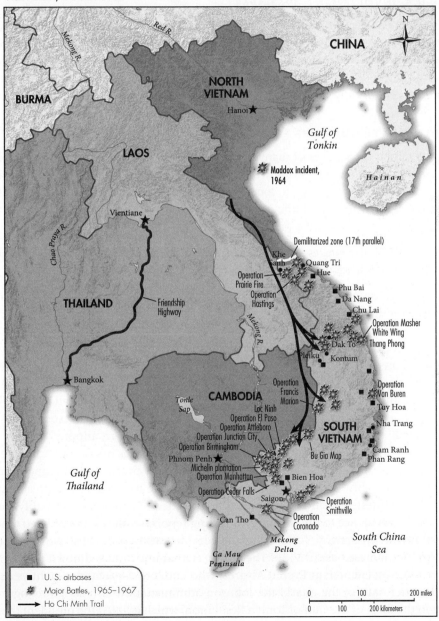

MAP 15.2 Vietnam, 1965–1967

The United States now faced an uncertain situation, as ARVN officers led by General Nguyen Khanh took power. Unfortunately for Kennedy, his time to deal with the transformation lasted less than three weeks. On November 22 the president was assassinated in Dallas. His vice president, Lyndon Johnson, inherited a mess in Vietnam.

THE BIG JUICY WORM ON THE HOOK:
MAJOR U.S. INVOLVEMENT, 1963–1968

Early in his presidency, Johnson told his advisor Bill Moyers on Vietnam, "Right now I feel like one of those catfish in your part of Texas. I feel like I just grabbed a big juicy worm with a right sharp hook in the middle of it." Of course, he had choices. Nonetheless, his decisions sent more U.S. troops to South Vietnam, especially in the summer of 1965. By the time of the Tet Offensive in early 1968, more than 550,000 U.S. troops occupied South Vietnam.

SLIDING INTO THE QUAGMIRE

Johnson retained the services of many of Kennedy's closest foreign policy advisors, including McNamara, Rostow, and Taylor, with the latter becoming U.S. ambassador to Vietnam. While the new president wanted to focus on domestic affairs, events conspired against him. The Texan originally took a middle-of-the-road approach to South Vietnam, even as the Republican challenger in the 1964 presidential race, Barry Goldwater, complained:

> "Failures infest the jungles of Vietnam . . . and now the Commander-in-Chief of our forces . . . refuses to say, mind you, whether or not the objective over there is victory."

Problems also arose in Vietnam as successive South Vietnamese governments failed against the Viet Cong. In addition, South Vietnamese actions provoked the North Vietnamese. OPLAN-34 operations designed to sabotage enemy facilities as well as DESOTO missions, reconnaissance and mapping operation of North Vietnamese defenses, increased the potential for conflict.

These actions had consequences. On the night of August 2, 1964, North Vietnamese torpedo boats attacked but did not damage the USS *Maddox* in the Gulf of Tonkin. The *Maddox* returned fire, and planes from the nearby USS *Ticonderoga* damaged three attackers. Johnson, knowing of *Maddox*'s relationship to OPLAN-34, showed restraint in his response but noted: "The other side got a sting out of this. If they do it again, they'll get another."

Two nights later, the *Maddox*, joined by the *Turner Joy*, was operating in the area, battling heavy seas. Suddenly, SONAR operators reported an attack, and the captain radioed an account of a confrontation. McNamara delivered the message to the president, who immediately requested verification. The navy responded that an attack probably had happened, despite evidence to the contrary, including reports from pilots overhead that there had been no enemy activity. To retaliate, the administration ordered sixty-four sorties on the North Vietnamese base at Vinh. The North Vietnamese knocked down two American planes, capturing Lieutenant Everett Alvarez, who endured captivity for eight years.

In the aftermath of the attack, the Johnson administration also sought congressional support in the form of the Gulf of Tonkin Resolution, which granted the president the power to take "all necessary measures to repel any armed attacks against the forces of the United

IMAGE 15.3 Gulf of Tonkin In August of 1964, news spread that American Navy destroyers, the U.S.S. *Maddox* (above) and U.S.S. *Turner*, were attacked by North Vietnamese patrol boats. The incident prompted Congress to pass the Gulf of Tonkin Resolution, providing President Johnson the authority to formally enter the United States into the Vietnam War.

States." Only two senators, the independent Wayne Morse of Oregon and Democrat Ernest Gruening of Alaska opposed the measure, fearing it amounted to a de facto declaration of war. Nevertheless, the resolution passed 88–2 in the Senate (unanimously in the House), and the administration gained a near blank check in Vietnam.

President Johnson's approval rating skyrocketed after U.S. forces pounded the enemy. Behind the scenes, however, Johnson worried about entering "the patient in a 10-round bout, when he was in no shape to hold out for one round." Most important, North Vietnamese hard-liners led by Le Duan began infiltrating more regular People's Army of Vietnam (PAVN) units in the South, hoping to achieve a victory before the United States fully engaged. The administration's forceful response persuaded Hanoi that Johnson would do whatever was necessary to sustain the Saigon government.

HITTING THEM HARD FROM ABOVE

With a virtual blank check from Congress and an overwhelming victory in the presidential election of November 1964, the Johnson administration explored various ways to sustain the South Vietnamese while limiting U.S. involvement. How to achieve that goal remained as elusive as ever, and over time, the military pushed for more manpower for its mission, paralleling its increasing reliance on advanced technology.

In early 1965, the air war expanded despite the vigorous protests of Undersecretary of State George Ball and others who warned about its potential negligible effects and feared it

IMAGE 15.4   US Troops landing in 1965   A young Marine at the landing of Da Nang, Vietnam, 1965. Although the law required that men be no younger than seventeen years old to enlist, cases have surfaced of underage soldiers as young as fourteen who lied about their age in order to join the war effort.

would lead to the introduction of more U.S. ground forces. However, war "hawks" led by McNamara, Secretary of State Dean Rusk, and NSC advisor McGeorge Bundy swayed the president toward firmer actions.

The drive for more American troops increased after the Viet Cong attacked the air base at Pleiku on February 2, 1965, destroying U.S. aircraft, killing 6 Americans, and wounding 126 others. Hard-liners pressed for heavier airstrikes on the North. When opposition arose, Johnson responded: "We have kept our guns on the mantel and our shells in the cupboard for a long time now. I can't ask our American soldiers out there to continue to fight with one hand behind their backs."

The hawks, including General William Westmoreland, the hard-nosed World War II and Korean War veteran who commanded MACV, won the day. Johnson unleashed Operation Rolling Thunder, a four-year heavy aerial bombardment of enemy positions and infrastructure. He insisted on tight control over targets, stressing, "They can't even bomb an outhouse without my approval." This restraint would anger many in the military, especially pilots who were limited in action by their orders. By the time the operation ended, the United States had dropped more than 7.6 million tons of ordnance on Vietnam.

BOOTS ON THE GROUND

As the air war expanded, General Westmoreland worried about security at U.S. air bases and the anemic abilities of ARVN troops. In late February, he requested that U.S. Marines be sent to the air base at Da Nang, noting a short time later that to avert a disaster, there was "no solution . . . other than to put our finger in the dike." Johnson agreed to send a large force on March 8, 1965, but he confined Westmoreland to only a few operational enclaves. One marine wading ashore observed that the forces "carried, along with our packs and rifles, the implicit conviction that the Viet Cong would be quickly beaten."

However, in May, a successful Viet Cong offensive in Binh Gia Province convinced more Americans that the ARVN could not defeat the Viet Cong and the ever-increasing number of North Vietnamese. General Nguyen Van Thieu and Air Marshall Nguyen Cao Ky seized control in Saigon, creating more uncertainty. Under intense pressure, Johnson approved a request for 100,000 more troops in the summer of 1965 and permitted operations to be conducted outside the enclaves. The president rationalized that if the United States retreated in South Vietnam, "it might as well give up everywhere else—pull out of Berlin, Japan, South America." He wanted to use force until the North "sobers up and unloads his pistol," an approach that he compared to a congressional filibuster, with "enormous resistance at first, then a steady whittling away, then . . . hurrying to get it over."

Much like the French before him, Johnson clearly underestimated the enemy. *"Chung ta nhat dinh thang* [We will ultimately win]" became an important rallying cry. While some like Giap and Ho pushed a strategy of guerrilla warfare, General Nguyen Chi Thanh, who headed southern military operations, argued that Westmoreland would fail because of a lack of resolve when directly challenged. One Communist leader crowed in the summer of 1965, "The liberation war of South Vietnam has progressed by leaps and bounds," with the American realizing "that he was in the process of being defeated."

BLEEDING THEM DRY IN THE VALLEY OF DEATH

With more troops, Westmoreland launched a war of attrition to try to force the enemy to capitulate or recognize the futility of resistance. He found it impossible to measure victory by common standards, as taking territory meant nothing when the Communists often willingly ceded ground and chose when and where to fight. For Americans fighting in Vietnam, the calculus of war became a matter of killing more of the enemy than were lost, relying on air mobility and other technology to inflict casualties while limiting American deaths.

The focus soon shifted to "search and destroy" as U.S. forces sought out the Viet Cong in hopes of bringing to bear their significant advantages in airpower and artillery. The Battle

IMAGE 15.5　Battle Photo　U.S. soldiers engaged in a battle north of Saigon in November, 1965. Three years later, Saigon would serve as a major target in the Tet Offensive.

of Ia Drang in late 1965 tested the new strategy. The 1st Cavalry Division (Airmobile) left South Carolina in October, at about the same time that the PAVN 66th Regiment started the treacherous trek along the Ho Chi Minh Trail into South Vietnam. Both converged at the Ia Drang Valley, southwest of Da Nang, in mid-November. On November 12, American helicopters swept into the valley after a major aerial and artillery bombardment to disembark troops. As they approached, one helicopter pilot complained, "We landed too close to some trenches the gooks dug. . . . The guys inside [the helicopter] didn't know Charlie was close. . . . They got us on our approach." Under the leadership of Lieutenant Colonel Hal Moore, a small force of about 450 Americans fought for two days against nearly 1,700 PAVN. Desperately, the Americans held on, inflicting heavy casualties. On November 14, the enemy withdrew after losing 634 dead and hundreds wounded. U.S. forces had lost 79 killed and 121 wounded. The following day, in a less reported part of the battle, another group replaced Moore's unit. On November 17, Lieutenant Colonel Robert McDade's units walked into a well-crafted ambush. The Americans and PAVN fought in close quarters in the elephant grass and dense foliage. That night, the American wounded, separated from two small perimeters, cried out for help. The next day, the PAVN left. Of the 450 Americans who had flown in, 155 died and 124 suffered wounds.

Both sides drew different conclusions from the battle. Westmoreland heralded it as a victory for his strategy, underscoring the proportional losses of nearly ten to one. McNamara, however, reacted differently. After receiving a briefing from Moore during a visit to Vietnam, he lamented: "It will be a long war." Some of the soldiers on the ground agreed. One member of the 1st Cavalry Division, Dennis Deal, talked about policing the battlefield and coming across a dead PAVN soldier with "his buttocks shot off and his insides . . . leaking out a large hole." He observed: "As he was lying there . . . he had taken a hand grenade, armed it, and wrapped it around the upper hand guard of his rifle stock. He had booby-trapped himself." Seeing that, Deal said, he had thought to himself: "Man, if we're up against this, it's going to be a long-ass year."

The Communists took away their own lessons. To many, the battle had proved that the PAVN could fight toe-to-toe with the Americans despite their superior mobility and firepower. Many believed that the U.S. population would not accept such heavy casualties. Some enemy strategists thought that the combination of guerrilla and conventional war would force the Americans out of their comfort zone and into eating "rice with chopsticks."

BLOW FOR BLOW

Throughout 1966 and 1967, both sides hammered away at each other. U.S. and ARVN forces tried to defend as much territory as possible, while the enemy typically chose when and where to fight. In response, Westmoreland continued to request more troops. By January 1967 the number of U.S. military personnel in Vietnam had climbed to 385,000. Casualties had also mounted, from 1,928 killed in action in 1965 to 6,350 in 1966.

U.S. commanders often relied on large-scale missions to draw out the enemy because they needed "body counts" (the number of enemy killed) to demonstrate success. From January 8 to January 28, 1967, MACV sought to root out enemy forces working in the

"Iron Triangle" near Saigon in Operation Cedar Falls. The effort began with the forced resettlement of people within a perimeter. In the villages at Ben Suc, Lieutenant Colonel Alexander Haig roared in on a helicopter as his troops set up loudspeakers warning: "You are surrounded by Republic of South Vietnam and Allied forces. Do not run away or you will be shot as V.C." Then U.S. forces swept the area and interrogated any young men they found, arresting suspected Viet Cong and drafting others into the ARVN. Shortly thereafter, they transported more than 6,000 people out, burning and bulldozing the villages behind them. For nearly three weeks, the Americans searched for enemy troops, some of whom stood and fought when discovered, and others hiding in an elaborate tunnel system that also housed hospitals and armories. At one point, Westmoreland visited a site, but the excursion ended abruptly when the senior noncommissioned officer died after tripping a booby trap.

Ultimately, Allied forces claimed that Operation Cedar Falls had led to more than 700 Communists killed and the capture of 600 weapons while sustaining 100 killed. MACV declared a victory. However, some commanders questioned the operation's effectiveness. Brigadier General Bernard Rogers observed: "We had insufficient forces . . . to permit us to continue to operate in the Iron Triangle and War Zone C and thereby prevent the Viet Cong from returning. In neither instance were we able to stay around, and it was not long before there was evidence of the enemy's return." Another commander grumbled that within a couple of weeks, "the Iron Triangle was again literally crawling with what appeared to be Viet Cong."

Cedar Falls encompassed several key aspects of the ground war in South Vietnam. First, the relocation effort constituted an attempt to win the "hearts and minds" of the local population. In an effort to reduce support for the enemy, the U.S. government provided housing, food, medical care, and education to evacuees. These activities had some success, but they were small scale and often reflected little understanding of local cultures and traditions. Promised financial support for refugees often failed to materialize, as corrupt South Vietnamese officials siphoned off funds and people found themselves short of food and sanitary living conditions. This situation left people angry and disillusioned, often driving them into the enemy's camp.

Second, the operation incorporated the use of chemical weapons such as Agent Orange and other defoliants to reduce enemy hiding places. In an earlier operation in 1962, code-named Ranch Hand, U.S. forces had ultimately sprayed more than 19 million gallons of herbicide, clearing more than 4.5 million acres of land. Flying in specially fitted C-123 planes and helicopters, Americans dumped compounds that destroyed wide swaths of the country equivalent in size to the state of Massachusetts. These chemicals poisoned water sources, crops, and people, including U.S. soldiers on the ground.

Third, the enemy constantly adapted to changing U.S. tactics. In many cases, Communist intelligence knew details of an attack in advance, to such a point that U.S. forces began withholding information from the South Vietnamese. In response to such intelligence, enemy fighters often left the area or blended in with the local populace. When they chose to fight, they often selected when and where to inflict the most damage before drifting back into the

IMAGE 15.6   Operation Ranch Hand   Operation Ranch Hand was a controversial form of chemical warfare used to strip the Viet Cong of food and cover. The over-spraying of herbicides during the Vietnam War not only caused lasting ecological and impacts to South Vietnam, but also exposed civilians to a variety of long-lasting ailments.

jungle or retiring to Cambodia. This proved a maddening game of whack-a-mole for the Americans and their allies, who by 1966 included a large contingent of South Koreans as well as smaller groups of Australians and New Zealanders. With only statistics to determine victories and casualties rising significantly, some Americans began to question their presence in Vietnam. While they often praised their foreign allies, the Americans rarely did the same for the ARVN. Many never trusted the South Vietnamese, fearing that they had been infiltrated by the Viet Cong or simply would not fight. Most grunts held them in contempt. Reflecting on preparing for an operation, one complained that "as often was the case with the South Vietnamese units, the ARVNs never showed up." Such events led another to grumble, "I started hating ARVNs because they were so unreliable and a couple of times in ambushes the ARVNs disappeared."

ARVN officers recognized their problems. General Ngo Quang Troung observed that the "permanent danger was that the ARVN had become psychologically and materially too dependent on Americans." The lack of an end date to service, the often-arbitrary conscription system, and a host of other problems further limited the force's effectiveness.

ROLLING IN FROM THE CLOUDS

Many of the same problems that plagued the ground war hampered air operations. In the earliest stages of the war, the United States had relied heavily on bombing to force the North Vietnamese to reduce support for the Viet Cong. The number of sorties over the North rose from 25,000 in 1965 to 108,000 in 1967, with the tonnage of bombs dropped increasing from 63,000 to 226,000 during that same period. Targets included factories, power plants, fuel depots, and transportation hubs.

While the aerial war enjoyed some successes and inflicted heavy casualties on civilians, it was also hampered by significant limitations. The scale of civilian deaths created an international outcry, while the North Vietnamese simply dug tunnels, moved factories to isolated areas, and endured, driven by patriotism and propaganda. Politicians also regulated targets, fearful that overzealous commanders would incite an international incident. Johnson consistently worried about bringing China and Russia into the conflict. His worst fear was an American plane dropping "a bomb down some smokestack of a Russian freighter in Haiphong Harbor, and the pilot will be from Johnson City, Texas, and we've got World War III going on."

Too, while curtailing some North Vietnamese capabilities and causing hardship, bombing failed to stop enemy resupply of war material and manpower. Nearly 300,000 Chinese helped North Vietnam with infrastructure and logistics, while the Soviets and their allies sent huge caches of arms. The Soviets also provided surface-to-air missiles as well as training to Vietnamese pilots who flew MiG jets in combat. Soon, such efforts took a toll on Americans; one pilot characterized North Vietnam as the "center of hell with Hanoi as its hub." This foreign support proved very expensive for the United States, both in manpower and in money. In 1965 and 1966, the United States lost at least 500 aircraft (excluding helicopters) at an estimated cost of $1.7 billion. Between 1966 and 1968, the numbers increased as enemy defenses improved, becoming capable of knocking down aircraft and highly trained pilots and crews, some of whom became POWs and extremely valuable propaganda tools. One report estimated that for every $1 of damage inflicted, the United States spent $9.60. Such losses not only drained the national treasury but also incited a public outcry against the war.

Most important, bombing failed to deter the North Vietnamese. While having some effect, it did not significantly alter the amount of soldiers and aid flowing south. In 1965, more than 35,000 PAVN troops headed south, a number that increased to 90,000 in 1967. The amount of supplies moving south also swelled as hundreds of thousands of workers repaired the Ho Chi Minh Trail and other routes, usually right after an attack.

Finally, the American reliance on aerial bombardment early on as well as the strategy of limiting ground operations frustrated U.S. commanders. Technology had limits, and interservice rivalry exacerbated long-simmering tensions between the air force, army, and marines, causing both political and military leaders to struggle to explain the stalemate developing in South Vietnam, where the Viet Cong and increasing numbers of PAVN soldiers inflicted casualties on the Americans and their allies. Stateside, many people began questioning the morality as well as practicality of fighting a war thousands of miles away, costing billions of dollars and the lives of thousands of Americans.

THE YEAR OF THE CONTINUOUS NIGHTMARE: 1968

As 1968 rolled around, there were significant concerns on the home front about the war. Its rising costs concerned policymakers as well as average citizens, who took to the streets to protest, led by prominent individuals such as Martin Luther King, Jr., and Dr. Benjamin Spock. The war threatened to rip apart the nation. Nonetheless, some people remained committed to the cause in Southeast Asia, although those numbers dwindled appreciably in 1968.

THE ROAD TO TET

Even as many Americans questioned U.S. involvement in Vietnam, Westmoreland and Johnson continued to appear publicly confident in the war effort. In November 1967, the general told reporters, "We have reached an important point where the end begins to come into view. . . . Whereas in 1965 the enemy was winning, today he is certainly losing." During a surprise visit to Vietnam in December, Johnson proudly announced that the United States "had come from the valleys and the depths of despondency to the heights and the cliffs, where we know now that the enemy can never win." But despite this optimism, the fighting actually escalated. In January 1968, all eyes focused on a lonely marine base at Khe Sanh near the Demilitarized Zone, where more than 30,000 PAVN troops encircled 6,000 marines and some ARVN rangers. U.S. leaders feared another Dien Bien Phu, so they poured massive resources into defending the base.

Other issues also distracted the Johnson administration, including the seizure of an American intelligence ship, the USS *Pueblo*, off the North Korean coast on January 23, 1968. The lightly armed spy ship offered little resistance when North Korean patrol boats demanded its surrender. As the North Koreans boarded the *Pueblo*, the crew frantically tried to destroy sensitive documents and coding machines but were ultimately hauled into harbor and imprisoned, charged with espionage. While some Americans called for an immediate attack in retaliation, Johnson knew that such a move would ensure the crew's death and also possibly start another war, distracting the United States from Vietnam. Instead, he chose to

"Everything's Okay —— They Never Reached The Mimeograph Machine"

IMAGE 15.7 Tet Offensive Political Cartoon
Editorial cartoon providing commentary on the Tet Offensive. News coverage of the major offensive triggered outcry and distrust in government that forever shaped the public's view of the Vietnam War.

THE HO CHI MINH TRAIL

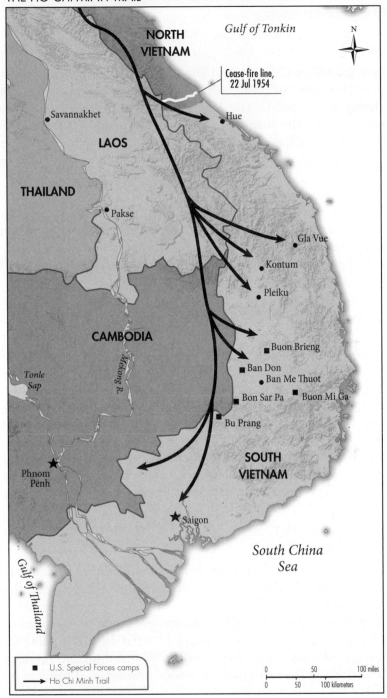

MAP 15.3 Tet Offensive

negotiate for the crew's release, which occurred just before Christmas 1968. Still, in January, it constituted a major distraction.

THE BIG SURPRISE

With Americans focused on the *Pueblo* and Khe Sanh, enormous numbers of PAVN and Viet Cong prepared for a major offensive. As the South Vietnamese and Americans respected a cease-fire during the Tet holiday (the Vietnamese New Year), the Communists suddenly launched massive attacks. The offensive caught American and ARVN forces, many of whom had gone home for the holiday, completely off guard. One American officer noted, "If we'd gotten the whole game plan, it wouldn't have been believed. It wouldn't have been credible to us."

The enemy hit almost every major base and provincial capital in South Vietnam. Viet Cong sappers even penetrated the outer sector of the American embassy, one of the most fortified positions in South Vietnam. Throughout Saigon, heavy fighting erupted as the American and ARVN soldiers fought off the onslaught. At home, Americans watched in horror as the dead piled up and reporters even captured a photograph of a South Vietnamese police official publicly executing a captured Viet Cong operative in Saigon. U.S. troops held on precariously in many areas. In Can Tho, a helicopter pilot watched the enemy flooding through the lines and remembered: "We had cooks and typists and whoever could carry a gun out there" to plug the holes. A heavy fog kept the Americans' Cobra gunships grounded, so pilots jumped in and hovered their craft a few feet off the ground, firing their machine guns and rockets. They "managed to blow Charlie right back out of the perimeter, but not before he blew up just about every helicopter on the flight line."

The heaviest fighting took place in Hue, where Viet Cong units overran the city's defenders, hoisting their flag above the citadel in the imperial city. ARVN forces and U.S. Marines subsequently counterattacked in a battle that lasted nearly six weeks. In vicious house-to-house fighting, enemy snipers slowed progress. A dark black cloud hung over the formerly beautiful city as American gunships and planes pounded the Viet Cong into submission, but only after they inflicted heavy casualties and murdered thousands of Saigon government supporters.

A CRISIS IN CONFIDENCE

After the initial surprise, U.S. and ARVN troops successfully turned the tide of the battle, forcing many enemy units to retreat into Cambodia. Yet the heavy fighting that arrived in American living rooms each night via television caused a severe crisis in confidence in the United States' military strategy in South Vietnam. Even long-time supporter of the war and respected journalist Walter Cronkite quipped: "What the hell is going on? I thought we were winning." After returning from a visit to Vietnam, he told millions of viewers that it was "more certain than ever that the bloody experience of Vietnam is to end in a stalemate."

Even more important, the president and his advisors wavered. The war weighed heavily on Johnson, who publicly stated, "The nights are very long. The winds are very chill.

Our spirits grow weary and restive as the springtime of man seems farther and farther away."
The president recognized the American people's growing frustrations. When a speechwriter
underscored Alexis de Tocqueville's observation that Americans "grow tired of a confusion
whose end is not in sight," Johnson put his head in his hands and said, "That's sure as hell
right." This new wariness of the war manifested itself in a sudden challenge against Johnson
from Senator Eugene McCarthy of Minnesota in the New Hampshire Democratic primary in
February, one the incumbent barely won.

When military advisors requested an additional 206,000 troops, Johnson was both shaken
and skeptical. McNamara noted growing American fatigue with "requests from the Wheelers
of the world" for more men and complained that the military had "no plan to win the war."
"When we add divisions, can't the enemy add divisions?" he asked. "If so, where does it all
end?" Ultimately, the president only approved a small portion of the request. On March 31,
he went on national television and announced his commitment to seeking peace in Vietnam.
He told viewers, "With America's sons in fields far away . . . with the world's hopes for peace
in balance every day, I do not believe that I should devote an hour or a day of my time to personal causes." Then the Texan paused and shocked almost everyone: "Accordingly, I shall not
seek, and I will not accept, the nomination of my party for another term as your president."

Formal peace talks began in May in Paris, but fighting continued across the country, even
near Khe Sanh, until U.S. forces abandoned the base that summer. In the South, the enemy
fought on despite the beating administered during Tet. Casualties mounted on both sides,
reaching nearly 17,000 killed in action for 1968 for the Americans, the highest of any year
of the war.

Tet proved a tactical victory for the United States but a strategic defeat. It initiated the
peace process and ultimate withdrawal of American combat troops, whose number peaked
in 1968 at nearly 550,000, the vast majority of whom served in noncombat roles reflective
of the massive logistical commitment the war required. But no one, including the new president, Richard Nixon, thought the United States could win at a reasonable price. He merely
wanted peace with honor. The enemy, while mauled, continued fighting while preparing for
a final struggle against the ARVN after American withdrawal. Ultimately, many more would
die, and the war would spill over into Laos and Cambodia with devastating effects—an outcome that became clearer by the end of 1968.

WE'VE GOTTA GET OUT OF THIS PLACE: VIETNAMIZATION AND WITHDRAWAL, 1969–1975

Once in office in January 1969, Nixon announced plans for "Vietnamization," a process
of shifting responsibilities to the ARVN and gradually withdrawing U.S. troops. Relying
on heavy bombing and U.S. soldiers when necessary, Nixon and new commander General
Creighton Abrams sought to push the North Vietnamese and Viet Cong to the negotiating
table. It took four more years and many casualties, but in January 1973, the United States
and the North Vietnamese signed a peace accord. Americans then watched as the enemy
went on the offensive and defeated the South Vietnamese in April 1975. It was a long five
and a half years for everyone involved.

IMAGE 15.8 U.S. Bombing The F-4 Phantom II was a highly popular fighter-bomber during the Vietnam War. Here, four of these fighters are seen dropping bombs on North Vietnam in 1966.

THE WAR OF SURVIVAL

Life for American soldiers changed dramatically after 1968. Problems related to racial strife, drugs, and a decline of discipline escalated in the military. More draftees arrived, many with college degrees, as graduate school deferments ended. The implementation of a draft lottery system in 1969 further changed the military's demographics. More grunts, while often fighting bravely, increasingly sought to avoid risking their lives in a quixotic crusade. The overall attitude was characterized by one marine who compared the American experience in 1968 to that of the British campaigning on the Indian frontier in the late nineteenth century. "They were just trying to manage the unwinnable," he said. "In a sense, we were only biding time until we pulled out of Vietnam." Increasingly, American soldiers became more disenchanted with the war, not wanting to be the last to die in a losing cause. Some infantrymen began writing "UUUU" on their helmets, meaning "The unwilling, led by the unqualified, doing the unnecessary for the ungrateful."

THE RACIAL TINDERBOX

The U.S. military in Southeast Asia inherited many problems from stateside, especially after Tet. In 1968 simmering racial tensions erupted in race riots all over the United States in cities such as Los Angeles, Detroit, and Newark. The conflict spilled over into the military, ultimately creating divisions and undermining combat effectiveness.

In Vietnam, problems often arose on base camps and in rear areas as segregation returned and tempers flared. When an assassin killed Martin Luther King, Jr., in April 1968, some whites paraded around Cam Ranh Bay in white sheets to celebrate his murder. Others flew racist symbols, including the Confederate battle flag, outside their quarters and spewed racial epithets. Others endured ignorance and prejudice. One Native American veteran recalled being on patrol when a white platoon sergeant told his unit, "The gooks are all out there and we're here. This is Fort Apache, and out there is Indian country." The veteran commented, "I should have shot him right then and there. Made me wonder who the real enemy was." However, on the frontlines, where lives depended on others, close relationships between soldiers were largely unaffected by race. One veteran observed: "Out in the field blacks and whites got along a whole lot better than in the unit that was way back." The shared burdens and dangers ensured that "people would go out and risk their lives for each other."

At the same time, rising racial tensions prompted African Americans and other minorities to band together. Over time, more came to identify with radical movements like Black Power. They increasingly challenged white officers and showed solidarity through symbols and greetings. Tensions flared, and violence ensued, causing many disciplinary problems. These incidents undermined morale and effectiveness at a stage of the war when everything appeared to be going off the rails.

THE ENEMY WITHIN

With racial issues affecting morale, another stateside phenomenon weakened the war effort: drug use. Soldiers' use of marijuana, LSD, and heroin became more prevalent as the war progressed. While alcohol continued to be the drug of choice and remained a constant companion for many in Vietnam, these new options created significant problems. Later in the war, an estimated 28 percent of American GIs regularly used hard drugs, creating 500,000 addicts, although some disputed those numbers, characterizing them as too high. The real numbers remained elusive, because soldiers hid their drug use. One medic observed, "When I was there you could see one or two vials just sitting there of white powder. . . . You'd see the guys smoking all the time." A marine returning for his second tour in 1968 recalled how things had changed: "Now there was a drug problem that I hadn't seen before. . . . Grunts were getting stoned on it, on hash and other drugs—you name it, and you could buy it. . . . I made up my mind not to trust the men screwed up on drugs. I would do my duty, but I intended to come out alive."

Most soldiers limited their drug use to the rear echelon areas. One marine stressed, "You didn't have time for drugs for the simple fact that if you were on drugs you couldn't make your mind work right in the jungle. . . . If they were on drugs they could get everyone killed." While many men relied on methamphetamines, sometimes provided by medics, to stay alert on patrols, the majority of soldiers avoided drugs in the field. Still, their use had a very deleterious effect on the war effort.

ADDING A NEW WORD TO THE DICTIONARY

Drugs also contributed to attacks on people who enforced rules against their use. As discipline declined, a new term entered the American lexicon: "fragging." While fratricide had occurred throughout military history, the numbers of such incidents increased in Vietnam. There, the weapon of choice was a grenade thrown into a tent where the victim lay sleeping. From 1969 to 1972 the Defense Department reported 788 fraggings in Vietnam. Other estimates claim that more than 1,000 officers and noncommissioned officers died at the hands of their own men. In one case, an African American sergeant, Woody Wanamaker, who hailed from the tough streets of Jersey City, developed a close relationship with Al, a fellow noncommissioned white officer from rural Vermont. They became so inseparable that others called them "salt and pepper." One night, they uncovered drugs during a search of living quarters. As they left, some soldiers muttered, "We're going to get you, motherfuckers." A few nights later, as Woody and Al relaxed in their quarters, the pair heard the sound of a pin being pulled from a grenade, which moments later landed near Al. Instinctively, Al covered it with his body to save his friend. "He wasn't blown to bits, but there wasn't too much left of a human being," Woody recalled. He was never able to find the culprit. When he escorted Al's body back to Vermont, he lied and told Al's wife that an enemy mortar had killed him. Later, he remembered that he had hated being unable to tell the truth to Al's son: "Your father wasn't killed in combat. Your father got killed by another American over stupidity."

Al wasn't the only one to suffer for his willingness to enforce the rules. Many murder attempts likely went unreported, as officers feared being labeled soft on discipline if fraggings occurred on their watch. Yet this type of violence demonstrated the decline of the American military. "Fragging" also became synonymous with the stereotype of the deranged Vietnam veteran who returned home with drug problems and violent proclivities. People feared such men, and those who fought in Vietnam never received the public honor granted veterans of previous wars.

THE BABY KILLER

Although negative stereotypes of soldiers abounded throughout much of the war, the most damaging was that of the veteran as a "baby killer." While most Americans performed their duties honorably, some perpetrated horrible atrocities. As one officer concluded:

> You put those kids in the jungle for a while, get them real scared . . . and let a few incidents change some of their fears to hate. Give them a sergeant who has seen too many of his men killed by booby traps . . . and who feels that the Vietnamese are dumb, dirty, and weak. . . . Add a little mob pressure, and those nice kids . . . would rape like champions. Kill, rape and steal is the name of the game.

Efforts to ensure that such perpetrators were brought to justice were often hampered by the rotation system and cover-ups. The violent nature of guerrilla warfare laid the groundwork for these atrocities, as did the dehumanization of the Vietnamese that began in basic training. "Free-fire" zones that allowed Americans to kill anyone in an area also ensured carnage, as did the sheer enormity of the weapons employed in Vietnam.

The iconic episode of U.S. brutality in Vietnam unfolded on March 16, 1968. That day, Charlie Company of the 1st Battalion of the 23rd Infantry disembarked from helicopters near My Lai. Incensed by earlier casualties due to booby traps and snipers and having been promised contact with the enemy, the force landed under the command of Captain Ernest Medina and Lieutenant William Calley. Once the soldiers arrived in the village, the situation quickly deteriorated, and the grunts murdered everyone they could, including women and children, with casualties ultimately amounting to more than 500 civilians. Calley led the mass executions, shooting one small child at point-blank. A few soldiers refused to participate, but most turned into cold-blooded killers. For four hours, the slayings continued, with bodies piling up in ditches and the rice paddies. Only the heroic actions of helicopter pilot Hugh Thompson, Jr., who landed his chopper in between fleeing Vietnamese and the Americans, helped stem the carnage.

In its final report, on the incident the army listed 128 enemy killed and three weapons collected. Only one American had suffered a wound, self-inflicted from an accidental discharge. Thompson reported the massacre, but commanders buried his story, and Medina ordered his men "not to do anything stupid like write [his] congressman." The cover-up efforts extended to the highest positions of the army, including General Samuel Koster, who led the Americal Division. Briefly, the attempts succeeded in hushing up what had happened.

However, a young soldier, Ron Ridenhour, overheard members of Charlie Company bragging about My Lai and wrote his congressman, Democrat Morris Udall of Arizona, and others, including Secretary of Defense Melvin Laird, to call on each to "press forward a widespread and public investigation on this matter."

In response, the army appointed Lieutenant General William Peers to investigate. He ultimately found that 224 serious violations had occurred at My Lai. Simultaneously, a young journalist named Seymour Hersh pieced together the story. In November 1969, he broke the story, and soon after, *Life* published photos of the massacre. A major firestorm erupted, and the army transitioned to damage control, characterizing the episode as an isolated event caused by Calley's poor leadership.

ISSUES IN MILITARY HISTORY

THE DESCENT INTO DARKNESS: A MILITARY ATROCITY AND THE VIETNAM WAR

When the members of Charlie Company landed in the area around the hamlet of My Lai and subsequently massacred more than 500 Vietnamese civilians, including women and small children, the army kept the atrocity quiet. However, when the news broke a year later, a major debate erupted in the United States over the barbarism of the act. For many antiwar activists, it confirmed the immorality of the American intervention in Southeast Asia. Some saw William Calley and his men as representative of the worst of the American involvement, young men turned loose in a foreign land to terrorize and murder civilians. Others blamed not the soldiers, but the militarized system that had thrown them into a quagmire where it was often impossible to identify the enemy. In this view, tactics such as free-fire zones, training that dehumanized the enemy, and an emphasis on body counts had helped lay the groundwork for the actions of Charlie Company. At the same time, some members of the military and its allies in Congress and the press defended the actions of Calley and his men as a result of the fog of war. They argued that most of those criticizing the company's actions had not served and did not understand the pressures of war, especially one in which the enemy rarely showed himself. Some even praised Calley, declaring that the United States needed to more forcefully wage the war in Southeast Asia to ensure victory and not worry so much about those caught in the cross-fire because the ultimate goal justified the means.

This debate continued throughout the war and was revived during the Winter Soldier hearings by Vietnam veterans in Detroit in 1971, by the Vietnam Veterans Against the War, and in response to other revelations about groups such as the Tiger Force. The My Lai incident and similar events in Vietnam caused a reevaluation by the U.S. military of the damage done to its men, who were often publicly branded "baby killers." Military leadership worked to create clearer rules of engagement, strengthened command structures to include people specializing in the rules of warfare, and incorporated training efforts to try to reduce future incidents like My Lai.

The debates over My Lai continue today, often following the original lines of argument. Some Vietnam veterans call the incident an anomaly and point out that Calley should never have held a command position. Others highlight that such problems have continued in Iraq and Afghanistan, although not on the scale of My Lai. In conflicts in both Vietnam and the Middle East, problems have remained with identifying the enemy and ensuring that a strong leadership prevents an event like what occurred in April 1968 from ever happening again.

In 1970, Calley and Medina went on trial for the massacre, with the latter represented by the famous F. Lee Bailey. Ultimately, a military jury found Calley guilty of twenty-two murders and gave him a life sentence. Most of the soldiers involved avoided prosecution after leaving the military. Others involved in the cover-up received punishments: General Koster was demoted to brigadier general and removed as superintendent of West Point. Only Calley served any time, a short stint in Fort Leavenworth, before being pardoned by President Nixon.

The My Lai massacre reinforced commonly held perceptions of American soldiers as "baby killers." Despite the fact that most American soldiers never perpetrated atrocities in Vietnam, My Lai and other incidents further cast the U.S. military in a very negative light and led to greater disillusionment among many Americans.

LOOKING INTO THE MIRROR

The issues of drugs, race relations, and atrocities all shaped perceptions of the U.S. involvement in Vietnam inside and outside the military. Many Americans fought hard even during the withdrawal, distinguishing themselves during the invasions of Cambodia in 1970 and the repulsion of the Easter Offensive in 1972. However, the handwriting was on the wall for the war's ultimate outcome, and many worried about the long-term consequences for the U.S. military.

A respected marine, Colonel Robert D. Heinl, was one of the first to question publicly the effects of U.S. involvement in Vietnam. In a biting and controversial critique in *Armed Forces Journal* in June 1971 he wrote, "The morale, discipline and battle worthiness of the U.S. Armed Forces are, with a few salient exceptions, lower and worse than at any time in this century and possibly in the history of the United States." Ultimately, he concluded that the military's prestige had fallen to its lowest point ever, adding that the "fall in public esteem . . . is exceeded by the fall or at least enfeeblement of the hierarchic and disciplinary system by which they exist."

But while many shared Heinl's appraisal, some saw hope in other armies that had experienced similar tragedies. Lieutenant Colonel William L. Hauser, while acknowledging Heinl's conclusions, pointed to how European armies had learned to adapt after crisis and declared, "The Army will survive. It is learning how to cope with problems of racial tension, political and anti-establishment dissent and drugs." In response to these challenges he called for the military to evolve by creating a "fighting Army" and "supporting Army" and instituting other changes reflective of the nature of modern warfare. His pleas for reform corresponded with many others originating from Vietnam veteran officers such as Colin Powell and Norman Schwarzkopf, Jr., who would lead the military forward during the 1980s and 1990s.

THE LOST CAUSE

In early 1973, the United States removed its combat forces from South Vietnam following the signing of the Paris Accords in January. In return, the United States received its POWs, and the North Vietnamese promised to restrict their activities in the South. The United States left behind billions of dollars in equipment for the ARVN but established restrictions on providing new materials and replacement parts. Despite the massive aid and years of U.S. training, the ARVN collapsed quickly after the U.S. withdrawal. In April 1975, enemy tanks crashed through the gates of the presidential palace in Saigon. Millions of Americans watched as helicopters airlifted Americans and some Vietnamese to ships in the South China Sea. On the USS *Denver*, one marine simply said, "Well, that's one country we don't have to give billions of dollars anymore." The cynicism of his statement summed up what many veterans and Americans felt about the whole episode. After spending billions of dollars and losing 58,000 American lives, the United States had left its longest war (to that point) wounded and disillusioned, not unlike the hundreds of thousands of surviving Vietnam veterans who bore physical and psychological wounds. Many wondered how a Third World country had expelled the most powerful military in the world. Vietnam ensured that much soul searching and calls for change would continue over the next two decades.

CONCLUSIONS

From the end of the Korean War to the American withdrawal from Vietnam, U.S. global commitments dramatically expanded as a result of the Cold War. Citizen-soldiers, many ensnared by the peacetime draft, manned new weapons, including the prolific M-16 rifle, jet aircraft, helicopters, and long-range high-altitude bombers. Others hunkered down in missile silos. Tactics evolved to deal with nationalist- and communist-inspired insurgencies in the Third World. Simultaneously, U.S. forces focused on fighting potential conventional wars in Europe against Warsaw Pact forces and on the Asian mainland against China.

Many observers worried about the dramatic expansion of the military in peacetime, particularly the rising expense of maintaining large forces globally. Frustrations over Vietnam exacerbated existing tensions over the role of the United States and its military in the global arena. Ultimately, these divisions played a significant role in the decline of American military power in the postwar era, leading to a major reenvisioning of how to organize and deploy U.S. forces after 1975.

TIMELINE

May 1954	Viet Minh emerge victorious in Indochina
September 1954–May 1955	First Taiwan Strait Crisis
January 1961	Eisenhower warns about the "military-industrial" complex
October 1962	Cuban Missile Crisis
August 1964	Gulf of Tonkin incident
March 1965	Operation Rolling Thunder launched
January 1967	Operation Cedar Falls
January–March 1968	Tet Offensive
March 1968	My Lai massacre
January 1973	Paris Peace Accords signed
April 1975	Saigon captured by the North Vietnamese and Viet Cong

SUGGESTED READINGS

Appy, Christian. *American Reckoning: The Vietnam War and Our National Identity.* New York: Penguin Books, 2015.

Daddis, Gregory. *Westmoreland's War: Reassessing American Strategy in Vietnam.* New York: Oxford University Press, 2014.

Herring, George. *America's Longest War: The United States and Vietnam, 1950–1975,* 5th ed. New York: McGraw Hill, 2014.

Kuzmarov, Jeremy. *The Myth of the Drug-Addicted Army: Vietnam and the Modern War on Drugs.* Amherst: University of Massachusetts Press, 2009.

Longley, Kyle. *Grunts: The American Combat Soldier in Vietnam.* New York: Routledge, 2008.

Martini, Edwin A. *Agent Orange: History, Science, and the Politics of Uncertainty.* Amherst: University of Massachusetts Press, 2012.

McMaster, H. R. *Dereliction of Duty: Lyndon Johnson, Robert McNamara, the Joint Chiefs of Staff, and the Lies that Led to Vietnam.* New York: Harper Perennial, 1997.

Nashel, Jonathan. *Edward Lansdale's Cold War.* Amherst: University of Massachusetts Press, 2005.

Spector, Ronald H. *Advice and Support: The Early Years, 1941–1960.* Washington, D.C.: Department of the Army, 1983.

Westheider, James E. *Fighting on Two Fronts: African Americans and the Vietnam War.* New York: New York University Press, 1997.

CHAPTER 16

THE ENDLESS WARS: THE COLD WAR AND BEYOND

1975–PRESENT

Ghosts of Vietnam • The Carter Interregnum • The Iranian Morass • A New Day Dawning
• Beyond the Cold War, 1989–2001 • Iraq 1.0 • From Juggernaut to Peacekeeper
• The Endless Wars, 2001–Present • Iraq 2.0 • Back to Afghanistan

In April 2008, marine sergeant Travis Twiggs visited the White House, where President George W. Bush honored the thirty-six-year-old veteran of four tours in Iraq and one in Afghanistan. When the president approached the gregarious marine with tattoos of "Gladiator" on one forearm and "Spartan" on the other, instead of shaking his hand, Twiggs bear-hugged Bush, exclaiming, "Sir, I've served there many times—and I would serve for you anytime."

Yet less than a month later Twiggs went absent without leave. Suffering from PTSD, he often took fourteen pills a day to battle his anxiety and depression. Ever since his second deployment, his doctors and family had warned the Marine Corps about his condition. While stateside, he stayed up late at night watching for incoming motor vehicles and fell to the ground when he heard cars on gravel roads, because to him the noise sounded like machine gun fire. In one case, his wife woke up to him pointing a gun to her head, saying, "Iraqi."

Twiggs recognized his problem, something he underscored in his January 2008 *Marine Corps Gazette* article, "PTSD: The War Within." He had all the classic symptoms of the condition, including dissociation and flashbacks to his second tour. On arrival home, he wrote, "I was more irritable, paranoid for no reason, unable to sleep." However, he recalled, when he learned of an upcoming deployment, "my symptoms went away. After all, I was going back to the fight, back to the shared adversity, where the tempo is high and our adrenaline pulses through our veins like hot blood." But he never healed. The ghosts of fallen soldiers haunted him, especially two young lance corporals who died under his command in 2005. On a virtual wall honoring one, he wrote, "I wish that I could erase that horrible day from my memory . . . but I can't." He spent time in Bethesda Naval Hospital, waking up at night in cold sweats and hallucinating. The drugs used to treat his condition sometimes turned him into a zombie, but they did not dampen the pain. Ultimately, he reached the conclusion, "PTSD was nothing more than an acronym created for weak Marines."

While his wife Kalee sought better care at a facility in New Jersey specializing in PTSD, Travis went back to Bethesda once more. It did not work. Only a short time after meeting the president, Twiggs jumped into his Toyota Corolla and headed to his hometown of New Orleans. There, he picked up his brother Willard and drove west. Within a few days, the two brothers had arrived at the Grand Canyon. Near the Twin Overlooks, he gunned his car and headed straight toward the edge, but a fir tree stopped the fall of 5,000 feet. The brothers then stole a vehicle from some tourists. Several days later, at a Border Patrol checkpoint near Yuma, Travis bolted when an agent directed him toward a secondary inspection. After careening down Interstate 8 for more than 100 miles, spike strips crippled the stolen Dodge Caliber near Gila Bend. Surrounded, Travis, according to observers, began waving a revolver. As authorities watched, he put a bullet in his brother's brain and then shot himself. Afterward, his wife said: "He really left us a long time ago. He tried to come back. But he couldn't. That was not my husband out there." Angry, she also declared: "When he got sick, got saddened, his government, his Marine Corps, let him down."

Twiggs represented a large number of veterans of the long Iraq and Afghanistan wars who fought as a part of the Global War on Terror (GWOT) after the attacks of September 11, 2001. Many of these soldiers endured multiple tours, which were often extended as a result of stop-loss policies. Others found themselves in a war zone after joining the Reserves and National Guard as a way to supplement their income or secure college educations. This small segment of the population bore the brunt of the wars, and many like Sergeant Twiggs carried the scars of service years after leaving the battlefields.

In many ways, the period from 1975 to 2018 brought the U.S. military full circle, from the lows of Vietnam to victories in the First Persian Gulf War and then back to complex and frustrating combat among civilian populations. Without any foreseeable end, Afghanistan replaced Vietnam as America's longest war. Ultimately, the United States' long and costly engagements during this time drained the American treasury and sapped the will of many to engage in future low-intensity wars.

GHOSTS OF VIETNAM

By the time of the fall of Saigon in April 1975, the U.S. military reflected the general cleavages in American society related to racial divides, drug use, and criminal behavior. Early manifestations of these problems appeared in the sabotage of the USS *Ranger* in 1972 and the race riots that gripped the USS *Kitty Hawk* that same year. By the mid-1970s, the military appeared to be in disarray, much like many other national institutions, including the office of the presidency after the Watergate scandal. Recognizing the deleterious effects of Vietnam

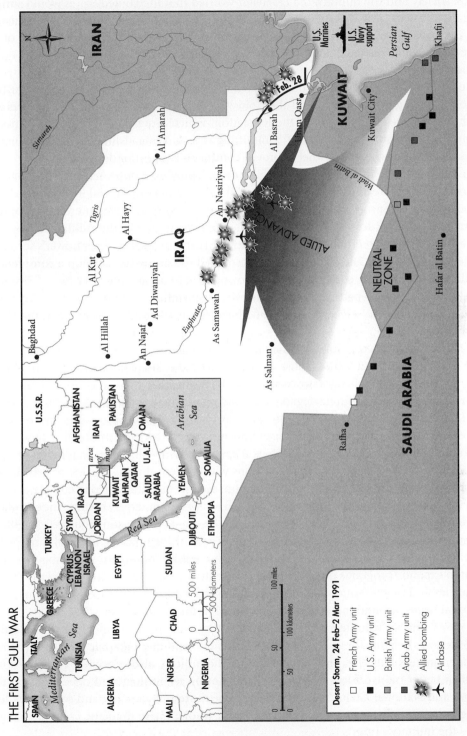

MAP 16.1 The First Gulf War

on U.S. society and the military, the *Economist* worried that the United States would simply withdraw from its global responsibilities, affecting Europe as well. As one distinguished historian noted after Vietnam, "A people accustomed to having their way in the face of re-current failure felt frustrated and impotent and vented their fury on their tormentors—and their leaders."

During the Watergate crisis, Congress tried to rein in the imperial presidency that had developed during World War II and the Cold War. In 1973, it passed the War Powers Act and then overrode Nixon's veto of the legislation, which required the president to notify Congress within forty-eight hours of committing U.S. forces and limited deployments to sixty days until Congress had either approved continued support or declared war.

As Congress and the president wrangled over deploying troops, military and civilian leaders focused on creating an all-volunteer military. The social and racial inequalities of the draft caused the Johnson and Nixon administrations to explore ending the very unpopular institution. In 1969, despite heavy opposition from many within the military, Nixon ap-pointed a Commission on an All-Volunteer Armed Force, headed by Eisenhower's secretary of defense, Thomas S. Gates. The president instructed the group to "develop a comprehen-sive plan for eliminating conscription and moving toward an all-volunteer force." Simulta-neously, the Defense Department created its own organization, Project Volunteer. Superiors ordered its members to serve as a "check and balance" to what became known as the Gates Commission.

For months, the two groups outlined a series of plans to create an all-volunteer army. While the Pentagon and White House sought to keep the discussions secret, word leaked out. Opponents of the changes, worried about the manpower drain if conscription ended and the costs associated with having to recruit and retain an all-volunteer force, used various media outlets to try to sabotage the process. For months, various proposals and counter-proposals circulated as stakeholders waged bureaucratic battles to promote their positions.

Finally, in late April 1970, President Nixon approved a middle course that reflected a po-litical compromise acceptable to many factions within the military and U.S. society. While accepting most findings of the Gates Commission, the president hesitated to end the draft by June 1971. Instead, he decided to continue it for a few more years, largely because the end of the war would be accompanied by reduced quotas. At the same time, Nixon requested $2 billion to support volunteer force development and more money for housing, medical care for de-pendents, moving expenses, and pay raises for those willing to remain in combat. He also sought to expand "programs designed to increase enlistments and retention" and to "review the policies and practice of the military services to give new emphasis to recognition of the individual needs, aspirations, and capabilities of all military personnel."

In 1973, the all-volunteer force became a reality with the retirement of the Selective Service system. Benefits for service members increased, and demographic changes occurred as women increasingly filled military positions. The military also concentrated on creating a smaller, better-trained force that was more reliant on technology and dependent on the Reserves and National Guard. The military became more self-selecting and sometimes less demographically representative of the society as a whole. These dramatic cultural changes shaped the military's future.

WOMEN IN THE MILITARY AFTER VIETNAM

The role of women in the military remained relatively static during most major conflicts of the twentieth century. Outside of nursing and support roles such as those adopted in World War II, women remained in noncombatant roles in rear areas away from the frontlines. This policy was maintained despite the fact that other countries, including the Soviet Union and Israel, allowed women into combat roles. However, as the women's movement gained momentum in the 1960s and 1970s, people increasingly challenged existing gender roles. West Point admitted women for the first time in July 1976, and over time, the military began allowing them to fly aircraft and perform other specialized duties typically carried out by men. Still, the military refused to put women in traditional combat roles. Some argued that women lacked the necessary physical or emotional strength to endure the rigors of combat. Others feared that the fraternization of women and men in frontline areas would limit combat effectiveness. Still others worried about the rape culture, both within the military and by the enemy, that could potentially result if women entered the frontlines.

However, changes kept occurring because of several factors, including the move toward an all-volunteer army that increasingly relied on women to fill positions. The army, navy, and air force all began using women to handle staff and technical duties. Others pointed out the active combat roles women played in other countries and argued that the United States should do so as well, a proposition that was reluctantly considered. Furthermore, during the wars of the twenty-first century, particularly the conflicts in Iraq and Afghanistan, insurgencies often blurred the distinction between frontlines and rear areas, which led more women to be placed in harm's way. Early in the war in Iraq, the enemy ambushed a convoy and killed Lorl Ann Piestewa and captured several others, including Jessica Lynch. Pilot Tammy Duckworth lost both legs after her helicopter went down after insurgent fire in 2004. She later became a U.S. senator from Illinois. Ultimately more than 160 women died in Afghanistan and Iraq.

The debates over women's role in the military continue today, although they have significantly changed since Vietnam and even the First Persian Gulf War. Some women have completed the rigorous ranger training, while an increasing number have assumed more direct combat roles, including as pilots and officers. Today, more than 15 percent of active-duty members of the military are female, and while conversations persist on what roles women should have in war, change marches on and likely will continue.

IMAGE 16.1 Tammy Duckworth Tammy Duckworth, a veteran of the Iraq War, currently serves as a United States Senator for Illinois. She has served as a legislative champion for veteran issues, with an emphasis on Veteran mental health.

THE CARTER INTERREGNUM

In 1976, the American people elected Jimmy Carter, a Naval Academy graduate and former nuclear submarine officer, as president. The election of the Washington outsider and former governor of Georgia reflected a general distaste for the endless series of scandals that had plagued the Nixon administration. By this time most Americans opposed foreign adventures and sought less military spending while they dealt with high inflation and interest rates, stagnant wages, and the general malaise of the 1970s.

Once in office, Carter, a born-again evangelical, pushed morality into foreign and military policy by focusing on human rights. This reorientation affected military operations, including the programs of the School of the Americas (SOA). Founded in 1946 and located at Fort Gulick in the Panama Canal Zone, the SOA trained individuals for leadership roles in Latin American militaries. By the early 1960s, its primary mission was counterinsurgency training. Large numbers of Salvadorans, Nicaraguans, Chileans, and Colombians cycled through the SOA, many becoming officers who developed reputations for ruthlessness during the 1960s.

The SOA gained special notoriety during the 1970s when Chilean graduates worked with General Augusto Pinochet to murder tens of thousands of their own people after a coup in 1973. Other graduates became identified with the murderous Operation Condor, in which agents from Latin American dictatorships collaborated in assassinating political dissidents around the world. SOA commanders declared that they created soldiers who respected democratic traditions, but the record often contradicted their claims.

With the Carter administration's heightened focus on human rights, the SOA came under increasing scrutiny. In 1984, the SOA moved to Fort Benning, where human rights activists increasingly protested its operations. While the institution remained open under various names, congressional and human rights organization oversight reined in its activities.

THE IRANIAN MORASS

As the Carter presidency unfolded, global challenges affected military priorities. In Iran in 1978, Muslim theocrat Ayatollah Ruhollah Khomeini deposed pro-U.S. dictator Shah Reza Pahlavi. Equally disturbing, the Soviets invaded Afghanistan in December 1979. When combined with perceived Soviet aggression in Central America, these events constituted significant threats. The administration increasingly became more hawkish and began a large-scale military buildup. Carter asked for a 5 percent increase in military spending, ordered the development of advanced weapons systems, and requested a possible reimplementation of draft registration. He also worked with the NSC on a new statement for U.S. nuclear strategy. In January 1980, as a challenging presidential campaign loomed on the horizon, Carter approved Presidential Directive 59 (PD-59), which called for U.S. strikes against civilian as well as military targets in response to perceived Soviet advances in weapons. The document clearly contradicted the dominant mutually assured destruction paradigm and pushed one of the largest expansions of conventional and nuclear arms since the Truman years.

IMAGE 16.2 **Operation Eagle Claw** The wreckage left behind from the disaster that was Operation Eagle Claw. The tragedy prompted organizational reform within the U.S. Military, with the creation of the United States Army Special Operations Command.

Despite increased budgets, the U.S. military continued to struggle. No maneuver demonstrated its challenges more than Operation Eagle Claw. Soon after Islamic fundamentalists took control of Iran, they seized the U.S. embassy there and captured more than fifty Americans. The Carter administration vainly tried to negotiate their release but grew frustrated and asked the military to free the hostages. The Pentagon charged army general James B. Vaught with coordinating efforts between the air force and Delta Force team members as well as CIA operatives working in Tehran. After weeks of planning and training, teams prepared for what one marine major characterized as an operation that was "tactically feasible, operationally vacant, and strategically risky."

On April 24, U.S. forces in Oman headed toward a clandestine airstrip just outside Tehran codenamed Desert One. The operation started poorly when incoming helicopters experienced mechanical problems and a sandstorm engulfed the area. In the confusion, one of the large planes crashed into a helicopter, killing eight Americans. Shortly after, the president aborted the mission. The next day, Carter acknowledged the failure, leading the Iranians to disperse the captives as the ayatollah praised Allah for sending the sandstorm.

Subsequent investigations showed that U.S. forces had lacked good equipment for the mission and highlighted major deficiencies in command structure, mission planning, and interservice cooperation. For many, Operation Eagle Claw showed the ineptness of the post–Vietnam War military and renewed calls for more investment in it, recommendations Carter heeded, but not soon enough to help his reelection chances. The episode also sparked the creation of the U.S. Special Operations Command, which increasingly provided specialized training and coordination of operations for units like the 160th SOAR.

A NEW DAY DAWNING

During the 1980 presidential race, Republican nominee Ronald Reagan and his supporters pilloried Carter for letting the United States fall behind the Soviet Union in military spending. Reagan promised increased investments in the military as well as cuts to taxes and government programs. To primary opponent George H. W. Bush, the numbers of these promises never added up, leading him to characterize Reagan's ideas as "voodoo economics." Nonetheless, Reagan won the presidency by a fairly small margin, given the country's frustrations with Carter over Iran and a sputtering economy.

Once in office, the administration started a large military buildup led by Secretary of Defense Caspar Weinberger, who in the Nixon administration had earned the nickname of "Cap the Knife" for his tendency to cut domestic spending. However, in his new position, Weinberger oversaw a budget expansion unmatched since the Vietnam War. Defense spending rose by 8 percent a year, with money pouring into defense contracts.

One of the most controversial programs launched under Weinberger was the Strategic Defense Initiative (SDI), under which the Reagan administration spent billions of dollars creating a missile defense shield to protect the United States from ICBMs. Dubbed "Star Wars" by both supporters and critics, the program supported scientific research into new space-based platforms that were primarily designed to use lasers to knock down incoming ICBMs and received much criticism. Most scientists questioned its feasibility, and politicians, including Democratic senator J. Bennett Johnston of Louisiana, complained that the program was "an ideological substitute for science." Others questioned its cost, estimated at $1 trillion, arguing that it diverted funds from practical defense systems. Still others feared that it would undermine deterrence and lead to a first strike by the enemy. Finally, some critics believed that SDI merely heightened the belief that a nuclear war could be won.

Ultimately, the research produced very little by way of an operational system. Some Reagan supporters bragged that SDI had forced the Soviets to spend more on the development of similar resources, bankrupting the country, but those structural problems existed long before SDI. Decades later, nothing approximating the vision of Star Wars exists, and something that started as science fiction has remained largely in the fantasy world.

FLEXING MUSCLES

During the Reagan administration the Middle East became a testing ground for the U.S. military. The Iranian Revolution and tensions between the Israeli Defense Forces (IDF) and the Palestine Liberation Organization (PLO) spilled over into Lebanon in the early 1980s. Militant Muslim and Christian sects, many backed by Iran and Syria, operated with relative impunity as the Lebanese government collapsed and disorder wracked the country.

In the summer of 1982 marines landed in Lebanon to evacuate U.S. citizens from Beirut. In September, the Reagan administration deployed 1,800 marines in what one person characterized as "an indistinct mission called 'presence.'" The U.S. forces established a base at Beirut International Airport and soon found themselves caught in the cross-fire between rival militias and the IDF and PLO. They provided training and equipment to the government to battle Muslim forces but faced significant challenges. The enemy, many Palestinian militants, relied on guerrilla tactics, including the use of car bombs. On April 18, 1983, one such attack killed sixty-three people, including eighteen Americans at the U.S. embassy. Sniping was common, and rocket attacks struck the marine compound throughout the year. By September, five marines had been killed and another forty-nine wounded. With an ill-defined mission and orders not to return fire unless under severe threat, the marines complained:

> They sent us to Beirut
> To be targets who could not shoot
> Friends will die into an early grave,
> Was there any reason for what they gave?

While the commanders on the ground opposed further aid to the Lebanese army, the Reagan administration ignored their warnings. The U.S. Navy bombarded Muslim fighters, infuriating them and driving them to increasingly attack the Americans, who were still bound by restrictive operational parameters. The confrontation reached a tipping point on Sunday, October 23, 1983, when a terrorist drove a five-ton truck loaded with explosives into the marine compound. More than 240 marines and sailors died when the building collapsed in the worst day of casualties for the corps since 1945. The Defense Department and Congress launched investigations, concluding that lax security, poor planning, and a muddled mission had caused the debacle. The incident foreshadowed future challenges that the United States would face in the Middle East related to sectarian violence, terrorism, and regime change. In February 1984, U.S. forces withdrew from the region.

While the Reagan administration was still reeling from the Beirut attack, it decided to invade the conflict-ridden island nation of Grenada, ostensibly to protect the lives of American medical students there. The administration had also received a request from the Organization of Eastern Caribbean States to help restore order on the island. In reality, the administration sought to confront what it considered a rising communist threat in the region. While some planners recommended only using special forces to extricate the Americans, others wanted a bigger show. The latter prevailed, and on October 25, 1983, Operation Urgent Fury began when 1,900 U.S. Marines stormed

IMAGE 16.3 Bombing of Marine Barracks, 1983 A cartoon criticizing commanders for the disorganization resulting in the terrorist attack on Marine barracks on October 23, 1983.

ashore. For six days, U.S. troops (later supplemented by an additional 4,000 soldiers) battled members of the small Grenadian military and Cuban construction workers. After some heavy fighting, the resistance collapsed in a few days, allowing President Reagan to crow: "I can't say enough in praise of our military . . . army rangers and paratroopers, navy, marine and air force personnel, those who planned a brilliant campaign and those who carried it out." Afterward, the military handed out more than 8,000 medals to the participants of the invasion. The operation ultimately cost more than $75.5 million. Eighteen Americans died, and 116 more suffered wounds. A comparable number of Cubans also died, as well as nearly fifty Grenadian soldiers. Soon, the United States expelled all Communists from the island, declared victory, and installed a pro-U.S. government before departing.

Many argued that the invasion served as a warning to the Sandinistas in Nicaragua. While Congress restrained future adventures in Latin America, the president and his supporters heralded the triumph of Grenada as a sign of the resurgence of American power and its ability to roll back communist threats. This group subsequently channeled unauthorized funding and military support to opposition forces in Nicaragua called the Contras, who waged a devastating war against the leftist Sandinista regime.

The lack of cooperation and command oversight in Lebanon and, to a lesser degree, Grenada pushed congressional leaders and military leaders to call for changes to reduce interservice rivalry, create a more coherent chain of command, and reform the Joint Chiefs of Staff. Legislation came in the form of the Goldwater-Nichols Act, named for Republican senator Barry Goldwater of Arizona and Democratic senator William Nichols of Alabama, which passed in 1986 with unanimous support in the Senate (95–0) and only twenty-seven votes opposed in the House. The most sweeping reworking of the Department of Defense since the National Security Act of 1947, the act pushed for more education and training for officers to better prepare for joint operations and rewarded leaders who promoted interservice collaboration. In addition, it made the chair of the Joint Chiefs of Staff the primary advisor to the president. Before, the chair had gathered recommendations from the various chiefs of the different branches, but now he became the primary conduit to the president and voiced his opinion directly to the commander-in-chief. Finally, the act gave full command over troops to theater commanders and encouraged "joint" command structures and operations. While some critics argued that the chairman became overly powerful in the reorganization and others feared that the chairman and theater commanders would favor their own service branches, the new system was soon used to face a series of challenges in Latin America and the Middle East.

A NEW DAY DAWNING

As predicted, massive deficits plagued the Reagan administration as it increased defense spending and issued massive tax cuts. However, during its last three years in office, the administration mothballed several weapons systems and flattened military spending. These changes were made possible by the rise in the Soviet Union of Mikhail Gorbachev, who took power in 1985. Dramatically different from his predecessors in style and substance, Gorbachev succeeded in ending the deadly Soviet involvement in Afghanistan, reduced funding for revolutionary movements, and generally acted as a modern leader.

Despite early frosty relations, Reagan and Gorbachev developed a good working relationship, especially on the issue of reducing nuclear weapons. By the end of Reagan's presidency in 1989, the two had made significant agreements that Reagan's successor, George H. W. Bush, would complete. When Bush entered the presidency, he confronted a very different world than had existed in 1981.

BEYOND THE COLD WAR, 1989–2001

In 1989, the Berlin Wall fell and the Soviet Union collapsed soon after as Gorbachev lost power and independent republics emerged. U.S. military planners found themselves without a major enemy. Thus, military tactics shifted toward fighting limited wars and conducting humanitarian interventions. It was a tough readjustment, both for the military and for the economy, but it lasted until a potent international terrorist threat arose in the 1990s.

A COMBAT PILOT IN THE WHITE HOUSE

After John Kennedy, no president brought more combat experience into the White House than George H. W. Bush, who had served as a pilot during World War II. The former congressman, director of the CIA, and vice president had impressive credentials. However, his critics accused him over the years of lacking aggressiveness, something some characterized as the "wimp factor." When asked about the label, he quipped: "People say I'm indecisive. Well, I don't know about that."

Bush inherited a rapidly changing world transformed by the dissolution of the Soviet Union, a resurgent China, and rising terrorism in the Middle East. To deal with these shifts he built a very experienced team, including National Security Advisor General Brent Scowcroft, Secretary of Defense Richard Cheney, and JCS chairman General Colin Powell. The administration soon formulated plans for a "New World Order" that would pivot the U.S. military away from its focus on the Soviet Union and toward other priorities.

GETTING PUBLIC ENEMY #1

Alliances shifted quickly as the Cold War ended, and none more quickly than in Panama. During the 1980s, the Reagan administration had nurtured a close relationship with dictator Manuel Noriega as he provided support for the Contras in Nicaragua. The CIA gave him a retainer of $10,000 per month, despite repeated warnings about his illegal activities and human rights abuses. Reagan eventually lost interest in Central America, but Bush focused attention on the region through his efforts to restrict the drug trade, which he declared "the gravest domestic threat to our nation today."

By 1988, the U.S. government seriously focused on Noriega as a grand jury indicted him on drug charges in 1988. Tensions intensified when Noriega overturned an election in 1989 and publicly beat his opponents. Some Americans called for action, but Bush vacillated. Fanning the fires, Noriega publicly declared a "state of war" between the two countries and brandished a machete at anti-American rallies. But he overplayed his hand when his forces killed an off-duty Marine and accosted another, threatening to rape his wife. At this point, Bush announced: "Enough is enough. This guy is not going to lay off. It will only get worse."

On December 20, 1989, the U.S. military launched Operation Just Cause. More than 20,000 troops, supported by the latest technology, including stealth bombers, attacked. U.S. officials hoped that "if there was a lot of noise outside of the front door, they would go out the back." However, heavy fighting erupted in Panama City, killing hundreds of civilians and twenty-three American servicemen and causing more than $1 billion in damages. Noriega evaded capture for fifteen days but ultimately surrendered to Drug Enforcement Administration agents, who took him to Miami to stand trial.

The operation received bipartisan praise. Republican senator Robert Dole of Kansas, a decorated World War II combat veteran, crowed that the invasion proved that "America won't cave in to anyone, no matter how powerful and corrupt." Another person noted that both parties "liked the old-fashioned display of American muscle." The quick and relatively painless victory in Panama underscored the ability of the U.S. military to flex its muscles when necessary.

IRAQ 1.0

Another quick reversal of alliances occurred in Iraq as the Cold War ended. Throughout the 1980s, the Reagan administration had strongly supported Iraqi strongman Saddam Hussein in a brutal war against Iran (1980–1988). Officials had hoped to counterbalance Soviet influence in the region and, more important, to contain rising Iranian fundamentalism. One observer characterized the policy as one in which "shortsighted opportunism prevailed." U.S. officials had even tolerated Iraq's use of poison gas against Hussein's Kurdish opponents and a devastating missile attack on the USS *Stark* in which thirty-seven Americans died.

But as the Cold War subsided, the Iranians and Iraqis exhausted themselves and stopped fighting. With the war over, Hussein found himself under fire internationally after he zeroed in on his southern neighbor of Kuwait. The small oil-producing nation's vast resources and strategic location provided an opportunity for Hussein to pay off debts and reestablish Iraqi prominence in the region.

On August 2, 1990, Iraqi forces swarmed across the border and easily occupied the country. In response, President Bush told reporters on August 5: "This will not stand, this aggression against Kuwait." Soon, the administration launched Operation DESERT SHIELD to stop further invasion, especially into oil-rich Saudi Arabia. Within a short time, American troops, joined by allied forces from Great Britain and France as well as Egypt and other Arab states, had flooded into the Saudi kingdom, reaching more than 100,000 in two months. The president and his advisors wanted "no excuse possible for anybody in the military to say that the civilian side of the house had not supported them."

The intervention came with a price, however, as Osama bin Laden, a young Saudi veteran of the war against the Soviets in Afghanistan and the scion of a prominent family, denounced Saudi Arabia's decision to let the American "infidels occupy the country and act as arbiters in an Arab dispute." He offered to raise an army of *mujahedin* to expel Hussein's forces, but the Saudi government rebuffed the offer and exiled him. In response, he vowed to bring down the House of Saud and to punish the American "infidels."

IMAGE 16.4 Massacre of Iraqi Military in 1990 Highway 90, a six-lane highway running from Kuwait and Iraq, became known as the "Highway of Death" after Iraqi forces fleeing Kuwait City were massacred by American and allied forces in Operation Desert Storm.

Over time, U.S. commanders moved into position, relying heavily on the new U.S. Army that had evolved in the 1980s with the introduction of the Field Manual 100-5 and Air-Land Battle models, as well as weapons developed in preparation for a ground war with the Soviets. These leaders soon shifted from a defensive posture to planning an invasion to expel the Iraqis codenamed Operation DESERT STORM. Under the command of Vietnam veteran General Norman Schwarzkopf, Jr., U.S. troops trained for worst-case scenarios, including Hussein's use of chemical weapons.

In Washington, JCS Chairman Powell led U.S. preparations. A Vietnam veteran, the ghosts of that conflict haunted him. Thus, he formulated what came to be known as the Powell Doctrine. This standard precept of planners posed a series of questions about a potential engagement, including: Was U.S. national security really threatened? Were there clear and attainable objectives? Was there support at home? Had all diplomatic endeavors been exhausted? Was there a clear exit strategy? Powell sought affirmative responses to all of these questions before putting U.S. troops in harm's way, an approach that influenced many around him.

Throughout the fall, the United States built up its forces, working through the United Nations to secure a resolution allowing the use of force (granted on November 29). Soon after, Congress approved, by fairly small margins, a resolution allowing for military action. With Hussein refusing to budge, President Bush gave the go ahead to begin operations on January 17, 1991. Coalition planes led by F-117 stealth fighters pounded important installations all over Iraq, creating a massive fireworks show in downtown Baghdad. Air defenses quickly collapsed, and most Iraqi pilots fled into neutral countries. Within short order, the coalition had established complete air superiority.

For the next six weeks, its air force pounded the Iraqis. Hussein desperately lashed out, dumping oil into the Persian Gulf and lighting hundreds of Kuwaiti oil wells on fire. He even launched SCUD missiles into Saudi Arabia and Israel, hoping to provoke a response, but Israel in particular showed remarkable restraint.

Throughout this time, Schwarzkopf held his forces for the right moment, already enjoying a three to one superiority in troops. The delays aggravated the men, with one Marine complaining: "Two or three deadlines have passed, Iraq is still in Kuwait, supposedly raping and killing, we're still ready to go. . . . We want to get there, we're tired of the rumors and false starts; we're exhausted from constantly training."

Finally, at 4 a.m. on February 24, coalition forces ripped through the Iraqi lines in a classic enveloping move. Many Iraqi units collapsed as conscripts surrendered in large numbers. The rapid advance surprised many who had expected a fiercer resistance from the vaunted Iraqi Republican Guard. Advancing with few casualties, coalition forces soon moved deep into Kuwait while pilots continued to pound the hapless Iraqis, who surrendered en masse. Within a few days, Powell reported: "Mr. President, it's going much better than expected. The Iraqi army is broken. All they're trying to do is get out." Soon after, the president decided to stop the slaughter. The ground war had lasted only 100 hours.

The cost of the war was surprisingly light. The United States lost 148 killed in action and 145 in noncombatant roles, as well as 278 wounded. Coalition forces lost 92 dead and 318 wounded, while the Iraqis lost an estimated 100,000 soldiers and 2,000 civilians. It was a complete victory and seemed to validate the massive U.S. military buildup as well as the all-volunteer army. The conflict also offered vibrant confirmation of U.S. technical superiority in armor, aircraft, and missiles and allowed President Bush to firmly announce: "By God, we've kicked the Vietnam syndrome once and for all."

Veterans of the short conflict returned to a hero's welcome, despite many being plagued by a host of maladies blamed on vaccinations and exposure to the environmental devastation wrought by Hussein. The country rejoiced in its victory with ticker tape parades and heaped praise on Schwarzkopf and Powell. A renewed vigor characterized the public's belief in America's ability to shape the world. It contrasted significantly with attitudes two decades before, and it differed sharply from those one decade later.

FROM JUGGERNAUT TO PEACEKEEPER

The victory in Kuwait and the dissolution of the Soviet Union created a power vacuum. As a result, some began calling for reductions in the U.S. military, a request labeled a "peace dividend." This aim proved elusive, however, as arms manufacturers and communities across the country that were dependent on bases fought to limit such effects. Ultimately, slight reductions occurred in troop levels and military contracts, and some bases closed.

With few identifiable enemies, Bush and military leaders employed military power in different ways, including peacekeeping efforts. No episode represented this shift better than the intervention in Somalia, where a civil war erupted in 1991, causing a breakdown of civil government and initiating power struggles between competing factions. As starvation threatened many Somalis, the international community tried to provide humanitarian assistance, only to see those efforts sabotaged by warlords.

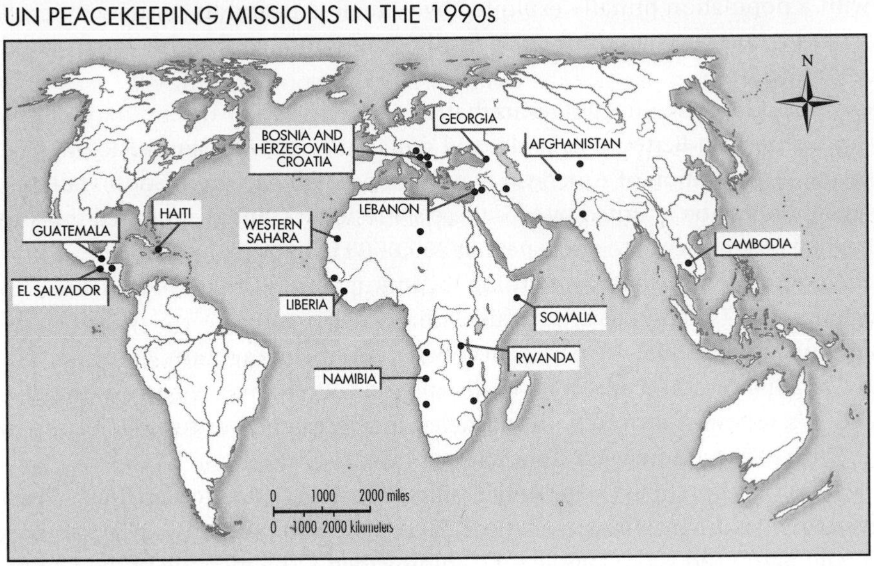

UN PEACEKEEPING MISSIONS IN THE 1990s

MAP 16.2 UN Peacekeeping Missions in the 1990s

In response, the Bush administration dispatched a relatively large number of U.S. troops to collaborate with UN peacekeepers to distribute food and provide security to relief workers in Operation Restore Hope. However, "mission creep" developed, especially after President Bill Clinton took office in early 1993. Increasingly, U.S. forces in Somalia began to confront the warlords, particularly around the large coastal capital city of Mogadishu, where the former Somali general Mohamed Farrah Adid ruled.

Clashes soon broke out between U.S. troops and Adid's forces. In the fall of 1993, U.S. commanders formulated plans to capture or kill Adid. However, on October 3, disaster struck after more than 150 rangers went after two of Adid's chief lieutenants. They left base in nineteen aircraft and twelve vehicles, tearing through the war-torn city.

Planners expected the operation to last only an hour, but trouble struck early when the Somali militia shot down two Blackhawk helicopters. U.S. commanders scrapped their original mission and diverted men to rescue the survivors. A running gun battle broke out, raging through the night and into the morning as a combined force of American, Pakistani, and Malaysian troops converged on the survivors from the Blackhawk. Fierce fighting continued before coalition forces finally retreated after rescuing several comrades.

The failed operation came at a steep cost of eighteen men killed and seventy-three wounded. Estimates of the number of Somalis killed ranged from several hundred to more than 1,000, with many civilians caught in the cross-fire. The American public recoiled as Somalis dragged the bodies of dead Americans through the streets. Within a short time, President Clinton ordered a withdrawal, and suspicions of future humanitarian efforts in war-torn areas spread among U.S. policymakers.

While the United States proved reluctant to commit troops in Africa, it acted more forcefully closer to home in Haiti. For years, Haiti had been one of the poorest nations in the world, with a population brutally exploited by a small elite and its military allies. Poverty, illiteracy, and crime ran high, ultimately leading thousands to flee the country and try to enter the United States.

A constitutional crisis in 1991 exacerbated problems when the military deposed the elected president, Jean-Bertrand Aristide, and replaced him with General Raoul Cédras. In response, the Organization of American States imposed an embargo. Soon Haitians began fleeing again, only to be returned by U.S. vessels. President Clinton inherited this problems in 1993, when reports began to circulate that 200,000 Haitians planned to flee. Clinton continued the policy of immediately returning the immigrants, leading one Aristide supporter to characterize the U.S. effort as a "floating Berlin Wall."

Finally, in October 1993, the parties negotiated for Aristide's return. However, when 200 U.S. and Canadian peacekeepers tried to disembark in Port-au-Prince to enforce the agreement, Cédras's followers arrived with machetes and threatened to turn Haiti into another Somalia. The troops withdrew amid the cheers of Cédras's allies.

For nearly a year, the United States and its allies pressured Cédras to step down. Pugnacious Secretary of State Madeleine Albright warned: "You can depart voluntarily and soon, or you can depart involuntarily and soon." President Clinton added: "The message of the United States to the Haitian dictators is clear: Your time is up. Leave now, or we will force you from power."

Initially, Cédras refused to relent. However, when he received intelligence about an imminent U.S. invasion, he relented, with one of his advisors acknowledging, "We'll have peace, not war." Soon, 15,000 U.S. troops landed on the island in Operation UPHOLD DEMOCRACY, dubbed by one journalist the "Immaculate Invasion." After a year, U.S. troops left, although one U.S. peacekeeper summed up the lingering problems: "We still gonna have a shitload of people in boats wanting to go to America."

WADING BACK INTO DEEP WATERS

Other challenges for the Clinton administration lurked in the Balkans. The dissolution of Yugoslavia in 1990 had unleashed ethnic tensions built up over the years between Serbs, Bosnians, and Croats. Heavy fighting erupted as the Serbs began ethnic cleansing. For several years, the United States avoided involvement, afraid of becoming bogged down in an intractable guerrilla war. However, some leaders called for forceful action. Secretary Albright groused to Secretary of Defense Colin Powell, "What's the point of having this superb military if we can't use it?" President Clinton stood somewhere in between the two positions, hoping that diplomacy and limited actions, including the imposition of a no-fly zone and assistance to the Muslim Bosnians and Croats, would stop the fighting.

However, when the Serbs massacred 7,000 men in Srebrenica in July 1995, Western resolve to mount an intervention strengthened. NATO began a two-week air campaign called Operation DELIBERATE FORCE that pushed the warring parties to the bargaining table. By the end of 1995, NATO had deployed more than 50,000 peacekeepers, including Americans, to Yugoslavia as part of the peace accord.

But problems continued in Kosovo in the late 1990s. When heavily armed Serb forces began the systematic destruction of Kosovar villages, the Clinton administration and NATO responded. When diplomacy failed, NATO launched an air war on Slobodan Milosevic's government on March 24, 1999. By April 3, the air war, dubbed Operation Nobel Anvil, had intensified, with forces pounding Belgrade and infrastructure throughout Serbia. After two months, the Serbs agreed to withdraw and allow international troops into Kosovo to monitor a cease-fire. By that time, NATO forces had conducted more than 38,000 sorties with few casualties and inflicted heavy losses, including 121 Yugoslav warplanes and billions of dollars in damage, especially in Belgrade. The operation was a major victory for airpower and reignited debates over its value in projecting U.S. power.

TWO STEPS FORWARD, ONE STEP BACK

If Clinton provoked controversy in Africa and the Balkans, he really stirred the pot when he attempted to fulfill a campaign promise in 1993 to allow gays to openly serve in the military by overturning the longstanding tradition of discharging men and women from the military for being homosexual.

A firestorm developed as some military leaders openly complained about the new Clinton policy's effect on morale and combat readiness. One naval commander declared that "homosexuals are notoriously promiscuous" and expressed fears that sailors sharing showers would have an "uncomfortable feeling of someone watching." General Powell, in a speech at the U.S. Naval Academy, warned that the presence of homosexuals "would be detrimental to good order and discipline, for a variety of reasons, principally relating around issues of privacy."

Others soon joined the fray, including Democratic senator Sam Nunn of Georgia, chairman of the Senate Armed Services Committee, who sided with the Clinton opponents. Still others argued that the military was no place for "social engineering," echoing arguments from the 1940s regarding African-Americans. Opponents rallied Christian conservatives and some veteran groups to defeat Clinton. However, there were supporters of the change, including Senator Goldwater, who told an interviewer: "I see no harm at all with having gays in the military. . . . I think it's high time to pull the curtains on this charade of a policy." He added: "I don't care if a soldier is straight, as long as he can shoot straight."

After months of wrangling, a compromise evolved in the form of the "Don't Ask, Don't Tell, Don't Pursue, Don't Harass" (DADT) policy, which prevented homosexuals from

IMAGE 16.5 Afghanistan War Now in its seventeenth year, The War in Afghanistan has joined the ranks of the Vietnam War as the one of the longest foreign conflicts in American history.

openly serving in the military but prohibited commanders from dismissing or harassing them as long as they did not make their sexual preferences public. It also tried to rein in over-zealous officers seeking to root out homosexuals and emphasized due process.

The controversial decision pleased neither side, and homosexuals in the military continued facing discrimination and living in fear of being outed throughout the 1990s. Each year, the military removed an average of 1,000 soldiers for being gay, although the number dropped significantly after September 11, when manpower challenges intensified. However, DADT remained in place until 2011, when the Obama administration, upheld by federal courts, repealed it with the support of many in the military, both active and retired. Afterwards, gays openly served in the U.S. military, although problems of discrimination continued.

THE ENDLESS WARS, 2001–PRESENT

On September 11, 2001, terrorists hijacked several planes and used them as weapons to slam into the World Trade Center in New York City and the Pentagon. More than 2,700 Americans died, sparking outrage. Afterward, U.S. troops invaded Afghanistan to root out the Taliban, which had supported the terrorist attack. Two years later, the Bush administration invaded Iraq, arguing that regime change was part of the new GWOT. Both wars proved costly in terms of gold and blood. The United States withdrew from Iraq in 2011, but the subsequent void allowed for the rise of new terrorist organizations. In Afghanistan, most U.S. troops left by 2014, but the ultimate outcome of the conflicts there remain uncertain.

CRASHING TOWERS

George W. Bush assumed the presidency in January 2001 after losing the popular vote but winning the Electoral College. While inexperienced and with little interest in foreign affairs, he tapped several Republican hawks, including Vice President Dick Cheney and Secretary of Defense Donald Rumsfeld, to occupy important positions in his administration.

Early on, the Bush administration concentrated on China and its resurgence, but September 11 changed its focus. Suddenly, the GWOT became an obsession. Unlike the nation-states the United States had battled in previous wars, terrorists were more amorphous and elusive and relied on irregular warfare.

Initially, the United States zeroed in on Afghanistan, where al-Qaeda and its leader, Osama bin Laden, maintained a base of operations protected by the Taliban government. In late September, the CIA and U.S. special forces initiated Operation Enduring Freedom, during which the United States provided support to the anti-Taliban Northern Alliance, spread around millions of dollars to buy the tribal leaders' loyalties, and called in airstrikes that decimated enemy convoys and fortified positions.

Within eight weeks, the Northern Alliance had captured most of Afghanistan's major cities and pushed the remaining al-Qaeda fighters, including bin Laden, into a small area near the Pakistani border known as Tora Bora. President Bush declared in October: "We'll smoke him out of his cave" and pledged that bin Laden would be taken "dead or alive."

But while CIA officers and soldiers on the ground called for encircling Tora Bora with newly arriving U.S. troops, operational commander General Tommy Franks hesitated.

Those on the ground knew that bin Laden and his aides were there, with one CIA operative even talking directly with bin Laden on a captured phone. Franks thought that the Afghan forces could conduct the capture, although they showed more interest in securing territory than killing the terrorist leader, and so he took no action.

Finally, on December 15, bin Laden went on the radio to thank his soldiers for battling the "crusaders" and to promise to continue the fight. After a prayer, he and his top lieutenant, Ayman al-Zawahiri, headed into Pakistan. One expert suggested that "had bin Laden been surrounded at Tora Bora, he would have been confined to an area of several dozen square miles; now he could well be in an area that snakes across 40,000 square miles." The United States had lost the chance to capture the September 11 mastermind.

With the Northern Alliance in control of the country by January 2002 and coalition troops arriving to train the Afghan security forces and pursue the remnants of the Taliban, victory seemed complete. U.S. forces captured many al-Qaeda fighters and transported them to Guantanamo Bay, the American naval base in Cuba. Most Americans greeted the defeat

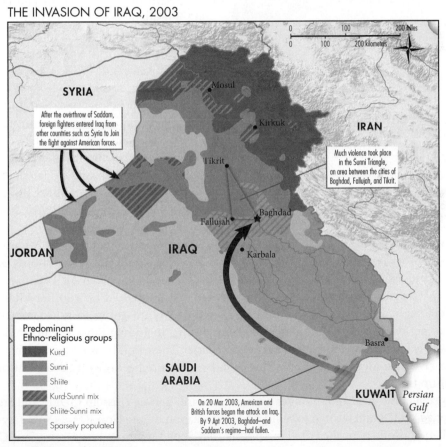

THE INVASION OF IRAQ, 2003

After the overthrow of Saddam, foreign fighters entered Iraq from other countries such as Syria to join the fight against American forces.

Much violence took place in the Sunni Triangle, an area between the cities of Baghdad, Fallujah, and Tikrit.

Predominant Ethno-religious groups
- Kurd
- Sunni
- Shiite
- Kurd-Sunni mix
- Shiite-Sunni mix
- Sparsely populated

On 20 Mar 2003, American and British forces began the attack on Iraq. By 9 Apr 2003, Baghdad—and Saddam's regime—had fallen.

MAP 16.3 The Invasion of Iraq

IMAGE 16.6 Pat Tillman Pat Tillman left his career as a professional football player in the NFL to enlist in the Army following the September 11 attacks. When he died in April of 2004, his family was notified that he was struck down by enemy fire in an act of bravery, and was posthumously awarded the Silver Star and Purple Heart. A month later, it was revealed the true cause of his death was covered up by the Army, and that in reality, he was shot and killed by fellow soldiers who mistook him for the enemy.

of the Taliban with great joy and resumed flying under much heavier security. However, cautious observers warned that much remained to be done in Afghanistan, where the Taliban remained a potent force.

IRAQ 2.0

Once the Bush administration had installed Hamid Karzai in power in Kabul, its attention turned elsewhere. Even before September 11, some members of the administration had wanted to oust Saddam Hussein. The ultimate drumbeat of war against him began with the accusations that he had provided aid to al-Qaeda and possessed weapons of mass destruction (WMDs). In late January 2002, President Bush in a speech included Iraq as part of the "Axis of Evil," along with Iran and North Korea. Singling out Hussein, he stressed: "This is a regime that has something to hide from the civilized world." Months before, he asked Rumsfeld: "What kind of a war plan do you have for Iraq? How do you feel about the war plan for Iraq?" Even in the middle of the Tora Bora operation, Bush had declared: "I want to know what the operations are [for Iraq]."

Calls for war grew steadily in 2002. As President Bush sold his ideas of "preventative war" (also known as "anticipatory self-defense") and remaking the Middle East in America's image, Rumsfeld pushed for an attack that would put fewer "boots on the ground" and avoid a time-consuming and costly air campaign. When Air Force Secretary Jim Roche asked Rumsfeld, "Don, you do realize that Iraq could be another Vietnam?" Rumsfeld replied, "Of course it won't be Vietnam. We are going to go in, overthrow Saddam, get out. That's it." Others joined his chorus, including Powell, who told Bush that Iraq "is like crystal glass. . . . It's going to shatter. There will be no government. There will be civil disorder. . . . You'll be the proud owner of the hopes and aspirations of 25 million Iraqis."

Consequently, Bush and his aides plunged forward, linking Hussein to 9/11 and arguing that he had WMDs and wanted to build a nuclear weapon. White House Press Secretary Scott McClellan and others pushed "talking points" developed by the White House Iraq Group (WHIG), headed by national security advisor Condoleezza Rice and presidential advisor

IMAGE 16.7 **Invasion of Iraq, 2003** On March 20, 2003, President George W. Bush announced the launch of Operation Iraqi Freedom, the effort to remove Saddam Hussein from power. U.S. troops engaged in the operation stand under the "Hands of Victory" in Iraq, in Ceremony Square, Baghdad.

Karl Rove, "to coordinate the marketing of the war to the public." By Labor Day 2002, the campaign to sell the war had fully began.

Early on, strong opposition developed in some quarters of the military. Army Chief of Staff Eric Shinseki, a decorated Vietnam War veteran, pushed back in early 2003 when he told members of the Senate Armed Services Committee that Iraq was a big country "with ethnic tensions that could lead to other problems." The United States, he declared, would need "something on the order of several hundred thousand soldiers" to invade it. Pentagon planners wanted at least 400,000. Rumsfeld balked, envisioning only half that number. Ultimately, Shinseki lost influence and retired early, as the administration marginalized and punished its critics in the Pentagon.

Despite vocal opposition in the military, Congress, and the country, the Bush administration steamed ahead. Soon, troops flooded into forward bases in the Middle East. There, much as they had in the first Gulf War, they trained and maintained their gear, including chemical protection suits. Many were from the Reserves and National Guard units. As one embedded journalist noted: "Culturally, these marines would be virtually unrecognizable to their forebears in the 'Greatest Generation.' They are kids raised on hip-hop, Marilyn Manson and Jerry Springer. For them, 'motherfucker' is a term of endearment. For some, slain rapper Tupac is an American patriot whose writings are better known than the speeches of Abraham Lincoln."

Some groused about the conditions, as well as their reason for being there. One medic told his compatriots after reading an article, "Gents, this is a very cognizant way of explaining what we are doing here. We're going to be fighting a war for oil." Despite such complaints, the soldiers anxiously waited for the final command to attack.

THE ROAD TO BAGHDAD

By March 2003, Bush was ready to pull the trigger. Mid-month, the bombing began as coalition forces (largely composed of British troops) pounded the depleted Iraqi army. In a shock and awe campaign that began on March 21, 2003, coalition forces launched more than 1,500 sorties a day, as well as hundreds of cruise missiles, into Iraq.

On March 22, the forces invaded Iraq and moved rapidly toward Baghdad. As they progressed, most of the Iraqi army disappeared, its conscripts simply discarding their weapons and uniforms and marching home. Some Republican Guards fought ferociously, despite their aged tanks and weapons. U.S. forces also encountered the *Fedayeen* (martyrs), a zealous pro-Hussein militia who wore no uniforms and attacked in civilian vehicles armed with rocket-propelled grenades (RPGs) and AK-47s. But overall, superior coalition firepower easily overcame the Iraqis. One U.S. commander bragged: "We weren't marching to Baghdad, we were sprinting there."

By April 3, U.S. forces neared the city after covering more than 300 miles. On April 4, the international airport fell to U.S. forces. Not long after, thirty M-1 Abrams tanks and fifteen Bradley fighting vehicles rushed toward downtown Baghdad, even while Iraqi officials cried: "The American louts fled." The resistance collapsed as the nation's leaders, including Hussein, went into hiding. As Iraqis tore down the huge statue of Hussein in Firdaus Square, Rumsfeld waxed poetic: "Watching them, one cannot help but think of the fall of the Berlin Wall and the collapse of the Iron Curtain." The fighting had only claimed 122 Americans, many victims of friendly fire and accidents. Thousands of Iraqi fighters died, as well as civilians caught in the cross-fire. It was a crushing defeat for a once-strong army.

In Washington, Bush supporters criticized doomsayers in Congress. One bragged that the "crushing win" had resulted from the White House's development of "a most creative and detailed war plan." Conservative columnist Fred Barnes declared that "setting up democracy is hard, but not as hard as winning a war." He was wrong.

On May 1, Bush took a victory lap. He flew in a navy warplane onto the USS *Abraham Lincoln* in the Pacific Ocean, exiting the plane in a military flight suit. Later, standing in front of a huge banner that read "Mission Accomplished," he told the crew: "Major combat operations in Iraq have ended. In the battle of Iraq, the United States and our allies have prevailed. And now our coalition is engaged in securing and reconstructing that country." He admitted that more work remained but clearly reveled in the victory.

INSURGENCY

Despite the White House's optimism, the situation in Iraq deteriorated quickly. The Pentagon's Office of Reconstruction and Humanitarian Assistance (ORHA) existed only several weeks before the war began and had little time to prepare to administer a country torn apart by years of fighting. NSC advisor Rice observed: "The concept was that we would defeat the army, but the institutions would hold, everything from ministries to police forces." An ORHA member believed that Iraqi government officials merely "would all be in their offices, at their desk, pen and paper at the ready. And we would come in and essentially . . . take them off the pause button."

They were completely wrong. Most Saddam loyalists simply walked away. Soon, the undermanned U.S. forces found themselves unable to provide basic services, including electricity and running water. One U.S. officer in Baghdad complained: "Banks were robbed, assassinations were common, and young, attractive women were snatched from their homes. It was as though we'd popped the cork on Iraqi society after decades of repression, and it was ugly. . . . I felt like Wyatt Earp in Tombstone."

The occupation unleashed longstanding animosities between religious and ethnic groups, sparking fears of a civil war. Simultaneously, the Bush administration suffered a public relations nightmare when it became apparent that no WMDs had ever existed and the OHRA had failed. The White House then disbanded the OHRA and created the Coalition Provisional Authority (CPA) under Paul Bremer, a former State Department official who came out of retirement to lead it.

Bremer was a poor choice for the role, with little knowledge about Iraqi culture and no experience in reconstruction. Soon, he alienated many in the military, telling commanders: "I'm the CPA administrator, and I'm in charge." With Bush's support, he purged the Iraqi government of members of Hussein's Baath Party, who simply blended back into society with their weapons and training.

The situation worsened over time. While many CPA officials lived comfortably inside Baghdad's heavily fortified Green Zone, patrolling soldiers saw tensions rise as angry Iraqi nationalists and displaced Baathists began attacking U.S. patrols and convoys, relying on ambushes and improvised explosive devices (IEDs) that could be detonated remotely when Americans passed. Ultimately, these attacks accounted for nearly 60 percent of U.S. deaths. In June, General Ricardo Sanchez stressed: "The undeniable fact was that we were still at war."

In response, on July 1, Bush boldly promised justice for anyone who harmed Americans. "There are some who feel like . . . conditions are such that they can attack us there," he declared. "My answer is, Bring them on. We got the force necessary to deal with the security situation." In response one army officer in Baghdad lamented: "My soldiers and I were searching for car bombs . . . and scanning rooftops for snipers, and our president was in Washington taunting our enemies and encouraging them to attack us." He added: "The enemy was already 'bringing it on' all over Baghdad."

By late 2003, those on the ground instinctively knew that the loose coalition of fighters had become an insurgency. Increasingly, the Iraqi people lost confidence in the CPA, which even American commanders snidely said stood for: "Can't Provide Anything." International relief organizations along with the World Bank and the International Monetary Fund began withdrawing their personnel as the violence escalated. Insurgents increasingly coordinated IED attacks and introduced new weapons, including suicide bombers and huge truck bombs. These attacks targeted not only Americans, but also rival groups, including Shiites and leaders like Muqtada al-Sadr, who unleashed his militia against rival factions and the Americans. Muslim fighters from all over the world poured into the country to wage war against the Christian occupiers. As the country spiraled out of control, Marine general Tony Zinni observed: "I have seen this movie. It was called 'Vietnam.'"

FIGHTING IN THE RUBBLE

The situation went from bad to worse in 2004 as the Americans and their allies became increasingly involved in a complex insurgency. Besides facing a classic guerrilla war, with the enemy hard to identify and the lines between friend and foe blurred, soldiers rarely understood the language or cultural norms. No place symbolized the challenges U.S. forces faced more than the Sunni stronghold of Fallujah. In late March, private security contractors for Blackwater USA (many of whom were former special forces or Navy SEALS making $1,000 a day) drove through the town in sport-utility vehicles. Suddenly, insurgents sprang an ambush, peppering the vehicles with bullets and RPGs. In a short time, they had killed three and pulled another from his vehicle, stoned him with bricks, and dismembered the body. They then burned all four bodies and hanged the remains from a bridge amid chants of "Allah Akbar!" ("God Is Great!"). When photos of the event appeared, an angry Rumsfeld declared: "We've got to pound these guys. We need to make sure that Iraqis in other cities receive our message." Some military commanders urged caution, arguing that their Marines were already making headway in peacefully engaging the Sunnis in Fallujah, but Bush emphasized, "We know it's going to be ugly, but we are committed."

On April 4, Marines attacked Fallujah, where they encountered an estimated 3,000 battle-hardened Sunni and al-Qaeda fighters in heavily fortified strongholds. One journalist wrote: "This was the classic immemorial labor of infantry, little different from the way it had been practiced in Vietnam, World War II." The Americans advanced into heavy RPG fire and encountered numerous IEDs and car bombs. Insurgents often used civilians as shields and hid in mosques, making progress slow.

IMAGE 16.8   Battles of Fallujah   This photo captures the moment before members of the 1ˢᵗ Cavalry Division enter and search a building at the Second Battle of Fallujah. The battle, which took place from November 7ᵗʰ to December 24ᵗʰ, 2004, is remembered as the bloodiest battle of the Iraq War. It is estimated that eighty-two of 12,000 U.S. troops entangled in the conflict died.

As images of the destruction and death spread through Arab media outlets, public opinion in the Muslim world turned against the Americans. One Muslim cleric screamed: "They are killing our children. They are destroying everything! The people can see through all the American promises and lies!"

On April 9, Bremer ordered the Marines to stop advancing while he negotiated. In early May, the Americans agreed to withdraw and allow the Fallujah Brigade, composed of former Iraqi soldiers (and some insurgents), to take over and impose a cease-fire. The decision angered many soldiers who had fought to take the city, especially after losing 27 dead and 100 wounded. One bitterly complained: "Does this remind you of another part of the world in the early 1970s?" Another observed that the enemy would "use Fallujah as a base to hit us." As the Americans withdrew, many citizens jeered them. One Iraqi noted: "They lost. They should leave." Another commented: "We believe God saved our city . . . and we believed they learned a lesson . . . not to mess with Fallujah." Signs on storefronts appeared: "We have defeated the devil Marines!" and "Jihad has triumphed!"

Soon another battle loomed as Fallujah remained a hotbed of enemy activity. By November, with an election on the horizon, Iraqi prime minister Ayad Allawi, under pressure from the Bush administration, agreed to work with the Americans to retake the city. To do so, commanders formulated Operation PHANTOM FURY, or what Allawi named Operation Al FAJR (Dawn). For months the Americans mapped the city and its fortifications. Determined not to repeat the scenes of the April offensive, U.S. forces warned Iraqi citizens to leave. This time, 90 percent left, including several top terrorist leaders. The United States then marshaled a larger force and prepared a series of feints to confuse the enemy, who remained reliant on small bands operating in limited areas.

On November 9, the Americans stormed into the city. They encountered heavy resistance in areas rife with booby traps and car bombs. The Marines, supported by heavy armor from the army, went house to house, often fighting in the kitchens and living rooms of the deserted homes. Within a week, they had gained the upper hand, although it would take more than a month to completely clear Fallujah.

The second Battle of Fallujah was more costly than the first. The Americans lost 95 killed and 560 wounded, for an 11 percent casualty rate (one company received eighty-four Purple Hearts). They killed more than 2,000 enemy combatants and captured another 1,000. It was a victory, but one that destroyed more than 60 percent of Fallujah's buildings. When Iraqis complained about the destruction, one Marine noted: "You never want to destroy a city like this . . . but this was the only way to eliminate those fanatics."

TO CONTAIN AN INSURGENCY

Despite the victory in Fallujah, the insurgency grew as the United States became embroiled in several major scandals. One involved the prison at Abu Ghraib, where U.S. forces faced accusations of torturing Iraqi detainees. Another involved the murder by Marines of twenty-four Iraqi men, women, and children in the village of Haditha.

As the situation deteriorated, the U.S. death toll climbed to 2,182, with 16,155 wounded by December 2005. Yet some administration officials remained optimistic. Vice President

Cheney said in May 2005, "I think they're in the last throes, if you will, of the insurgency." Most soldiers disagreed, as bomb attacks rose to 1,800 a month and militias and terrorist groups continued to control large parts of the country. One reporter noted: "Iraq belonged to militias, the resistance, terrorists, any man with a gun. The roads leading to Baghdad were a terror zone. The streets of Baghdad were war zones. . . . Iraqis continued to live in a republic of fear."

Deaths piled up among the coalition forces, mostly impacting Americans. In the period from 2006 to 2007, more than 1,800 Americans died. Many others suffered wounds, including major head injuries and the loss of limbs, from IEDs, surviving only thanks to advanced treatment in the field and improved transportation to critical care facilities.

Stateside, support for the war waned as it became more obvious that the administration had misled the nation into war. Many people began asking questions about those benefiting financially from the war, especially large companies like Halliburton, which had close ties to Cheney. By 2006, nearly 60 percent of Americans wanted to withdraw from Iraq, and public approval of President Bush's handling of the war had plummeted.

Such dissatisfaction exacerbated the isolation felt by many in the armed services, particularly those shouldering the heaviest burden by serving multiple tours. One soldier complained: "The fatal flaw was when right after September 11 the president asked everyone to

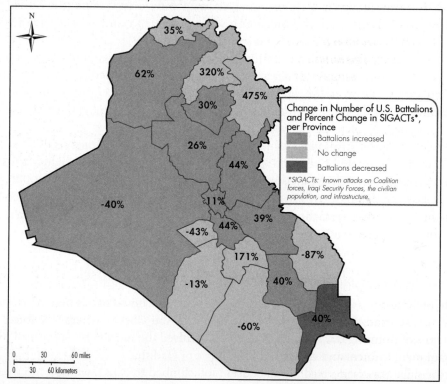

MAP 16.4   Surge Efforts in Iraq, 2006–2007

go on with their lives. That set the stage for no one sacrificing. That's why they aren't behind it, because they don't have a stake in this war." He concluded: "The military went to war. America went to the mall."

As the insurgency raged, the military sought ways to make the best of the situation. Some officials pushed counterinsurgency as an answer, producing some successes, including those led by Colonel H. R. McMaster in Tal Afar, on the Syrian border. In a policy described as "Clear, Hold, Build," McMaster ordered his officers and some enlisted men to start studying Iraqi culture and language, banned the use of racist terms for Iraqis, apologized to local leaders for past excesses, and built promised infrastructure. The efforts paid dividends as locals joined security teams and even called to report insurgents laying IEDs.

In support of such efforts, in December 2006, General David Petraeus and other officers at the Command and General Staff College published a new counterinsurgency field manual. The document stressed security for the local populace as a primary goal, questioned the targeting of suspected enemies' families, and made the point that "an operation that kills five insurgents is counterproductive if collateral damage leads to the recruitment of fifty more insurgents."

Those pushing change received a boost when Rumsfeld resigned in 2006. His replacement, former CIA director Robert Gates, brought a steady hand to the Pentagon. Unlike Rumsfeld, Gates was not an ideologue, and in one of his first appearances before Congress, he stressed that Osama bin Laden was responsible for 9/11, contradicting White House claims about Hussein's role in the attacks. When questioned whether the United States was winning in Iraq, he strongly replied, "No, sir."

Other changes appeared on the horizon in Iraq. Increasingly, U.S. troops began buying the allegiance of sheiks and militias. As one American observed, "We're paying them not to blow us up." Another emphasized: "Once a tribal leader flips, attacks on American forces in that area stop almost overnight." Both the payments and indiscriminate local attacks by al-Qaeda on anyone perceived to be cooperating with the Americans coalesced to reduce the violence.

Petraeus and Gates pressured Bush to open himself up to new strategies. Soon, he threw his support behind a plan to increase the number of troops in Iraq by 20,000 by June 2007, a policy characterized as "the surge." With support from 400,000 trained Iraqis, the expanded U.S. forces focused on ensuring the safety of the population against militants. Priorities also changed from building a fully

IMAGE 16.9 David Petraeus David Petraeus assumed an influential role in Iraq by leading the American military surge in 2007. He went on to become director of the CIA during President Barack Obama's Presidency in 2011; however, a year later resigned amid controversy of providing classified information to writer Paula Broadwell.

functioning democratic state to creating one that was "reasonably representative and broadly responsive to citizens." "We're not after a Jeffersonian democracy," Petraeus told Congress in April 2008. "We're after conditions that would allow our soldiers to disengage."

Ultimately, the surge allowed talks that led to the Status of Forces Agreement, under which the United States agreed to withdraw its forces from Iraqi cities by June 2009 and from the entire country by December 2011. This agreement gave the various factions an end date for U.S. involvement, so insurgents chose not to engage the heavily armed Americans, waiting to fight a weaker Iraqi government and its security forces. The Iranians, who had aided Shiite fighters during the conflict, also saw the value of waiting out the Americans so that their Shiite brothers in Iraq could prepare for the next stage of their fight, aiming to extend their influence even further after the U.S. removal of their mortal enemy in 2003.

When President Barack Obama took power in 2009, he honored Bush's agreements, and U.S. troops began withdrawing from Iraq. On August 31, Obama announced that "the American combat mission in Iraq has ended. Operation Iraqi Freedom is over." The withdrawal went as scheduled, but in the power struggle afterward (exacerbated by Syria's civil war), a potent new enemy emerged in the form of the Islamic State of Iraq and the Levant (ISIL, also called the Islamic State of Iraq and Syria, or ISIS), which controlled much of Iraq and brought U.S. forces back into the country by 2015.

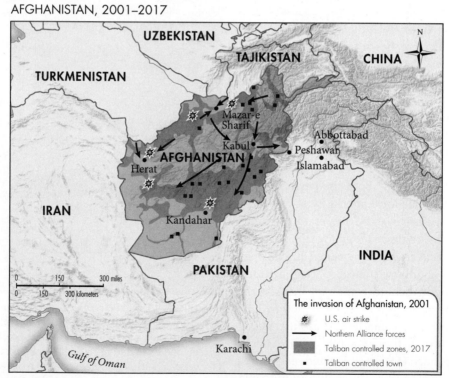

AFGHANISTAN, 2001–2017

MAP 16.5 Afghanistan, 2001–2017

BACK TO AFGHANISTAN

When President Obama took office, he committed the United States to finishing the job in Afghanistan. In 2008, he told the Veterans of Foreign Wars: "After eight years . . . it is my intention to finish the job. . . . I feel very confident that when the American people hear a clear rationale for what we're doing there and how we intend to achieve our goals, that they will be supportive." He listened to top advisors, including Petraeus and General Stanley McChrystal, who pushed for a replication of the Iraq surge in Afghanistan. Secretary of State Hillary Clinton also emphasized the importance of counterinsurgency, declaring, "We found out how to do it in Iraq."

But Obama was wrong. Few Americans, already exhausted by Iraq and the lack of progress in Kabul, backed the decision to build up U.S. forces in Afghanistan. One analyst asked: "How can American forces protect the population, let alone help build a functioning nation in a tribal narco-state consisting of some 40,000 mostly rural villages over an area larger than California and New York combined?"

Nonetheless, the Obama administration increased the number of troops in the country and worked to improve the Afghan army. It poured billions into building schools and hospitals, tried to root out endemic corruption, and battled the opium trade with substitute crops, all the while fighting the resurgent Taliban. In this fight the military increasingly relied on the use of drones to strike the enemy and limit U.S. casualties. While these strategies allowed the United States to gain some ground, the prescient words of a captured Taliban fighter summed up the challenges that faced Americans: "You have the watches, but we have the time."

CONCLUSIONS

While the Obama administration scored some successes in tracking down people responsible for 9/11 and killing bin Laden in a raid in Pakistan, the situation in Afghanistan remained tenuous. However, on December 28, 2014, Obama declared that "the longest war in American history" had come "to a responsible conclusion." While the number of U.S. forces in Afghanistan has decreased, the fighting there never abated and continues today.

In Iraq, ISIL insurgents and many former Sunni fighters have created chaos in the region and threatened Europeans and Americans with terrorist acts. While the Obama administration eventually pivoted toward a focus on Asia, the challenges of Iraq have remained, despite the billions spent and tens of thousands of casualties, including Sergeant Travis Twiggs, whose death did not occur on the battlefield but resulted from his time fighting in the GWOT.

The period after Vietnam highlighted significant changes in the American military as the world increasingly shrank and the United States became more involved in areas such as the Middle East. The military also became less oriented toward the civilian soldier after the end of the draft, becoming more professional and exclusive, in opposition to the general demographic trends of American society. At the same time, science and technology altered the new military establishment, as some officials advocated a smaller force reliant on new (very costly) weapons systems to reduce the human footprint and casualties. However, this

TIMELINE

June 1973	Draft ends
January 1980	Presidential Directive 59 released
October 1983	Suicide bomber attack on marine barracks in Beirut
October 1986	Goldwater-Nichols Department of Defense Reorganization Act signed
August 1990–February 1991	Operation DESERT STORM in Kuwait and Iraq
October 1993	Major operations in Somalia
February 1994	"Don't ask, don't tell" policy implemented
September 2001	Global War on Terror begins
March 2003	War in Iraq begins
November–December 2004	Second Battle of Fallujah
August 2009	President Obama announces end of U.S. combat mission in Iraq
May 2011	Special forces kill Osama bin Laden in Pakistan

approach has created problems, as the wars after Vietnam have largely been fought against guerrillas in inhospitable conditions.

Finally, politics, including the end of the Cold War and the embrace of new foci such as humanitarian relief and peacekeeping, strongly shaped the military of the post-Vietnam era. September 11 initiated a new period of domestic considerations, changing the military's mission to the fight against global terrorism. Finally, the need to protect access to natural resources and the United States' inability to reduce the size of the military-industrial complex have definitely altered perceptions of the military and its role in society, both of which continue to evolve in the twenty-first century.

SUGGESTED READINGS

Anderson, Terry H. *Bush's Wars.* New York: Oxford University Press, 2011.

Bacevich, Andrew. *America's War for the Greater Middle East: A Military History.* New York: Random House, 2016.

Bowden, Mark. *Black Hawk Down: A Story of Modern War.* New York: Atlantic Monthly Press, 1999.

Filkins, Dexter. *The Forever War.* New York: Alfred A. Knopf, 2009.

Fitzgerald, Frances. *Way Out There in the Blue: Reagan, Star Wars and the End of the Cold War.* New York: Simon & Schuster, 2000.

Gill, Lesley. *The School of the Americas: Military Training and Political Violence in the Americas.* Durham, NC: Duke University Press, 2004.

Griffith, Robert K., Jr. *The U.S. Army Transition to the All-Volunteer Force, 1968–1974.* Washington, D.C.: U.S. Army Center of Military History, 1997.

Mann, James. *Rise of the Vulcans: The History of Bush's War Cabinet.* New York: Penguin, 2004.

Packer, George. *The Assassin's Gate: America in Iraq.* New York: Farrar, Straus, Giroux, 2006.

CREDITS

Page 6: Frontispiece to 'Nova Reperta' (New Discoveries) engraved by Theodor Galle (1571–1633) c.1600 (engraving) (later colouration), Straet, Jan van der (Giovanni Stradano) (1523–1605) (after) / Private Collection / The Stapleton Collection / Bridgeman Images

Page 9: Preservation Virginia

Page 11: Illustration of Algonkian Indian Village, 1587 / Universal History Archive / UIG / Bridgeman Images

Page 29: National Museum of the American Indian, Smithsonian Institution, Catalog Number 23/9269

Page 35: North Wind Picture Archives / Alamy Stock Photo

Page 46: Jefferys, Thomas, – 1771, George, III, King of Great Britain, George, IV, King of Great Britain, and Roberts, William, active 1763. "PLAN of the TOWN and HARBOUR of S.T AUGUSTIN." Map. 1763. *Norman B. Leventhal Map & Education Center*, https://collections.leventhalmap.org/search/commonwealth:hx11z547c (accessed September 25, 2018).

Page 48: Courtesy of American Antiquarian Society

Page 53: Library of Congress Washington Washington, D.C. LC-DIG-pga-08972

Page 62: Jefferys, Thomas, d. 1771. "An authentic plan of the River St. Laurence, from Sillery to the Fall of Montmerenci." Map. 1759. Norman B. Leventhal Map & Education Center, https://collections.leventhalmap.org/search/commonwealth:8049g924s (accessed September 11, 2018).

Page 65: The Death of General Wolfe (1727–59), c.1771 (oil on panel) , West, Benjamin (1738–1820) / Private Collection / Phillips, Fine Art Auctioneers, New York, USA / Bridgeman Images

Page 78: GRANGER / GRANGER — All rights reserved.

Page 80: Library of Congress Prints and Photographs Division Washington, LC-DIG-ds-03379

Page 89: King George III, c.1762–64 (oil on canvas), Ramsay, Allan (1713–84) / Guildhall Art Gallery, City of London / Bridgeman Images

Page 93: 'Common Sense: Addressed to the Inhabitants of America', new edition by Thomas Paine (1737–1809) printed in Philadelphia, 1776 (print), American School, (18th century) / Private Collection / Photo © Christie's Images / Bridgeman Images

Page 102: Charles Willson Peale (1741–1827) George Washington. Ca. 1779–1781. Oil on canvas, 95 × 61 3/4 in. (241.3 × 156.8 cm). Gift of Collis P. Huntington, 1897 (97.33). Location: The

Page 401: (1944) Grenade hurls toward Japanese. Northern Mariana Islands Saipan, 1944. [Photograph] Retrieved from the Library of Congress, https://www.loc.gov/item/94500709/.

Page 402: Library of Congress Prints and Photographs Division Washington, D.C. 20540 USA LC-USZ62-105217

Page 405: (1945) This section of Osaka, Japan was levelled by fire-bomb attacks by Superfortresses in a long series of heavy raids during the months that preceded Japan's capitulation / Credit U.S. Army A.A.F. photo, Wash. D.C. Japan Osaka, 1945. [Photograph] Retrieved from the Library of Congress, https://www.loc.gov/item/91482334/.

Page 411: (1945) Second atomic bombing of Nagasaki, Japan. Japan Nagasaki, 1945. [August] [Photograph] Retrieved from the Library of Congress, https://www.loc.gov/item/98506956/.

Page 420: Library of Congress Prints and Photographs Division Washington, D.C. 20540 USA

Page 425: From the Photograph Collection (COLL/3948), Marine Corps Archives & Special Collections

Page 429: Copyright Unknown, Courtesy of Harry S. Truman Library

Page 431: Library of Congress Prints and Photographs Division Washington, D.C. 20540 USA http://hdl.loc.gov/loc.pnp/pp.print

Page 433: National Museum of the US Air Force

Page 435: Library of Congress Prints and Photographs Division Washington, D.C. 20540 USA http://hdl.loc.gov/loc.pnp/pp.print

Page 436: USAF photo 83980 AC

Page 445: O'Halloran, T. J., photographer. (1958) U.S. Marine sits in a foxhole and points a machine gun towards Beirut, Lebanon, in the distance / TOH. Beirut Lebanon, 1958. July. [Photograph] Retrieved from the Library of Congress, https://www.loc.gov/item/2003654381/.

Page 448: Cecil Stoughton. White House Photographs. John F. Kennedy Presidential Library and Museum, Boston

Page 453: Library of Congress Prints and Photographs Division Washington, D.C. 20540 USA http://www.loc.gov/pictures/item/2002695242/

Page 454: National Archives and Records Administration

Page 455: AP Photo

Page 458: National Museum of the U.S. Air Force photo 071002-F-1234P-022

Page 460: "Commanders are responsible for their troops – except when those sneaky terrorists fail to remind us that they have lately been using bigger bombs" — Published April 17, 1997. A 1997 Herblock Cartoon, © The Herb Block Foundation

Page 464: Official U.S. Air Force photo no. 020903-o-9999r-007 [1]

Page 475: U.S. Senate Photographic Studio; Renee Bouchard

Page 477: Bettmann/Getty Images

Page 479: "Everything's okay – they never reached the mimeograph machine" — Published February 1, 1968 A 1968 Herblock Cartoon, © The Herb Block Foundation

Page 483: Wikimedia Commons https://commons.wikimedia.org/wiki/File:Highway_of_Death_2. JPEG

Page 487: Steve Cavalier / Alamy Stock Photo

Page 490: AP Photo/Photography Plus via Williamson Stealth Media Solutions

Page 491: Technical Sergeant John L. Houghton, Jr., United States Air Force – https://arcweb .archives.gov/

Page 494: Photo by SFC Johancharles Van Boershttps

Page 497: Wikimedia Commons

INDEX

Note: Page references in *italics* indicate photo, "*f*" indicate figure, "*t*" indicate table.

A

AAF. *See* Army Air Forces
Abenaki Indians, 18, 37, 41–42
Abercromby, James, 59–61
Abraham Lincoln (USS), 492
Abrams, Creighton, 463
Abu Ghraib, 495
Acheson, Dean, 424, 448
Act of Union (1707), 43, 73
Adams, John, 89, 131, 138, 146
Adams, John Quincy, 178, 193
Adams–Onís Treaty, 193
Adid, Mohamed Farrah, 485
adoption ceremony, 10
AEF. *See* American
        Expeditionary Forces
Afghanistan War, *487*, 498*f*, 499
Africa, 365*f*
African Americans, 156, 166 197,
        283*f*, 329–30, 464–65
    in Great War, 333–34, 343–44
    Harlem Hellfighters, 344*f*
    as soldiers, 258, 278
    U.S. military relations with,
        376–77
African Squadron, 183
Agent Orange, 457
Aguinaldo y Famy, Emilio,
        314–17
Air Force, U.S., *433*
airpower
    in Great War, 345
    in Korean War, 432–34
    Mitchell, W., pursuing, 353–54

over Europe, 370–72
over Vietnam, 453–54, 459
in World War II, 367–69,
        372–73
Aisne-Marne Offensive, 343
Alabama Indians, 41
Alamo, the 194–95
Albany congress, 52–54
Albright, Madeleine, 486
Aleutian Islands, 395
Alexander, Harold, 365
Alexander VI (pope), 33
Algerine War, 173
Algonquian Indians, 35*f*
Algonquian Village, 11*f*
Alien and Sedition Acts, 148
Allen, Ethan, 84
Allerton, Isaac, 22
Allied forces, *377*
    civilian targets of, 385
    in Great War, 345–47
    Hitler's goal of dividing,
        384–85
    Japanese invasion force and,
        394–95
    Operation Dragoon of, 382
    Patton and, 345
Almond, Edward, 427
Almonte, Juan, 195
Alperovitz, Gar, 410
ambushes, small-scale, 11
Amelia Island, 177
American Expeditionary Forces
        (AEF), 338–43

American Revolution, 87.
        See also Virginia
    in Carolinas, 124–26
    Continental Army suffering in,
        109–13
    Iroquois Confederation in,
        116–17
    Philadelphia campaign of,
        107–9
    Saratoga campaign of, 102–7
    in Savannah and Charleston,
        118–20
    Spanish conquests in,
        117–18
    Treaty of Paris, 131–32
    troop morale in, 96
    Yorktown war of, 128*f*,
        129–31, 130*f*
The American Way of War
        (Weigley), 15
Amherst, Jeffrey, 59–60, 81
ammunition, 214, 237, 280–81,
        312–14, 329
"Anaconda Plan," 225
Anderson, Robert, 222
Andersonville stockade, 259
André, John, 122
Anglo-Dutch Wars, 36–37
Anglo-Powhatan War, 11–16
annexation, of Texas, 196
antinavalists, 149–50
antisubmarine campaign, 337–38
Apache Indians, 217
Apalachee Indians, 41

Appomattox Campaign,
240, 268–69
Appomattox Court
House, 268, 269f
Arista, Mariano, 198
Aristide, Jean-Bertrand, 486
Arizona (USS), *390*, 391
Arkansas Territory, 186
Armand, Jean, 55
Armistead, Walker K., 192
Armstrong, James, 175
Armstrong, John, 158–60, 162
army, U.S. *See also* standing army
  black troops in, 258
  Buffalo Soldiers in, 283f
  Burgoyne in, 103
  Canadian invasions failed
    by, 156
  Civil War fighting of, 225–27
  Civil War officers of, 276–77
  Confederate forces and officers
    of, 225
  Congress ordering expansion
    of, 148
  demobilization of, 275–77
  Indians massacre by, 145
  military manuals from, 208
  postwar configuration of,
    212–13
  Washington, G., needing
    national, 101
  as western frontier
    constabulary, 284
Army Air Corps, U.S., 367
Army Air Forces (AAF), 370
army officers, 276–77
Army of Northern Virginia
  (Confederate), 240,
  247, 252, 254
Army of the Cumberland,
  257–58, 264
Army of the Ohio, 244
Army of the Potomac, 229–30,
  250, 254, 260–62, 274
Army of the Republic of Vietnam
  (ARVN), 440, 443, 457–58
Army of the Shenandoah, 263
Army of Tennessee
  (Confederate), 256, 259
Army of the Tennessee,
  244, 257, 264
Army of the United States, 349
Army of Virginia, 247
Army Topographical Corps, 181
Arnold, Benedict, 84, 90–91,
  106–7, 122–23

Arnold, Henry "Hap," 372, 405
Arsenal of Democracy,
  356, 361, 363
Arthur, Chester, 280
Articles of Confederation, 136
ARVN. *See* Army of the Republic
  of Vietnam
asymmetrical warfare, 2, 15, 318
Atkinson, Henry, 181, 187
atomic bombs, 410–12, *411*, 419.
  See also nuclear weapons
Atomic Diplomacy (Alperovitz), 410
Attucks, Crispus, 77
Austin, Stephen F., 193
aviation, in U.S. military, 327
axis of evil, 490

B
B-29 Superfortress, 404, 412
baby killer, 466–67
Bacon, Nathaniel, Jr., 23–25
Bacon's rebellion, 21–26
Baghdad, 492–93
Bailey, F. Lee, 468
Bainbridge, William,
  135, 151, 157
Baker, Newton, 333, 340
Balangiga Massacre, 317
Baldwin, Hanson, 412
Ball, George, 453
Baltimore, 168–69
  Battle of, 167–168
Banks, Nathaniel, 239
Barbary Pirates, 150–52, 183
Barbary Wars, 135–36, 151f
Barclay, Robert H., 161
Barlow, Francis C., 239
Barnes, John, 359
Barney, Joshua, 166
Barras, Conte de, 129–30
Barrin, Roland-Michel, 50, 58
Barron, Samuel, 151
Battle
  of Antietam, 248f, 249, 250f
  of Anzio, *377*
  of Bad Axe, 188, 189f
  of Baltimore, 167f, *167–168*
  of Beecher's Island, 289
  of Brandywine, 123
  of Britain, 355
  of Bud Bagsak, 318
  of the Bulge, 377, *383*, 384
  of Bull Run, 229
  of Bunker Hill, 83f
  of Camden, 120–121, 121f,
  of Caporetto, 337

  of Chalmette, 171
  of Chancellorsville, 252
  of Chapultepec, 205, 206f
  of Charleston, 119–120
  of Chateauguay, 162, 163f
  of Chattanooga, 257–58
  of Chickamauga, 257
  of Chippawa, 164–165
  of Chosin Reservoir, *429*
  of the Coral Sea, 395
  of Cowpens, 121f,
    124–125, 125f
  of the Crater, 262f, 263
  of Detroit, 156
  of Fallen Timbers, 145
  of Fallujah, *494*, 494–95
  of Five Forks, 268
  of Fort Bowyer, 170, 172
  of Fort Henry, 235
  of Frenchtown, 159–160
  of Gettysburg, 239, 253f, 254
  of Great Bridge, 91
  of Guilford Court House, 121f,
    126–127
  of Horseshoe Bend, 169f, 170
  of King's Mountain, 121f, 124
  of Ia Drang, 455–56
  of Lake Borgne, 170
  of Lake Champlain, 168
  of Lake George, 55
  of Lexington, 92
  of Leyte Gulf, 407
  of Little Bighorn, 293–95,
    294f, 301
  of Lundy's Lane, 165
  of Midway, 393, 393f, 397, *397*
  of Moncks Corner, 119
  of Monmouth, 123
  of New Market, 262
  of New Orleans, 169f, 170–173
  of Okeechobee, 192
  of Palo Alto, 198
  of Palo Duro Canyon, 292
  of Philippines Sea, 403
  of Plattsburgh, 168
  of Puebla, 274
  of Queenston, 156
  of Resaca de la Palma, 198
  of the Rosebud, 293
  of Saipan, *401*, 401–2
  of the San Gabriel River, 200
  of San Jacinto, 195
  of Santiago de Cuba, 313
  of Savannah, 118–119
  of Second Bull Run, 247
  of Seven Pines, 246

of Shiloh, 242–44, 243f
of the Somme, 335
of Stalingrad, 372
of Stillman's Run, 188
of Tenaru, *398*
of Tippecanoe, 155
of Trevilian Station, 261
of the Verdun, 335
of the Virginia Capes, 129
of Waxhaws, 120
of Washington, D.C., 166
of the Wilderness, 260
of Wilson's Creek, 230
of Wood Lake, 286
of Wounded Knee, 281f
of York, 159
of Yorktown, 127–129, 128f
Baugh, William B., 429
Bay of Pigs, 447
Bear Flag Revolt, 199–200
Beauregard, P.G.T., 204,
    222, 229, 242
Beecher, Frederick, 289
Beirut attack, 479–80
Bell, John, 221
Belvidera (HMS), 156–57
Bendiner, Elmer, 371
Bennington, colonial
    victories at, 104–5
Benteen, Frederick, 293
Benton, Thomas Hart, 199
Berkeley, William, 16, 21–24, 25
Berlin, Germany, 419–20
Berlin airlift, *420*
Berlin Decree, 153
Bernard, Francis, 77
Bernard, Simon, 181
The Best Years of Our Lives
    (films), 417
Bevin, Ernest, 421
Biddle James, 182
Big Foot, 299
Bill of Rights, England, 56
Bingham, Arthur, 154
bin Laden, Osama, 482, 488–90
Birth of a Nation (films), 266
bison, 282
Black Codes, 277
Blackhawk helicopters, 485
Black Hawk War, 187–89
Black Kettle (chief), 287, 289
black soldiers, 46–47, 46f, 156,
    166, 258, 278
Blainville, Pierre-Joseph
    Céloron de, 50
Blair, Francis P., 227

Bleeding Kansas, 220
Bloody Island Massacre, 218
Bloody Morning Scout, 55
Blue Jacket (chief), 143–45
Bock's Car (aircraft), 412
Bolton, Herbert Eugene, 40
bombing attack, on Japan, 394
Bonaparte, Napoleon,
    148, 153, 164
Bonhomme Richard (American
    ship), 114, 115f
Bonneville, Benjamin, 181
Bonus Army, 350
Boot, Max, 15, 318
Booth, John Wilkes, 268
Boscawen, Edward, 60
Boston, Massachusetts, 76,
    80–81, 80f
  massacre in, 77–79, 78f
  siege of, 83f
Boston Port Bill, 80
Bougainville, Louis-Antoine de, 64
Bouquet, Henry, 72
Bowdoin, James, 138
Bowie, James, 194
Boxer Rebellion, 318, 319–20
Boyd, John, 162
Bozeman Trail, 287–88
Braddock, Edward, 54–55, 89
Bradley, Omar, 384, 428
Bradstreet, John, 61, 72
Bradstreet, Simon, 38
Bragg, Braxton, 203, 244, 256–57
Brant Joseph, 104
Brazil Squadron, 183
Breckinridge, John C., 221
breech-loading rifles, 214
Breed's Hill, 85–86
Bremer, Paul, 493
Brent, George, 22
brigades, 226
Britain. *See also* England;
    Great Britain
  battle of, 355
  Braddock's defeat setback
    to, 55
  campaigns of, 55–56
  colonial rebellion and, 81–84,
    97–98
  colonial support by, 49
  colonial taxation by, 73
  colonies and, 66–67
  colonies and authority of, 70
  colonies and reforms from, 69
  colonies and tyranny of, 74–75

Continental Congress and peace
    negotiations with, 131
France's war with, 153
French territorial claims and, 70
Indians supplied by, 144–45
ministerial turnover in, 75t
North America and, 60–62, 66
public's hunger for fighting
    in, 114
Québec captured by, 65f
seapower of, 43
as superpower, 66
U.S. relations with, 154–55
British Band, 187–88
British forces
  colonial forces battling, 86–90
  Fort Niagara seized by, 159
  French forces fighting, 62–66
  Lexington march of, 82
  Royal Navy reinforcing, 101
  sailing out of New York, 133
  U.S. and forces of, 164
  Washington, D.C. victory of,
    166–67
  Washington, G., and retreat
    of, 97
British Mutiny Act (1765), 74
Brock, Isaac, 156
Broke, Philip, 160
Brooke, Arthur, 167
Brown, Charlie, 371
Brown, Jacob, 164–66
Brown, Jesse L., 433
Brown, John, 69, 221
Brown Bess musket, 88
Browning machine gun,
    326, 327f
*Brown v. Board of Education of
    Topeka, Kansas*, 334
Buchanan, Franklin, 231
Buchanan, James, 218, 222
Buchanan-Pakenham Treaty, 196
Buckner, Simon Bolivar, 235, 268,
    Buckner, Simon Bolivar,
    Jr., 408–409
Buell, Don Carlos, 242, 244
Buffalo Soldiers, 283–84,
    289, 303, 325
  San Juan Hill and, 312
  in U.S. army, 283f
  in WWII, 376–77
Buford, John, 252
Bullard, Robert, 343
Bull Run, 229, 247
Bundy, McGeorge, 454
Bunker Hill, 85

Bureau of Indian Affairs, 290
Burgoyne, John, 82, 101–3
  army of, 103
  Saratoga arrival of, 106
  surrender by, 107
Burnett, David, 195
Burnside, Ambrose, 231,
  249–50, 257
Bush, George H. W., 478, 481–85
Bush, George W., 471
Bushmasters, 408
Butcher's Hall, 78*f*
Butler, Benjamin, 228,
  239, 245, 267
Butler, Smedley, 305–6,
  321–22, *322f*
Byng, John, 58

C
Cadillac, Antoine de la, 39
Cajuns, 56
Calhoun, John C., 179, 181
California, U.S. incorporating, 200
Calley, William, 466–68
Calling Forth Act (1792), 144
Calvert, Cecilius, 21
Calvin, John, 18, 87
Camel Corps, 213
Campbell, Archibald, 118
Campbell, William, 145
Camp Grant Massacre, 298
Camp Logan, 330
Camp Verde, 213
Canada, 42, 156
Canby, E.R.S., 296
Candy Bombers, 419–20
cap-and-ball revolvers, 214
Cape Trafalgar, 153
Capone, Al, 306
Carden, John, 157
Caribbean, 321*f*
Carignan-Salières Regiment, 37
Carleton, Guy, 90, 94, 133
Carr, Eugene, 298
Carranza, Venustiano, 324–25
Carrington, Henry B., 287
Carson, Christopher "Kit," 286
Carter, Jimmy, 476–77
Cass, Lewis, 188
Castle of Chapultepec, 205
Castro, Fidel, 447
Castro, José, 199
Catton, Bruce, 266
CCC. *See* Civilian
  Conservation Corps
Cédras, Raoul, 486

Cemetery Hill, 253
Central American, 321*f*
Central Intelligence Agency
  (CIA), 418
Cervera y Topete, Pascual, 312
Chaffee, Adna, 317, 319
Chamberlain, Joshua
  Lawrence, 239–40
Chamoun, Camille, *445*
Champlain, Samuel, 34–35, *35f*
Charles I (king of England), 21
Charles II (king of
  England), 25, 36–37
Charles II (king of Spain), 39
Charles III (king of Spain), 117
Charleston, 118–20
Charles VI (Emperor of
  Austria), 47
Château-Thierry, 341–43
Chattanooga, 257
Chauncey, Isaac, 159, 164, 165
checks and balances, 139–40, 474
chemical warfare, *458*
Cheney, Richard, 481, 488, 496
Cherokee Indians, 44–45, 186
Chesapeake (USS), 154, 160–61
Chesapeake, colonizing of, 23*f*
Chesapeake Bay, 107–8, 166–68
Chew House, 108
Cheyenne Indians, 217
Chiang Kai-shek, 390, 406, 431
China, 319–20
Chinese Communist army, 432
Chivington, John, 287
Choctaw Indians, 186
Chosin Reservoir, *429*
Chowder Society, 418
Christianity, 27, 29*f*
Church, Benjamin, 30
Churchill, Winston, 376
CIA. *See* Central
  Intelligence Agency
Cisneros, Leroy, 439–40
Citadel, 225
citizen-soldiers, 112, 136
Civilian Conservation Corps
  (CCC), 351, *351*
civilian control, over military, 2,
  14, 112
civilian targets, 385
Civil War
  Appomattox Court House end
    of, 268
  army fighting in, 225–27
  army officers after, 276–77
  campaigns of, 241*f*

conscription laws during, 255
death and destruction of, 270
decisive battles rare in, 229, 257
early battles of, 228–30
Eastern Theater of, 233–36
in England, 21
Fort Sumter in, 223, 223*f*
Grant after, 276–77
military campaigns, 95*f*
Overland Campaign, 260
prisoners of war in, 258–59
professional soldiers of, 239–40
reconstruction after, 277–78
Sand Creek Massacre, 287, 300
secession and, 224*f*
Sherman after, 276–77
slavery and, 211
Southern campaigns in, 121*f*
technology after, 280–81
technology during, 233, 237
Vicksburg, 245, 255–56
Western Theater of, 233–36
Claiborne, William, 21
Clark, George Rogers, 116
Clark, J. Reuben, 351–52
Clark, Mark, 374–75
Clark, William, 152–53
Clay, Lucius, 445
Cleburne, Patrick, 258, 265
Cleveland, Grover, 279
Clinch, Duncan, 191
Clinton, Bill, 485
Clinton, Henry, 82, 86, 91, 101
  Charleston seized by, 119–20
  Howe, W., command
    going to, 110
  New York controlled by, 116
  troops needed by, 118
Clinton, Hillary, 499
Coalition Provisional Authority
  (CPA), 493
coastal fortification, 181
Cochise, 298
Cochrane, Alexander,
  166, 170, 172
Cockburn, George, 166
Coercive Acts, 80, 81
Colbert, Jean, 37
Cold War, 420–21, 500
Collins, Lawton, 443
Colmery, Harry W., 417
colonial forces
  Arnold victory for, 106–7
  Bennington victories of, 104
  British forces battling, 86–90
  cause questioned by, 111–13

Cornwallis surrender to, 124,
  129–30
Fort Ticonderoga retreat of, 103
independence fight of, 93
Québec and invasion of, 90–91
shrinking, 102
struggle of, 122–23
troop morale of, 96
colonies
  Britain and, 66–67
  Britain and rebellion of,
    81–84, 97–98
  British authority of, 70
  British reforms and, 69
  British support of, 49
  British taxation of, 73
  British tyranny and, 74–75
  Continental Navy of, 113–16
  economic controls of, 74–76
  George III and, 88–89, 92
  Howe, W., and independence
    of, 101
  laws of, 14
  Puritan, 26
  Revenue Act and, 76
  Stamp Act and, 74–76
Comanche Indians, 218
combat, in Korean War, *433*
Common Sense (Paine), 92, 93*f*
companies, 226
Compromise of 1850, 218
compulsory militia, 6
Conciliatory Resolution, 88
Confederate army
  Grant and destruction of,
    259–61
  of Lee, R., 226
  Petersburg fortifications
    of, 262*f*
  U.S. Army officers joining, 225
  U.S. navy and, 231
  Western Theater challenges
    of, 234
Confederate forces, 224
Confederate States of America,
  221–23, 223*f*
Confederation, 26–27
Confiance (HMS), 168
Congress
  Albany, 52–54
  army expansion ordered by, 148
  Calling Forth Act from, 144
  Continental Army problems
    and, 111
  distilled spirits excise tax passed
    by, 145

Embargo Act passed by, 154
Indian Removal Act passed by,
  185–86
intercolonial, 53–54
military appropriations of,
  155, 212
National Defense Act from,
  349–51
Navy Department created
  by, 146
navy formation approved
  by, 88–89
Non-Intercourse Act passed
  by, 154
Selective Service Act from,
  338–39
slavery declaration of, 183
standing army objections
  of, 137
Uniform Militia Act from, 144
Washington, G., growing army
  and, 101–2
Congress (USS), 231
Coningham, Arthur, 368
Connecticut, 29–30
Connecticut (USS), 328*f*
Conner, David, 202, 203
conscription laws, 255, 338–39
conspiracy of silence, 330
Constellation (USS), 148, 160, 166
Constitutional
  convention, 139–40
Continental Army, 88
  American Revolution suffering
    of, 109–13
  Congress and problems of, 111
  Steuben's training of, 109–11
  suffering of, 111–13
  Trenton victory of, 96–97
  of Washington, G., 89, 92
Continental Congress, 90,
  92–93, 122–23
  British peace negotiations
    and, 131
  first, 81
  national standing army rejected
    by, 140–41
  second, 88
  U.S. navy beginnings by, 113
  Washington, G., appearance
    at, 100
Continental Navy, 113–16
Contras, 480
Contrecoeur, Claude-Pierre
  Pécaudy de, 51
Conyngham, Gustavus, 114

Cook, James, 63
Corinth, Mississippi, 241–42
Cornwallis, Charles, 97, 108
  colonial forces surrounding,
    124, 129–30
  Greene's battle with, 126–27
  Jamestown peninsula and, 101
  offensive-minded, 120
  surrender of, 129–30
  Washington, G., battling, 96
corps, 226
Cortéz, Hernán, 204
Cowpens, 125, 125*f*
CPA. *See* Coalition
  Provisional Authority
Cranford, Mike, 440
Crazy Horse, 293, 295
Creek Confederation, 43–45
Creek Indians, 41, 170
Creek War (1836), 186
Crimean War, 220, 233
Crockett, Davy, 194
Cromwell, Oliver, 21
Cronkite, Walter, 462
Crook, George, 273, 276,
    292*f*, 293, 295
  Crazy Horse attacking, 293
  unconventional tactics of, 298
Cuba, 310–313
Cuban Missile Crisis, 447,
    447*f*, 448–49
Culp's Hill, 253
Cumberland (sloop-of-war), 231
Currency Act (1764), 74
Custer, George Armstrong, 275,
    289, 293–95
Custer's Last Stand, 295, 302
Custis, Martha Dandridge, 89
Cyane (USS), 175, 220

D

Dacres, James, 157
Dade, Francis L., 190
DADT. *See* Don't Ask, Don't Tell
Dahlgren, John A., 215
Dale (USS), 175
Dale, Richard, 151
Dale, Thomas, 12
Daly, Daniel, 322
Davis, Benjamin O., 378
Davis, Charles, 245
Davis, Jefferson, 203, 213–14, 296
  as Confederate State
    president, 221
  Lee, R., as general-in-chief, 267
  strategic approach of, 279

Dawes, William, 82
D-Day, 381f
Deal, Dennis, 456
Dean, William, 424
Dearborn, Henry, 159
death
   Civil War rates of, 270
   highway of, 483
   Iraq War rates of, 495–96
   island of, 400
   of Jackson, T., 252
   submarines rates of, 403
Decatur, Stephen, 135,
      157, 172–73
Declaration of Causes, 193
Declaration of Independence, 93
Declaration of Rights, 81
Declaration of the Causes and
      Necessities of Taking
      Up Arms, 88
Declaration of the People, 24
Declaratory Act (1766), 75–76
Deep South, 245
Delaware River, 96
Demilitarized Zone, 460
demobilization, of U.S.
      Army, 275–77
Denton, Earle, 436
Denver (USS), 469
desertion rates, 217
Desert One, 477
desert warfare, 365–67
d'Estaing, Charles Hector, 119
Devil Texans (Tejanos), 202
Dewey, George, 311
Díaz, Porfirio, 298, 323
Dick, Charles, 328
Dick Act, 328
Dickinson, John, 76
Dieskau, Baron de, 55
Dinwiddie, Robert, 50–51
disabled veterans, 417
A Discourse on Western Planting
      (Hakluyt), 5
diseases, 17
Distinguished Service Cross
      (DSC), 377
divisions, 226
doctrine of the broken voyage, 153
Dodge, Grenville, 227, 315
Dodge, Henry, 188
Dodge Commission, 315
Dole, Robert, 482
Doniphan, Alexander, 199–201
Dönitz, Karl, 372
Don't Ask, Don't Tell (DADT), 487

Doolittle, Jimmy, 372, 394
Dornin, Thomas A., 175
Double V Campaign, 376–378
Douglas, Stephen, 221
Douglas C-54 Skymaster, 420
Douglass, Frederick, 266
Douhet, Giulio, 353
Downie, George, 168
draft boards, 338
draft lottery system, 464
Dragging Canoe, 117
Drake (HMS), 114
Drake, Francis, 4–5, 7, 34
Draper, Bobby, 439–40
Draper, Frank, 360
Dresden attack, 385
Drucor, Chevalier de, 60
drug use, in Vietnam, 465
Drummond, Gordon, 165
DSC. See Distinguished
      Service Cross
Du Bois, W.E.B, 333
Duckworth, Tammy, 475, 475
Dudingston, William, 69–70
Dulles, John Foster, 441
Dull Knife, 295
Dummer, William, 43
Dunmore, Lord, 91, 114
DuPont, Samuel, 231
Duquesne, Marquis, 50
Durnford, Elias, 117
Dutch, 35–36

E
Eagle (USS), 168
Early, Jubal, 262, 266
Eastern Theater (Civil War),
      233–36, 245–46,
      251–58, 260–63
East India Company, 35, 79, 97
East India Squadron, 183
Eaton, William, 151–52
economics
   colonial controls of, 74–76
   Englishmen and, 14
   U.S. depression and, 137
   U.S. navy expansion and, 182–83
Eisenhower, Dwight D., 350, 365
   military restructuring by, 440–41
   Operation Overlord command
      of, 380
   South Vietnam obstacles of,
      442–43
Eisenhower Doctrine, 444
Elements of Military Art and Science
      (Halleck), 208

Elizabeth I, (queen of England), 4
Elliot, Jesse, 161
Elliot, Joel, 289
Elrod, Henry T., 392
Emancipation
      Proclamation, 249, 258
Embargo Act, 154
Empire Javelin (troopship), 359
Empire of Liberty, 207
Endicott, John, 19
England
   Bill of Rights of, 56
   Canada and plans of, 42
   Civil War in, 21
   Indian beliefs of, 7
   North America explored by, 4–5
   North American outposts of, 7
   St. Augustine attack by, 46–47
   Virginia support of, 21–22
Englishmen
   economic foundations and, 14
   Indians annihilating, 13
   Indians attacking, 13–14
   North American travels of,
      20–21
   Pamunkey Indians reliance
      of, 9–10
   violent practices of, 11–12
Enola Gay (aircraft), 410–12
Ericsson, John, 232
Essex Case, 153
Europe
   airpower over, 370–72
   diseases brought from, 17
   Germany invading, 354–55
   military blocs in, 416f
   United States Air Force over, 368
   wars of, 37
   western, 380, 380f
   World War II in, 362
Eustis, William, 158
Ewell, Richard, 252
exploding shells, 180
exploration
   of North America, 4–5
   U.S. expeditions of, 184f
   by U.S. navy, 220
   of western frontier, 181–82

F
Fallujah, 494, 494
Farías,Valentín Gómez, 202
Farragut, David G., 245, 265
Fat Boy bomb, 411
Fedayeen (martyrs), 492
federal government, 140

Federalists, 141, 146, 148–49
Fellers, Taylor, 360
Ferdinand, Franz, 335
Ferebee, Thomas, 411
Ferguson, Patrick, 124
Fetterman, William, 287
Fetterman Massacre, 287
field armies, 226
fighter planes, of U.S. navy, *397*
The Fighting Sullivans (film), 389
fire bombing, of Japan,
    405, 405–6
1st American Regiment, 137, 141
1st U.S. Volunteer Cavalry (Rough
    Riders), 310–12, 313*f*
first Anglo-Powhatan War, 11–12
First Continental Congress, 81
First Gulf War, 473*f*
First Seminole War, 179
flat-bottomed bateaux, 193
Fletcher, Frank, 394
Flipper, Henry O., 283
Florida, 177–78
Floyd, John, 235
flying artillery, 198
flying columns, 54
Foch, Ferdinand, 341
Foch, Marshal, 347
food supply, 10
Foote, Andrew, 234
Forbes, John "Iron Head," 59–61
foreclosures, 137–38
Forgotten War, 437
Forrest, Nathan Bedford, 227,
    235, 239, 267
Forrestal, James, 418
Forsyth, George "Sandy," 289
Forsyth, James, 299
Fort
    Albion, 166
    Armstrong, 187
    Atkinson, 181
    Bowyer, 170
    Brooke, 189
    Caroline, 33–34
    Castillo de San Marcos., 41
    Charlotte, 117, 169
    Crescent, 118
    Detroit, 71, 116
    Detroit, (HMS), 161
    Donelson, 234–35, 270
    Duquesne, 52, 60–61, 89
    Edward, 55
    Erie, 164–66
    Frontenac, 61
    Gaspereau, 56

Henry, 234, 270
    Kaskaskia, 50
    King, 189
    Laramie, 217
    Leavenworth, 181, 200, 218
    Le Boeuf, 50
    Lee, 96
    McHenry, 167, 167*f*
    Meigs, 160
    Mosé, 46–47
    Nassau, 35
    Necessity, 52
    Niagara, 52, 62, 116, 159
    Oswego, 55–57
    Pillow, 245
    Pulaski, 231
    Recovery, 144
    Saint Frédéric, 52, 55
    Saint-Jean, 90
    San Juan de Ulúa, 204
    Santa Elena, 33–34
    Stanwix, 104, 106
    Stedman, 268
    Stephenson, 160
    St. Philip, 172
    Sumter, 222–23, 223*f*
    Texas, 197–98
    Ticonderoga, 61–62, 84–85,
        90, 103
    Washington, 96
    William Henry, 55, 56–57
Fox, John, 377
fragging, 465–66
France
    Britain and territorial claims
        of, 70
    Britain's war with, 153
    British campaigns and, 55–56
    British fighting forces of, 62–66
    campaigns of, 59*f*
    fall of, 355–56
    Louisbourg surrender by, 48–49
    New, 56, 62
    Normandy, 380–82, 381*f*
    North America control by,
        60–62
    North American power of,
        38–39
    U.S. independence recognized
        by, 109
    U.S. navy and vessels from, 148
    U.S. relations with, 146–47
Franco-American forces, 129
Franklin, Benjamin, 53, 72,
    79, 115*f*, 131
Franks, Tommy, 488

Frederick II (of Prussia), 47
Fredericksburg, 250–51
Frederick the Great (of
    Prussia), 57, 60
Freedmen's Bureau, 277
Freeman, Douglass Southall, 266
Freeman, John, 106
Frémont, John C., 199–200
French Revolutionary Army, 164
"From the Halls of
    Montezuma," 206, 206*f*
Frontenac, Louis de Buade de, 38
Funston, Frederick, 317, 324
fur trade, 36–37, 49–50

G
Gadsden Purchase (1853), 211
Gage, Thomas, 74, 77, 80–82, 85
Gaines, Edmund Pendleton, 191
Galisonnière, Comte de La, 50, 58
Gálvez, Bernardo de, 117–18
Garcia, Clive, 440
Gaspee (HMS), 79, 97
Gates, Horatio, 103, 105–7, 120
Gates, Robert, 497
Gates, Thomas S., 474
Gatewood, Charles, 273–74, 299
Gatling, Christopher, 280
Gay, George "Tex," 396
General Assembly of Virginia, 12
Geneva Accords, 442
Geographical positioning, 2
George II (king of
    England), 45, 57–58
George III (king of England),
    75–76, 80–81, 87, 89*f*
    colonies and, 88–89, 92
    royal proclamation by, 72
George Washington (USS), 151
Germain, George, 101–2
German tank, *383*
Germantown, 108
Germany, 354–55, 362
Geronimo, 273, 286*f*, 298–99
Gerry, Elbridge, 146
Ghormley, Robert, 399
Ghost Dance movement, 299
Gibbon, John, 226, 293, 297
Gibbs, Samuel, 172
G.I. Bill, 417
Gilded Age, 279–80
Giles, Barney, 373
global war, for North
    America, 57–66
Global War on Terror
    (GWOT), 472

Glorious Revolution, 38
Glover, John, 94–96, 113
Go For Broke (film), 379
Goldsborough, Louis, 231
Goldwater, Barry, 452, 480
Goldwater-Nichols Act, 480
Gone with the Wind (film), 266
Good Neighbor Policy, 352
Gorbachev, Mikhail, 480–81
Gordon, John Brown, 240, 268
Gorgas, William, 320
government spending, 148–49
Gracia Real de Santa Teresa de
    Mosé, 46, 46f
Grant, Ulysses S., 234, 260f
    at Appomattox Court
        House, 268
    Army of the Tennessee, 244
    in Battle of Shiloh, 242–44
    after Civil War, 276–77
    Confederate field army and,
        259–61
    Corinth objective of, 241
    Fort Donelson surrounded
        by, 235
    Indian reservations and, 290
    Lee, R., surrender and, 266
    Lincoln, A., getting victories
        from, 259
    Military Department of the
        Shenandoah from, 263
    Pemberton battle with, 256
    Vicksburg objective of, 245,
        255–56
de Grasse, François-Joseph Paul,
    123, 128–30
Grattan, John, 217
Graves, Thomas, 129
Great Britain, 155
Great Depression, 350, 353, 356
Greatest Generation, 384
Great Lakes, 160–62
The Great Marianas Turkey
    Shoot, 402
Great Meadows Run, 52
Great Migration, 18
Great Sioux War, 295
Great Swamp Massacre, 28–29
Great U.S. Exploring
    Expedition, 183
Great War
    AEF during, 338–43
    African Americans in, 333–34,
        343–44
    airpower in, 345
    allied offensives of, 345–47

armistice ending, 347
Passchendaele Offensive, 335
Pershing in, 346
Saint-Mihiel Offensive, 345
U.S. navy in, 337–38
western front of, 342f
Great White Fleet, 328f, 329
Green Beret promotions, 447
Greene, Nathanael, 109,
    124, 126–27
Grenada, 479–80
Grenier, John, 15
Grenville, George, 72, 75
Grenville, Richard, 4, 7
Grenville ministry, 74
Grierson, Benjamin, 256, 275, 283
ground war
    in South Vietnam, 457
    in Vietnam, 454–55
    in World War II, 406–8
Groves, Leslie, 410
Gruening, Ernest, 453
Guadalcanal, 398, 398–400
Guam, 314–15
Guerrière (HMS), 154, 157
guerrilla war, 317, 318
Guilford Court House, 126
Gulf coast, 177f
Gulf of Mexico, 169
Gulf of Tonkin
    Resolution, 452, 453
gunboat diplomacy, 320
gunboats, 150f
Gutiérrez de Lara, Bernardo, 176
GWOT. *See* Global War on Terror

H
Haig, Alexander, 457
Hakluyt, Richard, 5
Halberstam, David, 450
Half King, 52
Halifax Squadron, 155
Hall, Charles B., 378
Halleck, Henry W., 208, 242, 259
Halsey, William "Bull,"
    395, 400, 421
Hamilton, Alexander, 129, 140
Hamilton, Paul, 157
Hamilton, William, 116–17
Hampton, Wade, 162,
    227, 239, 261
Hancock, John, 76
Hancock, Scott, 287
Hannah (fishing
    schooner), 69, 113
Hansell, Haywood, 405

hara-kiri, 399
Harkins, Paul, 449
Harlem Heights, 94
Harlem Hellfighters,
    344, 344f, 376
Harmar, Josiah, 137, 141–43
Harmon, Johnson, 43
Harpers Ferry, 221, 249
Harrison, Benjamin, 279
Harrison, William Henry,
    154–55, 159–62
Harrison's Landing, 247
Harrold, Thomas, 436
Hartford (USS), 265
Hat Act (1732), 73
Hauser, William L., 468
Hawkins, John, 7
Hay, John, 315, 319
Hayes, Rutherford B., 278
Hayfield Fight, 288
Hays, Mary, 110
Hearst, William Randolph, 309
HEAT. *See* high-explosive anti-tank
heavy bombers, 354
Heinl, Robert D., 468
helicopters
    in Afghanistan war, 487
    Blackhawk, 485
    in Korean War, 436
Heredia, Jose A., 201
Hersh, Seymour, 467
Hess, Earl J., 233
high-explosive anti-tank
    (HEAT), 424
Highway of Death, 483
Hill, A. P., 249, 252, 268
Hillsborough (Lord), 76–77
Hiroshima, 410, 412–13
Hitler, Adolf, 354, 362,
    384–85, 386
H. L. Hunley (CSS,
    submarine), 231, 265
Hoback, Raymond, 360
Ho Chi Minh, 441–42
Ho Chi Minh Trail, 456, 461f
Ho-Chunk Indians, 188
Hodge, John R., 423
homosexuality, 487
Hood, John Bell, 213,
    247, 264–65
Hood, Samuel, 129
Hooker, Joseph "Fighting Joe,"
    251, 252, 257
Hoover, Gilbert, 388
Hoover, Herbert, 350
Hopkins, Esek, 88, 113–14

Hornets Nest, 242
Hotchkiss gun, 280, 281*f*, 299
Housatonic (USS), 265
House of Burgesses, 24
Houston, Charles Hamilton, 334
Houston, Sam, 194–95
Houston Riot (1917), 330
Howard, O. O., 277, 296–98
Howe, Richard, 93
Howe, William, 82, 85–86, 90, 93
    in Chesapeake Bay, 107–8
    colonists independence and, 101
    in Philadelphia, 108
    resignation of, 110
    Washington, G., battle with,
        94–97
Hudson, Henry, 35
Huerta, Victoriano, 323
Hull, Isaac, 157
Hull, William, 156
Hunter, David, 262
Hussein, Saddam, 482, 490, 492
Hutchinson, Anne, 18
Hutie, Oscar von, 341

I
ICBMs. *See* intercontinental
    ballistic missiles
IDF. *See* Israeli Defense Forces
IEDs. *See* improvised
    explosive devices
imperialism, 31, 218–20,
    305–6, 320
impressments, of Royal
    Navy, 153–55
improvised explosive devices
    (IEDs), 493
Inchon, South Korea, *425*, 426
Indian-English conflict, 22
Indian Removal Act, 185–86
Indians. *See also specific Indian tribe*
    armored Englishmen attacked
        by, 13–14
    Bacon war with, 24–25
    British agents supplying,
        144–45
    Christianity introduced to, 27
    English beliefs about, 7
    Englishmen annihilated by, 13
    Grant and reservations for, 290
    militia challenges against, 30–31
    Native Americans, 40
    North American interior
        controlled by, 53
    in northern plains, 292–95
    praying, 27

property ideas of, 12
Puritan colonies encroaching
    on, 26
removal of, 187*f*
retaliatory violence against, 30
settlements destroyed by, 28
Sheridan fighting, 291
slave trade of, 57*f*
in Southern Plains, 288–90
in Texas, 290–92
Trail of Tears, 186
of Trans-Mississippi West,
    284–85
vacuum domicilium and, 17
Wayne's army massacre of, 145
western frontier and, 212,
    286–87, 296–99
westward expansion
    influencing, 185
Indian Territory, 215–18, 285
Indian wars, 10
    campaigns of, 59*f*
    end of, 281–83, 302
    Jackson, A., and, 176
    in North America, 36
    small-scale ambushes in, 11
    in Southwest desert, 298–99
    in U.S., 142*f*, 299
Indochina, 441–42
industrial revolution, 2
infantry's journalist, 409
*The Influence of Sea Power upon
    History, 1660–1783*
    (Mahan, D.), 307
Ingle, Richard, 21
Inouye, Daniel, 379
insurgency, 493, 495–98
intercolonial congress, 53–54
intercontinental ballistic missiles
    (ICBMs), 441
internal combustion engine,
    329, 335, 352
Interstate Highway
    System, 445–46
interwar years, 348–49, 415
Intolerable Acts, 80, 97
Intrepid (American converted
    Turkish vessel), 135
Iran, 476–77
Iraqi military, *483*
Iraqi Republican Guard, 484
Iraq War
    death rates in, 495–96
    Duckworth in, *475*
    Highway of Death in, *483*
    insurgency in, 495–98

invasion, 489*f*, *491*
military massacre in, *483*
military surge in, 496*f*, 497–98
Operation DESERT SHIELD
    in, 482
Operation DESERT STORM in,
    483–84
Tillman in, *490*
troop deployment to Baghdad
    in, 492–93
U.S withdrawing troops
    from, 498
war for oil, 491
WMDs and, 490
Ireland, 3
ironclad warship, 231–33, 270
Iroquois Confederation, 116–17
Iroquois-English alliance, 39
Iroquois Indians, 11, 35, 35*f*, 37
Islamic State of Iraq and Syria
    (ISIS), 498
Island Hopping campaign, 401–3
Island of Death, 400
Island # 10, 244
Ismay, Hasting, 421
Israeli Defense Forces (IDF), 478
Italian campaign, 373–76, 374*f*
Italy, 373–76
Iwabachi, Sanji, 408
Iwo Jima, 408
Izard, George, 164

J
Jackson, Andrew, 170,
    172, 176–78
Jackson, Thomas J. "Stonewall,"
    229, 246, 249, 251–52
Jacobite Rebellion, 49
James Fort, 8
James II (king of England), 38, 40
Jamestown, 8–10, 8*f*, 9*f*, 34, 101
Japan, 390–91
    Allied forces and invasion force
        of, 394–95
    Battle of Midway defeat of, 397
    bombing attack on, 394
    fire bombing, *405*, 405–6
    Island Hopping battles with,
        401–3
    MacArthur, D., and postwar, 414
    Mitchell, W., and vulnerabilities
        of, 404
    Osaka, *405*
    Perry, M., mission to, 183, 219*f*
    U.S. interest in, 219
    warships of, 392, 395–97

Japan (*continued*)
World War II airwar over, 403–6
World War II final push to,
408–9
Japanese Americans, 378–79
Japanese navy, 407
Java (HMS), 157
Jay, John, 131
Jay's Treaty, 144, 146
Jefferson, Thomas, 93, 100, 127
military academy created
by, 152
military reduction sought
by, 149
as president, 136
tree of liberty comment
of, 138
Jeffreys, Herbert, 25
Jenkins, Robert, 45
Jesup, Thomas S., 186, 191
Johnson, Andrew, 277
Johnson, Guy, 82
Johnson, Louis A., 421
Johnson, Lyndon, 452, 454
Johnson, Richard Mentor, 162
Johnson, William, 55, 62, 72
Johnston, Albert Sidney, 125,
218, 241–242
Johnston, J. Bennett, 478
Johnston, Joseph, 229, 245–46,
256, 263–64
Join or Die, 53*f*
joint-stock company, 7, 17
Jomini, Antoine Henri, 208, 215
Jones, John Paul, 114, 115*f*
Jones, Sam, 192
Jones, Thomas ap Catesby,
170, 175, 200
Jones, William, 158
Joseph (chief), 285*f*
Juárez, Benito, 274
Jumonville, Joseph Coulon de
Villiers de, 51–52
Juneau (USS), 388

K
Kalb, Baron de, 120
kamikazes, 407
Kansas, 217–18
Kansas-Nebraska
Territorial Act, 220
Kasserine Pass, 365–66
Keane, John, 172
Kearny, Stephen, 198, 200
Kearsarge (USS), 265
Kennan, George, 417–18

Kennedy, John F., 443,
446–49, *447*
Kennedy, Robert, 448
Kent, Jacob F., 312
Kesserling, Albrecht, 374–75
Key, Francis Scott, 167*f*
Khomeini, Ayatollah
Ruhollah, 476
Khrushchev, Nikita, 447, *448*
Kim Il-Sung, 414, 423
Kimmel, Husband, 391
King, Ernest, 397, 421
King, Martin Luther, Jr., 460, 464
King, Stan, 439–40
King Cotton diplomacy, 230
King George's war (1744),
47–49, 48*f*
King's Mountain, 124
King William's war, 38–39
Knox, Henry, 85, 90, 141
Korean War, 422*f*
air war in, 432–34
combat in, *433*
as Forgotten War, 437
helicopters in, *436*
North Korean aggression in,
423–24
Operation Chromite in, 426
peninsula, 434*f*
Pork Chop Hill in, 435–36
POWs of, 435*f*
strategic blunders of, 422
38th Parallel in, 423, 427,
430–32
U.S. Air Force in, *433*
U.S. marines in, 428–30
Yalue River in, 427
Kościuszko, Tadeusz, 105
Koster, Samuel, 466, 468
Kuwait, 482, 484

L
Lafayette, Marquis de, 123, 127
Lafitte, Jean, 171
Laird, Melvin, 467
Lake Champlain, 168–69
Lambert, Henry, 157
Landgrave, Frederick, II, 97
Lane, Ralph, 4
Lansdale, Edward, 443
Larkin, Thomas Oliver, 196, 199
Laurens, Henry, 131
Lawrence (USS), 161
Lawrence, James, 160
Lawrence, William L, 172
Lawton, Henry, 312, 317

League of Nations, 348, 355
Lebanon, 478
Lee, Charles, 61, 91, 96, 110
Lee, Fitzhugh, 310
Lee, Henry, 109, 145
Lee, Richard Henry, 92
Lee, Robert E., 204–5,
253, 255, 260*f*
at Appomattox Court
House, 268
Army of Northern Virginia, 240,
247, 252, 254
Brown, John, captured by, 221
Confederate army of, 226
Davis, J., appointment of, 267
Grant and surrender of, 266
one-sided victory by, 250–51
rise of, 246–51
Sharpsburg focus of, 249
slow promotions and, 213
surrender comments of, 266
Legion of the United
States, 144, 146
Le Gris (chief), 142
Lejeune, John, 321–22, *322*
LeMay, Curtis, 371, 405–6, 419
Le Moyne, Pierre, 39
Lend-Lease program, 361
Leopard (HMS), 154
Lévis, François-Gaston de, 65
Lewis, Meriwether, 152–53
Lexington, 82, 83*f*, 92
Liberty (American
merchant ship), 76
Library of Congress, 279
Liggett, Hunter, 343
Ligonier, John (Jean Louis), 59
Lincoln, Abraham, 188
Booth killing of, 268
Emancipation Proclamation
issued by, 249
Grant providing victories
for, 259
militiamen called up by, 225
reelection of, 264
spot resolution from, 198
Lincoln, Benjamin, 119–20,
130, 130*f*, 138
L'Insurgente (FS, French
frigate), 148
Little Belt (HMS), 154
Little Boy bomb, *411*, 411–12
Little Round Top, 254
Little Turtle (chief), 142–43
Locke, John, 87
Lodge, Henry Cabot, 450

Logan, John A., 227, 239, 264
London Company, 8
Lone Star Republic, 193–96
Long, Stephen H., 181
long-range rockets, 386
Longstreet, James, 226, 247, 257
Looking Glass, 297
Lookout Mountain, 257
Lossing, Benson J., 150*f*
Lost Battalion, 378
Lost Cause narrative, 266
Loudoun, Earl of, 56–57, 59–60
Louisbourg, 48–49, 60
Louisiana, 56
Louisiana Purchase, 176
Louis XIV (king of France), 38–39
Louis XVI (king of
    France), 109, 123
Lovett, Robert, 373
loyalists (king supported by), 91
Lucas, John P., *377*
Luce, Henry, 416
Ludendorff, Erich, 340, 348
Ludendorff Offensives, 343
Luftwaffe, 367–69, 373, 384
Lusitania (luxury liner), 336
Lynch, Jessica, 475
Lyon, Nathaniel, 228, 230

M
MAAG. *See* Military Assistance
    Advisory Group
MacArthur, Arthur, 316–17
MacArthur, Douglas, 350,
    356, 390, 407
    audacious maneuvers by, 425
    miscalculations by, 427
    negotiations opposed by, 432
    postwar Japan and, 414
    Truman firing, 428, 432
Macdonough, Thomas, 168, 178
Macedonian (HMS), 157, 160
machine guns, 326, 327*f*
Mackenzie, R. S., 275–76,
    290–92, 291*f*
MacLeish, Archibald, 416
Macomb, Alexander,
    164, 168, 192
MACV. *See* Military Assistance
    Command, Vietnam
Maddox (USS), *453*
Madero, Francisco, 323
Madison, James, 139, 155,
    178–79, 181
Magee, Augustus William, 176
Magruder, John B., 246

Mahan, Alfred Thayer, 150, 208
Mahan, Dennis Hart,
    208, 215, 307
Manchester, William, 428
Manchu empress, 319
Manhattan Island, 94
Manhattan Project, 410–12
Manifest Destiny, 176, 178, 211
    foundation of, 197
    territorial expansion in, 207
Mansfield, Mike, 418
Mao Zedong, 420
March, Peyton C., 340, 350
March to the Sea, 264
Marcy, Randolph, 210–11
Marcy, William, 198
Maria Theresa of Austria,
    47, 57
marine barracks bombing, 479*f*
Marine Corps, U.S., 146, 330,
    428–30, *429*, 445
Marion, Francis, 120
Marshall, George C., 341,
    346, 361, 416
Marshall, John, 146
Marshall, S. L. A., 435
Marshall, Thurgood, 334
martial law, 85
Martin, Joseph Plumb, 110
Martin, Joseph W., Jr., 432
Martin, Josiah, 91
Martin's Hundred, 13
martyrs (*Fedayeen*), 492
Maryland, 21
Mason, George, 22
Mason, James, 230–31
Massachusetts, 137–38
Massasoit (chief), 18, 27
mass demobilization, 417
Mathew, Thomas, 22
Mathews, George, 176
Maximilian, 275
Mayflower, 16–17
Mayflower Compact, 17
Mayo, Henry, 324
McCarthy, Eugene, 463
McCarthy, Joseph, 418
McChrystal, Stanley, 499
McClellan, George, 211
    apprehensions of, 236
    command removed from,
        249–50
    Harrison's Landing retreat
        to, 247
    as major general of Army of
        Potomac, 229–30

    reserves never committed
        by, 249
    slow Richmond advance of,
        245–46
    Union army led by, 228
McClellan, Scott, 490
McConnell, Joseph, 433
McCrea, Jane, 104
McCullough, David, 428
McDade, Robert, 456
McDowell, Irvin, 229, 246
McFarland, Ernest, 417
McGregor, Gregor, 177
McKinley, William, 308, 320
McMaster, H. R., 497
McNamara, Robert, 369, 447, 463
McPherson, James B., 259, 264
Meade, George G., 252,
    254, 259, 277
medallion, 29*f*
Medina, Ernest, 466–68
Mediterranean Squadron, 183
Memphis Belle (documentary), 369
Menéndez de Avilés, Pedro, 33–34
Menneville, Ange de, 50
mercantilism, 73
merchant groups, 7
merchant ships, 137
Merrill's Marauders, 406
Merrimack (USS), 228–231
Merritt, Wesley, 275–76, 314
Metacom (King Philip), 22, 26–30
metallic cartridge revolvers, 214
Meuse-Argonne Offensive,
    345–47, 348
Mexican Revolution, 323
Mexico
    Monterrey, 201–2
    Santa Anna as president of, 205
    Taylor, Z., campaign in, 201–3
    U.S. intervention in, 323–26
    U.S war with, 196–99, 199*f*, 207
Mexico City, 206
Micanopy (chief), 190
*The Middle Ground: Indians,
    Empires, and Republics in
    the Great Lakes Region*
    (White, R.), 40
middle ground thesis, 40
Midway, 395–97
Mifflin, Thomas, 100
Milan Decree, 153
Miles, Nelson A., 227, 239,
    273, 275, 299
    as Indian fighter, 291–92, 291*f*
    Puerto Rico campaign and, 314

military, U.S. *See also* Union army
  African Americans relations
      with, 376–77
  aviation in, 327
  civilian control of, 2, 14
  Congress appropriations for,
      155, 212
  Eisenhower, D., restructuring,
      440–41
  Iraq War surge of, 496f, 497–98
  Jefferson seeking reduction
      of, 149
  manpower mobilization of, 376
  Marshall, G., buildup of, 361
  mass demobilization of, 417
  midcentury, 211–15
  Okinawa secured by, 409
  Operation Eagle Claw of,
      477, 477
  Patton's leadership of, 366
  planning lacking of, 163
  policy implementation of, 1
  professionalism in, 301–2
  Québec operations of, 62f
  reforming, 178–81
  Roosevelt, T., and power of, 328f
  South Vietnam strategy of, 462
  technology, 180, 214–15, 312,
      326–27, 331
  U.S. lacking plan for, 163
  U.S. production of, 398
  U.S. strategy for, 462
  Washington, G., and civilian
      control of, 112, 133
  women in, 379, 475
  World War II preparedness of,
      360–61, 389–91
military academy, 152, 179–80
Military Assistance Advisory
      Group (MAAG), 442–44
Military Assistance Command,
      Vietnam (MACV), 449
military blocs, in Europe, 416f
military campaigns, Civil War, 95f
Military Department of the
      Shenandoah, 263
military-industrial complex,
      441, 445–46
military manuals, 208
*The Military Policy of the United
      States* (Upton), 301–2, 327
military reconstruction
      district, 278f
militia
  cavalry and infantry of, 15–16
  civilian control over, 14

compulsory, 6
Indian challenges against, 30–31
Lincoln, A., calling up, 225
Lincoln, B., raising, 138
Puritan forces of, 28
standing army compared to,
      140–41
Tryon County, 104
Virginia, 50–51
Militia Act (1792), 328
Miller, Doris, 391
Minié bullet, 214–15, 233
ministerial turnover, in
      Britain, 75t
Minnesota, 247
Minnesota (USS), 232
Minorca, 58
Minutemen, 82
missile defense, 478
Mission Accomplished, 492
mission creep, 485
Mississippi River, 256
Missouri, 230
Mitchell, William "Billy," 345,
      353–54, 370, 404
Mohawk Indians, 35–36, 79, 80f
Mohegans Indians, 20
Molasses Act (1733), 73
Moncayo, Robert, 440
Monckton, Robert, 55–56
Monitor (USS), 232–33, 232f
Monmouth Court House, 110
Monroe, James, 97, 175–76, 308
Monroe Doctrine, 175–76, 320
Montagu, John, 70
Montcalm, Marquis, 61–65
Monterey, seizure of, 175–76
Monterrey, Mexico, 201–2
Montesquieu, Baron, 87
Montgomery, Richard, 90–91
Montreal, War of 1812 in, 162–64
Moore, Hal, 456
Moore, James, 41, 44
Morenci Nine, 439
Morgan, Daniel, 106, 124–26
Morgan, Robert, 404
Morris, Robert, 137, 151
Morse, Wayne, 452
Mountain Meadows Massacre, 218
Mount Siribachi, 408
Mourning wars, 11, 36
Moyers, Bill, 452
Munemori, Sadao, 379
Murphy, Audie, 382–83
muskets, 88, 233
Muslims, turning against U.S., 495

Mussolini, Benito, 354
My Lai, 466–67

N

Nagasaki, 389, 410, 411, 412–13
Naguno, Chuichi, 395
Nancy (supply brig), 113
Napoleon gun, 214
Napoleon III (Emperor), 215, 274
Narragansett Indians, 18,
      20, 26, 28
Nasser, Gamal Abdel, 444
National Defense Act
      (1916), 336, 339
National Defense Act
      (1920), 349–51
National Defense Education Act
      (1958), 446
National Guard, 325, 331, 474
National Guard Association, 279
Nationalists, 406
National Parks Service 280
national security
  government spending and,
      148–49
  standing army and, 179
  of U.S., 417–19
National Security Act
      (1947), 418, 480
National Security Council
      (NSC), 418
Native Americans, 40
NATO. *See* North Atlantic Treaty
      Organization
Nauset Indians, 17
Navajo Indians, 217–18
Naval Academy, U.S., 207–8
Naval Act (1916), 336
naval battles, of U.S., 147f
Naval War College, 307
Navarre, Henri, 442
Navigation Act (1651),
      22, 36, 72–73
navy, U.S., 265–66
  Confederate garrison and, 231
  Congress approving, 88–89
  Continental Congress
      beginnings of, 113
  Deep South control of, 245
  economic expansion of, 182–83
  expanded reach of, 211–12
  exploration and diplomacy
      by, 220
  fighter planes of, 397
  French vessels and, 148
  in Great War, 337–38

Great White Fleet, 328*f*, 329
rebirth of, 149
Roosevelt, F., approving
    expansion of, 361
shipbuilding of, 180–81
steel-hulled warships for, 307–8
submarines of, 402–3, 402*f*
U.S. imperialism and, 218–20
warships, *364*, 407
Navy Department, 146
Necotowance (chief), 16
Negroe Fort, 46*f*, 177
Nelson, Horatio, 135, 153
Nemattanew (chief), 13
Neutrality Act (1939), 355
Newburgh Conspiracy, 90, 112
New Deal programs, *351*, 351–52
New England, 18–19, 19*f*
New England Confederation, 36
New France, 56, 62
New Jersey, military
    campaigns in, 95*f*
New Netherland colony (Dutch),
    18–19, 27, 36
New Orleans, 170–72, 245
Newport, Christopher, 8
New York
    British forces sailing out of, 133
    campaigns in, 105*f*
    Clinton, H., controlling, 116
    military campaigns in, 95*f*
    Washington, G., defenses of, 94
Nez Perce War, *285*, 296–97
Ngo Dinh Diem, 443, 451
Ngo Quang Troung, 458
Nguyen Cao Ky, 454
Nguyen Chi Thanh, 455
Nguyen Khanh, 452
Nguyen Van Thieu, 454
Niagara (USS), 161
Niagara stalemate, 164–66
Nicaragua, 480
Nicholas, Samuel, 114
Nicholls, Richard, 36
Nichols, William, 480
Nimitz, Chester, 391, 397
9/11 attacks. *See*
    September 11, 2001
Nipmuck Indians, 28
Nixon, Richard, 463, 468
Non-Intercourse Act, 154
Noriega, Manuel, 481–82
Normandy, France, 380–82, 381*f*
North, Frederick, 76–79, 88
North Africa, 136, 150–52, 366
North America

Britain and, 60–62, 66
competition for, 34
England's exploration of, 4–5
Englishmen traveling to, 20–21
English outposts in, 7
French control of, 60–62
French power in, 38–39
global war for, 57–66
imperial struggle for, 31
Indians controlling interior
    of, 53
Jamestown in, 8–10
Treaty of Paris and, 71*f*
wars for, 15, 37–49
North Atlantic Squadron, 311
North Atlantic Treaty
    Organization (NATO), 421
North Carolina, 44, 120
Northern Alliance, 489
Northern Barrage, 338
Northern plains, 292–95
North Korea, 414
    aggression, 423–24
    ferocious fighting by, 426
    Pusan offensive launched by,
    425–27
    Truman's condemnation of, 424
North Vietnamese, 459
Northwest Ordinance (1787), 141
Northwest Territory, 141–45, 162
no taxation without
    representation, 75
Nova Reperta, 6
NSC. *See* National
    Security Council
nuclear weapons, 419, 449
Nunn, Sam, 487

O
Obama, Barack, 498–99
Ocaneechee Indians, 24
O'Donnell, Rosie, 404
Office of Reconstruction and
    Humanitarian Assistance
    (ORHA), 492
officer defections, 131
Oglethorpe, James Edward, 45, 47
O'Hara, Charles, 130, 130*f*
Ohio River Valley, 49–51, 116–17
Okinawa, 409
Oldham, John, 19
Old Northwest Territory, 189, 189*f*
Omaha Beach, 359–60, 381
Onis, Luis de, 178
Onondaga Indians, 116
Opechancanough, 13, 16, 18

Operation
    AVALANCHE, 374
    BAYTOWN, 374
    Cedar Falls, 457
    Chromite, 426
    Condor, 476
    DELIBERATE FORCE, 486
    DESERT SHIELD, 482
    DESERT STORM, 483–84
    Dragoon, 382
    Eagle Claw, 477, 477
    Enduring Freedom, 488
    Iraqi Freedom, *491*, 498
    JUST CAUSE, 482
    Meetinghouse, 406
    Mongoose, 447
    Overlord, 380–82
    PHANTOM FURY, 495
    Ranch Hand, 457, *458*
    Restore Hope, 485
    Rolling Thunder, 454
    SHINGLE, 376
    TORCH, 365
    UPHOLD DEMOCRACY, 486
    Urgent Fury, 479
    Vulture, 442
Oppenheimer, Robert, 410
Ordnance Rifle, 3-Inch 215
Oregon trail, 216
ORHA. *See* Office of
    Reconstruction and
    Humanitarian Assistance
Ormond, earl of, 3
Orwell, George, 373
Osaka, Japan, *405*
Osmeña, Sergio, 407
O'Sullivan, John L., 176
Oswald, Richard, 132
Otis, Elwell, 315
Ottoman Turks, 10
Overland Campaign, 260
overmountain men, 124
Ozawa, Jisaburo, 402

P
Pacific Squadron, 175, 183
Pacific war, in World War II, 392
Pahlavi, Reza, 476
Paine, Thomas, 92, 93*f*
Pakenham, Edward
    Michael, 171–72
Palestine Liberation Organization
    (PLO), 478
Pamunkey Indians, 9–10, 12, 24
Panama City, 482
Parker, Earl, 360

Parker, John (colonial
  militia captain), 82,
Parker, John (U.S. Army
  officer), 312
Parker, Quanah, 292
Parrott, Robert P., 215
Passchendaele Offensive, 335
Patterson, Robert, 418
Patton, George S., 366,
  366, 368, 415
  in Allied offensive, 345
  Bonus Army and, 350
PAVN. *See* People's Army
  of Vietnam
Pawtuxet Indians, 17
Peace Establishment Act
  (1802), 152
Peacekeeping missions, of
  UN, 485f, 486
Peace of Paris, 66
peace settlement, 12
Peale, Charles Wilson, 102
Pearl Harbor, 362, *390*, 391
Peck, Gregory, 436
Peers, William, 467
Pelham, Henry, 73
Pemberton, John C., 226, 256
Pennsylvania (USS), 180
Pennsylvania, campaigns in, 105f
Pennsylvania Gazette, 53f
People's Army of Vietnam (PAVN),
  453, 456, 462
Pepperrell, William, 47
Pequot Indians, 20
Pequot War (1636–1637), 19–20
Percy, Hugh, 84
Perfecto de Cos, Martín, 195
Perry, Matthew Calbraith,
  183, 202, 219f
Perry, Oliver Hazard, 161, 182
Pershing, John J. "Black
  Jack," 318, 338f
  AEF led by, 339
  in Great War, 346
  Roosevelt, T., impressed by, 325
Petersburg, Virginia, 127, 240,
  261–62, 262f
Petersen, Frank E., Jr., 433
Petraeus, David, *497*, 497–99
Pham Ngoc Thao, 449
Philadelphia (USS), 135
Philadelphia campaign, 107–9
Philip (Metacom), 22
Philip II (king of Spain), 33
Philip of Anjou (king of
  Spain), 39

Philippine-American War,
  315–18, 316f, 322
Philippines, 390, 392, 408
Philippines Expeditionary
  Force, 314
Phillips, William, 127
Phipps, William, 38
Pickens, Andrew, 120
Pickett, George, 254
Pickett's Charge, 254
Pico, Andres, 200
*Pictorial Field Book of the War of
  1812* (Lossing), 150f
Piestewa, Lori Ann, 475
Pike, Zebulon, 152, 159
Pilgrims, 16–17
Pilgrim Separatists, 17–18
Pillow, Gideon, 235
Pinckney, Charles
  Cotesworth, 146
Pinochet, Augusto, 476
Piscataways Indians, 21
Pitcairn, John, 82
Pitt, William, 58–60
Pittsburg Landing, 241–42
Plains of Abraham, 65
Platt, Charles, 182
Platt Amendment, 315, 320
Plattsburg Idea, 340
Plauché, Jean, 171
Pleasanton, Alfred, 252
Plessy v. Ferguson, 329, 334
PLO. *See* Palestine Liberation
  Organization
Plymouth, 17, 29–30
Pocahontas, 12–13
political cartoon, 460f
Polk, James Knox, 196, 207
Polk, Leonidas, 227, 234
Pomo Indians, 218
Ponce de Leon, Antonio, 201
Pontiac (Ottawa chief), 70–72
Pope, John, 242, 247
population, of U.S., 309
Pork Chop Hill, 435–36
Pork Chop Hill (film), 436
Porter, David, 182,
Porter, David Dixon 245, 256
Porter, Fitz John, 247
Port Royal, 42
post-traumatic stress disorder
  (PTSD), 383, 471–72
POW. *See* prisoner of war camps
powder, smokeless, 312
Powell, Colin, 481, 483, 486
Powell, James, 288

Power, Colin, 468
Power, Francis Gary, 445
Power Doctrine, 483
Powhatan (chief), 9–10, 12
The Prairie Traveler (Marcy,
  R.), 210–11
praying Indians, 27
Preble, Edward, 151
precision bombing
  techniques, 369, 371
Prescott, William, 85
Preston, Thomas, 77
Prevost, George, 168
Price, Sterling, 200
Pride of the Marines (films), 417
prisoner of war (POW) camps,
  258–59, 366, 435f
privateers, 114
Privy Council, 7
Procter, Henry, 160, 162
professionalism, in U.S.
  military, 301–2
professional soldiers, of Civil
  War, 239–40
PTSD. *See* post-traumatic
  stress disorder
Pueblo (USS), 460, 462
Puerto Rico, 314–15
Puller, Lewis "Chesty," 323, 429
Pullman Strike, 279
Punitive Expedition, 325–26
Puritans
  barbaric tendencies of, 29
  Indians and encroachment
    by, 26
  militia forces of, 28
  in New England, 18–19
  Pequot Indians annihilated
    by, 20
Purple Hearts, 378
Pusan offensive, 425–27
Putnam, Israel, 56, 85–86
Pyle, Ernie, 367, 409

Q

al-Qaeda, 488–90, 494, 497
Quarles, Donald, 444
Quartering Act (1765), 74, 80
Quasi-War, 146–48
Québec, Canada, 34–35, 62–66
  British capturing, 65f
  colonial forces invasion of,
    90–91
  military operations around, 62f
Queen Anne's war, 39–43
Queen Charlotte (HMS), 161

R

racial prejudice, 197, 464
racial segregation, 329
racketeer, 305–6
Radford, Arthur, 421, 442
railroads, 212, 270, 282, 288
Raleigh, Walter, 3–4
Rall, Johann, 96–97
Ramsay, Logan, 391
Rawdon, Francis Edward, 119
Read, George, 343
Reagan, Ronald, 478–81
Rebel Yell, 229
reconstruction policy, 274
Red Cloud, 286*f*, 287
Red Stick Creeks, 170
Reed, Walter, 315
refugees, 16–17, 166
regiments, 226
Reno, Marcus, 293–95
Rensselaer, Stephen Van, 156
Republicans, 148–49, 221
Republic of Florida, 176
Reserve Officer Training Corps
    (ROTC), 336
retaliatory violence, 30
Revenue Act (1767), 76
Revere, Paul, 78*f*, 82
revolvers, 214
Rhee, Syngmun, 423, 426–27, 436
Riall, Phineas, 164
Ribaut, Jean, 33
Rice, Condoleezza, 490, 492
Richardson, Ebenezer, 77
Richmond, VA, 228–29,
    245–46, 261
Richmond-Petersburg
    front, 267–68
Rickenbacker, Eddie, 345
Ridenhour, Ron, 467
Ridgway, Matthew, 430–31, 441
Riedesel, Friedrich Adolphus
    Baron von, 103–4, 106
rifles, 88, 214–15, 233
Rigaud, Philippe de, 42
Righteous and Harmonious
    Movement, 319
River Raisin Massacre, 160
Roanoke Indians, 4
Roanoke Island, 5
Roberts, W. L., 423
Rochambeau, Jean-Baptiste
    Donatien de Vimeur, 123
Roche, Jim, 490
Rodgers, John, 154, 156
Rodman, Thomas J., 215

Rodney, George, 129
Rogers, Bernard, 457
Rogers, Edith Nourse, 379
Rogers, Robert, 56, 104
Rolfe, John, 12–13
Rommel, Erwin, 356, 366
Romney (HMS), 76
Roosevelt, Franklin D.,
    351–52, 361–62
Roosevelt, Theodore,
    309, 311, 313*f*
    McKinley assassination and, 320
    military power from, 328*f*
    Pershing impressing, 325
    Philippines war over, 317–18
Roosevelt Corollary, 320
Rosecrans, William, 244, 256–57
Ross, Robert, 166
Rostow, Walt, 449
ROTC. *See* Reserve Officer
    Training Corps
Rove, Karl, 490–91
Rowlandson, Mary, 28
Royal George (HMS), 84
Royal Navy, 363
    blockade of, 160
    British forces reinforced by, 101
    Cape Trafalgar victory and, 153
    colonial ships and, 115–16
    Halifax Squadron of, 155
    impressments of, 153–54
    warships of, 113
    Yorktown and, 129
royal proclamation, 72
Rule of 1756, 153
Rumsfeld, Donald, 488,
    490, 492, 494
Runaway Scrape, 195
Rusk, Dean, 454

S

SAC. *See* Strategic Air Command
al-Sadr, Muqtada, 493
Saigon, 469
Saint-Mihiel Offensive, 345
St. Augustine, 33–34, 46–47, 176
Saipan Island, 401, *401*
de Salaberry, Charles, 162
Samoset Indians, 18
Sampson, William, 311
Sanchez, Ricardo, 493
Sand Creek Massacre, 287, 300
Sandinista revolution, 321
Sandino, Augusto Cesar, 321
San Jacinto (USS), 230
San Juan Hill, 312

San Patricio (Saint Patrick)
    Battalion, 205
Santa Anna, Antonio López
    de, 193–95
    Mexican army reformed by, 204
    as Mexican president, 205
    retreat of, 203
    stone church fortification of, 205
    Taylor, Z., battle with, 202–3
Santa Fe trail, 216
Satanta (Kiowa), 290
Saratoga (USS), 168
Saratoga campaign, 102–7
Sassacus (chief), 20
Sassamon, John, 27
Saunders, Charles, 63
The Savage Wars of Piece:
    Small Wars and the
    Rise of American Power
    (Boot), 15, 318
Savannah, 118–20
Saybrook Indians, 19
Schlesinger, Arthur M., Jr., 449
Schofield, John M., 259, 265, 301
School of the Americas
    (SOA), 476
Schuyler, Philip, 103
Schwarzkopf, Norman, Jr.,
    468, 483–84
Scott, Winfield, 156, 159, 164
    "Anaconda Plan," 225, 235
    Mexico City occupied by, 206
    postwar military and, 179
    Seminole attacks by, 191
    Veracruz invasion by, 203–7
Scottish Highlanders, 172
Scowcroft, Brent, 481
SDI. *See* Strategic Defense
    Initiative
seagoing ships, of U.S., 149–50
Sea Gull (paddlewheel ferry), 182
seapower, 43, 306–7
secession
    Civil War and, 224*f*
    of South Carolina, 222
    states, 223
    from U.S., 221–23
    of Virginia, 223
Second Amendment, 140
Second Anglo-Powhatan
    War, 13–14
Second Continental Congress, 88
Second Seminole War, 189–93
Sedgwick, John, 252
Selective Service Act, 338–39, 474
self-defending ship, 354

Seminole Indians, 190–91
Seminole Wars, 190*f*
  first, 179
  second, 189–93
  third, 215
Semmes, Raphael, 265
Seneca Indians, 116
separation of powers, 139–40
September 11, 2001, 488–90
Serapis (HMS), 114, 115*f*
settlements
  Indians destroying, 28
  in New England, 19*f*
Seven Days Battles, 247
Seven Years War, 37, 58, 67
Seward, William H., 268
sexual harassment, 379
Shannon (HMS), 160
Sharpsburg, 249
Shawnee Indians, 154
Shay, Daniel, 138
Shays' Rebellion, 137–39
Sheaffe, Roger, 159
Sheehan, Neil, 450
Shenandoah Valley, 246, 262
Shepard, William, 138
Sheridan, Philip, 233, 263,
    274, 280, 292*f*
  Indian fighting of, 291
  Richmond raid of, 261
Sherman, William T., 227, 244
  Army of Tennessee, 257
  Confronts Indians, 290
  March to the Sea of, 264
  Post-Civil War, 276–277
  Professionalism, 301
  Retirement, 302
Shinseki, Eric, 491
shipbuilding, 158, 180–81,
    233, 337, 352
Shippen, Peggy, 122
Shirley, William, 47, 55
Short, Walter, 391
Sickles, Daniel, 239, 254
"The Significance of the Frontier
    in American History," 40
Sitter, Carl, 430
Sitting Bull, 285*f*, 295, 299
Slaughterhouse-Five
    (Vonnegut), 369
slavery, 25–26
  abolishing concerns about,
    220–21
  Civil War and, 211
  Congressional declaration
    on, 183

conspiracies about, 46
Emancipation Proclamation
    ending, 249
  Indians and, 57*f*
Slidell, John, 196, 230–31
Slovik, Eddie, 382–84
smallpox virus, 91, 102
small-scale ambushes, 11
Small Wars Manuel (Marine
    Corps), 318
smart bombs, 369
Smerwick, Ireland, 3
Smith, Brad, 414
Smith, Edmund Kirby, 244
Smith, Francis, 82
Smith, Holland, 402
Smith, John, 9–10
Smith, Joseph, 218
Smith, Oliver P., *425*, 429
Smith, Walter Bedell, 443
smokeless powder, 312
smoothbore musket, 88,
    214–15
Smyth, Alexander, 156
Snyder, Christopher, 77
SOA. *See* School of the Americas
Society of Cincinnati, 152
soldiers, U.S. *See also* Buffalo
    Soldiers; standing army
  black, 278
  citizen-soldiers, 112, 136
  desertion rates of, 217
  of Union army, *214*
  in Vietnam, *455*
sole survivor policy, 389
Solomon Islands, 398–99
Somalia, 484–86
Sons of Liberty, 69, 75, 85
Sorrelman, Joe, 440
the South, campaigns in, 121*f*
South Carolina, 44, 120,
    123, 222
Southeastern Indians, 57*f*
Southern Plains, 288–90
South Korea, *425*, 426
South Pacific Squadrons, 183
South Vietnam, 449–50
  Eisenhower, D., and obstacles
    of, 442–43
  ground war in, 457
  U.S. military strategy in, 462
  U.S. removing forces from,
    468–69
Southwest desert, 298–99
Soviet Union, 356, 417, 446, 484
Spaatz, Carl, 368

Spain
  conquests in south by, 117–18
  Cuba and surrender of, 313
  territorial claims of, 6–7
  war with, 5
Spanish-American War,
    308–15, 310*f*
Spock, Benjamin, 460
spot resolution proposals, 198
Spotsylvania Court House, 261
Spruance, Raymond,
    395, 397, 402
Sputnik (Soviet satellite), 446
Squanto Indians, 18
Stalin, Josef, 380, 415–16
Stamp Act (1765), 74–76
Stamp Act Congress, 75, 87
standing army
  Congressional objections
    to, 137
  Continental Congress rejecting,
    140–41
  militia compared to, 140–41
  national security and, 179
  public not interested in, 349
  of U.S., 224, 437
Standish, Miles, 18
Stanton, Edwin, 277
Stark, Harold, 389
Stark, John, 56, 104
Star of the West (transport
    ship), 222
"Star Spangled Banner," 167*f*
Star Wars missile defense, 478
State of Union address, 178–79
St. Clair, Arthur, 103, 141, 143–44
steamboats, 192
steam propulsion, 180,
    208, 219, 306
steel-hulled warships, 307–8
steel industry, 308
Steuben, F. W. A. F., 109–11, 128
Stevens, Roy, 359–60
Stigler, Franz, 371–72
Stillwell, Joe, 406
Stimson, Henry, 379
St. Lawrence River, 155–56
St. Leger, Barry, 103–4
Stoddert, Benjamin, 146
Stone, John, 19
Strategic Air Command
    (SAC), 419
strategic bombing
    doctrine, 354, 369
Strategic Defense Initiative
    (SDI), 478

Stribling, Cornelius K., 175
Stuart, J. E. B., 221, 252, 261
Stuart, John, 72, 82
Stuart Restoration (1660), 22
Stuyvesant, Peter, 26, 36
submarines, 329, 357, 386
    antisubmarine campaign, 337–38
    death rates, 403
    H. L. Hunley (CSS), 231, 265
    U.S., 402–3, 402*f*
Sugar Act (1764), 74
Sullivan, Alleta, 389
Sullivan, John (general),
    94, 96, 116
Sullivan, John L., 421
Sullivan, Thomas, 389
Sullivan brothers, 388–89
Sullivans (USS), 389
Sumner, Edwin V., 217
Sumner, Samuel, 312
Sumter, Thomas, 120
Supreme Court, Indians
    petitioning, 186
Susquehannock Indians,
    21–22, 24, 71
Sutter, John, 200
Sweeney, Charles, 412
Symington, Stuart, 421

T
Taft, William Howard, 317, 323
Taiwan, 444
Taliban, 499
Talleyrand, Maurice de, 146
Tampico Battalion, 198
Tampico, Mexico, 305, 324
Tanaka, Raizo, 400
tanks, German, *383*
Tarleton, Banastre, 119, 125, 127
Tarrantines Indians, 18
taxation, 73
Taylor, Maxwell, 441, 449
Taylor, Richard, 239, 268
Taylor, Zachary, 191, 196
    flying artillery of, 198
    Mexican campaign of, 201–3
    as Old Rough and Ready,
        198–99
    Santa Anna's battle with, 202–3
tea party, Boston, 79–81, 80*f*
Teass, Elizabeth, 360
technology
    during Civil War, 233, 237
    military, 180, 214–15, 312,
        326–27, 331
    in post Civil War years, 280–81

Tecumseh (Shawnee chieftain),
    144, 154, 161–62
Tedder, Arthur, 368
Tejanos (Devil Texans), 202
telegraphic communications, 270
Tennessee (ironclad), 267
Tenskwatawa, 154
Tenure of Office Act, 278
territory
    Arkansas, 186
    colonial laws defending, 14
    expansion of, 207
    Indian, 215–18, 285
    Northwest, 141–45, 162
    Old Northwest, 189, 189*f*
    Spanish claims of, 6–7
    Utah, 218
terrorism, 479, 479*f*, 481, 488
Terry, Alfred, 267, 293
Tet Offensive, 460*f*, 461*f*, 462–63
Texas, 193–96, 194*f*,
    206–7, 290–92
Texas National Guardsmen, 375
Thayer, Sylvanus, 179–80, 208
Third Amendment, 140
third Anglo-Powhatan War, 16
third fortification system, 181
38th Parallel, in Korean War, 423,
    427, 430–32
Thomas, George H., 213, 226,
    257, 259, 267
Thompson, Hugh, Jr., 466
Thompson, Wiley, 190–91
Thornton, Seth, 198
Throg's Neck, 94
Tibbets, Paul, 404, 411–12
Tilghman, Lloyd, 234–35
Tillman, Pat, *490*
timeline
    1850–1862, 237
    1890–1917, 331
    1862–1865, 271
    1864–1890, 303
    1585–1676, 31
    1954–1975, 469
    1914–1939, 357
    1941–1945, 413
    1944–1953, 437
    1973–2011, 500
    1939–1945, 386
    1787–1816, 173
    1763–1777, 98
    1609–1763, 67
Tirpitz (DKM, Nazi German), 363
tobacco, 12
Tocqueville, Alexis de, 463

To Hell and Back (Murphy), 383
Toledo y Dubois, Álvarez de, 176
Tories, 91, 107, 116, 124, 132
Townshend, Charles, 76–77
Tracy, Benjamin, 308
Trail of Tears, 186
training, 210–11, 340
transcontinental railroads, 212
Transcontinental Treaty, 178
Trans-Mississippi Theater,
    234, 284–85
Travis, William B., 194
treason, 69, 122–23
Treason Act (1543), 77
Treaty
    Adams–Onís, 193
    Buchanan-Pakenham, 196
    of Dover, 37
    of Fort Greenville, 145
    of Fort Moultrie, 189
    of Ghent, 169, 172
    of Guadalupe Hidalgo, 206,
        211, 218
    of Hartford, 26, 36
    Jay's, 144, 146
    of Kanagawa, 219
    of Montreal (1701), 41
    of Mortefontaine, 148
    of Paris, 71*f*, 131–32, 141,
        314, 315
    of Payne's Landing, 189
    of Ryswick, 39
    of Tordesillas, 33
    Transcontinental, 178
    of Utrecht, 43
    of Versailles, 348, 354
    Webster-Ashburton, 183
tree of liberty, 138
trench warfare, 263
Trent (British mail packet), 230
Trent, William, 51
Trenton, 96–97
Trist, Nicholas, 204–5
troop morale, 96
Truman, Harry S., 409
    atomic bomb decision of, 410
    Cold War and, 420–21
    Executive Order 9981 from, 434
    MacArthur, D., fired by,
        428, 432
    North Korea condemnation
        by, 424
Truman Doctrine, 418
Truscott, Lucian, 365
Truxtun, Thomas, 148
Tryon, William, 107

Tryon County militia, 104
Tucker, William, 13
Tullahoma Campaign, 256
Turner, Frederick Jackson, 40
Tuscaroras Indians, 43–44
Tuscarora Wars, 43–45
12 O'Clock High (film), 369
Twenty Negro Law, 255
Twiggs, David, 222
Twiggs, Travis, 471–72, 499
Tyler, John, 196

U

U-boats, 336–37,
    363–64, *364*, 372
Udall, Morris, 467
The Uncertain Trumpet
    (Taylor, M.), 441
Uniform Militia Act (1792), 144
Union army, 224
    McClellan leading, 228
    Petersburg advance of, 261–62
    soldier of, *214*
United Colonies of New
    England, 26
United Nations, 483, 485*f*, 486
United States (USS), 157, 160, 175
United States (U.S.). *See also*
    colonies; North America
    Adams–Onís Treaty of, 193
    Air Force, *433*
    Article of Confederation, 136
    British forces and, 164
    British military force
        against, 164
    British relations with, 154–55
    California incorporated
        into, 200
    Central American and, 321*f*
    citizen-soldiers in, 136
    Constitutional convention of,
        139–40
    economic depression of, 137
    exploring expeditions of, 184*f*
    Florida included in, 178
    France recognizing
        independence of, 109
    French navy and vessels to, 148
    French relations with, 146–47
    geographical positioning of, 2
    Gilded Age in, 279–80
    Hitler declaring war on, 362
    imperialism of, 305–6, 320
    Indian wars in, 142*f*, 299
    interventions reduced of,
        351–53

interwar years of, 348–49, 415
Iraq War troop withdrawal
    of, 498
Japan interest of, 219
Lewis and Clark expedition of,
    152–53
Marine Corps, 146, 330,
    428–30, *429*, *445*
Mexican intervention by,
    323–26
Mexican war with, 196–99,
    199*f*, 207
military plan lacking of, 163
military production of, 398
military reconstruction district
    in, 278*f*
military strategy of, 462
Muslims turning against, 495
national security of, 417–19
Naval Academy, 207–8
naval battles of, 147*f*
new federal government of, 140
North Africa declaring war
    on, 136
Northwest Territory of,
    141–45, 162
population of, 309
Puerto Rico and Guam ceded to,
    314–15
racial prejudice in, 464
reconstruction of, 277–78
seagoing ships of, 149–50
Somalia intervention of, 484
South Vietnam removal of forces
    by, 468–69
standing army of, 224, 437
states secession from, 221–23
submarines, 402–3, 402*f*
Texas control of, 206–7
Treaty of Paris and, 131–32, 141
U.S. navy and imperialism of,
    218–20
Vietnam bombing by, *464*
war industry of, 361
war ravaging, 173
warships of, 146–48
United States Air Force, *368*, 419
United States Colored Troops
    (USCT), 258
United States Military
    Academy, 273
United States Naval Academy
    (USNA), 220
Upton, Emory, 261, 301–2, 327
Urrea, José de, 194
U.S. *See* United States

USCT. *See* United States
    Colored Troops
Ushijima, Mitsura, 409
USNA. *See* United States
    Naval Academy
Utah Territory, 218

V

VA. *See* Veterans Administration
vacuum domicilium, 17
Vallejo, Mariano Guadalupe, 200
Valley Forge, 108
Van Buren, Martin, 195–96
Vandergrift, Alexander, 399
Van Dorn, Earl, 218, 245
Van Fleet, James, 432
Vann, John Paul, 450
Vaudreuil, Chevalier de, 42, 63, 66
Vaudreuil, Pierre de Rigaud de, 56
Vaught, James B., 477
V-E Day, 385–86
Veracruz invasion, 203–7
Vergennes, Comte de, 109, 131
Vernon, Edward, 45
Veterans Administration
    (VA), 417
Vicksburg, 245, 255–56
Victorio, 298
Victorio War, 273, 298
Viet Cong, 449, 450, 454, 462
Vietnam. *See also* South Vietnam
    airpower over, 453–54, 459
    drug use in, 465
    fragging in, 465–66
    ground troops in, 454–55
    middle-of-the-road approach
        to, 452
    My Lai massacre in, 466–67
    operations in, 451*f*
    PAVN, 453, 456, 462
    Saigon airlift in, 469
    Tet Offensive, 460*f*, 461*f*,
        462–63
    U.S. bombing of, *464*
    U.S. soldiers in, *455*
    Vann landing in, 450
    veterans, 466–67
    worsening conditions in,
        450–52
Vietnamization process, 463
Villa, Francisco
    "Pancho," 323, 325
Villiers, Louis Coulon de, 52
Vinson, Carl, 421
violent practices, of
    Englishmen, 11–12

Virginia, 129
　federal assets seized by, 228
　General Assembly of, 12
　militia, 50–51
　Petersburg, 127, 240,
　　261–62, 262*f*
　royal support in, 21–22
　secession of, 223
　war in, 126–28
　Washington, G., sending troops
　　to, 127–28
Virginia (CSS), 231–33, 231*f*
Virginia Company, 12, 13
Virginia Military Institute
　(VMI), 225, 262
Virginia militia, 50–51
VMI. *See* Virginia Military Institute
Von Donop, Karl, 96
Vo Nguyen Giap, 442
Vonnegut, Kurt, 369

W

WAAC. *See* Women's Army
　Auxiliary Corps
Wainwright, Jonathan, 392
Waldron, John C., 396
Walker, Hovenden, 42–43
Walker, Walton H., 424–25
Wallace, Lew, 242, 262
Waller, Littleton W. T., 322, *322*
Walpole, Robert, 73
Wampanoag Indians,
　17–18, 27–28
Wanamaker, Woody, 465
warfare
　asymmetrical, 2, 15, 318
　chemical, *458*
　desert, 365–67
　for independence, 87
　Jackson and, 176
　North American, 15, 37–49
　trench, 263
　U.S. ravaged by, 173
　in Virginia, 126–28
war hawks, 454
war industry, 361
Warner, Seth, 104
War of 1812, 150, 155
　Armstrong taking over,
　　158–60
　Baltimore and Lake Champlain,
　　168–69
　campaigns of, 163*f*
　in Canada, 156
　in Chesapeake Bay, 166–68
　on Great Lakes, 160–62

in Montreal, 162–64
in New Orleans, 170–72
Niagara stalemate of, 164–66
northern war of, 158*f*
River Raisin Massacre, 160
at sea, 156–57
southern campaigns of, 169*f*
in southwest, 169–70
Treaty of Ghent ending,
　169, 172
war of attrition, 455–56
War of Austrian Succession,
　37, 47, 81
War of Jenkin's Ear, 45–47
War of Spanish Succession,
　37, 41, 45
War of the League of
　Augsburg, 37–38
War Plan ORANGE, 352
War Powers Act, 474
War Production Board
　(WPB), 363
Warren, Gouverneur, 254
Warren, Peter, 47
Warren Wagon Train
　Massacre, 290
warships
　ironclad, 231–33, 270
　of Japan, 392, 395–97
　Pearl Harbor, 391
　Royal Navy, 113
　steel-hulled, 307–8
　U.S., 146–48
　U.S. navy, *364*, 407
Washburne, Elihu, 234
Washington, D.C., 166–67
Washington, George, 102*f*
　adversity faced by, 110
　armies survival by, 88
　British forces retreat by, 97
　civilian control of military and,
　　112, 133
　Congress authorizing growing
　　army of, 101–2
　as Constitutional convention
　　president, 139–40
　Continental Army of, 89, 92
　Continental Congress
　　appearance of, 100
　Cornwallis battling, 96
　Declaration of Independence
　　and, 93
　as first president, 140
　foodstuffs and supplies
　　confiscated by, 111
　Fort Necessity from, 52

Germantown advance of, 108
Howe, W., battle with, 94–97
Lee, C., dismissed by, 110
national army needed by, 101
New York defenses by, 94
officer defections prevented
　by, 131
retreat of, 108
surrender of, 52
tactical masterpiece of, 98
troop morale of, 96
in Valley Forge, 108
Virginia getting troops from,
　127–28
in Virginia militia, 50–51
Washington, John, 22
Washington, Lawrence, 49, 89
Washington, William, 125–26
Watergate, 474
Water Witch (USS), 220
Watson-Wentworth, Charles, 75
de Watteville, Louis, 162
Wayne, Anthony "Mad," 109, 118,
　127, 144–45
weapons-for-pelts trade, 35–36
weapons of mass destruction
　(WMDs), 490
Webster-Ashburton Treaty
　(1842), 183
Weigley, Russell, 15
Weinberger, Caspar, 478
Wellington, Duke of, 205
West, Benjamin, 65*f*
West, Larry, 440
West, Thomas, 12
Western Europe, 380, 380*f*
western frontier, 216*f*, 288*f*
　army constabulary of, 284
　exploration and surveying of,
　　181–82
　of Great War, 342*f*
　Indians and, 212, 286–87,
　　296–99
　Warren Wagon Train
　　Massacre, 290
Western Theater
　Civil War, 233–36
　Confederate army challenges
　　in, 234
　in 1862, 241–45
　in 1864, 263–65
　in 1863, 255–58
West Indies Squadron,
　182–83, 191
Westmoreland, William,
　318, 454–56

West Point, 152, 165, 179–80, 207
    Confederate officers from, 225
    training from, 210–11
westward expansion, 185
Weyler, Valeriano, 309
Wheeler, Joseph, 310
Whipple, Abraham, 119
Whiskey rebellion, 145–46
White, John, 5, 11f
White, Richard, 40
White, William Allen, 361
white migration,
        215–18, 216f, 285
White Plains, 94–96
Whitmer, Van, 439–40
Wickes, Lambert, 114
Wilkes, Charles, 183, 230
Wilkinson, James, 152,
        162–63, 169
William, John, 41
William III (king of
        England), 38, 40
Williams, Roger, 18
Williams, Samuel, 443
Wilson, Charles, 441, 442
Wilson, James H., 267
Wilson, Woodrow, 323, 324–25
Wilton, Grey de, 3
Winchester, James, 159–60
Winder, William, 166
Wingina (chief), 4
Winslow, Josiah, 28
Winthrop, John, 36, 38–39
WMDs. See weapons of mass
        destruction

Wolfe, James, 60, 62–65, 65f
women, in U.S. military, 379, 475
Women's Army Auxiliary Corps
        (WAAC), 379
Wood, Leonard, 311, 327
Wool, John, 198, 201
World War I. See Great War
World War II
    African campaign during, 365f
    airpower in, 367–69, 372–73
    airpower over Europe in,
        370–72
    in Atlantic ocean, 363–64
    Battle of Midway, 393, 393f
    Buffalo Soldiers in, 376–77
    desert warfare during, 365–67
    Dresden attack in, 385
    in Europe, 362
    Fat Boy bomb, 411
    final push to Japan in, 408–9
    ground war ending in, 406–8
    Guadalcanal in, 398, 398–400
    Island Hopping campaign in,
        400f, 401–3
    Italian campaign in, 374f
    in Italy, 373–76
    Japanese airwar in, 403–6
    Japanese Americans in, 378–79
    kamikazes in, 407
    Little Boy bomb in, 411, 411–12
    military preparedness for,
        360–61, 389–91
    Normandy, France, 380–82, 381f
    North Atlantic victory, 372
    Omaha Beach, 359–60, 381

    Operation Overlord in, 380–82
    Pacific war in, 392
    Pearl Harbor, 362, 390, 391
    prelude to, 354–56
    U-boats, 336–37, 363–64,
        364, 372
    V-E Day in, 385–86
    in Western Europe, 380, 380f
    women in, 379
Worth, William J., 192
Wounded Knee, 299–301, 300f, 302
WPB. See War Production Board

Y

Yamaguchi, Tamon, 397
Yamamoto, Isoroku, 391,
        395, 397–98
Yamasee Wars, 44–45
Yamashita, Tomoyuki, 408
Yaocomicos Indians, 21
yellow fever, 315
yellow journalism, 309
Yellowstone National Park, 280
Yellowstone River, 181
Yeo, James, 159
York, Alvin C., 346, 347f
Yorktown, 128f, 129–31, 130f
Young, Brigham, 218
Young, Charles, 333
Young, Samuel B. M., 276, 327

Z

al-Zawahiri, Ayman, 489
Zimmermann, Arthur, 337
Zinni, Tony, 493